GREAT
WOMEN
ARTISTS

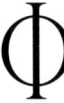

PREFACE
PAGE 6

INTRODUCTION
PAGE 7

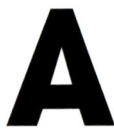

A
PAGE 16

Magdalena Abakanowicz
Berenice Abbott
Nina Chanel Abney
Marina Abramović
Tomma Abts
Carla Accardi
Etel Adnan
Hilma af Klint
Eileen Agar
Eija-Liisa Ahtila
Chantal Akerman
Njideka Akunyili Crosby
Anni Albers
Ellen Altfest
Olga de Amaral
Ghada Amer
Laurie Anderson
Mamma Andersson
Sofonisba Anguissola
Eleanor Antin
Janine Antoni
Ida Applebroog
Diane Arbus
Hrafnhildur Arnardóttir
Ruth Asawa
Dotty Attie
Gillian Ayres

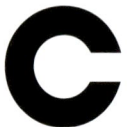

B
PAGE 44

Jo Baer
Fiona Banner
Phyllida Barlow
Tina Barney
Wilhelmina Barns-Graham
Anna Barriball
Yael Bartana
Uta Barth
Maria Bartuszová
Marie Bashkirtseff
Mary Beale
Vanessa Beecroft
Vanessa Bell
Rebecca Belmore
Lynda Benglis
Marie-Guillemine Benoist
Renate Bertlmann
Huma Bhabha
Zarina Bhimji
Dara Birnbaum
Maria Blanchard
Rosa Bonheur
Monica Bonvicini
Dineo Seshee Bopape
Pauline Boty
Pauline Boudry & Renate
Lorenz
Louise Bourgeois
Margaret Bourke-White
Carol Bove
Sonia Boyce
Geta Brătescu
Candice Breitz
Romaine Brooks
Cecily Brown
Tania Bruguera
Heidi Bucher

C
PAGE 81

Claude Cahun
Sophie Calle
Juno Calypso
Julia Margaret Cameron
Cao Fei
Janet Cardiff
Joan Carlile
Emily Carr
Rosalba Carriera
Leonora Carrington
Mary Cassatt
Jordan Casteel
Elizabeth Catlett
Vija Celmins
Helen Chadwick
Sarah Charlesworth
Constance Marie Charpentier
Judy Chicago
Saloua Raouda Choucair
Chryssa
Lygia Clark
Camille Claudel
Dana Claxton
Prunella Clough
Hannah Cohoon
Ithell Colquhoun
Grace Cossington Smith
Renee Cox
Petah Coyne
Cui Jie
Imogen Cunningham

D
PAGE 112

Hanne Darboven
Berlinde De Bruyckere
Elaine de Kooning
Tacita Dean
Jay DeFeo
Mary Delany
Sonia Delaunay
Agnes Denes
Rineke Dijkstra
A K Dolven
Tara Donovan
Rosalyn Drexler
Elsie Driggs
Rose-Adélaïde Ducreux
Marlene Dumas
Celeste Dupuy-Spencer
Mabel Dwight

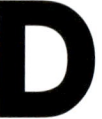

E
PAGE 130

Mary Beth Edelson
Nicole Eisenman
Tracey Emin
Alexandra Exter

F

PAGE 134

Monir Shahroudy
Farmanfarmaian
Lara Favaretto
Genieve Figgis
Rose Finn-Kelcey
Sylvie Fleury
Ceal Floyer
Lavinia Fontana
Martine Franck
Helen Frankenthaler
Andrea Fraser
Elisabeth Frink
Katharina Fritsch

G

PAGE 146

Anya Gallaccio
Ellen Gallagher
Yishay Garbasz
Gego
Artemisia Gentileschi
Isa Genzken
Marguerite Gérard
Vanessa L. German
Gluck
Nan Goldin
Natalia Goncharova

Eva Gonzalès
Dominique Gonzalez-Foerster
Catherine Goodman
Dora Gordine
Sheela Gowda
Lauren Greenfield
Katharina Grosse
Guerrilla Girls
Shilpa Gupta
Ike Gyokuran

H

PAGE 168

Elisabeth Haarr
Maggi Hambling
Ann Hamilton
Margaret Harrison
Rachel Harrison
Grace Hartigan
Mona Hatoum
Sharon Hayes
Jacoba van Heemskerck
Susan Hefuna
Mary Heilmann
Annemarie Heinrich
Catharina van Hemessen
Camille Henrot
Barbara Hepworth
Carmen Herrera
Eva Hesse
Sheila Hicks
Susan Hiller
Lubaina Himid
Hannah Höch
Candida Höfer
Nancy Holt
Jenny Holzer
Rebecca Horn
Roni Horn
Shara Hughes
Juliana Huxtable

I

PAGE 197

Cristina Iglesias
Graciela Iturbide
María Izquierdo

J

PAGE 200

Emily Jacir
Chantal Joffe
Gwen John
Joan Jonas
Loïs Mailou Jones
Louise Jopling
Birgit Jürgenssen

K

PAGE 207

Frida Kahlo
Hayv Kahraman
Kan Xuan
Katsushika Ōi
Angelica Kauffman
Mary Kelly
Iris Kensmil
Corita Kent
Bharti Kher
Kimsooja
Kiyohara Yukinobu

Emily Kam Kngwarray
Laura Knight
Běla Kolářová
Käthe Kollwitz
Eva Kotátková
Joyce Kozloff
Lee Krasner
Barbara Kruger
Shigeko Kubota
Agnieszka Kurant
Yayoi Kusama
Alicja Kwade

L

PAGE 230

Dorothea Lange
Greer Lankton
Maria Lassnig
Marie Laurencin
Louise Lawler
Deana Lawson
Lee Bul
Nikki S. Lee
Annie Leibovitz
Tamara de Lempicka
Zoe Leonard
Sherrie Levine
Helen Levitt
Edmonia Lewis
Judith Leyster
Liliane Lijn
Maya Lin
Linder
Hung Liu
Barbara Longhi
Sarah Lucas
Ana Lupas

M

PAGE 252

Dora Maar
Margaret Macdonald Mackintosh
Esther Mahlangu
Vivian Maier
Anna Maria Maiolino
Nalini Malani
Jeanne Mammen
Sally Mann
Britta Marakatt-Labba
Cinthia Marcelle
Teresa Margolles
Marisol
Helen Marten
Agnes Martin
Mary Martin
Julie Mehretu
Ana Mendieta
Marisa Merz
Angelica Mesiti
Annette Messager
Beatriz Milhazes
Lee Miller
Marilyn Minter
Marta Minujín
Aleksandra Mir
Joan Mitchell
Lisette Model
Paula Modersohn-Becker
Tina Modotti
Tracey Moffatt
Louise Moillon
Véra Molnar
Mariko Mori
Berthe Morisot
Mary Moser
Anna (Grandma) Moses
Marlow Moss
Zanele Muholi
Mrinalini Mukherjee
Vera Mukhina
Gabriele Münter
Elizabeth Murray
Wangechi Mutu

N

PAGE 295

Alice Neel
Plautilla Nelli
Senga Nengudi
Shirin Neshat
Rivane Neuenschwander
Louise Nevelson

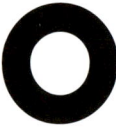

O

PAGE 301

Georgia O'Keeffe
Lydia Okumura
Yoko Ono
Maria van Oosterwijck
Catherine Opie
Meret Oppenheim
Orlan
Lucy Orta
Emily Mary Osborn

P

PAGE 310

Pan Yuliang
Gina Pane
Lygia Pape
Cornelia Parker
Katie Paterson
Clara Peeters
Beverly Pepper
Elizabeth Peyton
Susan Philipsz
Heather Phillipson
Patricia Piccinini
Cathie Pilkington
Howardena Pindell
Adrian Piper
Liubov Popova
Liliana Porter
Harriet Powers
Laure Prouvost
Pushpamala N

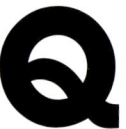

Q

PAGE 329

Lucrezia Quistelli

R

PAGE 330

Carol Rama
Anita Rée
Paula Rego
Lisa Reihana
Lili Reynaud-Dewar
Germaine Richier
Bridget Riley
Faith Ringgold
Pipilotti Rist
Marietta Robusti
Luisa Roldán
Tracey Rose
Martha Rosler
Properzia de' Rossi
Susan Rothenberg
Mika Rottenberg
Nancy Rubins
Rachel Ruysch
Hannah Ryggen

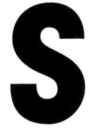

S

PAGE 349

Betye Saar
Natascha Sadr Haghighian
Kay Sage
Niki de Saint Phalle
Doris Salcedo
Charlotte Salomon
Zilia Sánchez
Augusta Savage
Jenny Saville
Miriam Schapiro
Mira Schendel

Hélène Schjerfbeck
Carolee Schneemann
Anna Maria van Schurman
Dana Schutz
Berni Searle
Tschabalala Self
Joan Semmel
Zinaida Serebriakova
Shen Yuan
Amrita Sher-Gil
Amy Sherald
Cindy Sherman
Mary Sibande
Amy Sillman
Laurie Simmons
Taryn Simon
Lorna Simpson
Dayanita Singh
Elisabetta Sirani
Sylvia Sleigh
Kiki Smith
Monika Sosnowska
Marie Spartali Stillman
Jo Spence
Nancy Spero
Frances Stark
Pat Steir
Irma Stern
Florine Stettheimer
Hito Steyerl
Jessica Stockholder
Michelle Stuart
Sturtevant
Maud Sulter
Alina Szapocznikow
Sarah Sze

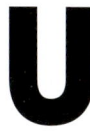

PAGE 408

Uemura Shōen
Mierle Laderman Ukeles
Amalia Ulman

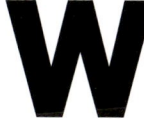

PAGE 422

Kara Walker
Rebecca Warren
Anna Waser
Michaelina Wautier
Gillian Wearing
Carrie Mae Weems
Marianne von Werefkin
Pae White
Rachel Whiteread
Faith Wilding
Hannah Wilke
Jane & Louise Wilson
Betty Woodman
Francesca Woodman
Rose Wylie

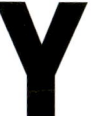

PAGE 439

Catherine Yass
Lynette Yiadom-Boakye
Yin Xiuzhen
Lisa Yuskavage

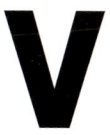

PAGE 411

Suzanne Valadon
VALIE EXPORT
Anne Vallayer-Coster
Remedios Varo
Joana Vasconcelos
Cecilia Vicuña
Maria Helena Vieira da Silva
Élisabeth Vigée-Lebrun
Marie-Denise Villers
Ursula von Rydingsvard

PAGE 443

Zarina
Fahrelnissa Zeid
Andrea Zittel

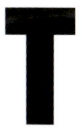

PAGE 397

Sophie Taeuber-Arp
Atsuko Tanaka
Dorothea Tanning
Tarsila
Lenore Tawney
Anna Dorothea Therbusch
Alma Thomas
Mickalene Thomas
Elizabeth Thompson, Lady Butler
Rosemarie Trockel
Anne Truitt

PAGE 437

Xiao Lu
Xing Danwen

INDEX
PAGE 446

PICTURE CREDITS
PAGE 456

When Phaidon published *The Art Book* in 1994, it offered a radical new approach to art history. Rather than a chronological journey, it presented artists from A to Z by name, enabling even the most familiar of artworks to be seen in a new context. This structure encouraged readers to put aside preconceptions about personally preferred styles and movements, with each turn of the page offering unexpected juxtapositions and connections between works from different points in history.

The Art Book was also notable for its inclusion of a number of women artists, at a time when some other popular art history books were still failing to do so. In the quarter century since then, diversity in art history – with regard to race, gender identity, disability, socio-economic background, and sexual orientation – has continued to expand. History is no longer perceived as a single narrative that represents and serves only one section of society, but rather a tangle of interwoven stories that coexist rather than compete for dominance. Sometimes they connect together along the well-trodden paths that we collectively share, but at other times they branch off into new directions, encouraging a rethink of long-held preconceptions and an appreciation of previously overlooked figures and their achievements.

This book shares stories of more than 400 women who have made art in the past five centuries – the earliest artist included in it was born in *c.*1490, the most recent in 1990. Many do not consider their gender identity a primary aspect of their artistic practice. This is not a survey of feminist art or a selection of art about 'female experience' and 'women's subjects'. The artworks chosen more often than not transcend issues of gender, and instead serve to demonstrate the widest variety of approaches to materials, technique, form and subject matter. Taken as a whole, it is a testament to the extensive work that has been undertaken over several decades to research artists who had been written out of history and it is also a celebration of the continuing creativity of women across the world today.

INTRODUCTION
BY REBECCA MORRILL

Any book of women artists is likely to be seen as a direct descendant of feminist art history, the discipline born in the 1960s alongside other social histories that challenged the dominance of the white male protagonist in accounts of the past. Yet women have been the focus of publications considerably further back in time. Giovanni Boccaccio's *De Claris Mulieribus* ('Concerning Famous Women'), 1361–2, for example, included several visual artists among its 106 biographies of important females, historical and mythological. Over a millennium earlier, the Christian theologian Clement of Alexandria in his *Stromata* ('Miscellanies'), *c*. AD 198–203, mentions the third-century BC Greek female artist Anaxandra within a chapter entitled 'Women as Well as Men Capable of Perfection'. And of course, some consider the first 'named' artist to have been a woman: Kora of Sicyon (*c*.650 BC), described by Pliny the Elder in his *Natural Histories* (AD 77), who drew the silhouette of her lover on a rock.

More recently, although still decades before the women's movement, the British writer Walter Shaw Sparrow (1862–1940) compiled and edited a substantial survey entitled *Women Painters of the World*. Seen from a twenty-first-century perspective, it is easy to be critical of this book: his notion of 'the world' encompasses only North America and parts of Europe, and his choice of vocabulary – with phrases such as 'the gentler sex' – now feels dated. However, in his preface, he touches on some of the fundamental issues that would come to concern feminists later in the century: the need to explore assumptions about the definition of 'genius' in art; the issue of whether a fundamentally feminine art style exists; and the question: 'Is a woman artist equal to any man among the greatest masters?'[1]

His book is also engaging for its fine period design and its multiplicity of printing techniques and paper stocks. Of particular interest is a small erratum slip attached into the binding within the contents pages. Printed on thick matte paper in red ink, it explains that images of works by nine additional – and at the time contemporary – painters had been featured in a supplement added after the rest of the book had gone to press. One can only imagine Sparrow's frustration, having finally completed his 332-page magnum opus, to have yet more artists to include. He hints that there were more than just those nine, stating, 'It is hoped that the Women Painters of Today may be studied again in the second volume ... there are thousands of ladies who now win a place in the art exhibitions of Europe and America.' No such

1. *Women Painters of the World from the time of Caterina Vigri, 1413–1463, to Rosa Bonheur and the Present Day*, edited by Walter Shaw Sparrow, (London: Hodder & Stoughton and New York: Frederick A. Stokes, 1905), p.11

volume was made, and Sparrow went on instead to author numerous mono-graphs on (male) artists in the 'Art and Life Library' series.

Sparrow's survey was published towards the end of the era of the 'lady painter' – a term used to describe ladies of leisure who undertook painting as an amateur, genteel pastime, as endorsed by etiquette guides. A number of those included in his survey had aristocratic titles. However, the willing-ness of the artists to have their work illustrated in the book suggests that they took their practice seriously and recognized the importance of their names being printed in an art historical publication. While acceptance of their work into exhibitions was a step forward compared to the experien-ces of previous generations of female artists, and while some exhibitions do make history, it is in books where history endures. Indeed, if it weren't for Sparrow's book, it is quite likely that several of the 200 or so artists he memorialized in print would have been completely forgotten in the interve-ning century.

WHAT'S IN A NAME?
Sparrow certainly understood the importance of names when it comes to art history: the book's subtitle mentions two: *From the time of Caterina Vigri, 1413–1463, to Rosa Bonheur and the Present Day.* The former indicates its historical scope,[2] important to evidence the fact that women being recog-nized as makers of high art was not simply a recent fad. The latter name was one of the best-known female artists of the time. Mention of Bonheur (p.65) offered a familiar name to catch the reader's attention and provide reassurance of the quality of the other artists within. In the history of art – of Western[3] cultures at least – the importance of the named producer took a firm hold after it became widespread for artists to sign their work. This practice grew in significance during the early Renaissance, a period that saw art production shift from cooperative guild systems towards the celebration of individual creativity (albeit often with extensive workshops behind the 'name'), meaning that successful artists needed to protect their personal brand. The perceived significance – and financial value – of art in the Western tradition is still almost entirely dictated by *who* made it, rather than *how* it was made.

The centrality of the 'authored' artwork has continued to hold sway des-pite expanding definitions of art in the early twentieth century – from the

2. Recently, scholars have rejected the attribution of artworks to Vigri and described her reputation as a painter as more legendary than factual, so she is not included in the present volume

3. 'Western' was originally a description or category of art produced in Europe or by those with European heritage (e.g. in North America) from Classical to modern times. Recently, it has been used more broadly to describe art with stylistic or cultural connections to the traditions of European art history, including art produced elsewhere in the world. Many contemporary artists and writers now question or reject the term entirely on account of the entrenched value judgements it is assumed to repre-sent, and thus the negative implications for any art outside of the 'Western' canon of art history

INTRODUCTION

employment of the 'ready-made' or 'found' object, to the extremes of Conceptual art in which nothing tangible need be made at all. Perhaps it is because of the move away from the *hand* of the artist to the *mind* of the artist, that the notion of a named artistic creator has become even more entrenched. Even in an era where increasing numbers of artists are working collaboratively, producing work under combined or assumed identities, the importance of their output having specified, authenticated 'creators' has endured. This obsession with names is epitomized in the opening line of E.H. Gombrich's introduction to *The Story of Art* (1950) – which went on to become the world's best-selling art history book – in which he stated, 'There really is no such thing as Art. There are only artists.'[4]

But if art history is an account of producers rather than products, who decides which names are included? And what does it mean if the names recorded and remembered are almost exclusively of one sex? Gombrich's telling of art history – which commences with some of the earliest-known demonstrations of human creativity: the prehistoric cave paintings in Lascaux, France – featured no female artists in the English edition, and only one in the German edition[5] (Käthe Kollwitz, p.221). Of course, Gombrich is far from the exception in this. There is precedence that goes right back to the birth of the discipline. The first edition of Giorgio Vasari's seminal *The Lives of the Most Excellent Painters, Sculptors, and Architects* (1550) included just one woman (Properzia de' Rossi, p.343), although the second edition (1568) featured a few more (Plautilla Nelli, p.296; Lucrezia Quistelli, p.329; and Sofonisba Anguissola, p.35). While this may seem a token gesture, it nevertheless proved important for researchers working centuries later who might otherwise have been led to believe, from the multitude of androcentric art books published in the intervening years that made no mention of female artists whatsoever, that women simply did not make art. Vasari's foundational text indicated that they did, and at the highest level – he quotes the divine Ariosto, 'Women have achieved excellence in every art they have given care to'.[6] This being the case, it seemed likely that there were others, lost to time, waiting to be rediscovered.

4. E.H. Gombrich, *The Story of Art* (London: Phaidon Press Limited, 16th edition, 1995), p.15

5. In 1995 Kollwitz was added into the English version, from the 16th edition onwards

6. Giorgio Vasari, *The Lives of the Most Excellent Painters, Sculptors, and Architects*, trans. Gaston du C. de Vere (London: Philip Lee Warner, 1912–14), v: 127–8

SOME ARE BORN GREAT...

This leads us to Linda Nochlin's celebrated 1971 essay, 'Why Have There Been No Great Women Artists?'[7] It would be remiss to introduce a survey of women artists without discussion of this polemical text (which is also referenced in this book's title). In this essay, Nochlin encouraged art historians to rethink their approach to unearthing forgotten female artists. She stated that while women artists could be 'interesting and very good' none was 'supremely great'[8] and to understand why, she urged consideration of what prevented women from attaining the same standard of greatness as their male peers. She argued that the institutions by which artists historically came to be educated and promoted had actively excluded women, and that this was because of the patriarchal ideologies out of which such institutions were created and whose needs they served to uphold. She further suggested that the notion of 'greatness' itself, which one might consider a neutral given, was itself a cultural construct, and for women artists, a vicious circle. Nochlin highlighted how the long-held art-historical ranking system by which different genres of painting were valued – 'history painting' (scenes from history, religion or mythology) being the highest, followed respectively by portraiture, genre (domestic scenes), landscape and still life – had the effect of excluding women from greatness, as they were denied access to the study of the nude figure via life classes, absolutely essential training for those aspiring to the highest-status genre. Her overall thesis is summarized in the much-quoted line:

> The arts, as in a hundred other areas, are stultifying, oppressive, and discouraging to all those, women among them, who did not have the good fortune to be born white, preferably middle class, and above all, male. The fault lies not in our stars, our hormones, our menstrual cycles, or our empty internal spaces, but in our institutions and our education.[9]

What Nochlin did not address, however, was the possibility that perceptions of 'greatness' in art could shift in time and space, rather than being fixed in perpetuity, and that there could be multiple definitions of greatness in existence at once. What is considered great in one era may not be valued in another. What is cherished and celebrated in one culture is not so highly prized elsewhere. If greatness is not inherent to art itself, but rather imposed upon it – in the eye of the beholder and through his institutions – then, rather than getting caught up in debates about whether any historical women artist can ever be as 'great' as the Old Masters, perhaps it is

7. First published as 'Why Are There No Great Women Artists?' in *Woman in Sexist Society: Studies in Power and Powerlessness*, edited by Vivian Gornick and Barbara Moran (New York: Basic Books, 1970), Nochlin's essay was revised and retitled 'Why Have There Been No Great Women Artists?' and published in *ARTNews*, January 1971, p.22

8. *Women Artists: The Linda Nochlin Reader*, edited by Maura Reilly (London: Thames & Hudson, 2015), p.45

9. Ibid., p.46

more meaningful to put aside the idea of a single, fixed standard and consider that there is a multiplicity of ways in which art can be appreciated and valued, depending in particular on who is looking.

A GREAT ARTIST, PERIOD

Nochlin's essay continues to divide feminist art scholars as to whether effort should be spent researching – and reattributing – art by women within the dominant (male) canon, or whether, once the obstacles women faced in pursuing an artistic career are taken into account, their art needs to be judged by other criteria, despite the risk that the latter approach implies some universal 'feminine essence' uniting their work.

Artists themselves, particularly those whose careers commenced after the late nineteenth century – once routes to becoming a professional artist became more open to women – have often resisted their work being categorized in relation to their own sex for fear of being ghettoized or belittled. In 1976, Georgia O'Keeffe (p.301) refused to lend a painting for the exhibition 'Women Artists: 1550–1950', curated by Nochlin, at the Los Angeles County Museum of Art,[10] and is said to have stated that she didn't want to be known as a great woman artist, but as a 'great artist, period'.[11] Similarly, in 1990, Dorothea Tanning (p.399) rejected the term 'woman artist', saying, 'It's just as much a contradiction in terms as "man artist" or "elephant artist".'[12] Artists generally consider themselves as more connected to their contemporary creative peers – male and female – than to any kind of universal womanhood that stretches across time and place.

In the twenty-first century, it might seem irrelevant to talk about artists in terms of gender at all. Women artists today are certainly no longer limited to making art about 'suitable' subjects (the domestic sphere, flowers, motherhood, etc.) or to using particular materials (as they were even in the otherwise radical Bauhaus School, see Anni Albers, p.29, where women were confined to 'feminine' arenas, such as weaving). However, while artworks themselves might not reveal whether their maker was male or female, in the surrounding structures of the art world – where art is exhibited, traded and written about – male artists are still likely to be more successful by any number of measures. They are more likely to have representation by a commercial gallery.[13] They achieve higher prices in the art market (at the time of writing, the top price paid at auction for a painting

10. Hilarie M. Sheets, 'Female Artists Are (Finally) Getting Their Turn', *The New York Times*, 29 March 2016

11. Jocelyn Murphy, 'A Bold Legacy', *Northwest Arkansas Democrat Gazette*, 27 May 2018

12. Dorothea Tanning interview with Carlo McCormick, *BOMB Magazine*, 1 October 1990

13. For a useful source of regularly updated statistics on these issues, see the National Museum of Women in the Arts: https://nmwa.org/advocate/get-facts

by a living male artist is $80m as compared with $12.4m for a living female artist;[14] for deceased artists it is $300m versus $44.4m[15]). They are more likely to be written about by critics and art historians (who are themselves, more likely to be male). More than forty years after Nochlin's essay, men artists continue to enjoy crucial institutional advantages, with their work more likely to be collected by – and actually put on display in – public museums, the ultimate destination for artists looking to secure their place in history.

REBALANCING ACTS

Museums, as the primary custodians of our cultural heritage, have long understood the importance of name recognition for blockbuster exhibitions to attract visitors. In displays of permanent collections, too, curators may find it difficult to justify allocating space to exhibit lesser-known artists' works among the usual 'old favourites'. As critic Jerry Saltz conceded, in one of many texts he has written about the problem of gender imbalance at New York's Museum of Modern Art, he states that curators are 'obliged to show MoMA's many icons, lest audiences feel cheated out of their $25 admission'.[16] Another critic, Helen Gørrill, believes that things are actually worse now for contemporary female artists than they were in the 1990s, putting the blame squarely at the door of museums' acquisition policies.[17] Yet for many commentators, things do seem to have improved in recent years, with significant shifts beyond mere tokenism, as Laura Cumming noted, in her art round-up of 2018: 'For the first time, artists who happen to be women were given the museum surveys they deserve without any implication that this was special, unusual, some kind of positive discrimination or curatorial bias.'[18]

Such shifts have occurred because of personnel changes within particular institutions, with new curators bringing fresh approaches, but in many cases have also been a result of deliberate policy changes within public museums seeking to better represent a wider range of artistic voices, to mirror the diversity of the populations they serve. These decisions can prove controversial: for example, in 2018 Baltimore Museum of Art de-acquisitioned seven works by white, male artists who were well represented in the collection, including Robert Rauschenberg and Andy Warhol, in order to fund the purchase of more works by women and artists of colour;[19] while in 2009 the Centre Georges Pompidou, Paris, removed

14. David Hockney vs Jenny Saville: both prices reached in 2018

15. Willem de Kooning vs Georgia O'Keeffe, prices reached in 2015 and 2014 respectively

16. Jerry Saltz, 'My Final Word on MoMA's Woman Problem', *Vulture*, 20 November 2013

17. Helen Gørrill, 'Are Women Artists Worth Collecting? Tate doesn't Seem to Think So', *The Guardian*, 13 August 2018

18. Laura Cumming, 'Best Art of 2018', *The Observer*, 30 December 2018

19. Julia Halperin, '"It Is an Unusual and Radical Act": Why the Baltimore Museum is Selling Blue-Chip Art to Buy Work by Underrepresented Artists', *artnet news*, 30 April 2018

male artists from the Musée National d'Art Moderne collection display for a year, making space to show the result of five years of proactively acquiring work by female artists.[20] Historic art museums have joined this rebalancing act, with both the Museo del Prado, Madrid, and Galleria degli Uffizi, Florence, promoting their commitment to show more female artists, starting with solo exhibitions by Clara Peeters[21] (p.315) and Plautilla Nelli[22] (p.296), respectively.

#WOMENARTISTS

As important as these institutional changes have been in raising the profile of female artists in recent years, the Internet, and social media in particular, have also played a big part. Cutting through seemingly infinite content, hashtags such as #womenartists, #femaleartist, #womensart have enabled burgeoning online communities of interested people to connect and disseminate information and images. There are a number of popular accounts on Twitter, Instagram and Facebook that focus solely on female artists – sharing hundreds, sometimes thousands, of photographs of artworks, and reinforcing both the quantity and quality of (often little-known) women art-makers past and present to an enthusiastic audience of followers.

While it is refreshing to see so many fresh and varied examples, as opposed to the same few names, it is nevertheless worth reflecting on the precarious nature of online content. Many social media accounts have no formal copyright clearance on the images they post, working on the basis that they can easily remove content if challenged later. Copyright holders such as artists, estates, galleries and museums have, to date, had a relaxed attitude regarding reproduction of artworks on social media, believing perhaps – for female practitioners in particular – that all exposure is good. But as the commercial potential of social media becomes more explicit and exploited, this may rapidly change. Indeed, the very existences of the platforms that host these accounts are by no means guaranteed – digital technologies change notoriously quickly and once-dominant software and brands can rapidly become obsolete, replaced by new platforms for user-generated content. This was demonstrated in 2017 when the video-sharing app Vine was unexpectedly withdrawn, with technology commentators noting that, 'Popular platforms can wither just as quickly as they bloom.'[23] Books, in comparison, are a technology that has already endured in the physical world for centuries. Furthermore, while they record history as a written

20. Emmanuelle Lequeux, 'Le Centre Pompidou glorifie les femmes au risque de les placer dans un ghetto', *Le Monde*, 28 May 2009

21. Alyssa Buffenstein, 'Museo del Prado Opens First Ever Exhibition Dedicated to a Female Artist', *artnet news*, 26 October 2016

22. Alyssa Buffenstein, 'Uffizi Gallery Launches Plan to Show More Women Artists', *artnet news*, 2 February 2017

23. Emma Jacobs, 'Death of Vine is a warning to social media stars and big brands', *Financial Times*, 18 January 2017

account on the page, they also capture and represent the moment in history from which they came, unlike their volatile online cousins, which can be modified repeatedly and without warning or declaration. In an era of fake news and retrospectively doctored Internet content, the constancy of the printed word has revitalized worth.

REMEMBER HER NAME

A book has its own inherent limitations, not least being of a fixed, physical nature. While presenting over 400 women artists, each illustrated with an artwork, represents a substantial undertaking by any standards of print publishing, this volume by no means makes claims to be comprehensive – the long-list of possible artists easily reached 2,000 names, all of whom would have been valid inclusions. The final selection was made with consideration of a number of factors, with the chief aim being to create as varied a representation of art as possible: from different historic periods, made by artists from across the world and created using diverse forms and materials. The very nature of the project (only known/named artists, and always featuring an image of their work) meant some inevitable exclusions: for example, women we know of from written accounts, including many pre-Renaissance, but where no artwork is extant; artworks where attribution is questioned and objects or images from cultures where the notion of attaching a name to a creative object is simply not part of their traditions. This also applies to work of great skill and value that was categorized separately as 'craft' or 'applied arts', for many centuries, excluded from art-historical accounts, the names of makers now lost to time even while the work itself has been carefully conserved and is valued highly.

In this book, we chose to include female-born artists who later adopted gender-ambiguous identities, and also the work of male-born artists who transitioned to identify as female, but excluded are artworks co-created by male and female artist duos or collectives. Such decisions were made to create boundaries for the selection rather than to comment on the quality of art made by any practitioners who are not included. Texts accompanying the images have also often faced the 'man question' – whether to mention the name of male artists at all, for fear that women may too easily become categorized as 'followers' rather than 'pioneers'. Other female-focused art books have taken the decision to strictly exclude any mention of males whatsoever, but to do this denies and misunderstands the way artistic circles, networks and relationships function, with exchanges of ideas being two-way and ongoing processes. The intention of this book is not to erase the reader's pre-existing knowledge of the art of the past, but to enhance and expand it.

The choice of just one artwork per artist was not an easy task. To help readers navigate such an extensive book featuring what may be a number of unfamiliar names, the selection of works has tended towards the best-known, most iconic examples – often those held in a public collection – although, in the case of living artists, their preference, when provided, was followed. A number of the accompanying texts also reference other important artworks to provide as broad an overview of the artist's practice as possible in these short essays.

Our overall hope is that readers will use this volume as an aide-mémoire and a point of departure, to prompt and support further explorations – to read more, see more and share more art made by women throughout history, until the names in this book are as well known as so many of their male counterparts, and until there is no need to ask whether an artwork is made by a male or a female because equality, across all institutions of the art world, has finally been reached. Until then, we encourage readers to let go of any narrow, singular definitions of greatness and to embrace every forgotten, overlooked or undervalued artist featured in these pages, and above all, to remember her name.

MAGDALENA ABAKANOWICZ

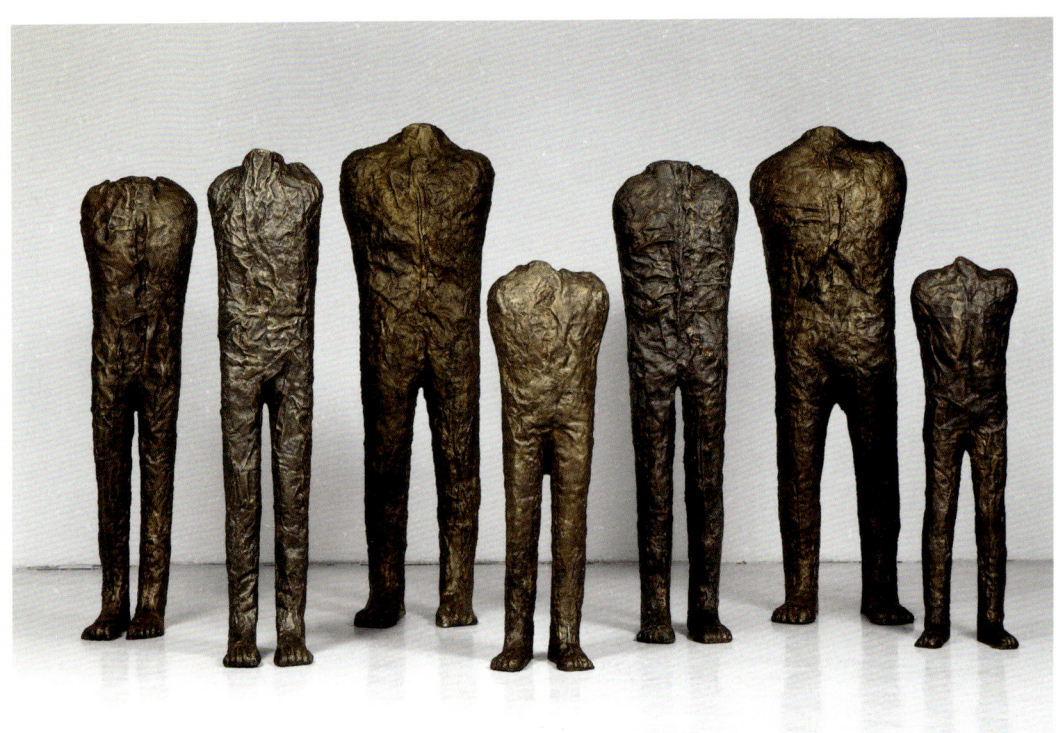

THE GROUP OF SEVEN

2012, bronze, overall: *c*.152.4 × 335.3 cm (60 × 132 in), each from h: 110.5 cm (43 ½ in) to h: 161.3 cm (63 ½ in), private collection
Magdalena Abakanowicz, born Marta Abakanowicz, 1930, Falenty, Poland. Died 2017, Warsaw.

Abakanowicz was just nine years old when her aristocratic family life on a country estate outside Warsaw was turned upside down by the outbreak of the Second World War. Her mother survived being shot by German soldiers but was severely wounded, and while working as a medical aide, Abakanowicz was caught up in the failed Warsaw Uprising of 1944. Under Soviet rule, the family left their home to avoid class recriminations, moving to a town near the coast. Changing her first name, Abakanowicz

enrolled at the Academy of Fine Arts in Warsaw in 1950, where creative freedom was curtailed under Stalinism. Enduring decades of repression, her sculptural practice addressed universal themes, including existence, oppression and corporeality. Exhibiting internationally from the late 1960s onwards, she achieved critical acclaim with abstract and figurative textile and mixed-media works, and later in her career worked increasingly with metal, creating monumental public works such as *Agora* (2006) for Grant Park, Chicago, comprising over a hundred bodies. This work, on a more domestic scale, demonstrates her ability to capture the existential essence of human experience, together with her mastery of the medium of bronze.

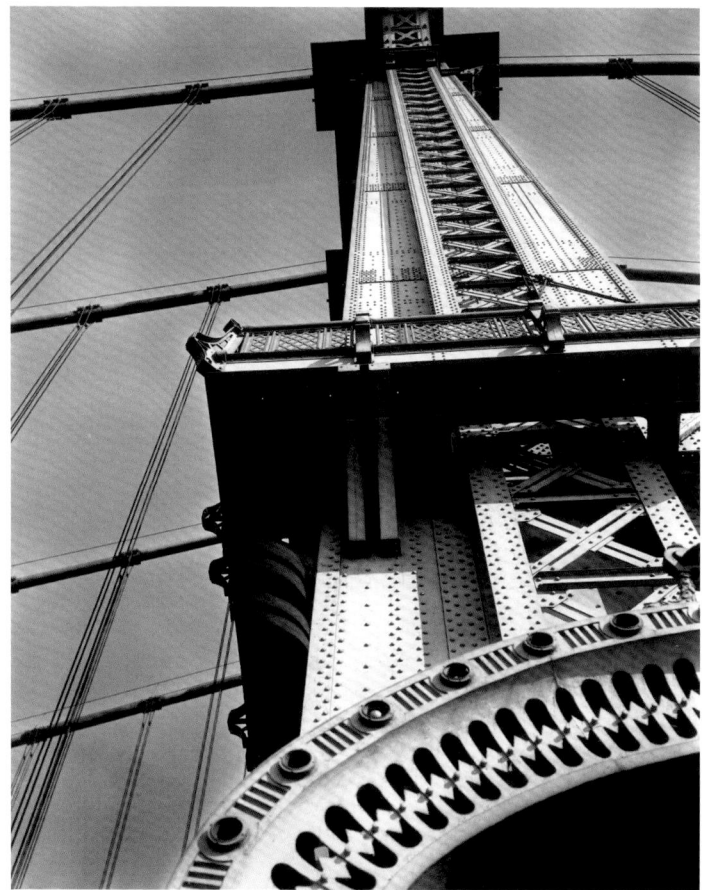

MANHATTAN BRIDGE LOOKING UP
1936, gelatin silver print, 24.5 × 19.4 cm (9 ⅝ × 7 ⅝ in), Metropolitan Museum of Art, New York
Berenice Abbott, born 1898, Springfield, Ohio. Died 1991, Monson, Maine.

Abbott was a noted portraitist of twentieth-century cultural figures, photographing the likes of Jean Cocteau, James Joyce and Peggy Guggenheim, but she has been remembered, above all, for her architectural studies. Part of the Straight Photography movement, her images were characterized by high contrast, sharp focus and attention to the form of the subject. Studying theatre and sculpture in Paris and Berlin, Abbott did not embark on photography until becoming a studio assistant to Man Ray (1890–1976). Introduced to the work of Eugène Atget (1857–1927), whom she photographed shortly before his death, Abbott became fascinated with his style and was instrumental in saving Atget's posthumous legacy, buying many of his glass slides and vintage prints, which she distributed among important museums. Returning to America in the 1930s she pursued documentary photography in New York, closely observing urban life and its aesthetics and people, and supporting herself with commercial work and teaching. This photograph – which provides a vertiginous perspective on the iconic suspension bridge over the Hudson River – is part of a series produced between 1935 and 1939 entitled 'Changing New York', which was produced for the Federal Art Project.

NINA CHANEL ABNEY

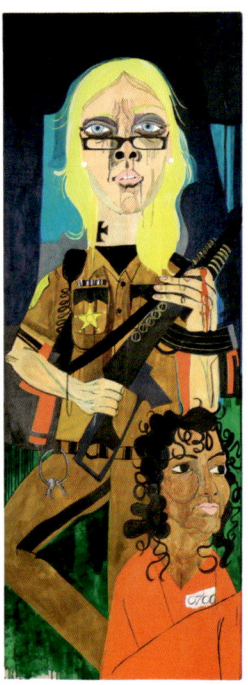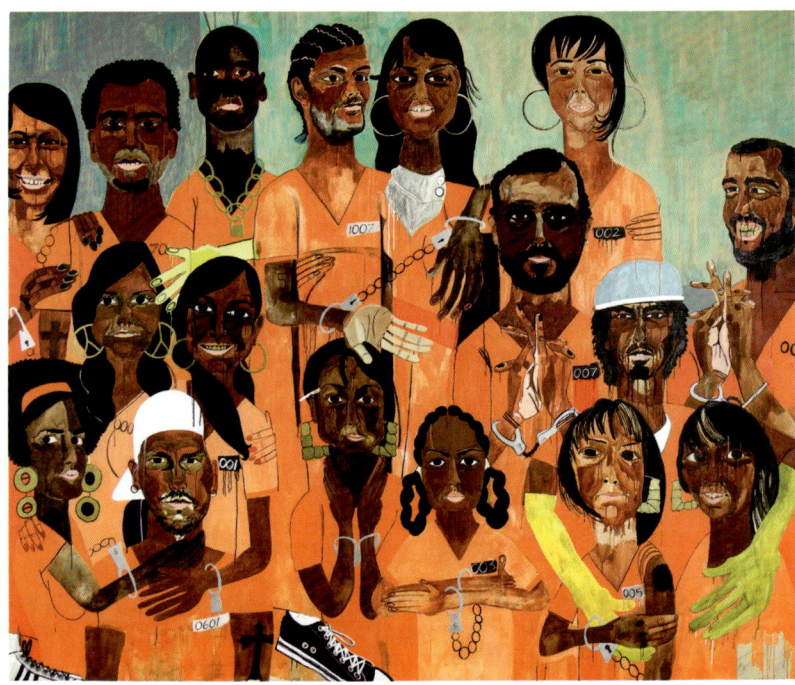

CLASS OF 2007

2007, acrylic on canvas, diptych, overall: 289.6 × 464.8 cm (114 × 183 in),
Rubell Family Collection, Miami
Nina Chanel Abney, born 1982, Chicago.

Exploring issues of ethnicity, gender and politics, Abney is an
African-American artist who explores race to subversive effect in
her paintings. Social injustice and contemporary protest movements
such as Black Lives Matter are reimagined by Abney; critique
and humour combine as satire, with works often featuring emoji
symbols and incomplete text. Her bright fragmented tableaux recall
early American modernist paintings, as well as public murals and
urban street art. Abney often uses spray paint and stencils, as exemplified by this painting, which was exhibited in her acclaimed MFA
exhibition at Parsons School of Design, New York. A race-swap
diptych depicts Abney as a white, blonde guard carrying a gun, while
her all-white classmates have become black inmates, corralled
together in orange uniforms. Abney highlights the racial imbalance
of mass incarceration in the United States and of achievement being
stifled along racial lines, black Americans statistically being less
likely to attend college and more likely to go to prison than their
white counterparts. Acquired by the Rubell Contemporary Arts
Foundation, it was subsequently included in its influential touring
exhibition '30 Americans', which travelled across the United
States for over a decade from 2008 onwards.

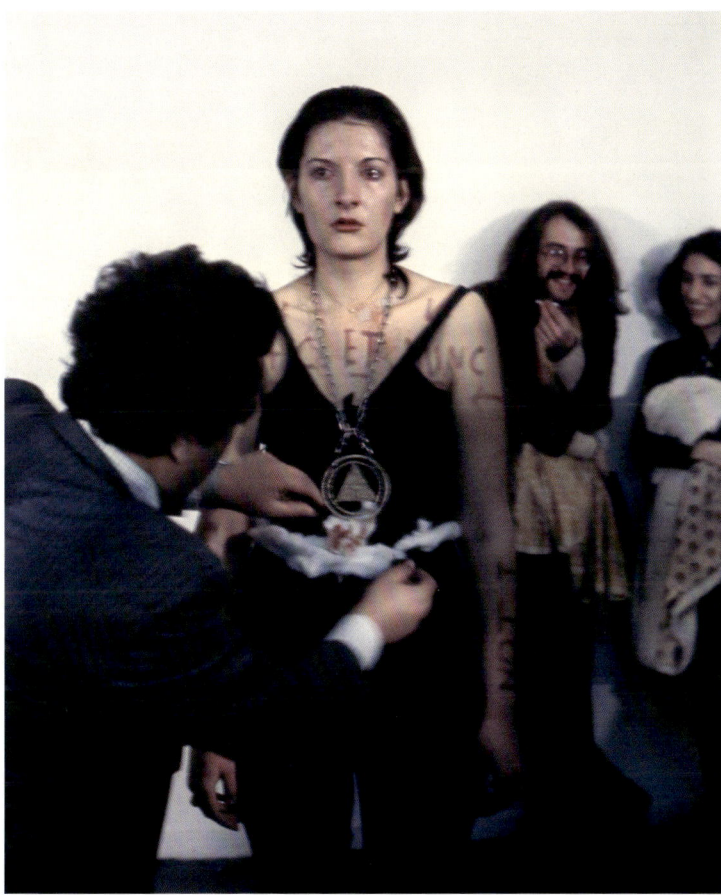

RHYTHM 0

1974, performance, 6 hrs, Studio Morra, Naples
Marina Abramović, born 1946, Belgrade, Serbia (then Yugoslavia).

One of the world's most famous performance artists following her 736.5-hour epic *The Artist is Present* at the Museum of Modern Art, New York, in 2010, Abramović initially studied painting at the Academy of Fine Arts in her home town of Belgrade from 1965 to 1970, and then in Zagreb from 1970 to 1972. As a student, she began to explore the possibilities of using her own body and mind as artistic materials. Her performances, whether for a live public or for the camera, have pushed at the limits of mental and physical endurance with their spiritual and emotional transformation of both artist and viewer. This is exemplified in *Rhythm 0*, where

Abramović stood motionless in a gallery and allowed viewers to interact with her body as they desired. Props were provided, ranging from food and a feather to more dangerous objects, including scissors and a loaded gun. The performance was stopped when someone held the pistol to her head. Abramović collaborated with her partner, the German-born artist Ulay (1943–2020), from 1976 until the end of their relationship in 1988. She has since opened her own school for performance art, the Marina Abramović Institute, dedicated to durational work using what she terms The Abramović Method.

TOMMA ABTS

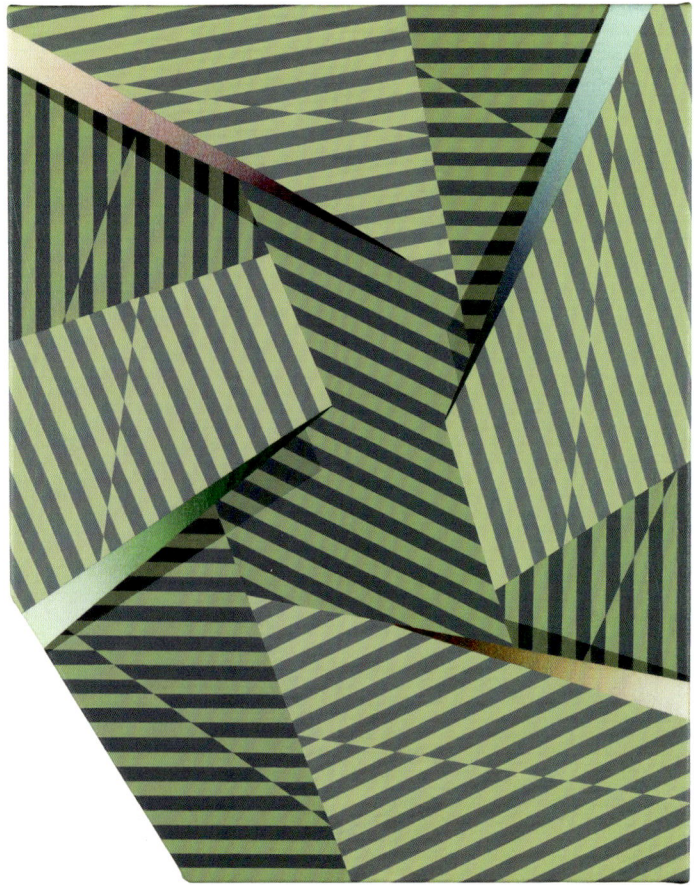

FENKE

2014, acrylic and oil on canvas, 48 × 38 cm (18 ⅞ × 15 in), promised gift to the Los Angeles County Museum of Art by Alice and Nahum Lainer

Tomma Abts, born 1967, Kiel, Germany.

Winner of the 2006 Turner Prize, Abts is a London-based abstract painter with a unique process of sustained engagement. 'When I start a painting,' she said in a 2007 interview in *The New Yorker*, 'I have no idea what it will look like. I invent the criteria as I go. Each painting is a remnant of thought processes I've gone through.' In its application of rules, Abts's formal practice is perhaps closer to poetry than painting, her images a lesson not only in looking but also in method. Beginning each work without preconceived ideas – only the scale and the materials are fixed – her abstraction feels controlled yet spontaneous. An heir to the visual games of Op art and its artists such as Bridget Riley (p.336), she constantly fractures their illusions. Compositions overlap and intersect, surfaces and patterns recede, and others reveal themselves. In *Fenke*, three layers are at work – the original wash, the *trompe l'oeil* folded and striped paper-like surface, and the wall behind the canvas, which is emphasized due to a slice cut from the corner of the canvas. The result is a painting that allows the viewer to appreciate the tension between improvisation and constraint.

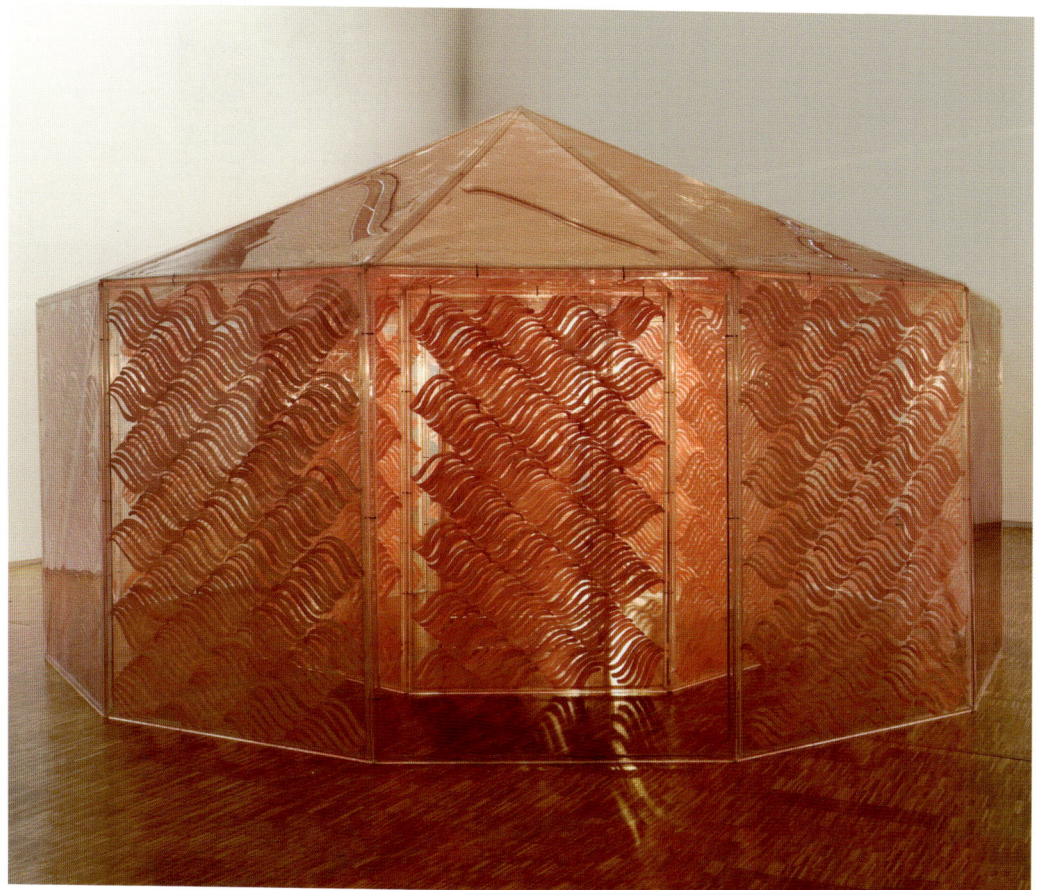

TRIPLE TENT

1969–71, varnish on Sicofoil mounted on Plexiglas, 255 × 438 × 438 cm (100 × 172 × 172 in), Musée National d'Art Moderne, Centre Georges Pompidou, Paris

Carla Accardi, born 1924, Trapani, Italy. Died 2014, Rome.

Educated at the Accademia di Belle Arti in Palermo and later in Florence, Accardi moved to Rome in 1946. Here she co-founded 'Forma 1', a group of abstract painters who defined themselves as Marxist Formalists. Their first exhibition took place the following year in Rome's Art Club, alongside which they published a journal on contemporary aesthetics. Initially making black-and-white paintings, by the mid-1960s she was experimenting with vibrant colour, and in a rejection of painterly tradition, began to use Sicofoil

– a transparent plastic – in place of canvas. Her series of painted tent pieces, such as *Triple Tent*, used this material sculpturally, creating intimate installations that demonstrate the tension between nomadism and homemaking. With her interest in simple everyday materials and a rough-edged aesthetic that did not conceal labour, Accardi was influential on the Arte Povera artists. A fervent supporter of the women's liberation movement, in the 1970s she co-founded the feminist collective and publishing house *Rivolta Femminile* ('Feminine Revolt') with critic Carla Lonzi. By the 1980s she had returned to using canvas, becoming interested in the use of signs and juxtapositions of colour in her later works.

ETEL ADNAN

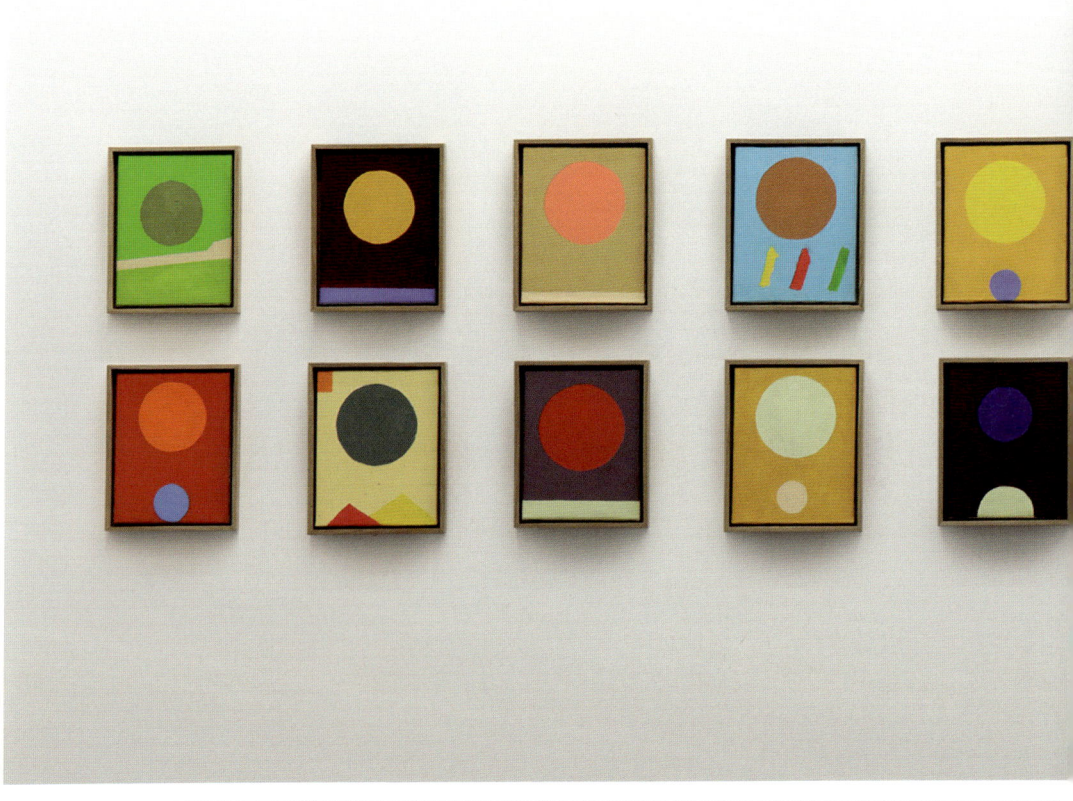

THE WEIGHT OF THE WORLD 1–20

2016, oil on canvas, each 30 × 24 cm (11 ¾ × 9 ½ in), installation view, 'Etel Adnan: The Weight of the World', Serpentine Sackler Gallery, London, 2016
Etel Adnan, born 1925, Beirut. Died 2021, Paris.

Colour is an elemental force in the compositions of this Lebanese-American artist, who is also celebrated internationally as a poet and writer. Adnan's intensely sensorial paintings, tapestries and verse are largely inspired by the natural world, as well as by her cultural experiences of childhood in a multilingual milieu and peripatetic life as an adult, moving between Beirut, Paris and Sausalito, California. For Adnan, images were an expression of pure feeling. Her early abstract paintings evoked landscapes using geometric blocks of colour, often anchored around a red square. On moving to Sausalito in the 1970s, she became fascinated with Mount Tamalpais, capturing its every mood in a patchwork of hues, just as Paul Cézanne (1839–1906) had done for Mont Sainte-Victoire in Provence. The work seen here distils composition itself into colour and form. Twenty compact canvases each feature a large disc floating above other shapes in a play of hues, suggestive of seas or mountains perhaps. While the title brings to mind the emotional impact of political conflict, which Adnan protested in her writings, these joyful paintings – executed by the artist at the age of ninety-one – exude lightness and sheer energy.

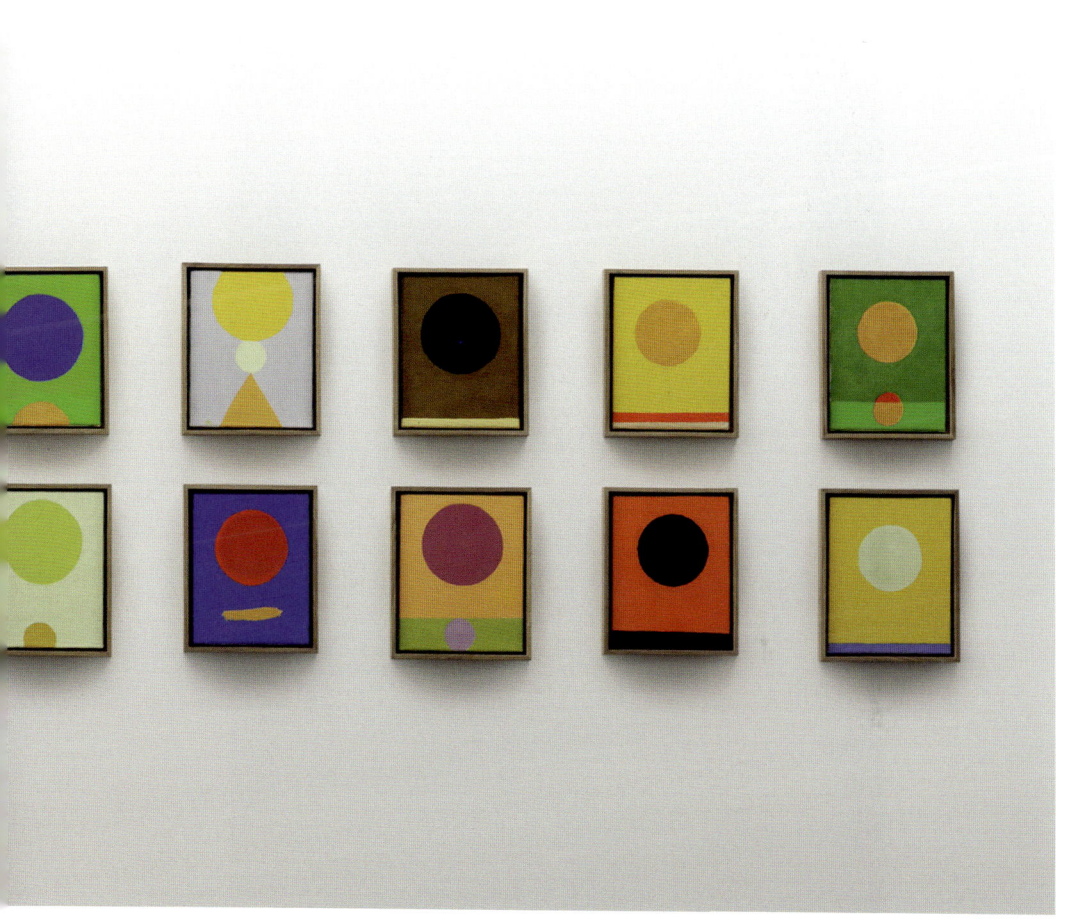

HILMA AF KLINT

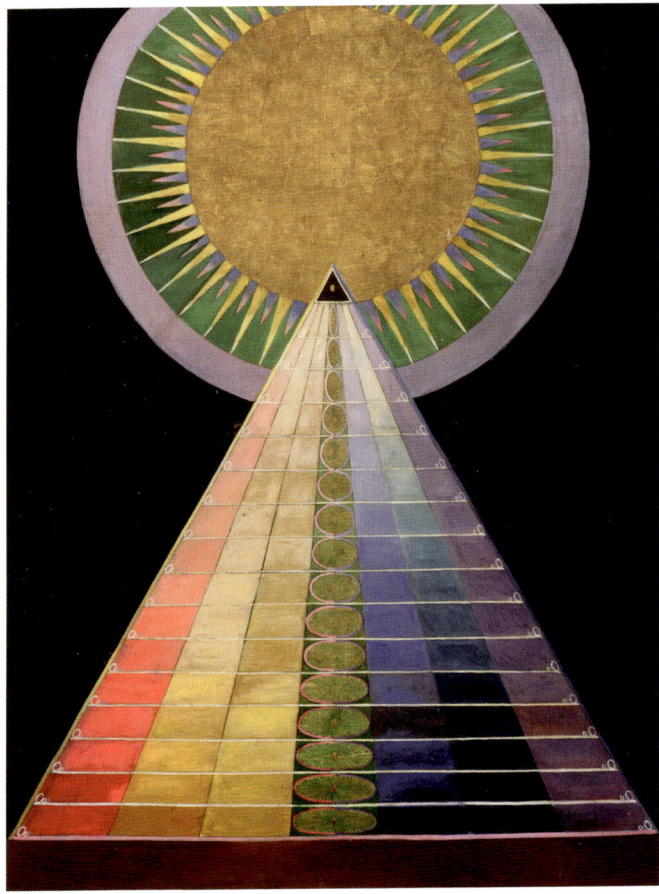

GROUP X, NO.1, ALTARPIECE
1915, oil and metal leaf on canvas, 237.5 × 179.5 cm (93 ½ × 70 ⅝ in), private collection
Hilma af Klint, born 1862, Solna, Sweden. Died 1944, Djursholm, Sweden.

Recent exhibitions have brought af Klint international recognition and acknowledgement that she – and not Wassily Kandinsky (1866–1944) – was the earliest exponent of abstract art. Aged twenty, she was admitted to the Royal Academy of Fine Arts in Stockholm. A public career as a painter of landscapes and portraits followed, while her hermetic work was done in secret. After the death of her sister in 1880, af Klint had been drawn to spiritualist ideas then much in vogue. Participating in séances with a group of fellow female artists called De Fem ('The Five'), she began to channel automatic drawings from 1896. She considered these as made 'through' her, with the artist as medium. Her magnum opus is 'Paintings for the Temple', a series of 193 compositions, including this work, a vibrant schema of spiritual evolution. Believing the world not ready to understand her practice, she stored away over 1,200 paintings, instructing her nephew to keep them secret for twenty years after her death. When they were offered to the Moderna Museet in Stockholm in 1970, the donation was declined. Only gradually has her mystical work come to attention.

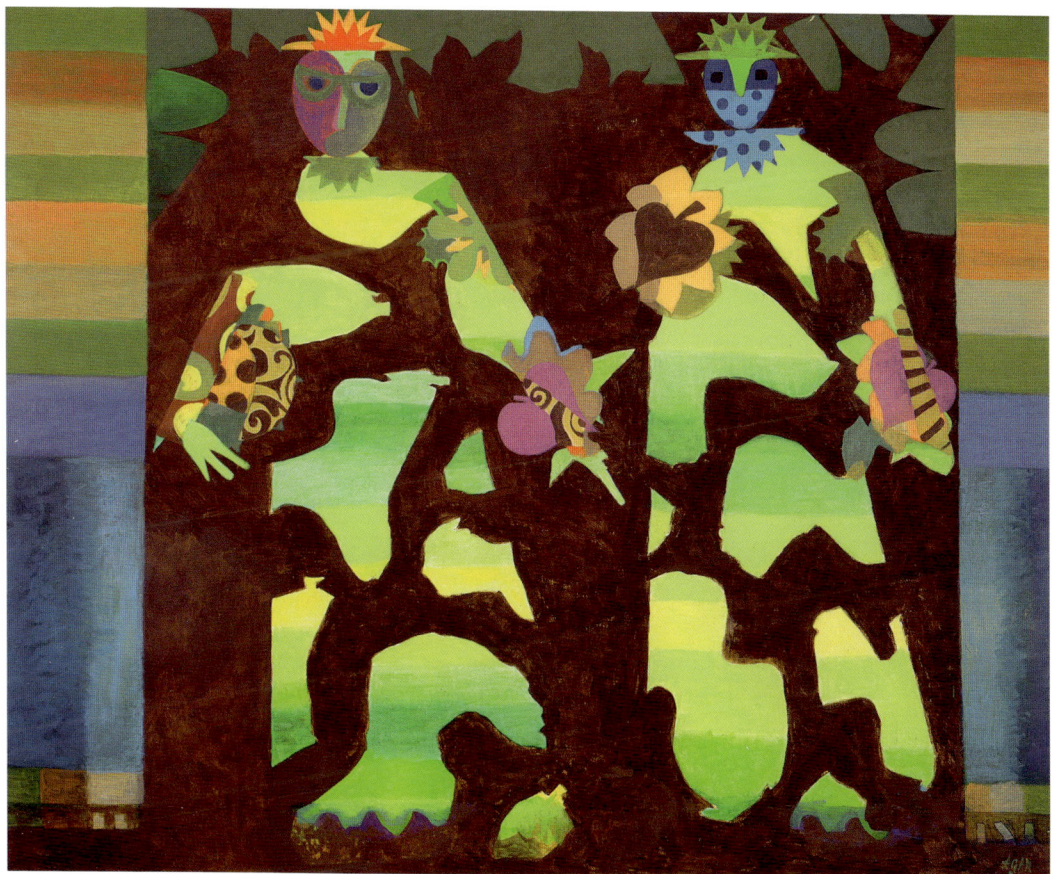

FIGURES IN A GARDEN

1979–81, acrylic on canvas, 122.5 × 153 cm (48¼ × 60¼ in), Tate, London
Eileen Agar, born 1899, Buenos Aires. Died 1991, London.

The daughter of British-American expatriates, Agar encountered Surrealism in Paris in the 1920s, later becoming a founder member of the British Surrealist Group. She had an intense affair with the artist Paul Nash (1889–1946) while holidaying in Dorset with her husband, Joseph Bard. Nash introduced her to the practice of appropriation, the use of found objects to make art. Working in collaboration in the mid-1930s, they made *Seashore Monster at Swanage*, based on a curious creature she discovered in the sand at Lulworth Cove. In 1936 Agar helped organize London's International Surrealist Exhibition at the New Burlington Galleries, becoming a key figure in a network that included Pablo Picasso (1881–1973) and his partner, the artist Dora Maar (p.252), Man Ray (1890–1976), Roland Penrose (1900–84) and Lee Miller (p.273). As well as assemblage, Agar experimented with automatic drawing, photography and collage, and by the late 1960s was painting, favouring acrylic as a medium that allowed for rapid work. This work shows figures dressed in masquerade, their bodies strange colourful fragments found floating in space. Using the techniques of collage, patches of camouflage-like pigment combine to reveal more than is really present on the canvas.

EIJA-LIISA AHTILA

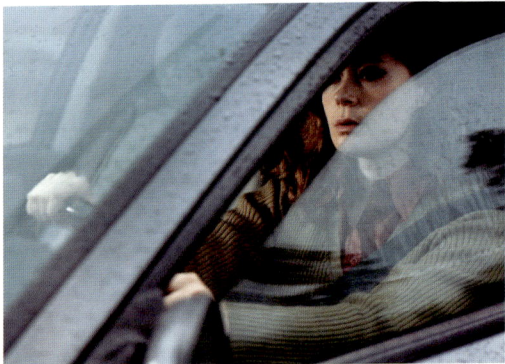
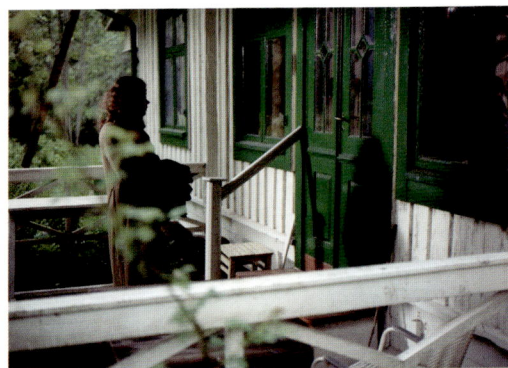
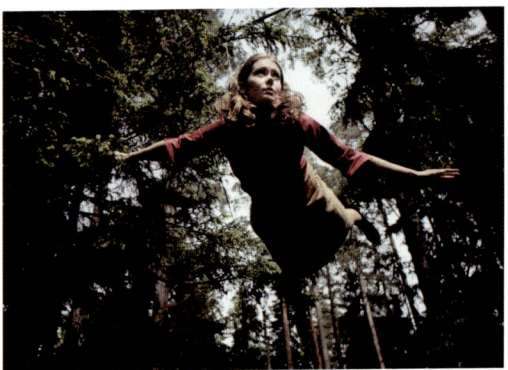
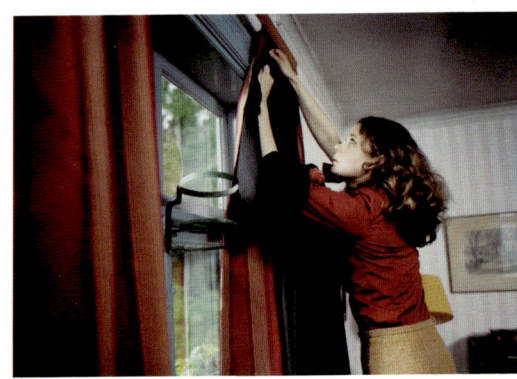

THE HOUSE

2002, 3-channel projected installation, 14 mins, looped, Finnish with
English subtitles
Eija-Liisa Ahtila, born 1959, Hämeenlinna, Finland.

Often presented on multiple screens, Ahtila's narrative-led video
installations cannot be understood from one position. Viewers must
navigate their way around the spaces she creates to make sense of her
unfolding fictions. In her early works the artist addressed the
complex emotions that underpin human relationships, exploring
family dynamics, teenage sexuality and mental health. More
recently she has tackled issues relating to perception and the ways
in which meaning is composed, touching on themes such as religious experience, post-humanism and the question of the animal.

Based on her own research into psychotic disorders, the three-
screen installation *The House* focuses on the experiences of a young
woman with schizophrenia. After entering a secluded house,
the female protagonist is affected by visual and auditory hallucina-
tions in which objects, creatures and sounds from outside appear
to invade her home. Mental fragmentation is evoked by the config-
uration of the screens in the gallery: displayed on separate walls,
they draw the viewer into a disorienting, dreamlike subjectivity
akin to the woman's.

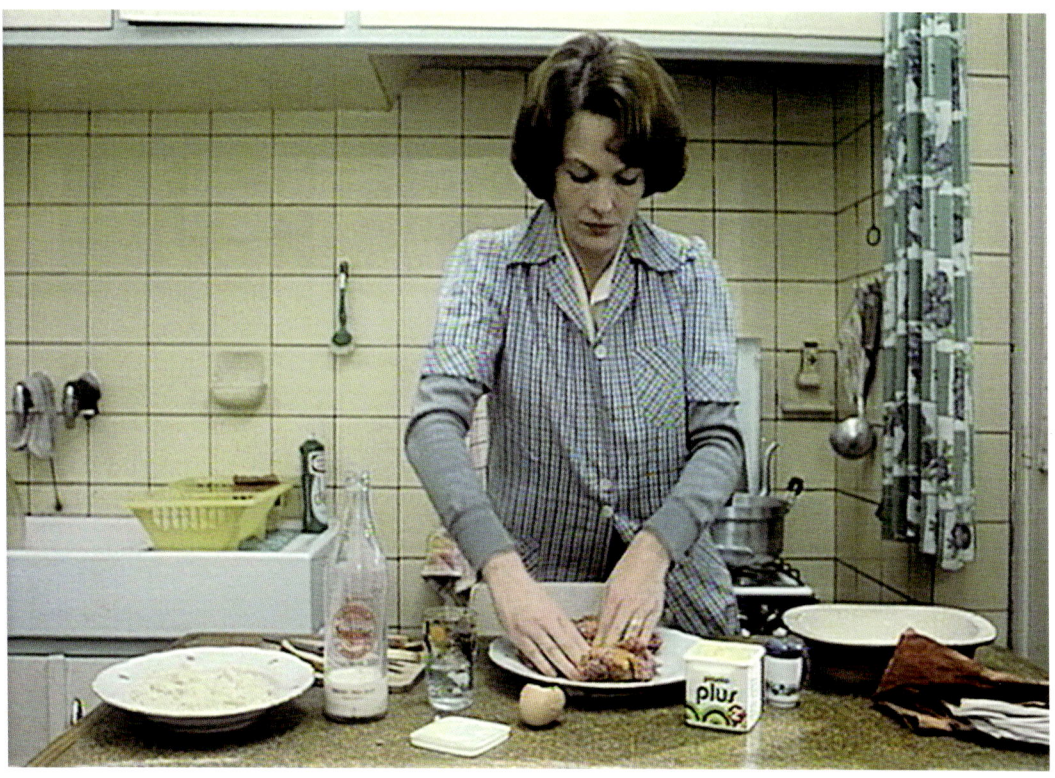

JEANNE DIELMAN, 23, QUAI DU COMMERCE, 1080 BRUXELLES
1975, (film still), 35mm film, colour, sound, 200 mins, production:
Paradise Films, Brussels
Chantal Akerman, born 1950, Brussels. Died 2015, Paris.

Renowned in her lifetime as an innovative filmmaker, Akerman's artistic career began at the age of eighteen. She had dropped out of film school after one term to make the short film *Saute ma ville* (1968), funding it by trading diamond shares on the Antwerp stock exchange. Maternal relationships, gender and the politics of domestic space are central themes in her work. She was close to her own mother, an Auschwitz survivor. Akerman moved to New York in 1971 to make short and feature-length films, experimenting with realist and avant-garde styles, and became recognized as a pioneer of feminist film. *News From Home* (1976) has a soundtrack derived from letters Akerman's mother wrote about everyday life, while *No Home Movie* (2015) is a meditation on her mother's death. The critically acclaimed three-hour piece *Jeanne Dielman* follows the banal and obsessive routines of a Brussels housewife whose quotidian life as a widow and mother is conducted with the same attention to detail as her work as a prostitute. This juxtaposition of female stereotypes becomes blurred and destabilized within a claustrophobic domestic sphere.

NJIDEKA AKUNYILI CROSBY

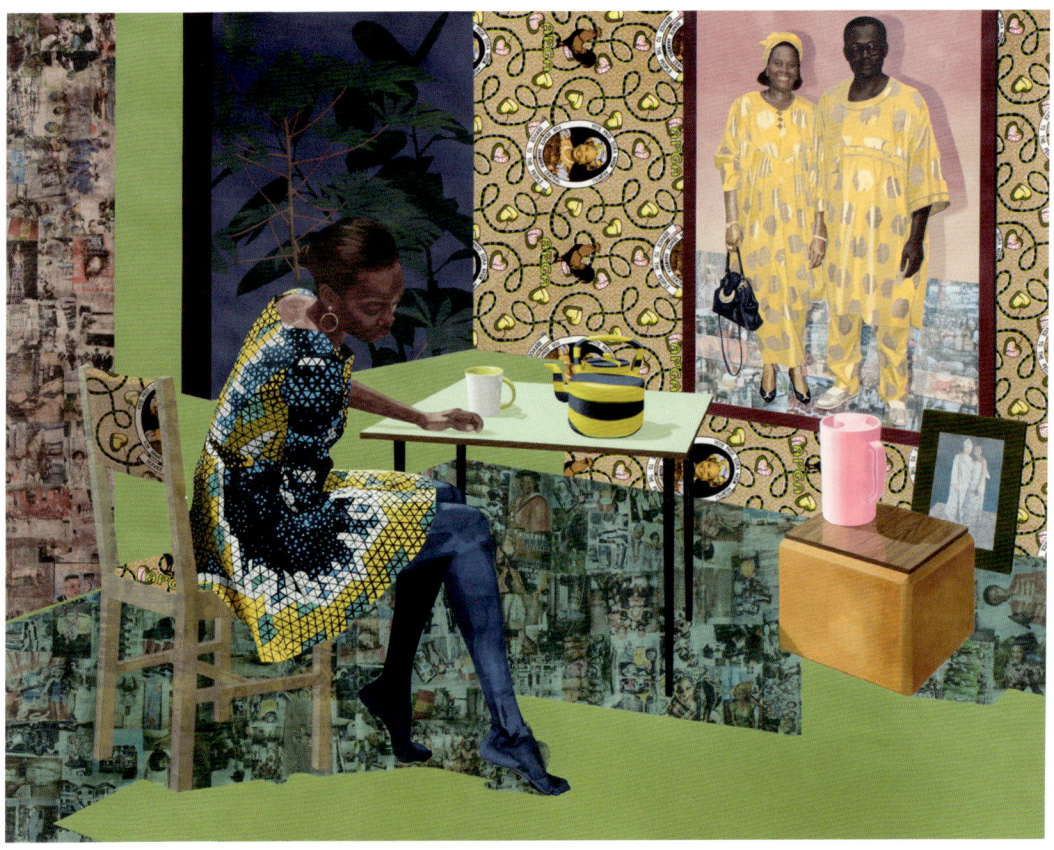

DWELL: ASO EBI

2017, acrylic, transfers, coloured pencil, collage and commemorative fabric on paper, 243.8 × 315 cm (96 × 124 in)

Njideka Akunyili Crosby, born 1983, Enugu, Nigeria.

Akunyili Crosby makes large-scale works on paper, which use detailed photo-transfers collaged as part of paintings. Growing up in Nigeria, she moved to the United States at sixteen to study, later gaining her MFA in 2011 from Yale School of Art. After a year as artist-in-residence at The Studio Museum in Harlem, New York, she moved to Los Angeles, and her first solo exhibition was mounted there at the Hammer Museum in 2015. In her depictions of domestic tableaux, walls and floors appear as densely patterned as people's clothing. The images used are sourced from family photo albums, Nigerian lifestyle magazines, advertisements, Nollywood films, the Internet and Akunyili Crosby's personal snapshots. *Dwell: Aso Ebi* was presented from 2018 to 2019 as a public billboard on London's South Bank; however, its symbolism is deeply intimate – the wallpaper comprises a political leaflet of her late mother. It speaks of the artist's transcultural identity: a woman sits at a dining table in Nigeria wearing Aso Ebi – a traditional West African uniform dress – while its companion piece, *Dwell: Me, We* (2017), shows the same woman in Los Angeles, each location signified with a patterned teapot and paper coffee cup respectively.

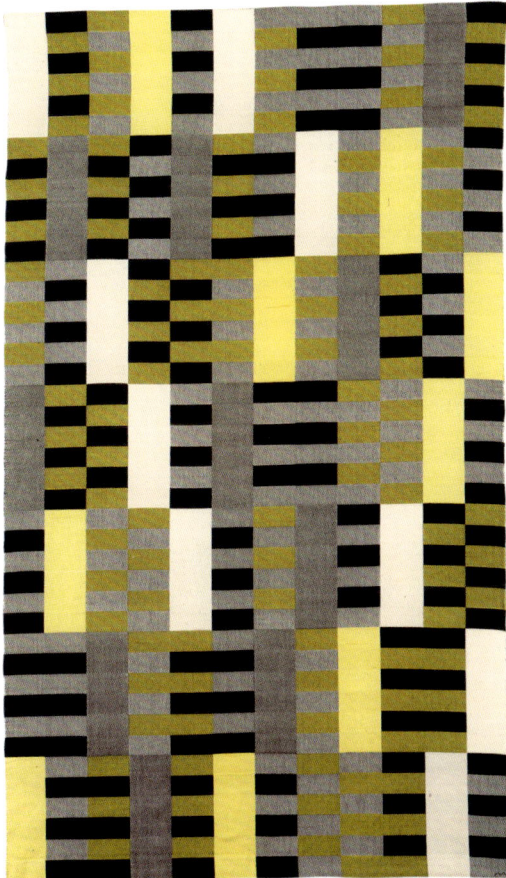

WALL HANGING

1926 (remade by Gunta Stölzl Workshop in 1965), mercerized cotton and silk, 203.2 × 120.7 cm (80¼ × 47⅜ in), Metropolitan Museum of Art, New York
Anni Albers, born Annelise Fleischmann, 1899, Berlin. Died 1994, Orange, Connecticut.

One of weaving's most innovative and internationally renowned artists, Albers was closely associated with the Bauhaus, the revolutionary and influential German art academy of the interwar years. While the school admitted students 'without regard to sex', women could not study architecture, metal- or glass-working, being directed instead towards 'feminine' subjects. Albers reluctantly took up weaving, which she called the 'least objectionable choice', and was instructed by Gunta Stölzl (1897–1983) the Bauhaus's first female master, before becoming head of the weaving department herself in 1931. As refugees from the Nazi regime, Albers and her husband, the painter Josef Albers (1888–1976), arrived in the United States in 1933, and both taught at the experimental art institute, Black Mountain College, North Carolina. Subsequently she was commissioned by design companies Knoll and Rosenthal, and in 1949 became the first designer to have a solo exhibition at New York's Museum of Modern Art. Her 'pictorial weavings', as Albers later called works such as this wall hanging, were not intended to be functional but, rather, purely aesthetic, the interlocking rectilinear patterns and grid structure, both hallmarks of the period's high modern style in art.

ELLEN ALTFEST

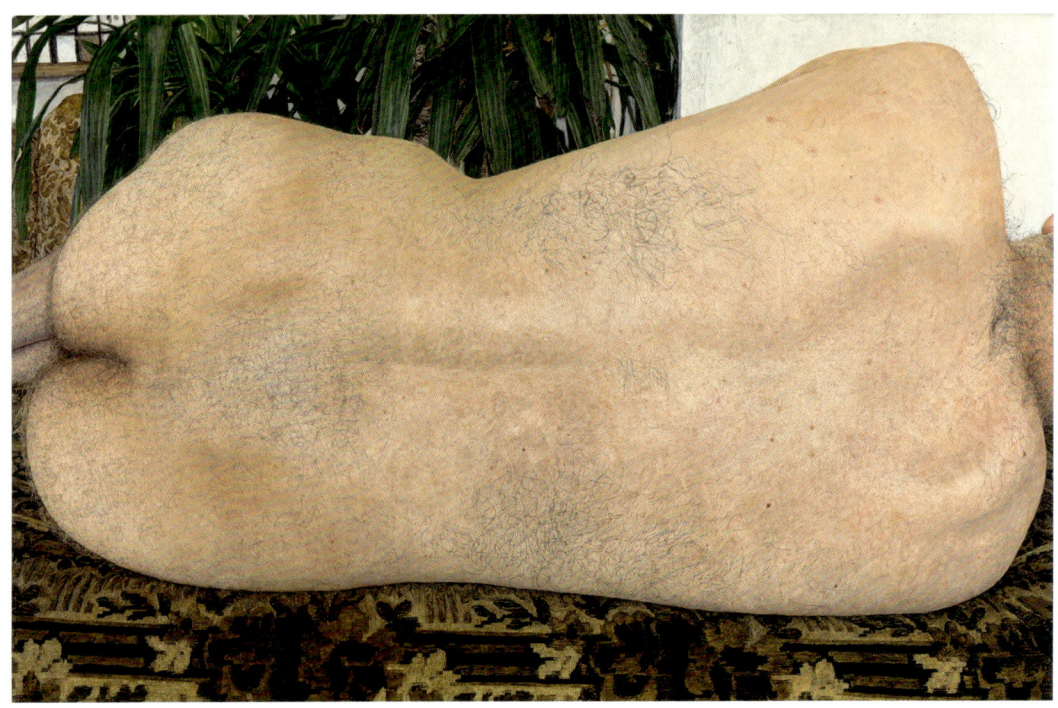

THE BACK

2008–9, oil on canvas, 40.6 × 63.5 cm (16 × 25 in), Olbricht Collection, Berlin
Ellen Altfest, born 1970, New York.

Known for her intimate, hyperreal paintings, a selection of which
were included in 'The Encyclopedic Palace' exhibition at the 55th
Venice Biennale (2013), Altfest changes perceptions of everyday
minutiae by shifting the viewer's perspective. Developing her style
during her MFA at Yale School of Art, which she completed
in 1997, she paints directly from life. Her close analytical approach,
enacted over hours of exhaustive observation, renders the nuances
of the physical world, both human and vegetal, in scrupulous detail,
with potted plants, gourds and body parts depicted close up and
tight against the frame, at times almost lost to abstraction. The work

seen here encroaches upon a male body in a domestic setting,
exemplifying Altfest's intense strategies of voyeurism and psychological scrutiny of her subjects. Turned away from the viewer and
curled up, the microscopic detail of the sitter's back includes every
individual hair. The body is objectified, treated with the same
approach taken to the nearby plant and inanimate rug upon which
it lies. The pores and pock-marked surface of the man's skin become
unfamiliar features on a surface, purposefully detaching the viewer
from the person within.

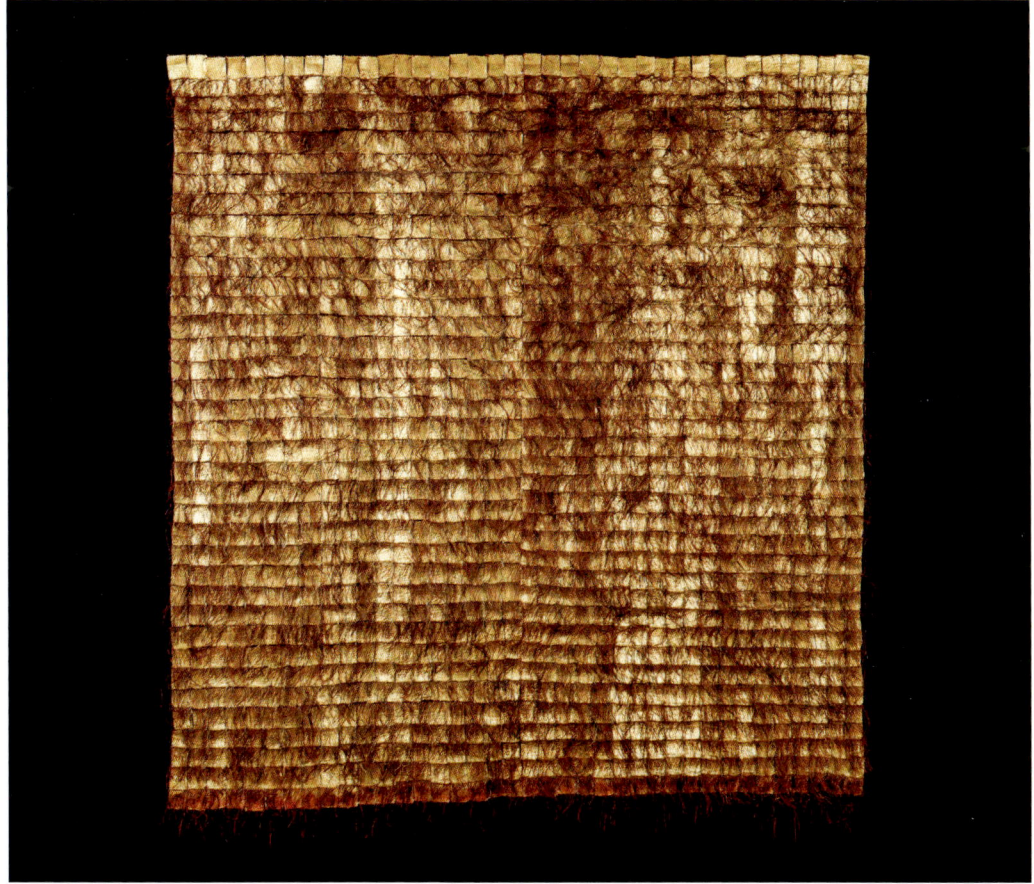

ALCHEMY 50

1987, canvas, gesso, gold leaf and acrylic paint, 165 × 150 cm (65 × 59 in),
Tate, London
Olga de Amaral, born Olga Ceballos Velez, 1932, Bogotá, Colombia.

Amaral initially studied architectural design in Bogotá and then briefly led her college's architectural drawing programme. Moving to Detroit, Michigan, she studied textile art from 1954, becoming a leading exponent of Latin American abstraction with her experiments in structure, surface and material. Vivid colour characterized her earlier work and by the end of the 1960s she had literally unravelled weaving's basic concepts; threads left as floating braids. In 1969 Amaral was included in the Museum of Modern Art's pioneering 'Wall Hangings' exhibition, with her first solo show in New York the following year. Based in Paris and travelling extensively in the 1970s, her work developed a rhythmic sculptural dimension, and also drew on painting as she applied acrylic and gesso to thread, an innovation that exposed how pigment on canvas is taken for granted. The ceramic artist Lucie Rie (1903–95) introduced Amaral to *kintsugi*, the Japanese practice of using gold leaf to mark cracks in repaired pottery, something she later witnessed at first hand. This work from a series is completely covered in gold leaf, a symbol of knowledge and the goal of alchemical transformation presented on a tangible human scale.

GHADA AMER

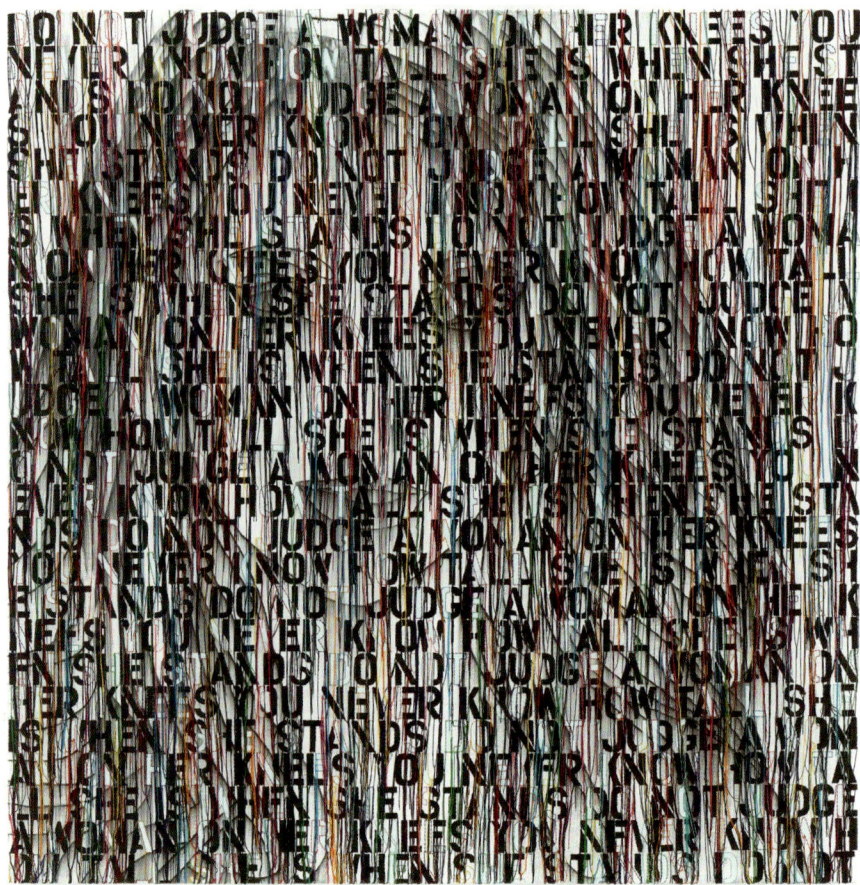

PORTRAIT WITH ONE EARRING
2016, acrylic, embroidery and gel medium on canvas, 106.7 × 106.7 cm (42 × 42 in)
Ghada Amer, born 1963, Cairo.

Amer moved with her family from Egypt to France at the age of eleven, relocating to the United States in 1995. While studying art at the Villa Arson in Nice, France in the 1980s, she discovered that some painting classes were reserved for male students; this exclusion fuelled her interest in making work about gender and sexuality. Using sewing and embroidery, as well as ceramic, collage and drawing, her mixed-media paintings refer to representations of women in pornography. Amer's eroticized line drawings have both figurative and abstract elements, her subjects either exposed or obscured to varying degrees among layers of stitched lines. Her images often contain feminist slogans, which are repeated over the work's surface. In this work, a female face is partially obscured by overlaid text that reads 'Do not judge a woman on her knees, you never know how tall she is when she stands', a quote from *Where Pain Thrives* (2017) by poet Mie Hansson. This combination of provocative imagery and empowering language sees Amer subverting the idea that women in pornography are simply one-dimensional sexualized beings, but rather thinking subjects too, with inalienable dignity.

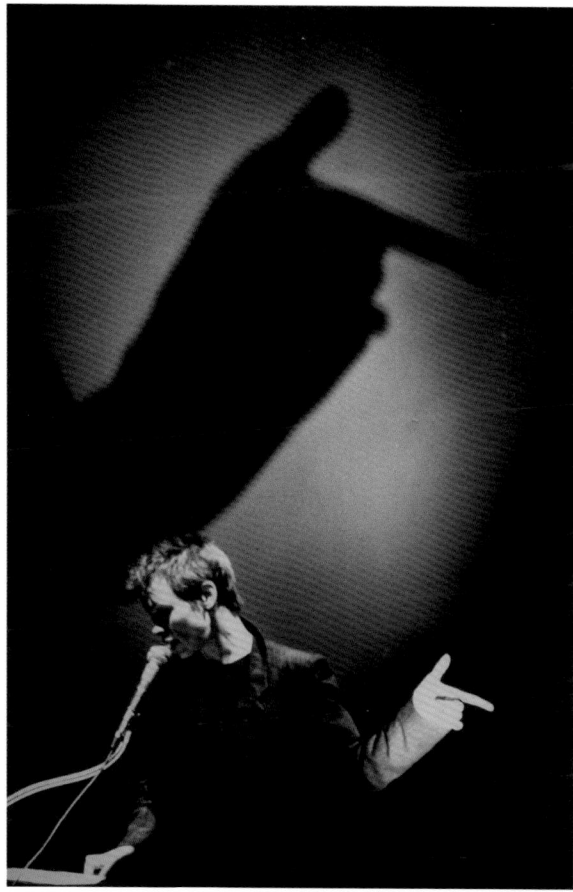

UNITED STATES 2: O SUPERMAN
1980, performance
Laurie Anderson, born Laura Phillips Anderson, 1947, Glen Ellyn, Illinois.

A pioneer in multimedia art and encompassing the roles of musician, composer, performance artist and filmmaker, Anderson made innovative sound pieces from the 1970s onwards. Initially studying classical violin, her early practice saw her pushing its boundaries, for example in her performance *Duets on Ice* (1974), in which she played the instrument while wearing ice skates that were frozen within a slowly melting block of ice. In 1977 she constructed a 'tape-bow violin', which used magnetic tape instead of horsehair and a magnetic pick-up on the bridge and was described as emitting 'eerie wolf howls'. Her numerous recordings, collaborations and live works have explored the limits of communication, remaining at the forefront of technological innovation. Her most famous piece, and perhaps the only artwork to have also been a hit single in the popular music charts, *O Superman* was a segment of the epic multimedia project 'United States'. Against a backdrop of synthesized music and looped sounds, Anderson's poetic lyrics explore themes spanning motherhood, nationhood and militarization. Her career has been recognized with major awards, including the prestigious Guggenheim Fellowship (1982) and in 2002 she became NASA's first artist-in-residence.

MAMMA ANDERSSON

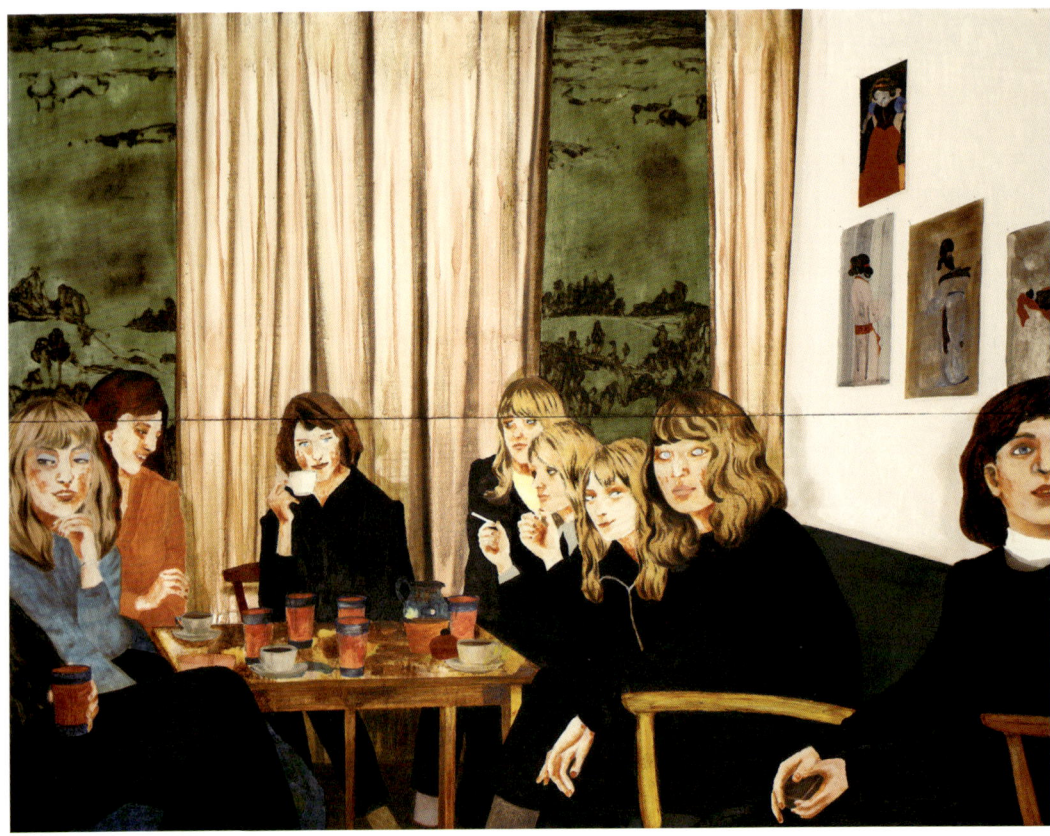

ABOUT A GIRL
2005, oil and acrylic on panel, diptych, overall: 122 × 160 cm (48 × 63 in)
Mamma Andersson, born Karin Andersson, 1962, Luleå, Sweden.

One of Sweden's most internationally well-known contemporary artists, Andersson creates dreamlike paintings that depict domestic scenes or expansive mountainous landscapes evocative of northern Sweden. Taking inspiration from modern theatre, Nordic folk art and period interiors, she lays out her paintings like cinematic compositions, some with remote roads overshadowed by dramatic skies, or empty elongated rooms. Blending the mysterious with the mundane, disjointed narratives are broken up further with obscured details or blocked out areas reminiscent of thick smoke. Reinforcing the strange familiarities in her work, her compositions include

recurring props such as lamps, tables and chairs. Reimagining a feature of seventeenth-century Dutch interior painting, she includes pictures within pictures, sometimes instantly recognizable: for example, in this work, Snow White above three traditional Japanese geishas. As the get-together is awkwardly interrupted, maybe by a decision to pose for a group photo, incongruous themes creep unbidden into the social space. With a sensuous approach to colour and style, Andersson creates juxtapositions and contrasts with the use of thick paint, wash-like textures and untouched surfaces, all of which add to her works' pervading air of mystery.

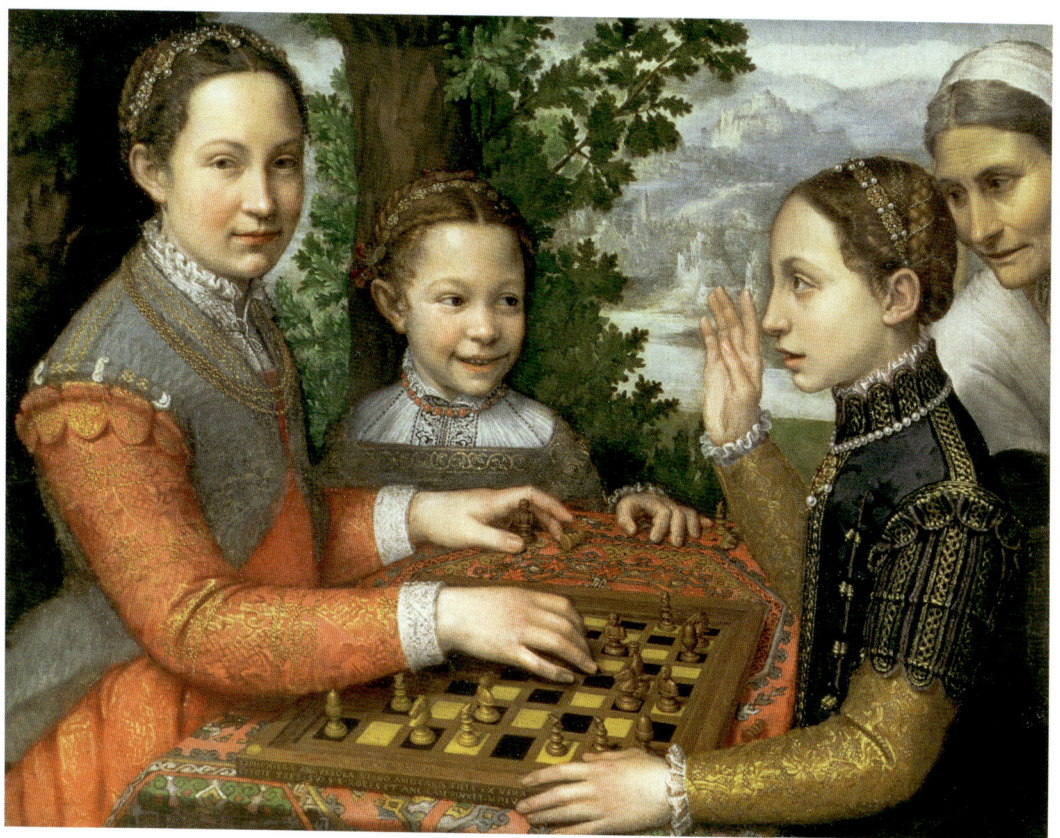

THE GAME OF CHESS

1555, oil on canvas, 72 × 97 cm (28 ⅜ × 38 ¼ in), National Museum, Poznań, Poland
Sofonisba Anguissola, born *c.*1532, Cremona, Italy. Died 1625, Palermo, Italy.

Anguissola's long and distinguished career, extending well into her nineties, spanned an extensive period of art history from Late Renaissance and Baroque. As a young woman, she received informal instruction from Michelangelo Buonarroti (1475–1564), who recognized her talent, while Anthony van Dyck (1599–1641) claimed to have learnt more from her about painting than anyone else. Born into minor nobility, she and her five sisters were encouraged by their father, Amilcare Anguissola, to undertake artistic training. Anguissola studied under Bernardino Campi (1522–91) and Bernardino Gatti (*c.*1495–1576). Later, she was herself a patron of the arts and encouraged other women artists, including Lavinia Fontana (p.140) and Artemisia Gentileschi (p.150). As Court Painter to Philip II of Spain for fourteen years, she gained considerable reputation and wealth. This privilege enabled her to paint an elite clientele, although she also used her family as models, as seen here in what is thought to be a portrait of three of her sisters – Lucia, Minerva and Europa. The painting was praised by the biographer and artist Giorgio Vasari (1511–74) for its vivid depiction of an aristocratic recreation – chess – more usually played by men.

ELEANOR ANTIN

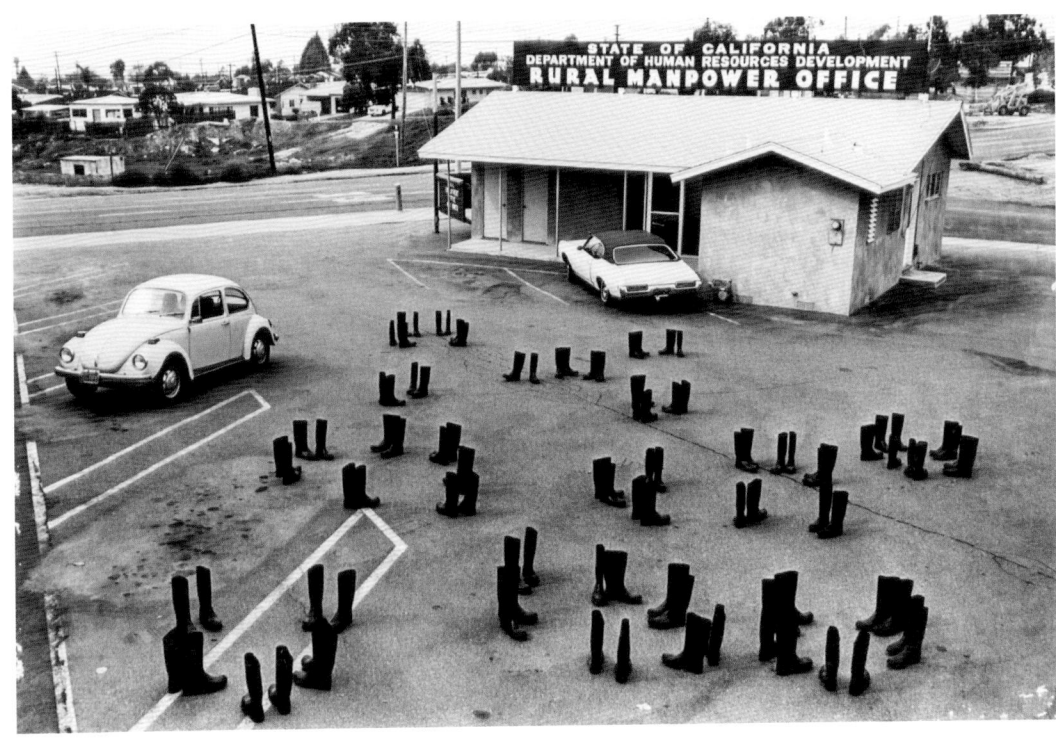

100 BOOTS LOOKING FOR A JOB, SAN CLEMENTE, CALIFORNIA

1972, vintage gelatin silver print mounted on board, 31.8 × 47.8 cm (12 ½ × 18 ¾ in)
Eleanor Antin, born Eleanor Fineman, 1935, New York.

After graduating from New York's City College in the late 1950s, Antin explored a multidisciplinary path that included acting, painting and poetry. In 1969, she moved to San Diego where she focused on themes of identity, feminism and history using video and photography. She employed her acting skills to take on personas of different races, genders and eras, referring to these as her 'Selves'. She also used props to suggest human presence, such as 100 black rubber boots, which she took on a two-and-a-half-year journey from California to New York's Museum of Modern Art (MoMA). Photographing them in different and often enigmatic situations

along the way – going to church, taking a lunch break, looking for work – she produced fifty-one photographs in total. A pioneering work of 'mail art': the project unfolded in real time, with one thousand recipients receiving postcard reproductions of the images as they were created. Conflating fact and fiction, and questioning the essence of the artwork, the photographs were finally exhibited, alongside the actual boots, at MoMA in 1973, the museum stating that Antin had sought to circumvent 'the spatial and temporal limits imposed on an artist whose work is shown in a gallery'.

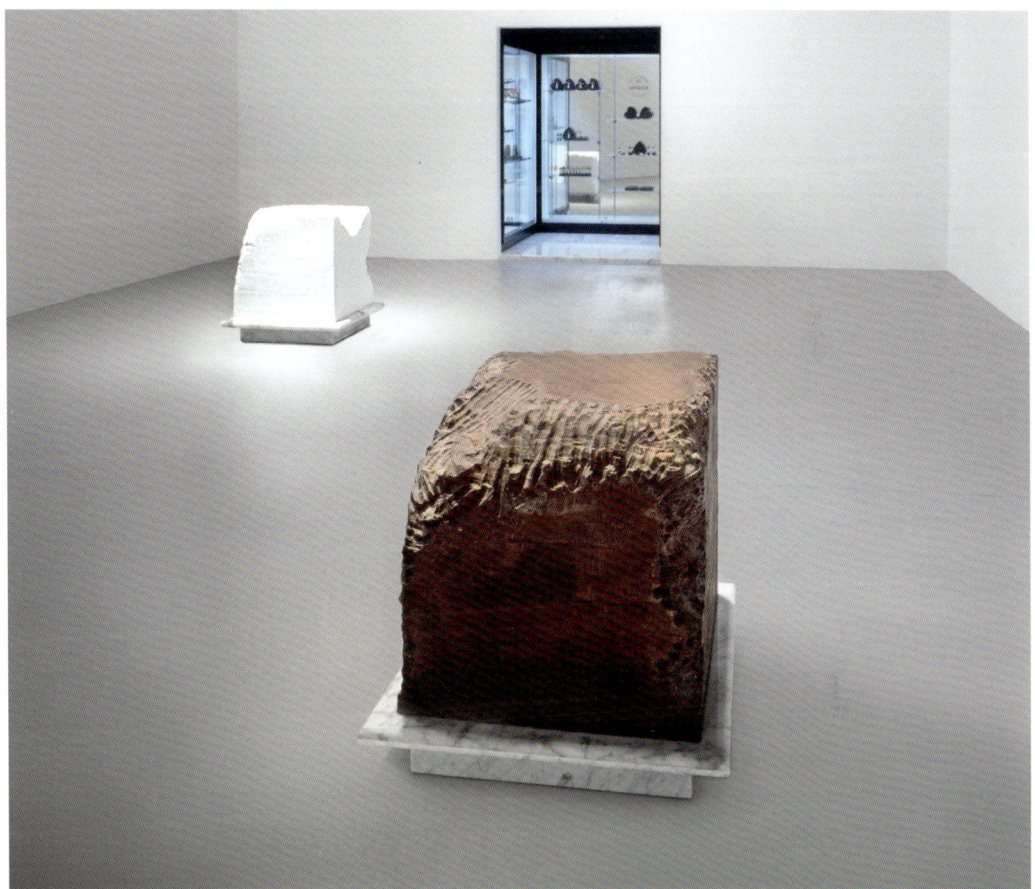

GNAW

1992, 3-part installation: 272 kg (600 lbs) of chocolate gnawed by the artist; 272 kg (600 lbs) of lard gnawed by the artist; display with 130 lipsticks made with pigment, beeswax and chewed lard removed from the lard cube; 27 heart-shaped packages made from the chewed chocolate removed from the chocolate cube, each cube: 61 × 61 × 61 cm (24 × 24 × 24 in), installation dimensions variable, installation view, Museum of Contemporary Art, Los Angeles. Collection Museum of Modern Art, New York

Janine Antoni, born 1964, Freeport, Bahamas.

Since completing an MFA at Rhode Island School of Design in 1989, Antoni has transformed everyday bodily activities, such as eating, bathing and sleeping, into art via performance, sculpture and photography. Often subverting archetypes of feminine beauty, she has made drawings using mascara-heavy eyelashes and painted/mopped the floor using her head as paintbrush, her long hair dipped in black dye. In *Gnaw*, two cubes – one chocolate, one lard – are presented like Minimalist sculptures, yet they are misshapen along the edges and corners, having been gnawed away by the artist's teeth. Displayed nearby are heart-shaped trays, resembling empty chocolate-box packaging, and red lipsticks, created using the chewed chocolate and lard. Gnawing is an important developmental stage for a child, a way of coming to know the world. But the act can also signal desire and anxiety. *Gnaw* blurs the distinctions between these associations by incorporating it into an artistic process whereby materials are both consumed and created. It is a work of opposites: the artist's mouth is both tool and subject, while chocolate, a food with romantic connotations, is placed next to lard, an abstracted stand-in for the body.

IDA APPLEBROOG

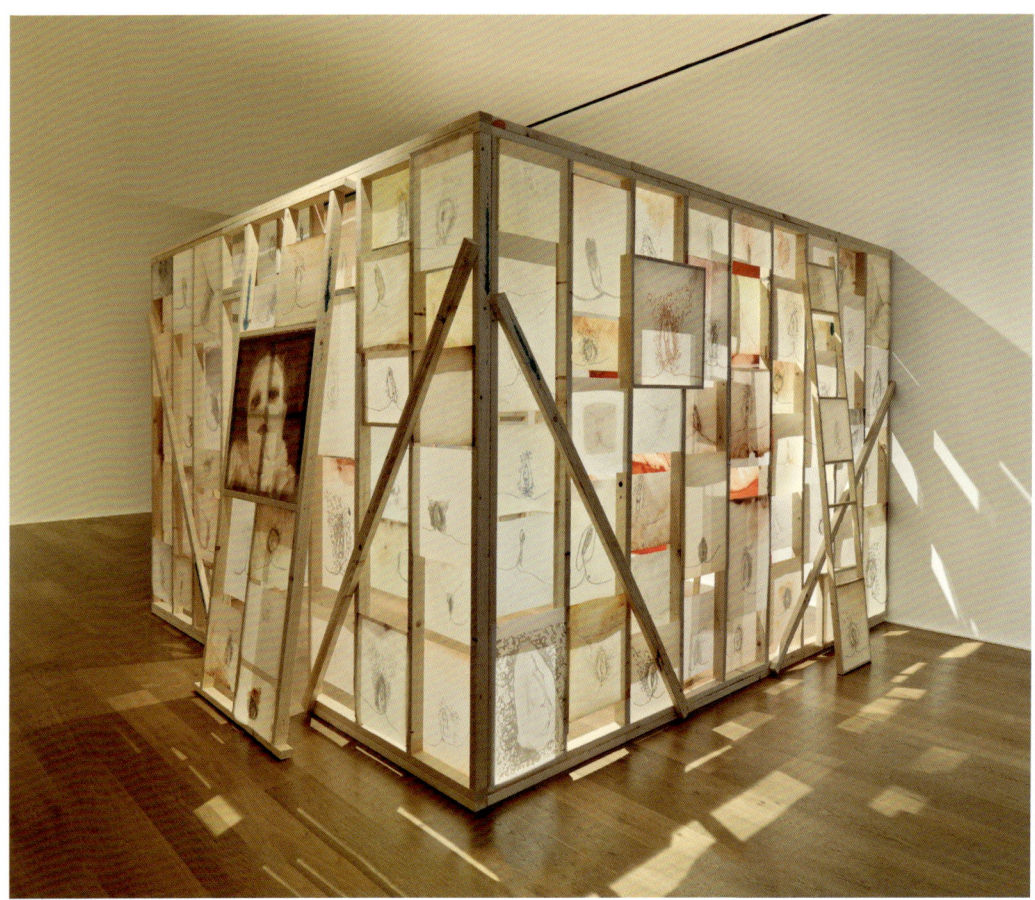

MONALISA

2009, gampi paper, Mylar, ultrachrome ink, pigment, oil, watercolour and wood, 279.5 × 366 × 372 cm (110 × 144 × 146 ½ in), installation view, 'Ida Applebroog', Hauser & Wirth, London, 2011
Ida Applebroog, born Ida Applebaum, 1929, New York. Died 2023, New York.

Applebroog made art that explores themes of gender, violence and sexuality. She initially studied graphic design and worked briefly in an advertising agency in New York before becoming disillusioned with the industry; she then worked for the New York Public Library Arts Department. In the 1960s she moved to Illinois to attend the Art Institute of Chicago, and then to Southern California with her husband and four children. Here she juggled her aspirations to be an artist in a new city with the demands of a family. Seeking solitude,

she would take refuge in the bathroom for several hours each evening, bringing a sketchbook and mirror to this daily ritual. Over a few weeks in 1969, she created more than 150 drawings of her body, specifically her vulva. These drawings moved with her to New York in 1974 and were rediscovered by her studio assistants in 2009. Seeing them afresh, Applebroog saw creative potential in the images. They were manipulated using oil and ink and then printed onto thin Japanese *gampi* paper. Presented together in a new work entitled *Monalisa*, the drawings are translucent and skin-like, stretched over a structure reminiscent of a domestic house.

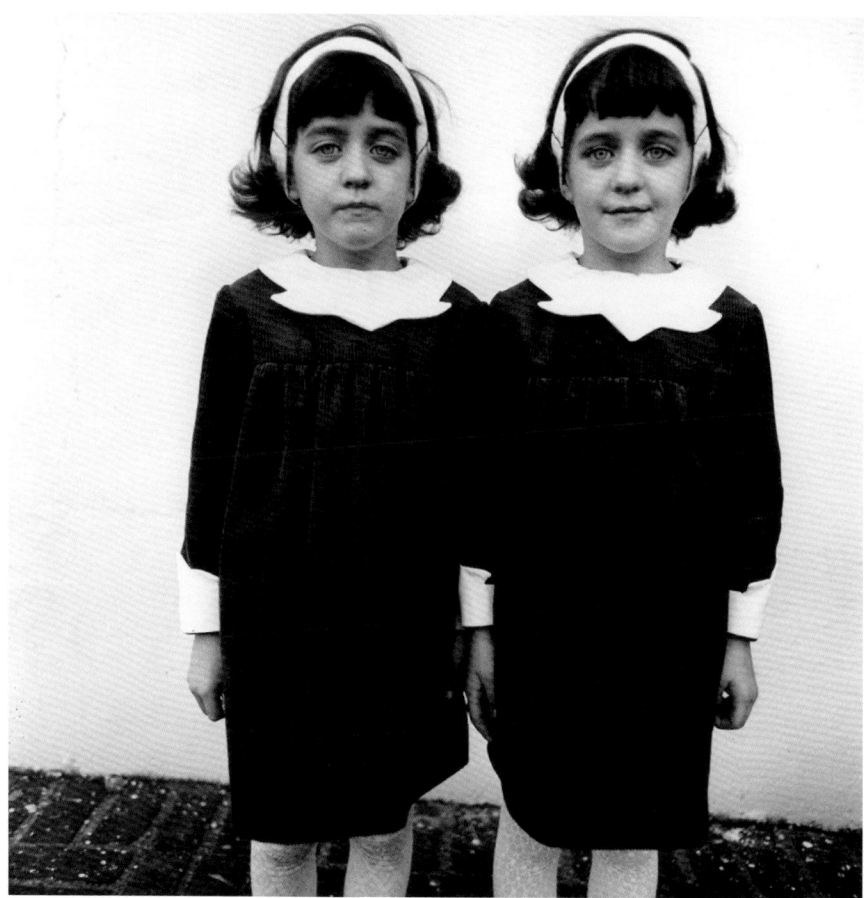

IDENTICAL TWINS, ROSELLE, N.J., 1966

1966, printed between 1967 and 1970, gelatin-silver print, image, sheet and aluminum mount, 36.2 × 36.2 cm (14¼ × 14¼ in)
Diane Arbus, born Diane Nemerov, 1923, New York. Died 1971, New York.

Arbus got her first camera in 1941, soon after she was married. She attended a brief technical course with Berenice Abbott (p.17), then started a fashion photography studio with her husband, Allan, where she provided art direction and he took the photographs. Their work appeared regularly in magazines such as *Glamour* and *Vogue*. In 1956, Arbus quit the studio and began studying with Lisette Model (p.278), known for her strange and intense street photography. Arbus, too, was fascinated by the uncanny within the everyday. She photographed nudists, transvestites, circus performers, giants and, as seen here, identical twins. It remains a mystery how Arbus found out about the neighbourhood Christmas party in New Jersey where she encountered the seven-year-old sisters, Cathleen and Colleen Wade. Set against a white wall, their matching dresses meet to suggest they are joined at the shoulders and plays on the mystical and psychic connection of identical twins. In 1972, the year after she took her own life, Arbus became the first photographer to be included in the Venice Biennale.

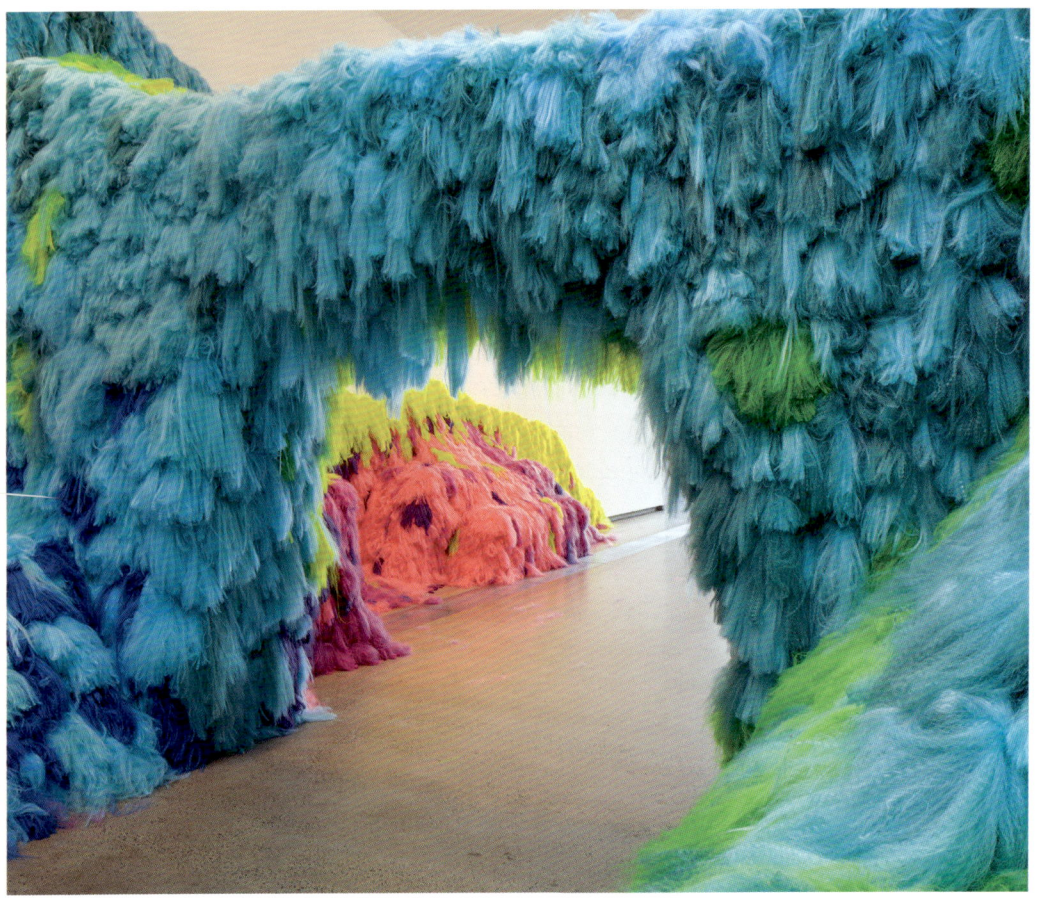

NERVESCAPE V

2016, (detail), Modacrylic fibre, nylon zip ties and steel staples, 500 sq m (5,380 sq ft), installation view, 'Sugar Spin: you, me, art and everything', Queensland Art Gallery|Gallery of Modern Art, Brisbane, Australia
Hrafnhildur Arnardóttir, born 1969, Reykjavik, Iceland.

As is evident in her self-given moniker – 'Shoplifter' – which derived from constant mispronunciation of her birth name, humour and playfulness are central to Arnardóttir's practice. She is best known for her use of synthetic and real hair in sculptures and installations: she investigates hair as a powerful signifier of culture and identity. A conventional standard of beauty and a measure of the unacceptable, especially for women, hair can represent comfort and nurture as well as connoting wildness and monstrosity. Her large-scale environments, of which *Nervescape V* is an example, are designed to stimulate the senses through their soft, tangible surfaces and a palette of fluorescent colours inspired by children's books, punk-rock aesthetics and the vivid sunsets of Iceland. Arnardóttir often underscores the multisensory nature of her installations by using them as settings for performances. Designing elaborate stage costumes and eccentric hairpieces, her outfits have been worn over the years by her friend and regular collaborator, the Icelandic musician, Björk. Arnardóttir, who has her studio in Brooklyn, New York, was selected to represent Iceland at the 58th Venice Biennale in 2019.

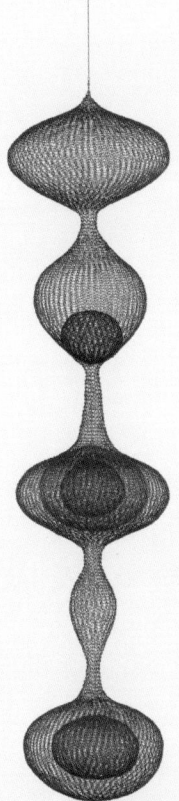

**UNTITLED (S.310, HANGING FIVE-LOBED CONTINUOUS FORM
WITHIN A FORM WITH SPHERES IN THE 2ND, 3RD AND BOTTOM LOBES)**

*c.*1954, copper and brass wire, 162.6 × 38.1 × 38.1 cm (64 × 15 × 15 in)
Ruth Asawa, born 1926, Norwalk, California. Died 2013, San Francisco.

The child of Japanese immigrants, Asawa and her family were interned with other Japanese-Americans in 1942–3 in Santa Anita, California, and Rohwer, Arkansas. While at Santa Anita, Asawa drew for up to five hours a day under the guidance of fellow internee Disney illustrators. After graduating high school at the Rohwer camp, she received a scholarship to Milwaukee State Teachers College. From 1946 to 1949 she attended the influential Black Mountain College in North Carolina, where she studied under Josef Albers (1888–1976), Merce Cunningham (1919–2009) and Buckminster Fuller (1895–1983).

Inspired by a 1947 trip to Mexico during which she observed a local craftsman weaving baskets in wire, Asawa began to work with wire as her primary medium. In their innovative use of material and form, her wire sculptures, which she continued to elaborate over the course of her lifetime, synthesize a wide range of aesthetic preoccupations at the heart of twentieth-century abstraction and challenge conventional notions of sculpture through their emphasis on lightness and transparency. An important advocate for arts education, Asawa campaigned for the founding of San Francisco School of the Arts in 1982 (renamed in her honour in 2010).

DOTTY ATTIE

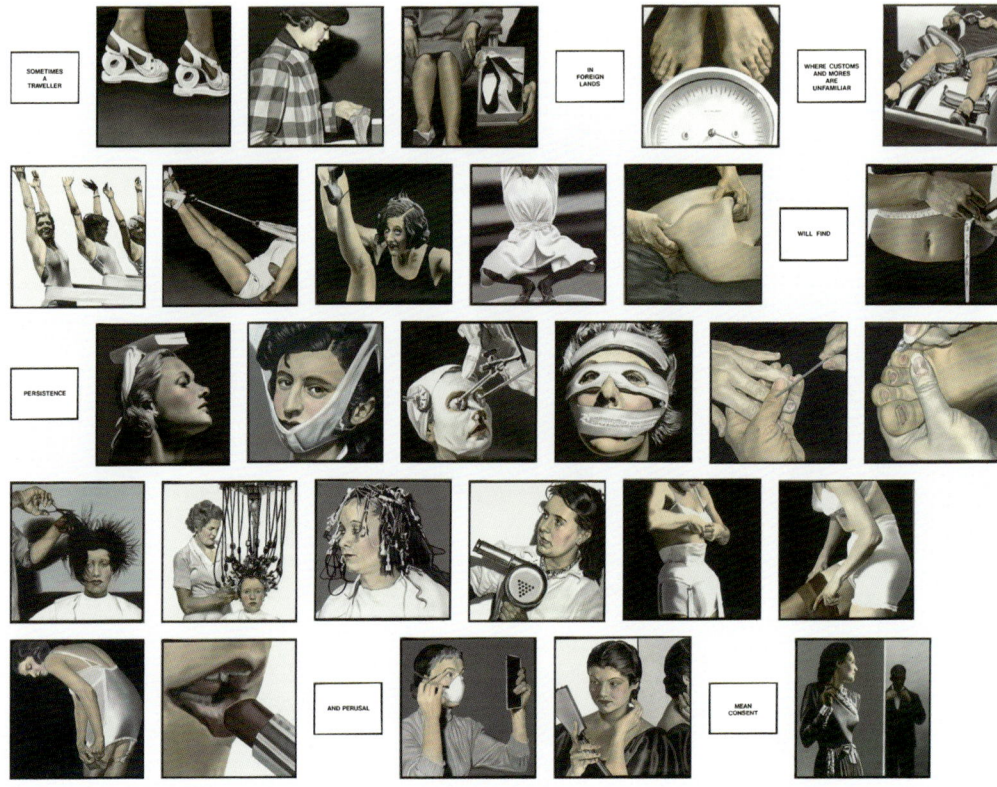

SKIN DEEP

2007, oil on linen, 28 panels, each 15.2 × 15.2 cm (6 × 6 in) and 7 panels, each 7.6 × 10.1 cm (3 × 4 in)

Dotty Attie, born 1938, Pennsauken Township, New Jersey.

A founding member of A.I.R. Gallery in 1972, a New York cooperative dedicated to women artists, Attie's work has a clear feminist stance. Studying fine art at Philadelphia College of Art in 1959, she initially painted in an Abstract Expressionist style, though subsequently returned to her first love: drawing. Developing a technique reminiscent of multi-panel, comic-strip narration – images interspersed with snippets of text – there is a graphic quality to her paintings, evident here in *Skin Deep*. Women are seen undergoing beauty procedures, a pseudo-medical regime of prodding,

measuring and weighing interspersed with scenes of exercises, hairstyling, applying cosmetics and wearing high heels – all signifiers of femininity, yet entirely superficial, as the work's title states. The text panels combine sequentially into a sentence, but the final one, 'MEAN CONSENT', establishes the work as a commentary about the pressures on women regarding their appearance. Often appropriating and recontextualizing art by historical figures – for example, Johannes Vermeer (1632–75) and Jean-Auguste-Dominique Ingres (1780–1867) – Attie exposes the subtle connotations in images of women that damage body-positivity.

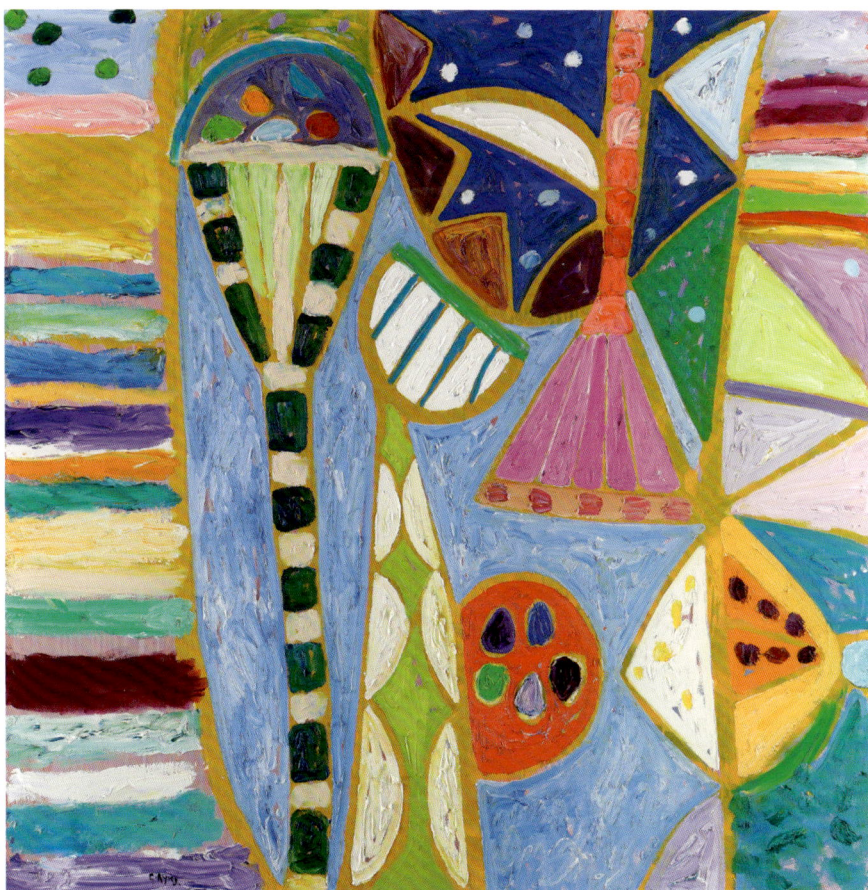

REMEMBRANCE OF THINGS PAST

2007, oil on canvas, 152.4 × 152.4 cm (60 × 60 in), private collection
Gillian Ayres, born 1930, London. Died 2018, North Devon, UK.

Gillian Ayres was instrumental to the development of British abstract painting throughout the second half of the twentieth century. Graduating from Camberwell School of Art in 1950, she exhibited the following year with the London Group, and had her first solo exhibition in 1956. In 1957 she received a significant commission to make a large multi-panel piece for South Hampstead High School's dining room, which was described in her obituary in *The Guardian* as 'the only true British contribution to American Abstract Expressionism'. That same year she participated in 'Metavisual, Tachiste, Abstract: Painting in England Today' at the Redfern Gallery, which cited her as one of the period's leading painters. She taught at art schools in Bath, London and Winchester for over twenty years before focusing fully on her studio practice from 1981 onwards. After a period living in North Wales there followed thirty years on the border of North Devon and Cornwall, where she devoted her practice to big, bold, bright abstraction, often using an impasto technique. *Remembrance of Things Past* is a joyful composition that suggests memories of objects, recalled using an abstract language of colour, shape and pattern.

JO BAER

BRILLIANT YELLOW #9
1964–5, oil on canvas, 121.9 × 152.4 cm (48 × 60 in), Art Institute of Chicago
Jo Baer, born Josephine Kleinberg, 1929, Seattle. Died 2025, Amsterdam.

Traversing notably different styles, Baer's seven-decade-long career developed from an interest in a strict formal vocabulary of painted abstractions to more 'meaningful' narratives conveyed through figurative subject matters. A key figure in twentieth-century art movements, from the 1970s she returned to possibilities of representation, in a style of painting she described as 'radical figuration'. Prior to this, Baer's uncompromisingly non-objective and sparse style attracted the attention of artists such as Donald Judd (1928–94) and Dan Flavin (1933–96), who invited her to participate in their 1964 Minimalist exhibition 'Eleven Artists'. Making

Abstract Expressionist paintings from the mid-1950s and experimenting with colour through the 1960s, she gradually expanded a Minimalist language by adding diagonal and curved paths of colour to predominantly white paintings. Later relocating to Ireland, Baer's dramatic break with her earlier practice introduced figurative elements derived from Palaeolithic art ancient symbols of female genitalia, her response to abstraction being a radically feminine figuration. Seen here is an earlier work, where a sparse white canvas is framed and intruded by a vibrant band of colour, which, the title suggests, this painting is 'about'.

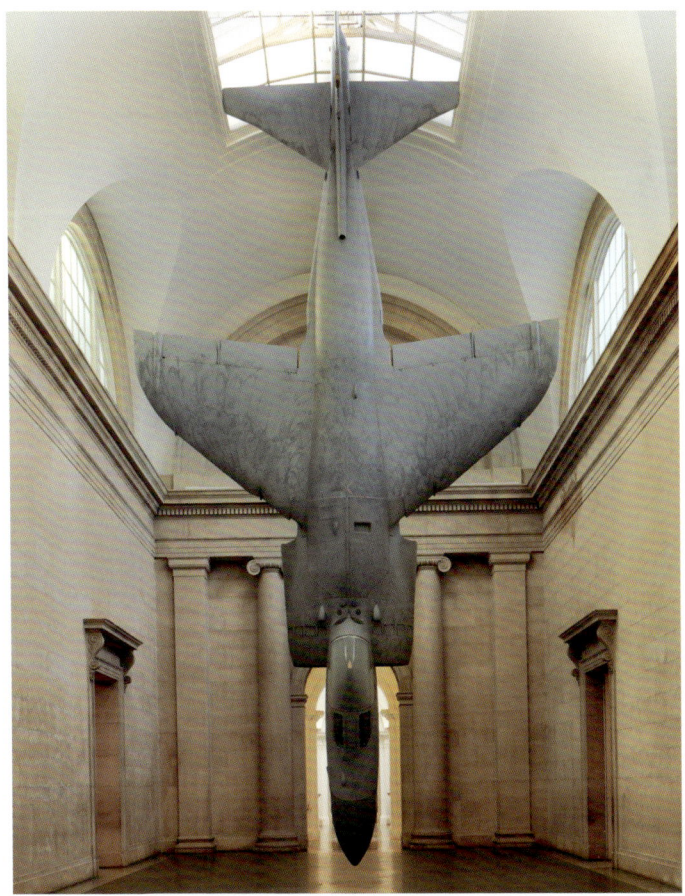

HARRIER

2010, BAe Sea Harrier aircraft and paint, 14.2 × 7.6 × 3.7 m (50 × 25 × 12 ft),
installation view, 'Fiona Banner: Tate Britain Duveens Commission 2010',
Tate Britain, London
Fiona Banner, born 1966, Liverpool, UK.

Banner's practice looks at communication and pushes it to its limits, either by playing with medium or timeframe, or by examining circumstances where it breaks down altogether, particularly during conflict. Many of her earlier works were 'wordscapes' – written retellings of Hollywood films, such as *Lawrence of Arabia*, *Point Break*, or a whole collection of Vietnam movies. These were manifested as dense text-filled paintings or in the case of *The Nam* (1997) as a 1,000-page book. That was the year she started her own publishing imprint, The Vanity Press, which has been a central aspect of her work ever since. Represented in a vast personal archive, the hardware of warfare – a technology of anti-communication – has gripped her imagination since childhood. *Harrier* is one of two decommissioned fighter aircraft presented with subtle yet suggestive alterations that Banner installed for her Duveens Commission. A polished Jaguar fighter, upturned like a vulnerable animal on the floor, offered viewers a distorted picture of their reflections, while the Sea Harrier seen here was suspended from the ceiling like a hanging piece of meat, its destructive function drained away. Made strange, abject and displaced, these machines of war become the objects rather than agents of history.

PHYLLIDA BARLOW

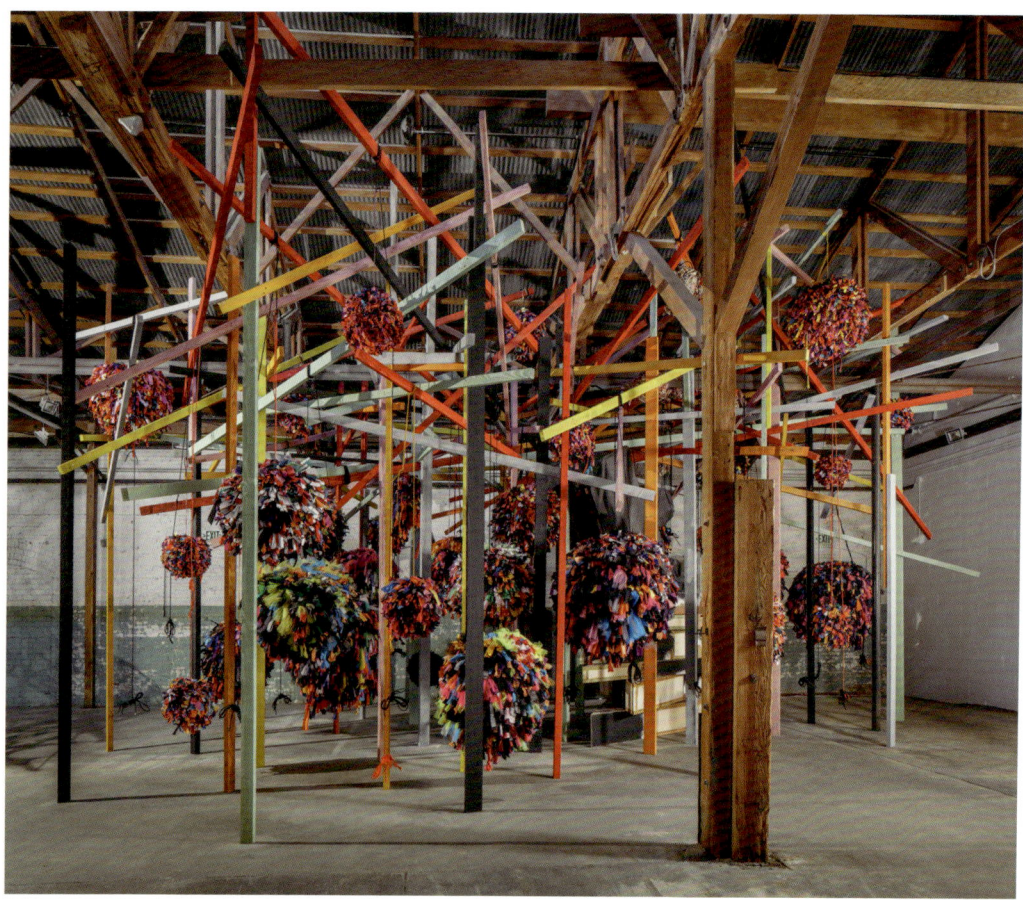

UNTITLED: GIG

2014, fabric, paper, cord, timber and paint, dimensions variable, installation view, 'Revolution in the Making: Abstract Sculpture by Women, 1947–2016', Hauser & Wirth, Los Angeles, 2016

Phyllida Barlow, born 1944, Newcastle upon Tyne, UK. Died 2023, London.

After the Second World War, Barlow's family moved from North East England to London, where she later attended Chelsea College of Art. During further studies at the Slade School of Art – where she would go on to teach for over forty years – she learnt traditional techniques of sculpture and discovered an affinity for the malleability of clay. Over subsequent decades she experimented with unconventional, and often inexpensive, materials such as cardboard, polystyrene, scrim and cement to create abstract sculptures and installations that have a tactile, contingent quality. Large-scale but decidedly anti-monumental, her work invites viewers to consider materials and means of construction – including cutting, folding, layering and arranging in precarious structures. Until she retired from teaching art aged sixty-five, Barlow's work went mostly unrecognized by institutions and collectors and she kept little of what she made beyond preparatory sketches. Subsequently, she was invited to exhibit work widely, and made ambitious and exuberant site-specific installations, like *untitled: GIG*, depicted here, and *folly* (2017), her commission for the British Pavilion at the 57th Venice Biennale.

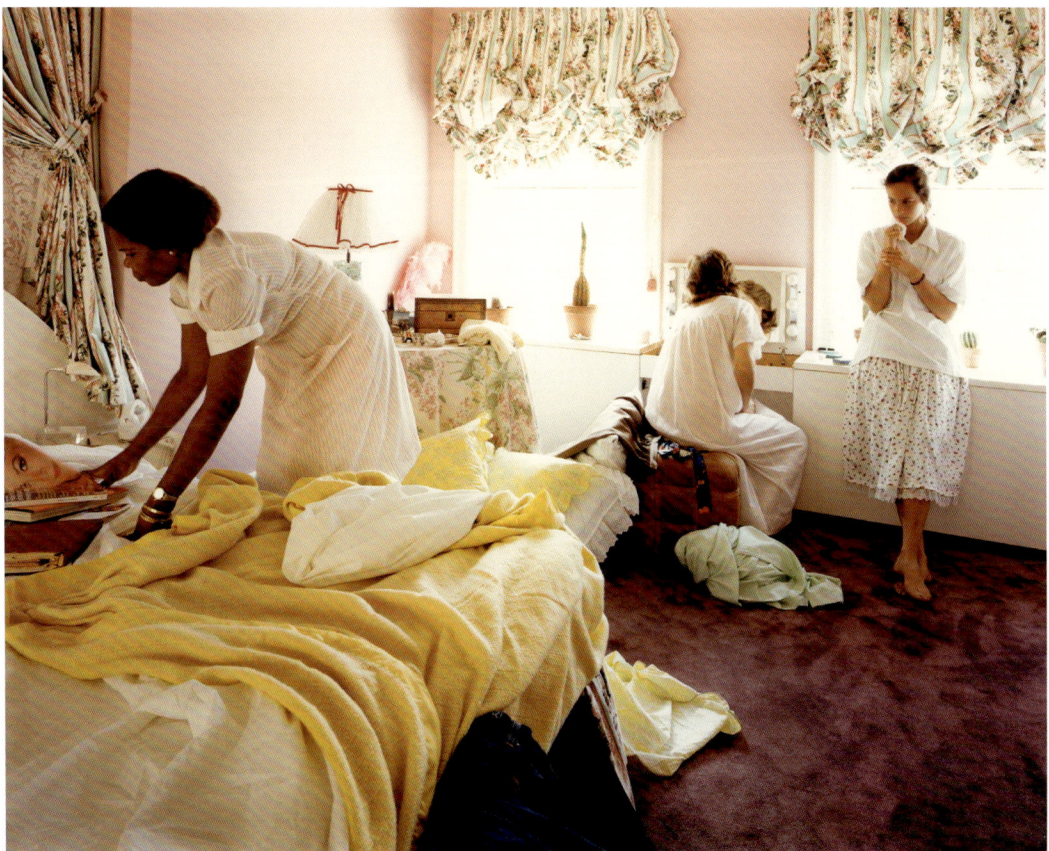

BEVERLY, JILL, AND POLLY

1982, chromogenic colour print, 121.9 × 152.4 cm (48 × 60 in), edition of 10
Tina Barney, born Tina Isles, 1945, New York.

Introduced to photography as a child by her grandfather, Barney is known for depicting her family, with her lens revealing intimate aspects of her own life and surroundings. The great-granddaughter of Emanuel Lehman, co-founder of Lehman Brothers bank, she studied art history at a secondary school in Manhattan, followed by further study in Italy. She collected contemporary art and photography as a way of learning about the medium. Despite this privileged start, it took many years for Barney to pursue her own art confidently. Volunteering at New York's Museum of Modern Art, she worked in cataloguing in the photography department, and later took amateur photography classes upon moving to Sun Valley, Idaho, in 1973. In her early thirties she embarked on a professional career in photography. This work is from the series 'Theater of Manners', in which Barney documented two decades of her family's life. Manhattan apartments and New England beach houses are the stages where they emerge as characters in an understated drama of affluence and affectation. Shot on large-format film, the mural-sized portraits seem candid, yet are the result of masterful orchestration and carefully considered composition.

WILHELMINA BARNS-GRAHAM

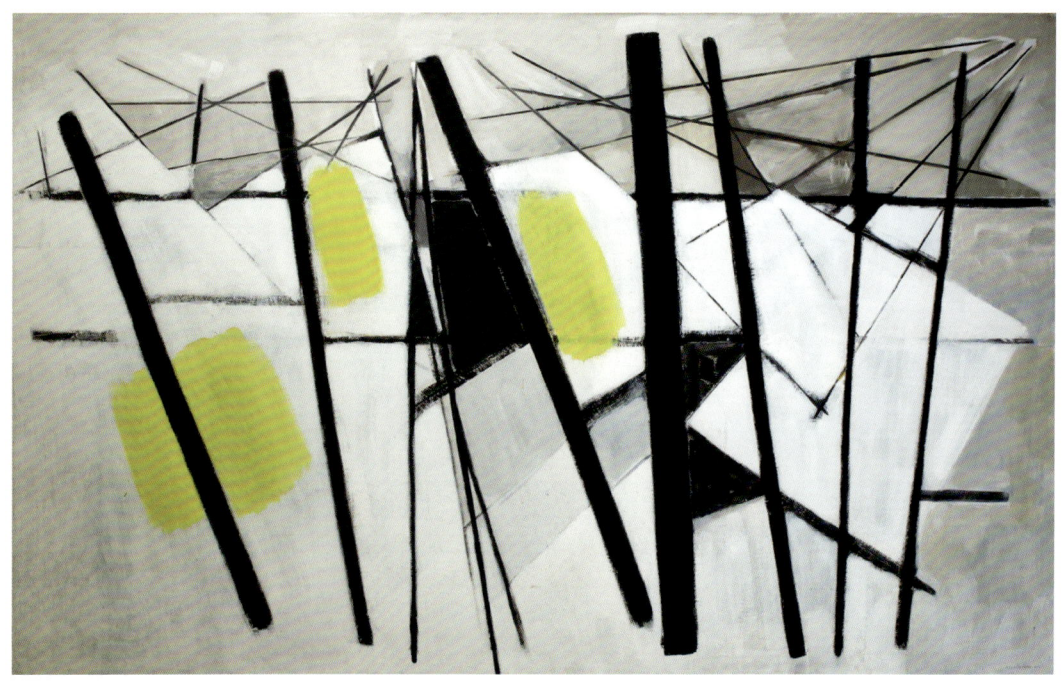

WHITE, BLACK AND YELLOW (COMPOSITION FEBRUARY)
1957, oil on canvas, 122 × 198 cm (48 × 78 in), Tate, London
Wilhelmina Barns-Graham, born 1912, St Andrews, UK. Died 2004, St Andrews, UK.

Raised in a conservative family in Scotland, Barns-Graham was determined to be an artist from an early age. Against her father's wishes, she attended Edinburgh College of Art from 1931, where her skill in painting and draughtsmanship earned her multiple scholarships. In 1940 she moved to the artistic hub of St Ives in Cornwall. Along with her friends Ben Nicholson (1894–1982) and Barbara Hepworth (p.183), she became part of a splinter group within the predominantly traditional St Ives' Society of Artists. The Crypt Group, later rebranded as the Penwith Society of Arts, was devoted to the exploration of a new vocabulary of modernist abstraction.

Barns-Graham was a key figure in this movement, although she frequently felt sidelined by its more prominent exponents. She later divided her time between Cornwall and Scotland. During her long career, Barns-Graham moved between representational and abstract modes, her work influenced as much by geometry as by natural and built environments – sometimes within a single piece, as in this painting, which was inspired by the moors of North Yorkshire.

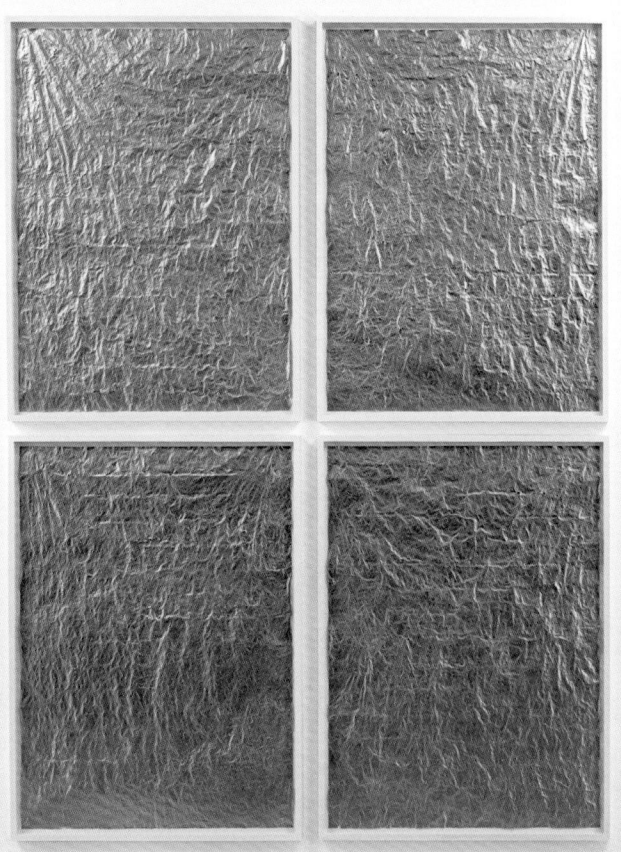

MIRROR WINDOW WALL III

2008, ink on paper, overall: 260.5 × 200.5 cm (102 ½ × 78 ⅞ in)
Anna Barriball, born 1972, Plymouth, UK.

After completing a master's degree at London's Chelsea College
of Art and Design in 2000, Barriball has evolved an artistic practice
that is rooted in drawing yet rarely involves making two-dimensional
pictures of things. Using the medium's processes and materials
she captures unseen or overlooked aspects of the day-to-day world
in work that includes sculpture, installation and video. Often taking
as her starting point architectural elements that are boundaries
between interior and exterior spaces – walls, doors and windows – her
best-known works are labour-intensive rubbings in pencil or ink
pen, which capture both the subject's form and texture, the paper

pressed into a relief-sculpture by the force of the action. Barriball
has described the resulting drawings as 'substitutes' – stand-ins
for the actual source, rather than a depiction of it made at a removed
distance. The work shown here simultaneously references three types
of objects: in abutting frames, it evokes an archetypal four-paned
window; the silver ink creates a mirror-like surface; this is interrupted
by the subtle yet recognizable pattern of a brick wall. A floating wall,
a window with no view and a mirror with no reflection – Barriball
invites the viewer to experience the poetic in the everyday.

YAEL BARTANA

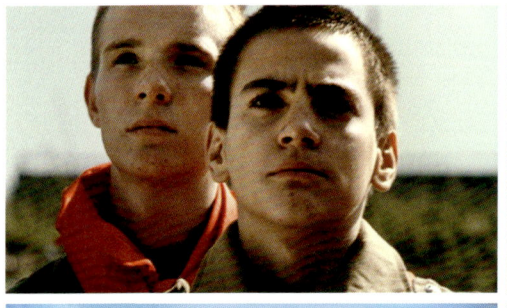
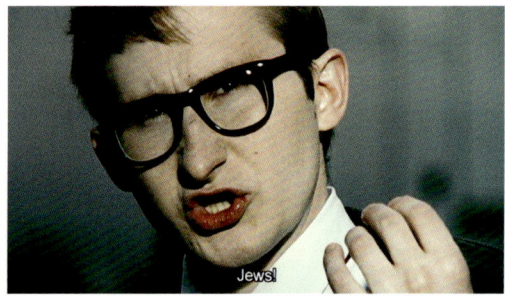
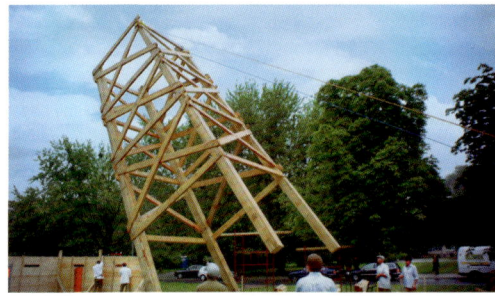
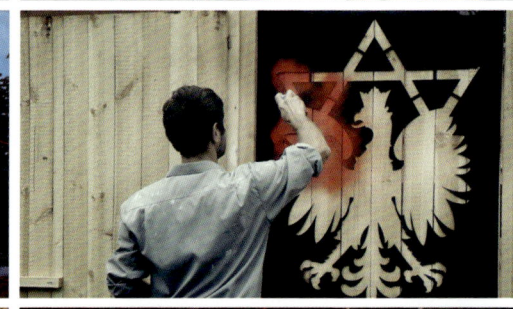
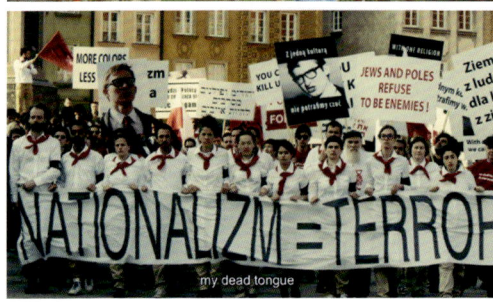
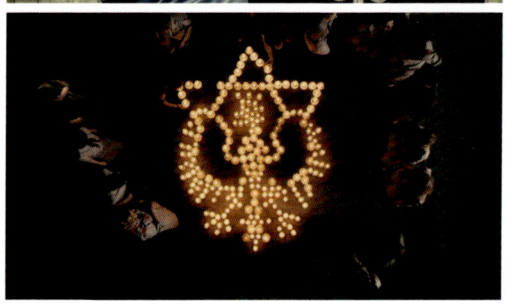

...AND EUROPE WILL BE STUNNED

2007–11, stills from trilogy of three video projections (top to bottom):
Mary Koszmary ('Nightmares'), 2007, transferred from 16mm film, colour, sound,
10 mins 58 secs; *Mur i wieża* ('Wall and Tower'), 2009, colour, sound, 15 mins;
and *Zamach* ('Assassination'), 2011, colour, sound, 39 mins 7 secs
Yael Bartana, born 1970, Kfar Yehezkel, Israel.

Bartana's installations, films and photographs explore the mechanisms that inform and affirm a country's collective identity and
consciousness, raising questions about contemporary geopolitics and
international conflict. Mixing fact and fiction, her works adopt the
aesthetics and performance of rituals, ceremonies and symbols associated with public displays of nationhood and ethnic unity, destabilizing such actions and the notions they promulgate. The year after

winning the 2010 Artes Mundi Prize, Bartana was the first non-
Polish-born artist to represent the country at the Venice Biennale,
exhibiting the dramatic film trilogy ... *And Europe Will Be Stunned*,
which presents the fictional narrative of a radical 'Jewish Renaissance
Movement in Poland' that lobbies for the return of 3.3 million Jewish
emigrants to their ancestral homeland. Her films are consciously provocative, a reversed Zionist utopianism presented via the seductive
tropes of propaganda cinema and with a resemblance to the work
of Nazi filmmaker Leni Riefenstahl. Bartana uses this to address
universal issues of diaspora communities and their right of return,
touching on assimilation and belonging and the questioning aspirations to nationhood.

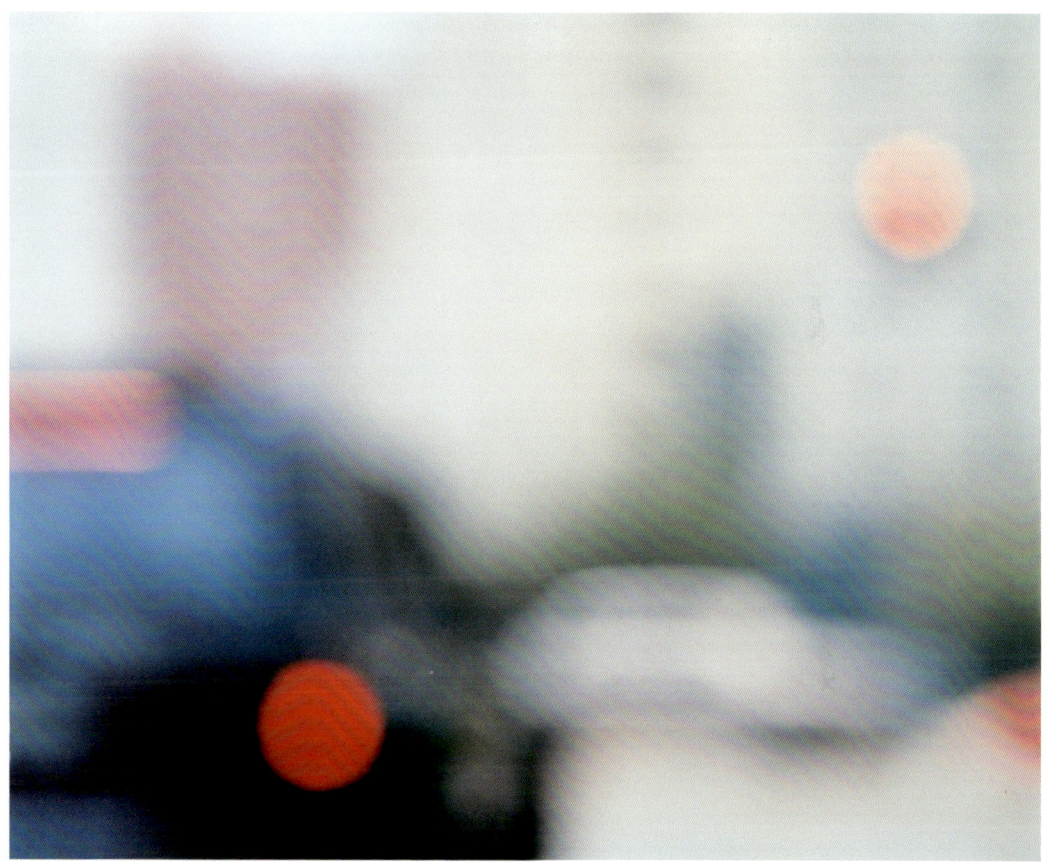

FIELD #3

1995, colour photograph on panel, 58.4 × 73 cm (23 × 28 ¼ in), edition of 8
Uta Barth, born 1958, Berlin.

Emigrating from Germany to the United States in the 1980s to study for a bachelor's and then a master's in fine art, Barth remained in Los Angeles and has taught in the art department of the University of California, Riverside, since 1990, remaining affiliated Professor Emeritus of art. She has won numerous major accolades, including a Guggenheim Fellowship (2004), MacArthur Fellowship and Anonymous Was A Woman grant (both 2012). Exploring the medium of photography, her early investigations were focused on self-portraiture and approaches to the gaze. Barth then became interested in abstraction. Typically out of focus or composed around non-specific objects, her photographs convey a sense of something glimpsed out of the corner of the eye. This work is part of Barth's best-known photographic series 'Field', which is based on visual devices from cinema. Driving through different neighbourhoods, she sought out neutral spaces that offered generic empty foregrounds, and aimed for a blurring effect within the resulting images. In doing so, the works become less about a subject – in this instance of a car and streetscape – and instead highlight atmosphere, the role of the viewer's perception in constructing meaning and the function of the subconscious mind.

MARIA BARTUSZOVÁ

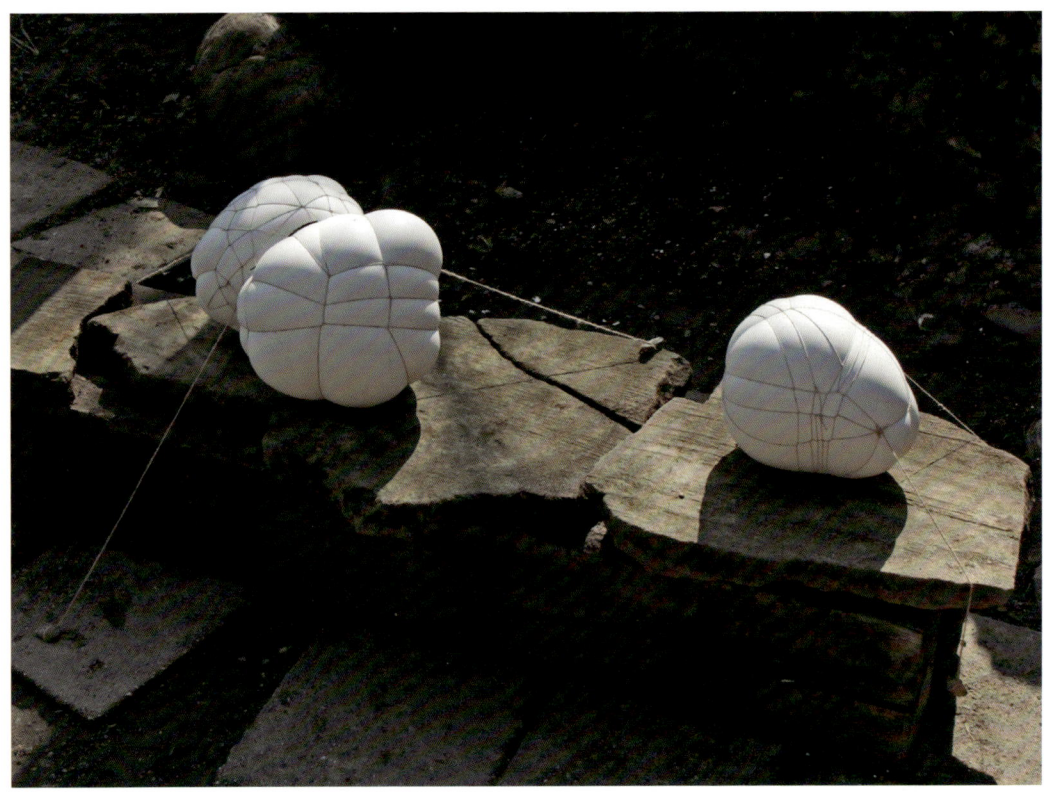

UNTITLED I AND UNTITLED II

1985–7, plaster, string, stone and pneumatic shaping, installed on stone plates,
private collections
Maria Bartuszová, born Maria Vnoučková, 1936, Prague. Died 1996,
Košice, Slovakia.

Bartuszová made plaster-cast sculptures with organic shapes that
reflect natural forms such as rocks or the curves of the human body.
She studied at the Academy of Art, Architecture and Design in her
home town of Prague, but moved to Košice in 1963, two years after
graduating, attracted by housing and work opportunities there.
Starting a family with her artist husband Juraj Bartusz (b.1933),
Bartuszová found artistic inspiration from play with her daughter,
sharing her fascination in the shapes of balloons and inflatables, and

she experimented with pouring plaster into them to create biomorphic casts. From the 1980s onwards, Bartuszová's works looked
at the fragility of fragmented or deformed objects, as seen in these
untitled pieces. Originally installed on stone plates to emphasize
its connection to nature, the cast form is weighted down as though
it might otherwise float away, and bound tightly with string, the
bulging surface seemingly constrained. Despite her art not being
widely appreciated during her lifetime, Bartuszová has since gained
critical acclaim and her work is included in major public collections,
including the Museum of Modern Art, Warsaw, East Slovak Gallery,
Košice and Tate, London.

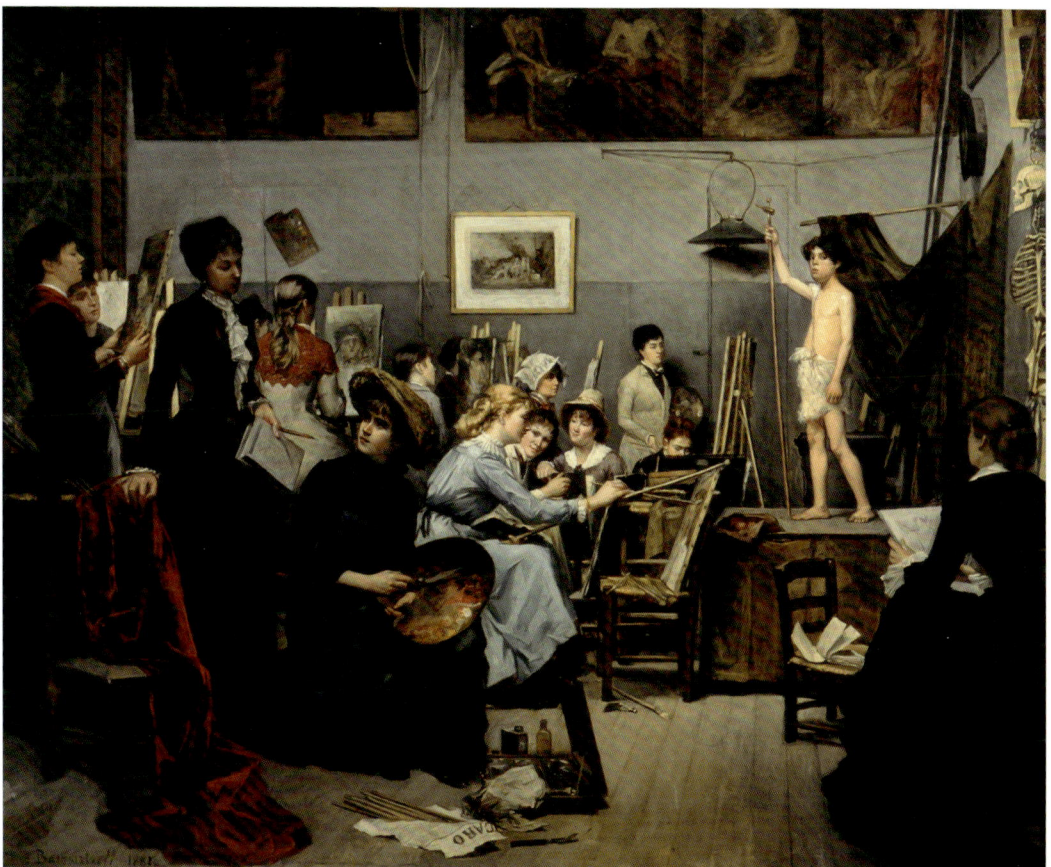

IN THE STUDIO

1881, oil on canvas, 154 × 188 cm (60 ⅝ × 74 in), Dnipropetrovsk State Art Museum, Dnipro, Ukraine
Marie Bashkirtseff, born 1858, Gavrontsi, Russian Empire (now Ukraine). Died 1884, Paris.

Bashkirtseff was inspired to become an artist at the age of fourteen while on a visit to Florence. Her mother had left Bashkirtseff's father when Marie was still a baby – a daring decision for a Russian noblewoman of the era – and from 1870 took her daughter around Europe. Bashkirtseff later attended the Académie Julian in Paris, one of the few art schools of the time that admitted women. This picture shows students painting a child posed as John the Baptist. Study of life models, through the prism of classical art, was the norm, while the skeleton shown reflects the importance of anatomy in artistic training. The artist recorded in her diary: 'As for the subject, it does not fascinate me, but it may be very amusing ... A woman's studio has never been painted.' This diary, posthumously released by her family in 1887, was only the second journal by a woman to be published in France. It bears witness to her aspirations as a professional artist and the challenges this posed in relation to society's expectations around femininity. It also documents her failing health: Bashkirtseff succumbed to tuberculosis at the age of twenty-five.

MARY BEALE

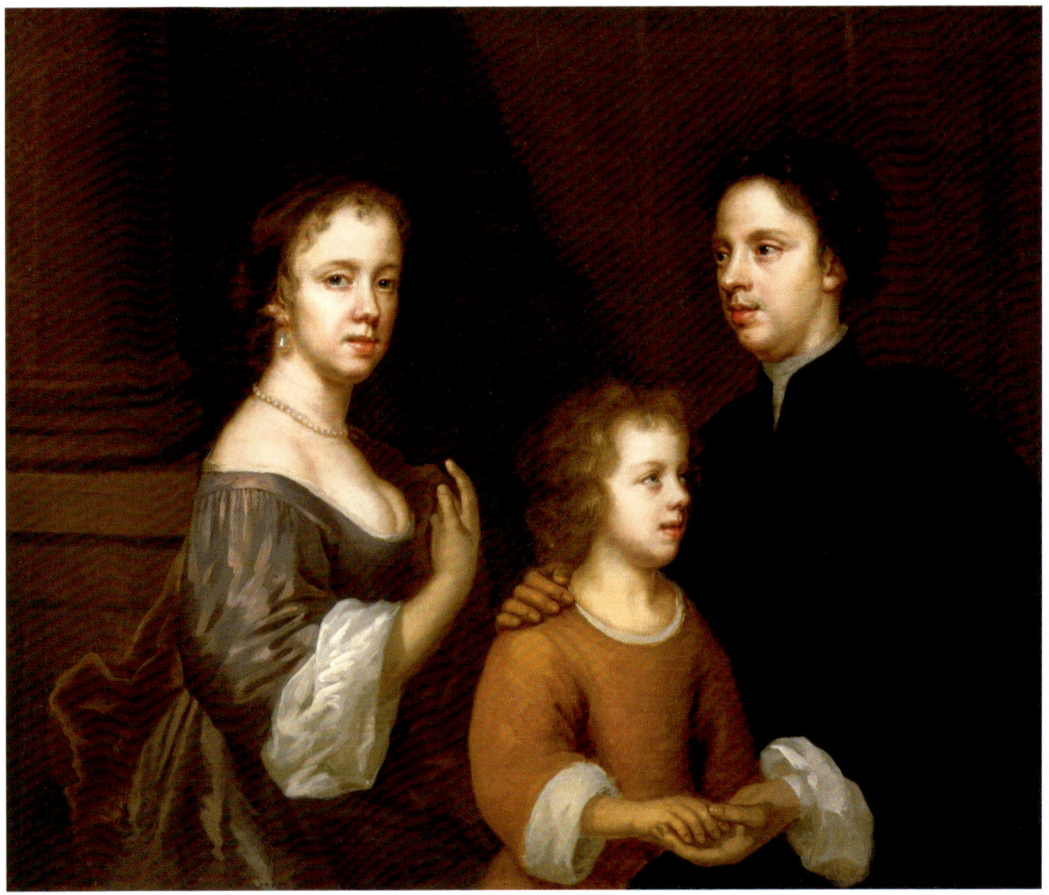

SELF-PORTRAIT WITH HUSBAND CHARLES AND SON BARTHOLOMEW

c.1660, oil on canvas, 60.2 × 74 cm (23 ¾ × 29 ⅛ in), Geffrye Museum
of the Home, London
Mary Beale, born Mary Cradock, 1633, Barrow, Suffolk, UK. Died 1699, London.

An established portraitist during the Stuart period, Beale was one
of the first women working as a professional artist from the mid-
1650s, and over the next twenty years built a profitable enterprise
among London's aristocracy. Her clientele included Henrietta
Maria, former Queen Consort of England as wife of King Charles I.
The graceful poses and flowing dress of her sitters echo the style
associated with Anthony van Dyck (1599–1641) and his successor
as court painter Peter Lely (1618–80), who was a strong advocate
of Beale's. Her *Observations by MB* (1663) made her the first woman

to write in English about her artistic practice, beginning with
an account of painting apricots. The treatise precisely describes the
skills applied to this group study of the artist with her husband and
studio manager, Charles Beale (1623–1705), and their child. In the
formality and elegance of this portrait, Beale identified herself with
the social elite that she was famed for depicting. Looking directly
at the viewer, the artist's accomplishment and authority is strongly
asserted, confirmed by the presence of a classical column symbolic
of worldly power and aesthetic excellence.

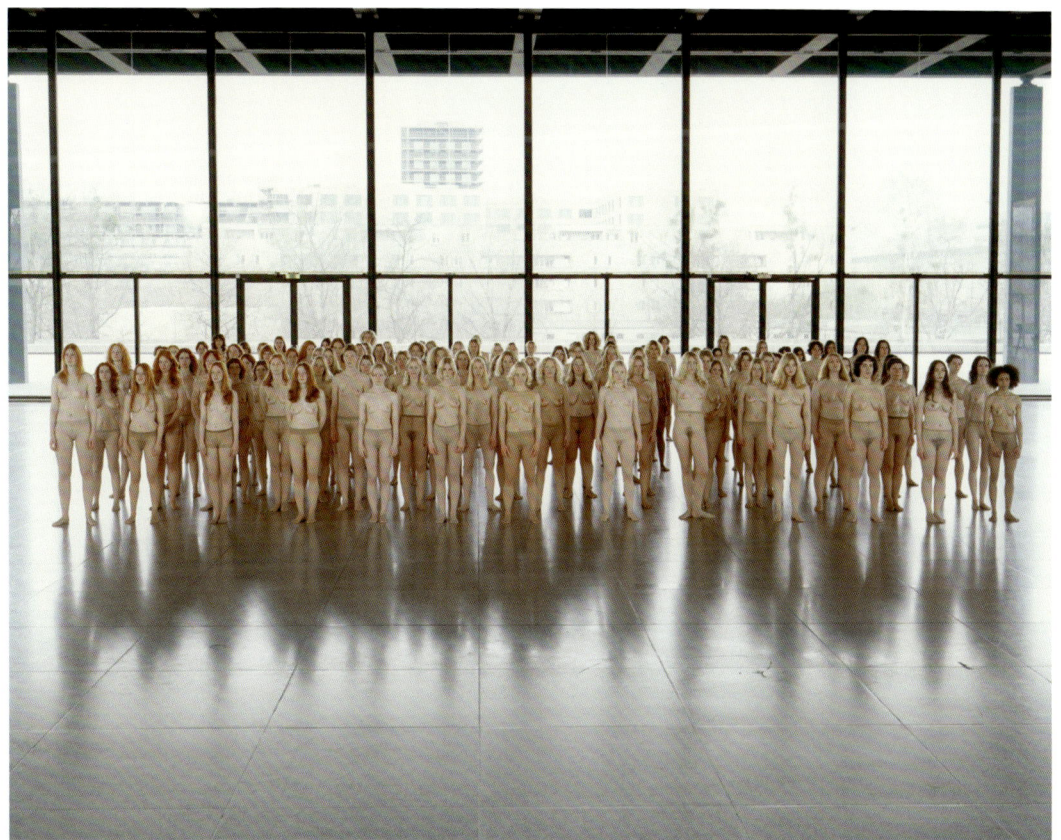

VB55 PERFORMANCE

2005, digital C-print mounted on Diasec, Neue Nationalgalerie, Berlin
Vanessa Beecroft, born 1969, Genoa, Italy.

Known for her highly choreographed *tableaux-vivants*, Beecroft's models are her medium, with large numbers of performers – mainly female, often semi-nude – displayed as living artistic objects. Instantly recognizable through her style, she regards each work as part of an unfolding series, titled sequentially with her initials and informed by her personal struggles with body image. Culturally engaged, and sometimes controversial, her work is a commentary on femininity in contemporary society. Alert to the fashion world – she has an ongoing collaboration with Kanye West's Yeezy label – *VB57* saw her placing nude models on shelves of handbags in a Louis Vuitton store.

Her explicitly political works have included *VB61*, a representation of the Darfur genocide, presenting thirty Sudanese women face down on a canvas, and *VB66*, featuring African immigrants to Italy in a reimagining of Leonardo da Vinci's *Last Supper* (1495–8). Seen here is one of her most famous performance pieces. In a modern art gallery, Beecroft arranged 100 female models dressed only in tights by hair colour. Standing motionless for three hours, her cast confronted objectification head-on, staring defiantly back at viewers and subtly challenging art-historical archetypes of a submissive feminine nude.

VANESSA BELL

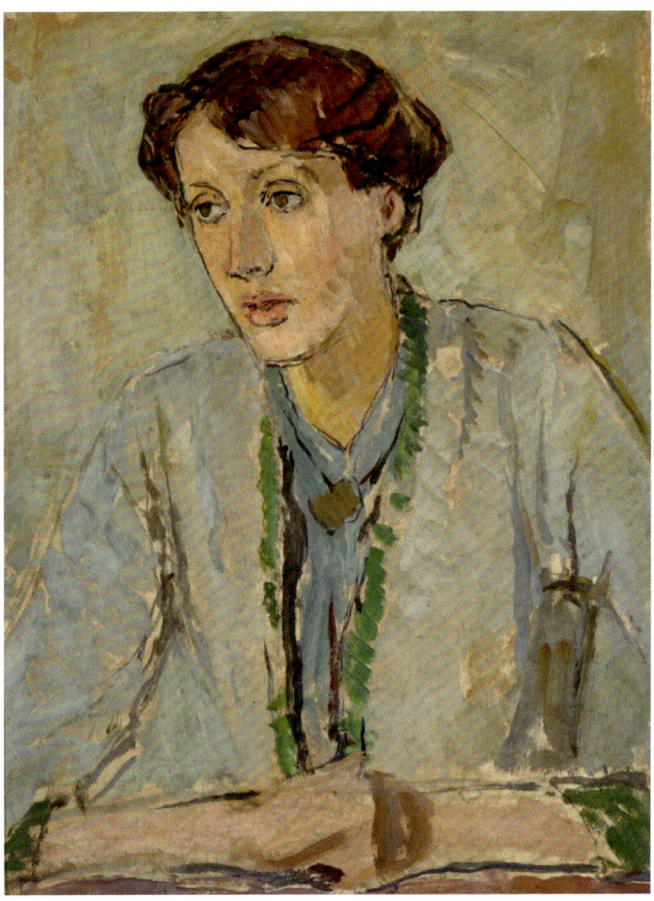

VIRGINIA WOOLF

*c.*1912, oil on panel, 41 × 31 cm (16 ⅛ × 12 ¼ in), Monk's House, Rodmell,
East Sussex, UK

Vanessa Bell, born Vanessa Stephen, 1879, London. Died 1961, Firle, East Sussex, UK.

A noted designer and celebrated member of Britain's Bloomsbury
Group, Bell was part of an intellectual circle that included writers,
poets and critics. Growing up in southwest London, she moved
to the Bloomsbury district after the death of her parents, living there
with her sister, the novelist Virginia Woolf, and their brothers.
Every Thursday evening, the group met at their Gordon Square home
to discuss art and culture. Her early paintings were inspired
by Post-Impressionism, using lively colours, strong shapes and a loose
painting technique. She abandoned figuration for abstraction
around 1914, a change already preempted in this work by the rapid
brushstrokes and constricted depth, the sitter's hands and arms
merging into one long, rectangular form. Bell lived in an open marriage with fellow Bloomsbury member Clive Bell, and when the couple relocated to rural Sussex before the First World War, they lived
in a complicated ménage with others from the group, including her
lover Duncan Grant (1885–1978). Bell and Grant made graphic
works for Roger Fry's Omega Workshops, commissioned in the spirit
of the group's aesthetics, and later designed book jackets for all her
sister's novels.

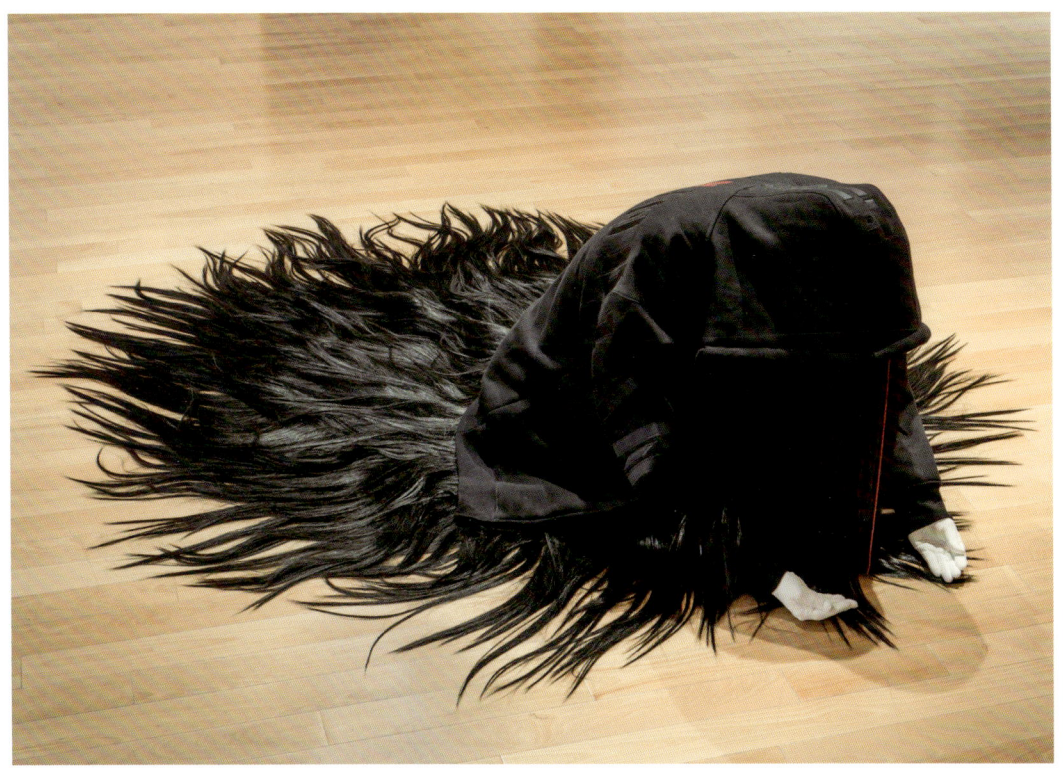

MIXED BLESSING

2011, mixed media, dimensions variable, installation view, 'KWE', Art Museum
at the University of Toronto, 2014
Rebecca Belmore, born 1960, Upsala, Ontario, Canada.

Belmore stands at the forefront of contemporary art made by indigenous artists in Canada and is renowned for her politically and
socially conscious performance and installation work. A member
of the Lac Seul First Nation community and the Anishinaabe
peoples, her art is primarily concerned with issues of colonialism,
oppression and dispossession. In 2005 Belmore became the first
aboriginal artist to represent a North American country at a Venice
Biennale. Her video performance *Fountain*, created for the exhibition, showed Belmore standing in a lake and filling buckets of water,
which she then hurled at the camera. The liquid turns red, seeming
to drench the viewer in an evocation of the colonial slaughter of her
ancestors. The sculpture *Mixed Blessing* embodies the tensions within
Belmore's own identity: a hunched, abject-looking figure with long
raven-black hair that fans out around her wears a black hoodie bearing the disdainful text 'Fuckin Artist, Fuckin Indian'. The words
intersect in the form of a cross, perhaps an allusion to Christianity's
role as a vehicle of colonization, while a red string of beads hangs
from the figure's forehead, suggesting both the bloodlines and blood-
shed of First Nation peoples.

LYNDA BENGLIS

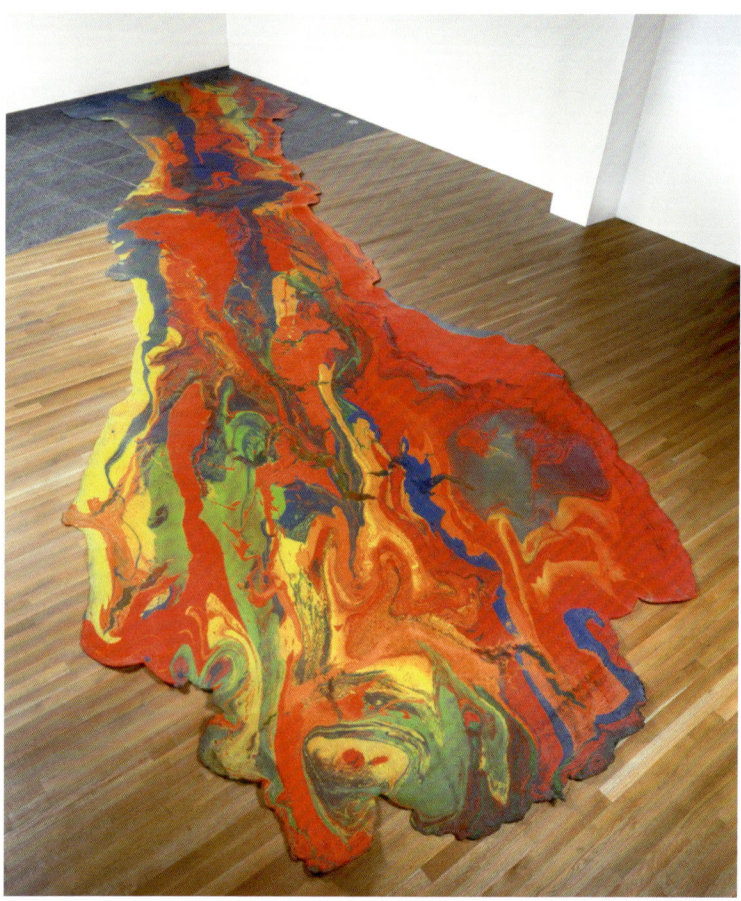

CONTRABAND

1969, Dayglo pigment and poured latex, overall (irregular): 7.6 × 295.3 × 1,011.6 cm
(3 × 116 ¼ × 398 ¼ in), overall thickness of latex: 0.3 cm (⅛ in), Whitney Museum
of American Art, New York
Lynda Benglis, born 1941, Lake Charles, Louisiana.

After studying ceramics and painting in New Orleans, Benglis briefly
taught in an elementary school before moving to New York in 1964,
where she attended classes at the Brooklyn Museum Art School. Over
the next few years, she experimented with materials, process and
form, making totem-like reliefs called 'wax paintings'. Benglis's feminist art upended gender norms, most infamously in *Centrefold* (1974),
the photograph she presented in *Artforum* magazine as an advertisement. Scandalous, above all, for what it ridiculed, the artist was
depicted naked, wearing sunglasses and provocatively holding a giant
flesh-coloured dildo: a challenge to the hyper-masculine art world
in the context of the women's movement. Although visually and mate-
rially very different, her earlier 'fallen paintings', such as *Contraband*,
are also parodies of machismo in the art world. Made by pouring,
flicking, smearing and dripping pigmented latex onto her studio floor,
her process echoed that of Jackson Pollock (1912–56), the artist seen
by many as the archetypal troubled creative genius. Experimenting
with vulgarity, kitsch and taste, Benglis stated that the legacy of feminist art lay in what it was not: not afraid of expression or of being too
pleasurable, too beautiful or too open.

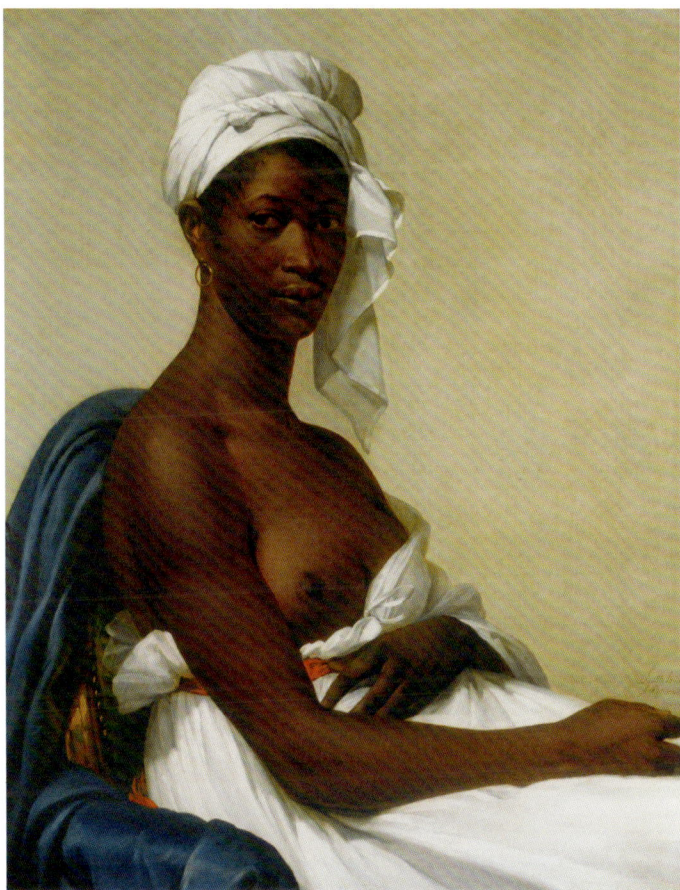

PORTRAIT OF A BLACK WOMAN

1800, oil on canvas, 81 × 65 cm (31 ⅞ × 25 ⅝ in), Musée du Louvre, Paris
Marie-Guillemine Benoist, born Marie-Guillemine de Laville-Leroux, 1768,
Paris. Died 1826, Paris.

Part of an elite circle of women painters, Benoist was mentored and
trained by Élisabeth Vigée-Lebrun (p. 418), who supported her
entry into the studio of Jacques-Louis David (1748–1825), an advocate for women's artistic training at a time when very few women
gained access to the French art academy. David and Vigée-Lebrun
encouraged Benoist to present her work at the annual Salon exhibition, which she did for the first time in 1791 with two history
paintings, including a gender-reversed depiction of Vice. During
the 1800s she received a number of commissions for official
portraits, including various paintings of Napoleon. *Portrait of a Black
Woman* has been described as an anomaly in her oeuvre and yet is the
work for which she is now most well known. In it, Benoist uses portraiture for political ends, the work being perceived as a statement
about the emancipation of women and people of colour, at a time
when advances in women's rights and the treatment of France's colonial subjects were about to be reversed by the Napoleonic regime.
After being presented at the Salon of 1800 – to mixed reviews – it was
purchased in 1818 by Louis XVIII for the nation. In 2019, the Musée
d'Orsay, Paris, temporarily changed its title to *Portrait of Madeleine*
– to emphasize the model's identity as an individual.

RENATE BERTLMANN

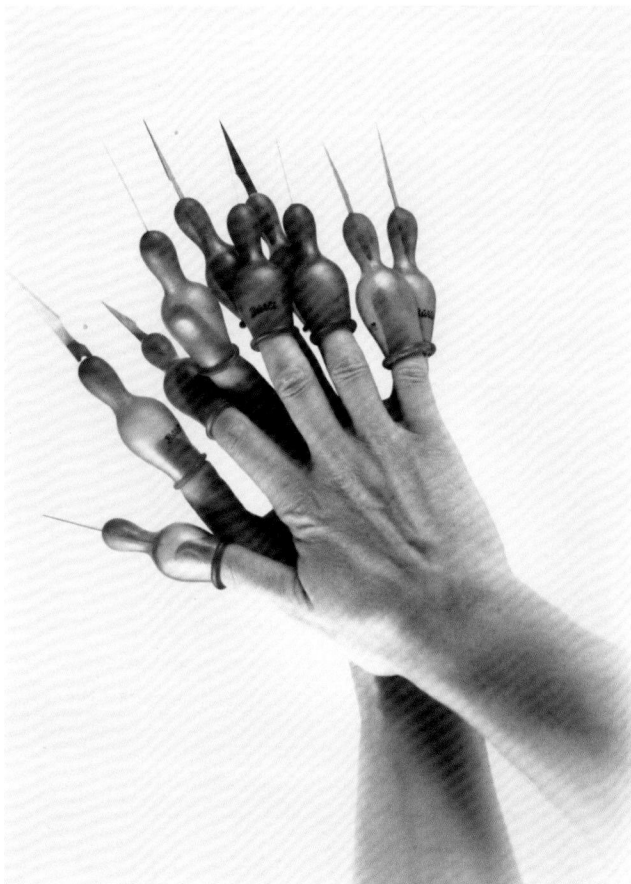

KNIFE-DUMMY-HANDS – AMBIVALENCE
1981, gelatin silver print on baryta paper, 24 × 17.8 cm (9 ½ × 7 in)
Renate Bertlmann, born 1943, Vienna.

In 1978, Bertlmann proclaimed her artistic philosophy as 'AMO ERGO SUM' ('I love, therefore I am'), identifying three dominant themes in her work: pornography, irony and utopia. At that stage, the Austrian avant-garde feminist had been using rubber teats and condoms as her art materials for three years, interested in their inflation, deflation and role in mutual penetration (enacted by pushing one into the other) and she also grafted them onto caps and masks. Exploring registers of tenderness, vulnerability and aggression, such works were part of a critique of patriarchy and, through the use of such sensual materials, explored the absurdity of the phallic order that dominated society. The series 'Tender Hands', in which Bertlmann covered her fingers with pacifier teats to allude to breasts and mothering, evolved into the more disturbing 'Knife-Dummy-Hands' series. The conflictual nature of desire is central to Bertlmann's oeuvre, naming the violence at the heart of sexuality and power at the core of love. Horror and nurture coexist in the prosthetic finger extensions that conjoin scalpels and dummies, symbolizing opposite poles of the care spectrum.

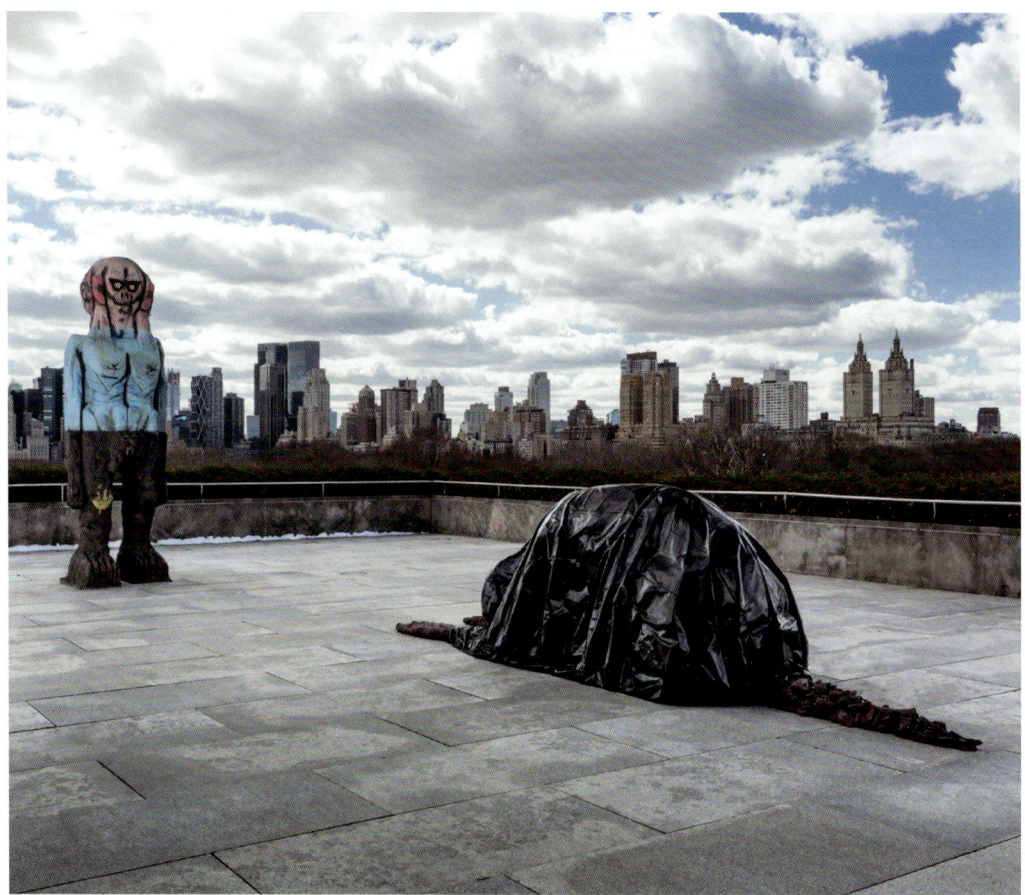

WE COME IN PEACE AND BENAAM

2017, painted and patinated bronze, 417 × 122 × 122 cm (164 × 48 × 48 in) and 139.7 × 457.2 × 147.3 cm (55 × 180 × 58 in), installation view, 'The Roof Garden Commission', Metropolitan Museum of Art, New York, 2018
Huma Bhabha, born 1962, Karachi, Pakistan.

Best known for making figures from everyday detritus, Bhabha imbues her work with a sense of mutation. The viewer is invited to project their own understanding of what Bhabha's 'characters' might be, or where they are from. Having worked as a taxidermist in the early 2000s, a sense of the macabre informs Bhabha's practice, with skulls incorporated into some sculptures. She draws on wide-ranging influences, from African, Classical and modernist sculpture to the tropes of science-fiction and horror movies,

notably the imagery of David Cronenberg. These strands can be detected in *We Come in Peace*, whose title suggests the arrival of alien life. Now a cliché of cinema, this line from *The Day the Earth Stood Still* (1951) conveys hope, trust and suspicion: is there peace and will it last? This is unclear in the indeterminate relationship between this ambiguously gendered colossus, erect and dominant, and a neighbouring piece on the roof of the Metropolitan Museum, *Benaam*, a prostate figure shrouded in plastic. The 'plastic' is in fact convincingly cast in bronze, as are the cork and Styrofoam of both sculptures, Bhabha's work playfully wrong-footing the viewer and upending perceptions of value and intent.

ZARINA BHIMJI

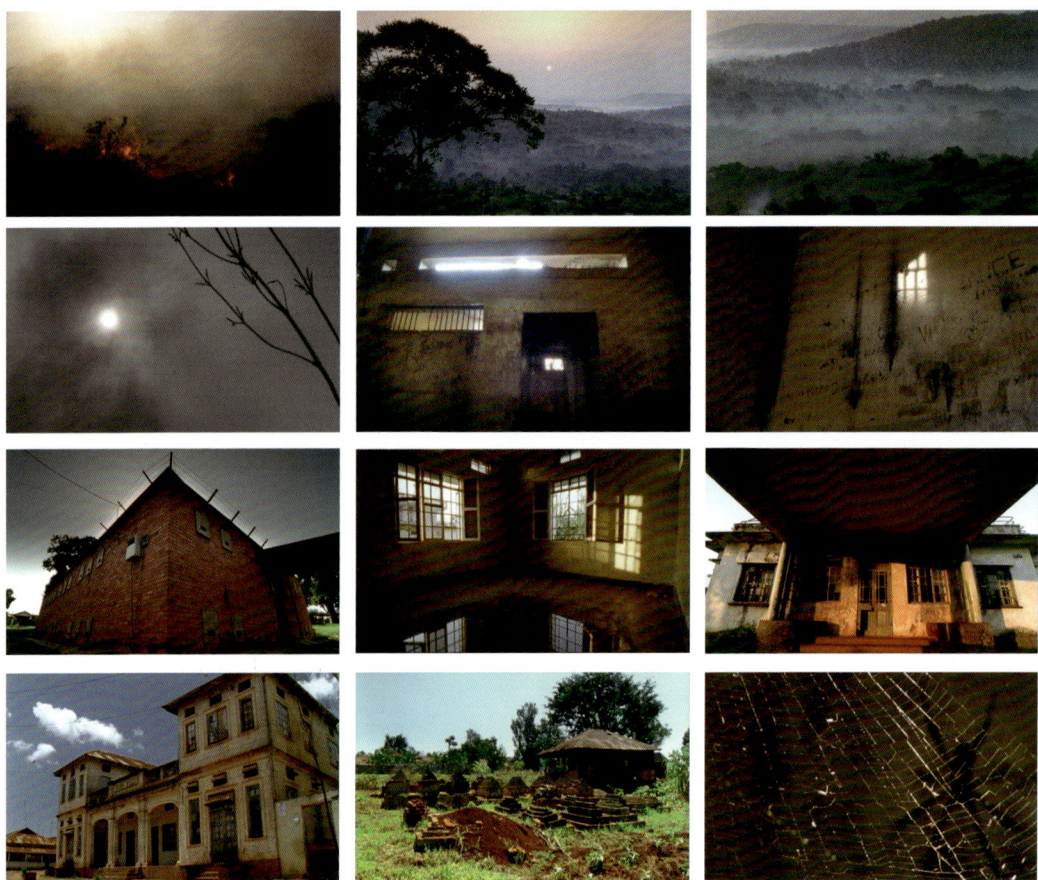

OUT OF THE BLUE

2002, screen grabs from super 16mm colour film, DVD transfer (single-screen installation with sound), 24 mins 25 secs, commissioned and co-produced by Documenta 11

Zarina Bhimji, born 1963, Mbarara, Uganda.

Bhimji studied at Goldsmiths College and the Slade School of Art in the 1980s and was nominated for the 2007 Turner Prize. Her work is held in major public collections including Tate, London, and the Art Institute of Chicago. Bhimji works primarily in photography and moving image, sometimes travelling to other continents to capture different atmospheres – lights, sounds, colours and shapes – which then feed into her artworks. *Out of the Blue* was Bhimji's first film and developed out of a photographic series she had shot during trips to Uganda in 1998, in which she aimed to express its beauty and poetry. Presented as an installation that immerses the viewer, the film unravels slowly. Verdant views of Uganda, inspired by the Romantic Sublime of British and German landscape painting, are shown alongside unpeopled shots of architecture and interiors, including prison cells, barracks and an airport. Bhimji created the soundtrack like a musical score, layering audio recordings that include babies laughing, people crying, old radio broadcasts, mosquito sounds, whispering, music and the tender singing of Abida Parveen. While not overtly political, she rigorously researched the project, and themes of elimination, extermination and erasure underpin it.

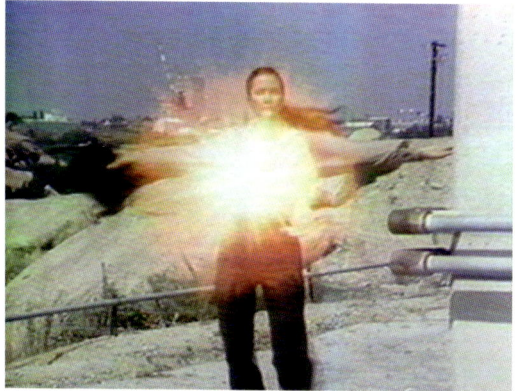 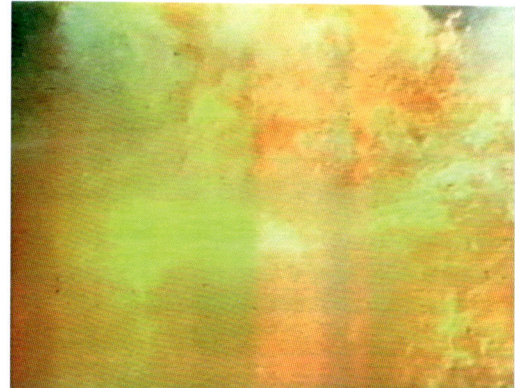

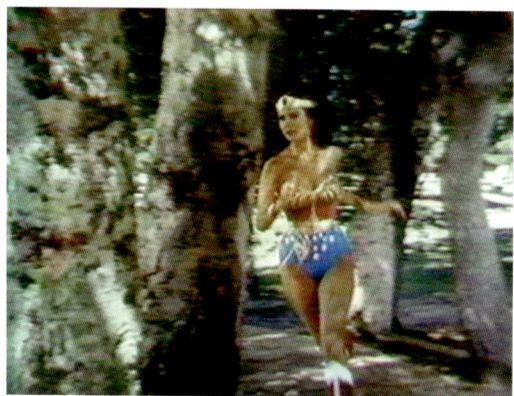 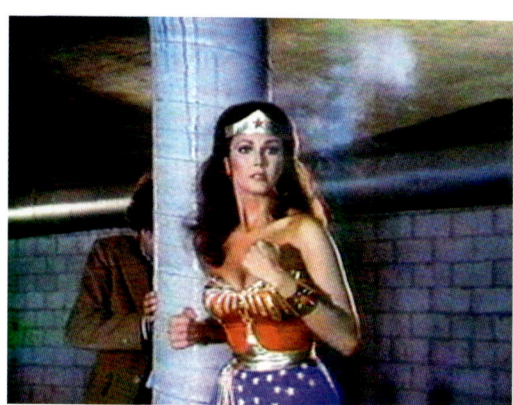

TECHNOLOGY/TRANSFORMATION: WONDER WOMAN

1978–9, stills from single-channel video, colour, stereo sound, 5 mins 50 secs
Dara Birnbaum, born 1946, New York. Died 2025.

With degrees in both architecture and painting, Birnbaum spent some time in Florence in 1974, where she encountered the pioneering gallery Centro Diffusione Grafica that was actively experimenting with the new art medium of video. Upon returning to the United States in 1975, she began working with moving image herself. By sampling television footage *Technology/Transformation: Wonder Woman* is one of the first artworks to use cultural appropriation to generate a mediated collage. Commenting on and subverting notions of gender, sexuality and identity, an alarm sounds as the professionally dressed Diana Prince, a US intelligence officer played by

Lynda Carter, begins to spin with a thunderous explosion, transforming into the iconic Amazonian superhero. Birnbaum uses technology to subject the footage to multiple looped edits that disrupt the narrative flow with Carter rotating over and over. Television of this era played a major role in constructing cultural identity, and young girls in the United States and beyond would enact the Wonder Woman spin. Birnbaum's work comments on representations of women in mass media and how these are reappropriated by audiences.

MARÍA BLANCHARD

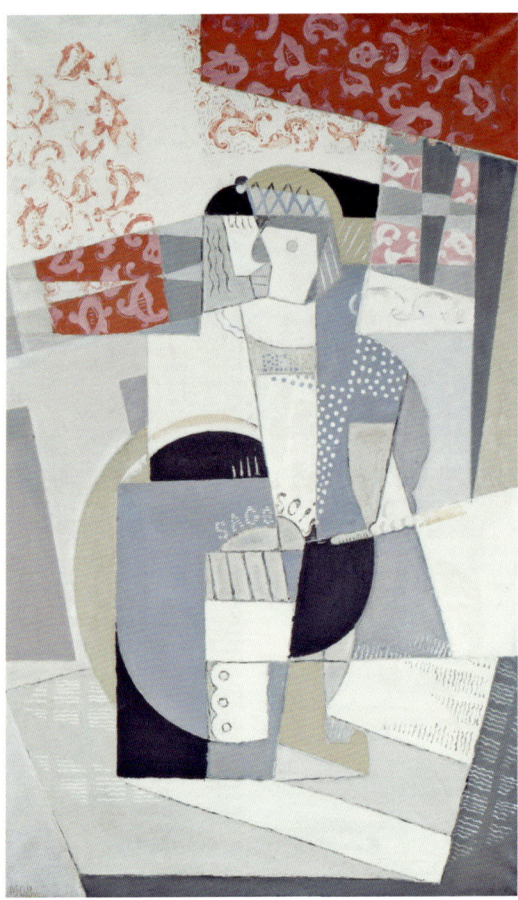

BE GOOD also called JOAN OF ARC

1917, oil on canvas, 140 × 85 cm (55 ⅛ × 33 ½ in), Musée National d'Art Moderne,
Centre Georges Pompidou, Paris
María Blanchard, born María Gutiérrez Cueto, 1881, Santander, Spain.
Died 1932, Paris.

Blanchard was born with a severe spinal deformity from which she
suffered all her life; as her friend the Spanish poet Federico García
Lorca noted, people saw the hunchback before they saw her. Nevertheless, she also gained recognition as a woman at the centre of revolutionary developments in Western art. After training in Madrid,
she continued her studies in Paris, settling there permanently in 1916,
and for the next three years was at the heart of Cubism. She worked
in symbiosis with her friend Juan Gris (1887–1927), sharing his calm

and luminous vision. Diego Rivera (1886–1957), with whom she
shared a studio, considered that Blanchard was second only to
Pablo Picasso (1881–1973) within the Cubist movement. The figure
in this painting, bearing the message '*sois sage*' ('be good', or 'behave
yourself'), has been interpreted both as a child with a hoop and stick
and as the fifteenth-century French heroine Joan of Arc, with a
shield and weapon. Though an image of childhood is more probably
what Blanchard intended – the word 'BÉBÉ' appears on the figure's
collar – the notion of courage is entirely appropriate to this artist and
her subject.

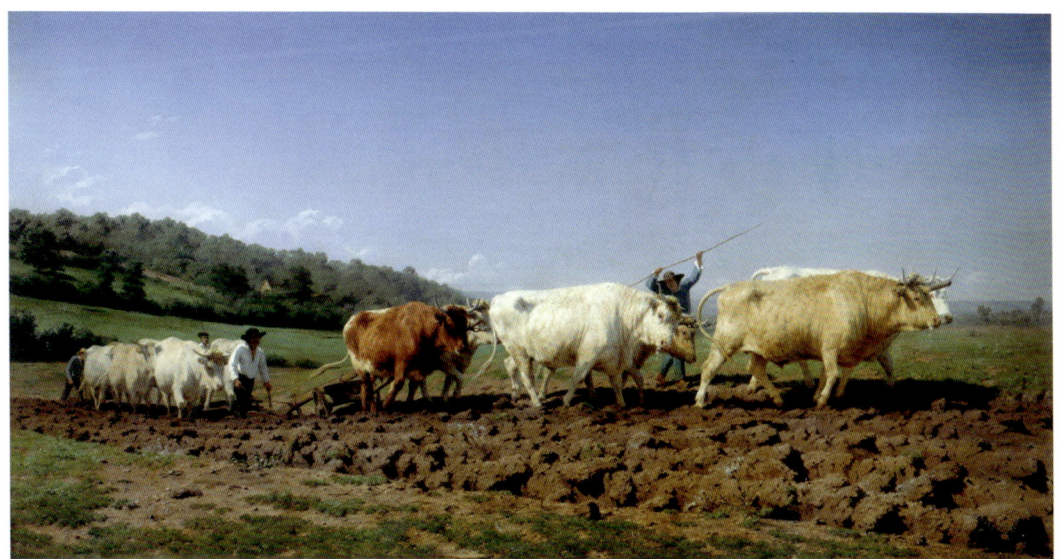

PLOUGHING IN NEVERS also called THE FIRST DRESSING
1849, oil on canvas, 134 × 260 cm (52 ¼ × 102 ⅛ in), Musée d'Orsay, Paris
Rosa Bonheur, born Marie-Rosalie Bonheur, 1822, Bordeaux, France. Died 1899, Thomery, France.

When, in 1865, Bonheur was the first woman to be invested with France's *Légion d'Honneur*, the Empress Eugénie remarked that 'genius has no sex'. As a painter and sculptor of animals, her immense success in both Europe and America afforded her social licence as well as artistic esteem. She gained financial independence and was officially permitted by the police to adopt male dress, which she argued was necessary for practical reasons in her professional life. Purchasing a château near the forest of Fontainebleau, she lived with her closest friend Natalie Micas and, later, the painter Anna Klumpke (1856–1942), the editor and publisher of Bonheur's memoirs. At a time when women were not formally trained in drawing nude subjects, she gained her exceptional knowledge of the anatomy of animals by visiting Parisian abattoirs and the city's Veterinary Institute. This study of a team of Charolais cattle, one of her best-known works, was commissioned by the government of the Second Republic and took first place at the 1849 Paris Salon. It was widely admired for its idealized representation of France's rural economy, but also for its exquisitely detailed physicality, right down to the spittle dripping from the oxen's mouths.

MONICA BONVICINI

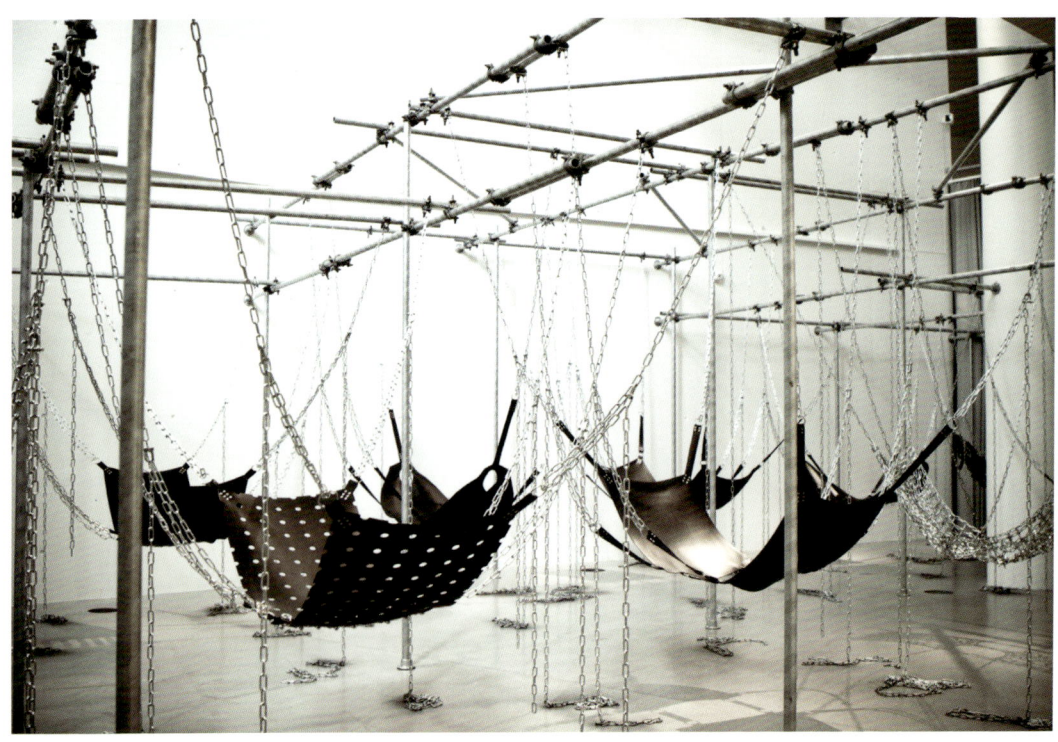

NEVER AGAIN

2005, galvanized steel pipes, black leather, black leather men's belts, galvanized chains and clamps, 3.5 × 16 × 11 m (11 ½ × 52 ½ × 36 ft), installation views, ARoS Aarhus Kunstmuseum, Denmark. Collection Städtische Galerie im Lenbachhaus und Kunstbau München, KiCo Stiftung, Munich
Monica Bonvicini, born 1965, Venice.

Bonvicini's works critically address the built environment, questioning expressions of power and the articulations of gender imbalance that exist in architecture and define most of our constructions of space. Since the beginning of her career, the Italian artist has been interested in the concept of authority, power and economic distribution. Formally, her practice spans different media: performance, film, installation, sculpture, painting and drawing and she works with industrial materials and structures, including drywall or scaffolding. Bonvicini creates large-scale thought-provoking installations, in which she pairs psychoanalytical concepts with fetish equipment; the imagery of gendered stereotypes with political protest. A typical example is *Never Again* – a collection of swings composed from various materials (mainly leather and chains), suspended from heavy steel chains. Evocative of sadomasochism, the playground jangles as the viewer navigates and physically engages with it, effectively changing the ingrained institutional politics of most gallery spaces where viewers are instructed to look but not touch. Bonvicini has been based in Berlin since the mid-1980s and, alongside her artistic output, has held academic positions as a professor of installation art and sculpture in Vienna and Berlin.

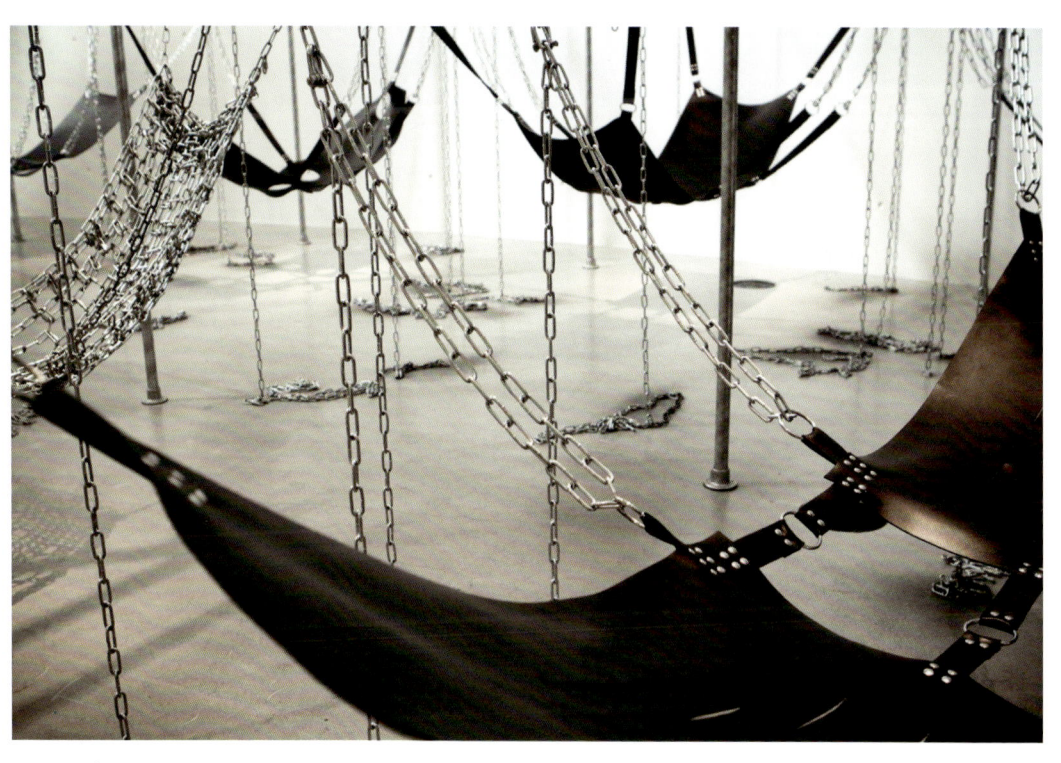

DINEO SESHEE BOPAPE

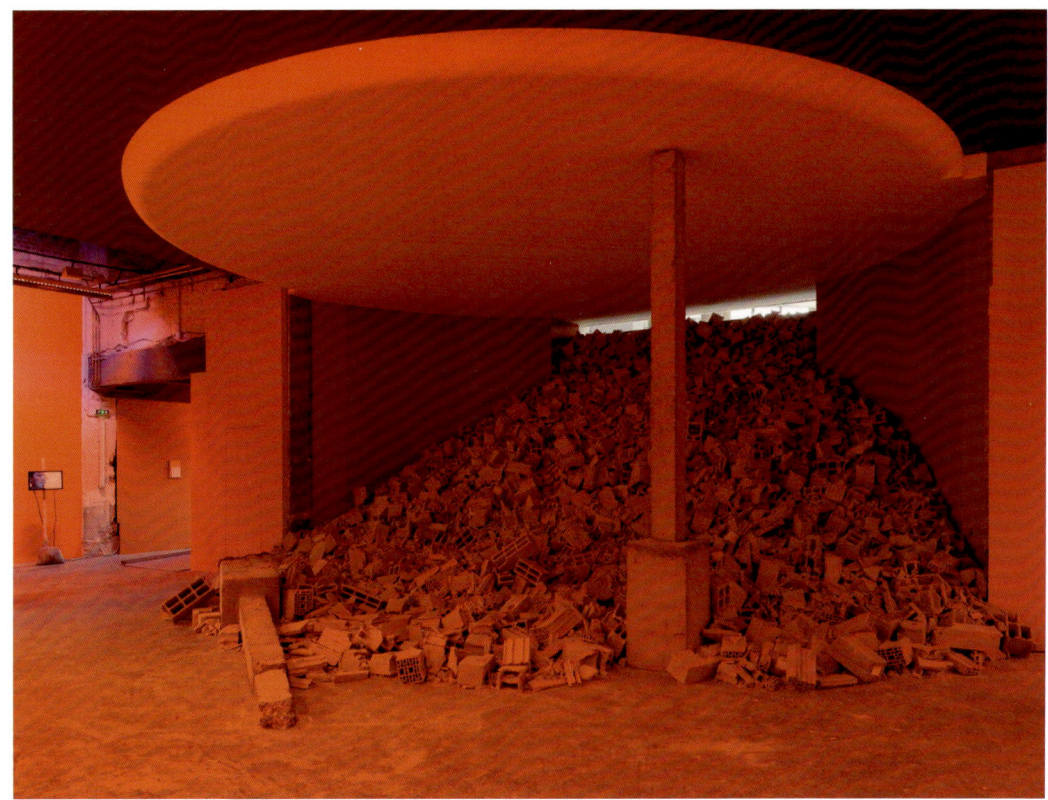

UNTITLED (OF OCCULT INSTABILITY) [FEELINGS]

2016–18, (detail), mixed-media installation: video and sound display of Nina
Simone's 1976 performance of 'Feelings', flat-screen monitors, plastic buckets,
water pumps, contact microphones and bricks. Also featuring the inclusion
of works by guest artists Jabu Arnell, Lachell Workman and Robert Rhee,
installation view, Palais de Tokyo, Paris, 2016
Dineo Seshee Bopape, born 1981, Polokwane, South Africa.

Bopape is a multimedia artist known for her installations and experimental video works that combine sound, photographs and found
objects collected throughout Africa, and which question how historic
places affect the present moment. Initially studying painting and
sculpture in Durban, South Africa, she continued her art education
in Amsterdam then New York before returning to live in Johannesburg.

Exploring socio-political notions of memory and heritage, Bopape's
work examines her own background in Limpopo Province while
remaining conscious of her wider experiences and the multiple, intersecting identities that define her – and every individual. The large-
scale installation seen here, with its heaps of rubble and deep-red
backdrop, evoke states of ruination and moods of madness and
psychic dissolution. It features a video depicting Nina Simone
singing 'Feelings' and consideration of Bessie Head's novel about
a woman's descent into insanity, *A Question of Power* (1973). The
'occult instability' of the title is a term used by psychiatrist and philosopher Frantz Fanon to describe colonialism's effect on the psyche
of the colonized, and Bopape has recalled her feelings of discomfort
visiting the Jardin Tropical de Vincennes in Paris, the site of a former colonial test garden.

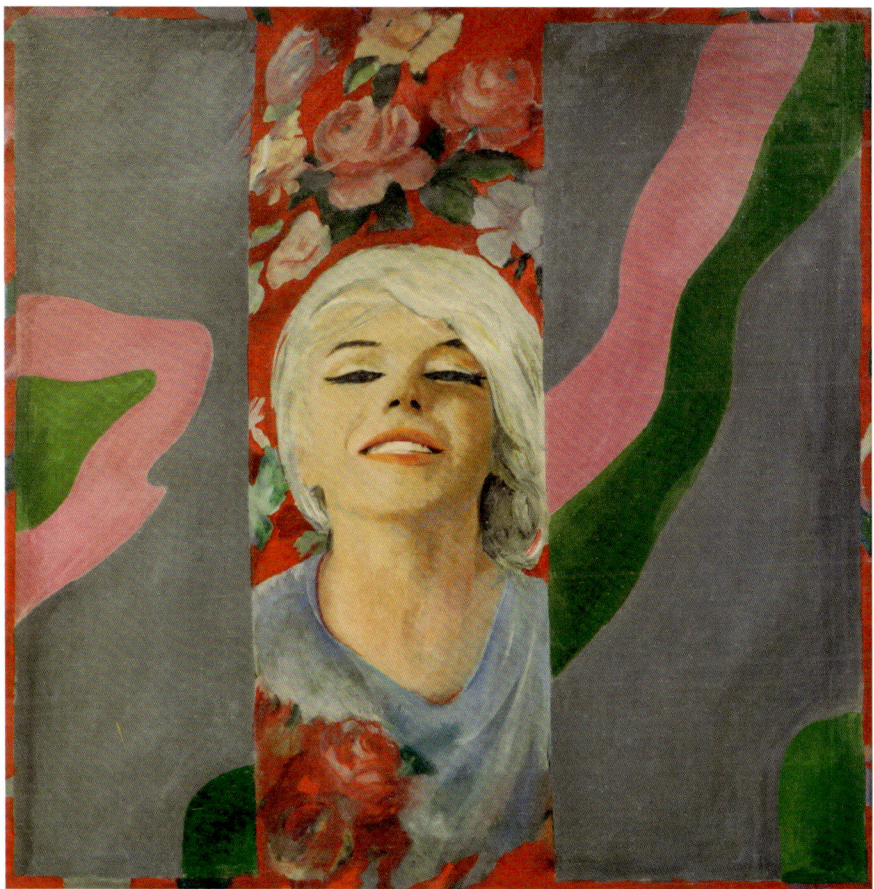

COLOUR HER GONE

1962, oil on canvas, 121.9 × 121.9 cm (48 × 48 in), Wolverhampton Art Gallery, West Midlands, UK

Pauline Boty, born 1938, London. Died 1966, London.

Awarded a scholarship to London's Wimbledon School of Art in 1954, Boty went on to study in the School of Stained Glass at the Royal College of Art. A central figure – and the only woman – in the nascent British Pop art scene, fame, beauty and sex were key themes in her figurative work, which she primarily executed using painting and collage. Also an actress appearing in films, television series and plays, she featured in Ken Russell's 1962 documentary *Monitor: Pop Goes the Easel*. Her life was cut tragically short at just twenty-eight; diagnosed with a cancerous tumour while pregnant, she chose to decline treatment in order to have the baby. This portrait was painted shortly after Marilyn Monroe's own premature death. Boty's work was largely forgotten for over thirty years, until many surviving pieces were located in her brother's barn by art historians David Alan Mellor and Sue Tate. Following a significant exhibition at Wolverhampton Art Gallery in 2013, and through the fiction of prize-winning writer Ali Smith, who pays tribute to Boty in her novel *Autumn* (2016), awareness of the artist's life and work has grown rapidly.

PAULINE BOUDRY & RENATE LORENZ

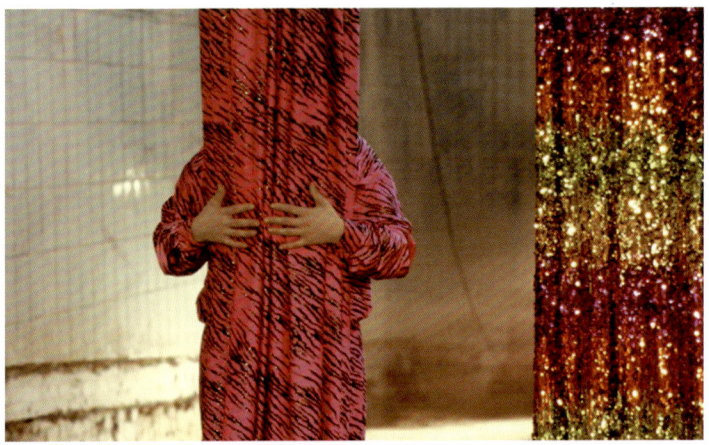

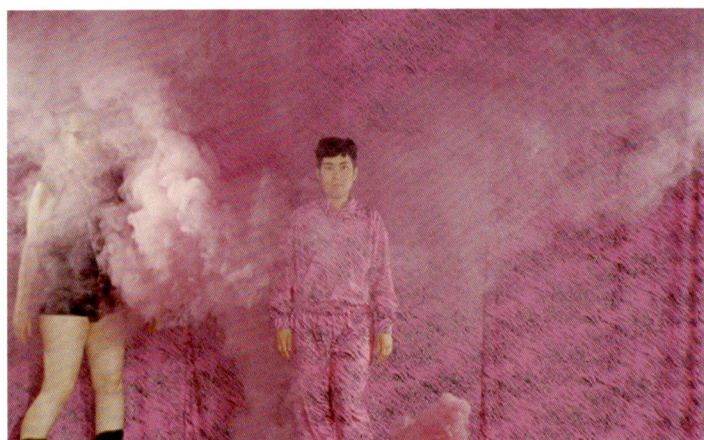

OPAQUE

2014, super 16mm film transferred to HD, 10 mins, Fond Régional d'Art
Contemporain Lorraine, Metz, France. Performance: Ginger Brooks Takahashi,
Werner Hirsch

Pauline Boudry, born 1972, Lausanne, Switzerland. Renate Lorenz,
born 1963, Berlin.

Based in Berlin, Boudry and Lorenz have collaborated since 2007,
working with performance, video and installation to reflect upon
the passage of time. Examining historical and cultural artefacts,
from literature to music and dance, they explore these in relation
to social conditions of the past and present. Highly staged scenarios
are played out and past events reformulated for future 'use'. Their
references are numerous and far-ranging: for example, the work

To Valerie Solanas and Marilyn Monroe, In Recognition of their Desperation
(2013) references a 1970 score by a pioneer of electronic music
Pauline Oliveros and was filmed in an East German radio studio
in Berlin called Funkhaus. Questions around visibility are key to their
practice, as in *Opaque*, a film of a performance in an abandoned
swimming pool. The scene evokes the idea, perhaps more relevant
than ever, of French-Caribbean theorist Édouard Glissant, who
spoke of the 'right to opacity': the quality of being unseen, unknown
and untraceable, which is crucial to the ability of the oppressed to
challenge systems of power and domination. Time's passing becomes
a mode of resistance.

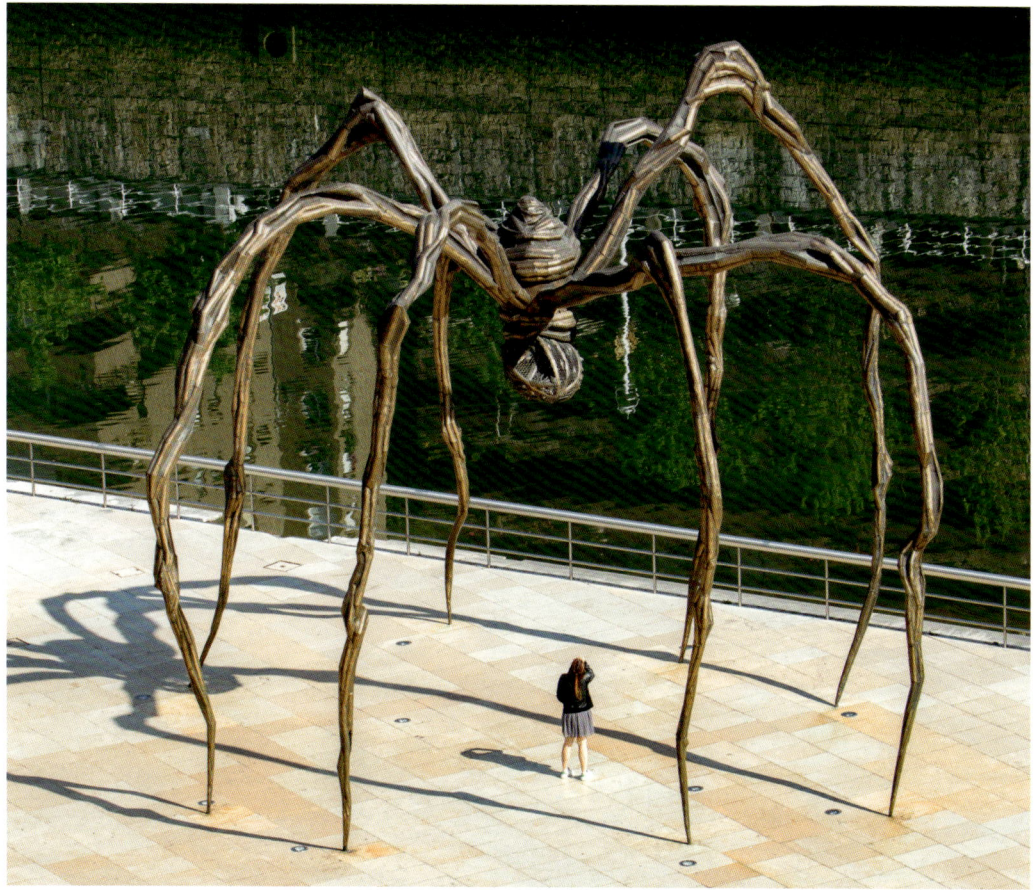

MAMAN

1999 (cast 2001), steel and marble, 9.3 × 8.9 × 10.2 m (30 ¾ × 29 ¼ × 33 ½ ft),
edition of 6, installation view, Guggenheim Museum Bilbao, Spain
Louise Bourgeois, born 1911, Paris. Died 2010, New York.

Now considered one of the twentieth century's greatest artists, Bourgeois did not receive international recognition until the age of seventy, following her 1982 retrospective at New York's Museum of Modern Art. The daughter of French tapestry restorers, she studied art in Paris before moving to New York in 1938, becoming an American citizen in 1951. Her first exhibition of paintings was held in 1945 at Bertha Schaefer Gallery and her sculptures debuted four years later at Peridot Gallery. Highly inventive, psychologically charged and often unsettling, her sculptural work – which ranges in material from bronze or marble to stitched, stuffed fabrics – has its roots in childhood memories and experiences and is at once visceral, precarious, fragile and full of subversive humour. In the 1990s, Bourgeois began a series of drawings and sculptures featuring spiders. This colossal iteration, versions of which have been presented around the world, was originally created for the inaugural programme of Tate Modern, London. Bourgeois described this towering arachnid as an ode to her beloved mother, who was a weaver, like a spider. Noting how clever spiders are, she also emphasized their protective qualities: walking beneath, visitors can see a woven sac, safeguarding seventeen marble eggs.

MARGARET BOURKE-WHITE

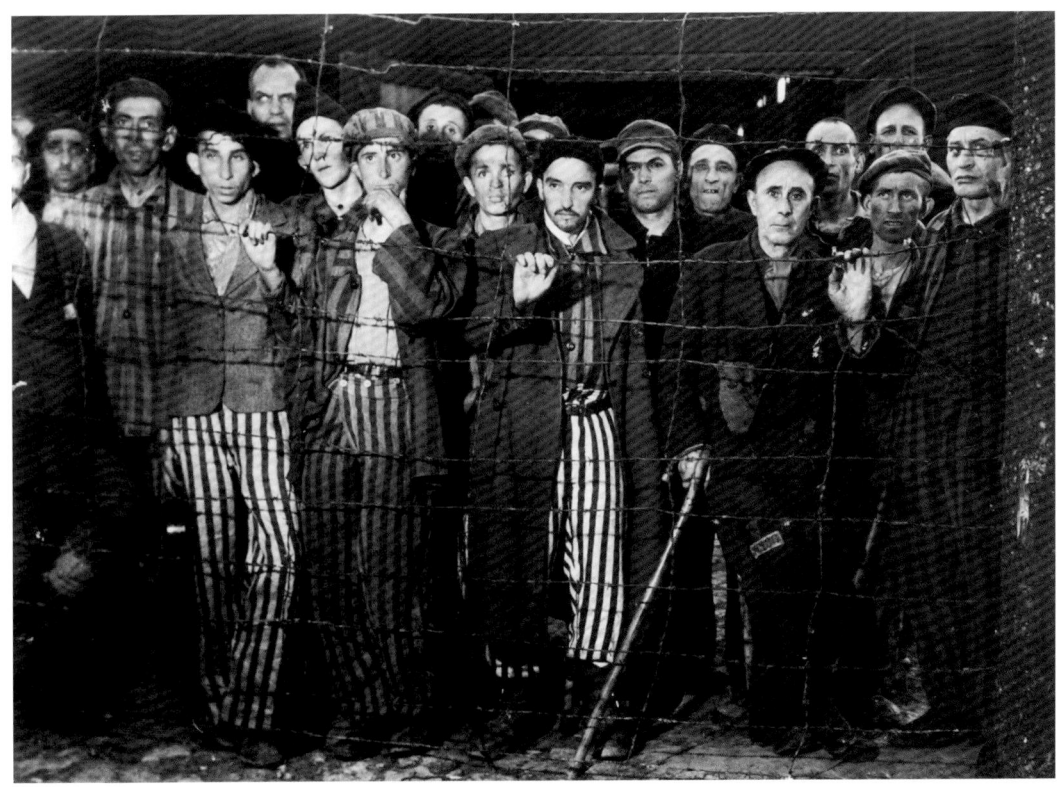

**PRISONERS AT THE GATES OF THE BUCHENWALD CONCENTRATION
CAMP NEAR THE END OF WORLD WAR II**

1945, black-and-white photograph
Margaret Bourke-White, born Margaret White, 1904, New York. Died 1971,
Stamford, Connecticut.

One of the most prolific documentary photographers of the twenti-
eth century, Bourke-White first picked up the camera as a hobby.
In 1929, she was hired by *Fortune* magazine to photograph the
Krupp Iron Works in Germany. On her own initiative, she then trav-
elled to the Soviet Union to document the first five-year plan – a list
of economic goals imposed by Joseph Stalin between 1928 and 1932.
In 1936, she was among only four staff photographers for the new
Life magazine, providing images for the launch issue's cover story.

The first woman documentary photographer to receive accreditation
from the US armed forces, Bourke-White covered the Second World
War and the Siege of Moscow for *Life* and crossed into Germany
shortly before the end of the war. This haunting image is one of many
she took following the liberation of the concentration camps,
recording gas chambers, corpses and survivors. She considered photography a witness to history, writing in her 1946 memoir *Dear
Fatherland, Rest Quietly*, 'I kept telling myself that I would believe the
indescribably horrible sight in the courtyard before me only when
I had a chance to look at my own photographs.'

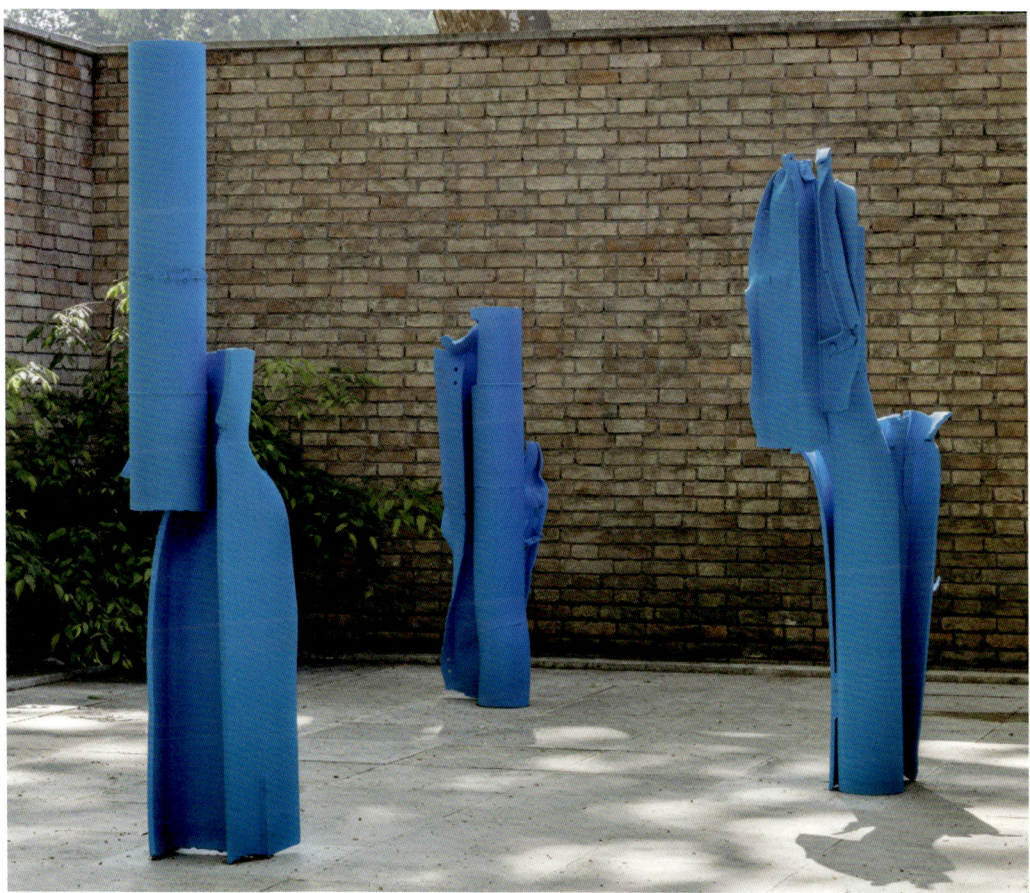

LA PLÉIADE

2017, steel, found steel and urethane paint, 208.2 × 55.9 × 38.1 cm (80 × 22 × 15 in), installation view, 'Women of Venice', Swiss Pavilion, 57th Venice Biennale
Carol Bove, born 1971, Geneva.

Growing up in Berkeley, California, the style of Bove's pieces is influenced by the public sculptures she encountered there as a child. She obtained her BA from New York University in 2000, and her work has steadily grown in scale since this time. Her practice also includes installations and assemblage – artworks made by grouping objects. In a May 2018 interview with *Wallpaper** magazine, she referred to her method of working as 'spontaneous' and 'expressionistic', rather than developing ideas in preliminary sketches. Her focus instead is on the way materials and objects connect to the themes she explores. Her installation for the Swiss Pavilion at the 57th Venice Biennale, of which these three sculptures formed a part, was inspired by a 1956 series of plaster figures by Alberto Giacometti (1901–66). A collection of seven sculptures is named after both the constellation of seven stars and also a mountain near her home in Switzerland. As such, it plays on ideas of identity and how individual circumstances can influence an outcome.

SONIA BOYCE

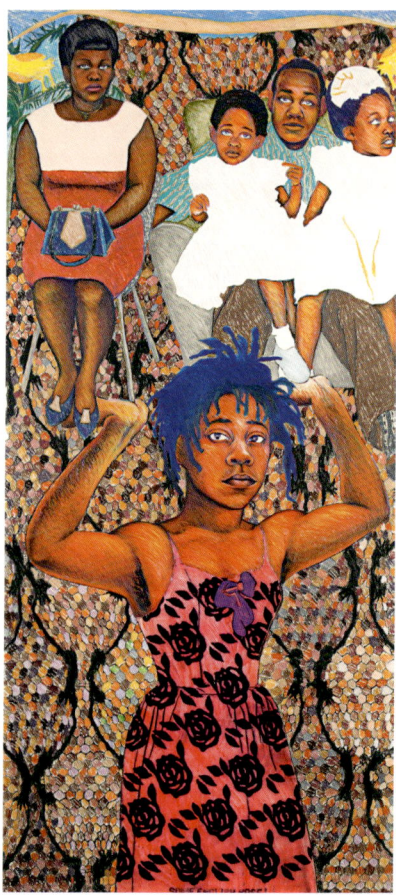

SHE AIN'T HOLDING THEM UP, SHE'S HOLDING ON (SOME ENGLISH ROSE)
1986, oil and pastel on paper, 227 × 113.5 cm (89 ⅜ × 44 ⅝ in), Middlesbrough
Institute of Modern Art, UK
Sonia Boyce, born 1962, London.

Boyce, who is of Barbadian and Guyanese heritage, emerged as part
of the British black arts movement – formalized in 1982 as the
BLK Art Group – alongside artists including Keith Piper (b.1960),
Lubaina Himid (p.188) and Maud Sulter (p.394). In parallel with her
artistic practice, Boyce now has prominent academic roles as professor at Middlesex University and University of the Arts London.
Her acclaimed early work in chalk and pastels explored the identities and positive representations of black women in art. Over time,
she has incorporated photography, collage, installation and video

into her practice and the themes of her work have progressively
broadened beyond race and gender identity to experiment with collaborative interactions between people, objects and spaces. In this
early self-portrait, Boyce appears to be physically supporting her
family, who are seated above her. However, the title both challenges this meaning – is she in fact holding onto them to sustain
a connection? – and invokes a stereotype of white femininity to subversive intent. Roses are set alongside tropical plants – allusions to
her English and Caribbean roots, respectively – a comment on Boyce's
layered identity as a black British woman.

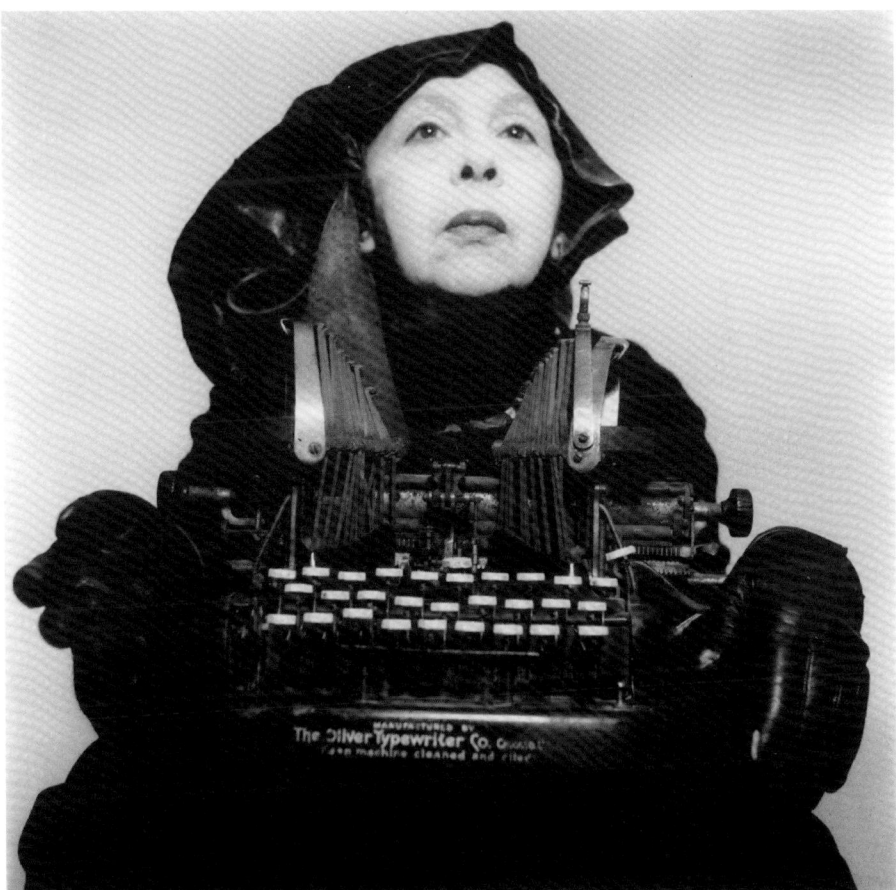

SELF-PORTRAIT – MRS OLIVER IN HER TRAVELING COSTUME

1980 (reprinted 2012), gelatin silver print, 38.9 × 39.5 cm (15 ⅜ × 15 ½ in)
Geta Brătescu, born Georgeta Comanescu, 1926, Ploieşti, Romania. Died 2018, Bucharest, Romania.

For Brătescu, art was alchemy, transforming everyday objects, experiences and materials. In her book *The Tree from the Neighbouring Courtyard* (2009) she described this as her mode of expression, infused with femininity – though she resisted the label feminist, seeing it as constrictive. Expelled from art school in 1949 after a Communist purge of Romania's middle class, she instead got a job sketching scenes of industrial life in the country. With a love of storytelling, she also worked as both a writer and illustrator. Much of her diverse practice, which spanned drawing, collage, textiles, performance and

film, took place in the studio. Here she had amassed a diverse collection of objects and materials, which appear as props or characters in her work. An old Oliver-brand typewriter, for example, features in this piece. The artist appears majestically in black, presenting the machine as if it were an extension of her body. A performance as much as a still image, portraits like this were taken in collaboration with her husband of over sixty years, photographer and engineer Mihai Brătescu, with the artist preferring to stand and play in front of the camera's lens rather than being behind it.

CANDICE BREITZ

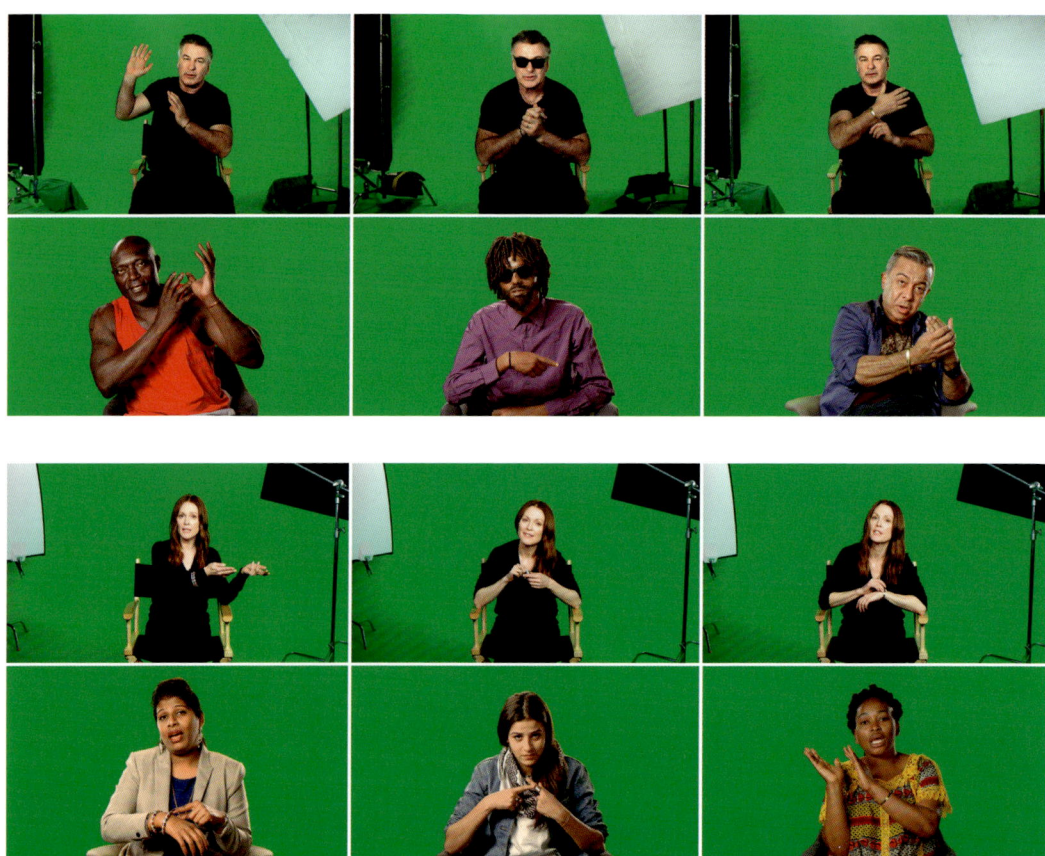

STILLS from LOVE STORY

2016, 7-channel installation: 7 hard drives. Featuring Julianne Moore and Alec Baldwin. Top: José Maria João, Farah Abdi Mohamed, Luis Ernesto Nava Molero. Bottom: Shabeena Francis Saveri, Sarah Ezzat Mardini, Mamy Maloba Langa. Commissioned by the National Gallery of Victoria, Australia; Outset Germany + Medienboard Berlin-Brandenburg

Candice Breitz, born 1972, Johannesburg.

Breitz makes photographs and video installations that explore the unspoken conditions of identity and community. Drawing on references from television, film and popular culture, she examines how individuals define themselves in relation to mainstream media. *Love Story*, for example, questions how empathy is generated for famous people in contrast to others. The work includes interviews with six people who have fled their home countries – Angola, the Democratic Republic of the Congo, India, Somalia, Syria and Venezuela – to escape persecution for a variety of reasons. Breitz then asked well-known American actors Alec Baldwin and Julianne Moore to perform excerpts from these testimonies in front of a green screen. Alternating shots of the two actors are projected on a large screen. In a second space, the complete original interviews with the six refugees can be viewed. The installation blurs the line between everyday reality and the cult of celebrity, asking viewers to reflect on their position within the attention economy. Originally from Johannesburg, Breitz currently lives in Berlin and has been a tenured professor at Germany's Braunschweig University of Art since 2007.

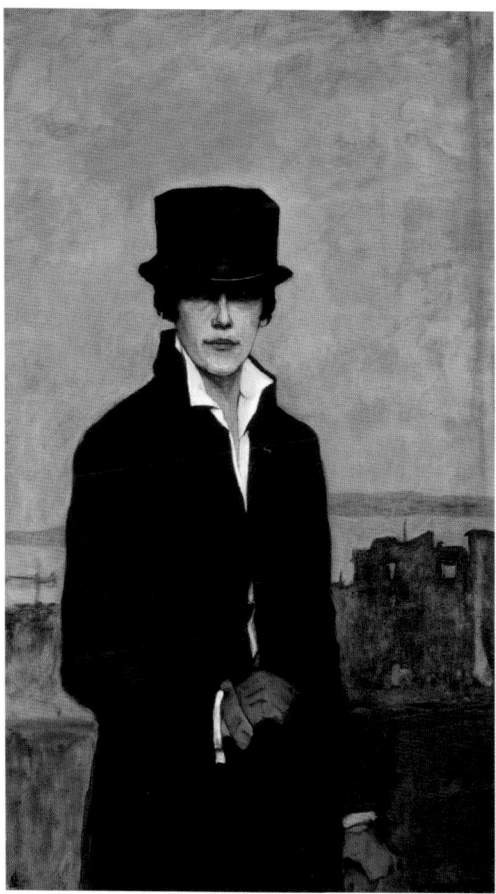

SELF-PORTRAIT

1923, oil on canvas, 117.5 × 68.3 cm (46¼ × 26⅞ in), Smithsonian American Art Museum, Washington DC
Romaine Brooks, born Beatrice Romaine Goddard, 1874, Rome (American national). Died 1970, Nice, France.

Brooks was born into an affluent but abusive family that was afflicted by alcoholism and mental illness. Wealth enabled her to live independently, which she did mostly in Paris and Capri. In her psychologically insightful portraits she challenged early-twentieth-century patriarchal representations of sexuality, gender and identity, typically painting in a muted palette of greys. Her sitters included the lesbian artist Gluck (p.154) as well as the bisexual performer Ida Rubinstein (1883–1960). Brook's own homosexuality and disregard for the avant-garde artistic styles of her time led to her exclusion from the art canon, yet recent years have seen a reappraisal of her work. In this painting, Brooks presents an androgynous figure sporting a masculine riding coat and hat typical of male aristocratic portraiture of the time. This costume worn as women's clothing would have made a powerful statement and her brooding, direct gaze suggests a quiet confidence in her identity. The only hint of colour, a red ribbon on her lapel – the Légion d'Honneur which she received in 1920 for her fundraising work during the war – suggests a self-contained but passionate nature.

CECILY BROWN

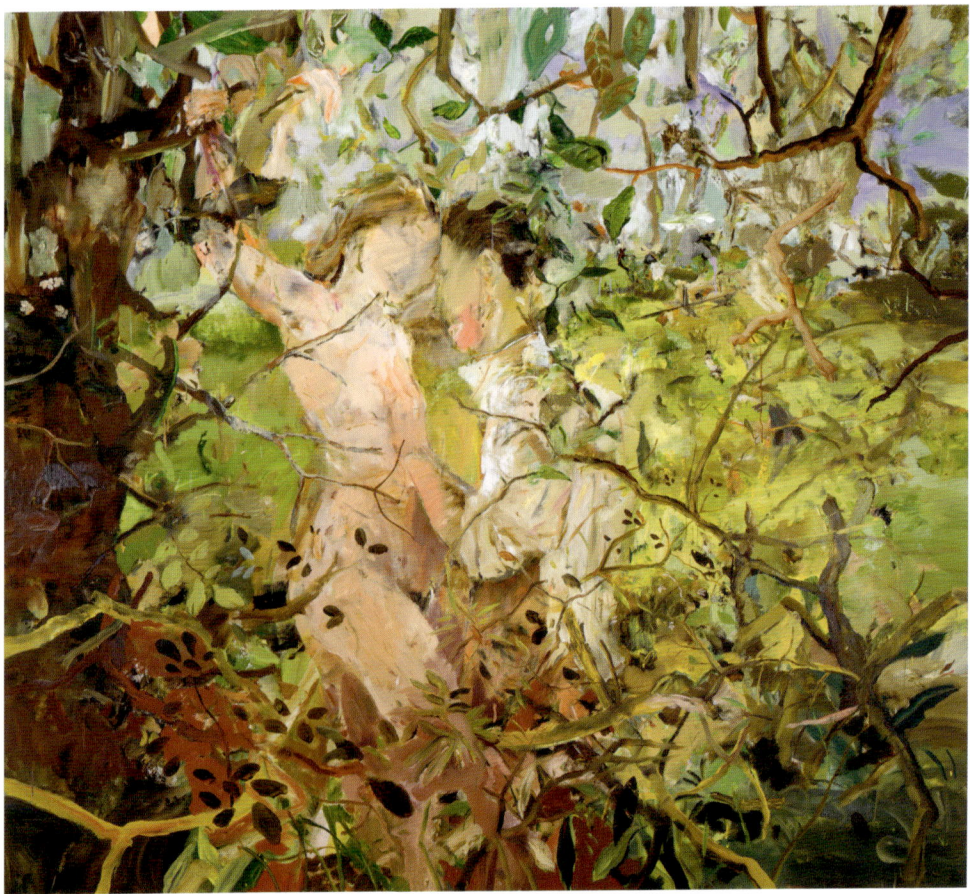

TEENAGE WILDLIFE

2003, acrylic and oil on linen, 203.2 × 228.6 cm (80 × 90 in)
Cecily Brown, born 1969, London.

Brown is from the same generation as the Young British Artists (YBAs) who dominated the country's art scene in the 1990s (such as Tracey Emin, p.132 and Sarah Lucas, p.250), she was never part of the group and moved to New York in 1994, a year after graduating from the Slade School of Art, London. Brown is known for her semi-figurative canvases that suggest themes of human attraction. Her influences are numerous, from the historic Old Masters of European art history, to the 'School of London' painters, to the transatlantic abstraction of the 1950s and 1960s. Her works have often been considered provocative, their erotic imagery verging on the explicit, albeit veiled by teetering on the edge of complete abstraction. Her dynamic use of paint is essential to her practice, her way of working expressing an emotional, psychological, physical and sexual vitality. Brown sometimes bases her paintings on photographs, but her method evolves without foreseeing a clear endpoint, reflecting the uncertainty and impetus of sexual and emotional relationships. This painting shows a young couple – whose genders are not entirely clear – embracing passionately in a wood. While perhaps voyeuristic, it is simultaneously intimate, tender and sensitive.

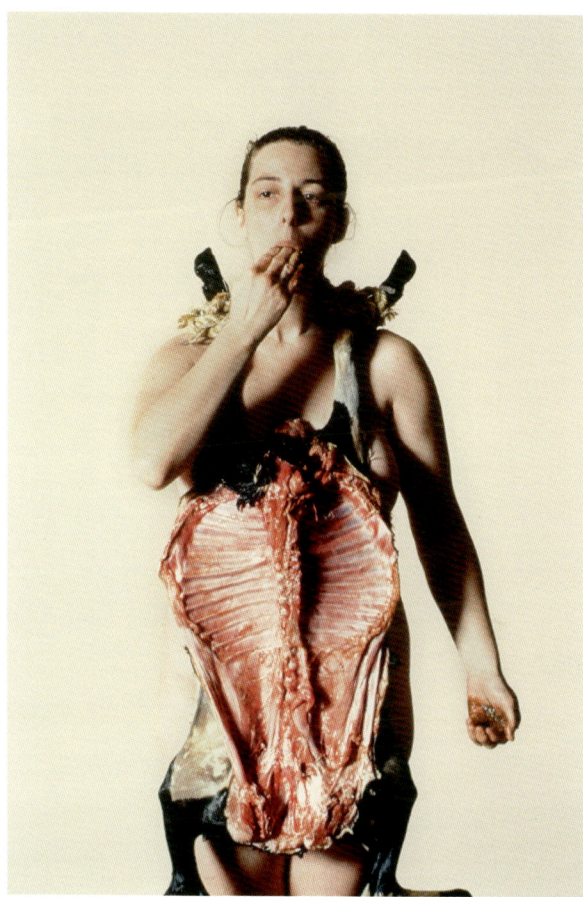

THE BURDEN OF GUILT
1997–9, performance with decapitated lamb, rope, water, salt and Cuban soil
Tania Bruguera, born 1968, Havana.

Using art as activism, Bruguera confronts discriminatory power relationships and engineers provocative performances and interventions
that create the possibility of destabilizing oppressive structures.
Consistently occupying the intersection of art and politics as a place
of productivity, her practice has moved from intimate body-based
work – including a ten-year-long project inspired by fellow Cuban
artist Ana Mendieta (p.268) – to large-scale interactive models where
the audience participates in her work. Bruguera sees herself as an ini-
tiator, with spectators transformed into users of art, her scenarios
evolving only with the viewer's engagement, an approach she calls

Arte Útil ('useful art'). In this earlier work the artist acted alone but
in solidarity with others, ingesting a thick mix of soil and salt water
as a lamb's carcass hung from her neck. For forty-five minutes,
Bruguera aligned herself with the plight of sixteenth-century Cuban
Indians, who consumed soil as an act of passive resistance against
the curtailment of their rights under Spanish rule. Her commitment
to addressing injustice and generating social change continues,
particularly in her homeland Cuba, where she founded the Instituto
de Artivismo Hannah Arendt (INSTAR) in 2015.

HEIDI BUCHER

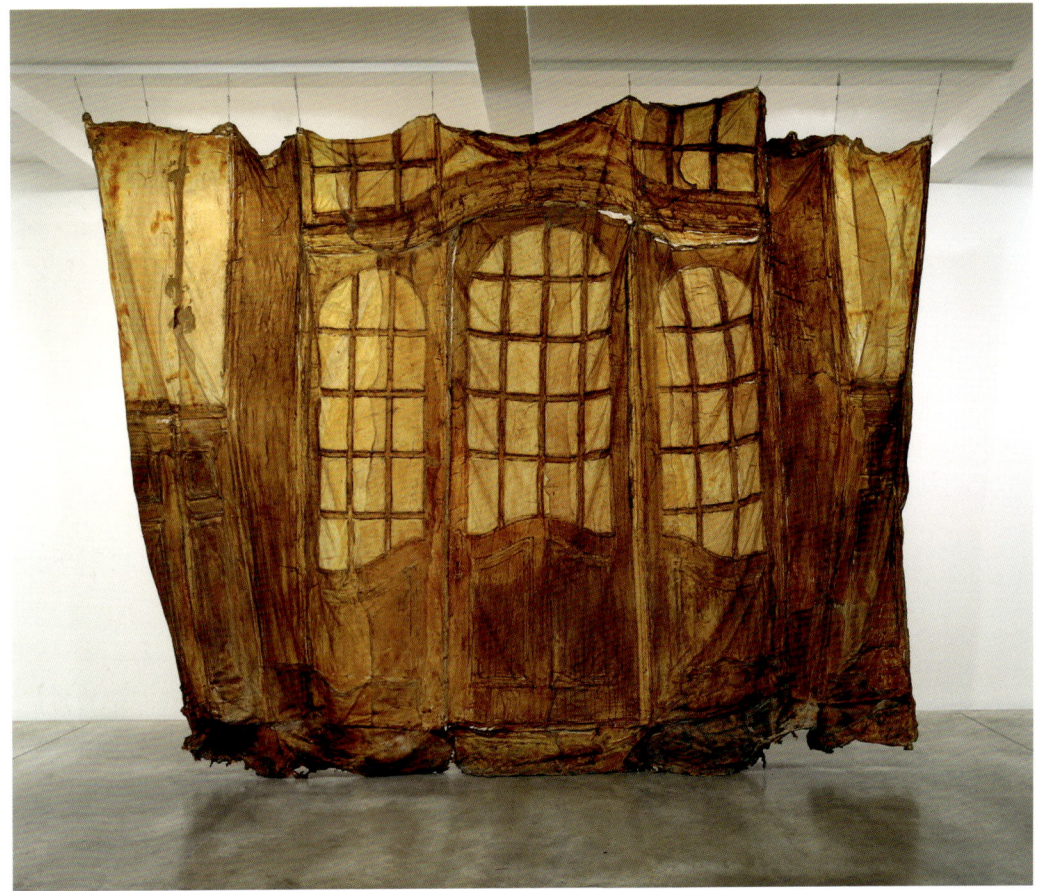

SMALL GLASS PORTAL, BELLEVUE KREUZLINGEN

1988, latex and gauze, 340 × 455 cm (133 ⅞ × 179 ⅛ in), installation view,
'Heidi Bucher', Parasol Unit, London, 2018
Heidi Bucher, born Adelheid Müller, 1926, Winterthur, Switzerland. Died 1993,
Brunnen, Switzerland.

After studying at the School of Applied Arts in Zürich, Bucher spent
time in London and New York before settling in California in 1972.
With her artist husband Carl Bucher (1935–2015), she created wearable foam and vinyl sculptures called 'Bodyshells', which were
exhibited at the Los Angeles County Museum of Art and documented on film being used in a performance on Venice Beach.
After separating from her husband, Bucher returned to Switzerland
in 1973 and developed a new artistic direction, which became her
signature technique. She used gauze sheets soaked in liquid latex
rubber to coat objects, clothing, the body and rooms. Once dry,
she carefully peeled away the material, creating translucent, skin-
like casts, which she sometimes painted with mother-of-pearl
pigments or glazes. The most ambitious of these, architectural
in scale, were called *Raumhäute* ('room skins') and are often
presented hanging in space, creating ghostly representations of
three-dimensional places. After casting her own studio in 1976,
she moved on to other buildings. This piece features the doors
of a derelict Swiss mental hospital that had functioned for over
120 years and was known for its role in the development of existential psychotherapy.

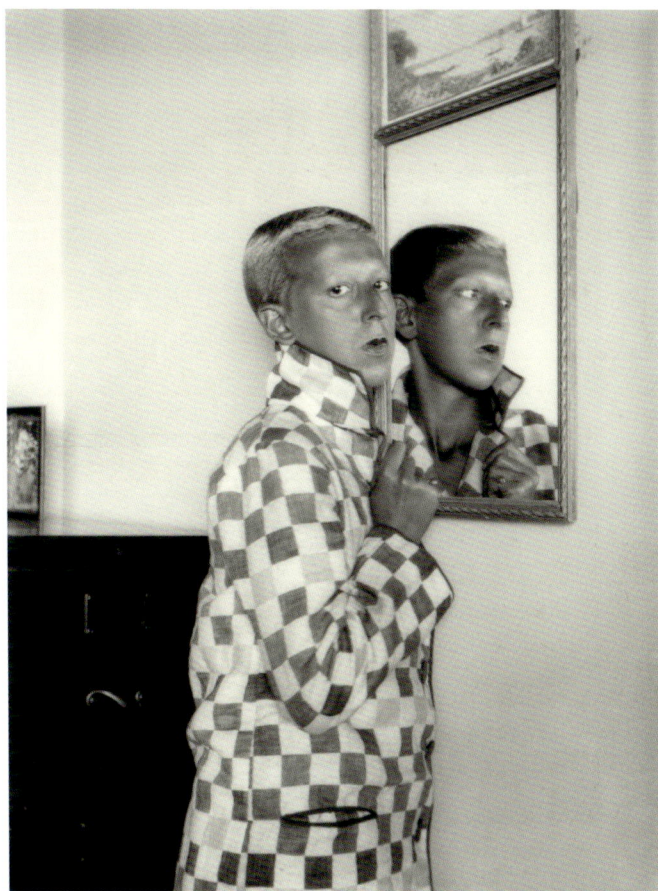

SELF-PORTRAIT

1928, black-and-white photograph, 10.7 × 8.2 cm (4¼ × 3¼ in), Jersey Heritage Trust
Claude Cahun, born Lucy Schwob, 1894, Nantes, France. Died 1954, Jersey,
Channel Islands.

Born into a prominent Jewish family, Cahun adopted this name in her
early twenties, an ambiguous pseudonym that expressed a radical,
often playful challenge to gender conformity. For similar reasons, her
stepsister, lover and collaborator, Suzanne Malherbe (1892–1972),
changed her name to Marcel Moore. Associated with the Surrealists
and their political activity in Paris, the couple later migrated to Jersey
in 1938, and during the German occupation of the island, they took
part in resistance activities. Arrested and sentenced to death in 1944
for making and distributing anti-Nazi leaflets, they survived only
because the war ended, although Cahun's health was broken. In this
self-portrait the artist's androgynous appearance and its reflection
complicate conventions of gender and identity. Gazing directly into
the camera, her appearance and confrontational stance are stereotypically masculine. Conversely, in the mirror image, her pose alludes to
traditions of femininity represented as coy or vulnerable. Assuming
both identities simultaneously was integral to her practice. In her
anti-realist autobiography *Disavowals* (1930) she stated: 'Shuffle the
cards. Masculine? Feminine? That depends on the case. Neutral is
the only gender that always suits me.'

SOPHIE CALLE

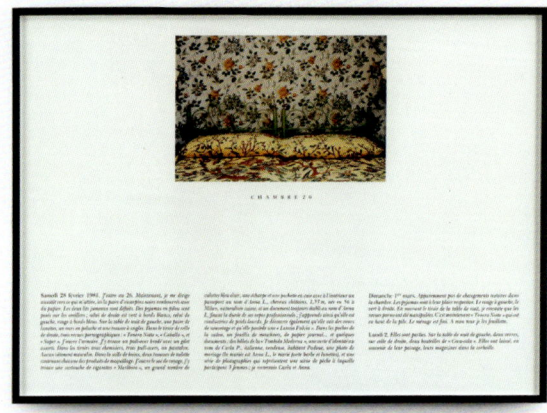

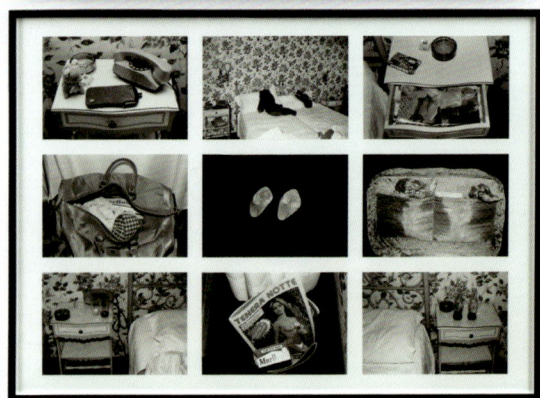

ROOM 26 (28 FEBRUARY) from the series 'THE HOTEL'
1981–3, colour and black-and-white photographs, framed, each 210 × 140 cm
(39 × 55 in)
Sophie Calle, born 1953, Paris.

After leaving school at nineteen, Calle travelled in the United States, China and Mexico, and never attended art school. Using writing, photography and installation, often tinged with humour and pathos, her practice is about identity, intimacy and the private details of daily existence. To begin a project, she limits her actions through self-imposed rules and directions, creating 'private games' and she frequently undertakes detectivelike investigations. In the early 1980s, for example, she conceived an identity for the owner of a lost address book, contacting those listed within it and writing accounts

of their conversations, which appeared as a serial in a French newspaper. 'The Hotel' – one of her best-known works – similarly involves creating portraits of persons unknown, but this time by more invasive means, as she explains in the text she wrote to accompany the project, 'On Monday, February 16, 1981 I was hired as a temporary chambermaid for three weeks in a Venetian hotel. I was assigned twelve bedrooms on the fourth floor. In the course of my cleaning duties, I examined the personal belongings of the hotel guests and observed through details lives, which remained unknown to me. On Friday, March 6 the job came to an end.'

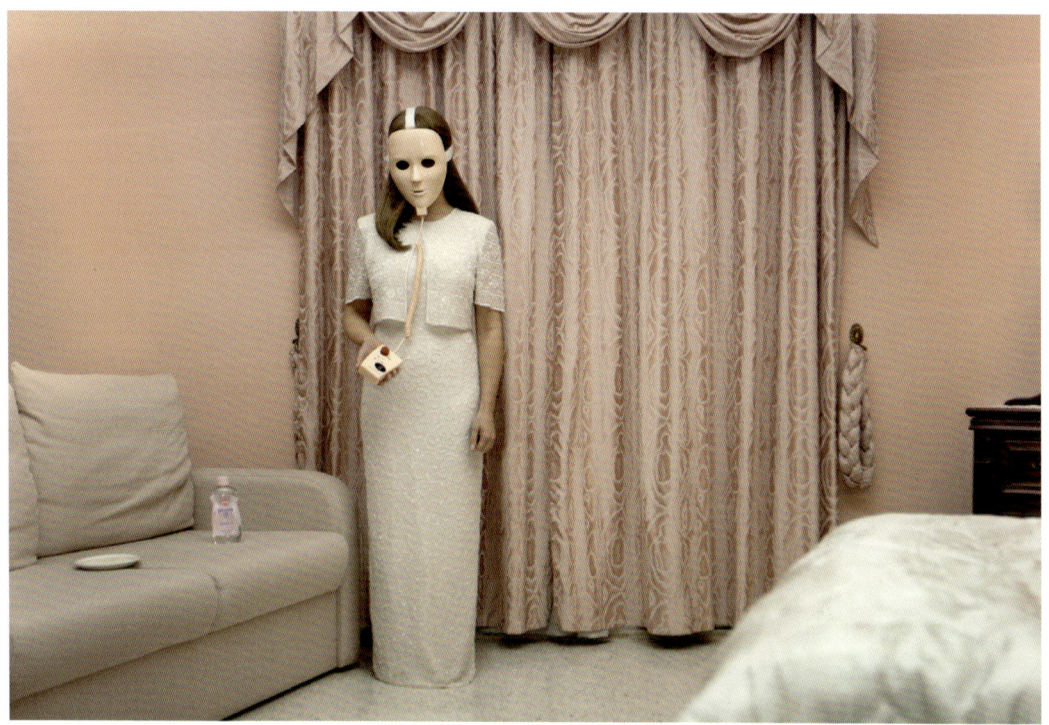

12 REASONS YOU'RE TIRED ALL THE TIME
2013, archival pigment print, 152.4 × 101.6 cm (60 × 40 in)
Juno Calypso, born 1989, London.

Growing up in the early Information Age, Calypso was intrigued by the proliferation of Internet images and noted society's obsessions with youth and beauty, and the pressures placed upon women to achieve an idealized appearance. Her photographs focus on the labour involved in constructing femininity, while also exploring what people do when alone, with an aesthetic that is simultaneously sinister and darkly humorous. Performing for the camera she inhabits the fictitious character, 'Joyce', a seemingly bored, lonely woman with a fanatical commitment to beauty regimes, from beauty masks to cosmetic surgery. The title of the image shown here is derived from a women's magazine and depicts Joyce wearing a mask that functions by electrocuting the face. The artist intensively researches settings in which to stage her images, and they range from her grandmother's bathroom to a kitsch Pennsylvania 'love hotel', complete with heart-shaped bathtubs. In the latter, she created 'The Honeymoon' (2015), a series for which she was awarded an international prize by the *British Journal of Photography*. More recently, for 'What to Do With a Million Years' (2018) she gained access to a pink, bombproof bunker outside Las Vegas, built by Avon cosmetics founder Jerry Henderson in the 1960s.

JULIA MARGARET CAMERON

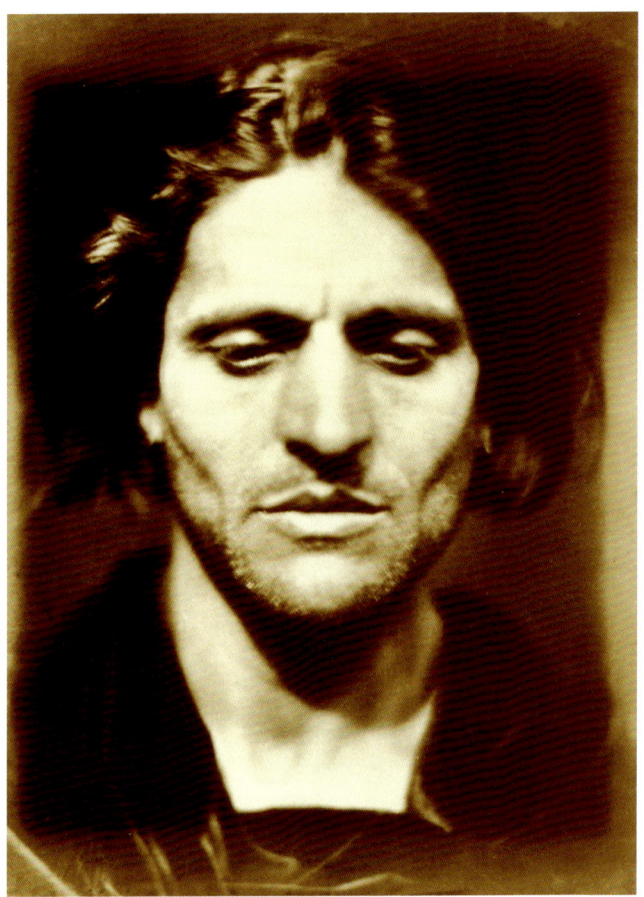

IAGO – STUDY FROM AN ITALIAN

1867, unique albumen print, 33.4 × 24.8 cm (13 ⅛ × 9 ¾ in), National Science and Media Museum, Bradford, UK
Julia Margaret Cameron, born 1815, Calcutta (now Kolkata), India. Died 1879, Kalutara, Ceylon (now Sri Lanka).

Cameron grew up in colonial-era India, though was educated in France. Marrying a man twenty years her senior, the couple moved to London in 1848 when he retired. She picked up the camera aged forty-eight, having received one as a present from her daughter. This was a formative time for the still-new medium of photography, and her innovative approach resulted in works of great beauty and intimacy, which are now held in major museum collections, including the Metropolitan Museum of Art, New York, and the Victoria & Albert Museum, London. Working with the wet collodion process, she became known for portraits in soft-focus, which was dismissed by some critics as rule-breaking. The artist's sister, Sara Prinsep, hosted a salon in Kensington, where Cameron met eminent Victorians who would become subjects. Among many others, she photographed naturalist Charles Darwin, actor Ellen Terry, poet Alfred Lord Tennyson and Pre-Raphaelite artists including John Everett Millais (1829–96) and Marie Spartali Stillman (p.382). Her work has immense documentary significance, together with an empathy that collapses the distance from these historical figures. She also photographed friends, sometimes in character for plays, as here – the villain in Shakespeare's *Othello*.

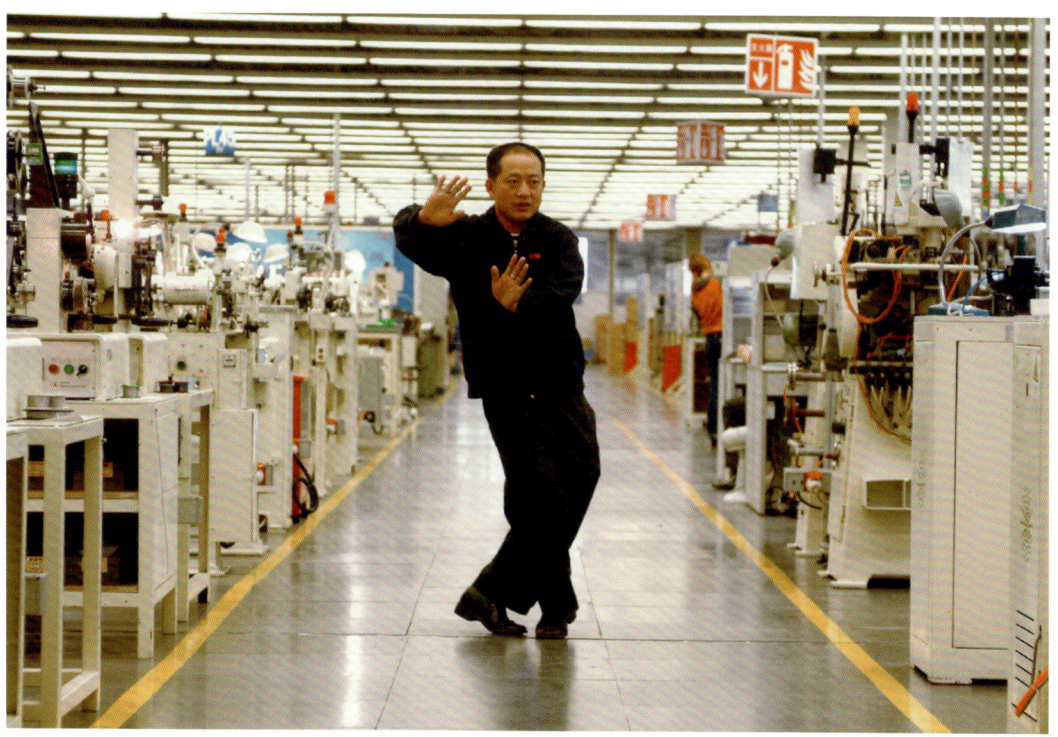

WHOSE UTOPIA?

2006, single-channel video, colour, sound, 20 mins 20 secs
Cao Fei, born 1978, Guangzhou, China.

The daughter of famed sculptor Cao Chong'en (b.1933), Cao earned her degree from the Guangzhou Academy of Fine Arts in 2001, producing short films examining the psychology of youth subcultures. Working in video, photography and digital media, Cao explores the effects of China's rapidly developing society on post-Cultural Revolution generations and their efforts at escapism through daydreaming, cosplay and adopting virtual online avatars. In 2005, she began a six-month residency as a part of the Siemens Art Program at the OSRAM lighting factory in her native Pearl River Delta industrial region. For *Whose Utopia?* Cao filmed workers' daily lives, documenting their time on the shop floor and in the dormitories provided. She also interviewed them about their future aspirations, asking some to act out these ambitions and fantasies for the camera – such as this factory worker who dances in an aisle while his colleagues around him continue to work. The film reflects on both the repetitive and depersonalized nature of the production process, while also offering a more intimate look at the individuals working within it, highlighting the individual sacrifices demanded of migrant workers as a reality of globalization.

JANET CARDIFF

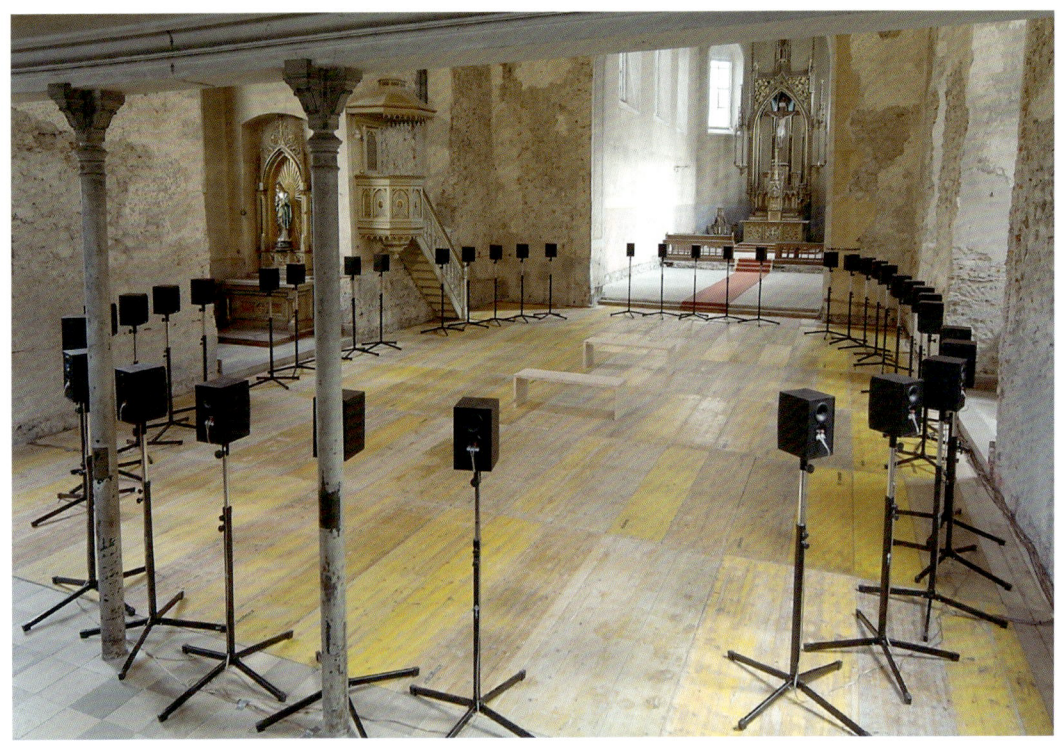

THE FORTY PART MOTET (A REWORKING OF 'SPEM IN ALIUM' BY THOMAS TALLIS 1556/1573)

2001, 40 loudspeakers mounted on stands and placed in an oval, amplifiers and playback computer, 14 mins, looped (music: 11 mins, intermission: 3 mins), dimensions variable, installation view, Johanniterkirche, Feldkirch, Austria, 2005. Originally produced by Field Art Projects with the Arts Council England; Canada House; the Salisbury Festival and Salisbury Cathedral Choir; BALTIC Gateshead; The New Art Gallery Walsall; and the NOW Festival Nottingham. Janet Cardiff, born 1957, Brussels, Ontario, Canada.

Cardiff's work bridges visual art, cinema and music. Her 'audio walks' starting in the mid-1990s involve the dimension of an interior monologue being transposed upon the visual world. Comprising site-specific narratives delivered through headphones, sometimes with photos, videos or digital video accompaniment, they garnered her international acclaim. She is also known for installations that simulate fantastical and dream-like environments. Often working collaboratively with her husband George Bures Miller (b.1960), the duo represented Canada at the 49th Venice Biennale (2001). Also from that year is this solo piece, which highlights Cardiff's ability to conjure affective, intellectually provocative experiences through a spare use of audio, deployed with rigorous attention to sound's sculptural qualities. Forty loudspeakers are arranged around a room at head-height, each emitting one vocal part from the sixteenth-century polyphonic choral piece *Spem in Alium* by Thomas Tallis. Presented as an installation rather than a performance (where audience and singers are kept separate), here the listener can move around the space and hear each line of harmony, gaining an intricate understanding of this epic Renaissance-era composition.

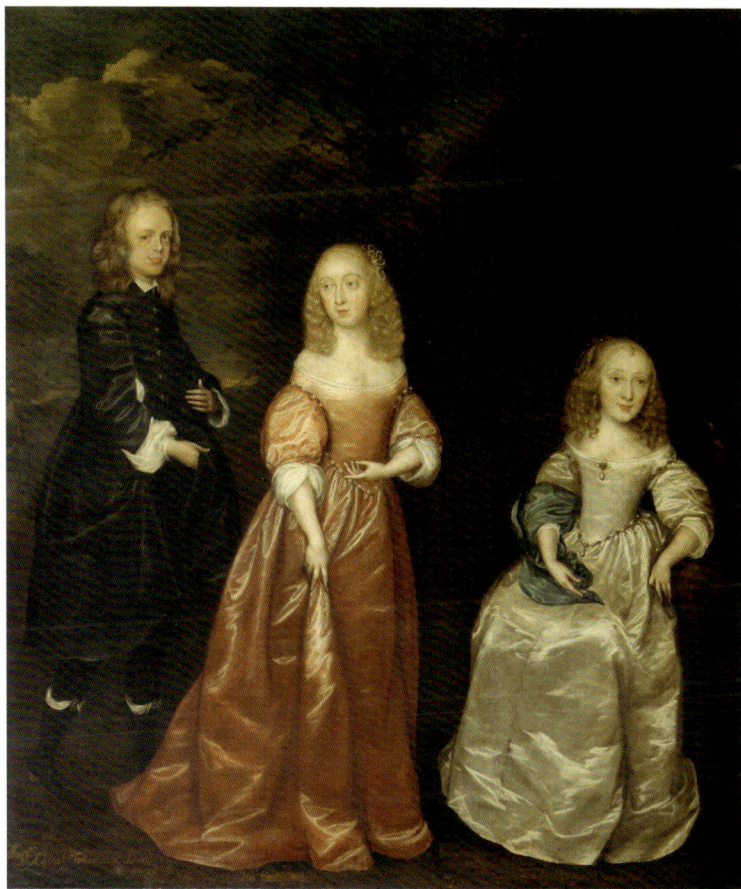

ELIZABETH MURRAY, COUNTESS OF DYSART, WITH HER FIRST HUSBAND, SIR LIONEL TOLLEMACHE AND HER SISTER, MARGARET MURRAY, LADY MAYNARD

*c.*1648, oil on canvas, 109.2 × 92.7 cm (43 × 36½ in), Ham House, Surrey, UK
Joan Carlile, born Joan Palmer, *c.*1603, London. Died 1679, Petersham, Surrey, UK.

Carlile was one of the very first women artists to work professionally in England in the medium of oil painting. William Sanderson's *Graphice* (1658), a record of noted contemporary artists in the seventeenth century, celebrated her use of colour, stating that: 'In Oyl colours we have a virtuous example in that worthy artist, Mrs Carlile.' Similarly to her peer Mary Beale (p.54), who was also mentioned by Sanderson, she was best known as a portraitist, specializing in full-length depictions of her sitters in landscape settings. She also is said to have worked as a copyist of Old Masters, probably for the court of Charles I, although she was described as such only after her death. This, one of her earliest-known portraits, depicts Carlile's neighbours in Richmond, Surrey. Despite the political upheavals of Civil War and a period of republican rule under the Commonwealth (1649–60), Carlile was able to prosper and be celebrated as an artist, moving to London's Covent Garden in 1654 in order to further her professional career, which she had considered constrained by living away from the city.

EMILY CARR

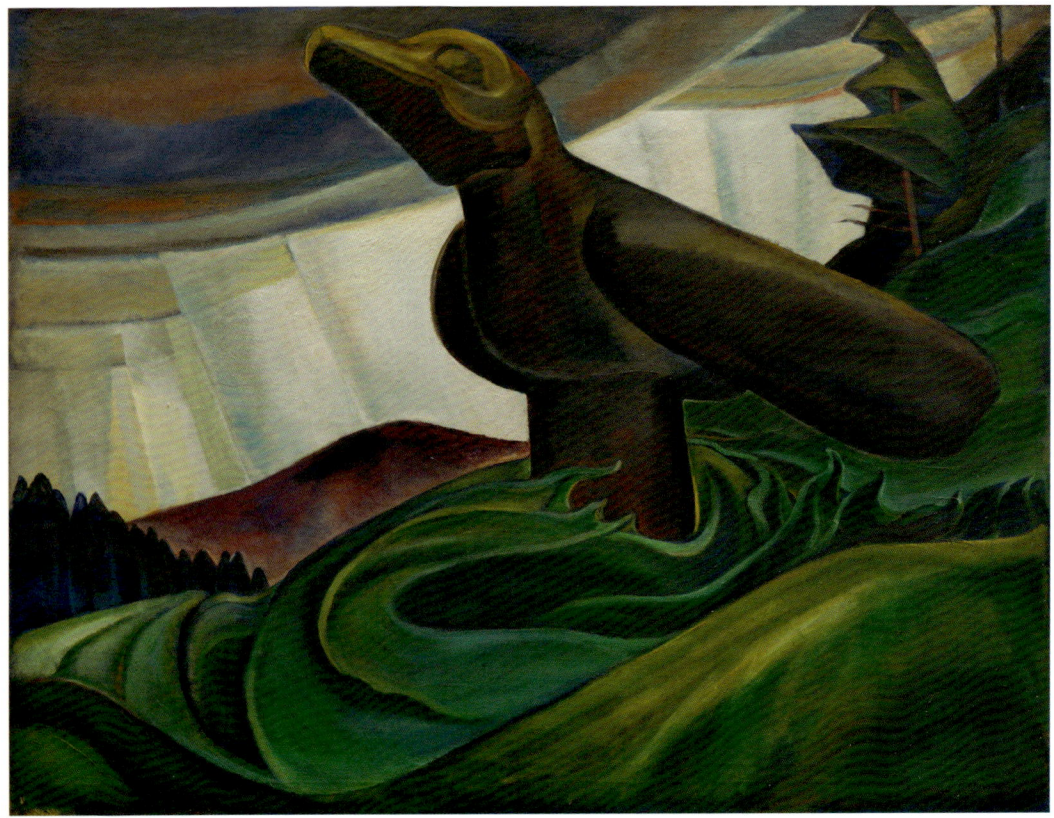

BIG RAVEN

1931, oil on canvas, 87 × 114 cm (34 ¼ × 44 ⅞ in), Collection of Vancouver Art Gallery, Emily Carr Trust
Emily Carr, born 1871, Victoria, British Columbia, Canada. Died 1945, Victoria, British Columbia, Canada.

Captivated by the wild landscapes of Canada's northwest coast and the cultures of its indigenous people, Carr was the first modern artist to make these her subjects. After studying painting in San Francisco and London, she spent time in Paris where she was inspired by the strong colours, dynamic brushwork and expressive depth of Fauve and Post-Impressionist paintings. Returning to Canada she applied this visual language to her paintings of boldly carved Gyáa'aang (totem poles) and native villages, bridging the gap between First Nations and European cultures. Ravens, an important element in aboriginal mythology, are a recurring motif in Carr's works. In this work, a carved bird surrounded by swirling foliage dominates the landscape. Each element has a majestic, weighty quality, emphasizing the power of the natural environment it represents. Based on a 1912 watercolour of a Gyáa'aang from the Queen Charlotte Islands (now Haida Gwaii), the painting was produced at a time when indigenous life in Canada was facing increasing threat from oppressive state policies. Though Carr pioneered modernist painting styles in Canadian art, her significant contributions were not recognized until late in life.

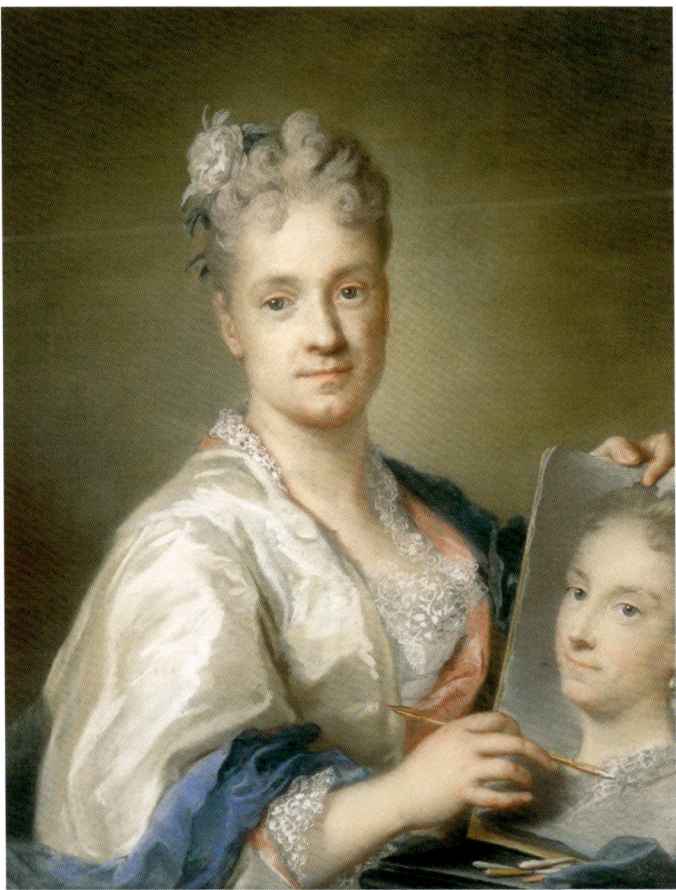

SELF-PORTRAIT HOLDING A PORTRAIT OF HER SISTER

1715, pastel on paper, 71 × 57 cm (28 × 22 ½ in), Galleria degli Uffizi, Florence
Rosalba Carriera, born 1675, Venice. Died 1757, Venice.

Carriera first trained in lacemaking, subsequently establishing a business as a miniaturist, creating tiny paintings on ivory that were included in keepsakes and jewellery for both women and men. Around the turn of the eighteenth century, this evolved into production of larger portraits. Her ground-breaking use of pastel became pivotal in the development of Rococo painting and her reputation grew rapidly, with many commissions and honorary membership of Rome's Accademia di San Luca. Encouraged by this, Carriera expanded her range of portraiture, culminating in a visit to Paris in 1720 where she introduced the Rococo style into France. This self-portrait of Carriera highlights her innovative use of soft colour and line, techniques that saw her credited as the first woman to introduce a new painting movement – one that was to dominate eighteenth-century Europe. Élisabeth Vigée-Lebrun (p.418) and Adélaïde Labille-Guiard (1749–1803) were among many artists inspired by her pioneering methods. Incorporating an image of her sister – one of the many women that Carriera tutored – and confidently facing the viewer, this composition is a powerful statement of Carriera's skill and status.

LEONORA CARRINGTON

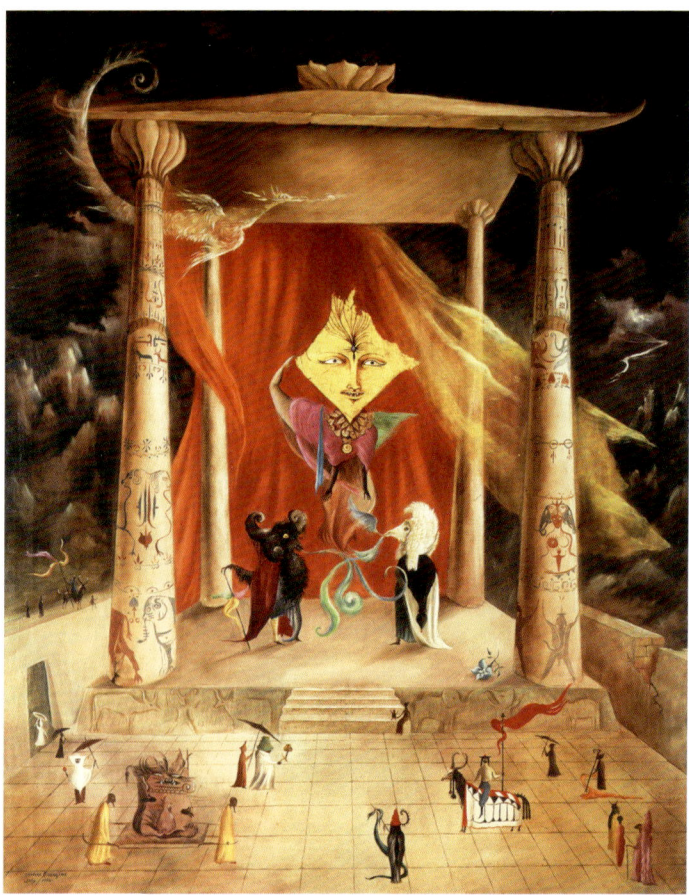

TEMPLE OF THE WORD

1954, oil and gold leaf on canvas, 100.3 × 80 cm (39 ½ × 31 ½ in), private collection
Leonora Carrington, born 1917, Clayton-le-Woods, Lancashire, UK. Died 2011,
Mexico City.

Carrington encountered Surrealist painting in Paris at the age of ten.
Her mother, who encouraged her to be an artist, later gave her a copy
of Herbert Read's 1936 book on the subject. The following year, she
met Max Ernst (1891–1976) and moved to Paris as his partner. With
the outbreak of war, Ernst was arrested (though he eventually escaped
to America) and Carrington fled to Spain in great emotional distress.
Here she had a breakdown and was committed to an asylum by her
parents, an experience she documented in her 1972 novel *Down Below*.
Fleeing again, she sought refuge in Mexico from 1943, and she

became a founding member of the country's women's liberation
movement. The first major exhibition of Carrington's Surrealist
paintings was held in 1947 at Pierre Matisse Gallery in New York.
In the following decade, she turned to stage design, creating sets and
costumes for her play, *Penelope*, in 1957. These theatrical preoccupations are evident in this painting, which also reflects her interests in
Mayan symbolism – the large sun-like masked figure is surrounded by
animals, regarded as archetypes in the beliefs of the Chiapas people.

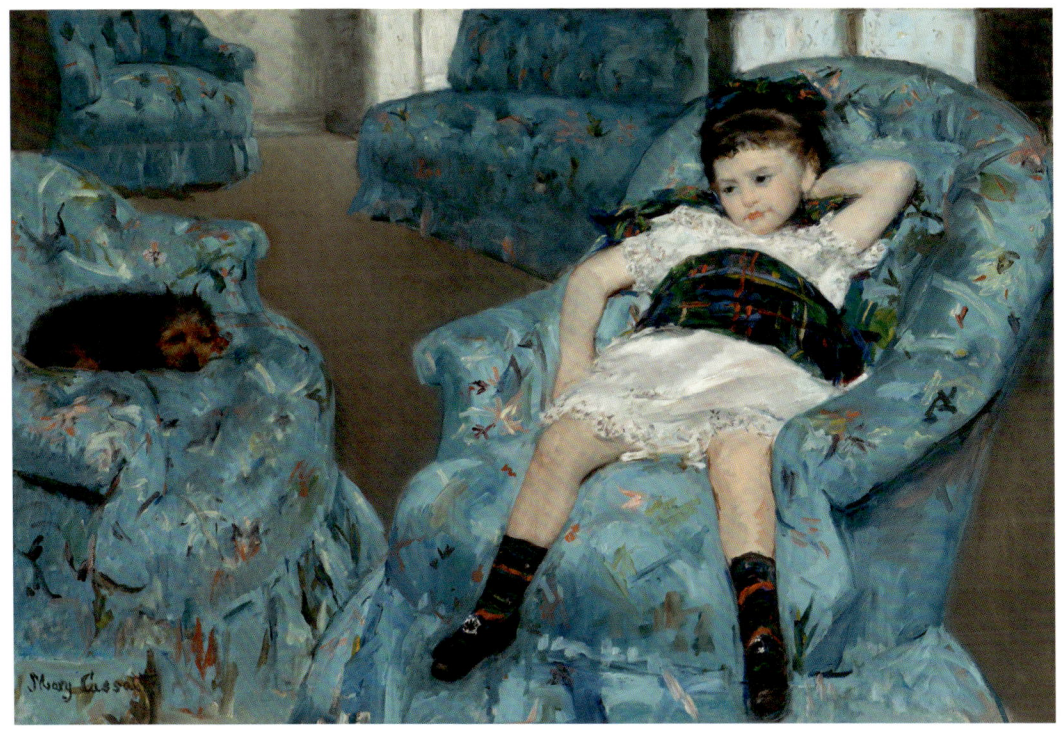

LITTLE GIRL IN A BLUE ARMCHAIR

1878, oil on canvas, 89.5 × 129.8 cm (35 ¼ × 51 ⅛ in), National Gallery of Art, Washington DC
Mary Cassatt, born 1844, Allegheny City, Pennsylvania. Died 1926, Le Mesnil-Théribus, France.

Cassatt spent most of her adult life in France, where she became one of the *grandes dames* of the Impressionist movement and one of the best-known female artists of the nineteenth century. She was one of the first Impressionists to exhibit work in the United States, influencing wealthy patrons and encouraging the formation of collections of Impressionism in America. When the work she submitted to the Paris Salon of 1877 was rejected by the French art establishment, her friend Edgar Degas (1834–1917) officially invited her to join the Impressionists, who had organized their own exhibitions since 1874. Both came from upper-class backgrounds and shared a visual sensibility for texture and pattern, as well as a love of Japanese prints, the asymmetrical compositions and high vantage points of which are echoed here. In fact, the artists' close working relationship extends to this very painting: the model was the daughter of Degas's friends, and in a letter that she wrote around 1903, Cassatt told Parisian art dealer Ambroise Vollard that Degas 'even worked on it.' The painting was included along with ten other works by Cassatt in her debut at the Impressionist exhibition of 1879.

JORDAN CASTEEL

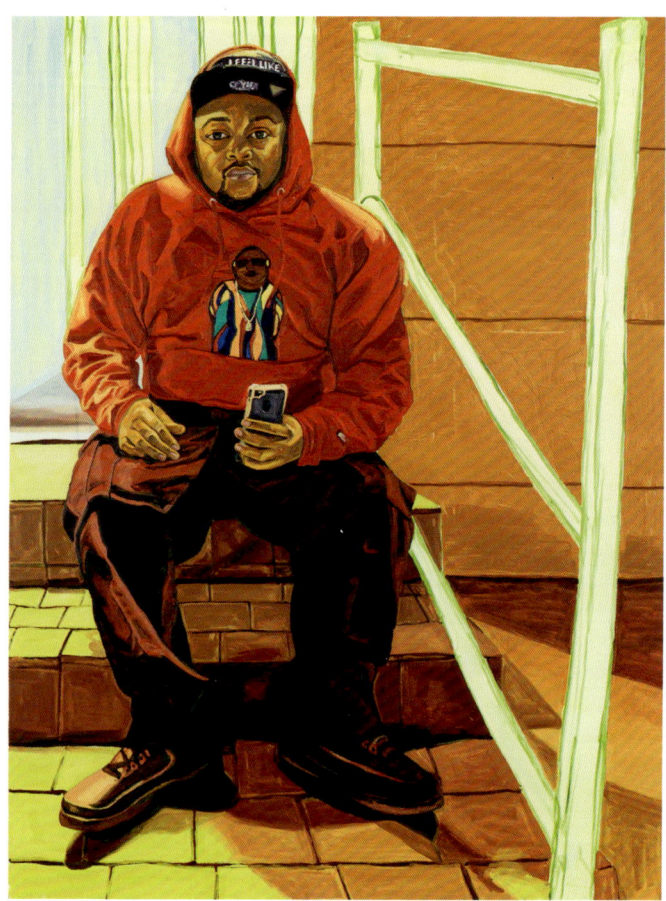

Q
2017, oil on canvas, 198.1 × 152.4 cm (78 × 60 in), Ann and Mel Schaffer
Family Collection
Jordan Casteel, born 1989, Denver, Colorado.

Casteel studied sociology and anthropology as an undergraduate
before switching to art and this interest is evident in her paintings
of African-American people in everyday settings of home, workplace
and on the street, the artist representing the stories of those who
often go unseen by society. In 2014, Casteel graduated from Yale
School of Art with a master's degree in painting and printmaking.
The following year she undertook a prestigious residency at The
Studio Museum in Harlem, New York, the city in which she continues to live. Casteel is known for her use of colourful expression in
painting large-scale, oil-on-canvas portraits. These are often titled
after the people she depicts: friends, relatives, lovers and even
strangers, as demonstrated in *Q*, which is based on a man Casteel
met on the streets of Harlem, who sits on a doorstep, mobile phone
in hand. Initially focusing on male figures, the artist's recent reper-
toire has expanded to include depictions of women. Such socially
engaged figuration places her in a tradition of artists using portraiture to accord visibility and subjectivity to the black experience.

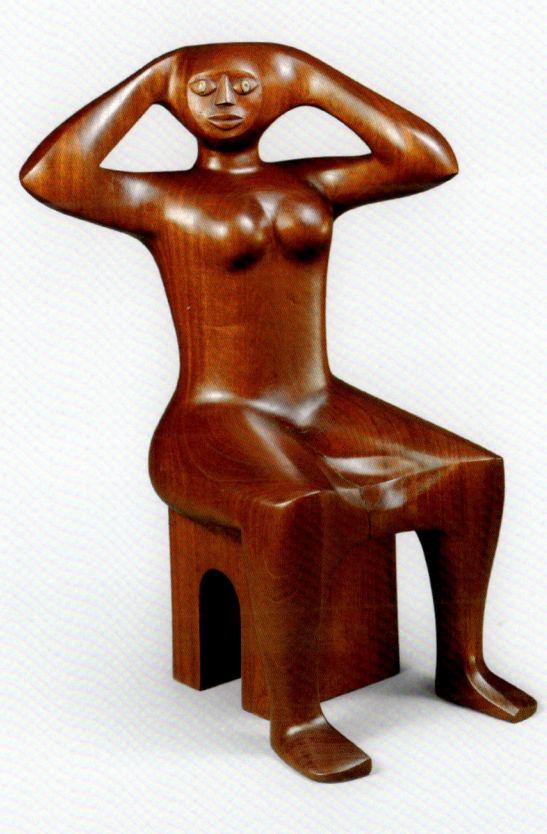

WOMAN FIXING HER HAIR

1993, mahogany and opals, 68.6 × 45.7 × 33 cm (27 × 18 × 13 in), Metropolitan Museum of Art, New York
Elizabeth Catlett, born 1915, Washington DC. Died 2012, Cuernavaca, Mexico.

As the granddaughter of freed slaves, to pursue an arts career as an African-American woman posed challenges for Catlett. Despite winning a scholarship to Carnegie Institute of Technology, she was refused admission when it was discovered she was black. She studied instead at Howard University in Washington DC and, later, the University of Iowa, where her painting professor was Grant Wood (1891–1942). Pursuing her interest in a figurative style through sculpture, further studies with the Russian-born sculptor Ossip Zadkine (1888–1967) introduced her to European modernism and led her away from strictly representational work. Throughout this time, Catlett was an art teacher, while also trying to exhibit. In 1946 she received a fellowship to go to Mexico City, where she settled for the rest of her life, becoming the head of the sculpture department in the Universidad Nacional Autónoma de México. Much of her art drew on the experience of African-Americans and on Mexican traditions. In this work, a woman tends to her appearance as if looking into a dressing table mirror. Catlett's treatment of her subject is an intimate celebration of femininity, rendered in rich materials.

VIJA CELMINS

UNTITLED (OCEAN)
1970, graphite on acrylic ground on paper, 36 × 48 cm (14 ⅛ × 18 ⅞ in),
Museum of Modern Art, New York
Vija Celmins, born 1938, Riga, Latvia (American national).

After fleeing the Soviet occupation of her homeland and surviving wartime in Nazi Germany, Celmins and her family arrived in America as refugees in 1948. Her earlier paintings drew on these experiences, reflecting on images of war and conflict, and using photographs and magazine clippings as source materials. Inspired by Pop art's preoccupation with everyday life and techniques of Photorealism, she also painted simple objects including lamps and pencils. From the late 1960s, Celmins concentrated on natural phenomena and environments, creating meticulously executed pencil drawings remarkable for their realism. Celmins sees the process of transforming the three-dimensional world onto the page or canvas as a type of abstraction. She is above all interested in what is physically present in a work itself, more than in the reality depicted. This is how she conceived of her 'Ocean Surface' drawings series, the earliest of which was made in 1968 and which she continued to develop throughout the 1970s. Speaking about this series in a 2017 interview with *Flash Art*, she stated: 'I'd like the viewers to forget that there's an ocean outside the work.'

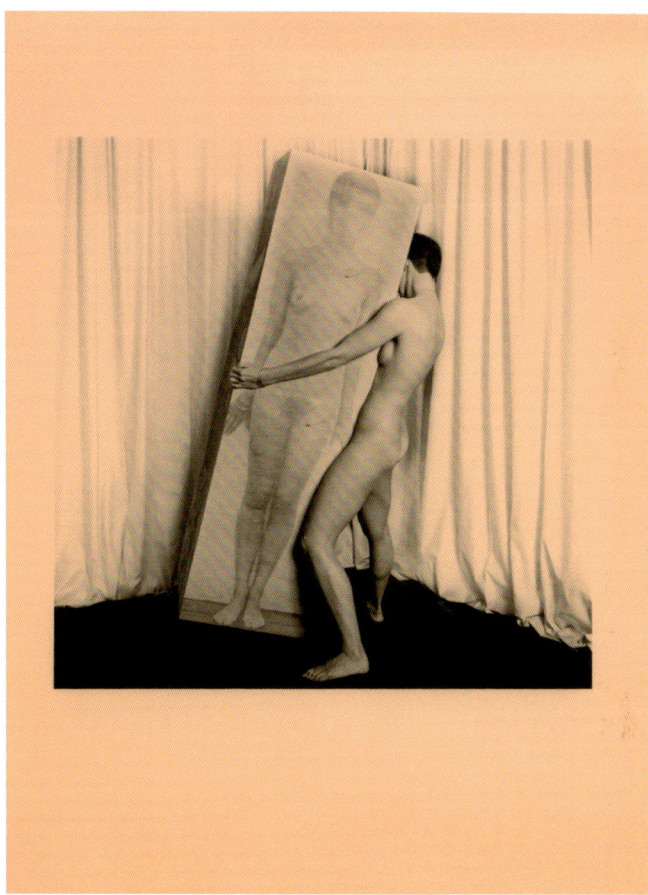

EGO GEOMETRIA SUM: THE LABOURS X
1982–3, gelatin silver print on paper, from a set of 10 black-and-white hand-tinted
photographs mounted on card, each 29.3 × 21 cm (11 ½ × 8 ¼ in)
Helen Chadwick, born 1953, London. Died 1996, London.

A sculptor, photographer and installation artist whose life was cut
tragically short by a fatal heart attack aged just forty-two, Chadwick
explored perceptions of the body and questioned the binaries con-
ventionally imposed on gender, beauty and existence. After graduating from Chelsea College of Art, she joined a number of other
artists in establishing a thriving artistic community in a squat in
Hackney, east London. Chadwick taught at a number of London's art
colleges through the 1980s and 1990s and her experimental work
inspired many of the next generation of artists. Chadwick was also

the first woman nominated for the Turner Prize in 1987. Using a pleth-
ora of unconventional materials to make art, including chocolate,
lambs' tongues, rotting vegetable matter and her own bodily fluids,
her works referenced nature, death and decay, alongside personal and
collective memory. In this key example of her varied practice, she
used images of her own body alongside geometric structures to chart
her development from birth to the age of thirty, ten stages of her life
represented in a set of ten photographs. Alluding to Greek myth,
the title suggests that recollection is a Herculean task.

SARAH CHARLESWORTH

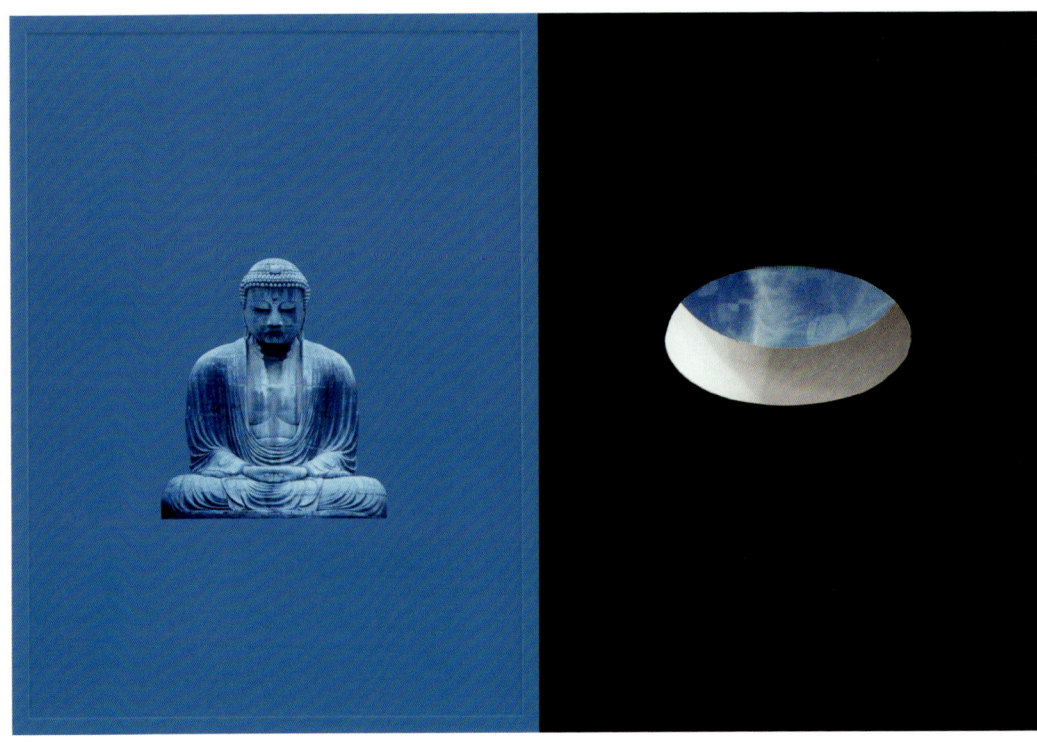

BUDDHA OF IMMEASURABLE LIGHT

1987, Cibachrome prints with lacquered wood frame, diptych, 106.7 × 157.5 cm
(42 × 62 in), Museum of Modern Art, New York
Sarah Charlesworth, born 1947, East Orange, New Jersey. Died 2013,
Falls Village, Connecticut.

Charlesworth's interest in Conceptual art was evident during her
undergraduate studies at Barnard College, New York. Later trained
in the studio of Lisette Model (p.278), she described herself as
'someone who makes art with photographs', rather than as a photographer, her works challenging the idea of 'capturing' images in the
outside world. Instead, questioning ideas of the authorship, authenticity and manipulation of images, she explored their power within
contemporary culture. These concerns associated her with the

Pictures Generation, a New York-based group of artists that included
her close friends Cindy Sherman (p.371) and Laurie Simmons (p.374).
Charlesworth co-founded the arts magazine *BOMB* in 1981 and was
involved in numerous collaborations. Typically, her work involves
re-photographed, enlarged images of objects that are immediately
recognizable yet detached from their original media context. The
meticulous reproduction and careful arrangement of isolated imagery
are demonstrated in this work from her 'Objects of Desire' series.
A picture of a devotional icon is connected with an ambiguous motif,
suggesting escape and enlightenment, the correspondence enhanced
by use of colour and emphatic framing reminiscent of religious diptych paintings.

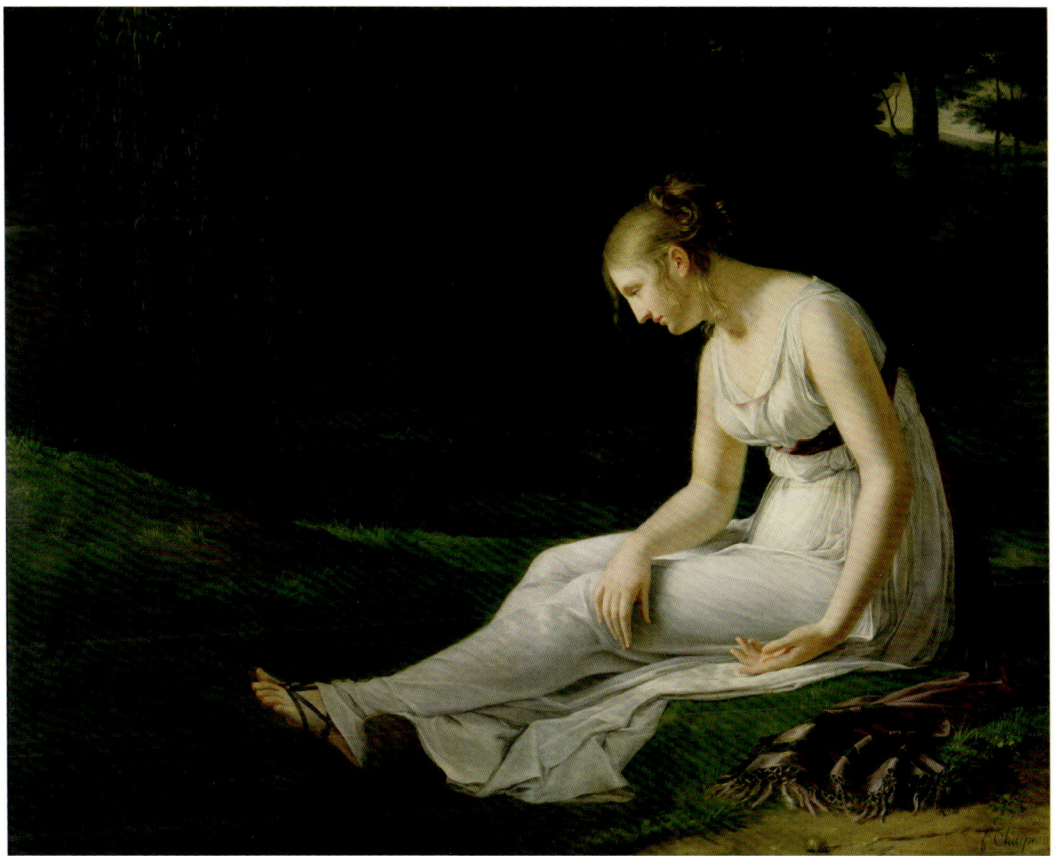

MELANCHOLY

1801, oil on canvas, 130 × 165 cm (51 ⅛ × 65 in), Musée de Picardie, Amiens, France
Constance Marie Charpentier, born Constance Marie Blondelu, 1767, Paris.
Died 1849, Paris.

Charpentier is thought to have been a student of various French painters, including the acclaimed Neo-Classical artist Jacques-Louis David (1748–1825) who was notably supportive of female artists at time when they were typically denied access to formal art training. She was considered one of the finest portrait painters of the era and several of her works were once misattributed to David. She regularly exhibited at the Paris Salons, receiving its Gold Medal in 1814 among other prizes throughout her career. While she worked predominantly in portraiture, she also painted small-scale scenes of everyday life – both genres that were deemed more 'suitable' for women than allegorical or mythological subjects. Women were not entirely prevented from tackling such themes, however, as Charpentier's best-known painting, *Melancholy*, demonstrates. A brightly lit woman in a white robe sits slumped upon the ground, her arms limp, while contemplating the encroaching darkness of the surrounding landscape. Exhibited in the Salon of 1801 to critical acclaim, the work demonstrated Charpentier's professional ambitions and her skill in creating an emblematic representation of melancholia, which was fashionable among the cultural elite of the time.

JUDY CHICAGO

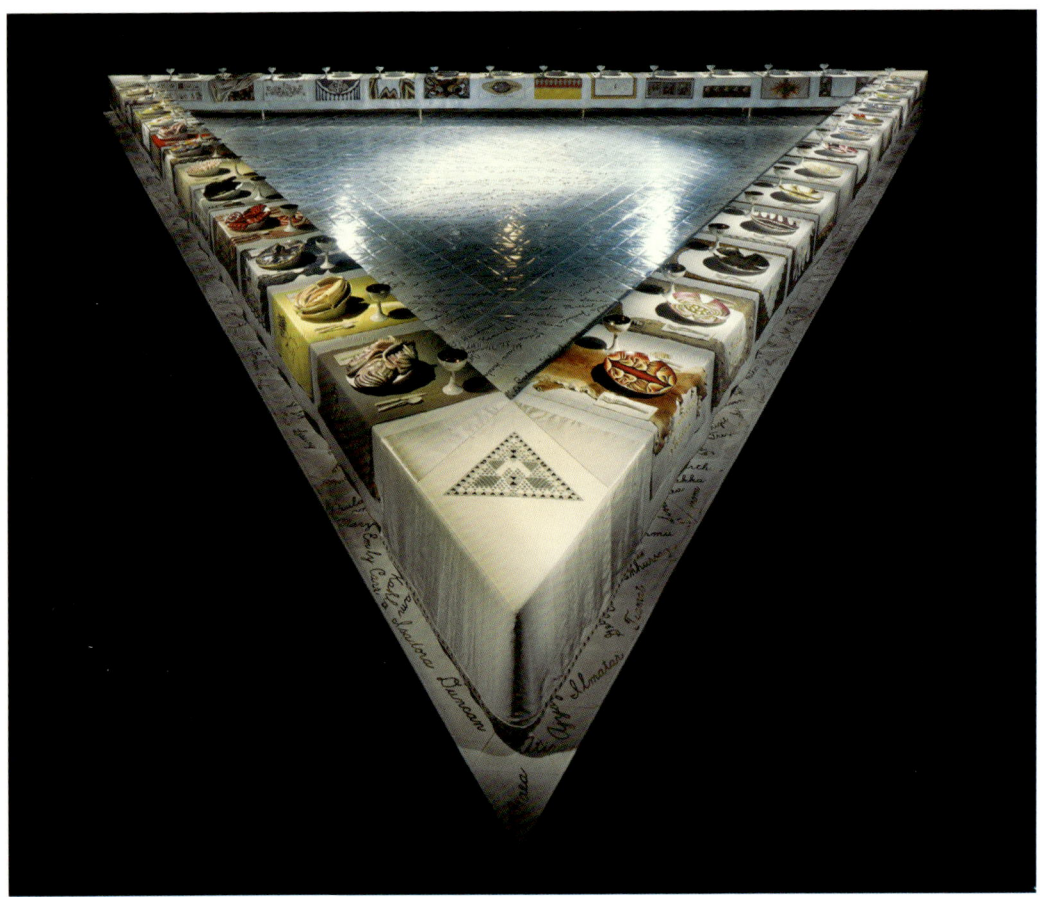

THE DINNER PARTY

1974–9, ceramic, porcelain and textile, 1,463 × 1,463 cm (576 × 576 in), Brooklyn Museum, New York
Judy Chicago, born Judith Cohen, later Judith Gerowitz, 1939, Chicago.

A leading figure among first-generation feminist artists, Chicago's work made and rewrote art history. In the aftermath of bereavement, she changed her surname to detach her identity from a man's. She chose 'Chicago' because of her strong regional accent, although much of her life has been spent in California. Politically active since her student days, in civil rights as well as feminism, she was identified in the 1960s as a Minimalist, being included in the landmark exhibition 'Primary Structures' (1966) at New York's Jewish Museum. By 1972 she was experimenting with performance art, using pyrotechnics and coloured smoke, and with Miriam Schapiro (p.358) co-organized *Womanhouse,* a CalArts installation and performance space. *The Dinner Party* is a monumental work of feminist art, a large triangular refectory whose ornate dinner service is dedicated to thirty-nine iconic women, among them Hildegard of Bingen (1098–1179), Artemisia Gentileschi (p.150), Anna Maria van Schurman (p.362) and Georgia O'Keeffe (p.301). Getting a seat at the table is a powerful metaphor for gaining access to patriarchal spaces, while the motifs on the ceramics themselves use vulva forms to boldly reflect women's subjectivity at an intimate level.

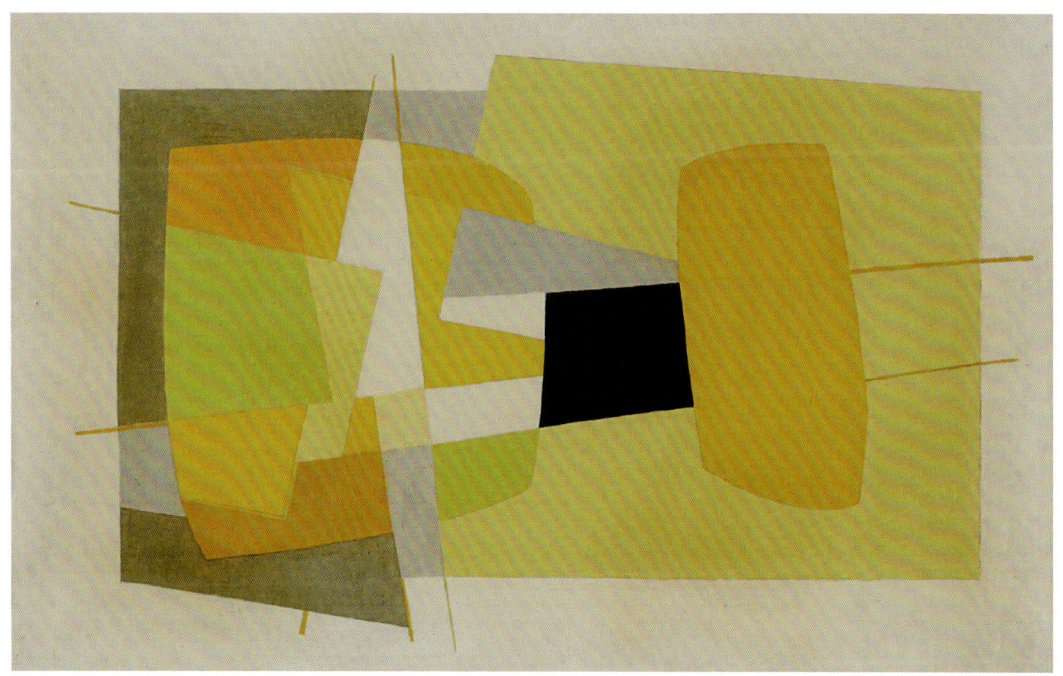

COMPOSITION IN YELLOW

1962–5, oil on panel, 51.5 × 81 cm (20 ¼ × 31 ⅞ in), Barjeel Art Foundation,
Sharjah, UAE
Saloua Raouda Choucair, born Saloua Raouda, 1916, Beirut. Died 2017, Beirut.

Exhibiting at the Arab Cultural Gallery in Beirut in 1947, Choucair
emerged as among the first Lebanese artists of the abstract movement. Little known through much of her life, she would eventually
be recognized as one of the foremost modernists in the Arab world.
Initially apprenticed to the renowned Lebanese Impressionist
painters Moustafa Farroukh (1901–57) and Omar Onsi (1901–69),
she travelled to Paris in 1948 to study at the École des Beaux-Arts,
spending time at the studio of Fernand Léger (1881–1955) and
encountering artists such as Sonia Delaunay (p.118), in whose

abstract Salon des Réalités Nouvelles she was included two years
later. Choucair's attention later turned to sculpture, although only
one large public commission survived the Lebanese Civil War
and her extant legacy is in painting, exemplified in this work.
Its colour palette informs a dynamic compositional arrangement
of geometric, organic shapes and intersecting lines. In its balance
and confidence, Choucair's work drew on the non-representational
traditions of Islamic art, although less from its familiar calligraphic
style. Aged ninety-seven, she had her first major international retrospective, at Tate Modern, London, which proved so popular that its
run was extended.

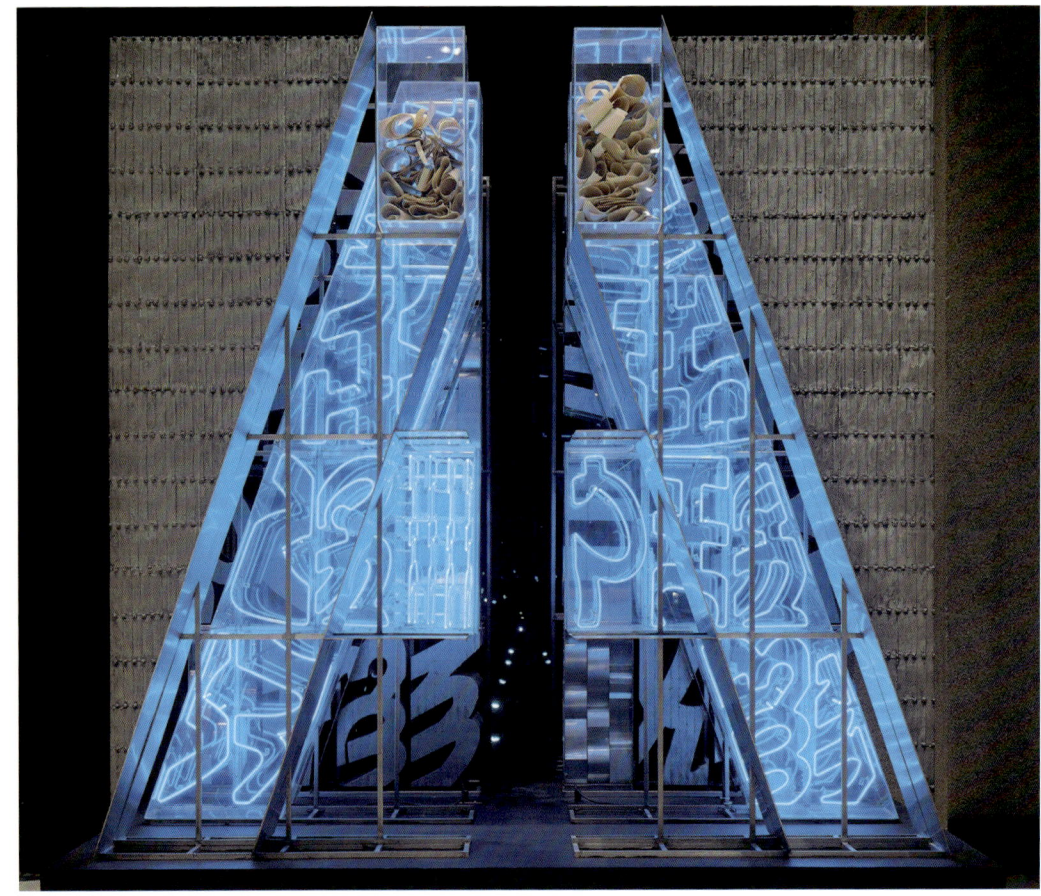

THE GATES TO TIMES SQUARE

1966, welded stainless steel, neon and Plexiglas, 304.8 × 304.8 × 304.8 cm
(120 × 120 × 120 in), Albright-Knox Art Gallery, Buffalo, New York
Chryssa, born Chryssa Vardea Mavromichali, 1933, Athens. Died 2013, Athens.

A descendant of the prominent Mavromichalis family, Chryssa's
upbringing was not wealthy but highly cultured. She studied for
a year in Paris alongside André Breton (1896–1966) and Max Ernst
(1891–1976) before moving in 1954 to continues her studies in
California, later settling in New York. Her breakthrough work,
Cycladic Books (1957) is a series of plaster reliefs formed from the
insides of cardboard packaging. Inspired by geometric reliefs
of ancient Greek art it also connected with Pop art in its use of everyday materials. Moving on to explore typography and lettering,

Chryssa apprenticed herself to a commercial sign writer. Intoxicated
by American life, on first experiencing Times Square, she imagined
it as a new Acropolis, finding its flashing signs of advertising and adult
theatres poetic rather than vulgar. Seeing potential in neon as a
creative material, her first major neon sculpture, made in 1962, was
a homage to what was then a somewhat seedy neighbourhood. The
monumental work shown here was begun two years later. Big enough
to walk through, the gateway is formed by two gigantic As, perhaps
standing for America (or Acropolis), filled with letters and symbols
that illuminate and immerse.

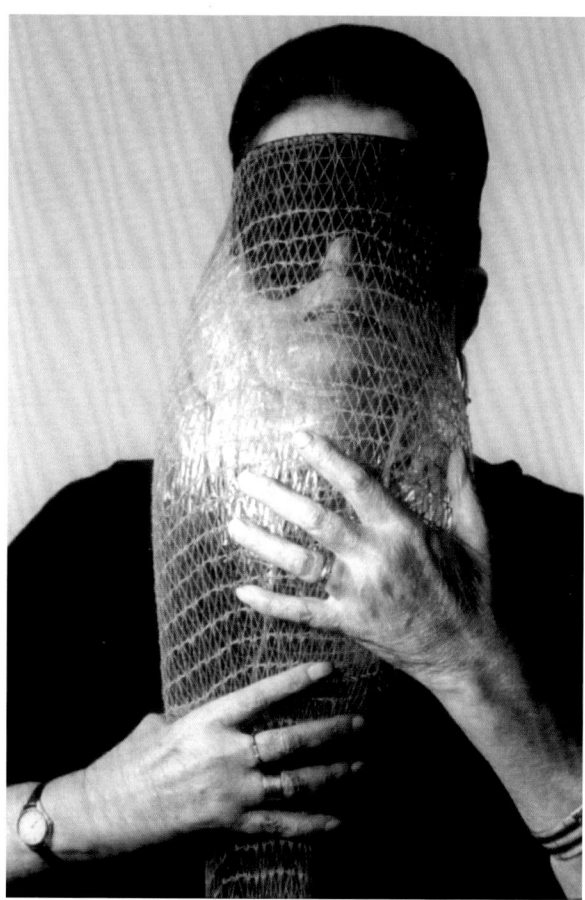

MÁSCARA ABISMO (ABYSS MASK)
1968, photograph, 110 × 60 cm (43 ⅓ × 23 ⅔ in)
Lygia Clark, born 1920, Belo Horizonte, Brazil. Died 1988, Rio de Janeiro.

A pioneering figure in the Brazilian avant-garde movement, Clark created works ranging from geometric paintings, drawings and collages to participatory experiences. She studied art in both Rio de Janeiro and Paris. Returning to Rio in 1954 she joined the *Grupo Frente* ('Front Group'), an artist collective that rejected figuration and nationalism, associating instead with a type of abstraction termed Concretism. Together with fellow *Grupo Frente* artist Lygia Pape (p.312) and several others, Clark co-founded the Neo-Concrete movement (1959–61), seeking to develop a more psychologically engaged and sensorial approach to abstraction. Clark explored the relationship between artwork and audience, with sculptures composed of moveable metal planes, which she termed 'relational objects'. These included *Abyss Mask*, a loosely woven mesh to be worn over the face along with an eye mask, which was intended to enable the wearer to gain awareness of the air's movement within their body. Increasingly, Clark saw her work less as an aesthetic form and more as a therapeutic process, creating multisensory environments and situations designed to engage the audience in a transformatory healing act.

CAMILLE CLAUDEL

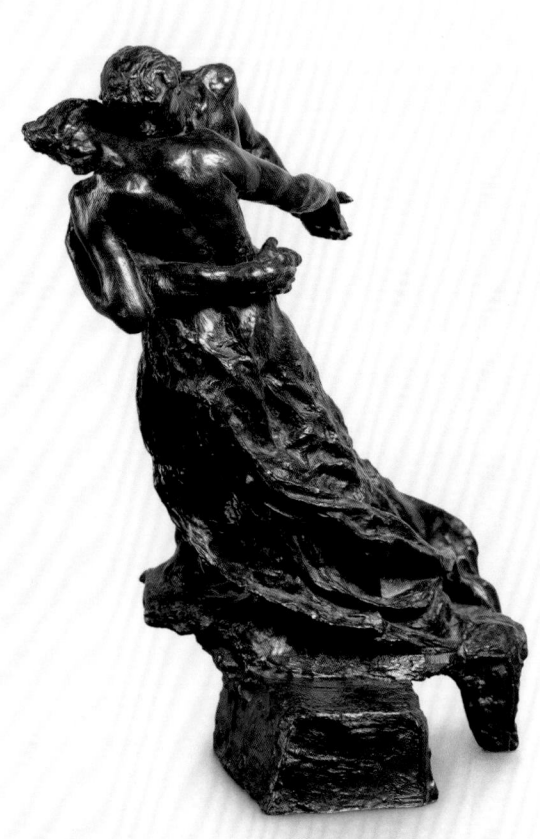

THE WALTZ

*c.*1893, bronze, 43.2 × 23 × 34.3 cm (17 × 9 × 13 ½ in), Musée Rodin, Paris
Camille Claudel, born 1864, Fère-en-Tardenois, France. Died 1943, Avignon, France.

Claudel studied sculpture at the Académie Colarossi in Paris at a time when women were barred from attending the École des Beaux-Arts. She rented a studio with a group of young female artists, and by 1884 was employed by Auguste Rodin (1840–1917), who became her lover in a stormy relationship that lasted until 1893. Her work has been repeatedly compared to his, yet Claudel distanced herself from his practice while continuing to seek large-scale public commissions. *The Waltz* was praised in literary circles, while the composer Claude Debussy kept a version in his study for the rest of his life. Her admirers found something shocking in her – the critic Octave Mirbeau describing her as 'a revolt against nature: a woman genius' – while an earlier, fully nude version of this work was deemed too explicitly sensual to be publicly displayed unless modified with drapes, and a large-scale marble was never made. Such institutional censorship exacerbated Claudel's bouts of depression. Isolated after her father's death in 1913, she was committed against her will to a psychiatric institution by her diplomat-poet brother, Paul. Without art materials, she lived a virtual prisoner until the end of her life.

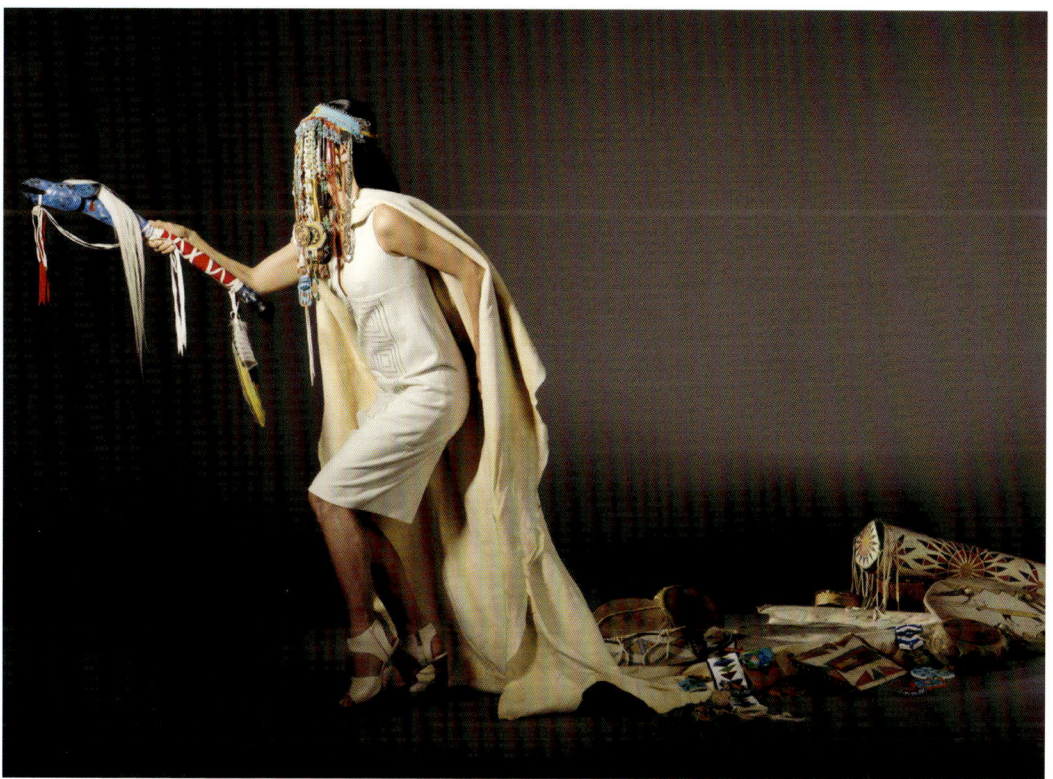

CULTURAL BELONGINGS

2016, LED Firebox with transmounted Lightjet Duratrans, 72 × 96 cm
(28 ⅜ × 37 ¾ in), Collection of Amir and Rosalind Adnani
Dana Claxton, born 1959, Yorkton, Saskatchewan, Canada.

Of mixed heritage, including the Native American tribe of Hunkpapa Lakota as well as European-Canadian ancestry, Claxton moved to Vancouver in the 1980s, where she continues to live and work. She has dedicated her photography, video and performance practice to critiquing Western stereotypes of indigenous identities, reclaiming these through alternative portrayals. In the 1990s, Claxton's role as a critic and teacher developed, with her co-founding the Indigenous Media Arts Group for training aboriginal artists in 1998, and she remains involved in education as associate professor at the University of British Columbia. Claxton's art projects at this time included *Buffalo Bone China* (1997), a video that explored the indigenous loss of the American bison due to the nineteenth-century colonial practices of the British – these animals being shot for sport and their bones also being used to make fine porcelain. Her more recent photographic series have explored the contemporary appropriation of indigenous culture, exemplified in this large-scale image, *Cultural Belongings*. It depicts a glamorously dressed model wearing a beaded headdress and holding a Lakota horse dance stick, pretending to run from the frame to leave behind an array of artefacts.

PRUNELLA CLOUGH

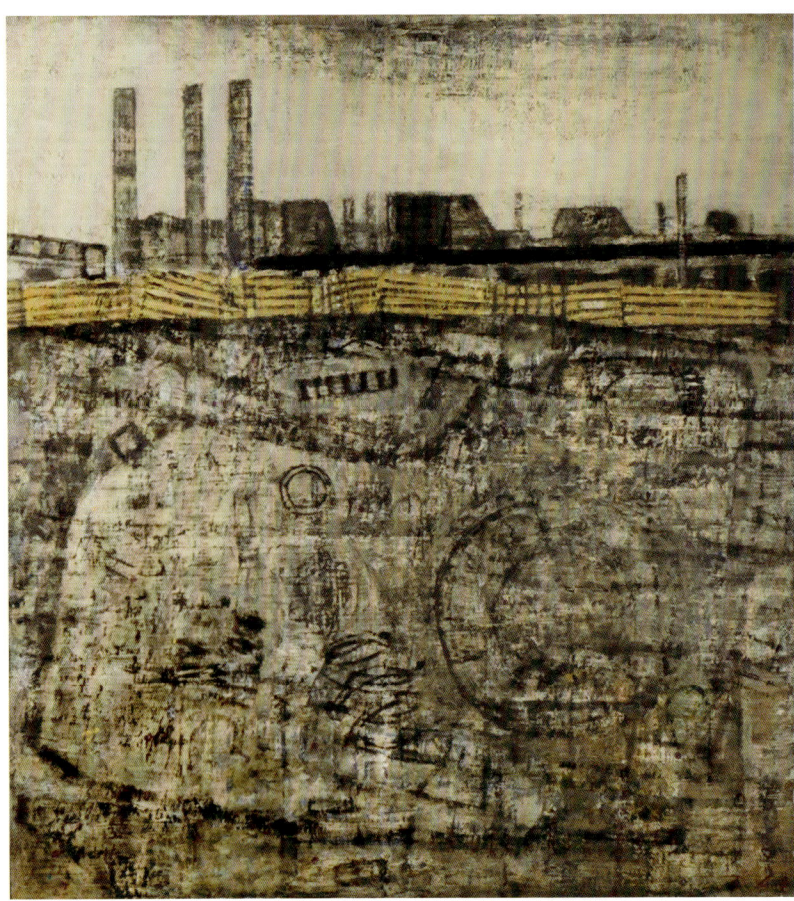

MIDLAND LANDSCAPE II
Undated (before 1965), oil on board, 81.3 × 75.2 cm (32 × 29 ⅝ in),
Sunderland Museum & Winter Gardens, UK
Prunella Clough, born Cara Prunella Clough-Taylor, 1919, London.
Died 1999, London.

Having studied at Chelsea College of Art, Clough remained in London for the rest of her career, though also based herself intermittently at her mother's house in the small town of Southwold, Suffolk, until 1966, where she enjoyed working. She developed a fascination with the urban and industrial areas in and around London, as well as travelling repeatedly to East Anglia and the Midlands, specifically the latter region's 'Black Country', named after both its abundance of coal and its heavily polluting forges and factories. During repeated visits, Clough would record extensive notes and diary entries rather than sketching, building up materials for future paintings where her recollections, rather than direct perceptions, would be represented. Incorporating the materials and colours of industry into her landscapes, she frequently placed found objects in her prints and paintings. In this landscape study, she pressed objects onto the work's surface to leave indented impressions, a connection to her parallel practice as a printmaker. The industrial skyline in the distance sits in contrast to the more abstract foreground, demonstrating Clough's mode of recording space and place by utilizing her visual memory.

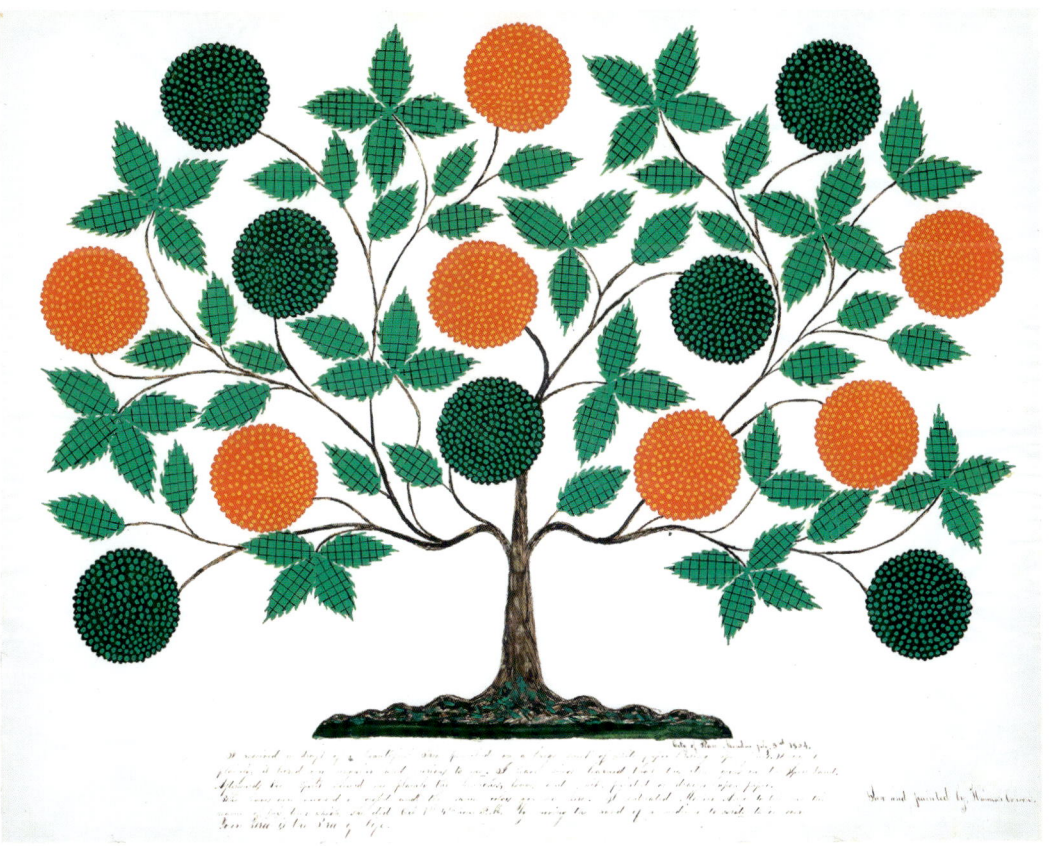

THE TREE OF LIFE

1854, watercolour and ink on paper, 62.9 × 75.6 cm (24 ¾ × 29 ¾ in),
Hancock Shaker Village, Massachusetts
Hannah Cohoon, born Hannah Harrison, 1788, Williamstown, Massachusetts.
Died 1864, Hancock, Massachusetts.

The Christian sect of the Shakers, to which Cohoon belonged, origi-nated in England and expanded to America in the late eighteenth century. So-called because of their ecstatic customs of worship, the movement was also known for its simple lifestyle in celibate, gender-equal communities. From 1830 to 1850 the Shaker movement experienced a spiritual reawakening when its followers received beatific visions, which they translated into drawing, dance and song. Among the most impressive of the 'gift drawings' were those

created by Cohoon, a member of the Hancock Shaker Village in Massachusetts, who was unusual for signing her work. Four sur-viving drawings of Cohoon's focus on forms redolent of both nature's bounty and the divine presence. One depicts a basket of wondrously luminous apples, another, a mystical tree, each leaf emitting a divine charge of wavy red lines. In the stylized image seen here, spindly branches defy gravity to support hefty red and green orbs of ripe fruit, which are arranged in perfect harmony among the foliage. An inscription beneath describes the vision that inspired the drawing. Despite their apparent simplicity, these works on paper radiate with an unexpected intensity born of religious fervour.

ITHELL COLQUHOUN

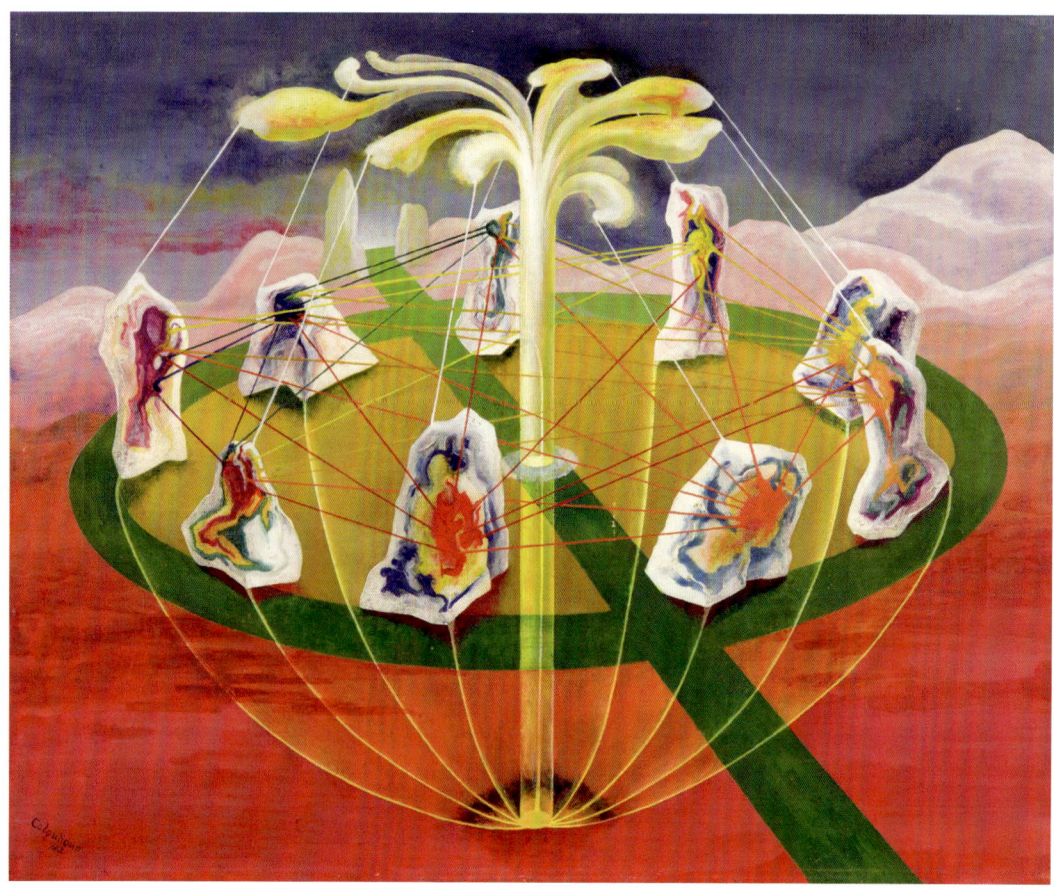

THE DANCE OF THE NINE OPALS

1942, oil on canvas, 54.5 × 68.5 cm (21 ½ × 27 in), Sherwin Collection, Leeds, UK
Ithell Colquhoun, born 1906, Shillong, India. Died 1988, Lamorna, Cornwall, UK.

The daughter of a civil servant in India, Colquhoun became interested in the esoteric arts during her teenage years at boarding school. She was largely self-taught as an artist, although she attended some classes at London's Slade School of Art in the late 1920s. Visiting Paris in 1931, she encountered for the first time the work of Salvador Dalí (1904–89), which influenced her decisively, and her first solo exhibition was in Cheltenham in 1936. Returning to Paris in 1939, she met the chief theorist of Surrealism, André Breton (1896–1966), after which she became part of the movement in London, exhibiting with Roland Penrose (1900–84) and formally joining the British

Surrealist Group. The following year she was expelled for research into the occult, and while continuing to develop innovative techniques of drawing, she focused more on automatic writing, and practices of Wicca and Druidism and alchemy. Made during these years, *The Dance of the Nine Opals* is a transformation of the outward, visible world into a symbolic space, resembling a kabbalistic diagram. Based on the Merry Maidens, a Neolithic stone circle near her home in Cornwall, the opals refer to the artist's birthstone.

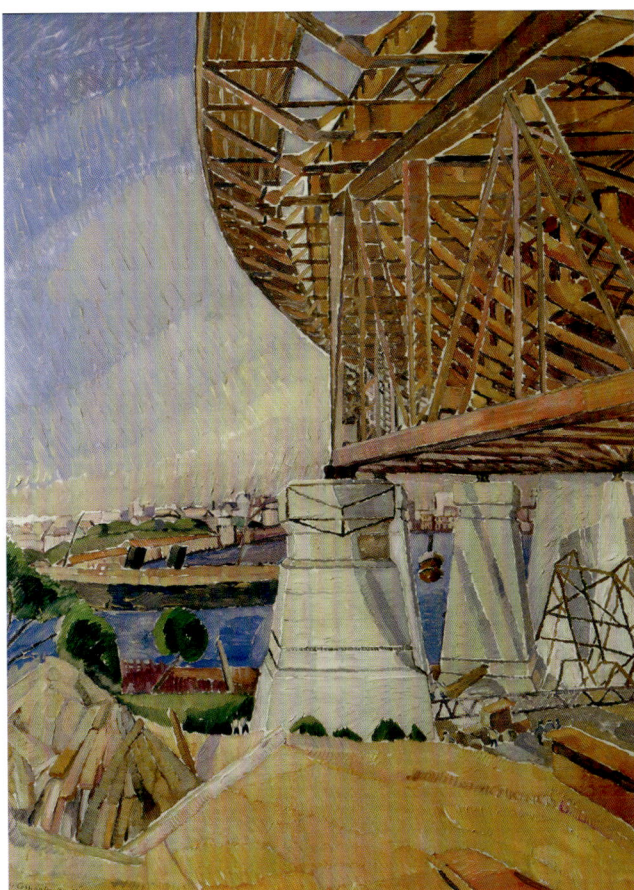

THE CURVE OF THE BRIDGE

1928–9, oil on cardboard, 110.5 × 82.5 cm (43 ½ × 32 ½ in), Art Gallery
of New South Wales, Sydney
Grace Cossington Smith, born Grace Smith, 1892, Sydney. Died 1984, Sydney.

Cossington Smith adopted her middle name to reflect strong family
connections with England, and in some ways her career represents
an evolution of Australian art and culture in the twentieth century,
with close adherence to European models giving way to a distinct
national identity. Cossington Smith studied in England and
Germany, with further training in Sydney from Italian-Australian
painter Antonio Dattilo-Rubbo (1870–1955). She subsequently
pioneered an Australian response to Post-Impressionism, developing
an unabashed colour palette that captured her experience of Sydney

life. As she stated, her aim was 'to express form in colour – colour
within colour, vibrant with light', seen in this study of a cityscape
in flux. Designed and fabricated in England before being shipped
to Australia for assembly, Sydney's Harbour Bridge provided the
artist with a hulking and hopeful subject. Instead of the overall, iconic
shape, this work shows the approaches of the bridge under construction. Light pours down in visible brushstrokes from a radiant sky
to meet concrete pylons and energetic steel framework. Conveying
the artist's optimism about this monumental engineering project,
it also illustrates a nation's growing self-confidence.

RENEE COX

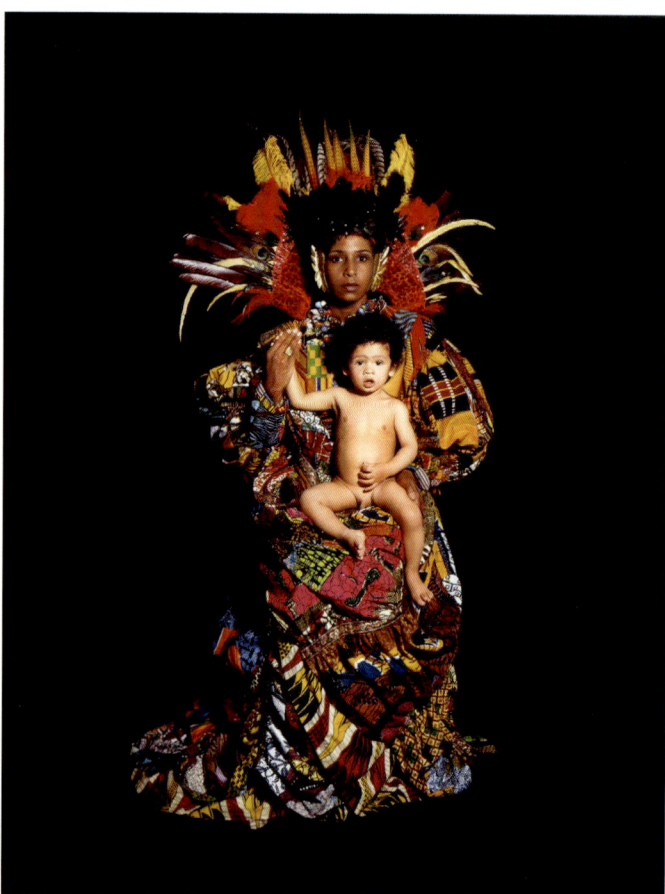

YO MAMADONNA AND CHILD
1994, archival digital inkjet print on cotton rag, 121.9 × 182.9 cm (48 × 72 in),
edition of 3. Costume: Januwa Moja
Renee Cox, born 1960, Colgate, Jamaica.

After working as a fashion photographer, Cox turned to making bold
and provocative photographs that challenge stereotypes and champion cultural representations of black people – women in particular.
Often appearing in her work as a model, she performs a sharp critique
of racist and sexist currents in contemporary society. Her first solo
show in 1998 included a series of self-portraits in character as Raje,
a black superhero and embodiment of Cox's activist intentions.
She has repeatedly addressed the lack of black figures in the history
of Western art – particularly their absence from images with

enduring religious significance – by restaging iconic works with
black subjects. While pregnant with her first child in the 1990s, Cox
began her 'Yo Mama' project, a group of often nude self-portraits
as a black Madonna, which includes this work. For her series 'Flippin
the Script' she remade European religious masterpieces such as
Michelangelo Buonarroti's sculpture *David* (1501–4). *Yo Mama's Last
Supper* (1996), a version of Leonardo da Vinci's *Last Supper* (1495–8),
proved especially controversial, featuring Cox as a nude Jesus surrounded by black apostles – apart from Judas, who is white.

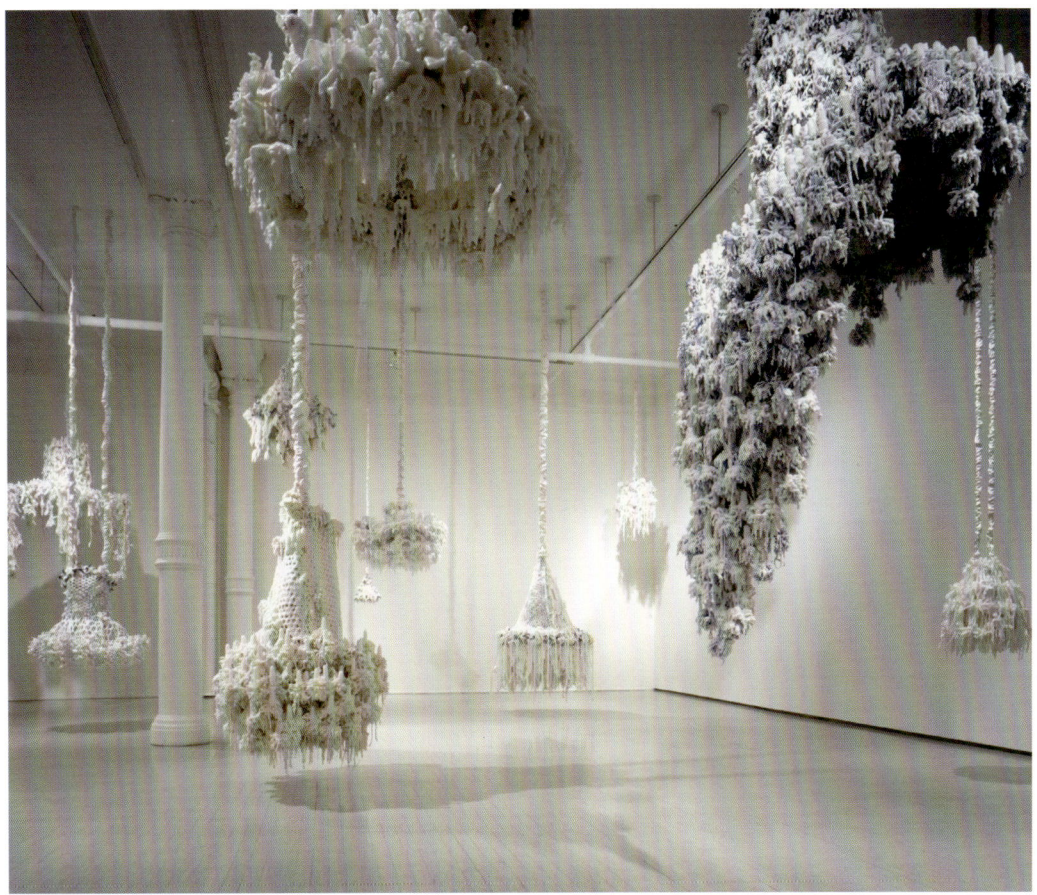

UNTITLED WORKS

1992–4, mixed media, dimensions variable, installation view, 'Petah Coyne: Recent Sculpture', Jack Shainman Gallery, New York, 1994. Collections: Addison Gallery of American Art, Andover, Massachusetts; Brooklyn Museum, New York; Minneapolis Museum of Art; Museum of Contemporary Art, North Miami, Florida; Museum of Modern of Modern Art, New York; Philadelphia Museum of Art; and private collections
Petah Coyne, born 1953, Oklahoma City.

Growing up in a military family, Coyne moved throughout the United States constantly as a child until settling in Ohio at age thirteen. She then attended Kent State University and the Art Academy of Cincinnati. By 1977, she had moved to New York and was receiving critical attention for her sculptures, which diverged from earlier twentieth-century approaches to the medium, both in form and materials. Coyne mixed industrial substances with an array of everyday items, from pearls, silk flowers and ribbons, to car parts, tree branches, taxidermied animals and human hair. These elements were often dipped in a specially formulated wax that can withstand high temperatures of up to 200 degrees Celsius (392 Fahrenheit), and layered to build up complex shapes full of intricate detail. The results, seen for example in this installation, are organic, fantastical forms that hang like chandeliers or recall stalactite formations found in caves. With its symbolic, baroque sensibility, Coyne's work reflects influences that are varied: from the drama of her own personal stories to, invariably, the imperfection of humanity and our changing relationships. As she puts it, 'those times that are almost perfect, but not quite'.

CUI JIE

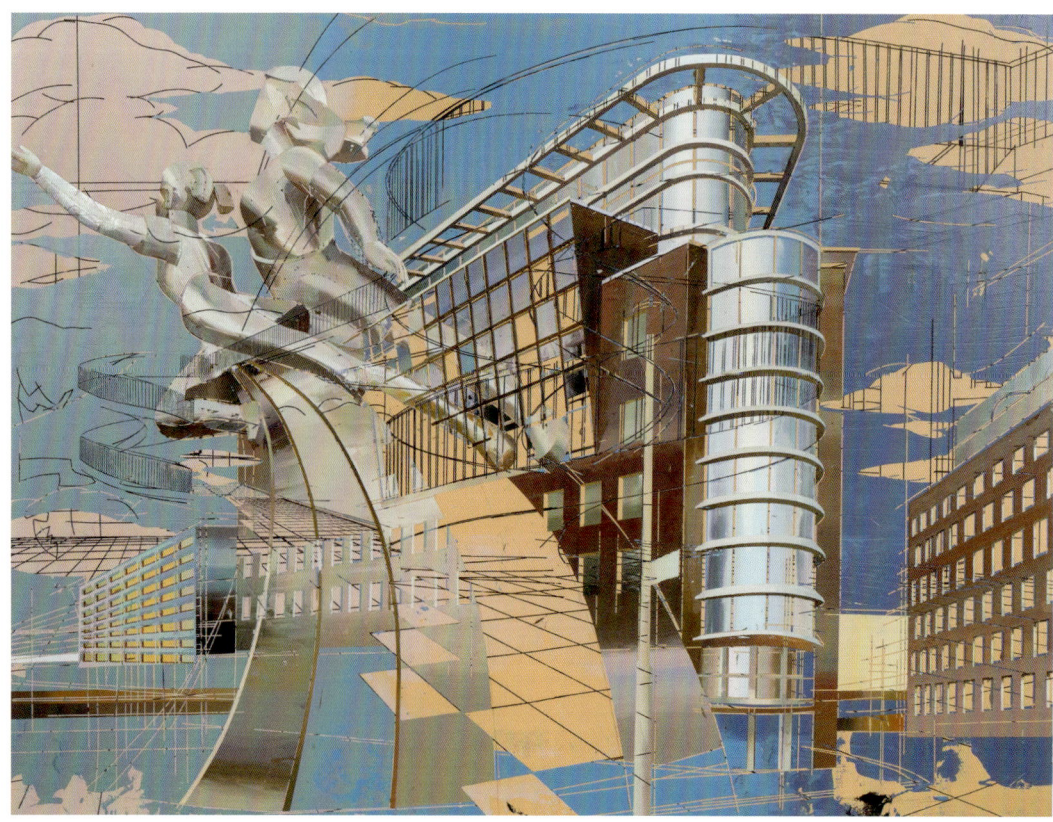

CORNER BUILDING

2017, oil on canvas, 150 × 200 cm (59 ⅛ × 78 ¾ in), The East West Bank Collection
Cui Jie, born 1983, Shanghai.

Cui makes paintings of architectural transformation that represent
particular elements of urban China. She has depicted scenes from
her native city, from Hangzhou where she studied oil painting at the
China Academy of Art, and from Beijing where she now lives and
works. While her early practice mixed disparate imagery to investigate
the truthfulness of reality, she later became interested in the specific
imagery of buildings influenced by Modernism. During Cui's lifetime
Chinese urban landscapes have been shaped by styles ranging from
Bauhaus and Soviet architecture to Japanese Metabolism, with urban
life affected by the confused impact of their progressive aims. Using
a style of layered paint and overlapping perspectives, she represents
the accelerated evolution and severe dislocations that have defined
Chinese cities over the past few decades. Showing Cui's interest
in science fiction, her paintings have a sense of the imaginary as
rooted in reality. In this otherworldly scene, numerous structures
come together, from utilitarian office blocks to a curved facade with
opalescent windows. Two pristine figures in a Socialist Realism style
seem to fly into the atmosphere, with gravity absent and time upended.

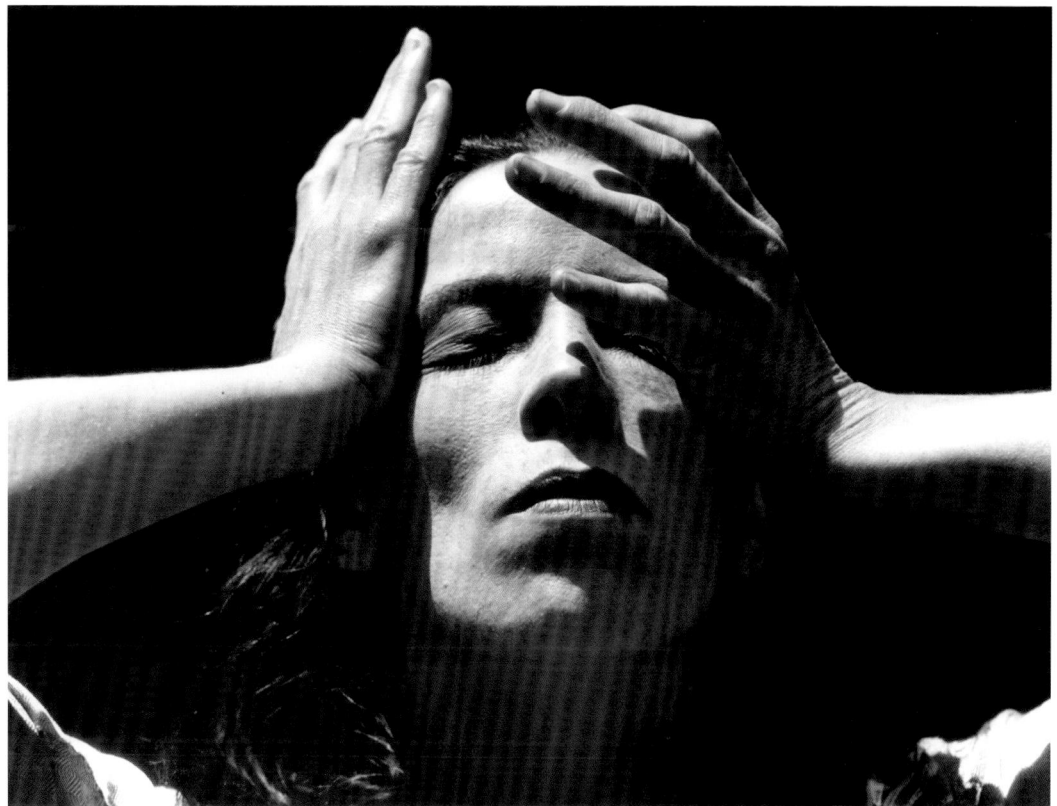

MARTHA GRAHAM
1931, gelatin silver print, 15.9 × 23.5 cm (6 ¼ × 9 ¼ in)
Imogen Cunningham, born 1883, Portland, Oregon. Died 1976, San Francisco.

One of America's first female professional photographers, Cunningham established her own studio in Seattle in 1910, when she was in her mid-twenties. Earlier, as a student of chemistry at the University of Washington, she had taught herself how to use a camera and earned money by photographing specimens in the botanical collection before writing her dissertation on the science of photography. Inspired by the work of Gertrude Käsebier (1852–1934) – an American portrait photographer who promoted the medium as suitable and fulfilling for women artists – Cunningham chose this path for herself. She proceeded to work and innovate with photography, a passion that remained strong until her death. Her subjects included plants, still lifes, nudes and everyday activities seen on the streets, though portraiture was at the heart of her practice. Her sequence of nearly ninety photographs of Martha Graham (1894–1991), the choreographer and pioneer of modern dance, was taken one summer afternoon, outdoors in strong sunlight. In this mask-like close-up, the hands framing Graham's disembodied head express the angular, theatrical gestures for which the dancer was renowned.

HANNE DARBOVEN

7 PANELS, II (PANEL 1)

1972–3, pencil on paper, 177.2 × 177.2 cm (69 ¾ × 69 ¾ in), Pinakothek der Moderne, Bayerische Staatsgemäldesammlungen, Munich

Hanne Darboven, born 1941, Munich. Died 2009, Hamburg, Germany.

Calculations, numerical units and formulas were the stuff of this German conceptual artist's works. Moving to New York for just two years, from 1966 to 1968, immediately after studying painting at the Hochschule für bildende Künste in Hamburg, Darboven quickly developed her esoteric language. She also enjoyed informative friendships with members of New York's art scene, including Sol LeWitt (1928–2007), Carl Andre (1935–2024) and Joseph Kosuth (b.1945). The conceptualization of time informed Darboven's expression; believing time was a universal measure and unit of existence, on a daily basis she systematically noted its passing using numerical constructs and cryptic codes that she referred to as 'mathematic prose'. It was these sheets of writing, framed individually or in groups, that comprised her expansive wall-based grid installations and, later in her career, were punctuated with images, texts and personal archival objects. This panel, which is the first of seven that constitute the work, holds thirty-five sheets of composition paper. Along faint blue lines, looping pencil marks, evocative of the letter 'i', repeat and appear infinite. Emblematic of her obsessive consistency, the text does not form readable words, but rather functions as a manifestation of her desire to trap and systematize time.

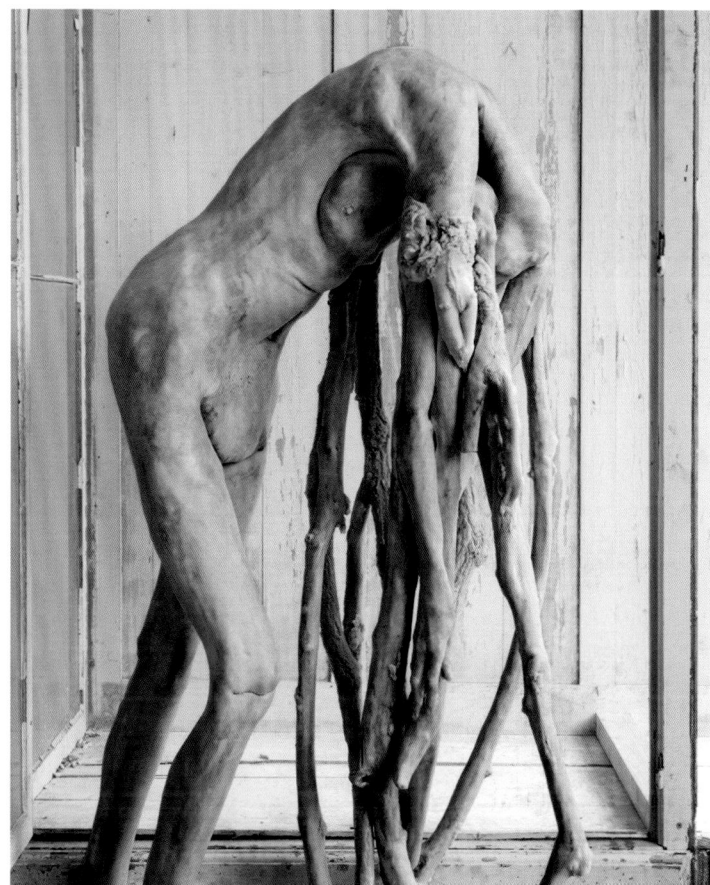

MARTHE

2008, wax, wood, glass, epoxy and iron, 260 × 177 × 199 cm (102 ⅜ × 69 ⅜ × 78 ⅜ in), Fondazione Sandretto Re Rebaudengo, Turin, Italy
Berlinde De Bruyckere, born 1964, Ghent, Belgium.

De Bruyckere has been making sculptures based on casts of human and animal forms since the early 1990s. Her disfigured and contorted creations, made with wax, textiles, animal skins, hair, metal and wood, find their inspiration in Flemish Baroque painting, as well as in European folklore and Christian iconography. These multiple reference points, layered with new narratives suggested by current events, invite diverse interpretation, but lying at the core of her haunting works is a concern with the vulnerability of the human body and the fragility of life – universal themes that have

preoccupied artists for centuries. Many of her sculptures address the dualities of the human condition – body and spirit, joy and suffering, life and death – but they are not literal representations; rather, they are an attempt to depict mental states. This headless, androgynous figure is typical of her approach. A chaotic tangle of withered limbs that gradually become branches underlines the fundamental human search for transformation and transcendence that De Bruyckere's work deals with. Accentuating its vulnerable state, the mutated, half-human form is displayed on a plinth in a semi-enclosed vitrine.

ELAINE DE KOONING

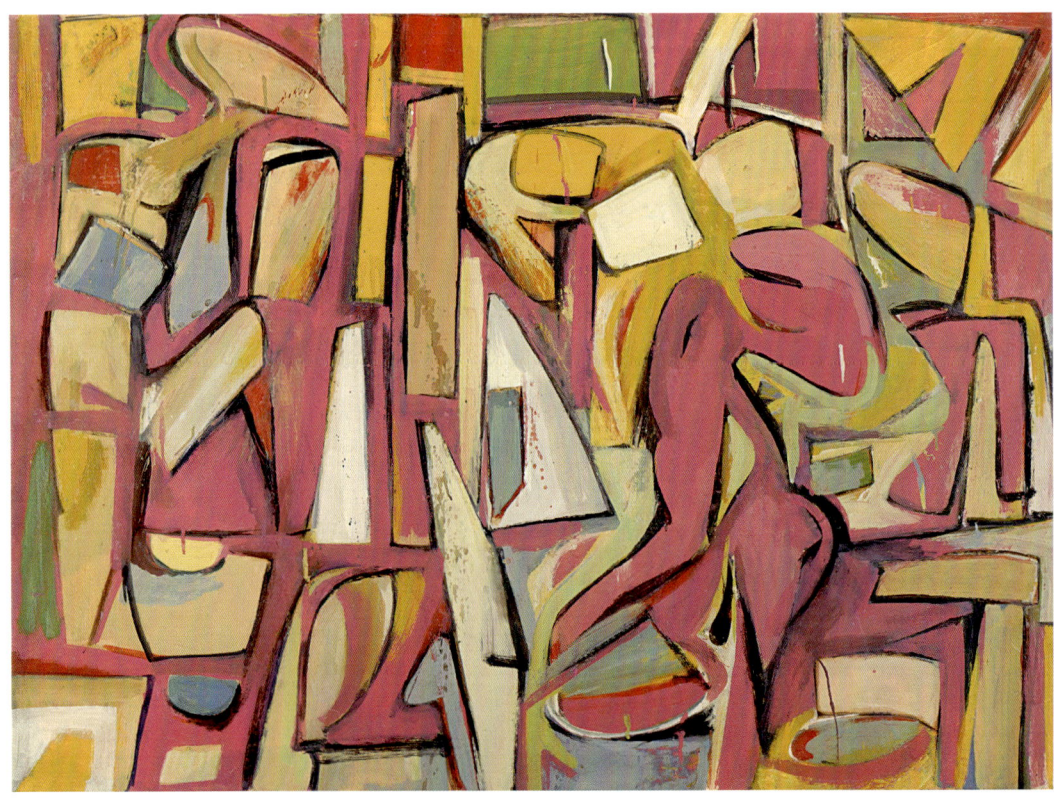

UNTITLED, NUMBER 15

1948, enamel on wrapping paper mounted on canvas, 81.3 × 111.8 cm (32 × 44 in),
Metropolitan Museum of Art, New York
Elaine de Kooning, born Elaine Fried, 1918, New York. Died 1989,
Southampton, New York.

Aged five, de Kooning was copying paintings she'd seen in the
New York museums and in elementary school was selling portraits of
her classmates. As a professional artist, her practice was chiefly a figurative expressionism, focusing on landscape, still lifes and, above all,
portraiture. Interested in movement, she sometimes blurred the faces
of her sitters in what she called 'gyroscope' paintings, to emphasize
how people are recognized as bodies-in-action. Commissioned in
1963 to paint John F. Kennedy, a work she completed after his death,
she worked from dozens of preliminary sketches to represent the
president in the midst of life as a recognizably restless figure,
not simply an iconic face. She is often associated with Abstract
Expressionism, partly due to her marriage to Willem de Kooning
(1904–97), and also to works like this painting – its flat composition
and bold use of colour reflecting the tenets of the movement a
response to a specific moment and location. It is part of a series she
produced while studying dance with Merce Cunningham (1919–
2009) at the experimental art school Black Mountain College, North
Carolina. Its unusual materials reflect her straitened circumstances
at that time.

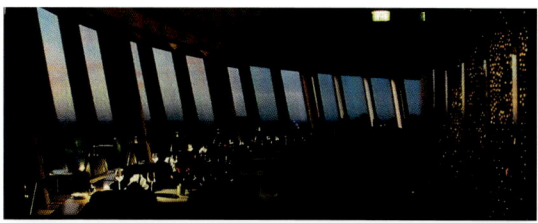

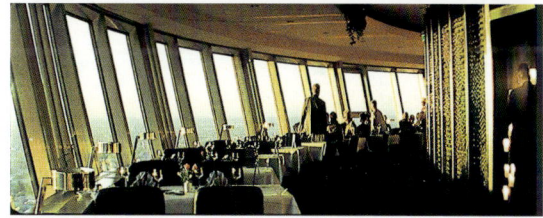

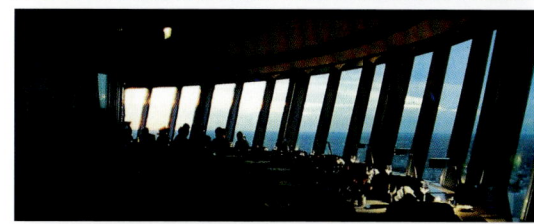

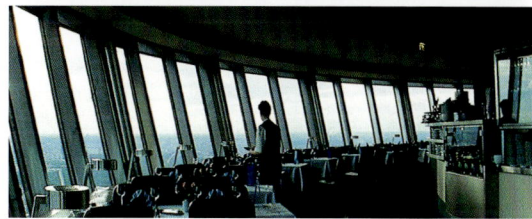

FERNSEHTURM

2001, stills from 16mm colour anamorphic film with optical sound, 44 mins
Tacita Dean, born 1965, Canterbury, UK.

Dean works with the mediums of drawing and photography, but is best known as a filmmaker. She shoots on 16mm and 35mm stock and has been a passionate advocate for celluloid as an artistic medium in an area when many moving-image artists have shifted to digital formats. Dean's work frequently touches on unsolved mysteries or the occult, with projects having explored themes of alchemy, solar eclipses and her collection of four-leaf clovers. Seen here are stills from one of her early films set in Berlin's giant television tower, the Fernsehturm. Perhaps the city's most recognizable landmark, Dean was captivated by the structure when first visiting the capital in 1987

– at which time, it stood in East Germany. Thirteen years later she created this work during her DAAD fellowship with the Berlin artist-in-residence programme. A single shot from inside the tower's revolving restaurant while the sun sets, the film focuses on the curved wall of windows overlooking the city, conveying a futuristic vision conceived in the past that cannot quite escape its historic location. In 2018, three major public galleries in London – the National Portrait Gallery, Royal Academy of Arts and National Gallery – staged concurrent presentations of Dean's work.

JAY DEFEO

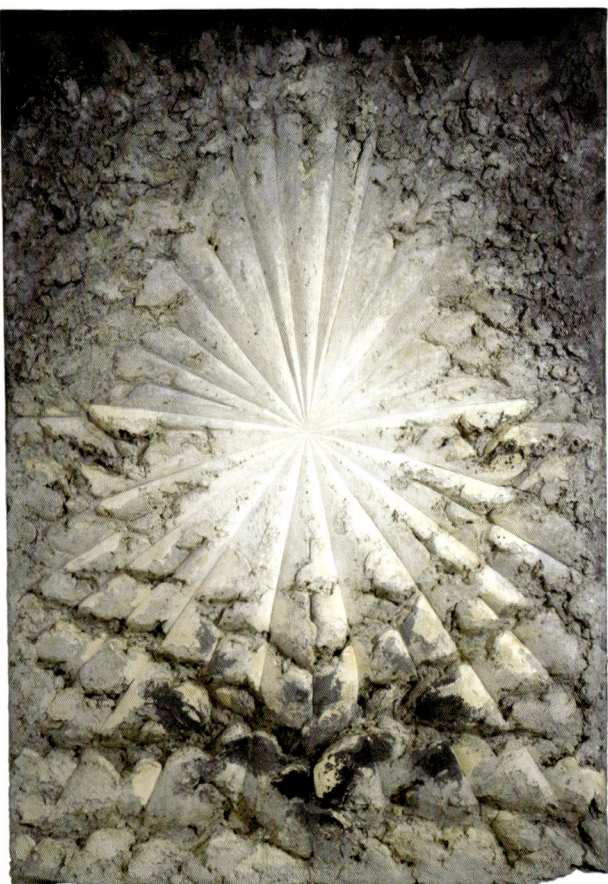

THE ROSE
1958–66, oil with wood and mica on canvas, 327.3 × 234.3 × 27.9 cm
(128 ⅞ × 92 ¼ × 11 in), Whitney Museum of American Art, New York
Jay DeFeo, born Mary Joan DeFeo, 1929, Hanover, New Hampshire. Died 1989,
Oakland, California.

Raised in the San Francisco Bay Area, DeFeo explored art movements including Abstract Expressionism while attending the
University of California, Berkeley, in the late 1940s and cultivated
an interest in creative experimentation there that would shape her
later career. Travels in Europe and North Africa in the early 1950s
awoke her fascination with African and prehistoric art, in addition
to Classical architectural design. An exploration of geometric and
organic forms and her fearless use of diverse media led to DeFeo

becoming a key figure within the Californian art scene. Her
first major solo show was held in 1959, the same year as her work
was included in the prestigious 'Sixteen Americans' exhibition at
New York's Museum of Modern Art. Reflective of DeFeo's challenges
to convention, her cross-disciplinary epic *The Rose*, built up with layers of oil paint and featuring a scored, star-like motif in relief, unites
the media of painting and sculpture. Her most celebrated work, the
colossal canvas weighs almost one tonne, itself the result of a monumental process of transformations during its eight-year creation.

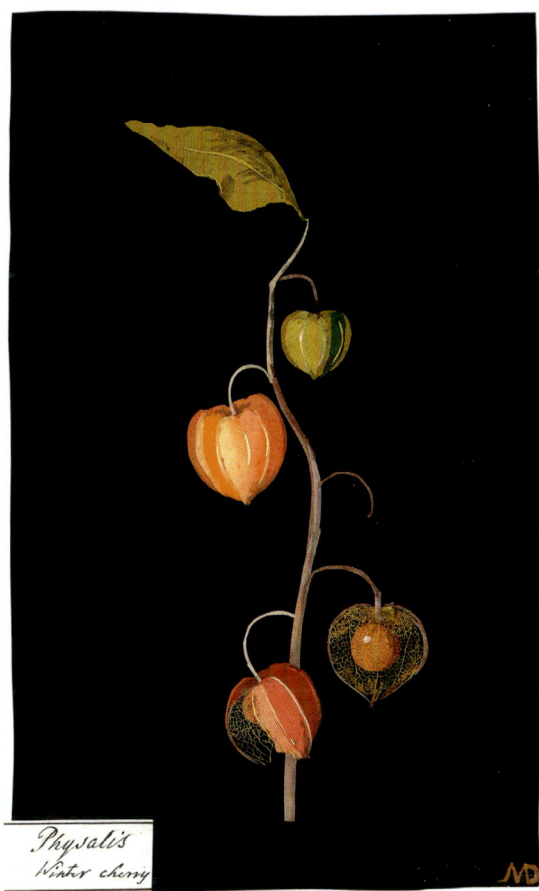

Physalis
Winter cherry

PHYSALIS (WINTER CHERRY) from 'FLORA DELANICA'

1772–82, collage of coloured papers with bodycolour and watercolour, and with plant fibre samples on black ink background, 29.2 × 17.9 cm (11 ½ × 7 in), British Museum, London

Mary Delany, born Mary Granville, 1700, Coulston, Wiltshire, UK. Died 1788, Windsor, UK.

From a genteel but not wealthy background, Delany moved to London as a child. Living with her well-connected aunt, Lady Stanley, she was schooled in subjects thought to befit a girl aspiring to courtly life, and became friends with the composer George Frideric Handel. The death of Delany's first husband, four decades her senior, in 1724 liberated her to travel and socialize, and it was during her second marriage, spent in Dublin, that she developed her artistic interests, making landscape drawings, silhouettes and lacquered objects. Widowed a second time, her close friendship with Margaret Cavendish Bentinck, Duchess of Portland, afforded regular access to the notable collection of natural history specimens on the Duchess's estate in Bulstrode, Buckinghamshire. Delany invented a method of depicting flowers by overlapping hundreds of minute pieces of coloured paper on a black background. Moving in intellectual circles including the 'Blue Stocking Society', she was spurred on to produce her magnum opus, which she started at the age of seventy-two. 'Flora Delanica' was a technically innovative and scientifically accurate collection of 985 botanical collages, of which this is one example.

SONIA DELAUNAY

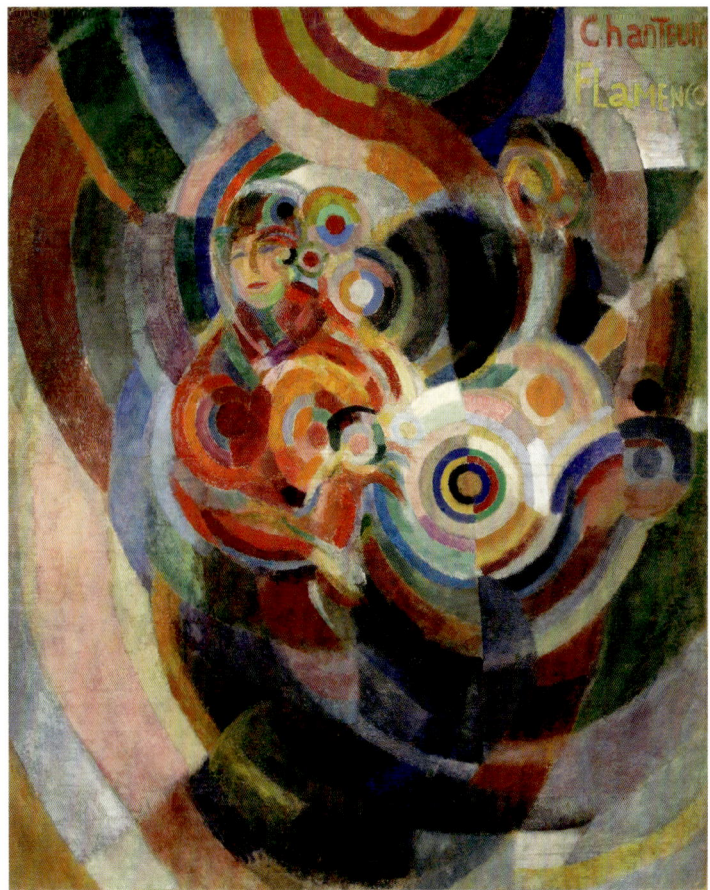

FLAMENCO SINGERS

1915–16, oil, wax and glue on canvas, 174.5 × 143 cm (68 ¾ × 56 ¼ in),
Museu Calouste Gulbenkian, Lisbon
Sonia Delaunay, born Sarah Stern, later Sonia Terk, 1885, Hradyzk,
Russian Empire (now Ukraine). Died 1979, Paris.

Raised in a cosmopolitan adoptive family in St Petersburg, Delaunay
was to become an influential member of the Parisian avant-garde
of the early twentieth century, Delaunay worked as a painter, illustrator and textile designer. In the 1910s, with her husband Robert
Delaunay (1885–1941) and others, she pioneered a new type of non-
figurative painting known as Orphism. Recognized as key to the
development of pure abstraction in painting, Orphism combines
strong colours and geometric shapes to produce pictures with

a sense of rhythm and movement. In its colourful semicircles and
semi-figurative elements, this lively painting captures the dynamism
of the Flamenco tradition. Painted in Portugal during the
First World War, it is one of many works for which Delaunay drew
inspiration from popular culture and entertainment, especially
music and dance. After the war, she expanded her practice to incorporate clothing and interior design, opening a boutique in Madrid,
'Casa Sonia', to sell her creations, and also produced costume
for ballet. In later life Delaunay received international recognition
for her work and, in 1964, became the first living female artist
to have a solo exhibition at the Louvre in Paris.

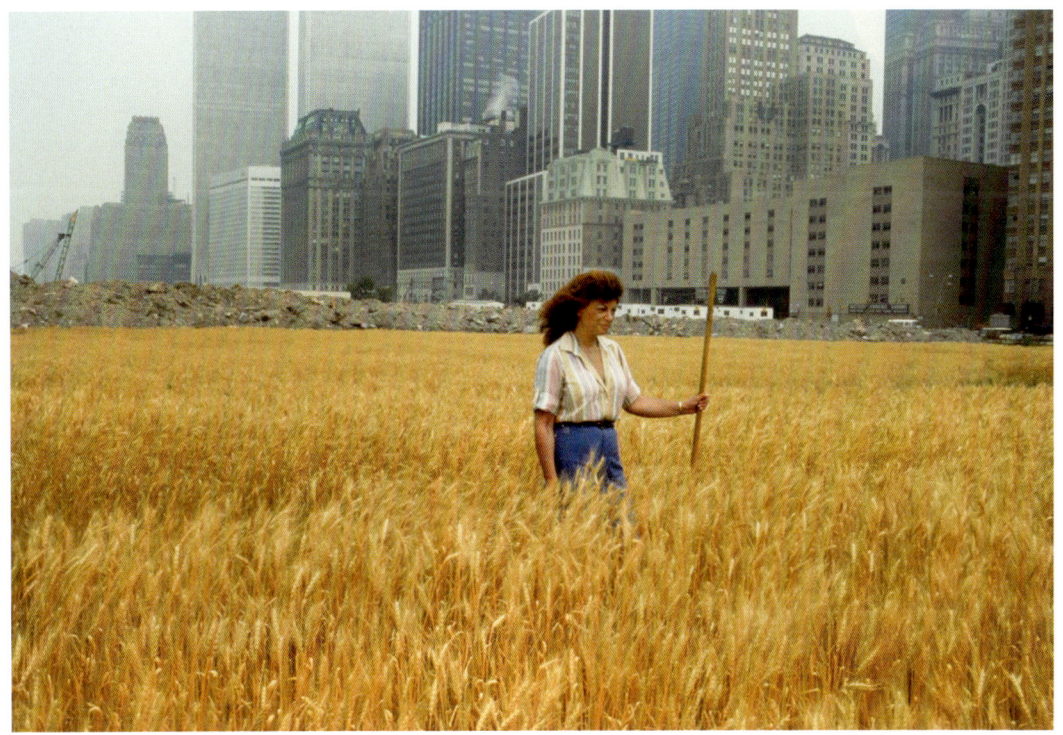

WHEATFIELD – A CONFRONTATION

1982, wheat planted and harvested by the artist, 0.8 hectare (2 acres),
Battery Park Landfill, New York
Agnes Denes, born 1931, Budapest.

Denes is concerned with celebration and repair of the environment. Having survived the Nazi occupation of Hungary, she migrated with her family as a teenager, firstly to Sweden and then to New York. There, she studied painting at The New School and Columbia University, but ultimately found the medium too confining and instead was drawn to the relatively new field of Conceptual art. Although her practice encompasses poetry, philosophical writing and computer-rendered drawing, she is best known for her lyrical environmental installations that are part of the Land art movement. For example, *Tree Mountain – A Living Time Capsule* (1992–6) saw her create a small hill in Finland on which she planted a virgin forest that will remain untouched for four centuries. Pictured here is a work of shorter duration – just four months. This 0.8-hectare (two-acre) plot of wheat creates a David-and-Goliath confrontation with the power represented by New York's financial district. The crop is a universal symbol of food and world hunger, but also a commercial commodity, so the juxtaposition is an indictment of capitalism's skewed values. The unexpected rural idyll temporarily occupied a patch of land newly created using rock excavated during construction of the World Trade Center.

RINEKE DIJKSTRA

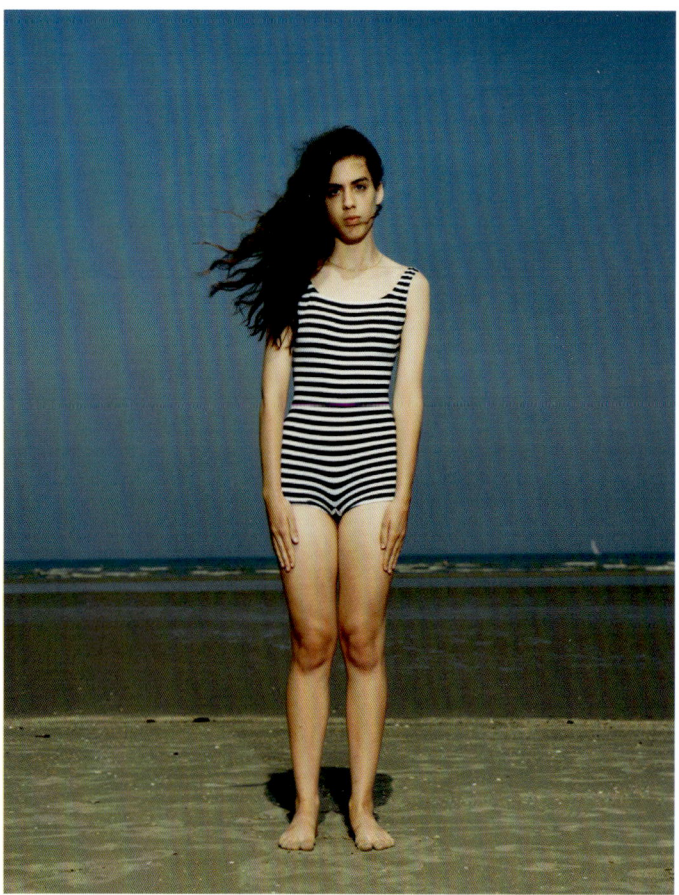

DE PANNE, BELGIUM, AUGUST 7 1992
1992, chromogenic print on paper, 137 × 107 cm (53 ⅞ × 42 ⅛ in)
Rineke Dijkstra, born 1959, Sittard, Netherlands.

Expanding a tradition of photographers energized by direct, psychologically charged encounters with their subjects, such as Diane Arbus (p.39) and August Sander (1876–1964), Dijkstra has been widely lauded since the early 1990s for a body of work marked by intense emotional acuity and vivid conceptual concerns. The artist's intimate photographic portraits, frequently comprising expansive, meticulously realized series, pierce the identity of usually anonymous subjects. Upending conventions of portraiture that have celebrated the appearance and deeds of great men throughout history, Dijkstra by contrast communes with teenagers. *De Panne, Belgium, August 7*

1992 is part of a series in which she photographed youths in swimwear on beaches around the world. The image of this young subject is tender and carefully conveys the effort put into maintaining her appearance. As in some of her other series – 'Bull Fighters' (1994–2000), which includes her portraits of matadors and new mothers; 'Tiergarten' (1998–2000); and 'Parks' (1998–2006) – the 'Beach Portraits' (1992–2015) do not name the individual depicted but are titled by location. In offering this fleeting view into a changing identity, the subject is less the specific human being depicted, but rather their state of becoming.

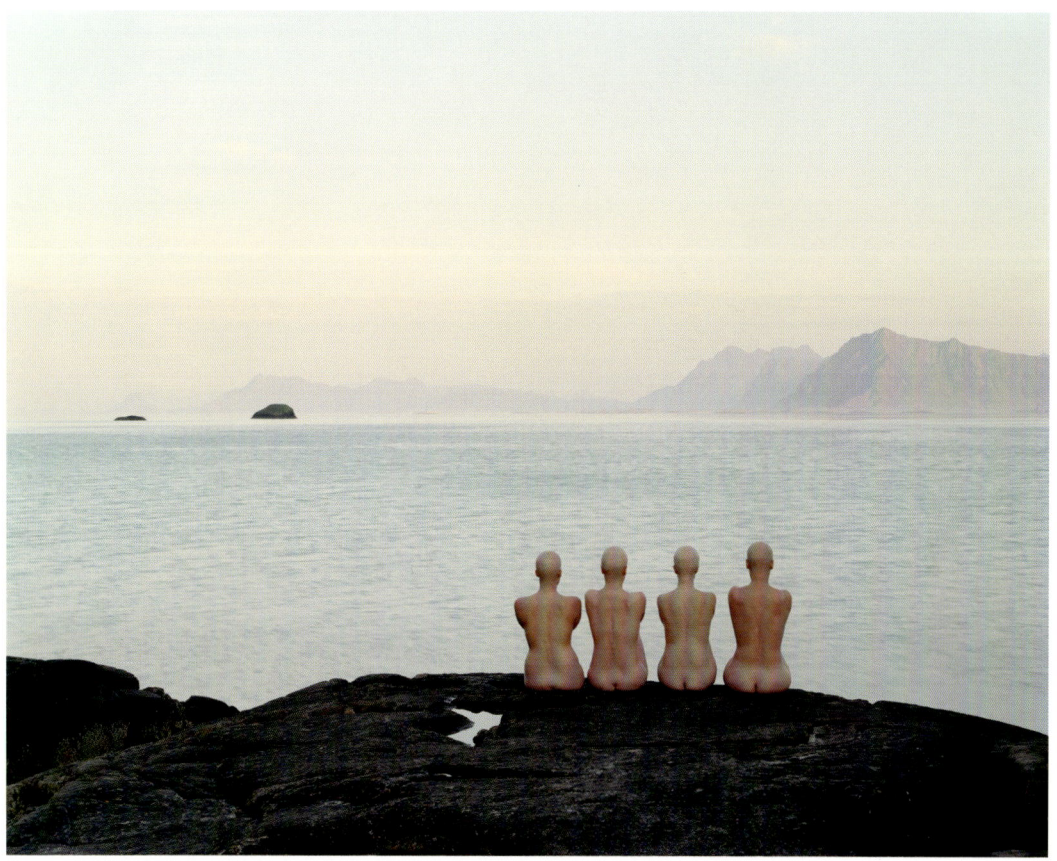

2 AM SOUTH

2003, Cibachrome print, 177 × 220 cm (69 ⅝ × 86 ⅝ in), Malmö Art Museum, Sweden

A K Dolven, born Anne Katrine Dolven, 1953, Oslo.

One of Norway's best-known contemporary artists, Dolven works across several mediums, including painting, photography and video art. She directly referenced her historical compatriot Edvard Munch (1863–1944), in earlier works, for instance in her videos *Puberty*, *Self-Portrait with Cigarette* and *The Kiss* (all from 2000). Having trained in France as a painter during the 1970s, in the following decade she lived between Berlin and on the Lofoten Islands of Arctic Norway. Establishing Atelier Kvalnes on the islands in 2005, Dolven has promoted public art as a way of connecting isolated communities across the country's far north, while her own practice explores the realities of life in the Arctic Circle. Pared down to the essentials of composition, Dolven's photographic works often depict barren, timeless landscapes of rock, sand, sea or ice, in the artistic tradition of the Sublime. Set against this she considers intimate moments of human life where dreams and reality merge, again reminiscent of Munch. Such characteristics are demonstrated in this work, in which four naked, bald-headed women sit gazing out over calm waters, the sky light despite the time, as the title reveals, being two o'clock in the morning.

TARA DONOVAN

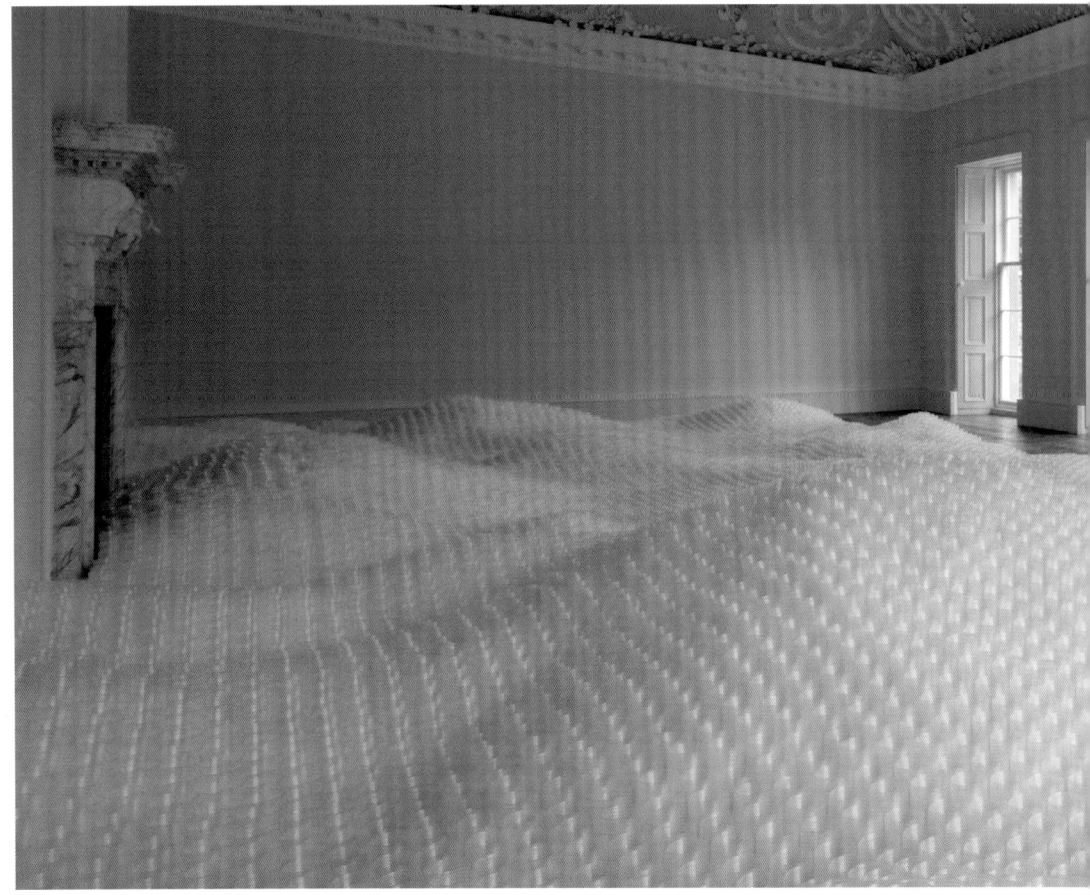

UNTITLED (PLASTIC CUPS)

2006/2015, plastic, dimensions variable, installation view, Jupiter Artland,
Edinburgh, 2015
Tara Donovan, born 1969, New York.

As a native New Yorker, Donovan has steadily gained recognition
since returning to the city to start her studio practice in Brooklyn
after completing her MFA at Virginia Commonwealth University,
Richmond, in 1999. Following her debut at the 2000 Whitney
Biennial, her ambitious solo exhibition at Ace Gallery New York
in 2003 earned widespread critical praise, which she was able to par-
lay into various museum projects and an ongoing relationship with
Pace Gallery. She soon received awards and accolades, including
the first annual Calder Prize in 2005 and the prestigious MacArthur

Foundation 'Genius' Award in 2008. Employing everyday materials
such as drinking straws, toothpicks or pencils, Donovan's process-
orientated approach to sculpture creates illusion through accumulation.
Untitled (Plastic Cups) is typical of the artist's alchemical transformation of mundane, mass-produced, disposable materials into sublime
natural forms, this work resembling a topographical landscape or the
soft curves of clouds. While she adheres to a rule-based system, working with single repeatable units, her sculptural language is distinctively organic in form and process, and sometimes recalls cellular,
fungal or bacterial structures.

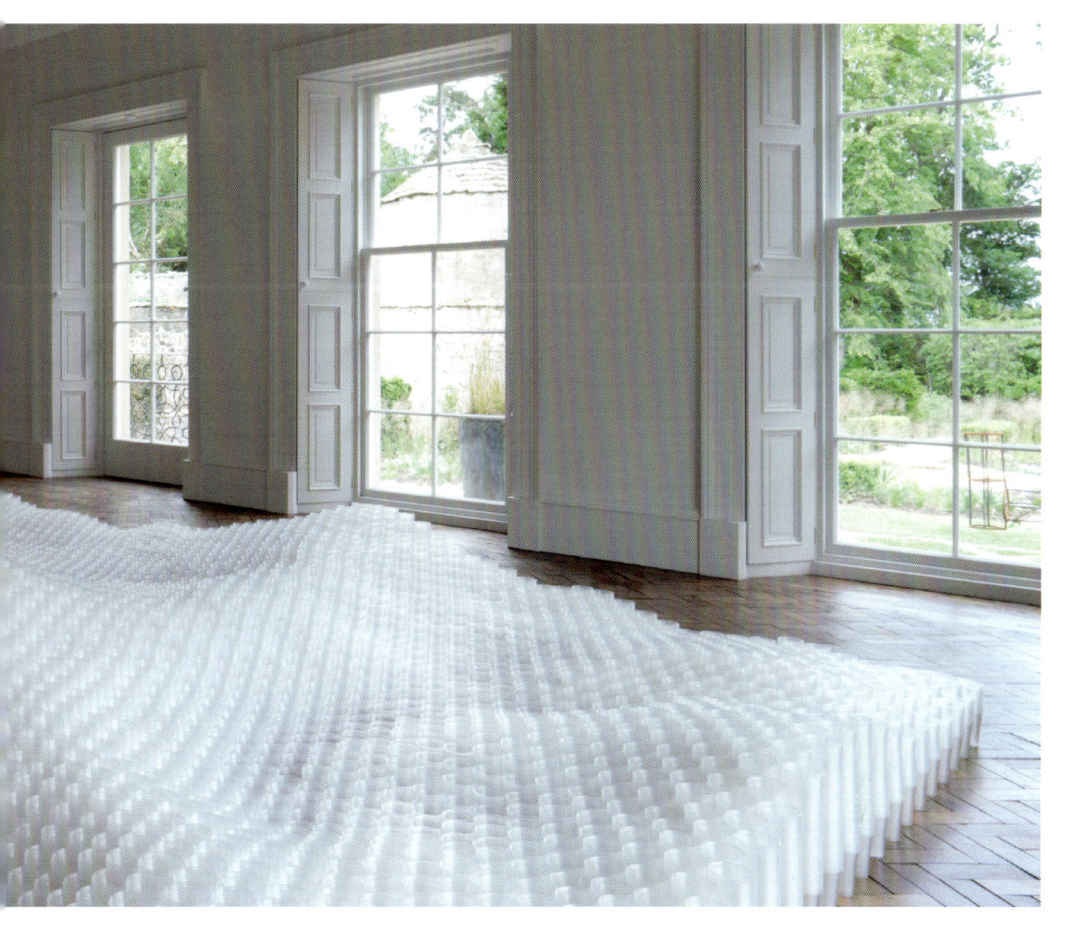

ROSALYN DREXLER

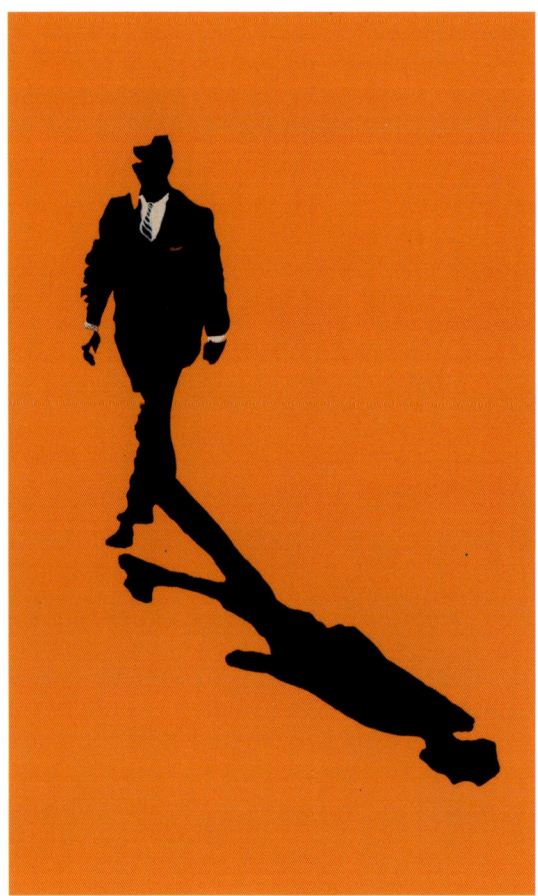

ME AND MY SHADOW

1966, acrylic and paper collage on panel, 121.9 × 76.2 cm (48 × 30 in),
private collection
Rosalyn Drexler, born Rosalyn Bronznick, 1926, New York.

Growing up in the Bronx and East Harlem, Drexler's parents encouraged her to make art, buying her crayons and posters to fuel her imagination. Steeped in popular culture, she became a true polymath, as an acclaimed playwright, novelist and even for a short time, a professional wrestler. Her art practice has been equally varied and accomplished. Drexler began making sculptures assembled from found objects. She switched to painting in the early 1960s and developed a 'DIY' style of collaging and painting onto canvas, using enlarged images from magazines, newspapers and posters as source materials. Her works addressed themes such as abusive relationships, violent crime, social alienation and racism. Drexler participated in major Pop art shows through that decade, being one of only two women artists in the exhibition 'First International Girlie Exhibit' at New York's Pace Gallery in 1964, where she showed collages of images from erotic magazines. Seen here, in a restrained graphic style, is Drexler's depiction of a besuited masculine figure with a seemingly feminine shadow, one of many works to explore the dynamics between men and women, and their role in the symbolism of power.

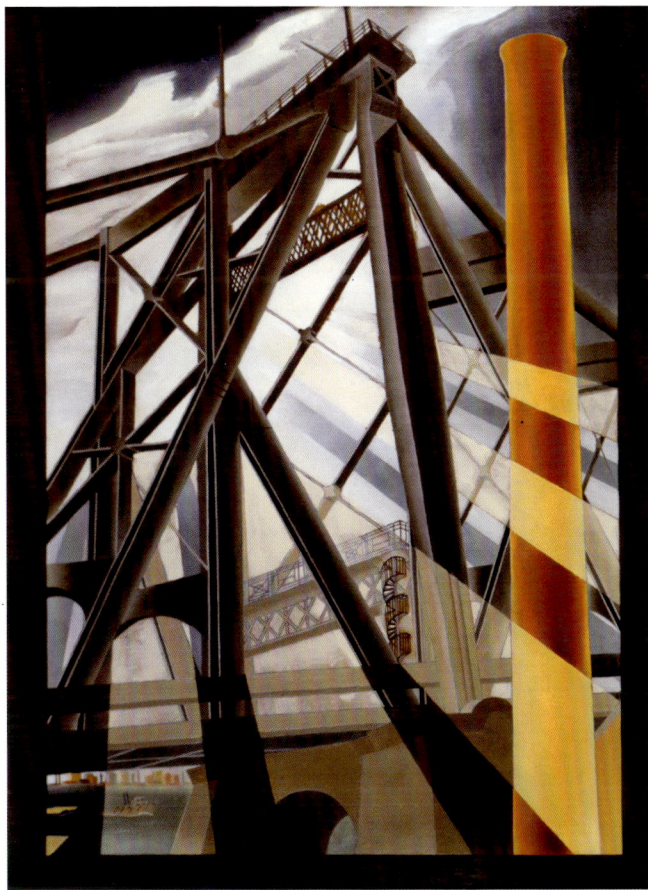

QUEENSBOROUGH BRIDGE

1927, oil on canvas, 102.2 × 76.8 cm (40¼ × 30¼ in), Montclair Art Museum, New Jersey
Elsie Driggs, born 1898, Hartford, Connecticut. Died 1992, New York.

Following her studies at the Art Students League of New York (1918–23), Driggs travelled to Europe where she experienced at first hand works of the Italian Renaissance, with Piero della Francesca (c.1415–92) in particular having a profound impact on her style. Driggs subsequently produced a group of paintings that placed her at the centre of Precisionism – the first art movement in the modernist canon to originate in the United States. Represented by Charles Daniel from 1913 to 1932, Driggs withheld her gender from the reportedly misogynistic dealer until he had offered her a place in the gallery's programme. Driggs and her Precisionist peers celebrated the Machine Age and American industry, capturing with geometric exactness the modern landscape and streamlined architecture of skyscrapers, factories and bridges. Referred to in the 1920s as the New Classicists or 'Immaculates', the Precisionists were indebted to European avant-garde movements of Cubism and Futurism. The view from Driggs's apartment is depicted in *Queensborough Bridge*, the window's frame visible on three sides and the bridge's industrial forms illuminated with bright beams of light.

ROSE-ADÉLAÏDE DUCREUX

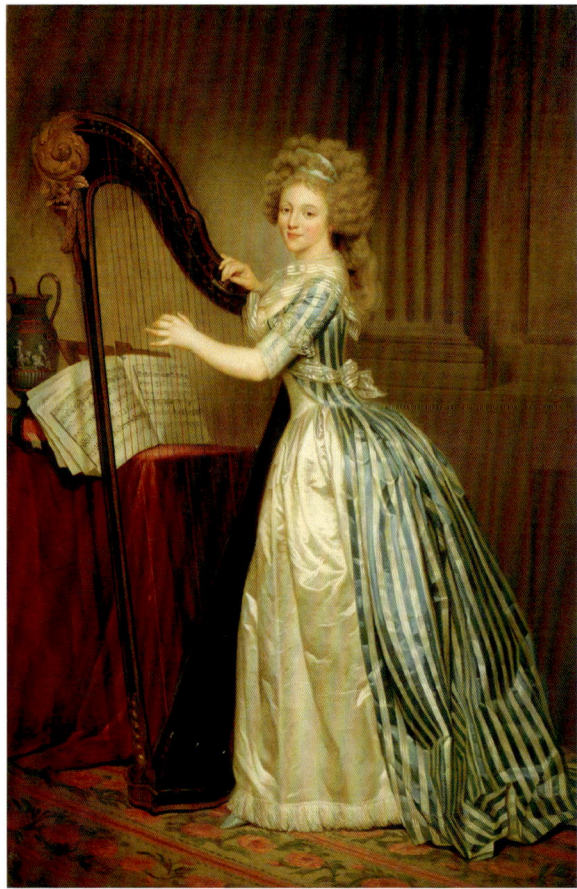

SELF-PORTRAIT WITH A HARP

1791, oil on canvas, 193 × 128.9 cm (76 × 50 ¾ in), Metropolitan Museum of Art, New York

Rose-Adélaïde Ducreux, born 1761, Nancy, France. Died 1802, Saint-Domingue (now Haiti).

Several female artists of the eighteenth century had access to training, materials and even clientele through male-artist relatives. This was the case with Ducreux, who studied with her father Joseph Ducreux (1735–1802), the principal portraitist to Marie Antoinette. Before the French Revolution, it was not possible for an artist to exhibit at the elite Paris Salon unless a member of the Académie Royale de Peinture et de Sculpture. In 1791 the Salon became open to other artists, and accordingly Ducreux made a joint debut with her father, entering this

painting. Critics singled out her talent as an oil painter – something her father, more adept in pastel work, was said to lack – and her skill stands out particularly in its delicate rendering of surface effects like silk and wood. The huge harp was not merely an accessory: it show-cased her additional talent as a musician and this bold, full-length depiction attracted a favourable reception in a period where presentation of female self-portraits was a rarity at the Paris Salon. After exhibiting at four further Salons, she became engaged to a maritime prefect and travelled to the French colony of Saint-Domingue, where he was posted to help restore order during a revolution. There Ducreux contracted typhoid fever and died.

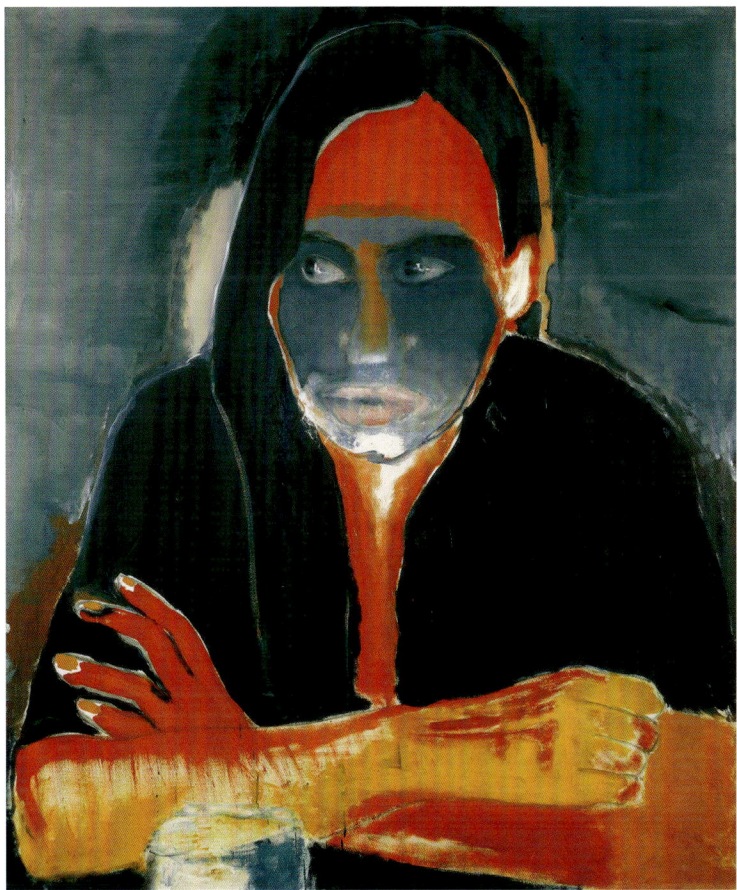

GENETIC LONGING

1984, oil on canvas, 130.4 × 110.6 cm (51 ⅓ × 43 ½ in), Van Abbemuseum, Eindhoven, Netherlands
Marlene Dumas, born 1953, Cape Town.

While studying at the University of Cape Town in the early 1970s, Dumas found painting to be frustratingly removed from reality. She loved photography but disliked the mechanics of that medium; enjoying the physicality of paint, she wanted to make figurative images with her own hands. Realizing that she could integrate the two by using found images as the basis for paintings, she began to collect pictures from magazines, newspapers and films, as well as taking Polaroids of friends and lovers. Since moving to Amsterdam in 1976, these resources have grown into a vast archive of images touching upon themes of politics, racism, religion, sexuality and death – her mid-career touring retrospective organized by the Los Angeles Museum of Contemporary Art in 2008 was titled 'Measuring Your Own Grave'. These themes are used to explore the ambiguities and problems of representation, its language, methods and ethics. The painting shown here was one of a number of large-scale portraits Dumas made in the mid-1980s, titled to reference the emotions or states of the subjects depicted. Employing bold colours and soft brushstrokes, the application of oil paint echoes the fluid spontaneity of her ink and watercolour works on paper.

CELESTE DUPUY-SPENCER

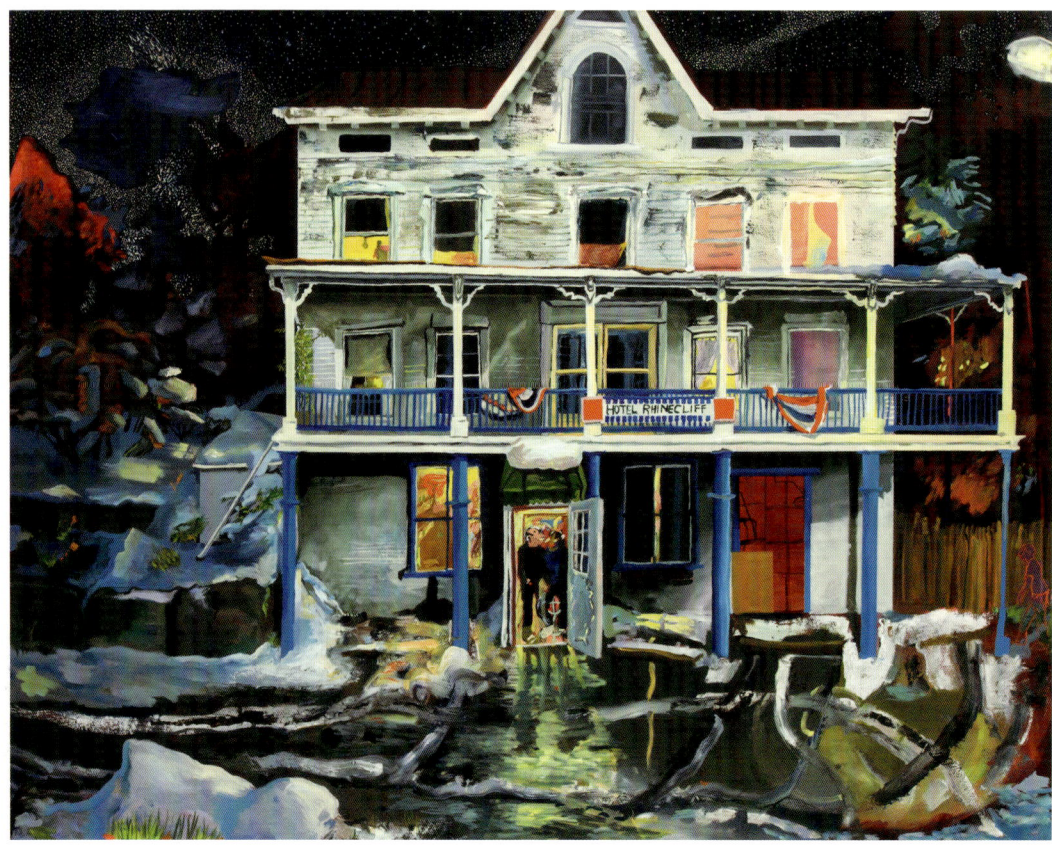

EARLY SNOW – RHINECLIFF HOTEL

2017, oil on canvas, 127 × 165.1 cm (50 × 65 in), private collection
Celeste Dupuy-Spencer, born 1979, New York.

Using the tropes of figurative painting, Dupuy-Spencer's canvases depict the everyday activities of America's queer communities. The artist identifies as transgender though without preference about which pronoun is used. Thematically complex, these images are raw and intimate in nature, delineating particular, intense socio-political narratives in ways that convey the shared human condition. Growing up in New York and moving briefly to New Orleans, Dupuy-Spencer now lives in Los Angeles, often painting people from an immediate circle of acquaintances but with a broad vision that encompasses American culture and history. Artistic precedents range from the Mannerism of the Renaissance to the geometric forms of modernism, interspersed with moments from comics, television, pop culture and pornography. Inverting gender clichés, the resulting images often undermine social conventions. *Early Snow – Rhinecliff Hotel* presents a scene viewed as if from a passing car and has an explicitly ambivalent vantage point. Bunting rests on the porch railings, as if decorated for a national holiday. There appears to be a snowstorm swirling on the banks behind, shaking up the banality of the festivities, a portent in the quotidian of something apocalyptic.

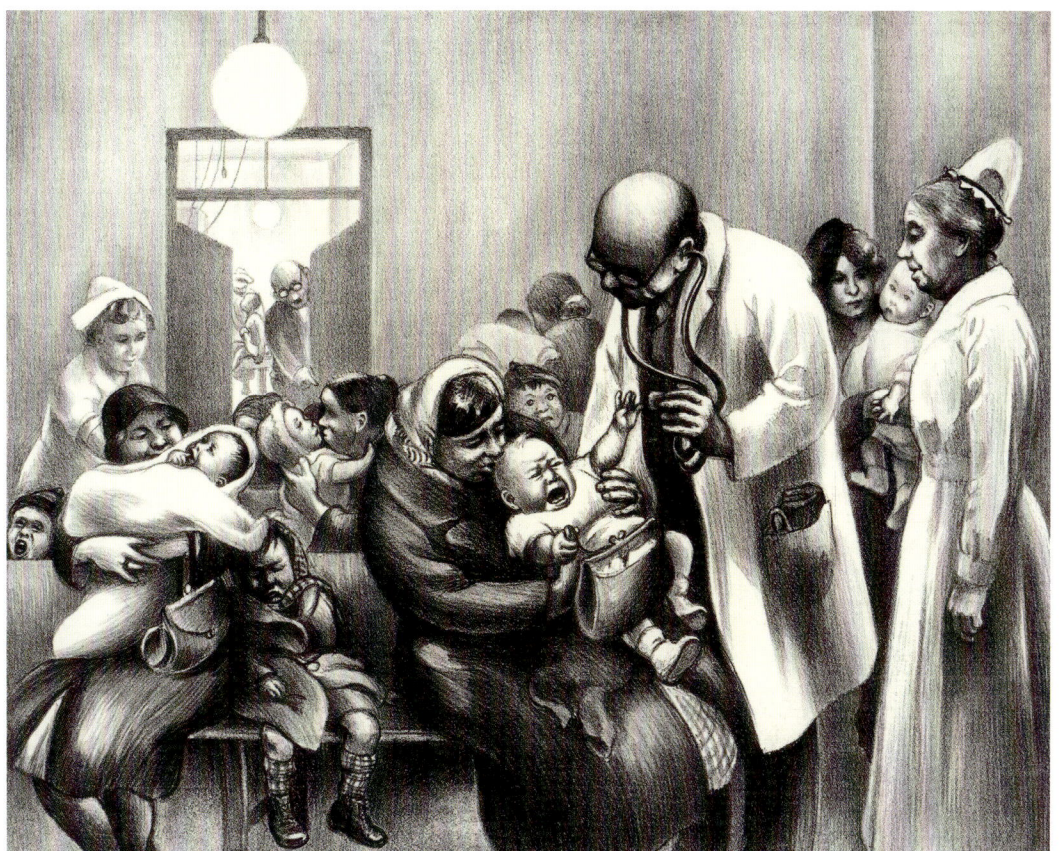

CHILDREN'S CLINIC

1936, lithograph, 24.5 × 30.2 cm (9 ⅝ × 11 ⅞ in), San Diego Museum of Art
Mabel Dwight, born Mabel Williamson, 1875, Cincinnati, Ohio. Died 1955,
Sellersville, Pennsylvania.

Perhaps the best-loved American printmaker of her day, Dwight
is remembered for lithographs depicting everyday life in the 1930s.
In 1917 she separated from her artist husband, Eugene Higgins
(1874–1958), and adopted a new surname, chosen for reasons she
never revealed. The following year she joined the Studio Club
of Gertrude Vanderbilt Whitney (1875–1942), a sculptor and collector
who would go on to found the Whitney Museum of American Art
in New York. Dwight moved to Paris in the mid-1920s where she
studied lithography and began to draw scenes of street life. By then

in her early fifties, it was with these humorous vignettes that she
made her name back in America. The demotic focus of her work
reflects her lifelong commitment to socialism, yet her images are
typically droll rather than doctrinaire. This print was commissioned
by the Federal Art Project – a New Deal programme to fund and
promote the arts in the 1930s – and dates from the period of Dwight's
greatest success. The image of a noisy, crowded paediatric ward
reflects the dual strands of social realism and cartoonish humour running throughout her work.

MARY BETH EDELSON

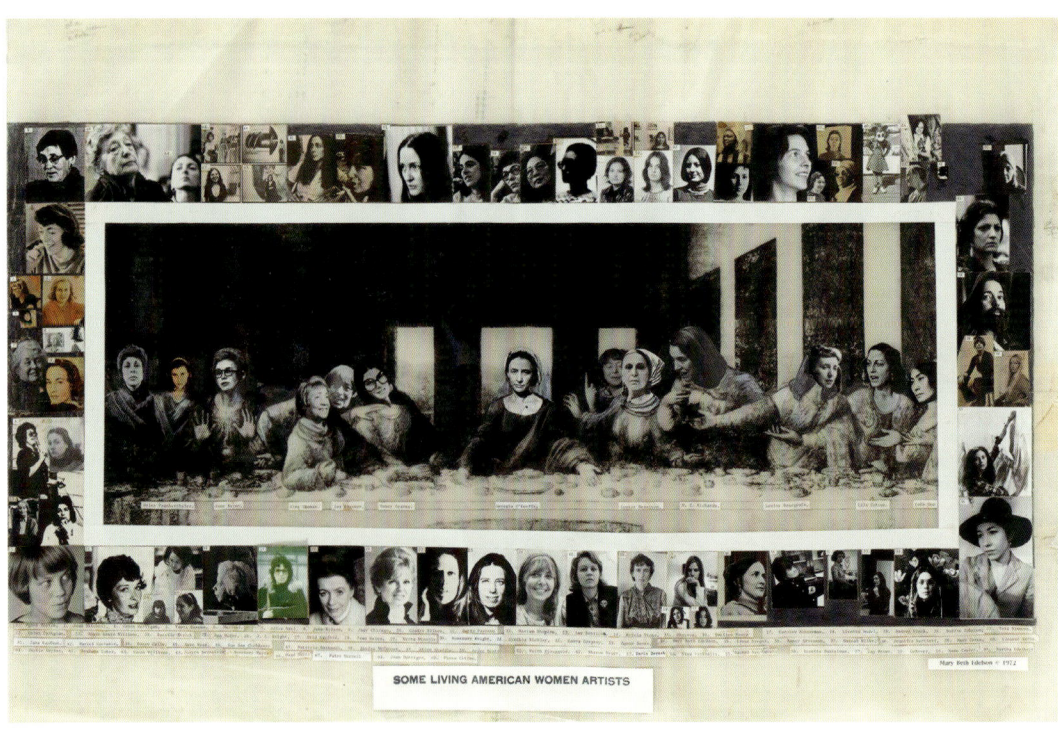

SOME LIVING AMERICAN WOMEN ARTISTS

1972, cut-and-pasted gelatin silver prints with crayon and transfer type on printed paper with typewriting on cut-and-taped paper, 71.8 × 109.2 cm (28¼ × 43 in), Museum of Modern Art, New York
Mary Beth Edelson, born 1933, Chicago. Died 2021, Ocean Grove, New Jersey.

During the revolutionary 1960s, Edelson was an activist in the civil rights movement and a champion of feminist art. Already in 1955, while studying at the Art Institute of Chicago, one of her paintings was removed from a student exhibition for being 'unseemly'. In 1968 she delivered her first feminist speech and that same year established the first Conference for Women in the Visual Arts in Washington DC. She was a founding member of A.I.R. Gallery and in 1976 she co-founded the Heresies Collective and its accompanying journal,

to open up discourse on art from a feminist and political perspective. In *Some Living American Women Artists*, an appropriation of Leonardo da Vinci's *Last Supper* (1495–8), Edelson enshrined women artists within a revised canon by collaging faces onto a reproduction of the fresco. Georgia O'Keeffe (p.301) takes the place of Jesus, Nancy Graves (1939–95) that of Saint John, with Lynda Benglis (p.58), Helen Frankenthaler (p.142) and Lee Krasner (p.224), among others, constituting the other disciples. The border around the central image includes further thumbnail images of living women artists, locating them at a turning point of history.

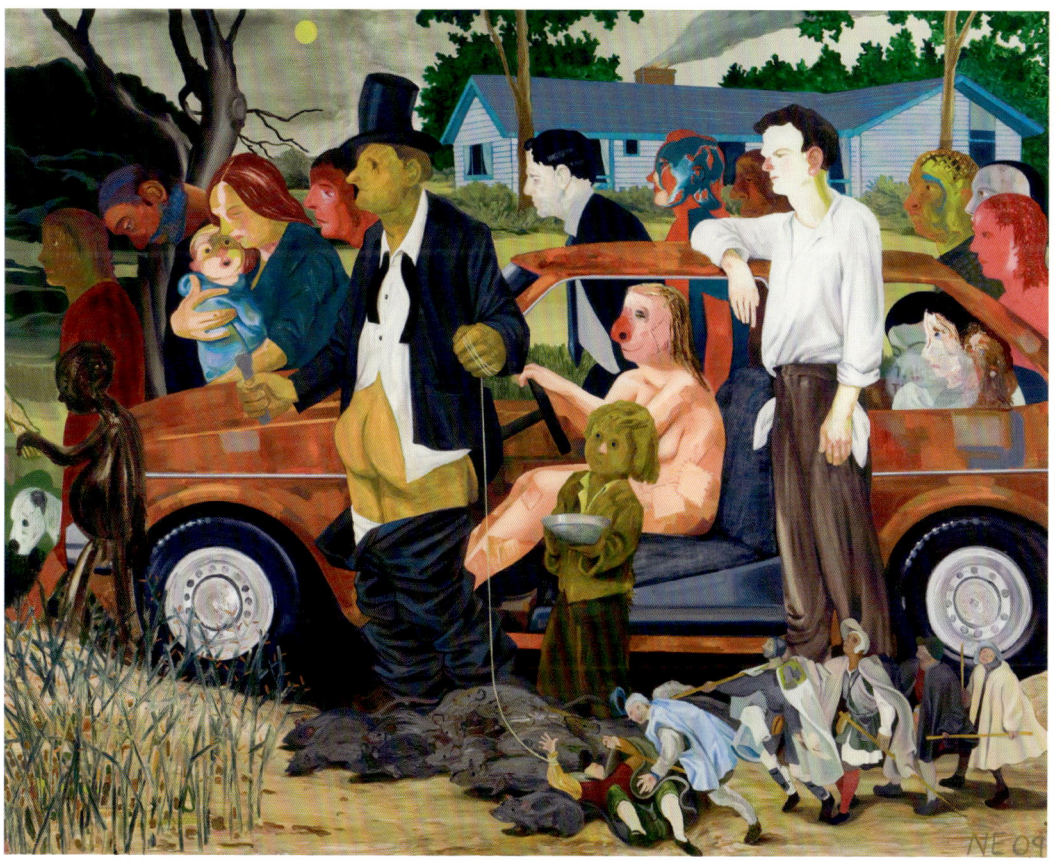

THE TRIUMPH OF POVERTY

2009, oil on canvas, 165.1 × 208.3 cm (65 × 82 in), private collection
Nicole Eisenman, born 1965, Verdun, France (American national).

After her studies at Rhode Island School of Design and a period
as a college professor, Eisenman's artistic talents were recognized
with honours including a Guggenheim Fellowship (1996), Carnegie
Prize (2013) and MacArthur Fellowship (2015). The latter
acknowledged the cultural relevance of her paintings, in her exploration of themes and subjects ranging from the bourgeois beer
garden to gender and homosexuality. Her work often incorporates
amusingly recast and contemporized versions of compositional
and thematic elements from art history, and her influences include
German Expressionism and contemporary cartoon strips.

Eisenman's painting is celebrated for its use of wit and a sense of
the absurd, combined with semiautobiographical insights into her
own circle of New York contemporaries. *The Triumph of Poverty*
exemplifies her busy and colourful figurative compositions, which
are, paradoxically, contemplations of human isolation. A rambling
parade of bizarre characters is depicted in vivid shades, the cartoonish style contrasting with an underlying sense of foreboding.
The prominent figure's contorted exhibitionism suggests the crude
irrationality of poor leadership and is indicative of Eisenman's darkly
humorous social commentary.

TRACEY EMIN

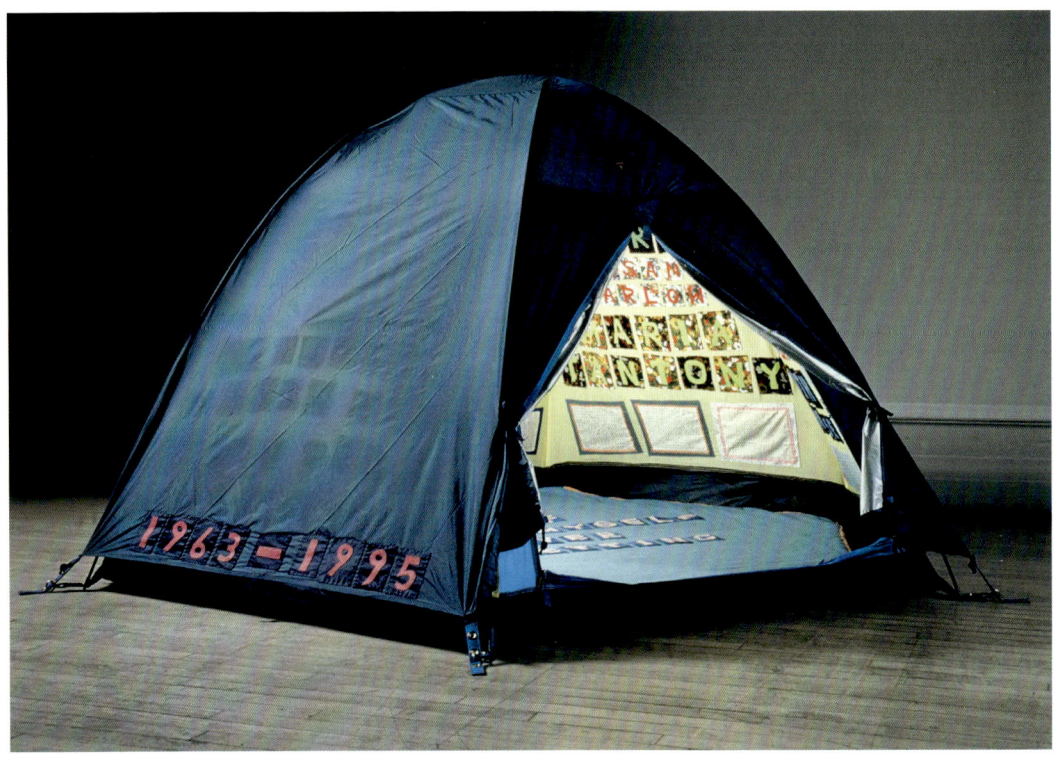

EVERYONE I HAVE EVER SLEPT WITH 1963–1995

1995 (destroyed by fire, 2004), appliquéd tent, mattress and light, 122 × 245 × 215 cm
(48 × 96 ½ × 84 ⅔ in)
Tracey Emin, born 1963, London.

Growing up in the seaside town of Margate, Emin moved to London
in the late 1980s to study at the Royal College of Art. She became
one of the leading lights of the Young British Artist (YBA) generation,
making art that is raw, intimate and confessional using a variety
of processes, particularly sewing, mono-printing and drawing. Early
in her career, Emin courted controversy with this work, which was
included in the notorious 'Sensation' exhibition (1997) at the Royal
Academy of Arts, London. Comprising a tent with the names of all
the people she'd 'slept' with appliquéd onto the interior, it implies
a list of sexual conquests, inviting a judgmental reponse. However,
Emin's choice of words for the title is nuanced – the 102 names are
revealed to be people she had shared a bed with, or literally slept next
to – including non-sexual partners such as her grandmother, her
twin brother Paul and her two aborted foetuses. It is less about sexual
intimacy than general human intimacy, emphasized by the small
size of the tent and the fact that the names were only fully readable
when inside. The work reinforces the idea of emotional connection
being gained from sleeping side by side.

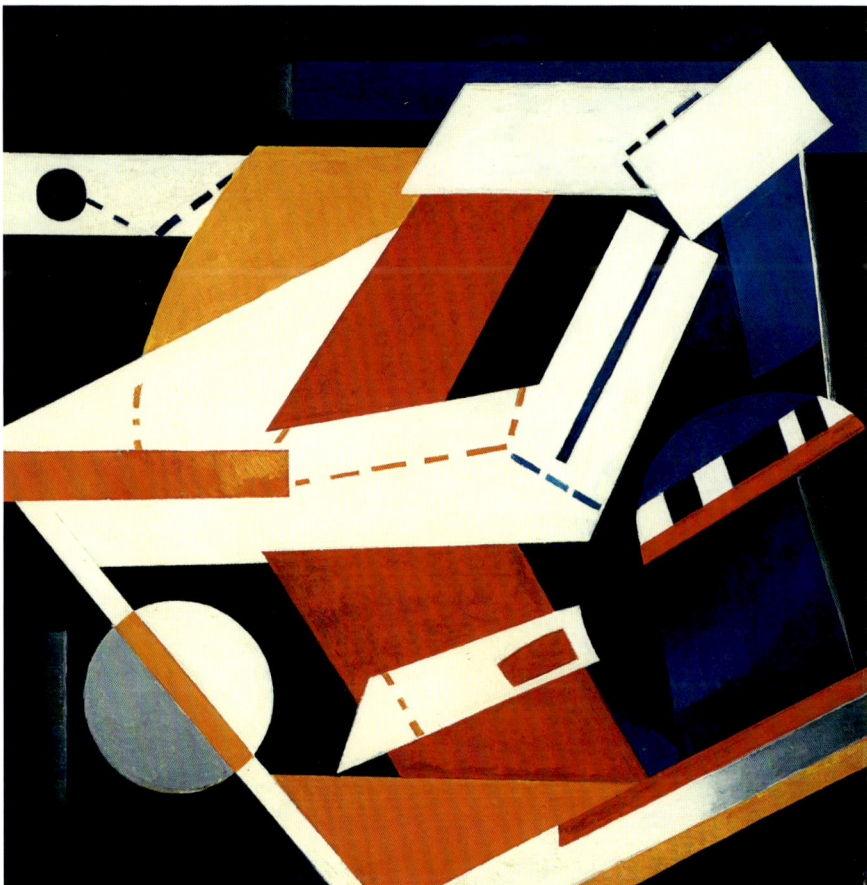

CONSTRUCTION

1922–3, oil on canvas, 89.2 × 89.9 cm (35 ⅛ × 35 ⅜ in), The Riklis Collection
of McCrory Corporation, Museum of Modern Art, New York
Alexandra Exter, born Alexandra Grigorovich, 1882, Białystok, Poland. Died 1949,
Fontenay-aux-Roses, France.

Travelling frequently to Paris between 1909 and 1914, Exter was
pivotal in the dissemination of Western European developments
in modern art among Russia's pre-revolutionary avant-garde and
participated in many important exhibitions in Russia and France.
A friend of the artists Pablo Picasso (1881–1973) and Georges Braque
(1882–1963), and acquainted with writers such as Guillaume
Apollinaire, Max Jacob and Gertrude Stein, she was part of a milieu
that had a profound cultural influence. After experimenting with
Cubist and Futurist approaches, she began developing her own visual
language and in 1916, inspired by the work of Kazimir Malevich
(1879–1935), started producing purely abstract canvases. The lively
mix of flat geometric shapes and hard edges that comprise this
work evinces her interest in shape, colour and rhythm. Its title reflects
her interest in Constructivism, a Russian art movement whose
proponents believed that art should imitate the dynamism of modern
technology. Exter is also celebrated for her bold and experimental
set and costume designs for Aleksandr Tairov's Kamerny Theatre
in Moscow. She emigrated to Paris in 1924, becoming an academic
colleague of Fernand Léger (1881–1955) and continuing with her
own art.

MONIR SHAHROUDY FARMANFARMAIAN

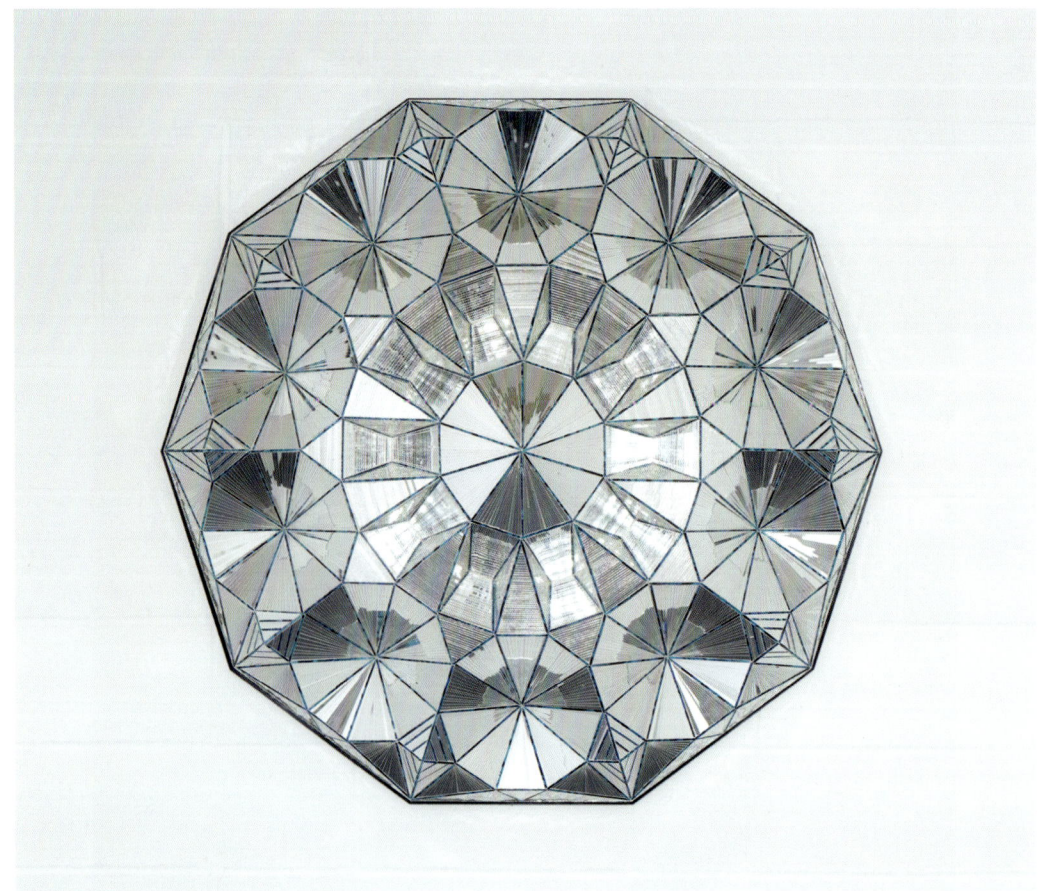

DECAGON (THIRD FAMILY)
2011, mirror and reverse glass painting on plaster and wood, diam: 120 cm (47 ¼ in),
private collection
Monir Farmanfarmaian, born Monir Shahroudy, 1924, Qazvin, Iran.
Died 2019, Tehran.

Born into a wealthy family, Farmanfarmaian studied fine art at the
University of Tehran before moving to New York in 1944 to undertake further education. Here she mixed with artists Louise Nevelson
(p.300), Willem de Kooning (1904–97) and Joan Mitchell (p.277),
and also met Andy Warhol (1928–87) while working as a fashion illustrator for the department store Bonwit Teller. Returning to Iran
in 1957, Farmanfarmaian was inspired by the mirror mosaics and
geometric forms that she encountered in ancient mosques. A brief

holiday to the United States in 1979 turned into long-term exile,
following Iran's revolution. Her innovation was to combine the
Islamic non-figurative tradition with the aesthetics of Western
Minimalism, using vernacular Persian techniques to make dazzling
reflective sculptures and paintings that employ mirror mosaic
and reverse glass painting techniques. This work's title relates to the
artist's way of describing these works as 'geometric families'.
It appears to present a portal into myriad worlds, the glittering facets
simultaneously beckoning and concealing. Farmanfarmaian
returned home in 1994, and in 2017 she became the first woman artist
to have a museum dedicated in her honour in Tehran.

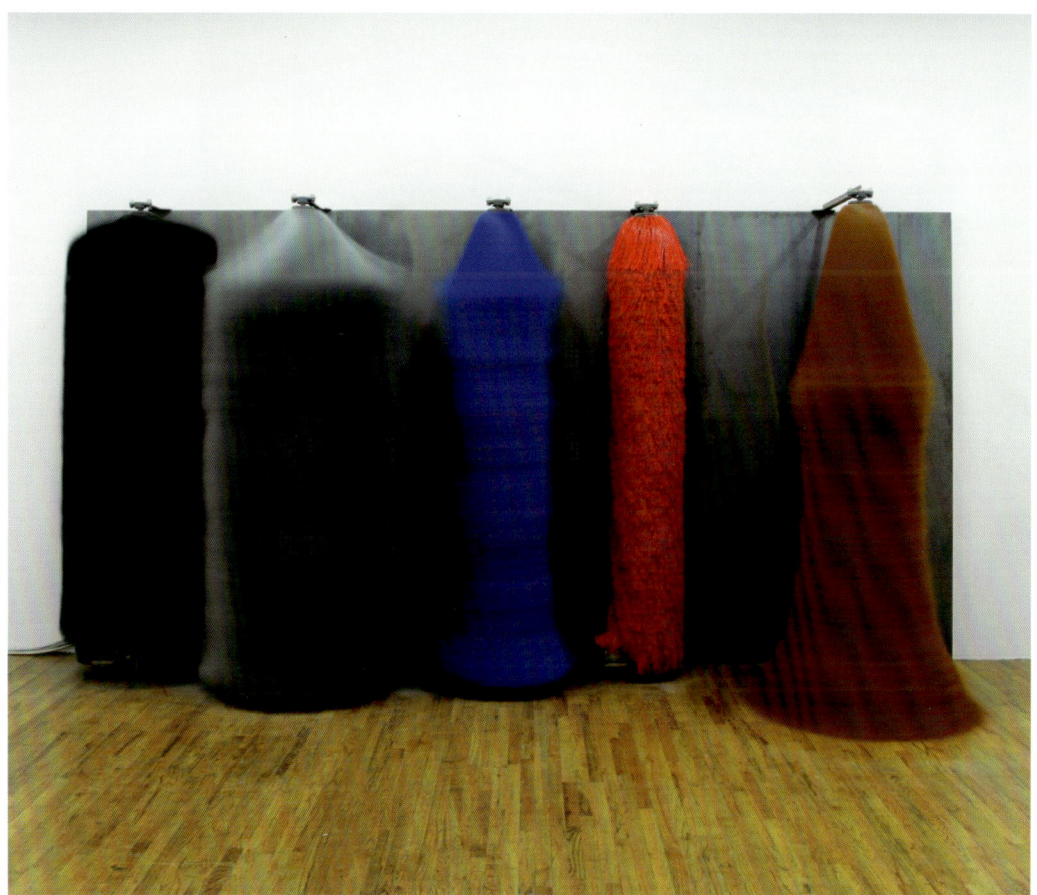

GUMMO V

2012, car-wash brushes, iron slabs, motors, electrical box and wires, 250 × 250 × 190 cm (98 ⅜ × 98 ⅜ × 74 ¾ in), installation view, 'Just Knocked Out', MoMA PS1, New York. Collection Fondazione Sandretto Re Rebaudengo, Turin, Italy
Lara Favaretto, born 1973, Treviso, Italy.

Making sculpture and site-specific installations, Favaretto questions the relationships between art, society and, particularly, time and memory – with a sense of loss, decay and obsolescence occurring throughout her practice. An example is the ongoing series 'Momentary Monuments', which explores memorialization and ephemerality in public space. The materials she employs are often industrial in nature – concrete, metal, motors and engines – and are regularly accompanied, or followed, by more transitory and immaterial phenomena such as steam, oxidation and the traces of actions past, including scuff marks, dents and holes. In the 'Gummo' series, which began in 2007, the artist presents large car-wash brushes of differing widths and colours, spinning side by side at various speeds. Energetically contributing to the legacies and discourse of both modernist sculpture and abstract painting, Favaretto's brushes gradually wear down during the course of an exhibition – a kinetic testimony to the entropy and decay that ultimately and inevitably confronts everything in life.

GENIEVE FIGGIS

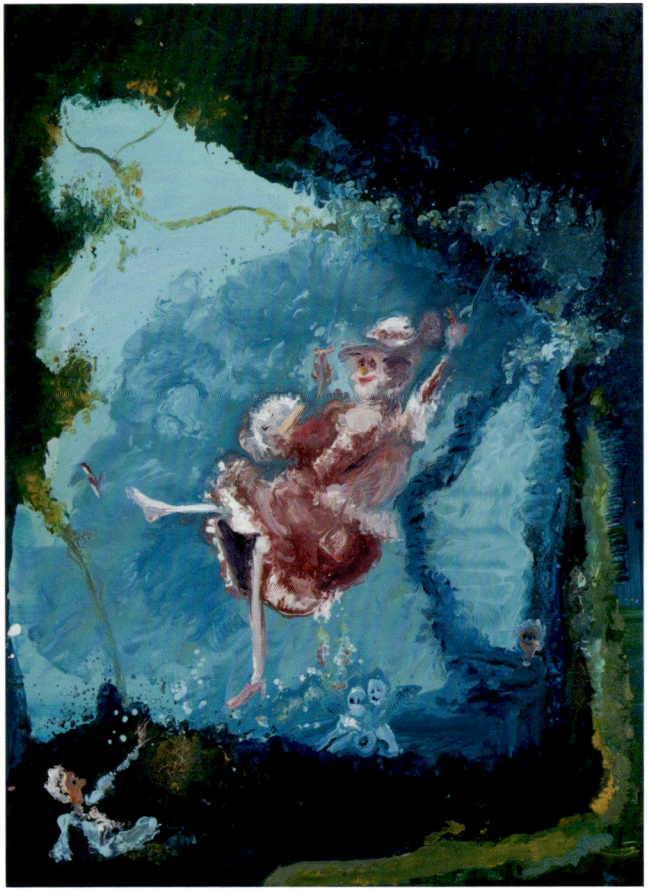

THE SWING AFTER FRAGONARD

2014, acrylic on canvas, 80 × 59.7 cm (31 ½ × 23 ½ in)
Genieve Figgis, born 1972, Dublin.

Figgis received an MFA from the National College of Art and Design in Dublin and has cited her artistic influences as including Marlene Dumas (p.127), Jenny Saville (p.357) and Lynette Yiadom-Boakye (p.440). It was through the use of social media and the Internet that her work was disseminated, notably after artist Richard Prince (b.1949) admired her paintings on Twitter and purchased one. Figgis uses thick acrylic paint to render dynamic figuration in cartoonish scenes that parody historic artworks such as Thomas Gainsborough's *Mr and Mrs Andrews* (1750) and Édouard Manet's *Olympia* (1863). Defined by their irony and wry humour, Figgis's canvases render her subjects unstable – melting or morphing into the monstrous. Appropriating the iconic masterpiece of French Rococo painting Jean-Honoré Fragonard's *The Swing* (1767), Figgis takes a sardonic view of his depiction of an encounter between two lovers. Spied on both by the viewer and figures in the background, a young lady in an elaborate pink dress flings off her slipper, revealing her legs, and perhaps more, to the man beneath. In Figgis's version, the crudely painted facial features make the scene ghoulish and unsettling.

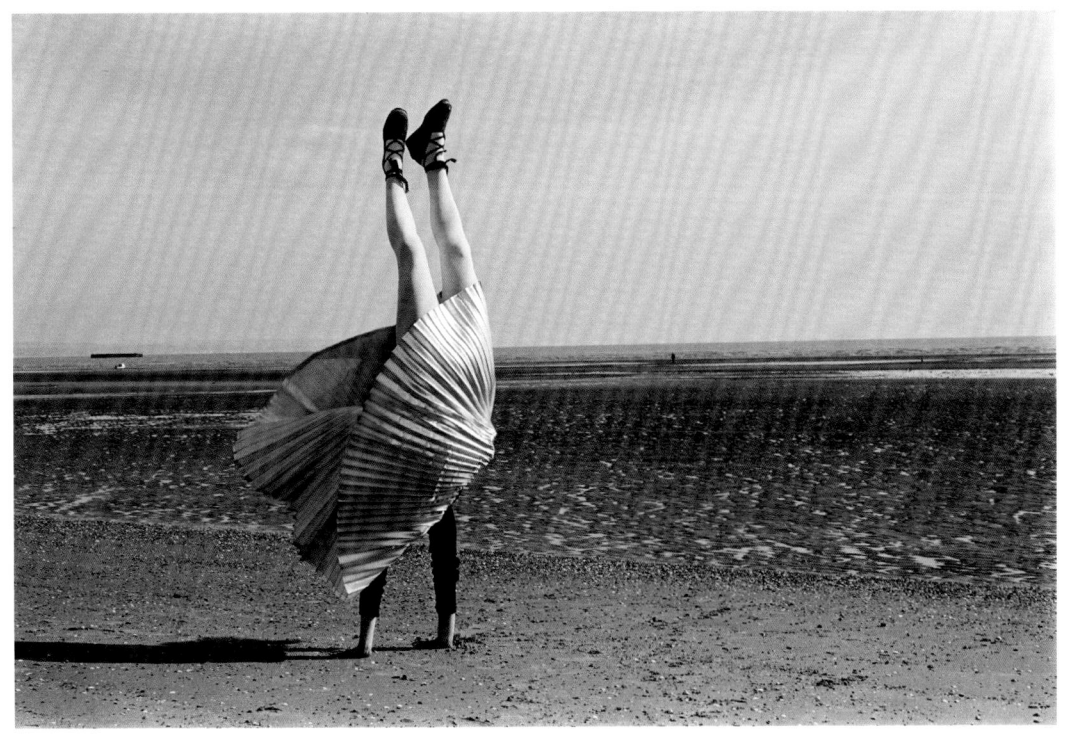

THE RESTLESS IMAGE: A DISCREPANCY BETWEEN THE FELT POSITION AND THE SEEN POSITION

1975, black-and-white gelatin silver print
Rose Finn-Kelcey, born 1945, Northampton, UK. Died 2014, London.

Ambivalence is a recurring theme in Finn-Kelcey's work, in relation to issues including identity, presence, value and belief. Growing up in a large family in the Home Counties of southeast England, followed by art studies in London, she came to prominence in the early 1970s. Her practice in performance, Conceptual and feminist art often combined ironic humour with deep seriousness and the element of chance, using widely different techniques with great accomplishment. Early works involved flags, which she flew above public and municipal spaces – most memorably, London's iconic Battersea Power Station – to question ideas of citizenship and authority. She staged inventive live works, pioneering a strategy that she called 'vacated performances', in which the artist's live participation in her work was inflected by recorded materials. Alongside feminist empowerment, Finn-Kelcey explored personal self-effacement, as seen in this work, a self-portrait and, a re-enactment of a snapshot taken of her mother as a young woman. Taken on the beach at Dungeness, Kent, where the artist had spent family holidays as a child, the image appears spontaneous but is in fact carefully staged, the title implying a discrepancy between action and affect.

SYLVIE FLEURY

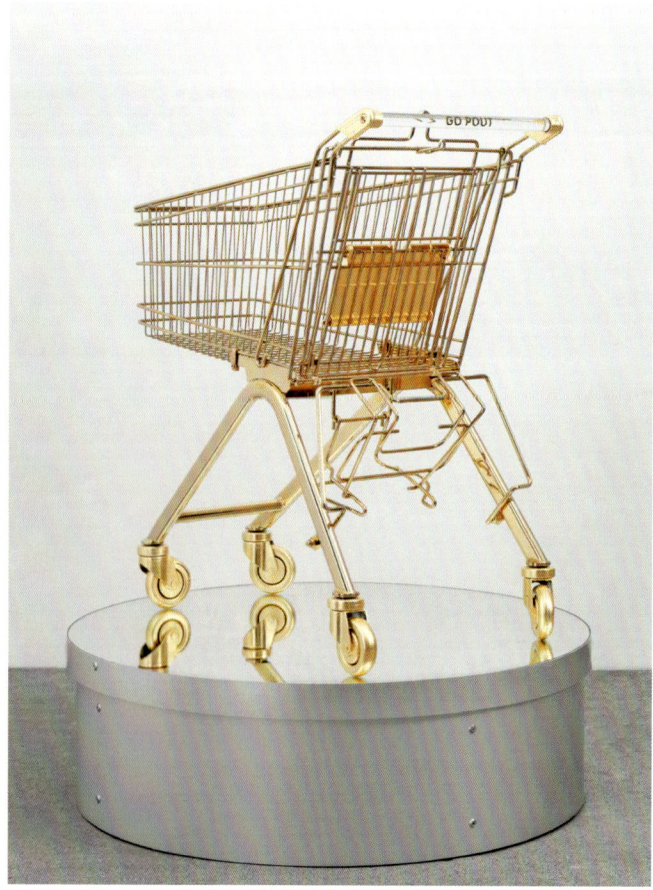

ELA 75/K (GO POUT)

2000, gold-plated shopping trolley, Plexiglas handle, vinyl text and rotating pedestal
Sylvie Fleury, born 1961, Geneva.

After graduating from the Germain School of Photography in New York in 1981, Fleury returned to Switzerland, initially working as an assistant to fellow Genevan John Armleder (b.1948), an artist connected to the Fluxus movement. Since her 'Shopping Bag' series of the early 1990s, with designer-label bags reconceived as 'ready-mades', her practice has focused on contemporary consumer culture. Her works have ranged from neon signs delineating punchy slogans to paintings inspired by the colours and shapes of make-up compacts. These conceptual strategies echo those of Marcel Duchamp (1887–1968), leading to her work being termed 'post-appropriationist'. She considers the fetishization of objects made specifically for purchase – from luxury fine art to products bought in shopping malls – through the lens of gendered consumption. Market-based society and its arguably shallow values are critiqued in sculptures such as *ELA 75/K (Go Pout)*, where an empty, gold-plated shopping trolley is placed on a pedestal like a modernist masterpiece, with the work's subtitle coming from a variety of lipstick. In a takedown of consumerism's vacuity and the hyper-elevation of artworks, Fleury conflates the two, calling into question the state of today's rampant cultural markets.

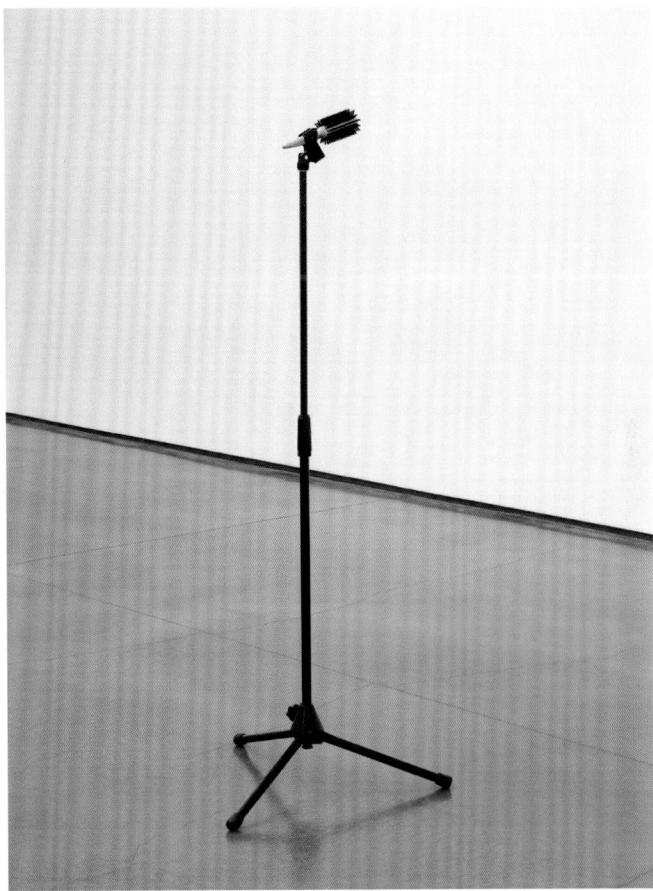

SOLO

2006, König & Meyer 'Proline' mic stand, 22mm mic holder and hairbrush, 138 × 64 × 64 cm (54 ⅜ × 25 ¼ × 25 ¼ in), edition of 3 + 2 APS
Ceal Floyer, born 1968 (British national).

After attending Goldsmiths College in London in the early 1990s, Floyer was awarded a scholarship in 1997 to the Künstlerhaus Bethanien, Berlin, and still lives in the city today. She has gained further accolades including the Preis der Nationalgalerie für Junge Kunst, Hamburger Bahnhof, Berlin (2007) and the Nam June Paik Art Center Prize, Yongin, South Korea (2009). Using humour and metaphor, her deceptively simple installations, sculptures and videos juxtapose everyday objects to render them unfamiliar and subvert their normal function or implied use value. Her work has a sense of the absurd and frequently evinces a 'double-take' whereby the viewer is disarmed into contemplation. Installed in an empty space, *Solo* features a stand supporting what might appear on first glance to be a normal microphone. Upon closer inspection, the playful aspect of the piece is revealed: a hairbrush in place of the expected apparatus. It suggests antics of singing songs into a mirror at home – stereotypically done by teenagers dreaming of careers as pop stars. Floyer's titles underline her interest in language and in semiotics and are often the key to unlocking the complexity of her conceptual artworks.

LAVINIA FONTANA

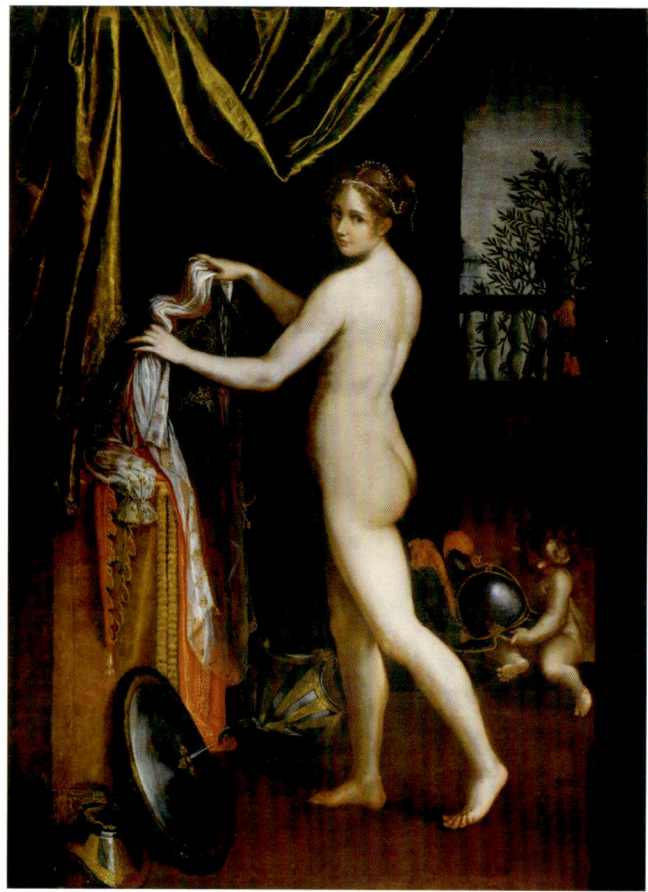

MINERVA DRESSING

1613, oil on canvas, 258 × 190 cm (101 ½ × 74 ¾ in), Galleria Borghese, Rome
Lavinia Fontana, born 1552, Bologna, Italy. Died 1614, Rome.

Fontana was the first female artist to achieve critical and commercial success in Counter-Reformation Italy. The daughter of a prominent painter, Prospero Fontana (1512–97), she trained in her father's studio in Bologna – a hub of intellectual life in the university city. In her youth she earned recognition for her portraits and went on to paint altarpieces and grand mythological scenes to rival those of male contemporaries of the Baroque movement, such as Annibale Carracci (1560–1609) and his cousins. In 1577 Fontana was married to the minor artist Paolo Zappi (dates unknown) without a dowry – an unusual arrangement made possible by her income as a painter –

and her husband became her assistant and agent. Fontana and her family moved to Rome in 1603, where her subjects included Pope Paul V. Seen here is her last-known painting, a ground-breaking instance of a female nude painted by a female artist. The mythological title and attributes (for example, the shield that lies beneath the martial goddess) do little to mask the fact that this is a contemporary Italian woman, although whether a courtesan or noblewoman is unclear.

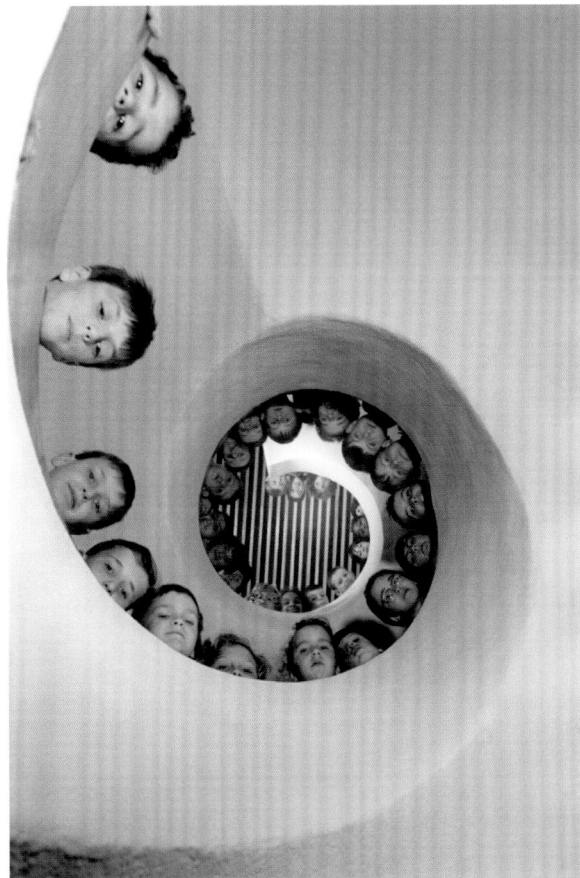

CHILDREN'S LIBRARY, CLAMART, HAUTS-DE-SEINE

1965, gelatin silver print, 34.9 × 26 cm (13 ¾ × 10 ¼ in)
Martine Franck, born 1938, Antwerp, Belgium. Died 2012, Paris.

While studying art history at the École du Louvre, Paris, Franck discovered that her true passion lay not in academia, but photography. During a trip across Asia in 1963, she borrowed her cousin's 35mm Leica camera to document her travels, developing a particular interest in recording fragile cultures, and finding her preference for shooting in black and white. On her return home, she was an assistant at *Time-Life* magazine for a period before becoming a freelance photographer for publications including *The New York Times* and *Vogue*. She was also a founding member and official photographer for the avant-garde Parisian theatre collective *Théâtre du Soleil*, where she met her husband, photographer Henri Cartier-Bresson (1908–2004). Her practice ranged from portraits of notable artists such as Marc Chagall (1887–1985) to her preferred theme, the lives of marginalized peoples, in which she was influenced to some extent by the American photojournalist Dorothea Lange (p.230). This image of a spiral staircase showcases her acute photographic eye, following with near-perfection the framing principle known as the 'rule of thirds', as well as exemplifying her empathy towards her young subjects.

HELEN FRANKENTHALER

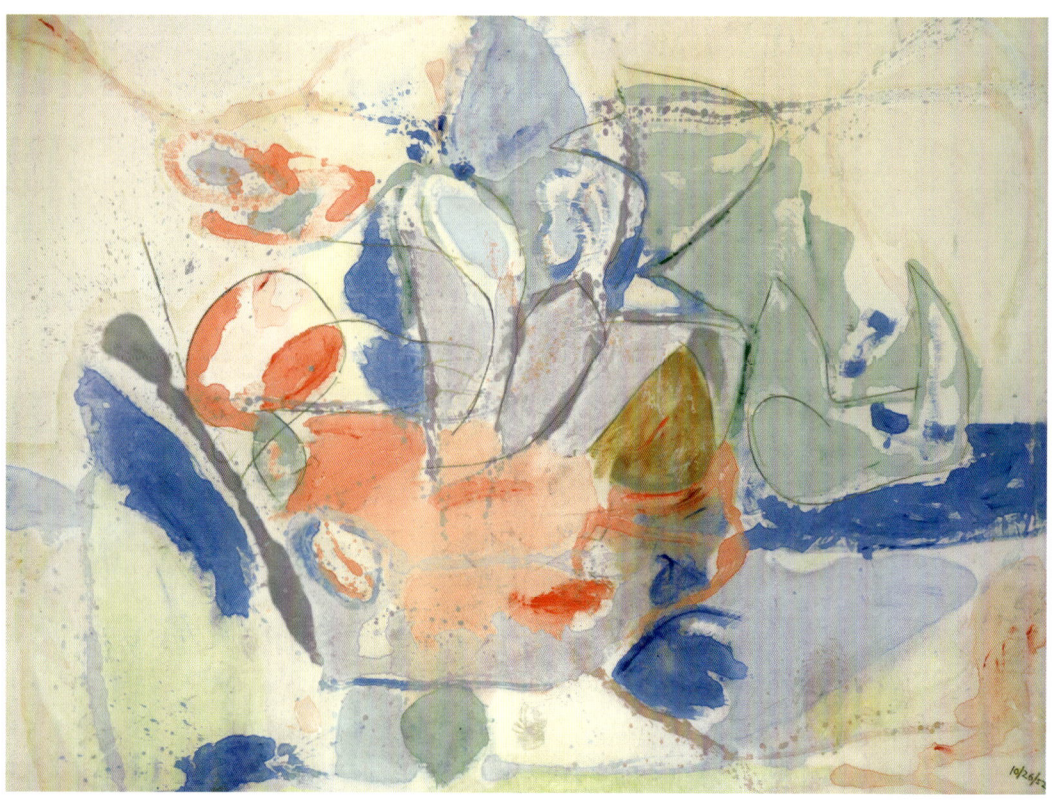

MOUNTAINS AND SEA

1952, oil and charcoal on unsized, unprimed canvas, 219.4 × 297.8 cm
(86 ⅜ × 117 ¼ in), Helen Frankenthaler Foundation, New York, on extended loan
to the National Gallery of Art, Washington DC
Helen Frankenthaler, born 1928, New York. Died 2011, Darien, Connecticut.

During her long artistic career Frankenthaler created some
of America's most original and poetic abstract paintings and
prints. As she observed in 1983: 'Anything is possible… It's all
about risks, deliberate risks.' On seeing her first solo exhibition
at New York's Tibor de Nagy Gallery in 1951, critics described
her as 'imaginative, fearless, and immensely talented'. The following year, aged twenty-three, she initiated a new form
of Abstract Expressionism. Frankenthaler had been introduced

to Jackson Pollock (1912–56) and she was impressed by his radical drip technique. In *Mountains and Sea* she took Pollock's
painting method further, pouring oil paint thinned to the consistency of watercolour onto unprimed canvas laid flat on the
floor. Frankenthaler called this innovatory technique 'soak-stain'.
This painting, which has attained legendary status, was inspired
by the coastal scenery of Nova Scotia in Canada. She began by
drawing her abstracted memory of the landscape, making sweep-
ing calligraphic gestures with charcoal, over which she then
poured colours, which bled into the canvas in more or less unpredictable ways.

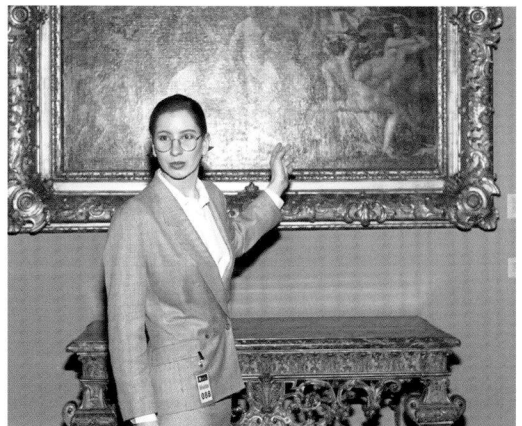

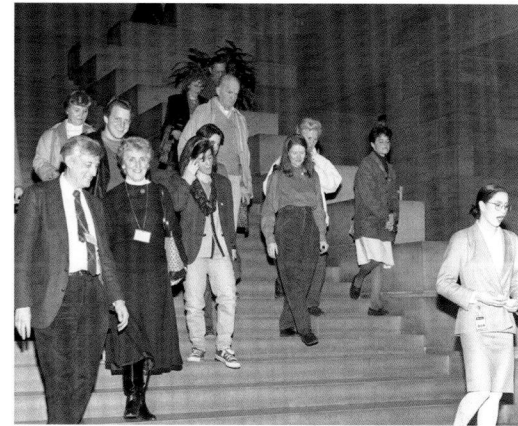

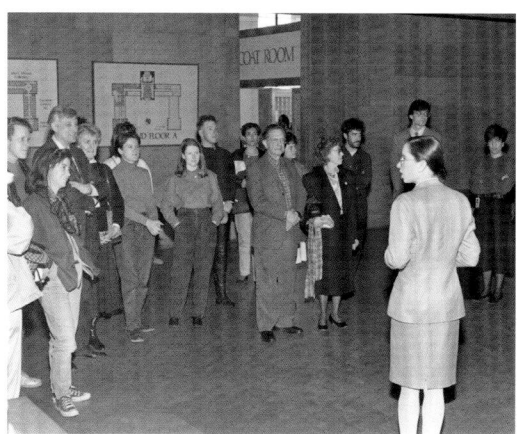

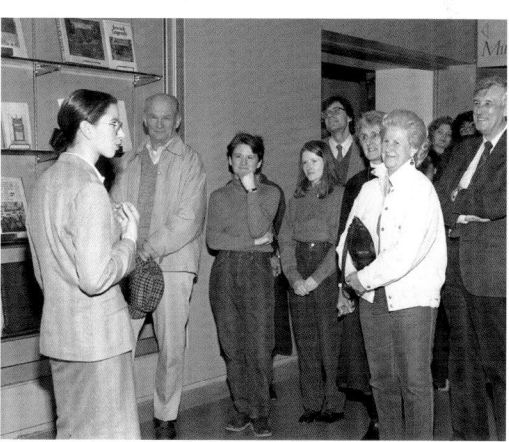

MUSEUM HIGHLIGHTS: A GALLERY TALK

1989, 30-min live performance, single-channel video and text
Andrea Fraser, born 1965, Billings, Montana.

Fraser's practice attends to the inner workings of art – its commerce, labour conditions and architectures – and relates to both feminism and the loose 'institutional critique' art movement, alongside Hans Haacke (b.1936), Adrian Piper (p.323) and others. Her practice encompasses performance, video and installation, as well as books and texts. She is also a collaborator in various initiatives: a founding member of feminist performance group The V-Girls (1986–96) and partner in the cooperative art gallery Orchard, New York (2005–8). One of her best-known and earliest works, *Museum Highlights* sees the artist assume the role of a volunteer museum guide named

Jane Castleton, who delivers a tour of the Philadelphia Museum of Art. Drawing from extensive research into the museum, her script is constructed using quotations from a range of sources including the city's archives, scholarly studies and social policy documents. As expected in a museum tour, she describes artworks in the collection, but she also mentions the cloakroom, exit signs, toilets, water fountain and gift shop, in language that exposes how class values and notions of an 'ideal visiting public' are subtly expressed by the museum and the social structures that surround it.

ELISABETH FRINK

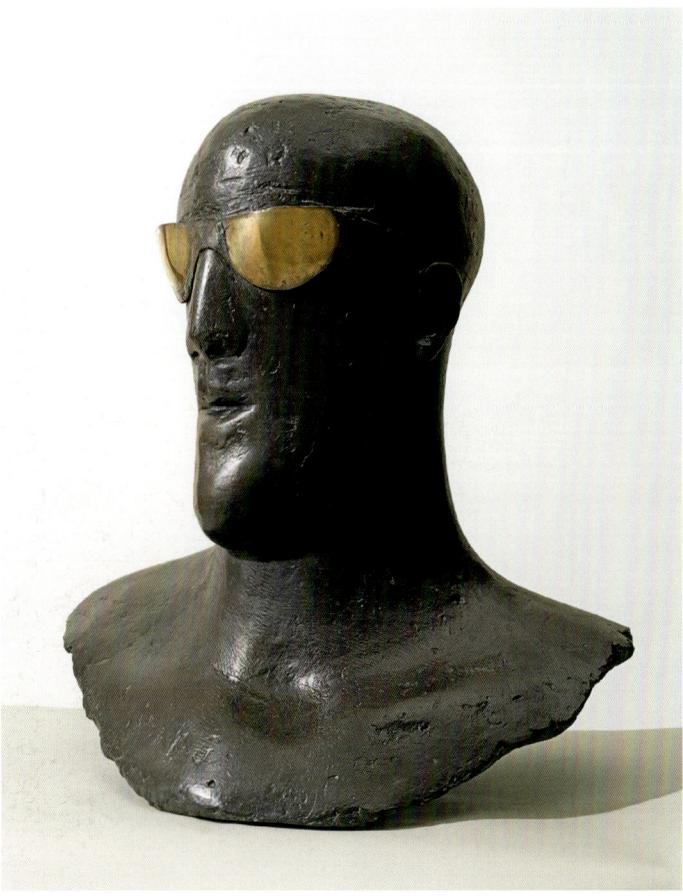

GOGGLE HEAD

1969, bronze, 60 × 56.5 × 44.5 cm (23 ⅝ × 22 ¼ × 17 ½ in), Tate, London
Elisabeth Frink, born 1930, Great Thurlow, Suffolk, UK. Died 1993, Woolland, Dorset, UK.

Trained in Guildford and Chelsea, Frink quickly became one of the leading post-war sculptors in Britain. Aged nine when the Second World War began, her father was later evacuated at Dunkirk and the family lived near a military airfield. Her drawings from this time often contained dark themes of wounded birds and falling figures, subjects she would revisit in her sculptural practice in works that often convey a sense of menace. One of her early sculptures, *Bird*, was acquired by the Tate in 1953, a raven-like creature with an alert posture and a predatory air. As well as birds, horses, dogs and male

figures were recurring motifs in her practice, usually executed in a distinctively rough, textured aesthetic. This was achieved by placing plaster on an armature, then chiselling and manipulating the material. One of her best-known series was of large male busts. In *Goggle Head* the eyes of the head are obscured by polished golden goggles, perhaps those of an aviator, but an archetypal man rather than an individual person. She later remarked that the heads had become a 'symbol of evil' for her.

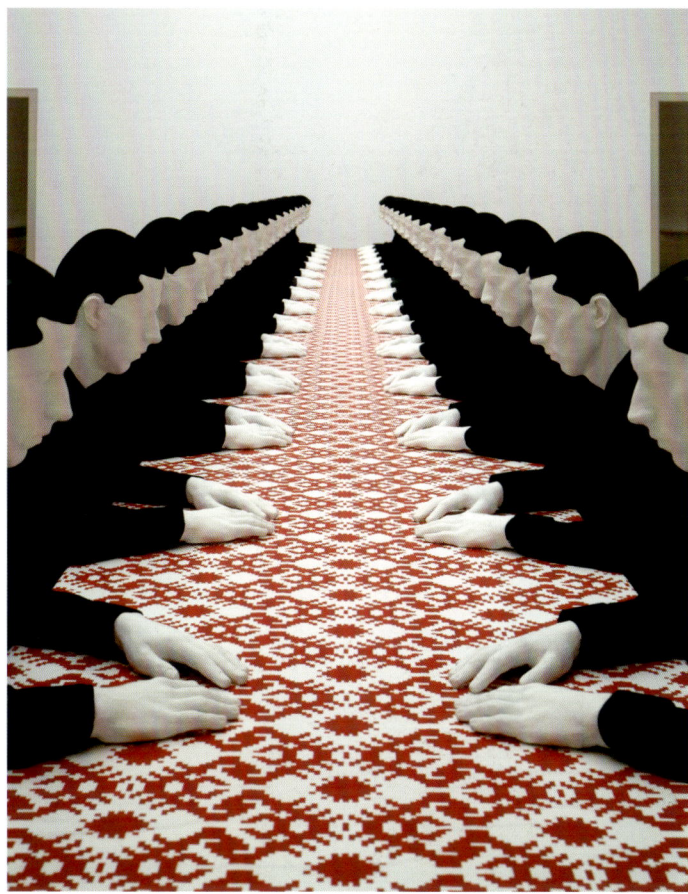

TISCHGESELLSCHAFT (COMPANY AT TABLE)

1988, polyester, wood, cotton and paint, 140 × 1,600 × 175 cm (59 × 629 ⅞ × 68 ⅞ in), Museum für Moderne Kunst, Frankfurt
Katharina Fritsch, born 1956, Essen, Germany.

Fritsch's work has been prominent in major exhibitions and collections for four decades, including her representing Germany at the 46th Venice Biennale (1995). She creates vividly detailed sculptures of figures and creatures – sometimes enlarged to giant-size – that are intensely painted, often in monochrome. Her iconic work *Rat King* (1991–3) comprises several three-metre (ten-feet) tall black rats in a circle with their tails tangled in a knot. It plays on a primordial fear of rodents – giant rats being many people's worst nightmare – but for the artist, who sees things from the creatures' perspective, the work represents being trapped in a hopeless situation. Other figurative works appear subtly humorous, such as *Hahn/Cock* (2010), the giant ultramarine cockerel first presented on the 'Fourth Plinth' in London's Trafalgar Square, which contrasted with the other more typical public statues. Fritsch's early work *Company at Table* features thirty-two identical male figures sitting at a long table, heads slightly bowed, staring at a patterned tablecloth, each withdrawn into himself. Fritsch considers it like a *Welträtsel* – an unanswerable riddle about the enigma of existence. Appearing like clones, the figures are a visual representation of an anxiety about losing one's individual identity.

ANYA GALLACCIO

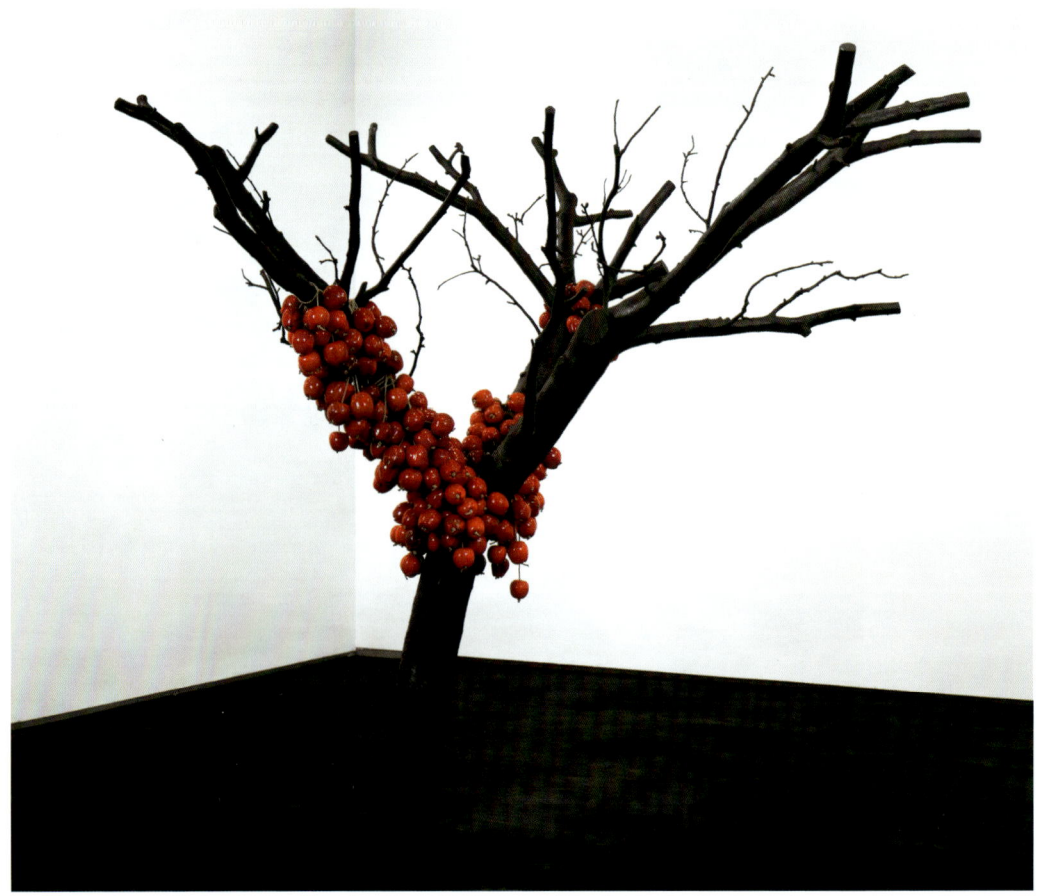

BECAUSE NOTHING HAS CHANGED

2001, cast bronze, 250 live apples and twine, *c.*280 × 200 × 150 cm
(*c.*110 ⅛ × 78 ¾ × 59 in), private collection
Anya Gallaccio, born 1963, Paisley, UK.

Working with unusual art materials such as chocolate, salt, ice, flowers and other organic and ephemeral substances, Gallaccio creates sculptures and site-specific installations that often undergo an unpredictable transformation and decay over time, ultimately becoming just a memory and leaving little or no physical trace. A graduate of Goldsmiths College in London and one of the Young British Artists (YBAs) whose work was included in the now legendary 'Freeze' exhibition of 1988, Gallaccio combines influences from Minimalism and Land art in her poetic practice. Revelling in the flux of the natural world, she gives its transitory processes space to perform. In *because nothing has changed*, a truncated tree is cast in bronze. From its branches, 250 shiny red apples are tied, appearing – to those who witness it at the outset – as a bountiful harvest. Over the course of its exhibition, the hanging apples shrivel and rot, eventually falling to the ground, creating a *memento mori* still life in which the inevitability of death is not just symbolized but actually demonstrated. In visualizing the impermanence of materiality, the work reveals the impossibility of the changelessness suggested in the title. Time shifts our experience of matter and, as such, existence.

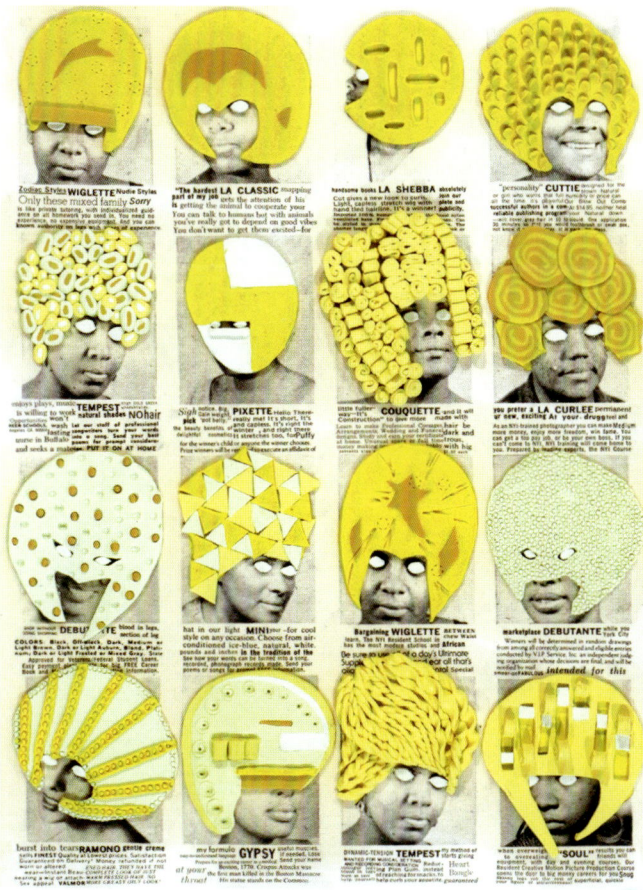

WIGLETTE FROM DELUXE

2004–5, from a portfolio of 60 etchings with photogravure, spitbite, collage, laser cutting, laser peeling, silkscreen, offset lithography, hand-painting and plasticine sculptural additions, overall framed: 214 × 444.5 cm (84¼ × 175 in), edition of 20
Ellen Gallagher, born 1965, Providence, Rhode Island.

Gallagher is an inventive builder. Born in the port city of Providence, she has long been an inspired and imaginative chronicler of large-scale marine paintings featuring science experiments, portraiture, abstraction and minstrelsy. Her exploration of visual culture covers a wide-ranging temporal terrain stretching from blackface minstrelsy to twentieth-century abstraction, and includes mining of vernacular forms as diverse as science fiction, advertising, mid-century race magazines, travelogues and scrimshaw in order to address and release the concealed threads that bind the visible. In her paintings, prints and film installations Gallagher modifies archival images from magazines including *Ebony, Sepia* and *Our World*, which relate to the construction of African-American identities, including advertisements for cosmetic transformations. She typically manipulates the images with painted marks, collage and lacerations, subversively reanimating the products to her own means. In *Wiglette from DeLuxe* the eyes of sixteen 1950s wig models are redacted leaving eerie voids and haunted exchanges: everyday people transformed by elastic prosthetic forms encroach on and subsume their faces, drawing attention to the fungibility of hair in female and black cultural identities.

YISHAY GARBASZ

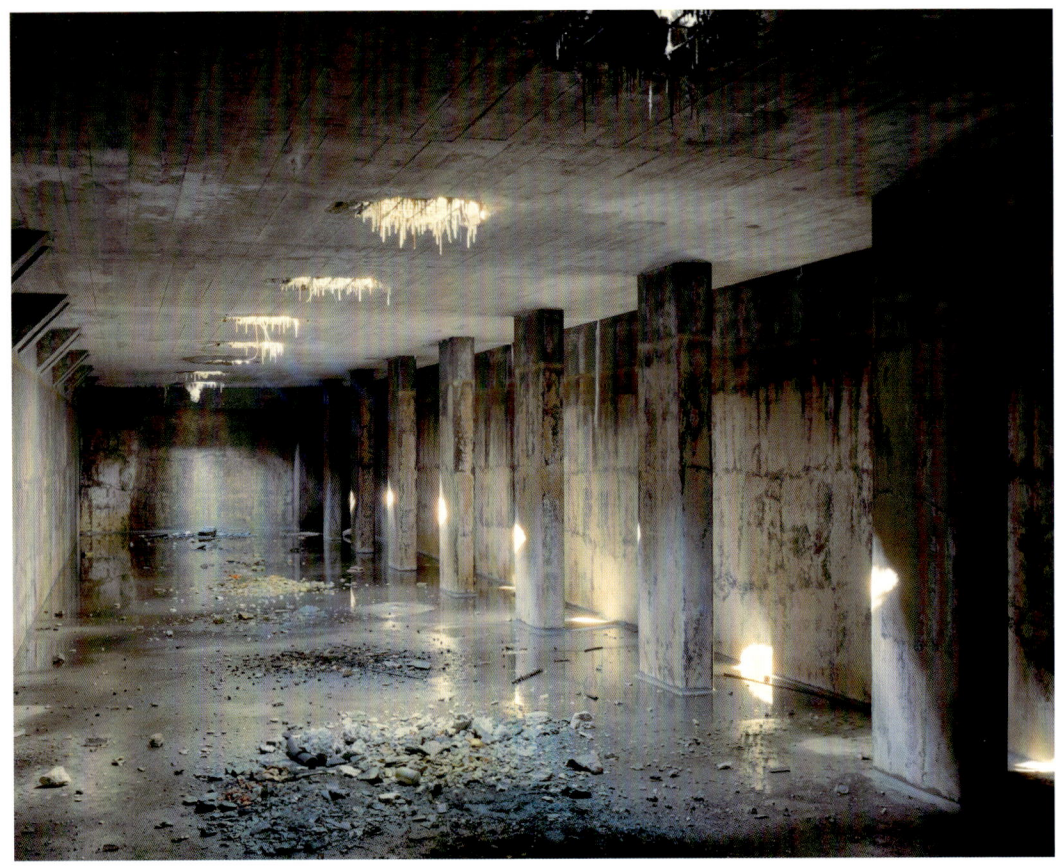

FOOTSTEPS (48) from 'IN MY MOTHER'S FOOTSTEPS'

2004–9, chromogenic photograph, 28 × 35.6 cm (11 × 14 in) Text panel reads:
'Many women in the camp started suffering from seizures. This was being caused
by all the chemicals used in the factories around us.'
Yishay Garbasz, born 1970, Israel.

Garbasz was initially unable to bring herself to read her mother
Salla's 10,000-word manuscript about her experiences of imprisonment in five concentration camps during the Holocaust. When,
much later, she did so, it became her mission to travel through
Germany, the Netherlands, the Czech Republic and Poland to visually document the sites that featured in her mother's account: from
childhood apartment interiors and schools, to hidden synagogues and
the bleak expanse of Auschwitz. Using a large-format camera

and making much of the year-long journey on foot, the artist intentionally slowed down this act of recollection. The resulting sixty-two
contemplative images, scenes devoid of people save for one portrait
and three sparsely populated urban landscapes, conceal memories
that are then revealed in accompanying text panels that are quotations from Salla's text. *Footsteps (48)* depicts a long-abandoned and
dilapidated German munitions factory where Garbasz's mother
and aunt were enslaved. 'In My Mother's Footsteps' reckons with
intergenerational responses to trauma and remembrance. Garbasz
has since photographed other sites of trauma, alienation and division,
such as the Korean Demilitarized Zone and the border between
Israeli and Palestinian territories.

SEVEN ICOSIDODECAHEDRONS

*c.*1977, stainless steel wire, 110 × 170 × 75 cm (43 ¼ × 66 ⅞ × 29 ½ in), installation
view, 'Gego: Line as Object', Henry Moore Institute, Leeds, UK, 2014
Gego, born Gertrud Goldschmidt, 1912, Hamburg, Germany. Died 1994,
Caracas, Venezuela.

Born into a German-Jewish family, Gego trained as an architect and
engineer at the Technische Hochschule in Stuttgart. Escaping the
Nazi regime, she emigrated with her family to Caracas in 1939,
working there initially as a freelance industrial and architectural
designer, before turning to art in the mid-1950s. Her professional
background is evident in her art, which often uses industrial materials to explore the relationship between line and space. Exploring
two and three dimensions, she produced works on paper, as well
as large-scale wire constructions. Particularly in her early career,
Gego was closely associated with prominent practitioners of geometric abstraction and kinetic art in Venezuela, such as Jesús Rafael Soto
(1923–2005) and Alejandro Otero (1921–90). A concern with both
geometry and movement is clear in this delineation of polyhedral
space, its delicate, suspended structures composed of steel wire.
Elsewhere in Gego's work a more personal, expressive element is seen
in the handcrafted lines and semi-organic shapes of what she called
bichos ('creatures'), a series that resists fitting into any of the period's
mainstream art-historical movements.

ARTEMISIA GENTILESCHI

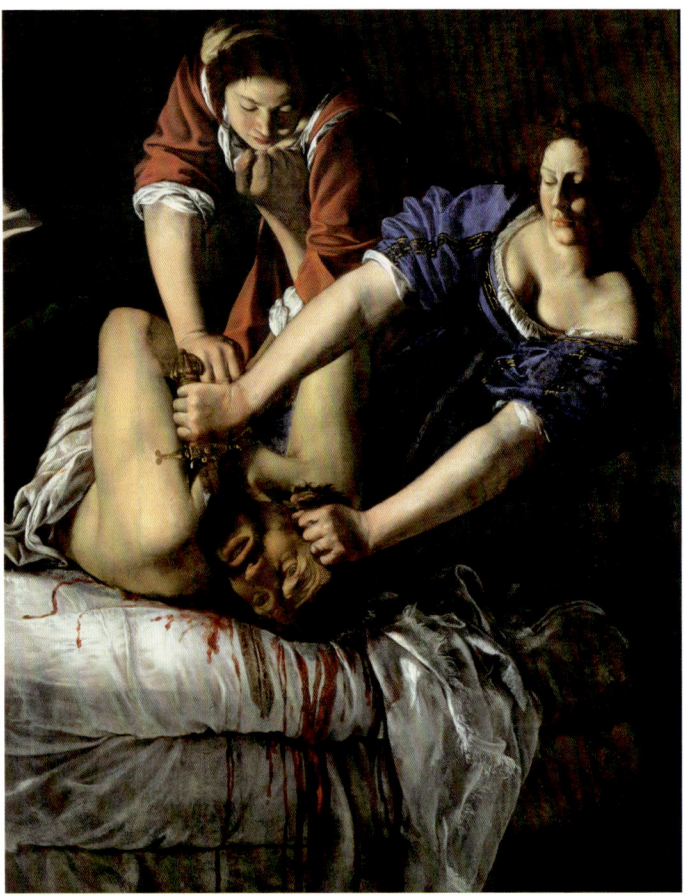

JUDITH BEHEADING HOLOFERNES

1611–12, oil on canvas, 163 × 126 cm (64⅛ × 49⅝ in), Museo Nazionale
di Capodimonte, Naples
Artemisia Gentileschi, born 1593, Rome. Died 1652/53, Naples.

The daughter of renowned Roman painter Orazio Gentileschi
(1563–1639), and regarded in her lifetime as a pre-eminent painter
of the Italian Baroque, the generation that followed Michelangelo
Merisi da Caravaggio (1571–1610), Gentileschi initially trained in
her father's studio. She was sent for further tutelage to the painter
Agostino Tassi (1578–1644), who raped her in 1612, resulting in a
lengthy trial and Tassi's eventual indictment. A witness in court,
Gentileschi was tortured to ensure the truth of her testimony.
These early traumas reverberate throughout her work, this painting

being one of two depictions of the Apocryphal story of the widow
Judith decapitating Holofernes. The noble Israelite heroine is shown
holding down the Persian general and driving a sword through his
neck, averting her face (but not her eyes) from the spray of blood. The
work sounds a note of proto-feminist outrage against corrupt masculinity and sexual violence, resonating with her experience of injustice
and suffering. Similar perspectives are traceable in her painting
of Susannah spied upon by leering elders. In 2018, London's National
Gallery announced that Gentileschi's work would be the subject
of the first solo exhibition by a female artist in the institution's almost
two-hundred-year history.

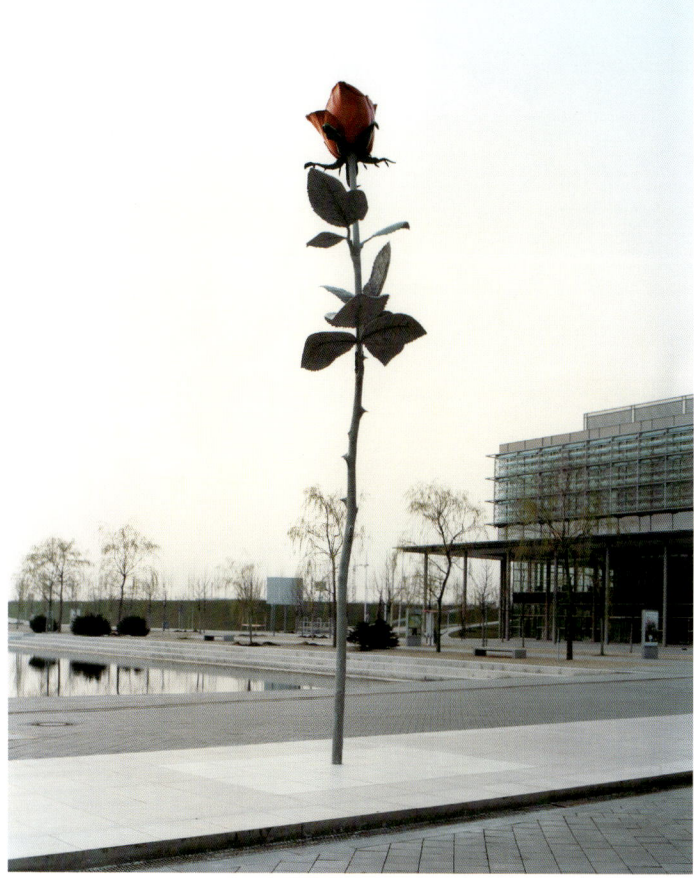

ROSE

1993/97, stainless steel, aluminium and lacquer, h: 800 cm (315 in), installation, Fair, Leipzig, 1997. Collection Leipziger Messe gmbh, Leipzig, Germany Isa Genzken, born Hanne-Rose Genzken, 1948, Bad Oldesloe, Germany.

Genzken studied fine art, art history and philosophy from the late 1960s, then developed a studio practice in Düsseldorf, working periodically in New York. She is known primarily for her sculpture and installations, making architectonic work that is influenced by twentieth-century movements, from Modernist architecture to Minimalism and Constructivism. Her practice investigates material and popular culture as well as the links between architectural design and urban space. Stylistic transformations and innovative use of materials – including ready-made objects, steel and cement

– have formed a diverse body of work, earning her awards such as the Wolfgang Hahn Prize in 2002 and the International Art Prize in 2004. *Rose*, a colossal single-stemmed flower, is permanently installed outside the Leipziger Messe, a major trade exhibition venue in one of Germany's largest industrial cities. Standing as a symbol for love, pain and the passing of time, *Rose* also hints of the promise that nature could reclaim the city, exemplifying Genzken's poetic response to the contemporary man-made environment.

MARGUERITE GÉRARD

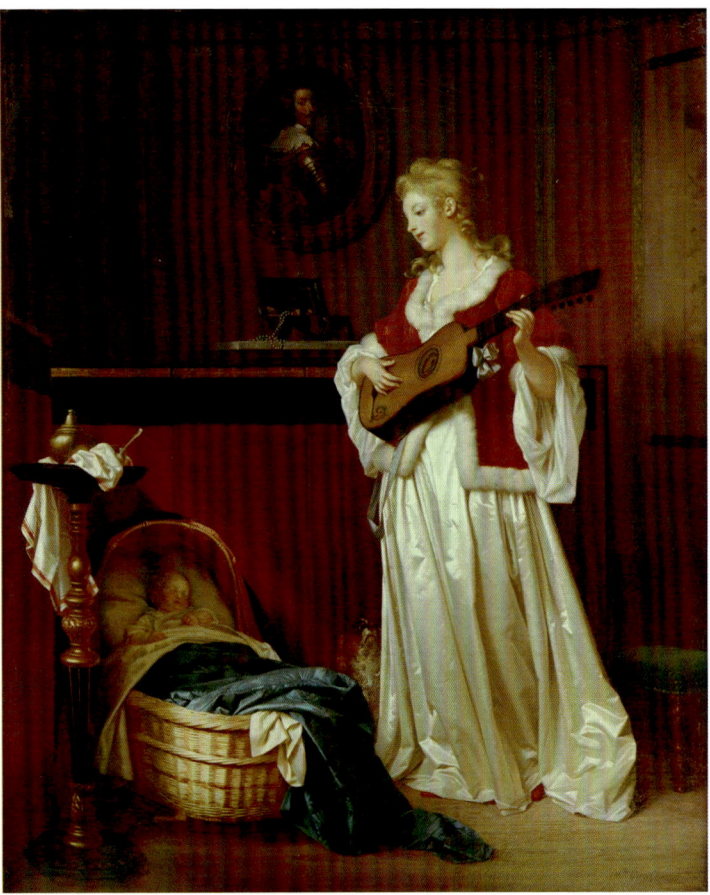

SLEEP, MY CHILD

*c.*1788, oil on canvas, 55 × 45 cm (21 ⅝ × 17 ¼ in), Staatliche Kunsthalle, Karlsruhe, Germany
Marguerite Gérard, born 1761, Grasse, France. Died 1837, Paris.

One of a creative family, Gérard was sister of miniaturist Marie-Anne Fragonard (1745–1823), herself the wife of famed late-Rococo artist Jean-Honoré Fragonard (1732–1806). She established a career spanning fifty years, specializing in genre painting – depicting finely rendered scenes of everyday life – which was prized by the burgeoning bourgeoisie of late-eighteenth-century Paris. As a result of her financial success, she secured a comfortable position in the city and never married, instead living for thirty years in the Louvre's artist accommodation, where her sister and brother-in-law also painted,

and where she benefited from Fragonard's instruction. As a woman, she was excluded from formal artistic training at the Académie Royale de Peinture et de Sculpture (whose successor institution did not admit female students until 1897). She studied the Louvre's collection closely, focusing on works by seventeenth-century Dutch painters, such as Gabriel Metsu (1629–67) and Gerard Ter Borch (1617–81), who had by that time become popular in Paris. Gérard's interpretation of this tradition – with its painting-in-a-painting – demonstrates her in-depth knowledge of the genre and technically skilful rendition of the costumes and furnishings of her time.

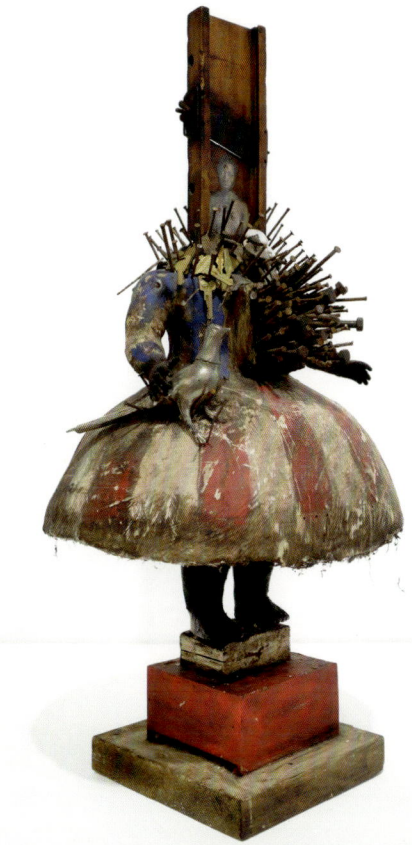

DELIA ON THE PLANE, OR CABBAGE SLICER

2012, mixed-media assemblage, 81.2 × 43.2 × 38.1 cm (32 × 17 × 15 in),
Spelman College Museum of Fine Art, Atlanta
Vanessa L. German, born 1976, Milwaukee, Wisconsin.

A multidisciplinary artist, poet and activist, German's handmade figurines are assembled from street detritus. Addressing the tragedy of slavery, she draws on folk art – and the form and intention of Congolese fetish idols in particular – to create what she calls 'contemporary power figures', totems of resistance against racial and patriarchal oppression. Growing up in Los Angeles, her artist mother taught her skills of making, encouraging German to sew her own clothes. Moving to Pittsburgh, she began making art on her porch, with children joining to watch; this developed into her community projects 'ARThouse' and 'Love Front Porch', where art becomes a healing force against violence. The horrors of slavery are encapsulated in this statuette, whose dress evokes the United States flag, locating this history of violence. Beneath the guillotine-like blade of her cabbage-slicer head is a reproduced daguerreotype image, made in South Carolina in 1850, of a slave called Delia, identifying this suffering to a real life. In an article written by German in 2016, she specifies its materials in more detail: together with 'nails', 'wood' and 'gauze' are 'rage', 'fire in her eyes', 'meanness' and 'the legacy, the legacy, the legacy'.

GLUCK

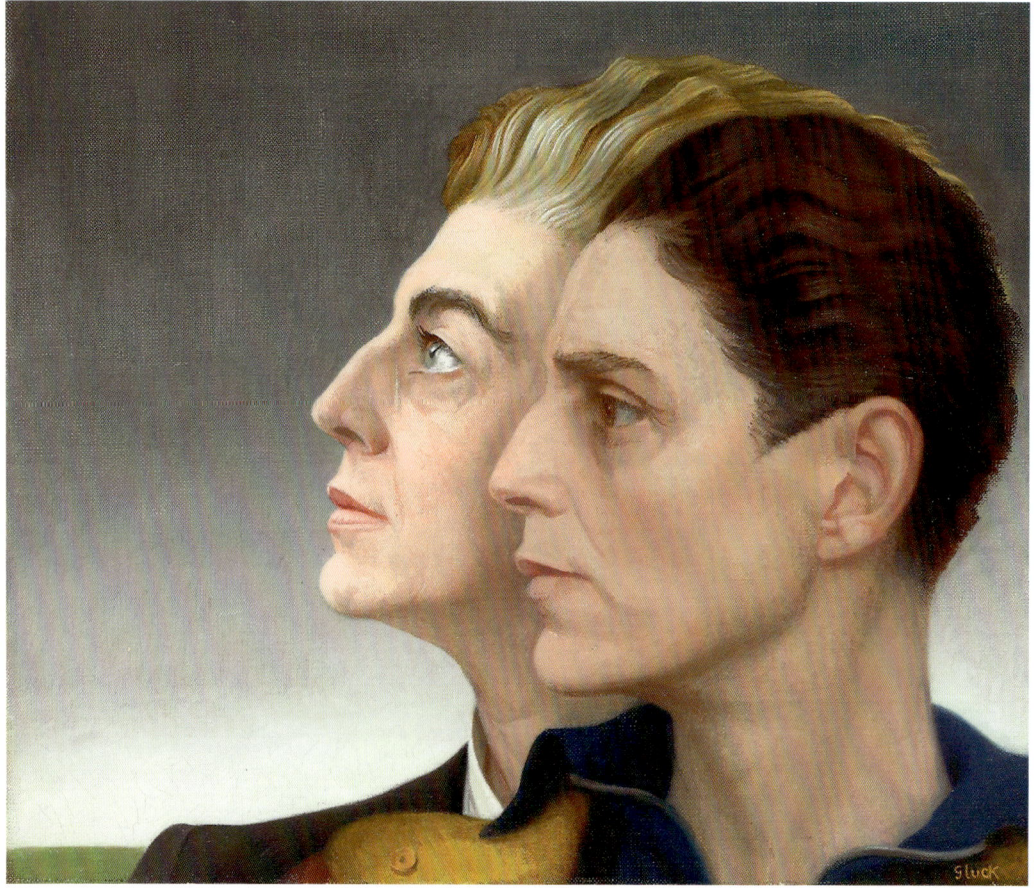

MEDALLION [YOUWE]

1936, oil on canvas, 30.5 × 35.6 cm (12 × 14 in), private collection.
Gluck, born Hannah Gluckstein, 1895, London. Died 1978, Steyning,
West Sussex, UK.

Born into the wealthy family who owned the Lyons catering empire,
Gluck pursued an independent course in her life and work. Rejecting
her given name in favour of a gender-neutral moniker, she likewise
eschewed formal association with any artistic movements or categories, although influences from Neo-Classicism and Surrealism may
be detected in the stylized gazes and preternatural light of *Medallion*.
This work was referred to by Gluck as *YouWe*, and portrays the
artist and her new lover, the American socialite Nesta Obermer.
It was painted following a trip to Glyndebourne to see Mozart's

Don Giovanni and commemorates what the artist considered their
'marriage'. With their profiles overlapping in the style of a coin portrait, the women appear doubles of one another. The work first
appeared at the Fine Art Society in 1937 alongside Gluck's flower
paintings and her portraits of society figures. Widely reproduced,
for example on the cover of the 1982 reprint of Radclyffe Hall's
The Well of Loneliness (the subject of a notorious obscenity trial upon
its 1928 publication), the picture has become emblematic of same-
sex love.

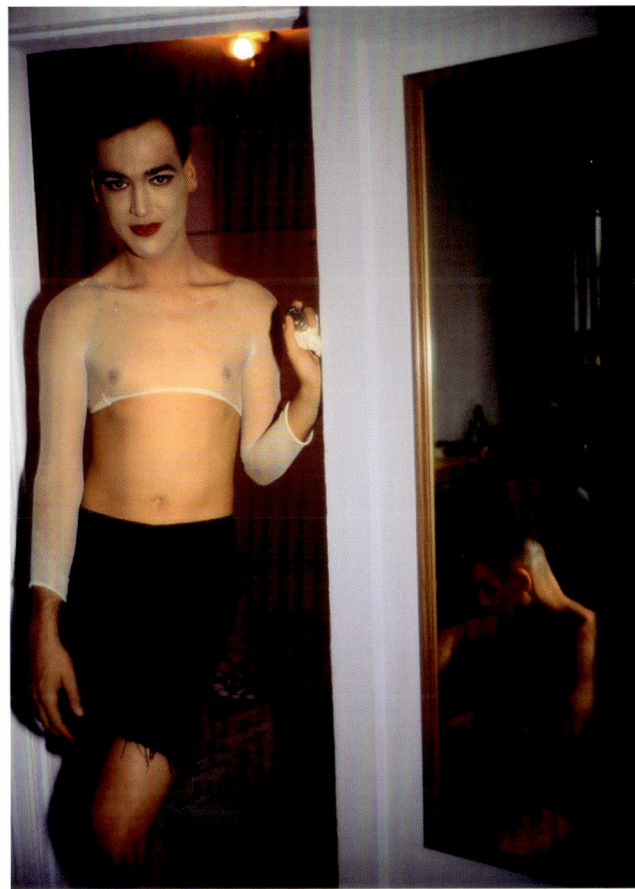

JIMMY PAULETTE AND TABBOO! UNDRESSING, NYC
1991
Nan Goldin, born 1953, Washington DC.

Responding to the suicide of her beloved sister, Goldin used photography to foster close relationships with her subjects, focusing on love, gender, domesticity and sexuality. She began taking photographs as a teenager, and documenting the drag queens of Boston's gay scene in the early 1970s. 'Part of my worship of them involved photographing them,' she later recalled in her book *The Other Side* (1993). Goldin went to study art at the School of the Museum of Fine Arts, Boston, in 1974, and chronicled New York's alternative scenes throughout the 1980s and 1990s, including its post-punk new-wave music scene, drug culture and AIDS crisis. Her treatment of queer subcultures in a tender, candid style has earned her work cult status. Her best-known series, 'The Ballad of Sexual Dependency' (1979–86), was a diary-like project that included autobiographical moments and portraits of close friends such as Greer Lankton (p.231). In this photograph, one of a large series shot in 1991 in New York, Paris and Berlin, Goldin depicted two drag queens in a New York apartment, Jimmy Paulette in the doorway and Tabboo! reflected in profile.

NATALIA GONCHAROVA

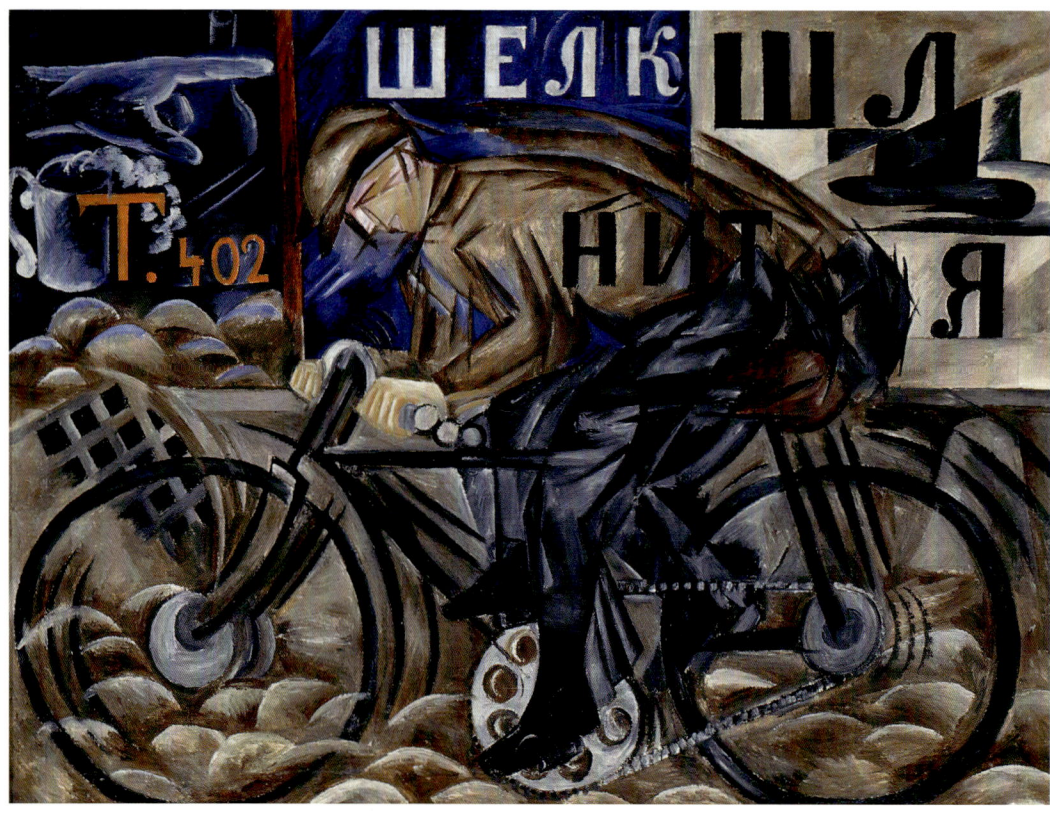

CYCLIST

1913, oil on canvas, 78 × 105 cm (30 ¾ × 41 ⅜ in), State Russian Museum, St Petersburg

Natalia Goncharova, born 1881, Nagaevo, Russia. Died 1962, Paris.

A leading figure in the pre-revolutionary Russian avant-garde, Goncharova worked as a painter and illustrator, and as a set designer for the Ballets Russes. She participated in many of the important exhibitions of modern art in Russia and, at the age of thirty-two, became the first woman and first avant-garde artist to have a retrospective in Moscow. Seen as a role model to other female artists in her country, she advised women to 'believe in yourself more, in your strengths and rights before mankind and God'. Involved in various European modernist movements, but also influenced by Russian folk art, Goncharova experimented in a range of styles. With her lifelong partner Mikhail Larionov (1881–1964), they founded Rayonism, a type of abstract art in which objects appear fragmented like splintered glass. Seen here is one of her most iconic paintings, echoing Italian Futurism in its representation of the speed, energy and dynamism of modern urban life. The contours of the cyclist's body and machine are repeated to suggest movement through space and time. In 1917, Goncharova fled the Bolshevik Revolution for the safety of Paris, where she lived until her death.

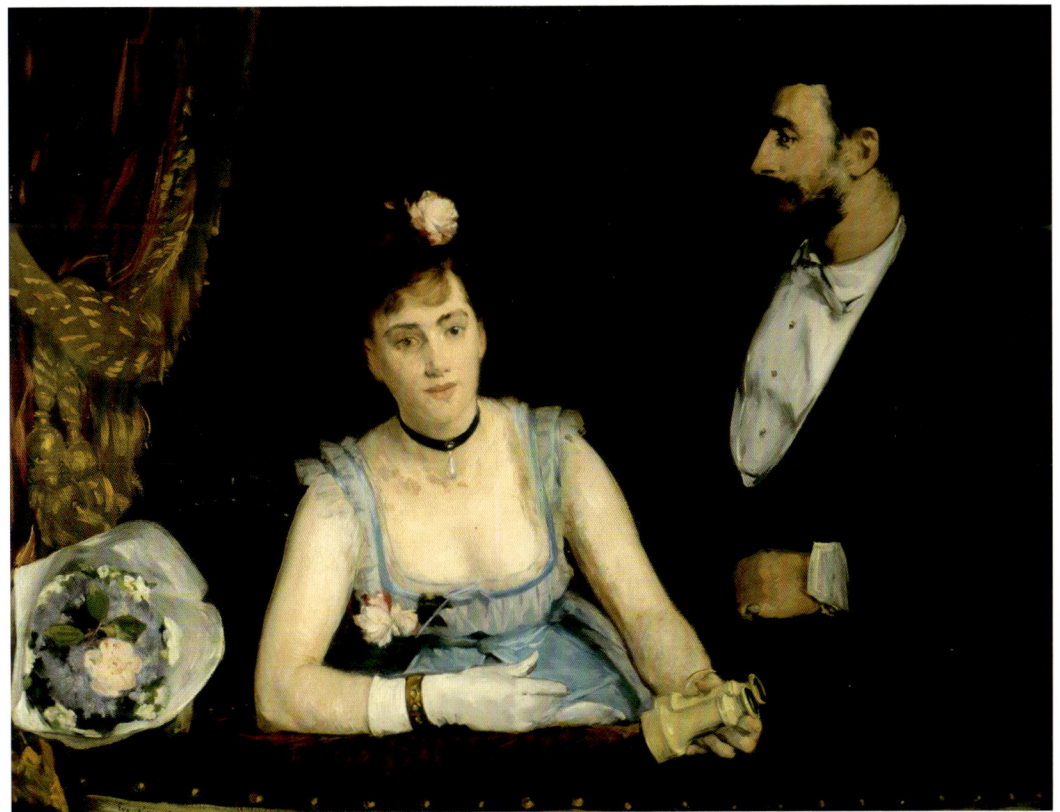

A BOX AT THE THÉÂTRE DES ITALIENS

1874, oil on canvas, 98 × 130 cm (38 ⅜ × 51 ⅛ in), Musée d'Orsay, Paris
Eva Gonzalès, born 1849, Paris. Died 1883, Paris.

Beginning her artistic training in 1866 at the age of seventeen and subsequently the only student Édouard Manet (1832–83) ever accepted, Gonzalès enjoyed success within a small but influential circle of artists and critics. Her career ended abruptly when she died in childbirth aged thirty-four. Like Manet, Gonzalès did not formally join the Impressionists but shared their interest in depicting contemporary scenes, as in this painting. Intended for the 1874 Paris Salon, the piece was rejected, only to be accepted five years later when slightly reworked and submitted together with the pastel drawing, *La Matinée Rose ('The Pink Morning')*. According to the

contemporaneous art critic and feminist activist Maria Deraismes the reason for this initial exclusion was because the committee associated Gonzalès with Manet, some suspecting that the painting could not have been made by a woman. Others in the male-dominated art establishment were threatened by Gonzalès's 'virility … firmness, energy and vigor', and would accept women artists only if they worked with 'soft, timid, niggling execution' and in 'soft pastels', a prejudice that had marked the Academy's attitude to women artists since the late eighteenth century.

DOMINIQUE GONZALEZ-FOERSTER

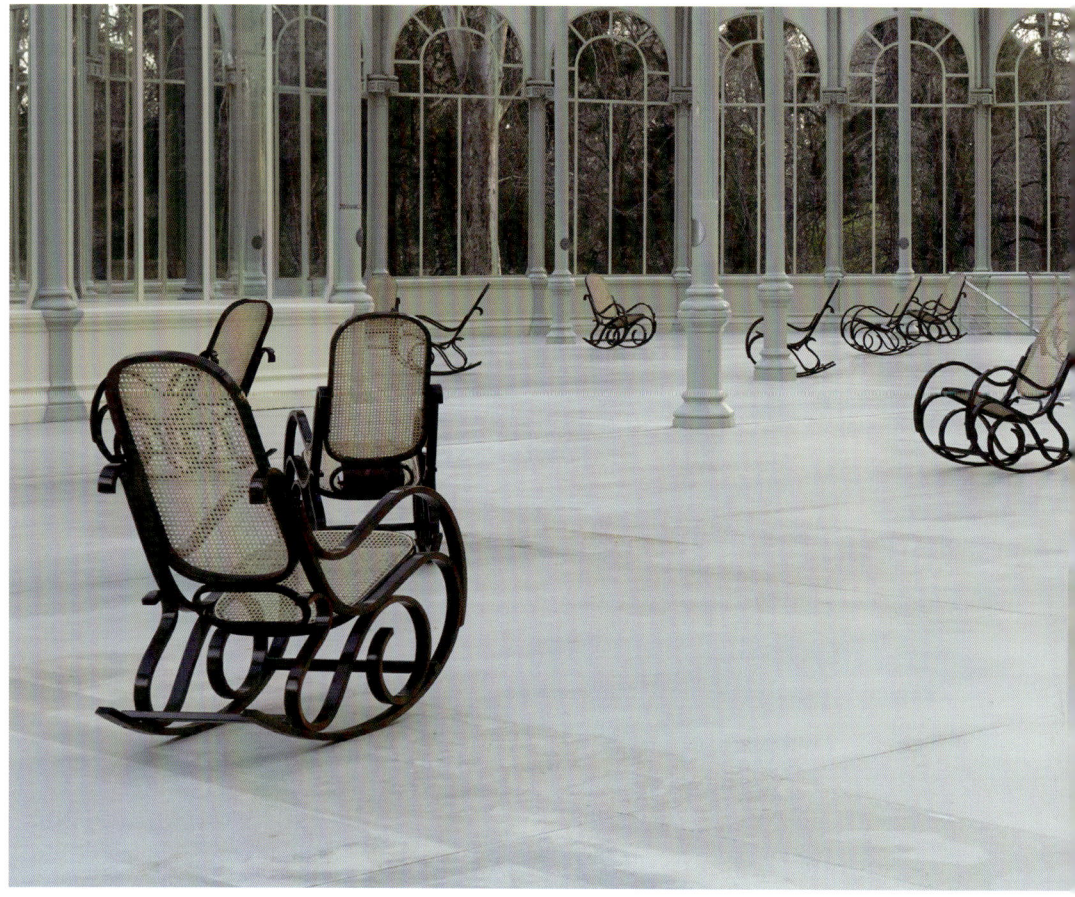

SPLENDIDE HOTEL

2014, rug, chairs, books and neon, installation view, Palacio de Cristal,
Museo Nacional Centro de Arte Reina Sofía, Madrid
Dominique Gonzalez-Foerster, born 1965, Strasbourg, France.

Gonzalez-Foerster is known for her interdisciplinary practice, which
spans film, architecture, philosophy, art history and literature,
although 'experience' has also been described as her chosen medium.
She studied in Grenoble, France, meeting artist Philippe Parreno
(b.1964) with whom she has since sometimes worked – the pair
co-writing a science fiction novel – and this exemplifies her frequently
collaborative approach. While a student, she worked as a museum
invigilator, a role that involved sustained presence and attention
amid juxtapositions of other makers' objects. This has extended to

installations involving the designer items of high-end fashion – for
example, in her project with Balenciaga. Space and time are themes
that recur throughout her oeuvre, their combination altering the
viewer's mood through techniques akin to psychological collage.
In *Splendide Hotel*, Gonzalez-Foerster transformed a large greenhouse,
the Palacio de Cristal in Madrid, into an imaginary space from 1877,
the year the building was constructed. Furnished with a historical
carpet, rocking chairs and literature by the writers H.G. Wells and
Fyodor Dostoyevsky, Gonzalez-Foerster encouraged visitors to sit
down in an airy, spacious environment and become swept up in
a constructed journey.

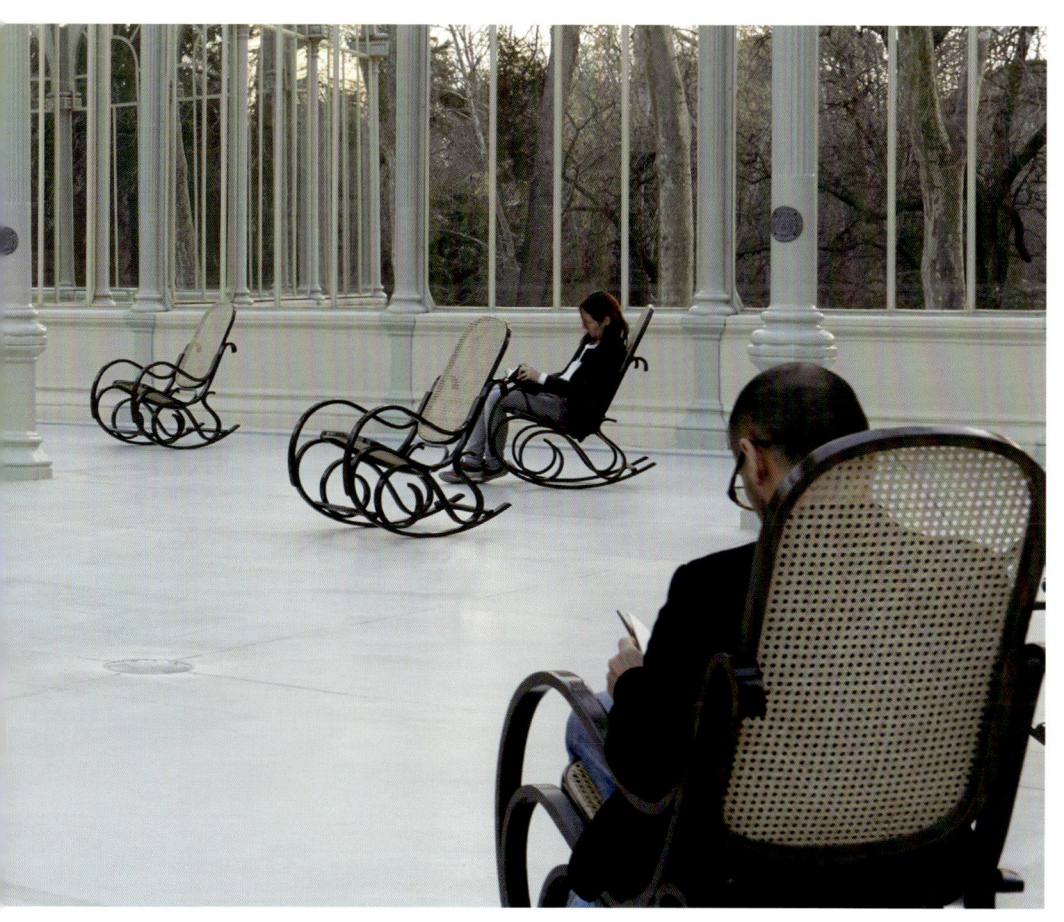

CATHERINE GOODMAN

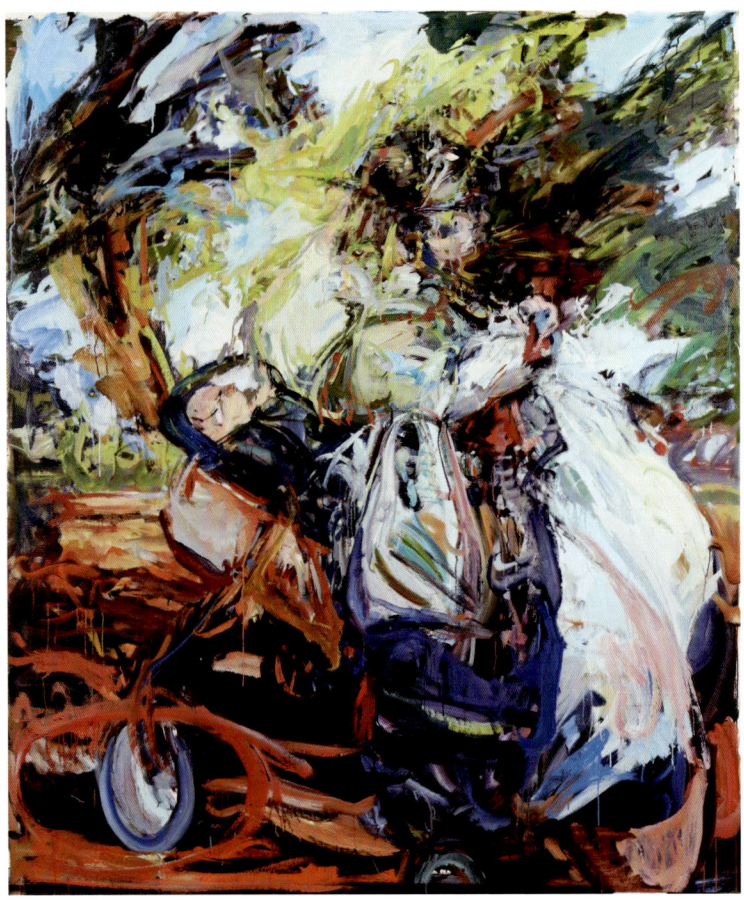

SISTER

2018, oil on canvas, 209.5 × 178 cm (82 ½ × 70 ⅜ in), Hauser & Wirth Collection, Henau, Switzerland
Catherine Goodman, born 1961, London.

Whether in portraiture for which she is best known, or in landscape or collage, Goodman's practice is rooted in the discipline of observation. She studied in London, at Camberwell School of Arts and Crafts followed by the Royal Academy Schools, where she won the Gold Medal in 1987. During these years, there was a resurgence of interest in figurative drawing and painting, with Goodman integral to this reappraisal of the British representational tradition, the so-called 'School of London'. Sustained practice in life-drawing and skills of draughtsmanship underpinned the work of artists such as Francis Bacon (1909–92), David Hockney (b.1937) and Paula Rego (p.332) and forms the basis of Goodman's compositions, such as this example, a vigorous and dynamic painting of her younger sister. In 2000, together with the then Prince of Wales, she co-founded the Royal Drawing School in London, becoming its artistic director, with the aim of furthering the skills of observational drawing in Britain's art schools. Two years later she won the BP Portrait Award at the National Portrait Gallery, London, and several of her works have since been added to its collection.

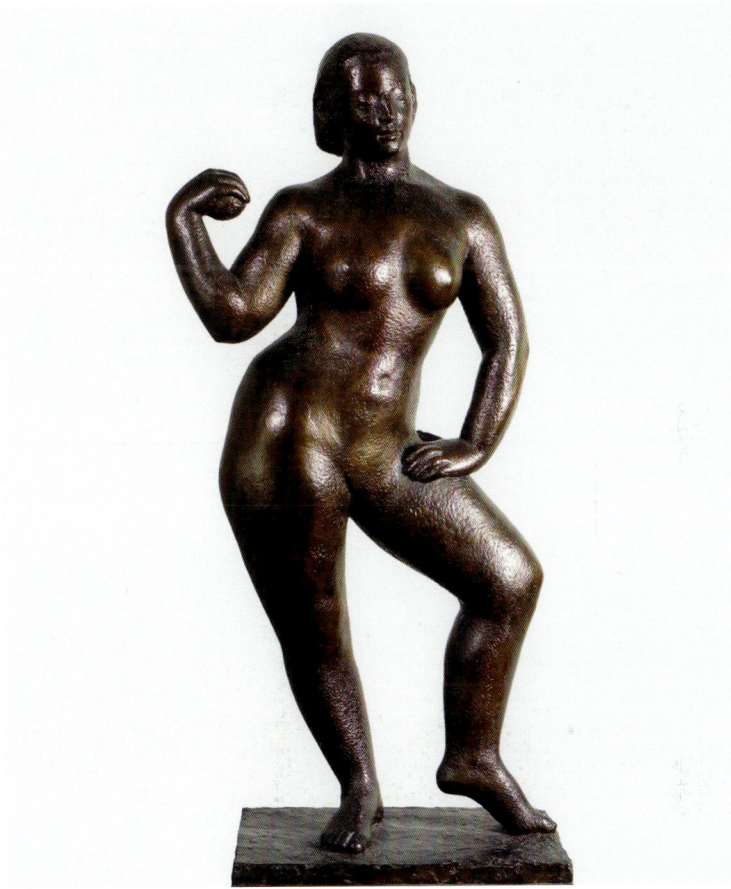

JAVANESE DANCER

1927–8, bronze, 143.2 × 65.1 × 37 cm (56 ⅜ × 25 ⅝ × 14 ½ in), Dorich House Museum, Kingston upon Thames, UK

Dora Gordine, born Dora Gordin, c.1895, Liepāja, Latvia. Died 1991, London.

Worldly, peripatetic and widely celebrated during her lifetime, Gordine spent her early years in Tallinn, Estonia, and was influenced by the Estonian Art Nouveau style. After early success in Paris she exhibited in London during the 1920s, before moving to Singapore and marrying her first husband in 1930. The marriage soon failed and, upon returning to London, Gordine married Richard Hare, a scholar of Russian art and literature. By 1936 the couple were living in a studio house designed by Gordine on the edge of Richmond Park. Built by and for a female artist and a notable example of Modernist architecture in its own right, the Grade II listed building is now Dorich House Museum (the combined first names of its original owners). The permanent collection incorporates the largest holdings of the artist's work as well as Russian art and artefacts acquired by the couple. This sculpture exemplifies the artist's consistently figurative style. Influenced by growing European interest art from other parts of the world, such as so-called Primitivism, Gordine was instinctively drawn to South East Asia as a source of subjects for her work.

SHEELA GOWDA

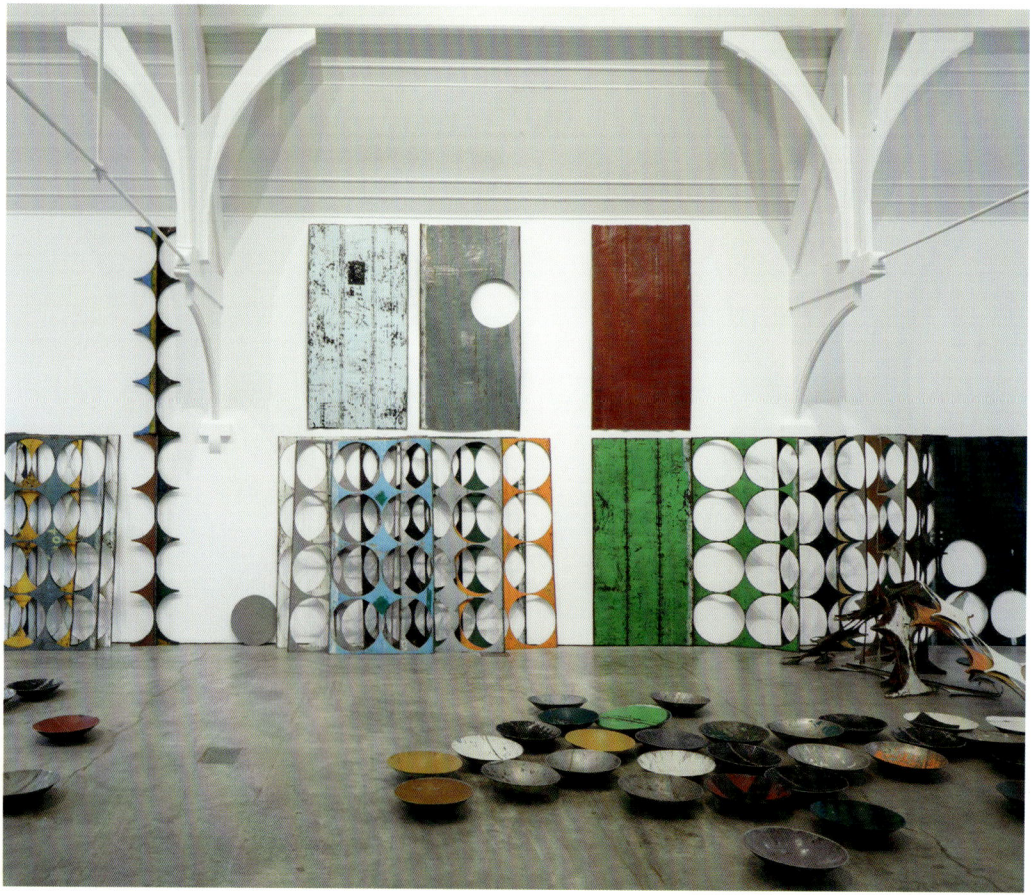

WHAT YET REMAINS

2017, recycled metal drums, dimensions variable, installation view, Ikon Gallery, Birmingham, UK

Sheela Gowda, born 1957, Bhadravati, India.

Gowda initially studied for an MFA in painting at London's Royal College of Art in 1986, but her artistic practice subsequently widened to encompass process-based sculpture, installation and photography. Much of her work focuses on the changing political landscape of India, and specifically the city of Bangalore (now Bengaluru) where she now lives. Fascinated by the subcontinent's rapid industrialization over recent decades, Gowda has used a variety of materials – including human hair, thread, cow dung and incense – to reveal the economic, social and cultural dynamics of her homeland. In this site-specific installation, the artist turns to industrial materials. From flat sheets of metal from recycled tar drums, eight circles were cut and hammered to form *bandlis* – small shallow bowls used by labourers to carry sand, cement and concrete slurry on construction sites. Presented as they might appear in reality, with offcuts of metal leaning nearby, their diminutive size is in stark contrast to the high-rise architecture they play a part in creating, and as such, become a reminder of the hard graft endured by India's manual labourers. Through simple means, Gowda powerfully highlights the realities of scavenging and subsistence life that underpins glossy, high-end developments and urbanization.

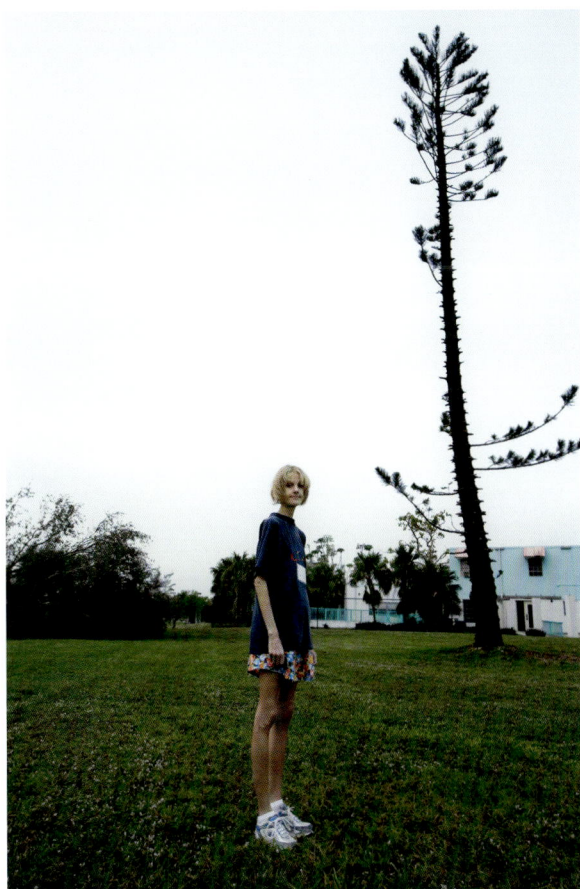

CARA, 31, FROM BATAVIA, ILLINOIS, LOST 60 POUNDS IN TWO MONTHS DURING HER FRESHMAN YEAR OF HIGH SCHOOL. AFTER 18 YEARS OF DISORDERED EATING, CARA SUFFERS FROM SEVERE INTESTINAL PROBLEMS AND HAS HAD A DIFFICULT TIME RE-FEEDING. from the project 'THIN'
2006
Lauren Greenfield, born 1966, Boston.

A chronicler of youth culture, gender issues and consumerism in the late capitalist era, Greenfield studied visual and environmental studies at Harvard University, graduating in 1987. After an internship at *National Geographic* magazine, she received a grant to support her first photographic monograph, *Fast Forward: Growing Up in the Shadow of Hollywood* (1997). Her work has subsequently been published and exhibited extensively, and is held in major museum collections including San Francisco Museum of Modern Art and the Art Institute of Chicago. Greenfield is also a celebrated documentary filmmaker: *The Queen of Versailles* won 'U.S. Directing Award: Documentary' at the Sundance Film Festival (2012) and *Generation Wealth* (2018) was nominated for the 'WGA Award for Best Documentary'. Her directorial debut, 'THIN', is a film and photographic essay about the treatment of eating disorders at the Renfrew Center in Coconut Creek, Florida, where she lived for six months to make the project. Revealing the subjects' struggles for recovery, Greenfield describes it as part of her 'decade-long exploration of body image and the way the female body has become a primary expression of identity for girls and women in our time'.

KATHARINA GROSSE

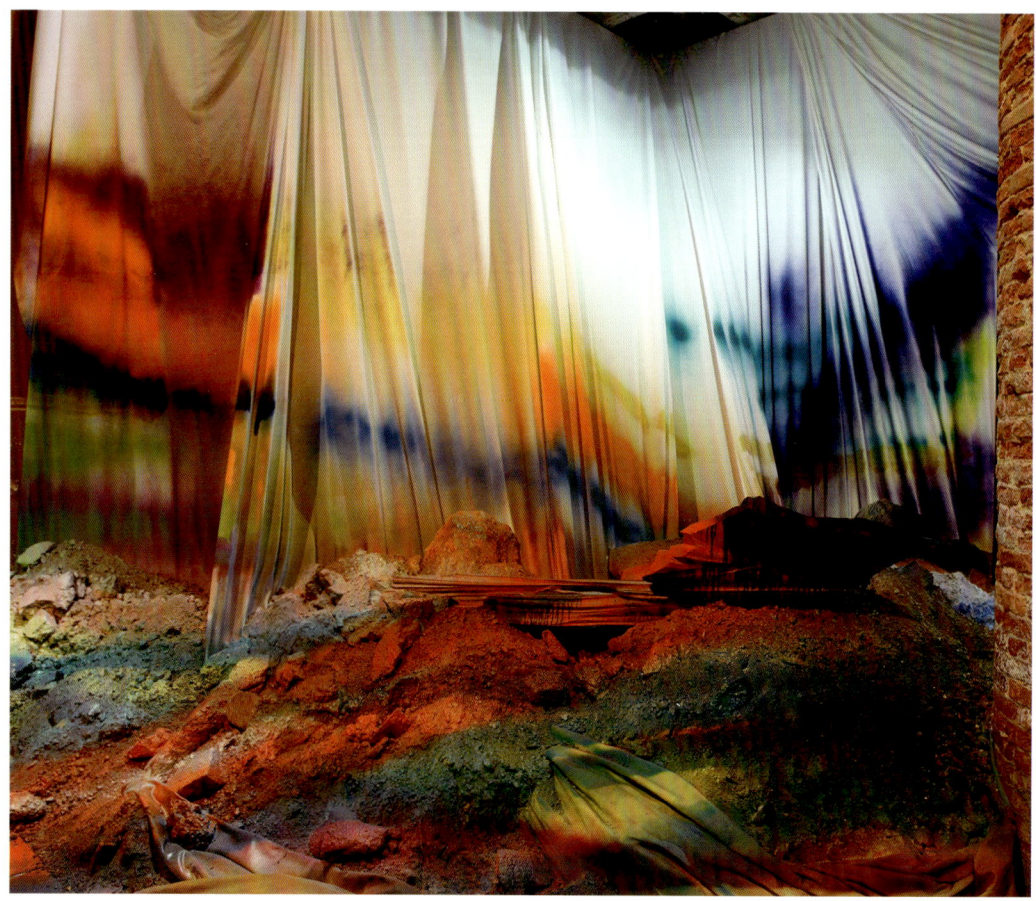

UNTITLED TRUMPET

2015, acrylic on wall, floor and various objects, 660 × 2,100 × 1,300 cm
(260 × 827 × 512 in), installation view, 'All the World's Futures', 56th Venice Biennale
Katharina Grosse, born 1961, Freiburg im Breisgau, Germany.

Redefining the boundaries that usually separate the categories of architecture, sculpture and painting, Grosse creates large-scale installations that blend all three. As she wrote in 2015: 'I do not see borders … between foreground or background, nor between the visible and the invisible.' Growing up in southern Germany, she moved north to study art in Münster and Düsseldorf, and since 2010 has been a professor at the Düsseldorf Kunstakademie. Reflecting the exuberance of expressionist painting, Grosse's installations also connect with artistic traditions of mural making and the subculture of graffiti art, recognizing their political meanings and emotional impact. With a vibrant colour palette, she uses high-pressure acrylic spray paints to psychedelic effect, a vortex of pigment covering materials including mounds of earth, balloons, furniture and fabric – often in very large quantities, draped from ceiling to floor to fill cavernous spaces. She has even tackled whole buildings, such as at *Rockaway!* (2016) at Fort Tilden in Queens, New York. *Untitled Trumpet* was a site-specific installation for the Arsenale exhibition at the 56th Venice Biennale, the red-brick columns of the historic industrial space punctuating a colourful landscape of fabric, soil and Styrofoam.

WHEN RACISM & SEXISM ARE NO LONGER FASHIONABLE, WHAT WILL YOUR ART COLLECTION BE WORTH?

The art market won't bestow mega-buck prices on the work of a few white males forever. For the 17.7 million you just spent on a single Jasper Johns painting, you could have bought at least one work by all of these women and artists of color.

Bernice Abbott	Elaine de Kooning	Dorothea Lange	Sarah Peale
Anni Albers	Lavinia Fontana	Marie Laurencin	Ljubova Popova
Sofonisba Anguisolla	Meta Warwick Fuller	Edmonia Lewis	Olga Rosanova
Diane Arbus	Artemisia Gentileschi	Judith Leyster	Nellie Mae Rowe
Vanessa Bell	Marguérite Gérard	Barbara Longhi	Rachel Ruysch
Isabel Bishop	Natalia Goncharova	Dora Maar	Kay Sage
Rosa Bonheur	Kate Greenaway	Lee Miller	Augusta Savage
Elizabeth Bougereau	Barbara Hepworth	Lisette Model	Vavara Stepanova
Margaret Bourke-White	Eva Hesse	Paula Modersohn-Becker	Florine Stettheimer
Romaine Brooks	Hannah Hoch	Tina Modotti	Sophie Taeuber-Arp
Julia Margaret Cameron	Anna Huntingdon	Berthe Morisot	Alma Thomas
Emily Carr	May Howard Jackson	Grandma Moses	Marietta Robusti Tintoretto
Rosalba Carriera	Frida Kahlo	Gabriele Münter	Suzanne Valadon
Mary Cassatt	Angelica Kauffmann	Alice Neel	Remedios Varo
Constance Marie Charpentier	Hilma of Klimt	Louise Nevelson	Elizabeth Vigée Le Brun
Imogen Cunningham	Kathe Kollwitz	Georgia O'Keeffe	Laura Wheeling Waring
Sonia Delaunay	Lee Krasner	Meret Oppenheim	

Please send $ and comments to:
Box 1056 Cooper Sta. NY, NY 10276 **GUERRILLA GIRLS** CONSCIENCE OF THE ART WORLD

WHEN RACISM & SEXISM ARE NO LONGER FASHIONABLE, WHAT WILL YOUR ART COLLECTION BE WORTH?

1989, offset lithograph on paper, 43.2 × 55.9 cm (17 × 22 in)
Guerrilla Girls, active from 1985.

Guerrilla Girls are an anonymous group of art activists, with a unified philosophy and strong visual identity, whose members use gorilla masks and take the names of historic female artists to disguise their identities. Deploying provocative language and direct humour, they highlight gender bias and racial inequality in the art world and beyond, to prompt a redressing of imbalances. The group originated in 1985 with a protest at New York's Museum of Modern Art exhibition 'An International Survey of Recent Painting and Sculpture'. Out of 165 artists only 13 were women and the show also featured very few artists of colour. Five years later, their most recognizable work, *Do Women Have to be Naked to Get into the Met. Museum?* applied their trademark mask to an image of the famous reclining nude of 1814, *La Grand Odalisque* by Jean-Auguste-Dominique Ingres. Using the aesthetics and media of propaganda and advertising – posters, fliers, stickers, books and billboards – as well as public protests and interventions, their practice is driven by and subverts the metrics and data of capitalism. This piece, produced at a time of soaring prices in the art market, highlights disparities and questions the very notion of 'value' in art.

SHILPA GUPTA

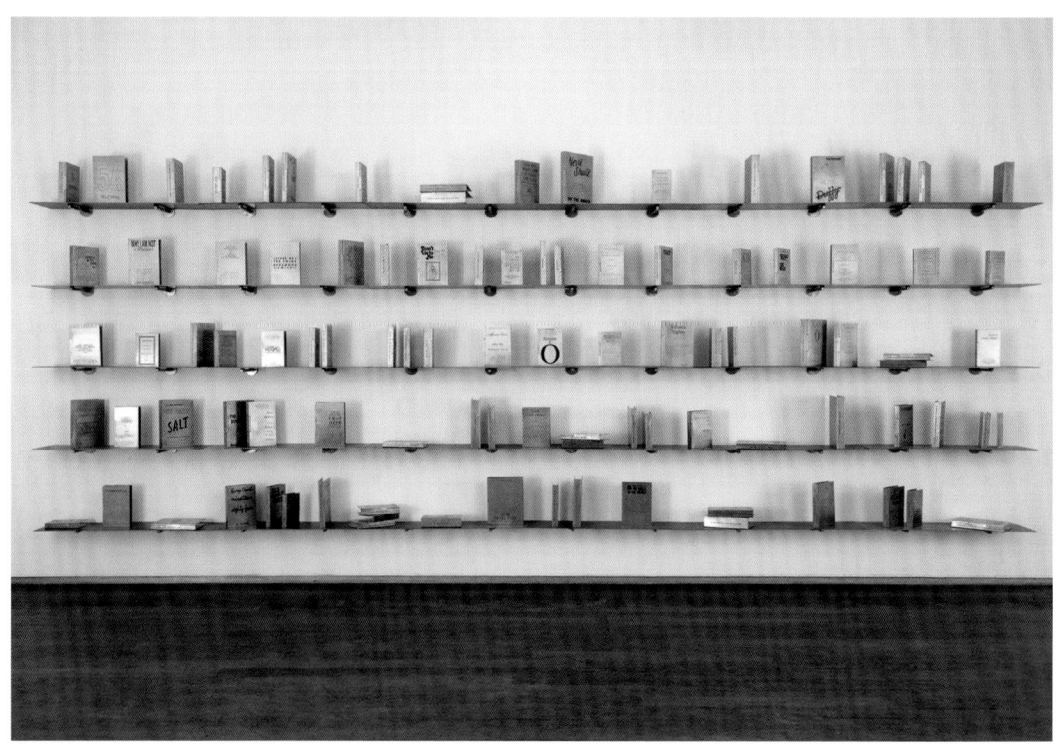

SOMEONE ELSE – A LIBRARY OF 100 BOOKS WRITTEN ANONYMOUSLY OR UNDER PSEUDONYMS

2011–13, etched stainless steel, 190 × 488 × 22 cm (72 × 192 × 8.5 in), Kiran Nadar Museum of Art, New Delhi
Shilpa Gupta, born 1976, Bombay (now Mumbai), India.

India's increasing global influence in the 1990s following economic reforms and entry into world markets coincided with the emergence of a young generation of artists on the international stage, Gupta among them. She deploys a range of media – including video, performance, sound and installation – to create participatory experiences that articulate social injustices. Often establishing an interactive relationship with her audience, she encourages the scrutiny of cultural discrimination and authoritarian infrastructures on both a local and international scale. Playing upon popular anxieties and imagined threats, Gupta attempts to reclaim and rearticulate the voices of those who are silenced or repressed. Presented at the 11th Sharjah Biennial (2013), *Someone Else…* exemplifies her drive to emancipate knowledge and stimulate flows of information within and across communities. On five shelves, 100 steel books appear in a library that spans time and nationality. They are re-creations of real titles by authors who all used pseudonyms or published anonymously. The text etched on the cover offers explanations for this; for example, J.K. Rowling used the initialized form to disguise her gender. Highlighting the burden of a name, the books memorialize the prejudices individuals face and the cost of expression.

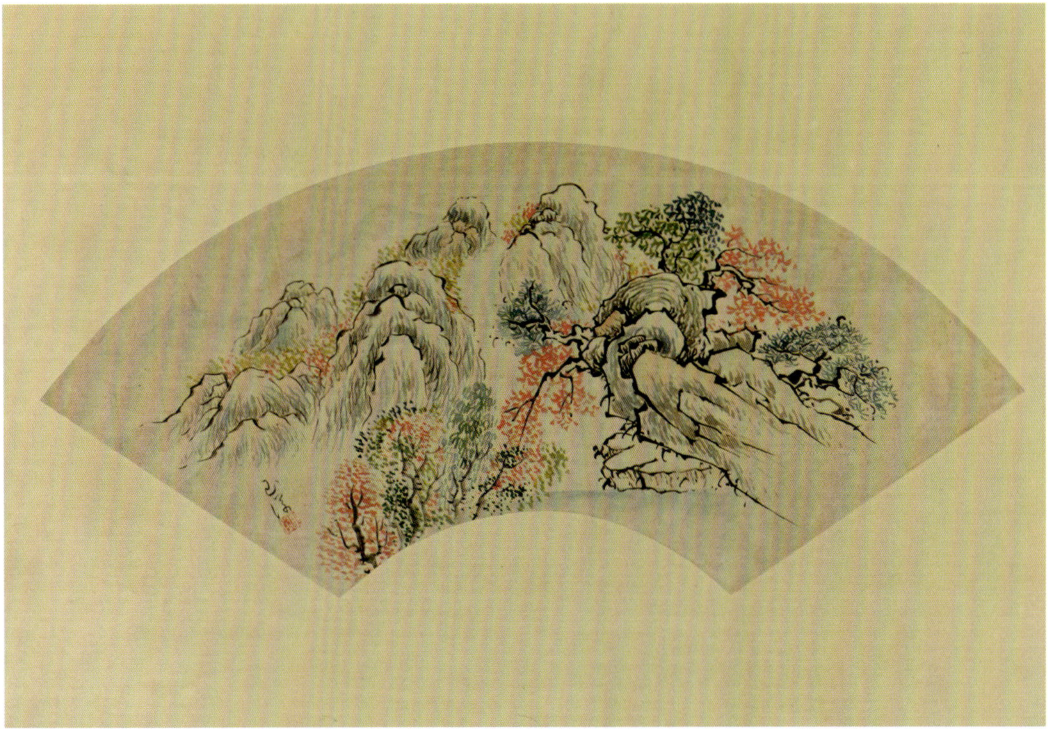

AUTUMNAL LANDSCAPE

18th century, fan mounted as a hanging scroll, ink and colour on paper, 19.1 × 52.3 cm (7 ½ × 20 ⅝ in), Metropolitan Museum of Art, New York
Ike Gyokuran, born Tokuyama Machi, 1727, Kyoto. Died 1784, Kyoto.

The wife of artist Ike Taiga (1723–76), Gyokuran achieved recognition at the height of Japan's Edo period, an age of significant cultural development despite the country's isolationist stance, with Chinese traditions of art and philosophy especially influential. As a girl she studied under the tutorship of the eminent artist Yanagisawa Kien (1703–58), who bestowed on her the name Gyokuran – the Eastern tradition of the 'art name' indicating continuity between teacher and student – and possibly introduced her to her husband. Their marriage was one of equals, unusual at the time, sharing a studio and playing music together. She taught him poetry in the *waka* style; in turn he introduced her to *nanga* – rarefied pen-and-ink landscapes characterized by delicate colours and an abstracted, almost calligraphic style that aimed to capture the rhythms of nature, not merely its appearance. Stemming from an intellectual movement that eschewed more commercial Japanese art, Gyokuran's paintings often incorporating her own poetry, they none the less also decorated practical objects like screens, sliding doors and fans. *Autumnal Landscape* shows her distinctive, unorthodox brushwork, its exaggerated lines and shading suggesting depth and texture.

ELISABETH HAARR

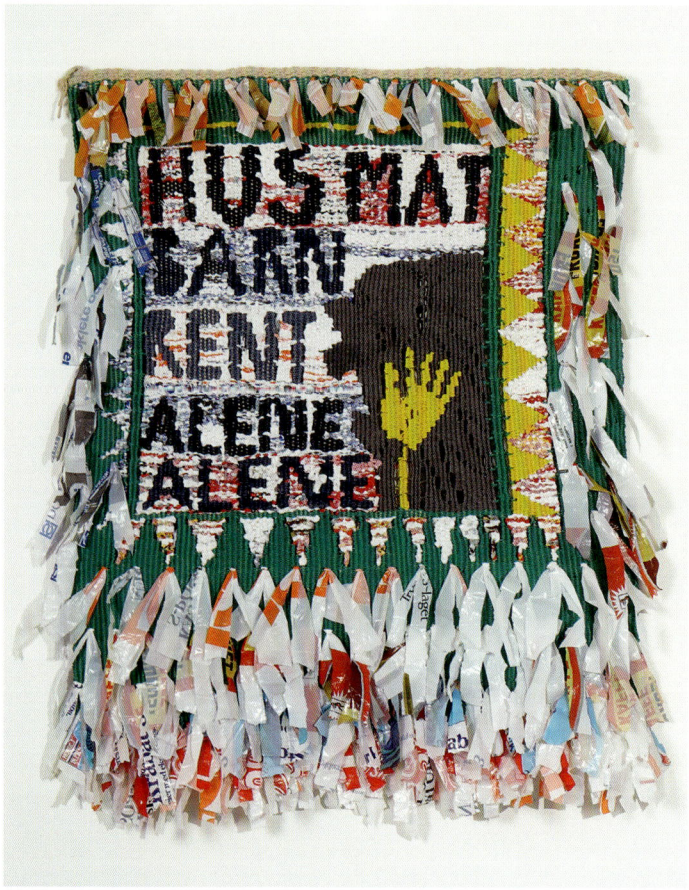

FRUSTRATION RUG
1982, strings, nappy bags, grocery bags, nylon and polyester, 150 × 120 cm (59 × 47¼ in), Nordenfjeldske Kunstindustri-museum, Trondheim, Norway
Elisabeth Haarr, born 1945, Hamar, Norway. Died 2025, Kristiansand, Norway.

Haarr's work addresses the politics of weaving, looking at how textiles play an essential role in every human culture, symbolizing status and identity as well as offering practical protection. Throughout her career she drew on this universal history, from pre-Columbian Andean traditions to the Bauhaus weaving of Anni Albers (p.29), and particularly, Scandinavian rya (knotted-pile woolen rugs). Studying in the mid-1960s at Oslo's National Academy of Crafts and Art Industry, at the end of that decade she participated in an experimental textile biennial in Spain, with her first solo show in 1973 at the Oslo Art Association. The Chilean coup of that year inspired her to confront contemporary politics, a theme that has continued up to the Syrian Civil War. Haarr's feminist work includes this hanging rug, which reads, 'HOUSE HOME / CHILDREN / CLEAN / ALONE / ALONE'. It expressed the artist's feelings of frustration while being a housewife and mother of young children in the early 1980s. Using materials including nappies and grocery bags, she highlights the materiality of domestic labour. The knotting of plastic strips recalls the tradition of *båtrya*, boat rugs crafted by women for their husbands going off to sea.

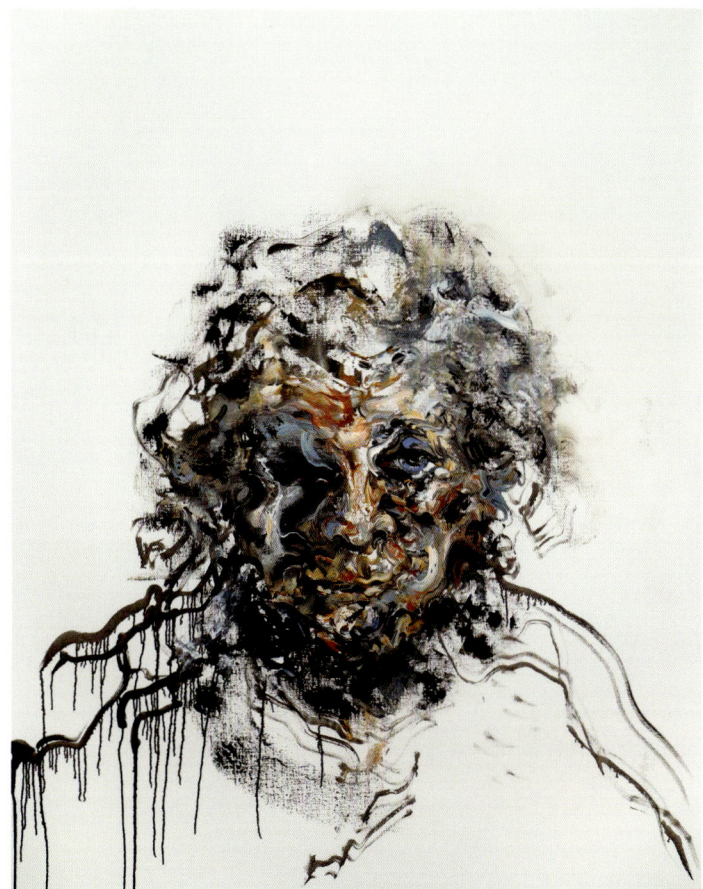

SELF-PORTRAIT

2017, oil on canvas, 152.4 × 121.9 cm (60 × 48 in), private collection
Maggi Hambling CBE, born 1945, Sudbury, Suffolk, UK.

Hambling is best known for her portraits, public sculpture and celebrated paintings of the North Sea, which were exhibited in 2014–15 upon the artist's return to the National Gallery, London, where she had inaugurated the 'Artist in Residence' programme back in 1980. Having been commissioned to create memorial sculptures to celebrate writer Oscar Wilde (completed 1998) and composer Benjamin Britten (completed 2003), in London and Suffolk respectively, in 2018 she was selected to make the first commemorative statue of eighteenth-century, feminist writer Mary Wollstonecraft. Hambling also paints portraits of people, living and dead, with underlying themes of human vulnerability and fragility. As a means of coping with death and grief, she depicted her mother and father as well as the muse, Henrietta Moraes, in their burial coffins. In this self-portrait, the artist's face dissolves into a frenzy of coloured curls and loops that connect rhythmically with an unkempt, monochrome thatch of hair. Her left eye stares intently out of the folds of wrinkled skin, while her right remains shrouded in the quivery mess of paint that delineates her other features, her mouth set between a scowl and a grin. The piercing blue eye conveys the force of Hambling's personality in a brutally candid portrait of ageing.

ANN HAMILTON

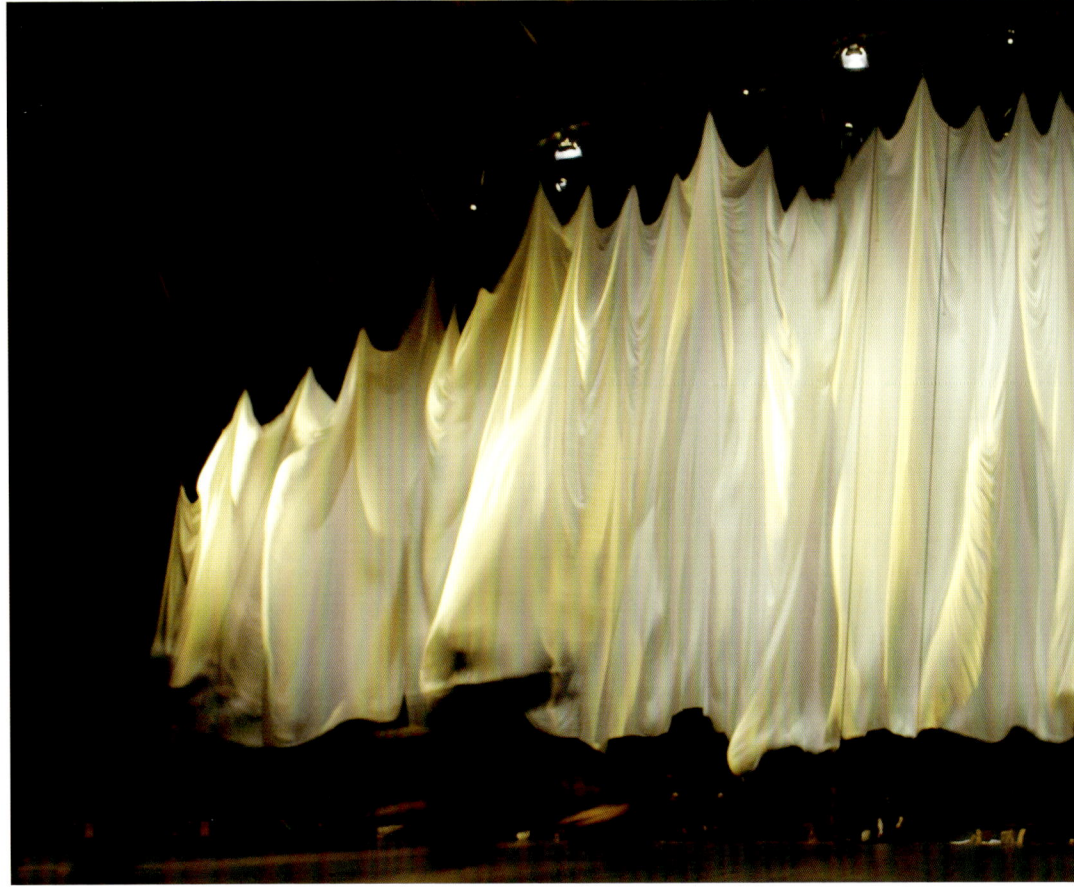

THE EVENT OF A THREAD

2012, silk fabric, swings, human voices, pigeons and recordings, dimensions variable, installation view, Park Avenue Armory, New York
Ann Hamilton, born 1956, Lima, Ohio.

After completing a BA in textile design at the University of Kansas, Hamilton lived in Canada before pursuing an MFA in sculpture at Yale School of Art in the early 1980s. Working with video, sound and interactive installation, she incorporates elements of time, change and decay into her multimedia art. Unsatisfied with the flatness of textiles, she increasingly made quasi-participatory works from the early 1990s, placing solitary performers in tightly controlled environments, asking them to conduct repetitive tasks and frequently incorporating sounds and smells into the performances. Her installations animate the spaces that contain them, often using objects that reflect the history and identity of these places. *The Event of a Thread* was a fully participatory work installed at Park Avenue Armory in New York. A large-scale intervention that enhanced the building's architecture by hanging an immense, diaphanous white curtain across the centre of the 5,110-square-metre (55,000-square-foot) Wade Thompson Drill Hall, visitors were invited to sit on swings attached to the curtain that, when in use, caused the fabric to billow and flutter. If people were not using the swings, therefore, the artwork was not complete.

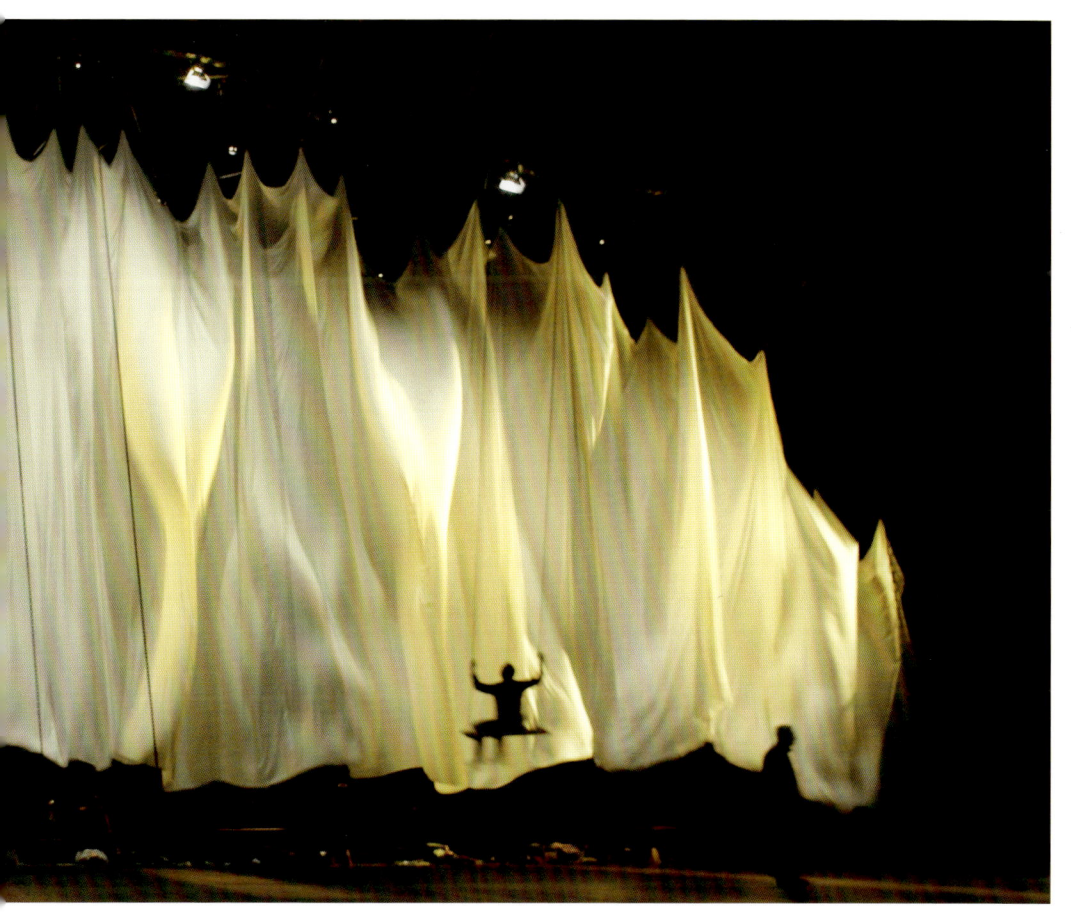

MARGARET HARRISON

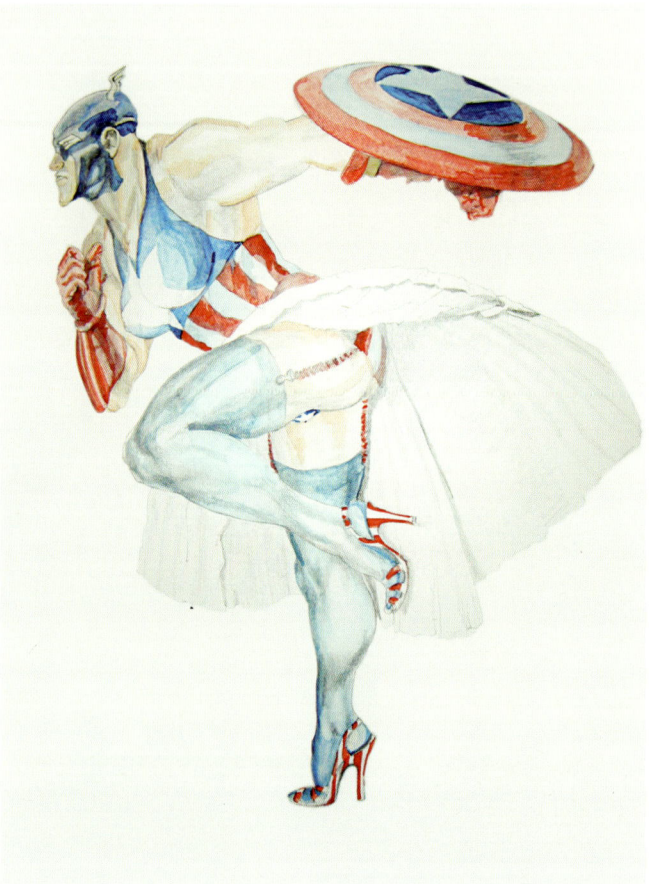

CAPTAIN AMERICA

1971/1997, watercolour and graphite on paper, 74 × 55 cm (29 ⅛ × 21 ⅝ in)
Margaret Harrison, born 1940, Wakefield, UK.

Harrison studied first in Carlisle and later, in the early 1960s, at the
Royal Academy Schools. Living in London's Notting Hill Gate,
she was able to browse American comic books and discovered the
underground cartoons of Robert Crumb (b.1943), Eric Stanton
(1926–1999) and *Oz Magazine*. The protests of 1968, with student
uprisings in Europe and continued opposition to the Vietnam War,
marked the point where the artist was politicized, and in 1970 she
founded the Women's Liberation Art Group. In this early example
of her work, she references comic culture alongside Pop art through
a feminist sensibility. Depicting Captain America with breasts and
wearing a stars-and-stripes basque, this work parodies a potent symbol of Western identity and challenges ideas of macho masculinity
as well as heteronormative sexuality. This work was first exhibited
in a solo show of Harrison's work at the Motif Editions Gallery,
London, the event being closed by police after just one day on grounds
of indecency and what was deemed a demeaning portrayal of men.
Harrison recalls that it was the reaction to this exhibition that
heightened the feminist politics that have underpinned her practice
ever since.

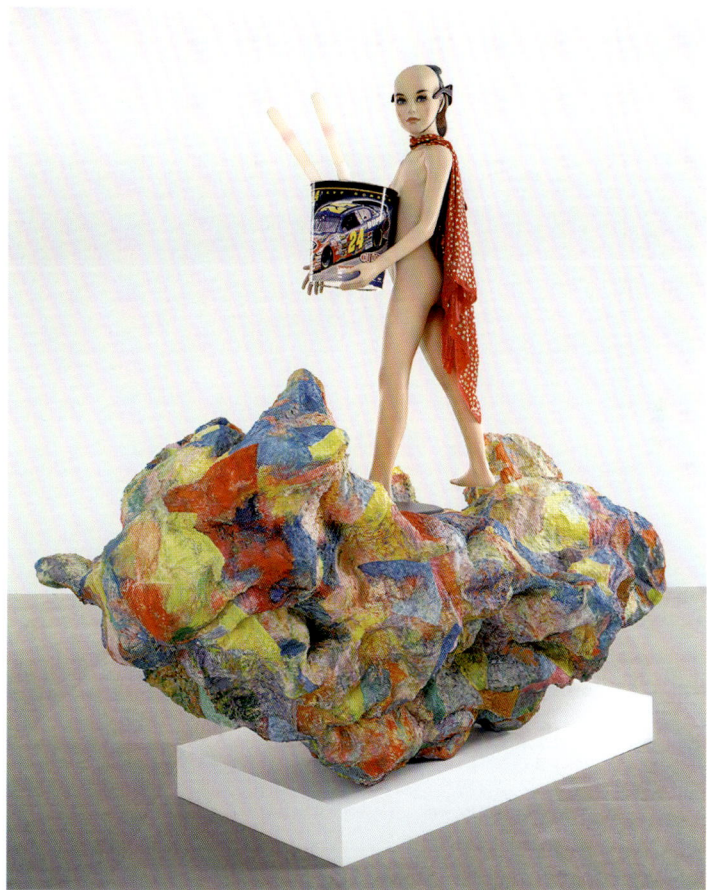

ALEXANDER THE GREAT
2007, wood, chicken wire, polystyrene, cement, acrylic, mannequin, Jeff Gordon
wastebasket, plastic Abraham Lincoln mask, sunglasses, fabric, necklace and
2 unidentified items, 231.1 × 221 × 101.6 cm (91 × 85 × 40 in), Museum of Modern
Art, New York
Rachel Harrison, born 1966, New York.

Lurid abstract forms and found objects combine in riotous polyphony
in Harrison's sculptural installations. Made of polystyrene covered
in cement, these often unwieldy assemblages are densely packed with
wry cultural references. They evoke Pop art and neo-Dada, yet
speak their own distinctive language that fuses high and low art, craft
and the ready-made, abstraction and representation. After gaining
a BA in Fine Art at Wesleyan University in Middletown, Connecticut,
in 1989, Harrison came to critical attention in the mid-1990s, evading categorization through her endlessly eclectic, multidisciplinary
practice. This work belongs to a series named after famous men,
from sixteenth-century explorer Amerigo Vespucci to contemporary
politician Al Gore and actor Johnny Depp. Each is loaded with seemingly random associations. Here, the titular warrior (356–323 BC) is
presented as a shop mannequin, holding a NASCAR-branded wastebasket. Standing astride a brightly painted rock-like form, on the
back of the head is a mask of Abraham Lincoln, wearing sunglasses.
The trajectory of masculine greatness across millennia is abruptly
stopped in its tracks by this contemporary gender-fluid Janus.

GRACE HARTIGAN

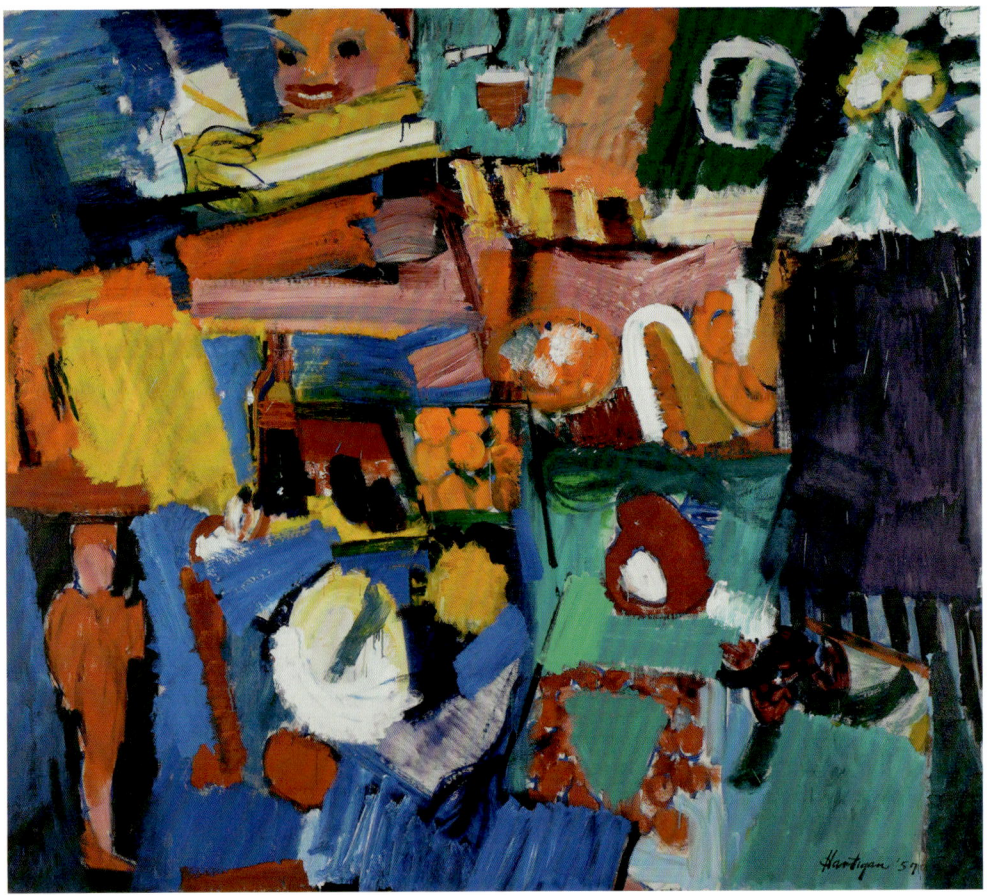

BILLBOARD

1957, oil on canvas, 199.4 × 221 cm (78½ × 87 in), Minneapolis Institute of Art
Grace Hartigan, born 1922, Newark, New Jersey. Died 2008, Baltimore.

Exploring themes of gender and popular culture, Hartigan was
a second-generation Abstract Expressionist painter whose work
anticipated Pop art in its use of motifs from everyday life. Trained
in engineering drawing during the Second World War, she experimented with watercolours in her spare time, before turning to oil
painting and full abstraction. Moving to New York in 1945 she
befriended artists including Lee Krasner (p.224), Elaine de Kooning
(p.114) and Willem de Kooning (1904–97). From the latter, she
developed an interest in Old Master painting, a tradition that overcame the divide between figuration and abstraction, leading her
to a more representational style. In 1950 influential art critic
Clement Greenberg included Hartigan in the seminal 'New Talent'
exhibition he co-curated at Kootz Gallery, although his support of her
cooled as she moved further from abstraction. Later that decade,
Hartigan was the only female painter selected for the prestigious 'New
American Painting' exhibition at the Museum of Modern Art.
Modelled on a collage of clippings from *Life* magazine, *Billboard*
demonstrates her signature style with its rich palette and bold
arrangement. Drawing on the brashness of American advertising,
the material transcends its commercial origins to transform into
something beautiful.

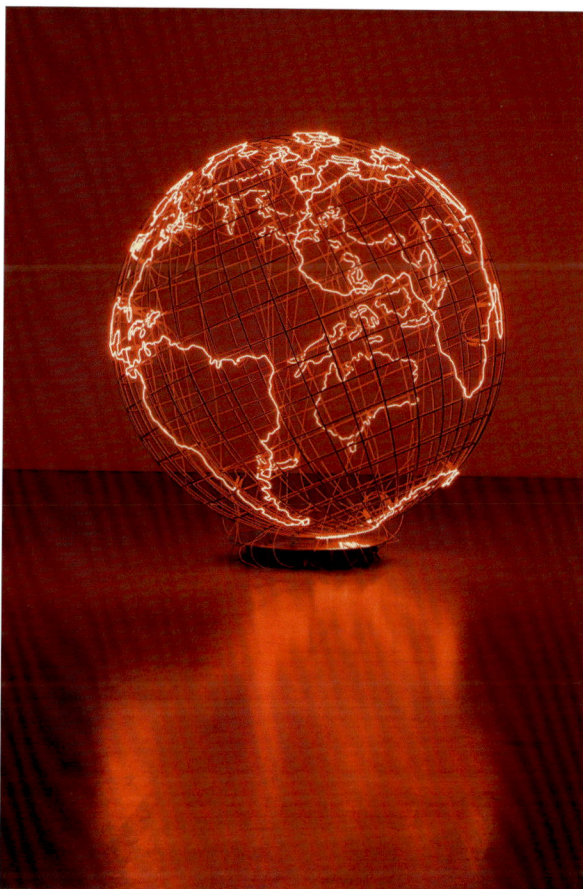

HOT SPOT III

2009, stainless steel and neon tube, 234 × 223 × 223 cm (92 ¼ × 87 ¾ × 87 ¾ in),
Sammlung Goetz, Germany
Mona Hatoum, born 1952, Beirut.

Known for sculptures made of menacingly oversized kitchen utensils
– such as *Greater Divide* (2002) with cheese graters scaled to the
size of a folding screen – Hatoum presents the entire globe as simultaneously threatened and threatening in her later series of works,
'Hot Spot' (2006–18). The title evokes sites of political unrest and
violence, a reality with which the artist is intimately familiar.
Hatoum, born in Beirut to Palestinian parents who were exiled
in Lebanon, was herself stranded in London during a visit in 1975
when the Lebanese Civil War broke out, preventing her return.

In an era of conflict and climate change, the whole world is becoming
a figurative, and in some cases literal, hot spot. Buzzing red neon
traces the outlines of landmasses and also radiates colour to saturate
the entire gallery space with an ominous glow. The globe, whose
lines of latitude and longitude are described in a stainless steel frame,
is large enough for a human to fit inside, suggesting that there
is no other planet to which we might escape; humanity is trapped,
as if in a cage, on an increasingly dangerous Earth.

SHARON HAYES

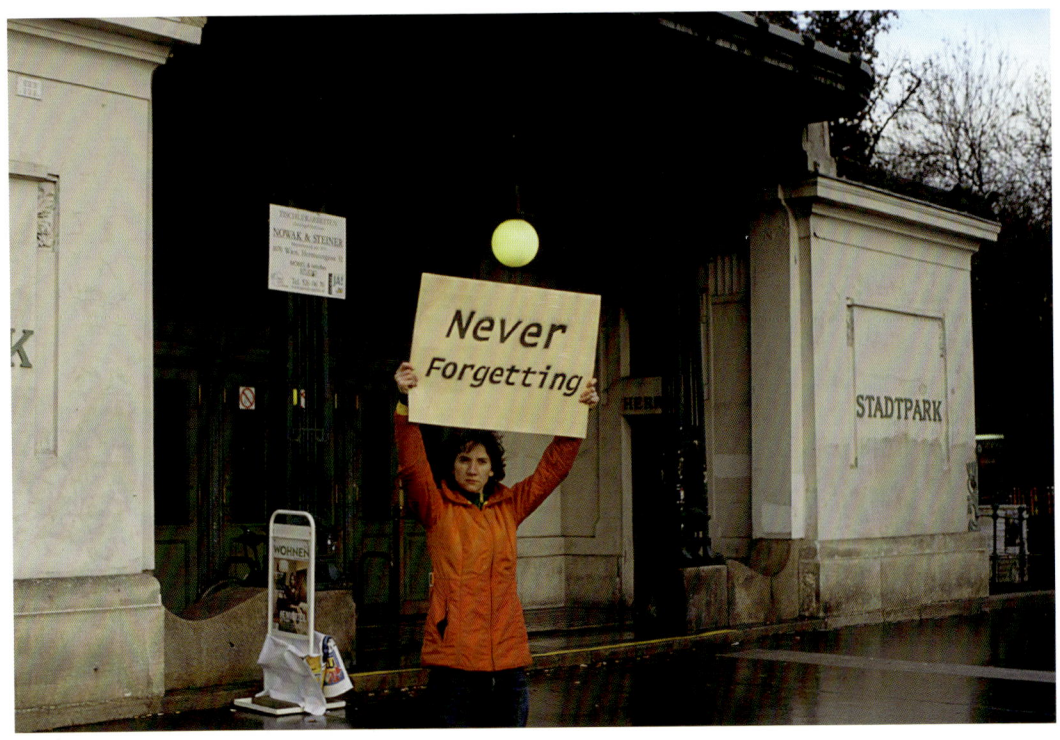

IN THE NEAR FUTURE

2009, 35mm multiple slide projection installation, 13 actions, 13 projections,
1,053 slides, dimensions variable
Sharon Hayes, born 1970, Baltimore.

Hayes's work invites the viewer to consider their relationship to social and political issues. Having studied anthropology at Bowdoin College, Maine, Hayes then attended the Whitney Museum's Independent Studio Program before completing an MFA at UCLA with foundational feminist artist Mary Kelly (p.212) in 2000. She described herself as becoming 'a feminist, a lesbian and then an artist, in that order' while at college. Moving to New York in 1991, she was involved in the downtown dance, theatre and performance scenes at the height of the AIDS crisis and came to a profound understanding of the epidemic's political nature as it impacted the queer community and individual lives. *In the Near Future* began in 2005, when for nine days in nine locations in New York, Hayes stood holding different protest signs. Many used wording from historic struggles – against the Vietnam War, gender inequality and race discrimination – which still had resonance in the present. Hayes undertook similar actions in other cities, including Brussels, London, Paris, Vienna and Warsaw, inviting the audience to visually document the performances, before combining the images in a multi-screen installation.

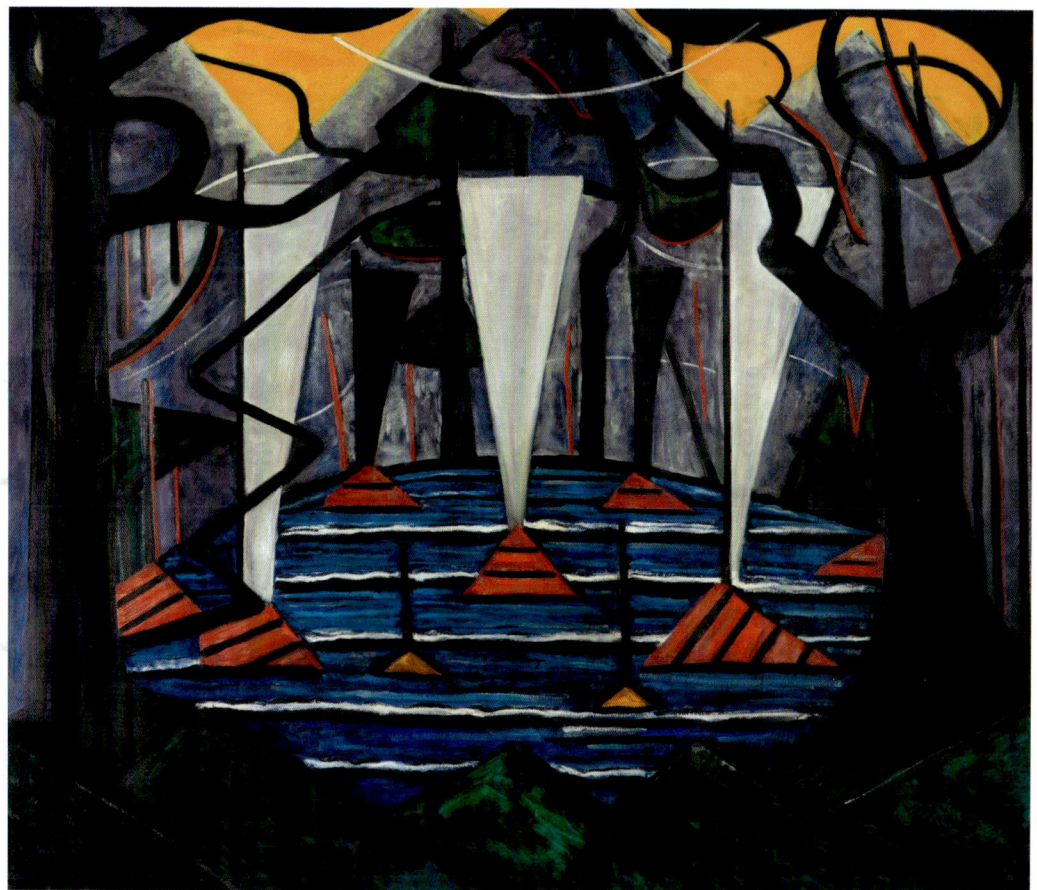

COMPOSITION NO. 23

1915, oil on canvas, 113.9 × 133.1 cm (44 ⅞ × 52 ⅜ in), Gemeentemuseum, The Hague, Netherlands
Jacoba van Heemskerck, born 1876, The Hague, Netherlands. Died 1923, Domburg, Netherlands.

After studying in The Hague, van Heemskerck travelled to Paris to train at the studio of Eugène Carrière (1849–1906), who also taught Henri Matisse (1869–1954) and Pablo Picasso (1881–1973). Returning to the Netherlands, she continued to engage with the artistic avant-garde through the collection of her friend and patron, Marie Tak van Poortvliet. The development of van Heemskerck's style followed a parallel path to that of her compatriot Piet Mondrian (1872–1944) in its gradual shift from naturalism to abstraction.

Both artists were influenced by anthroposophy – the philosophical teachings of Rudolf Steiner – and sought to express a spiritual element in their work, although while Mondrian ultimately adopted pure geometric abstraction, van Heemskerck maintained figurative elements in her compositions. This stylized painting, made the year she abandoned titling her work in favour of a numbering system, sees sailing boats and mountains rendered as simple triangular forms, while a glowing orange sky casts the foreground into near silhouette. The scene is framed by trees with heavy trunks and gnarled branches, a recurring motif in her work, which also included woodcut prints and, later, designs for stained glass.

SUSAN HEFUNA

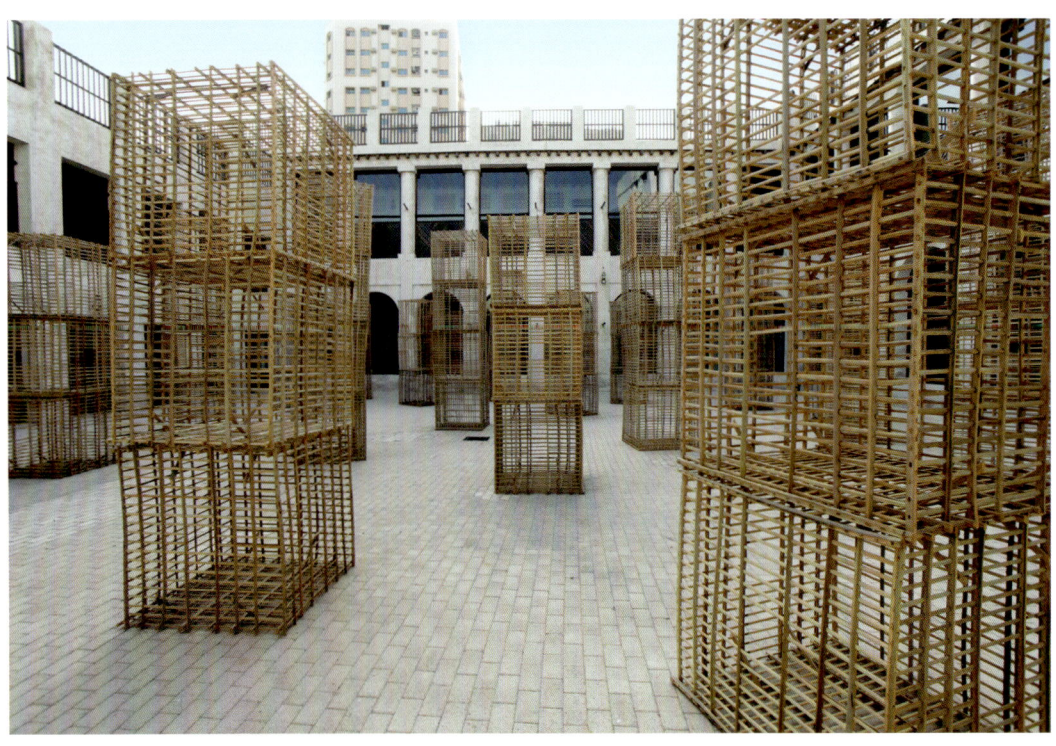

AFAZ DRAWINGS

2014, palmwood, dimensions variable, installation view, 'Another Place',
Sharjah Art Foundation, UAE
Susan Hefuna, born 1962, Berlin.

Reflecting on the relationship between architectural forms and
human connectivity, and how location and dislocation are connected,
Hefuna's drawings, digital prints and photographs explore diaspora
experiences, combining disparate imagery to negotiate multiple identities. Of German-Egyptian heritage, she lived near Alexandria
as a child before her family moved to Graz, Austria. She later studied
at Frankfurt's Institute for New Media at the Städelschule, followed
by a year's residency at Delfina Foundation, London. Urban imagery
suggestive of buildings, cages and grids populate her work, especially
the latticework *mashrabiya* screen, a recurring element in Egyptian
architecture. *Afaz Drawings* is a site-specific installation featuring
tall, open structures that nevertheless convey a sense of confinement, echoing the forms of the many skyscrapers that have recently
sprung up in the cities of the United Arab Emirates. The grid-like
imagery also represents the complexity of human networks, their
cultural boundaries and unreached interstices. Interested in the
sociopolitical actions of the Arab Spring, Hefuna exhibited at the
Serpentine Gallery in 2011 as part of 'On the Edgware Road', a
project connecting London's 'Little Cairo' community with those
tumultuous events.

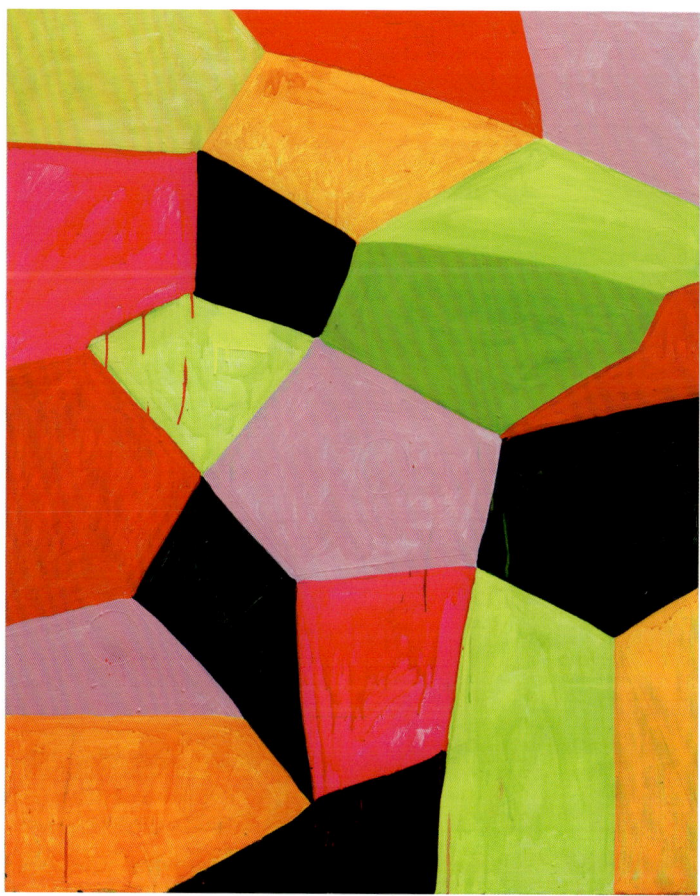

PRIMALON BALLOON

2002, oil on canvas on wood, 127 × 101.6 × 4.5 cm, (50 × 40 × 1 ¾ in),
private collection
Mary Heilmann, born 1940, San Francisco.

With a career spanning five decades, Heilmann is known for her playful and geometric approach to abstraction. She works with a variety of media including painting and ceramics, and also makes furniture. Her art is often autobiographical, including references to her personal relationships and friendships, films, music, popular culture and her artistic influences, including Henri Matisse (1869–1954) and Piet Mondrian (1872–1944). Heilmann studied poetry, then ceramics in California, before moving to New York in 1968, where she began to create paintings. Initially referring to the lines and shapes of Minimalism, using the square and grid, she integrated spots, stripes and amorphous patches of pigment from an eye-popping colour palette. In 2016 she had her first major survey exhibition in the UK, at the Whitechapel Gallery, London, displaying work from her entire career, including *Primalon Balloon*. The exhibition also featured her 1970s geometric and abstract paintings, later canvases that are shaped as if fragments of colour are conjoined, watercolour studies, wall-based ceramics and brightly painted plywood chairs, in which visitors were encouraged to sit and contemplate her work.

ANNEMARIE HEINRICH

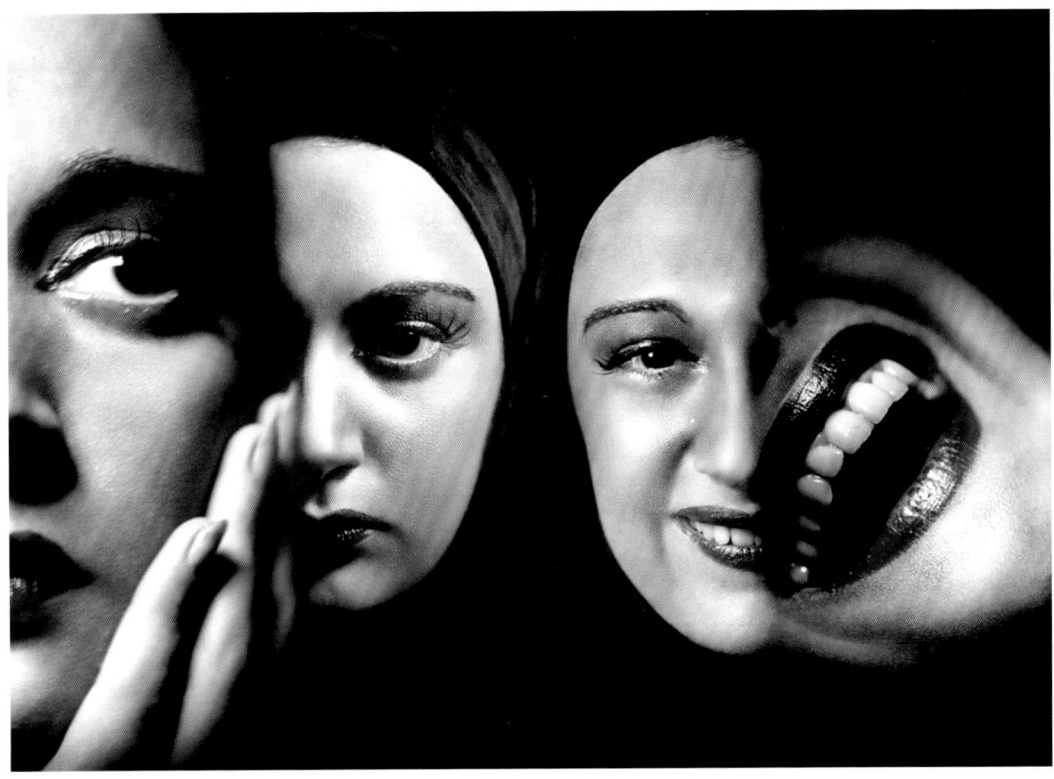

CAPRICHOS, ANITA GRIM

1936, gelatin silver print on paper (vintage print), 10 × 15 cm (3 ⅞ × 5 ⅞ in)
Annemarie Heinrich, born 1912, Darmstadt, Germany. Died 2005, Buenos Aires.

Having moved to Argentina with her parents in 1926, Heinrich grew
to become one of the country's most prominent photographers
by the early 1940s. Part of a group of modernists working under the
name *La Carpeta de los Diez* ('Group of Ten', 1952–9), she nurtured
a bold style that combined an experimental approach to the photographic image with a developed eye for portraiture – she had trained
as a high-society portrayer and a documenter of theatre, ballet and
other performing arts. In collaborative working sessions, the Group
of Ten forged an environment where modernist photography could
be discussed, analysed and exhibited, disrupting the conservative
understanding of photography that prevailed in Buenos Aires at the
time. Heinrich's use of extreme camera angles, contrasting lighting
and adjusted sharpness furthered her reputation as a pioneer of experimental portraiture, of which *Caprichos, Anita Grim* is an example.
In a photomontage of multiple-angled, close-up portraits, the sitter
is both being directly portrayed as an individual and being used
to depict the spectrum of human emotions. In 2015, a retrospective
at the Museo de Arte Latinoamericano de Buenos Aires paid homage
to her daring body of work.

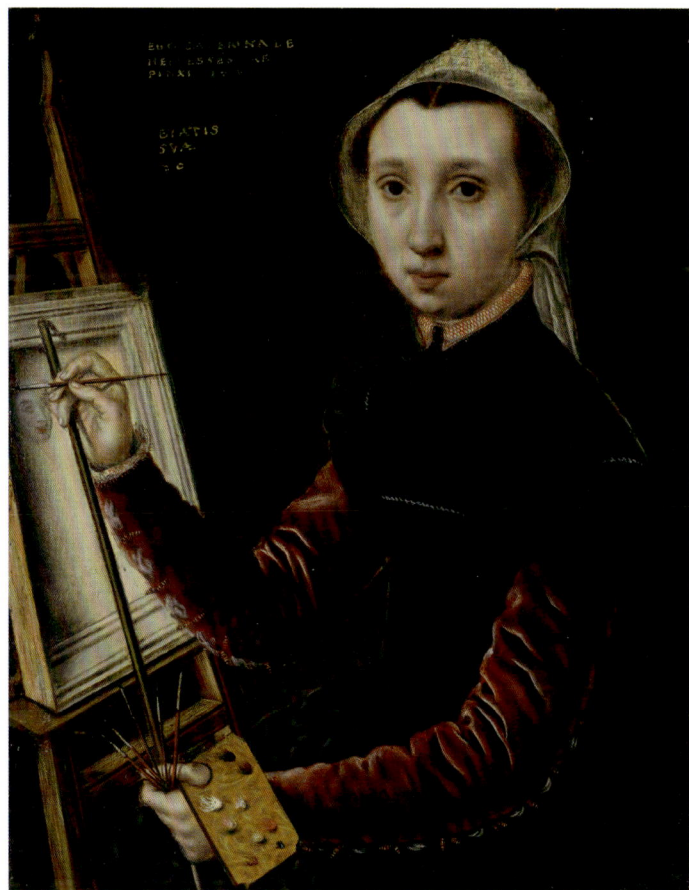

SELF-PORTRAIT AT THE EASEL

1548, oil on oak panel, 32.2 × 25.2 cm (12 ⅝ × 9 ⅞ in), Kunstmuseum
Basel, Switzerland
Catharina van Hemessen, born 1528, Antwerp, Belgium (then Duchy of Brabant).
Died after 1588, probably in Antwerp, Belgium.

A successful portraitist of the Flemish Renaissance, van Hemessen
was the daughter of painter Jan Sanders van Hemessen (*c*.1500–63).
She received training in his studio and collaborated with him on religious paintings before moving on to independent work. She had many
wealthy and noble patrons including Mary of Hungary, who was the
governor of the Netherlands on behalf of her brother, Emperor
Charles V. Indeed, Mary continued to employ van Hemessen after
abdicating her viceroyalty and the artist became part of her entourage
when she returned to Spain in 1556. This self-portrait is one of the
earliest examples in art history of an artist depicting themselves in the
act of painting – she steadies her hand on a mahlstick as she paints
the detail of a face. Her elegant clothes were not practical for painting,
but symbolized her social rank and demonstrated her skill in depicting cloths of different textures. The piece may have functioned
as an advertisement to demonstrate her abilities as a painter of portraits. As was customary at the time, she signed the back wall of the
scene in Latin, which roughly translates as: 'I Catharina van
Hemessen painted myself. 1548. Her age 20.'

CAMILLE HENROT

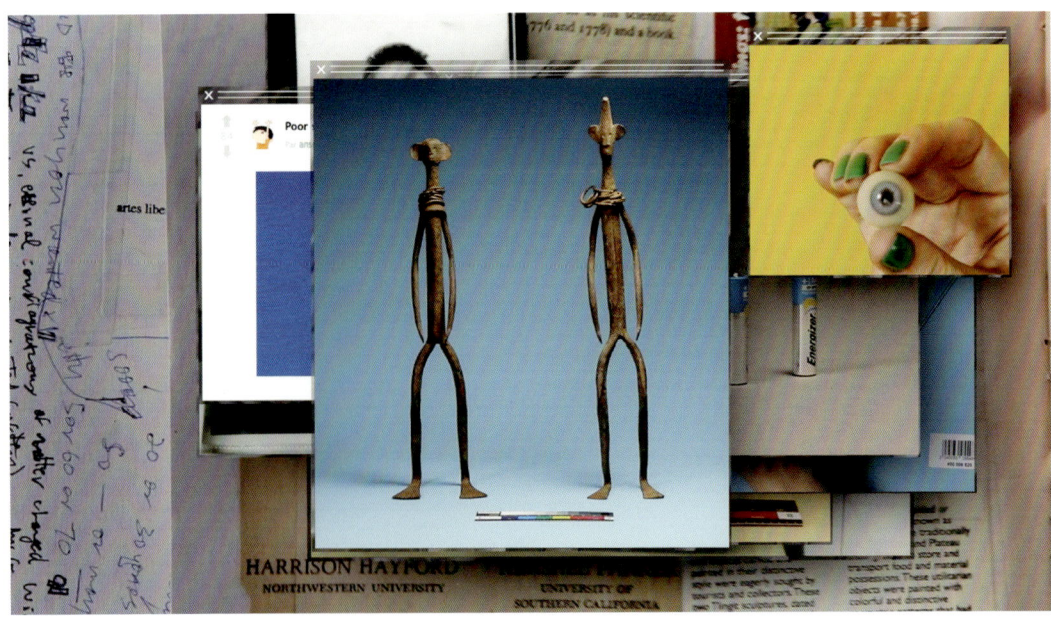

GROSSE FATIGUE

2013, video, colour, sound, 13 mins
Camille Henrot, born 1978, Paris.

With work ranging from drawing and sculpture to video installations, Henrot's diverse multimedia practice illustrates shifts in the status quo, suggesting that human agency resides in the imagination, thus enabling systems and cultures to be changed. After studying film animation in Paris, she subsequently worked in advertising, music video production and as an assistant to the artist Pierre Huyghe (b.1962). As an artist, she came to public attention for her video work *Grosse Fatigue*, for which she was awarded the Silver Lion at the 55th Venice Biennale (2013). Made during Henrot's fellowship at Washington DC's Smithsonian Institution, it depicts an everchanging cycle of overlapping computer windows, mixing footage of the Smithsonian with Internet images. A compelling audio narrative, accompanied by a driving musical beat, tells a story of the world's formation. In 2017, Henrot presented 'Days are Dogs' for the *Carte Blanche* programme at the Palais de Tokyo, Paris. The exhibition show explored the relationship between authority and fiction in shaping our existence. Each room opened up a world that represented a day of the week, a starting point for viewers to create a whole new mythology.

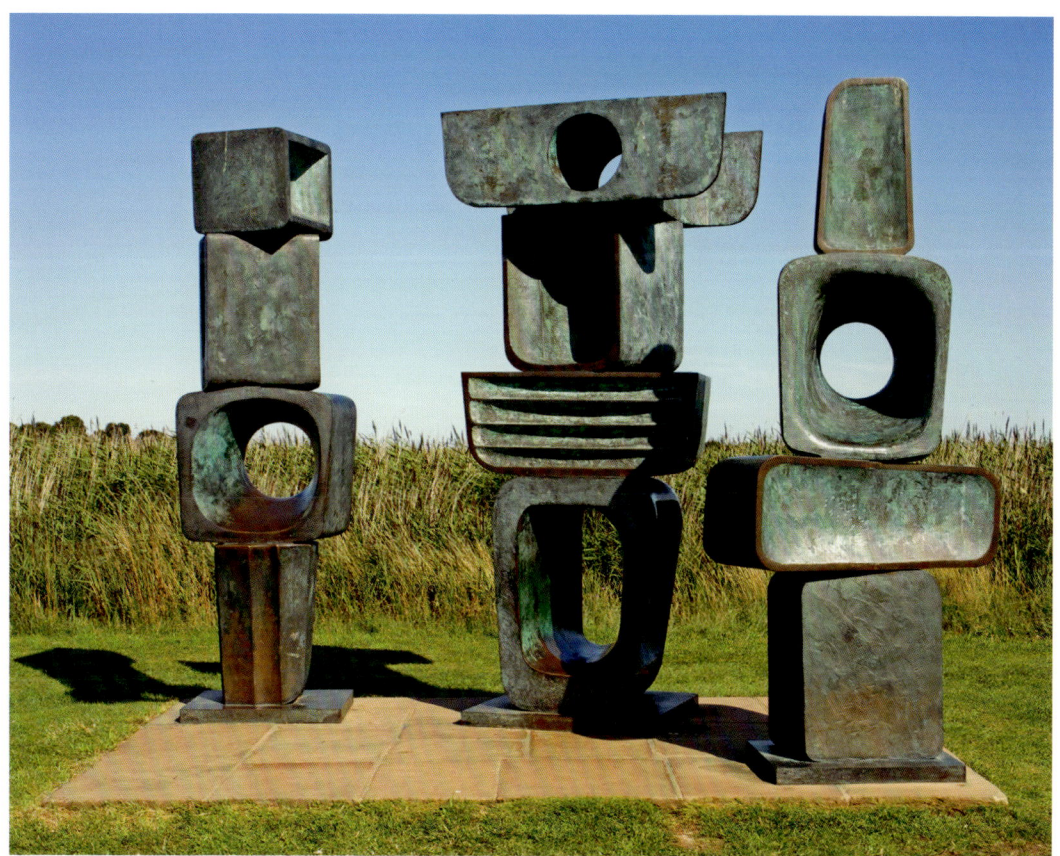

THE FAMILY OF MAN (ANCESTOR I, ANCESTOR II, PARENT I)

1970, bronze, left to right, h: 276.9 cm (109 in), h: 271.8 cm (107 in), h: 268.9 cm (105 ⅞ in), Snape Maltings, Suffolk, UK. Collection of The Fitzwilliam Museum, Cambridge, UK

Barbara Hepworth, born 1903, Wakefield, UK. Died 1975, St Ives, Cornwall, UK.

One of the best-known British sculptors of the twentieth century, Hepworth's large-scale works explore form and abstraction through methods of direct carving and casting. Having trained alongside Henry Moore (1898–1986) in Leeds from 1920 to 1921, she encountered the European avant-garde when visiting artist studios in Paris, including Piet Mondrian (1872–1944), whom she visited often and who lived as her neighbour in London from 1938 to 1939. When war broke out, Hepworth and her partner, the painter Ben Nicholson

(1894–1982) moved with their triplets from London to St Ives. Her work is primarily about human relationships at individual and societal levels, as well as between the figure and the landscape. Representing these interconnections, which for Hepworth are consciously gendered, are these three sculptures from the ensemble *The Family of Man*, one of her final works. The original title, *Nine Figures on a Hill*, points to the importance of the work's intended location. Influenced by megaliths of the ancient Cornish landscape, she wanted the components of this sculpture to appear as if they had 'risen out of the ground', making this striking example of modernism seem both pre-historic and rooted in present-day life.

CARMEN HERRERA

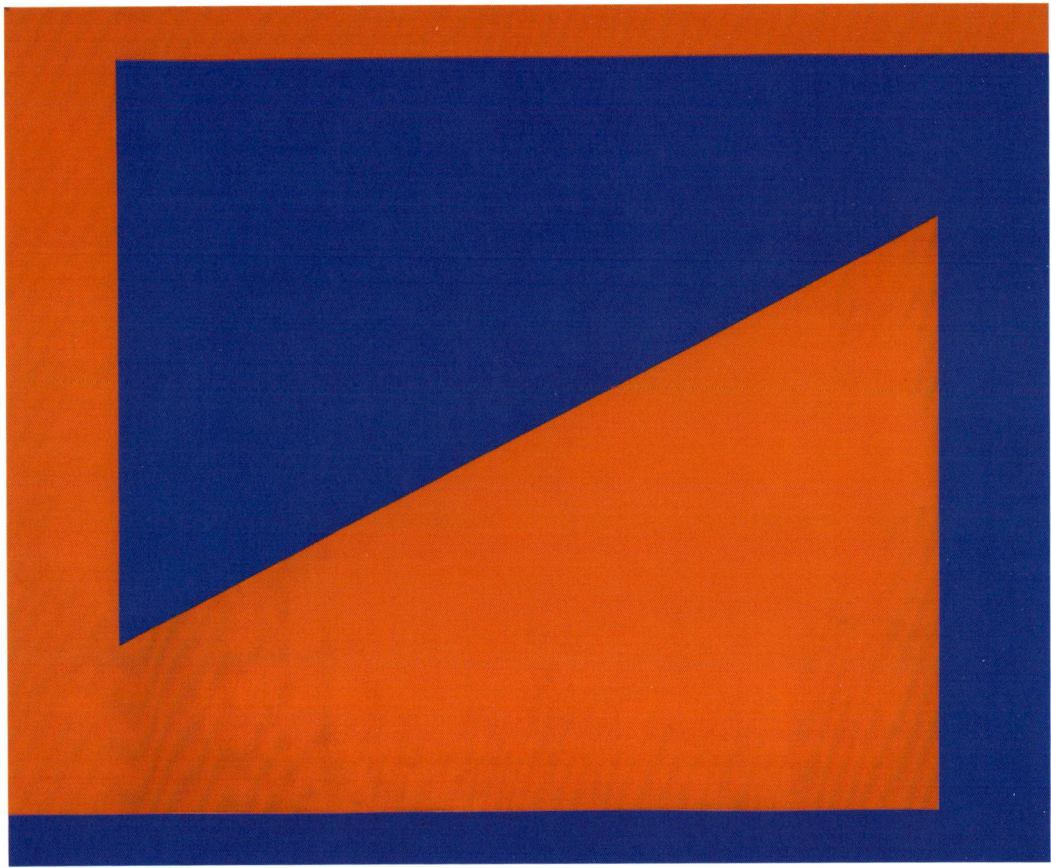

RED & BLUE

1993, acrylic on canvas, 121.9 × 152.4 cm (48 × 60 in)
Carmen Herrera, born 1915, Havana. Died 2022, New York.

Now celebrated internationally by museums, collectors and critics, Herrera did not sell a single work until the age of eighty-nine. Originally training in Havana as an architect, she began making art in earnest in the 1940s, after moving to New York with her husband, art teacher Jesse Loewenthal. Herrera's architectural training is evident in her paintings, sculptures and drawings, which primarily consist of geometric forms, rendered with mathematical precision. From 1948 to 1953 she lived in Paris, where she exhibited with the Salon des Réalités Nouvelles, an influential group of abstract artists co-founded by Sonia Delaunay (p.118). Returning to America,

however, critical and commercial recognition eluded Herrera, something she attributed to discrimination on the basis of gender at a time when painting in New York's avant-garde scene was overwhelmingly considered the preserve of the male artist. Over time, her compositions evolved towards an increasingly 'hard-edged', minimalist aesthetic characterized by straight lines and flat planes of two to three colours – this is exemplified in *Red & Blue*, which reveals Herrera's fascination with symmetry and vibrant contrast, made all the more powerful by the most essential formal schemes.

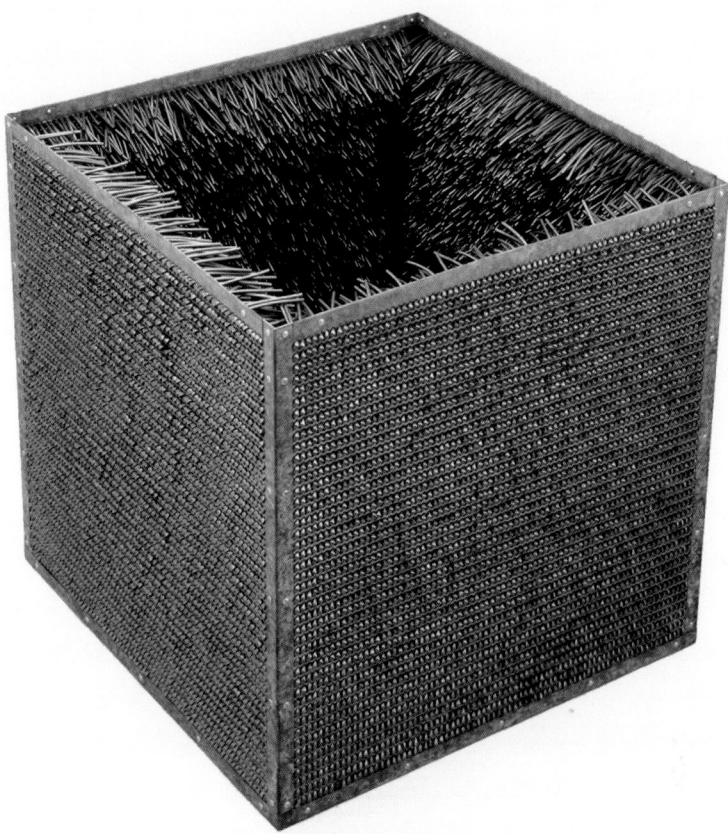

ACCESSION II

1969, galvanized steel and vinyl, 78.1 × 78.1 × 78.1 cm (30 ¼ × 30 ¼ × 30 ¼ in),
Detroit Institute of Arts, Michigan
Eva Hesse, born 1936, Hamburg, Germany. Died 1970, New York.

Born to a Jewish family, Hesse came to the United States as a refugee at the age of three, at the start of the Second World War, becoming an American citizen in 1945. She grew up in New York, and returned there after completing a bachelor's degree in fine art at Yale School of Art in 1959, before her untimely death from a brain tumour aged just thirty-four. Initially working as a textile designer, Hesse quickly became immersed in New York's artistic community. In 1962, she created costumes for 'happenings' – performances staged by Fluxus artist Allan Kaprow (1927–2006). From 1964 to 1965, she lived and

worked in a derelict factory in the Ruhr region of her native Germany. Inspired by her surroundings, she began making sculptures from unconventional and often industrial materials such as mesh, rubber, cord, latex and fibreglass. These works, celebrated for their fusion of contradictory elements, are exemplified in *Accession II*, a cube of perforated steel sheets filled with flexible hair-like tubes. Machine-like yet tactile, repetitive but exhibiting subtle differences, the work is at once geometric and organic in form, simultaneously applying and subverting the formal codes of Minimalist sculpture.

SHEILA HICKS

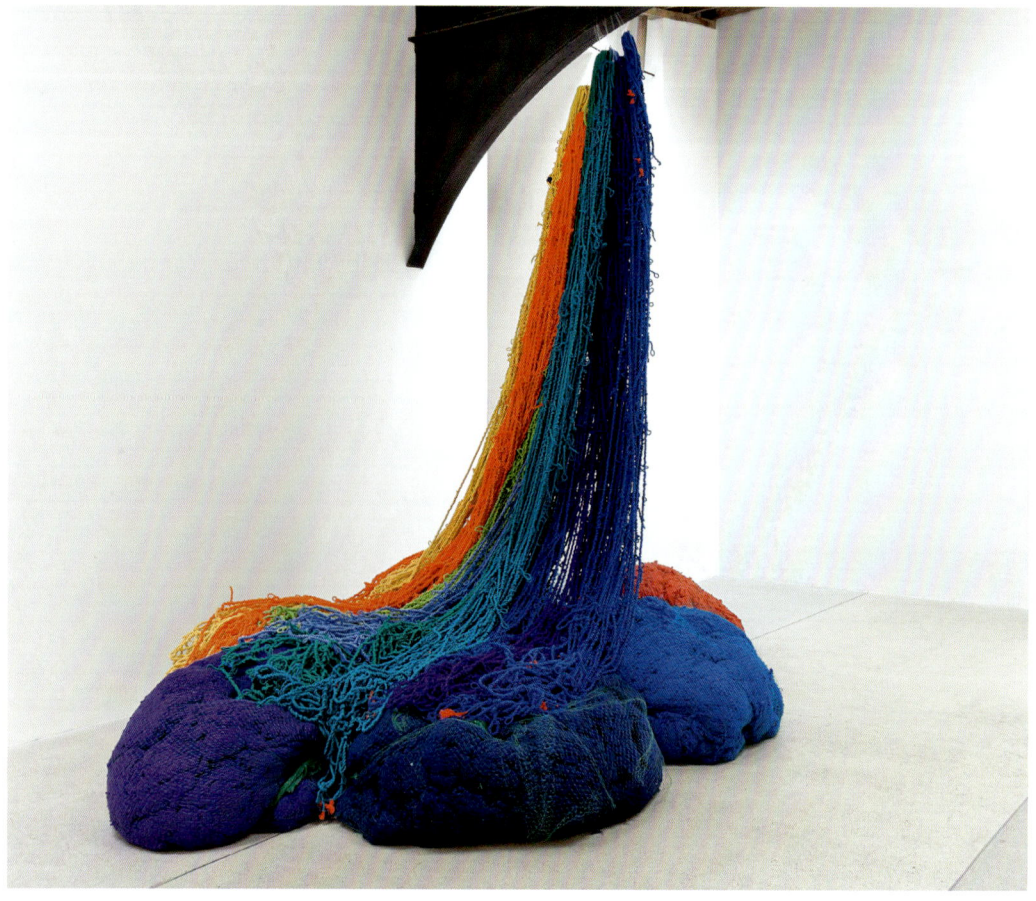

ATTERRISSAGE (LANDING)
2014, pigmented acrylic fibre and nylon fishnet, 480 × 430 × 260 cm
(189 × 169 ¼ × 102 ⅜ in), installation view, 'Unknown Data', galerie frank elbaz,
Paris. Collection Fondation Louis Vuitton, Paris
Sheila Hicks, born 1934, Hastings, Nebraska.

Using traditional textile methods in innovative ways, Hicks creates
large-scale fibre sculptures and installations, as well as intricate woven
works. Hicks initially worked in an Abstract Expressionist style while
at Yale School of Art, where she studied alongside Eva Hesse (p.185),
before becoming enthralled with Raoul d'Harcourt's book *Textiles
of Ancient Peru and Their Techniques* (originally published in Paris,
1934). Receiving a Fulbright scholarship to Chile in 1957, she toured
South America widely in order to study Andean textile traditions,
then lived in Mexico for a number of years. In 1964 she moved to
Paris, where she has remained ever since. Vibrant colour is a
recurring aspect of Hicks's work, as in this installation, where a spectrum of cords cascade from ceiling to floor, appearing to pool and
drip over biomorphic bundles that seem ready to burst from the net-
ting that confines them. The highly saturated hues, dynamism and
vast scale boldly assert the monumentality of textiles. A medium
largely ignored in the Western canon of art history due its lower status
by association with craft and objects traditionally made by women,
Hicks has pioneered its use as a viable sculptural material.

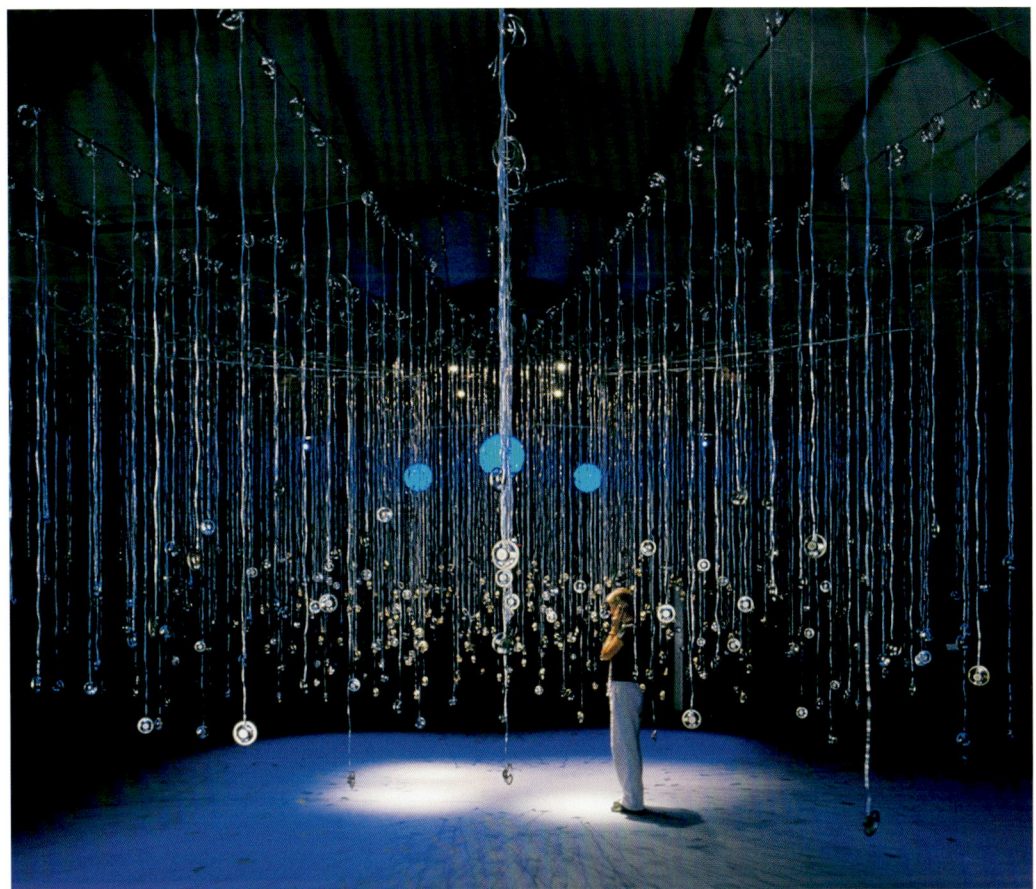

WITNESS

2000, audio-sculpture: 350 loudspeakers, 10 CD players, amplifiers, wiring, lights, etc, commissioned by Artangel, installation view, The Chapel on Golborne Road, London

Susan Hiller, born 1940, Tallahassee, Florida. Died 2019, London.

Trained initially as an anthropologist in the early 1960s, Hiller attended college in Massachusetts and Louisiana. Between her undergraduate and postgraduate courses, she spent a year in New York, studying film, photography, archaeology and linguistics. It was after gaining experience of anthropological fieldwork that she became disenchanted with the discipline's purported objectivity and decided instead to pursue a career as an artist. She moved to London in the mid-1960s, from then on producing works in video, photography and installation. Hiller draws on her academic background by referencing cultural and psychological phenomena into her pieces, also exploring parallel themes within their shadow spaces, the realms of the paranormal and the occult. In *Witness*, which was first presented in a disused chapel, Hiller created an unsettling environment: with an aesthetic akin to biomorphic sci-fi, intimate listening devices hang down to convey the testimonies of hundreds of witnesses reporting UFO sightings in the UK, Australia and the Philippines. Sounds reaching the visitor's ear reproduce the visual experiences of people across the world, the gap between these two senses giving room for the listener's imagination and interpretations to create a visualization of events.

LUBAINA HIMID

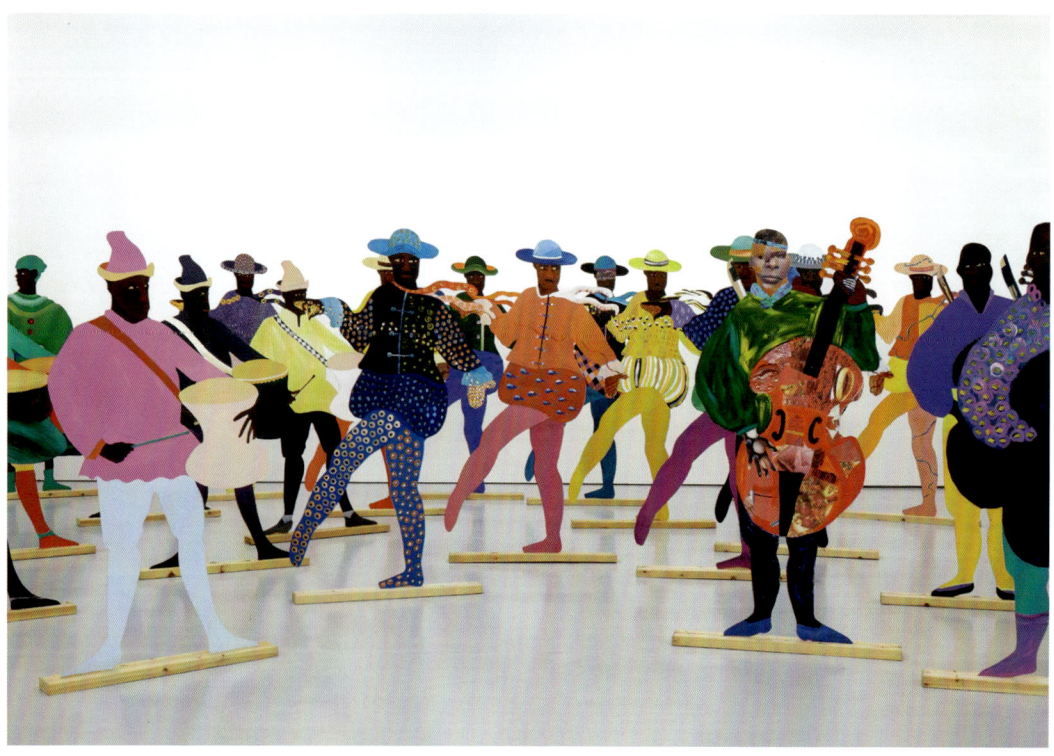

NAMING THE MONEY

2004, (detail), acrylic on wood, dimensions variable, installation view,
'Navigation Charts', Spike Island, Bristol, UK, 2017
Lubaina Himid, born 1954, Zanzibar, Tanzania.

A leading member of the radical British black arts movement in the
1980s, Himid promoted black women artists when they were largely
invisible. She curated ground-breaking exhibitions including 'Five
Black Women' at London's Africa Centre in 1983 and 'The Thin
Black Line' at the ICA in 1985, alongside continuing her own practice as a painter. Working for many years in higher education she is
Professor of Contemporary Art at the University of Central
Lancashire, UK, and in 2017 she became the first woman of colour
to win the Turner Prize. Trained as a theatre designer and cultural
historian, storytelling is at the centre of her work, especially in relation to the history of the transatlantic slave trade. *Naming the Money*
presents an exuberant crowd of 100 enslaved people, in the roles
they played in the princely courts of Europe: everything from
dog-trainers, toy makers and mapmakers to dancing masters, musicians and painters. They were bought as the 'property' of wealthy
Europeans at a time when Africans were regarded as units of cur-
rency and black servants were status symbols. Encountering these
victims of eighteenth-century human trafficking, the visitor learns
their original identities as well as those imposed on them.

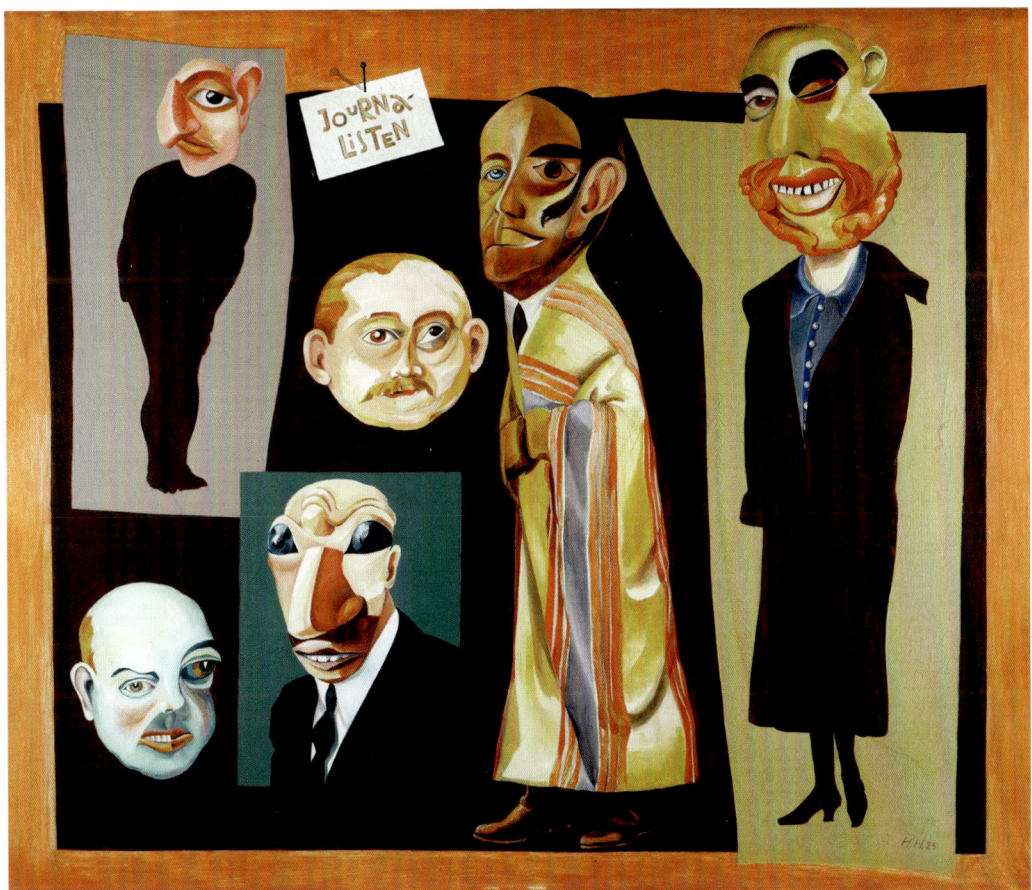

THE JOURNALISTS

1925, oil on canvas, 86 × 101 cm (33 ⅞ × 39 ¾ in), Berlinische Galerie, Berlin
Hannah Höch, born Anna Therese Johanne Höch, 1889, Gotha, Germany.
Died 1978, West Berlin.

The sole female member of Berlin's Weimar-era Dada group, Höch initially studied glassmaking at the city's applied arts school in 1912. Interrupted by the outbreak of war and service with the Red Cross, she returned three years later to study graphic design at the training institute of the museum of arts and crafts. Working on handicrafts features for Ullstein Verlag's publications from 1916 to 1926, Höch produced embroidery, lace and dress patterns, the influence of which can be seen in her collages from this period, which incorporate these designs. In her spare time, she created a radical new form of art: the photomontage. Juxtaposing found photographic images from the media, she ridiculed accepted social norms and critiqued identities as socially constructed. The grotesque painting-photomontage hybrid shown here acerbically depicts figures of the press establishment, their gender or even humanity rendered fluid and disturbed. Images like this earned Höch the Nazi label of a 'degenerate' artist and her work was banned during the Third Reich. Although exhibited in Germany and elsewhere in Europe up until 1935, her first major international retrospective did not take place until the artist was eighty-six.

CANDIDA HÖFER

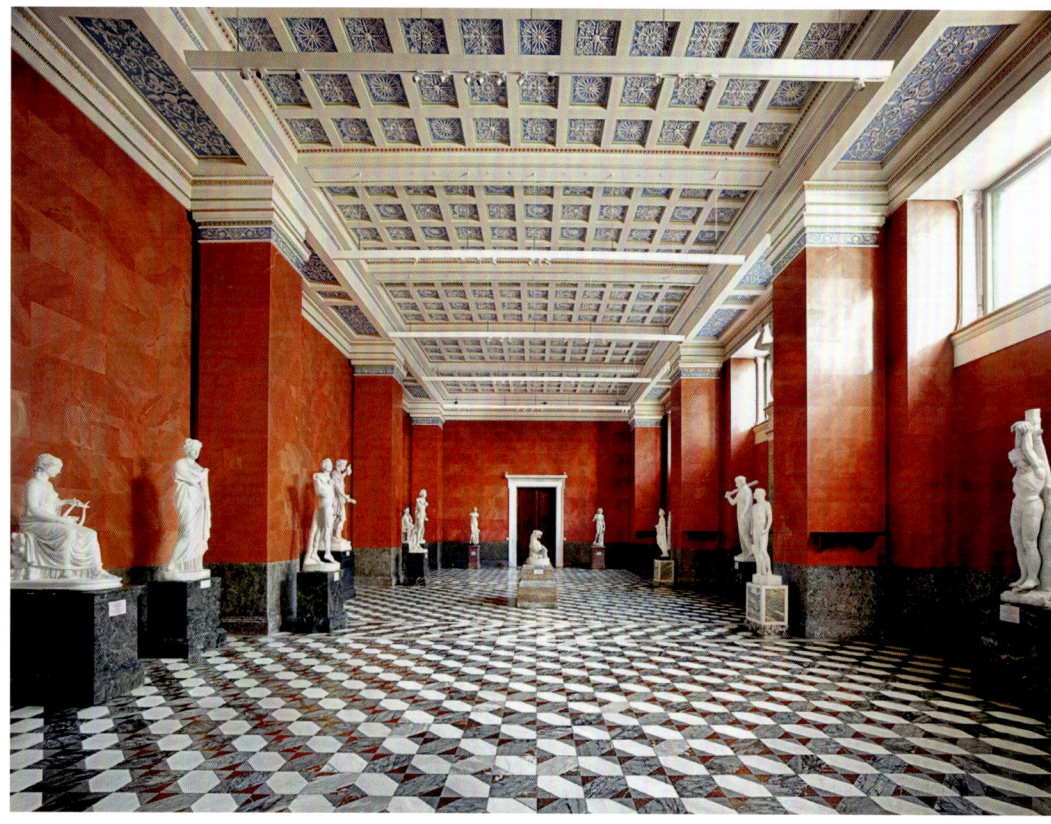

HERMITAGE, ST. PETERSBURG VIII 2014

2014, C-print, 180 × 226 cm (70 ⅞ × 89 in), edition of 6
Candida Höfer, born 1944, Eberswalde, Germany.

A student of the influential collaborative photography duo Bernd and Hilla Becher (1931–2007 and 1934– 2015) at the Kunstakademie Düsseldorf from 1976 to 1982, Höfer learnt a conceptual and technically exact approach to art-making, characterized by an objective, depersonalized and documentary aesthetic. Her long-exposure photographs, illuminated with existing light sources, depict public interiors – offices, banks, theatres and libraries – at times when they are conspicuously devoid of people. Photographed over two weeks, her 'Memory' series included historic sites in St Petersburg, including the Hermitage Museum where the photographs were premiered.

Her approach – working with the intrinsic symmetries of her subjects – offers a strong sense of compositional stability, allowing the viewer to slow down and experience the dramatic spaces and rich detail of what she calls her 'architectural portraits'. Here, marble statues set against intense red walls are a proxy for an absent public, taking on the role of inhabitants and perhaps even observers. Superficially straightforward, these conceptual works convey what in fact can never be seen, a completely empty room, and what we take for granted in photography, ourselves in an impossible frozen moment.

NANCY HOLT

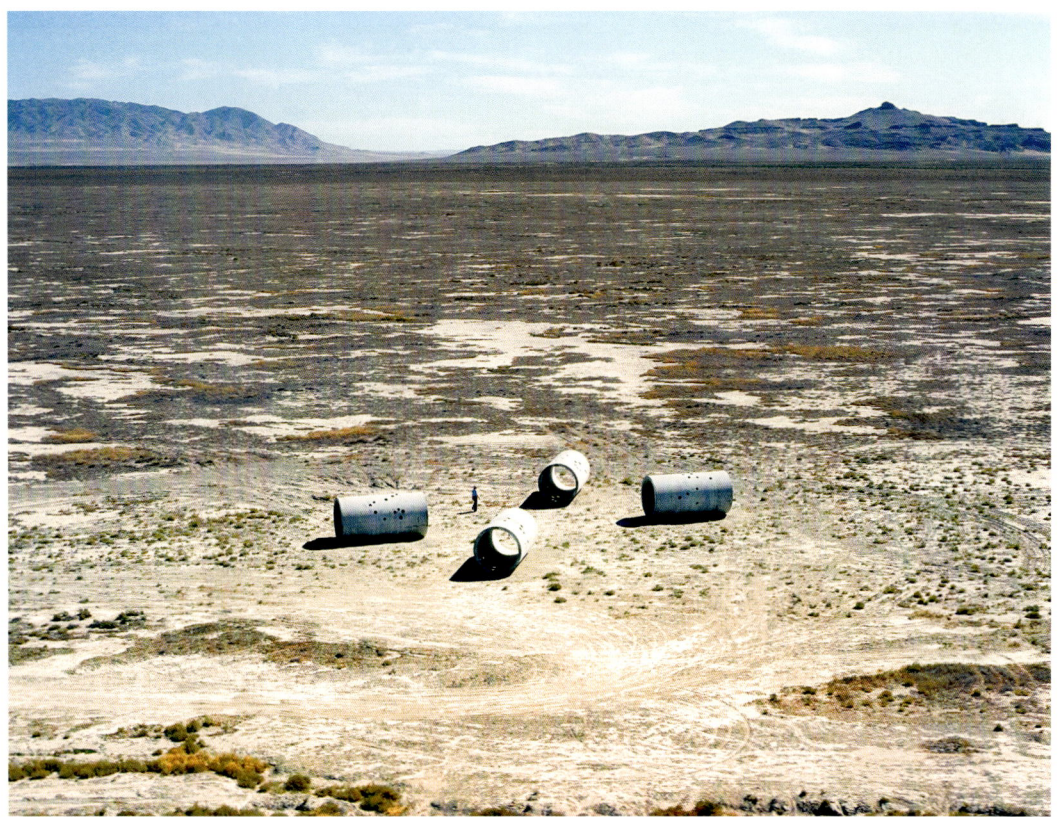

SUN TUNNELS

1973–6, concrete, steel and earth, overall: 2.8 × 20.9 × 16.2 m (9 ¼ × 68 ½ × 53 ft); each tunnel, length: 5.5 m (18 ft), diam: 2.8 m (9 ¼ ft), installation view, Great Basin Desert, Utah. Collection Dia Art Foundation with support from Holt/Smithson Foundation

Nancy Holt, born 1938, Worcester, Massachusetts. Died 2014, New York.

After studying for a degree in biology at Tufts University, Massachusetts, Holt emerged in the 1960s as a key figure in Conceptualism and a pioneer of the Land art movement. Considering humanity's physical relationship with the cosmos and its perceptions of time and space, she made earthworks, sculptures and site-specific installations, often in the form of astronomical monuments that allowed the positions of the sun and stars to be tracked. Holt's early practice used photography and video – for example, *Boomerang* (made in 1974 in collaboration with the artist Richard Serra, 1938–2024). Broadcast live on a TV station in Amarillo, Texas, it features Holt becoming disoriented by her own voice heard over headphones with a one-second time-delay. *Sun Tunnels*, in contrast, reflects the aim of Land artists to take sculpture out of the gallery or public square – and indeed out of the art market. Four huge concrete cylinders – normally used for major engineering projects – are arranged to align with the rising and setting sun at the summer and winter solstices. Viewed from a specific position at a given moment, the tunnels frame the sun, connecting human and celestial bodies in time, recurrence and eternity.

JENNY HOLZER

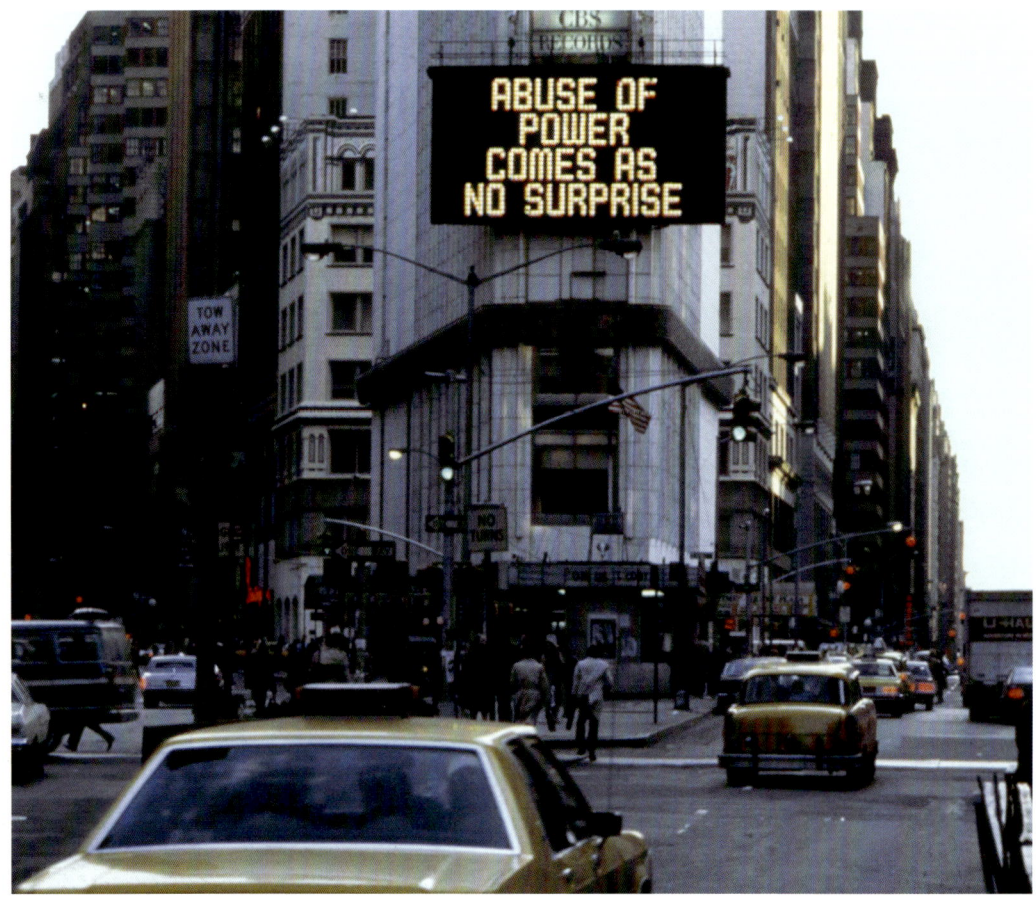

**UNTITLED ('ABUSE OF POWER COMES AS NO SURPRISE'),
from the series 'TRUISMS'**

1982, Spectacolor electronic sign, 6.1 × 12.2 m (20 × 40 ft), installation view,
Times Square, New York. Organized by Public Art Fund, Inc.
Jenny Holzer, born 1950, Gallipolis, Ohio.

Holzer gained public attention in 1977 for her 'Truisms' series
(1977–87), which at the time consisted of anonymous broadsheets
bearing concise statements being pasted on walls and fences around
Manhattan. Holzer derived these phrases from the reading list of
her studies in literature and philosophy – distilling each book into a
single line to concisely convey the message of its content. With an
implicitly acerbic or ironic tone, her pithy statements invited onlook-
ers to consider themes of sexuality, money and war, and structures
of power inherent to each of them. Further repurposing the strategies of advertising and marketing, Holzer had each aphorism
printed in unfussy, bold fonts on objects including mugs, caps and
pencils. Subsequently, Holzer embraced more ambitious technologies, presenting her texts on scrolling LED displays and 'news tick-
ers'. In 1982, 'Truisms' was delivered to a mass audience when it
was broadcast on the giant screen above New York's Times Square.
In 2017, at the height of the #MeToo movement, the phrase 'Abuse
Of Power Comes As No Surprise' gained renewed force when it
became the slogan of the allied campaign #NotSurprised, which
rallied against sexual harassment specific to the art world.

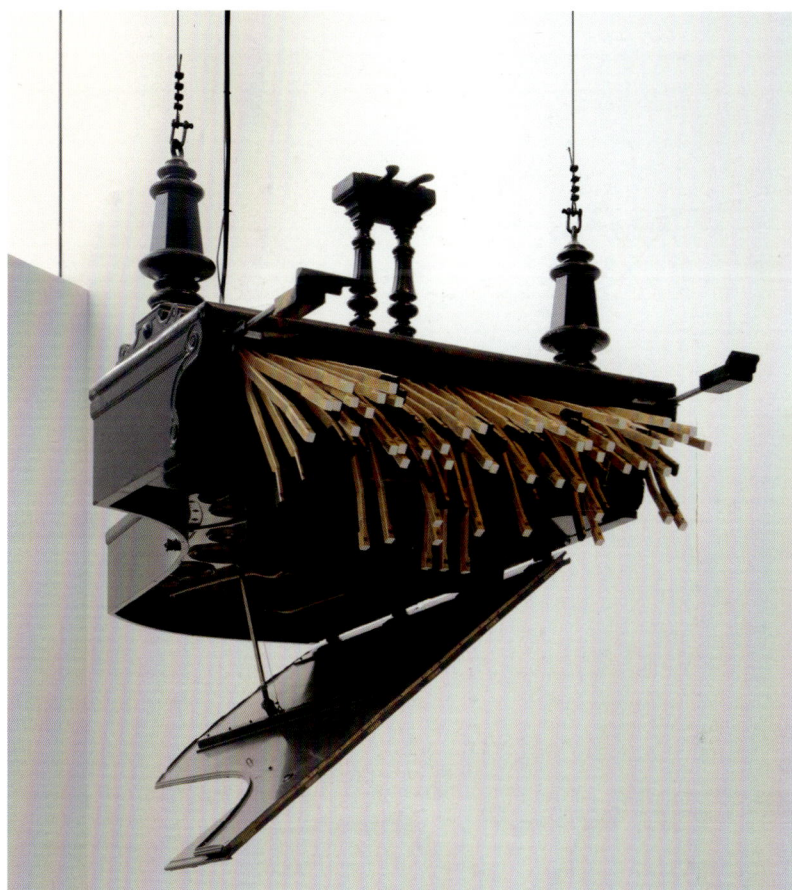

CONCERT FOR ANARCHY

1990, piano, hydraulic rams and compressor, 150 × 106 × 155.5 cm
(59 × 41 ¼ × 61 ¼ in), Tate, London
Rebecca Horn, born 1944, Michelstadt, Germany. Died 2024, Bad König, Germany.

Through sculptures, performance, photography and film, Horn investigates the intersections between objects, movements and the body. Her 'body extensions', begun in 1968 and which include, for example, metre-long rods attached to her fingers, serve both to restrict and amplify physical movement and reach. One such work, *Einhorn* ('Unicorn', 1968–9) – a wordplay on the artist's name – comprised a long tusk protruding from her head. Conversely, her kinetic sculptures render machines into bodies: for example, the tangoing table in the film *Der Eintänzer* ('One Man Show', 1978). The surreal absurdity of such works recalls those of Jean Tinguely (1925–91) and of Horn's friend and mentor Meret Oppenheim (p.306). In *Concert for Anarchy*, a grand piano is suspended overhead, out of reach and in an impossible orientation for playing. At timed intervals the keys abruptly thrust out like the earlier finger extensions, while the lid simultaneously opens, all of which generates a startling, discordant clamour. After several minutes the keys slowly retract and the lid closes to slow creaking and dissonant murmuring. In 1992, Horn became the first woman to receive the prestigious Kaiserring Goslar international art prize, and was also awarded the Medienkunstpreis Karlsruhe for art and technology.

RONI HORN

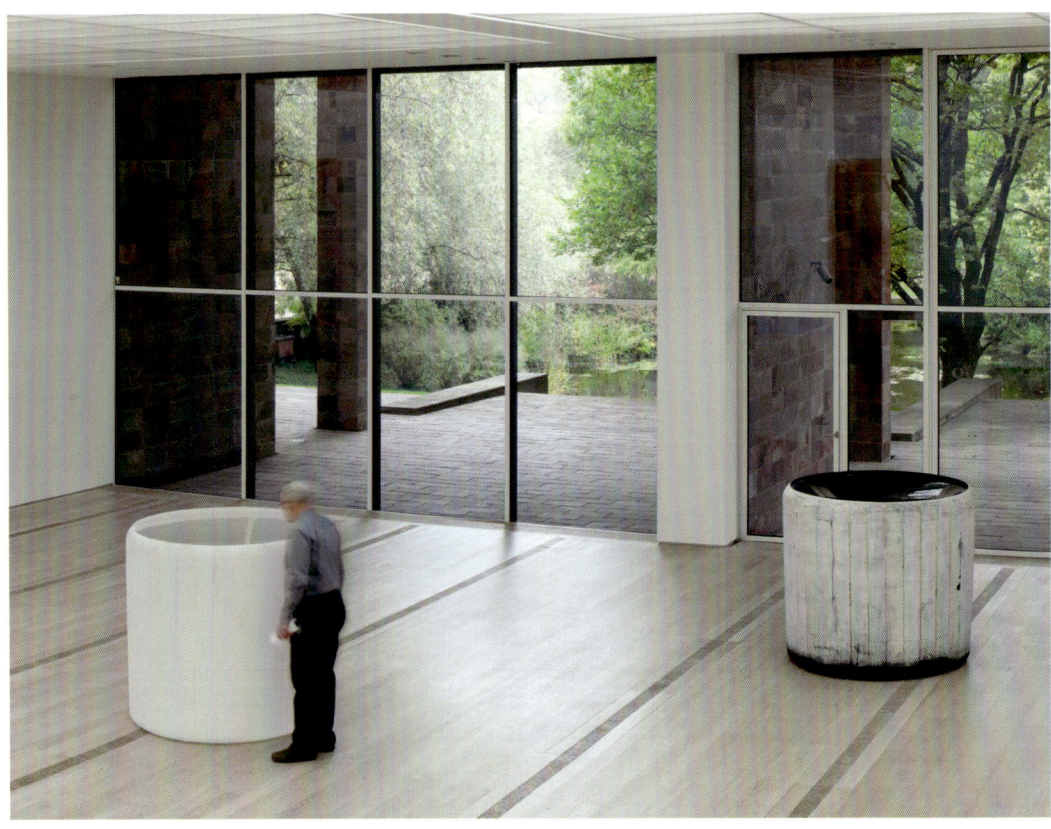

WATER DOUBLE, V. 3

2013–16, solid cast glass with as-cast surfaces, h: 127.3 cm (50 ⅛ in) × tapered diam:
134.6–142.2 cm (53–56 in), installation view, Fondation Beyeler, Basel, 2016
Roni Horn, born 1955, New York. Died 2024, Bad König, Germany.

Horn studied art at Rhode Island School of Design and Yale School
of Art, subsequently teaching for three years at Colgate University,
before returning to New York city. Her oeuvre comprises diverse
media, from drawing and photography to installation and performance. In the 1970s, she first travelled to Iceland, becoming enduringly fascinated by its landscape and geological formations. Her
ongoing series of artist's books, *'To Place'*, which she began in the
1990s, convey her passion for the country and include her photographs,
such as *You Are the Weather* (1994–5) – 100 images of a woman's face as
she bathes in the water amid changing atmospheric conditions.
Water as defined by time and space is a recurring theme for Horn,
who is interested in its mutable and illusory nature. Her photographic
series 'Still Water (The River Thames, for example)' (1999–2000)
captures London's river at different times of day and reveals vast
variations in its appearance. Her 'Water Double' sculptures also play
with illusion. Cylindrical (or sometimes cuboid) forms with rough,
translucent sides and a smooth, concave, meniscus surface appear like
pristine pools of water held in vessels, but are in fact entirely made
of cast glass.

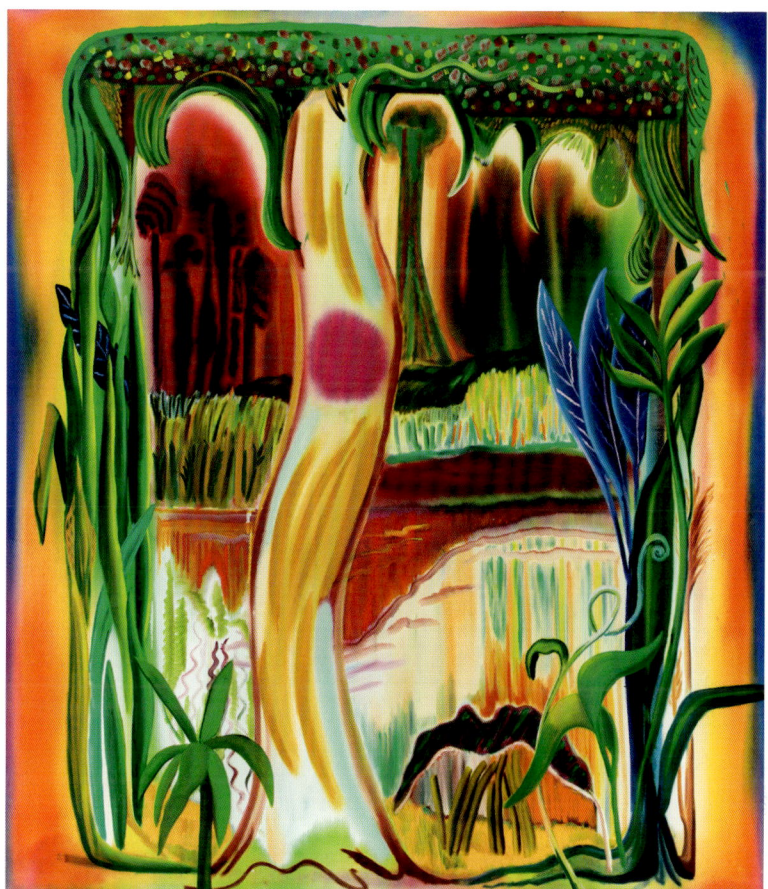

IN THE CLEAR

2016, oil, acrylic and dye on canvas, 172.9 × 152.1 cm (68 ⅛ × 59 ⅞ in),
Whitney Museum of American Art, New York
Shara Hughes, born 1981, Atlanta.

Hughes graduated with a BFA from Rhode Island School of Design in 2004 before studying at the Skowhegan School of Painting and Sculpture in Maine. Initially painting interior scenes, Hughes has subsequently turned to landscape and has widened her techniques to include printmaking. She creates images intuitively and without prior planning, often evolved from a title – words acting as her initial brush-strokes – or a feeling. Using raw and dyed canvas, with selected areas heavily coated in gesso, her rich colour palette and swirling gestures are expressionistic in style, with influences ranging from Renaissance art to Helen Frankenthaler (p.142), Elizabeth Murray (p.293) and David Hockney (b.1937). Hughes's paintings transport the viewer to a joyful place of the imagination, yet any journey into the subconscious crosses unnerving undercurrents too, with a push and pull between these opposites, as exemplified in this depiction of a lush landscape at sunset. Upon second glance, blood-red waters and an ominous haze in the air alter the mood. It was exhibited as part of an entire room of her paintings shown at the 2017 Whitney Biennial and the museum later acquired it for its collection.

JULIANA HUXTABLE

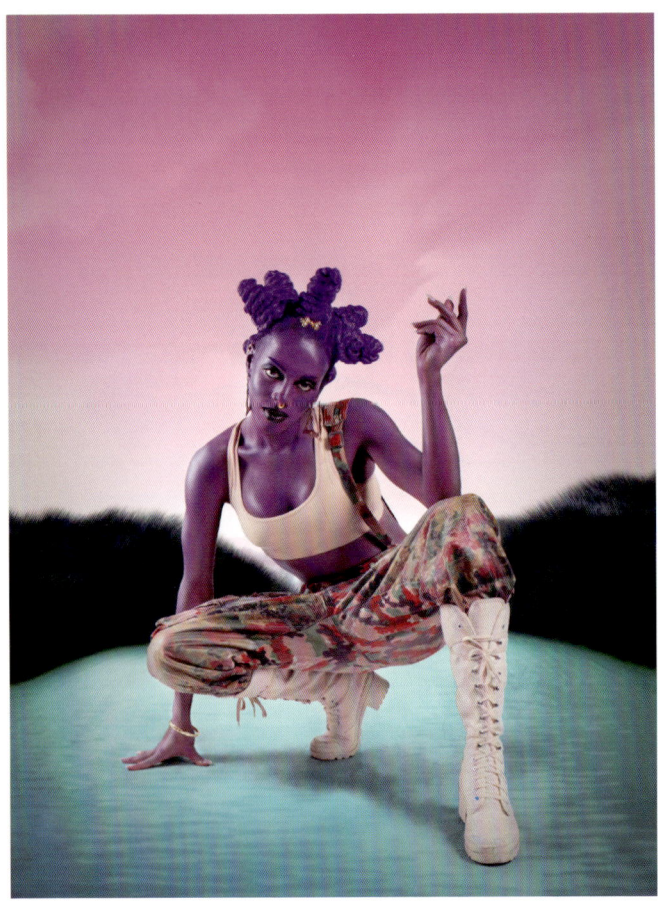

UNTITLED (PSYCHOSOCIAL STUNTIN') from the series 'UNIVERSAL CROP TOPS'

2015, colour inkjet print, 101.6 × 76.2 cm (40 × 30 in), The Studio Museum in Harlem, New York
Juliana Huxtable, born 1987, Bryan-College Station, Texas.

Artist, fashion icon, Internet celebrity, night-life impresario and DJ, Huxtable explores race and queer identity through her multifaceted oeuvre. Propelled to fame through social-media posts, particularly on Tumblr under the moniker 'BLUE LIP BLACK WITCH-CUNT', her photographs were included in the 2015 exhibition 'Surround Audience: New Museum Triennial' in New York. Experiencing racism as a child in her predominantly white home town, Huxtable defiantly interrogates and counters right-wing conspiracy theories with her own Afrofuturism fictions, which are often drawn from Nuwaubian mythology – a hybrid of Islam, ancient Egyptian aesthetics and extraterrestrial theories. She grew up as an intersex boy in a strict Baptist home and conservative community and practised breast binding after she was bullied over their appearance. In contrast, the 'crop-top' she wears in this series poignantly suggests Huxtable's acceptance and celebration of her body. The purple manifesto accompanying these pictures, written in uppercase letters, pays homage to those who do not conform to racial or sexual binaries and norms as reinforced by the fashion industry but forge their own. Colouring herself an otherworldly purple, she creates new visions that expand perceptions of the material body.

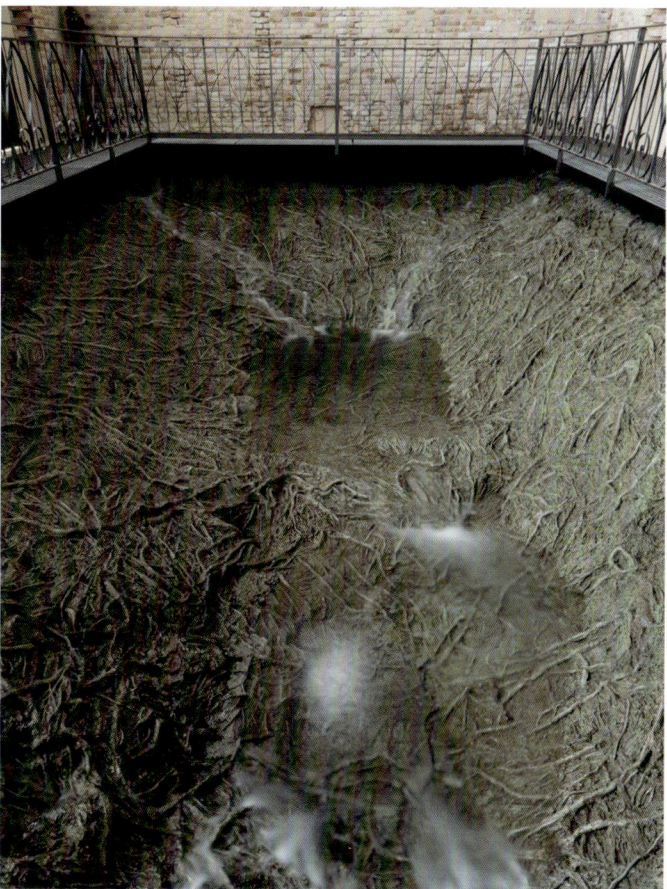

TRES AGUAS (WATER TOWER)

2014, stainless steel, hydraulic mechanism and water, installation, Toledo, Spain.
Commissioned by Artangel and Fundación El Greco
Cristina Iglesias, born 1956, San Sebastián, Spain.

Iglesias took a degree in chemical sciences at the Universidad del País Vasco, before studying sculpture at London's Chelsea College of Art from 1980. In her installations, sculptures and architecture, object and place are often interdependent and sometimes linked through the medium of water. She speaks of 'building' rather than 'sculpting' her work. Her first landscape intervention in Norway's Lofoten Islands, *Laurel Leaves* (1993–4), consisted of a portal into a natural rock formation. Two years later she completed a major permanent public water work, outside Antwerp's Royal Museum of Fine Arts.

Recurring motifs in her work include gates, passages, screens, rooms and truncated labyrinths, subterranean streams and submerged structures. Seen here is the opening section of a three-part sequence of works that link historic sites in Toledo with its river, the Tagus. Deep inside the ancient city's tall Mudejar-style water tower, Iglesias fashioned a dark pool, lined with matted vegetation made of steel. Water flows and bubbles before gradually draining away – a cycle that lasts for seventeen minutes. Its location and the summoning of water recall practices of Toledo's *La Convivencia* period, from the eighth to late fifteenth century, when Muslims, Christians and Jews lived a relatively peaceful coexistence.

GRACIELA ITURBIDE

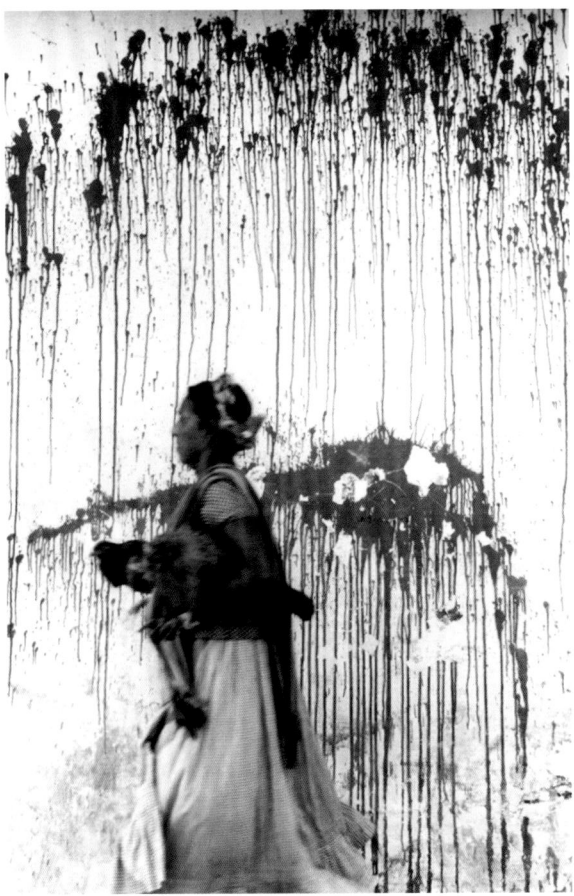

CHICKENS, JUCHITÁN, MEXICO

1979, gelatin silver print, 40.6 × 50.8 cm (16 × 20 in)
Graciela Iturbide, born 1942, Mexico City.

Intending to train as a film director, Iturbide became interested in still photography after seeing the work of Mexican photographer Manuel Álvarez Bravo (1902–2002). From 1970 to 1971, she worked as Bravo's assistant, accompanying him on trips throughout Mexico. She has continued to travel her country widely ever since, working to photograph its indigenous populations and always developing what she calls 'a complicity' with her subjects. In 1979, the artist Francisco Toledo (1940–2019) invited Iturbide to photograph the Juchitán people, a traditional matriarchal society from the indigenous Zapotec culture of Oaxaca in south-east Mexico, whose beliefs and superstitions are a hybrid of Catholicism and pre-Columbian ritual. The project took nearly a decade, resulting in the photo essay *'Juchitán of the Women'* (1989) of which this image is a part. It documents a milieu in which women dominate the social, economic and religious practices of public life. Their strength and agency are exemplified in this dynamic photograph, in which a woman carrying two chickens hurries past a paint-splattered wall. Pigment runs down the surface, recalling both bloodstains and Abstract Expressionist mark making, while the woman herself is blurred in the midst of action.

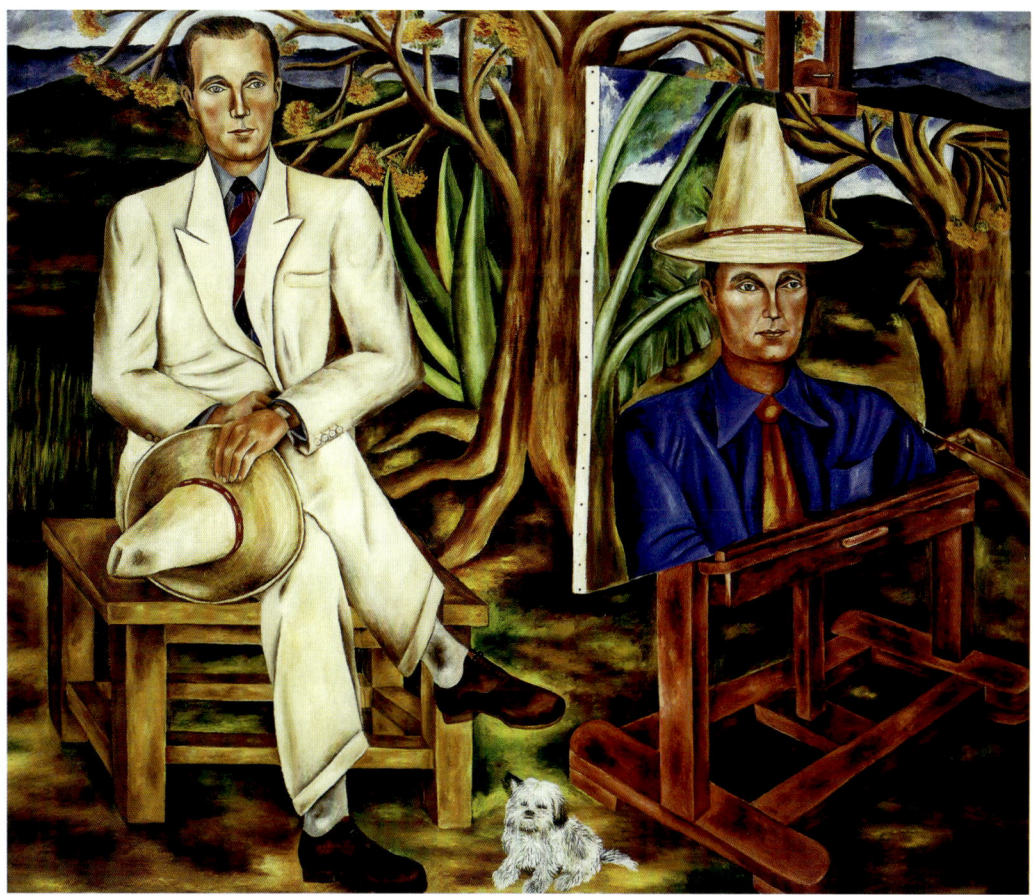

PORTRAIT OF HENRI DE CHATILLON

1940, oil on canvas, dimensions unknown, private collection
María Izquierdo, born 1902, San Juan de los Lagos, Mexico. Died 1955, Mexico City.

'It is a crime to be a woman and have talent,' wrote Izquierdo in her diary in 1953, two years before she died unexpectedly of a stroke. One of the few female Mexican artists to be internationally successful during her lifetime, alongside her contemporary Frida Kahlo (p.207), she became the first Mexican woman to have a solo exhibition in the United States. Izquierdo was a self-taught painter with an avid curiosity who depicted popular culture in her rich and colourful canvases, some of which border on Surrealist. Her compositions are loaded with unusual details, such as the small poodle sitting beside the figure of French fashion designer Henri de Chatillon in the portrait shown here. In other work, it is an aeroplane, fruit, flowers or a landscape full of distinctly Mexican detail, that add a local flavour, and testify to her sense of belonging in a particular time and place. However, a deep sensitivity towards her cultural heritage and a sharp sense of humour differentiated her stance from many of her contemporaries, who favoured social realism as depicted by Mexican Muralists. Izquierdo's fresh and bold work opened the door to many later female artists.

EMILY JACIR

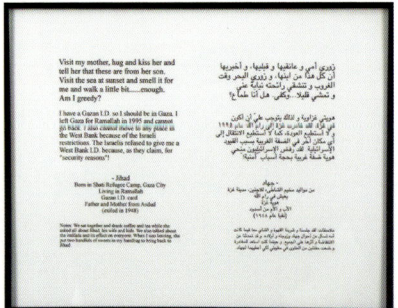

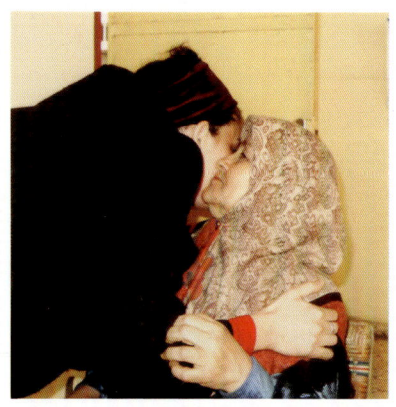

WHERE WE COME FROM

2001–3, detail (Jihad), American passport, 30 texts, 32 C-prints and 1 video
Emily Jacir, born 1972, Bethlehem, Palestine (American national).

The devastating effects of the Israeli occupation of Palestinian land is the main subject of Jacir's art. Her practice mediates social intervention using installation, performance, writing, video and sound work. As a Palestinian who was brought up in Saudi Arabia and educated in Italy and the United States, Jacir has had direct experience of life outside her country, as well as the privilege of being able to return without persecution. Her art concentrates on the dispossession of a people who are either exiled or face everyday resistance, with a special focus on the lack of freedom of movement within Palestine. This impulse motivates the series 'Where We Come From', an extended visual essay about fulfilling quotidian yet impossible requests. Jacir asked Palestinians living abroad and in the Occupied Territories the question: 'If I could do anything for you, anywhere in Palestine, what would it be?' Using her American passport, she endeavoured to carry out requests, including playing football, eating meals, looking at views, paying bills and meeting relatives – as in this example of a visit to someone's mother. Each of these successfully accomplished tasks is represented by an explanatory text and a colour photograph of the request being actioned.

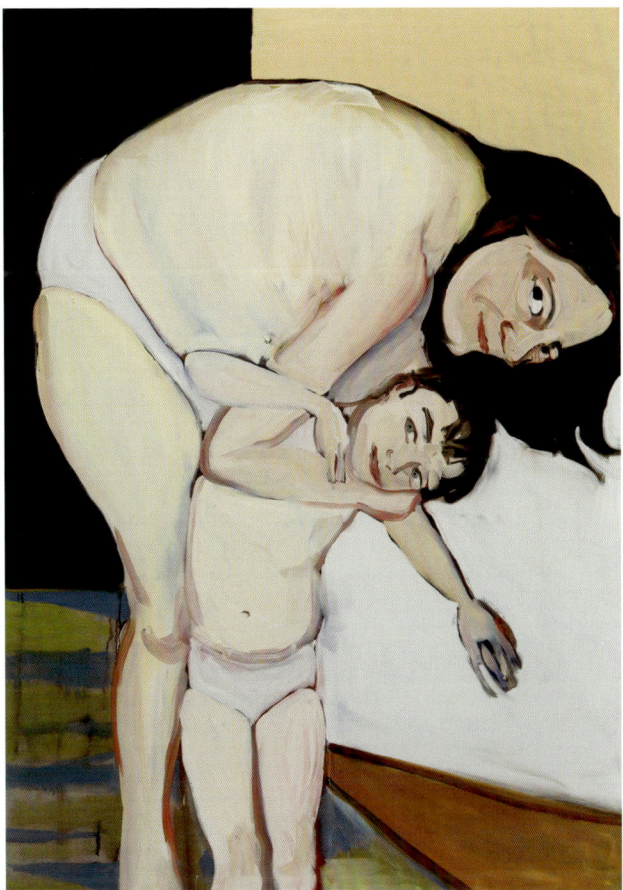

SELF-PORTRAIT WITH ESME

2009, oil on linen, 213.5 × 152.5 cm (84 ⅛ × 60 ⅛ in), Institute of Contemporary
Art, Boston

Chantal Joffe, born 1969, St Albans, Vermont.

After completing an MFA at London's Royal College of Art
in the early 1990s, Joffe's work was selected for the 1996 'New
Contemporaries' exhibition. Here her portraiture and erotic imagery
caught the attention of prominent collectors and the gallerist Victoria
Miro, who went on to represent her. Characterized by liquid pigment
running down the canvas, her recent paintings depict women –
herself, friends and family members. Neutral tones are punctuated
by moments of brilliant, sumptuous colour, her introspective
subjects appearing simultaneously confident and vulnerable. Joffe

painted self-portraits during her pregnancy and continues to depict
her daughter, Esme, born in 2004. Earlier artists including Mary
Cassatt (p.91), and Berthe Morisot (p.285) had demonstrated that
the everyday lives of women and mothers were subjects worthy of
serious representation, and Joffe extends this tradition by rendering
her figures often greater than lifesize, the stooped figure seen here
suggesting a monumental presence. Yet Joffe is candidly posed, wearing only underpants and huddling over her carefree daughter, this
intimacy underscored by its tactility – the coolness of exposed skin,
the warmth of intertwined flesh, the softness of free-flowing hair.
While the work is beautiful, the artist aims for unmediated honesty.

GWEN JOHN

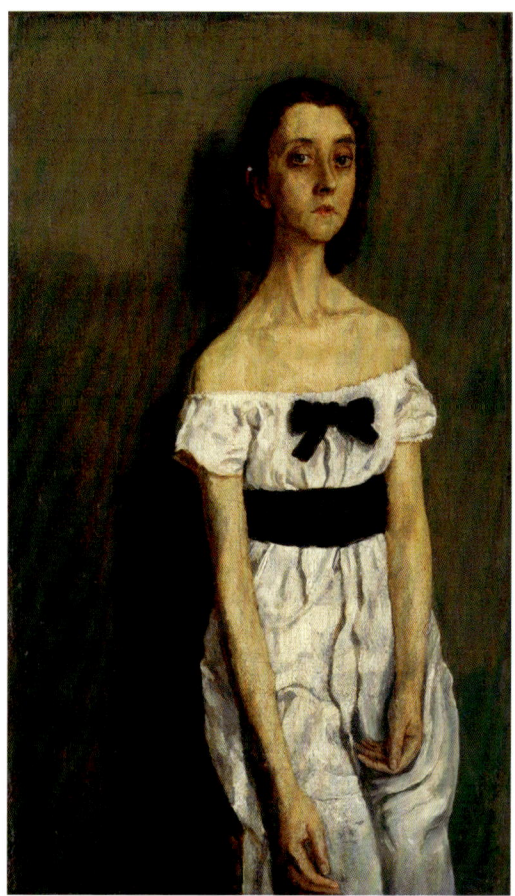

GIRL WITH BARE SHOULDERS

1909–10, oil on canvas, 43.4 × 26 cm (17 ⅛ × 10 ¼ in), Museum of Modern Art, New York

Gwen John, born 1876, Haverfordwest, Pembrokeshire, UK. Died 1939, Dieppe, France.

The elder sister of painter Augustus John (1878–1961), whose success overshadowed hers during their lifetime despite him stating that she was the better painter, John's reputation has grown steadily since. Both trained at the Slade in London, the only British art school of the time to admit both women and men. John settled in Paris in 1904, remaining in France for the rest of her life, initially working as a model for artists including Auguste Rodin (1840–1917) with whom she had a turbulent relationship. On close terms with leading lights of modernism, she was unmoved by their stylistic approach, her work instead having been compared to that of Francisco Goya (1746–1828) a century earlier. In contrast to her brother's society portraits, she sought to convey 'a more interior life'. Seen here is John's portrait of the model Fenella Lovell, whose blue eyes had first attracted the artist – Rodin rejected her as too thin. This is one of two paintings by John showing the model in the same pose, one clothed the other nude. Appearing forlorn and elongated, the lack of background detail and off-centred composition creates a sense of dislocation.

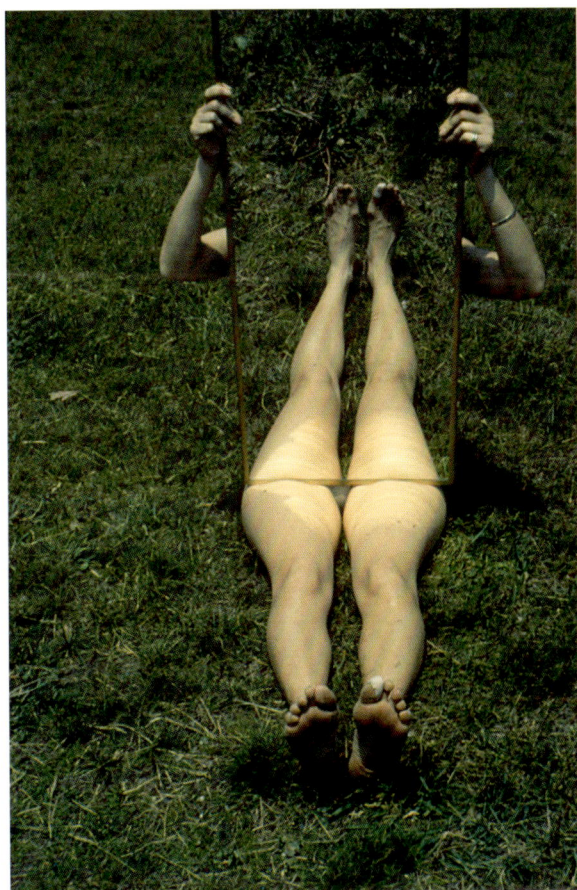

MIRROR PIECE I

1969, C-print, 101.6 × 56.5 cm (40 × 22 ¼ in)
Joan Jonas, born Joan Amerman Edwards, 1936, New York.

A trailblazer in video and performance art, Jonas was pivotal to the development of these new artistic media from the late 1960s onwards. While studying for her master's in sculpture at Columbia University (1965) Jonas was immersed in New York's art scene, learning about movement from choreographers Trisha Brown, Yvonne Rainer and Steve Paxton, who were also based in the city at this time. Her second home in Nova Scotia has also influenced much of her work, calling her back to deeply felt environmental issues and finding form in dreamscape theatre pieces. Recurring themes of disturbed representations and alter egos feature in her work, an early example,

simple yet ground-breaking, being *Mirror Piece I*. Performers moved slowly while holding large mirrors to reflect their surroundings and the audience – a meditation on the contingency of individual and collective identities. Drawing on the many metaphors that cluster around reflection and the uncanny reality we experience in a mirror, Jonas makes image and spectatorship her medium. In this photograph, shot by the artist, a single performer sits in the grass, creating a surreal visual effect as reflection merges with reality and feet appear to replace head.

LOÏS MAILOU JONES

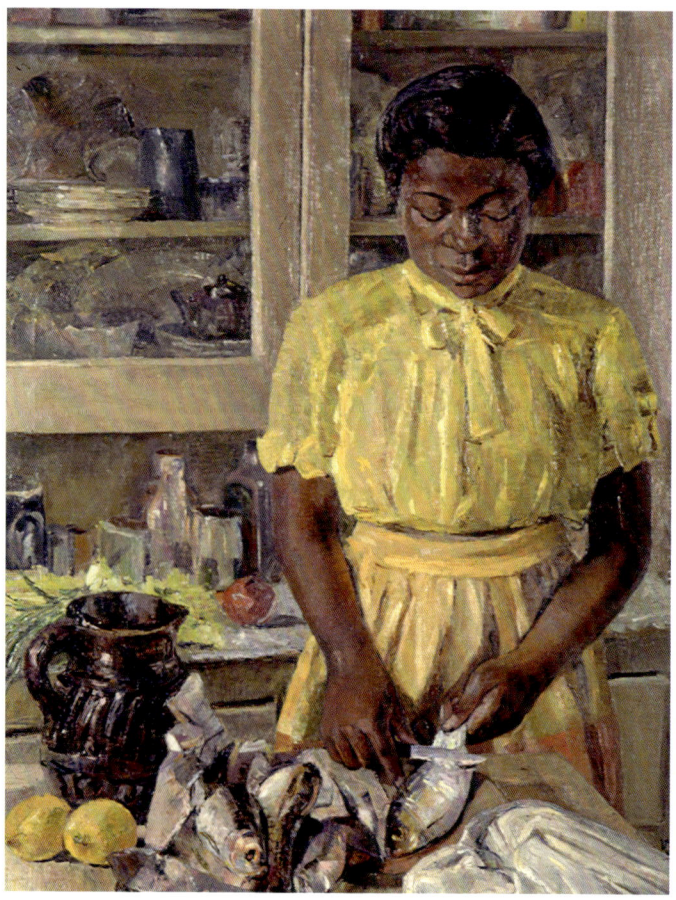

JENNIE

1943, oil on canvas, 90.8 × 73 cm (35 ¾ × 28 ¾ in), Howard University Gallery of Art, Washington DC

Loïs Mailou Jones, born 1905, Boston. Died 1998, Washington DC.

Encompassing Impressionist techniques and African-inspired abstraction, Jones's work spans a great breadth of styles. She began her career as a textile designer in the late 1920s, having studied at Boston's School of the Museum of Fine Arts, and, immediately afterwards, at the Designers Art School. Dissatisfied with the anonymity of her textile work, Jones turned to fine art and teaching – first in North Carolina, then at Howard University in Washington DC – and in 1937 undertook a formative journey to Paris to study painting at the Académie Julian, finding a far more racially tolerant climate than in America. Here, alongside Neo-Impressionist still lifes and landscapes, she began to introduce African motifs such as tribal masks into her work. On her return to the US, Jones met Alain Locke, a philosopher and leading figure of the black cultural movement known as the Harlem Renaissance. Encouraged by Locke, she concentrated her focus on black subjects, as demonstrated in *Jennie*. Her later work fused this type of realist portraiture with colourful, semi-abstract designs steeped in African and Caribbean culture while also recalling her early textiles.

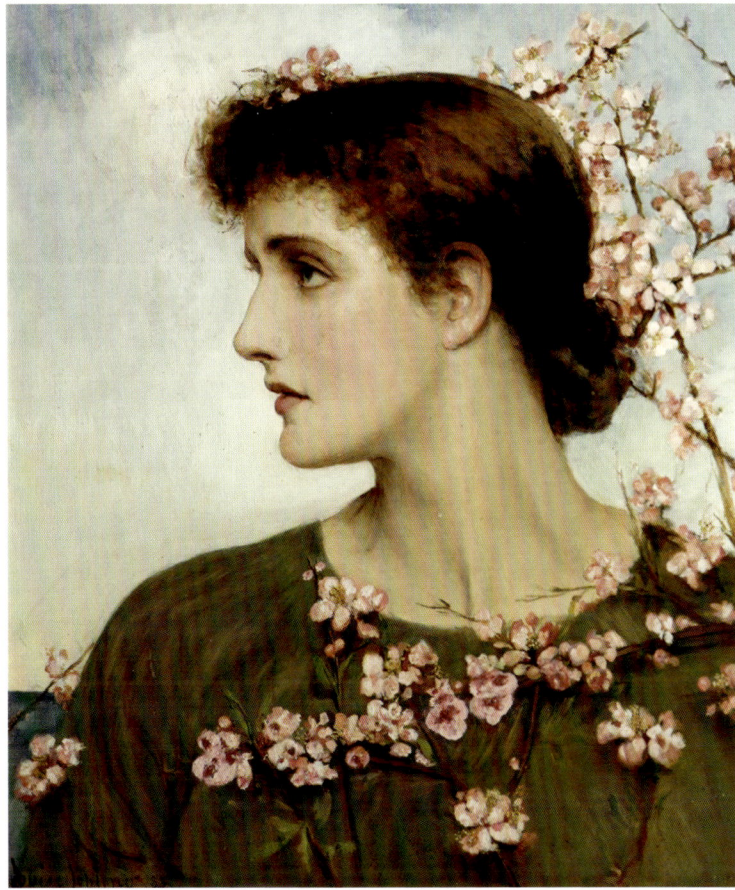

PHYLLIS

1883, oil on canvas, 52 × 44 cm (20 ½ × 17 ⅜ in), Russell-Cotes Art Gallery and Museum, Bournemouth, UK.
Louise Jopling, born Louise Goode, later Rowe, 1843, Manchester, UK. Died 1933, Chesham Bois, Buckinghamshire, UK.

Jopling was one of the most prominent female portrait and genre painters of the Victorian era. Studying in Paris in the 1860s, she entered her paintings to the Salon, and later to London's Royal Academy of Arts. A staunch supporter of women's suffrage and early feminist causes, she campaigned tirelessly for gender equality. In 1887 she established a women's painting school and in 1901 became the first woman admitted to the Royal Society of British Artists. Wife of a society caricaturist, she moved in circles that included Oscar Wilde and James McNeill Whistler (1834–1903), for whom she also modelled. Despite her husband's connections, she was the primary earner during their marriage, producing work constantly. Painting in oils, watercolours and pastels, her aristocratic subjects included Coutts and Lady Lindsay, the founders of London's Grosvenor Gallery. The influence of Pre-Raphaelite circle painters such as Edward Burne-Jones (1833–98) is evident in this work, which depicts the same tale from Ovid's 'Heroides' as his *Phyllis and Demophoön* (1870). Jopling portrays Phyllis as strong and determined as she emerges from a blooming almond tree, symbolizing triumph over adversity.

BIRGIT JÜRGENSSEN

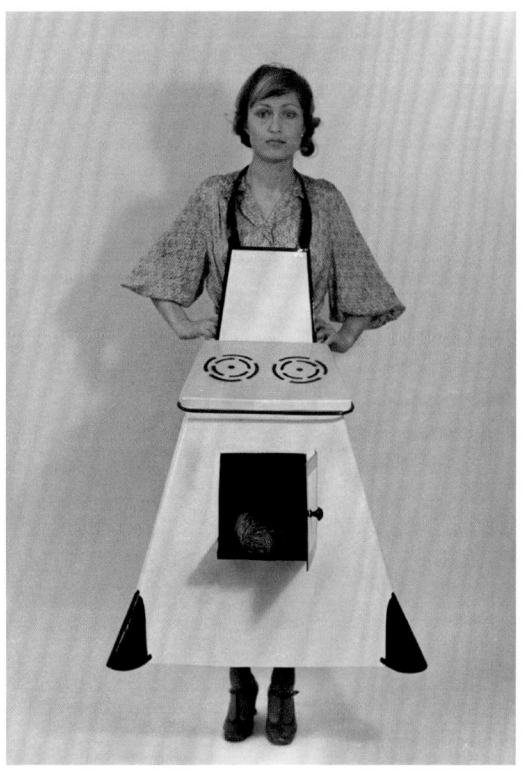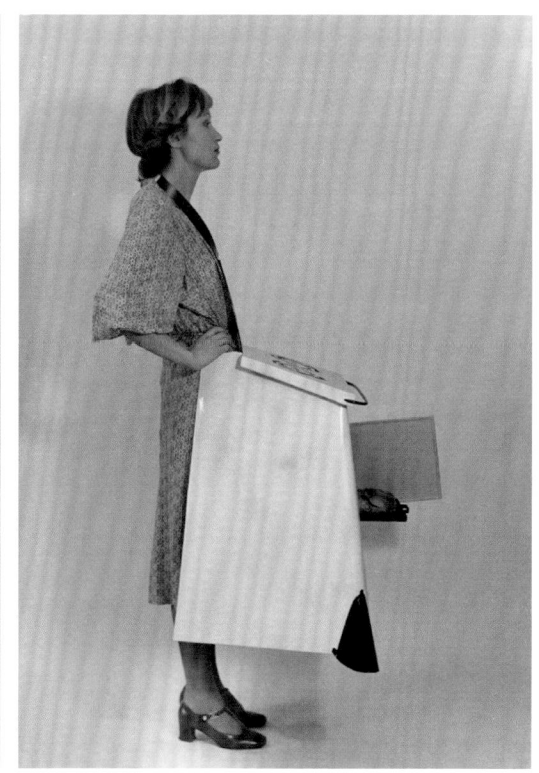

HOUSEWIVES' KITCHEN APRON

1975, black-and-white photographs, diptych, each 39.3 × 27.5 cm (15 ½ × 10 ⅞ in)
Birgit Jürgenssen, born 1949, Vienna. Died 2003, Vienna.

Through drawing, photography, collage, sculpture and performance, Jürgenssen's expansive oeuvre critiqued the social forces that confine women and regulate their bodies. Before her untimely death, she was for twenty years an influential and highly regarded teacher at the Academy of Fine Arts, Vienna, and her work was exhibited in numerous solo and group exhibitions, including 'MAGNA – Feminism: Art and Creativity' (1975), curated by fellow feminist artist VALIE EXPORT (p.412). Her posthumous reputation has continued to grow as art historians and curators have led a revival of her artwork. Many of Jürgenssen's drawings, almost Surrealist in style, depict women trapped in domestic spaces, while others blur the boundary between animal and woman through inventive hybrid forms. In this work, she models her wearable sculpture of an oven-apron. Shot from the front and in profile, the photographs resemble criminal mug shots and expose the kitchen as an institutional space of imprisonment. The cooking rings perhaps allude to breasts and the loaf of baked bread popping out of the oven to the womb and childbirth. Jürgenssen critically depicts the female body reduced to a machine with prescribed and limited functions.

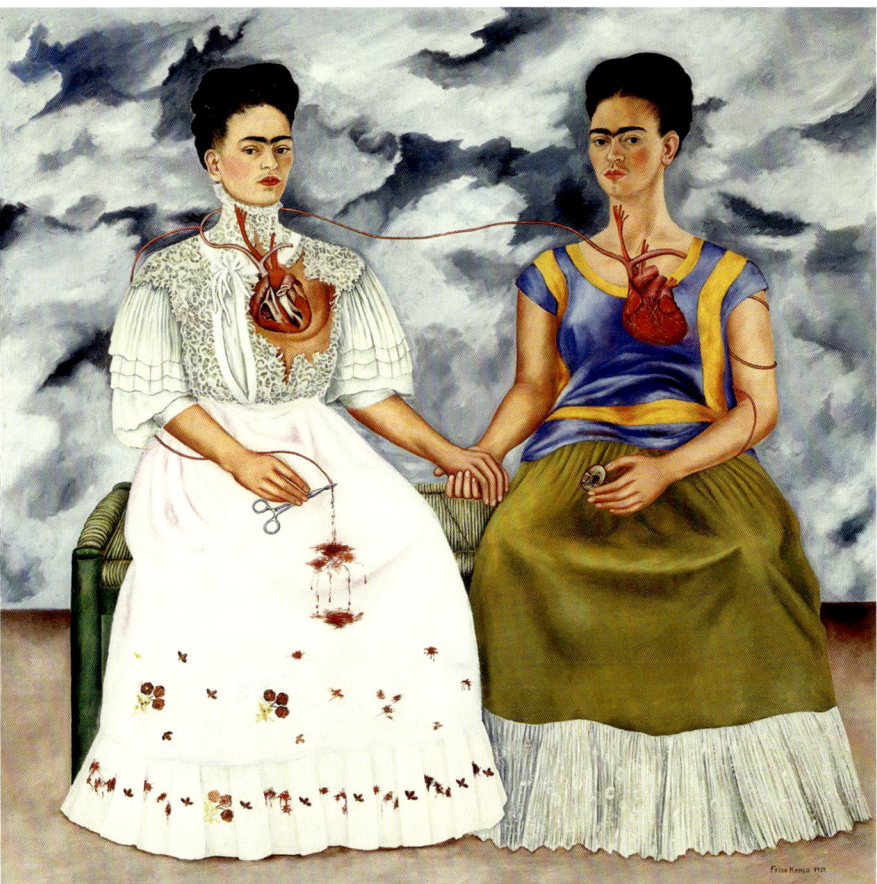

THE TWO FRIDAS

1939, oil on canvas, 171.8 × 171.8 cm (67 ⅝ × 67 ⅝ in), Museo de Arte Moderno, Mexico City
Frida Kahlo, born Magdalena Carmen Frida Kahlo y Calderón, 1907, Coyoacán (now in Mexico City). Died 1954, Mexico City.

One of the world's most well-known and beloved female artists, Kahlo began painting aged eighteen to distract herself from the pain of severe injuries sustained in a bus accident. She had been a medical student in Mexico City, a career she was forced to abandon as a result. Resting canvases on her body while in bed and positioning a mirror above so she could use herself as a model, Kahlo used bright colours and decisive brushstrokes reminiscent of Mexican folk art. This work, the first of her large-scale paintings, was made in the year that she divorced acclaimed mural artist and political activist Diego Rivera (1886–1957), although they were to remarry the following year. This twin self-portrait represents two states of being: holding hands and with a shared blood supply their conditions are nevertheless quite different: Frida on the right, in Tehuana dress, has a strong heart fed by a locket painted with Rivera's face, whereas the other, more European Frida is cut off, weakened and bloodied. Vulnerable and exposed but also defiant, this dual persona embodies the emotional upheaval of separation, presented in terms of physical distress.

HAYV KAHRAMAN

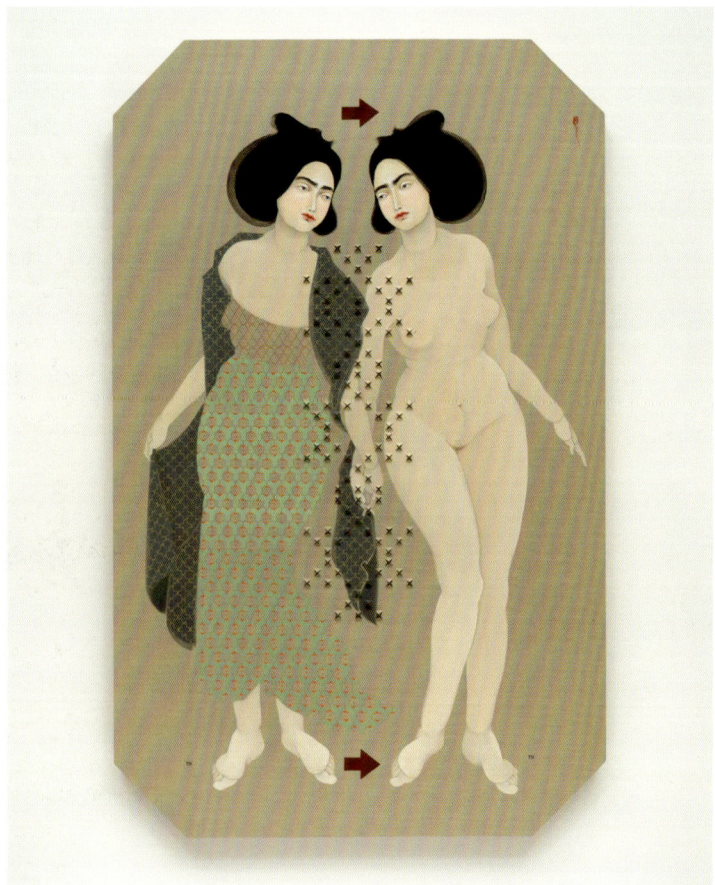

STRIP SEARCH

2016, oil on linen and acoustic foam, 193 × 121.9 cm (76 × 48 in), private collection
Hayv Kahraman, born 1981, Baghdad.

As a child, Kahraman fled with her family to Sweden to escape the chaos of the First Gulf War. She studied in Italy in 2005, then moved to the United States, settling in Los Angeles. Female identity and gender, seen through the lens of her experiences of exile and psychological upheaval, inform her paintings, which are populated by stylized solitary figures or small groups drawn from a restricted cast of women with pale flesh and dark hair. Painted on wood panels or raw linen, her figures float against flat backgrounds. Often incorporating geometry, symmetry and intricate patterns, Kahraman has also produced abstract wooden sculptures to accompany her oil paintings. In *Strip Search*, she depicts the realities of travel for the diaspora today. Two women are shown side by side with entwined arms – the arrow suggesting these as the before-and-after images from the invasive action of the work's title. Where the bodies meet, a pattern of small cross-shaped cuts perforates the linen, pierced by tiny pyramids of acoustic foam. This material is used to absorb sound and alludes to the harrowing noises of war of Kahraman's childhood, and to those who choose not to hear them.

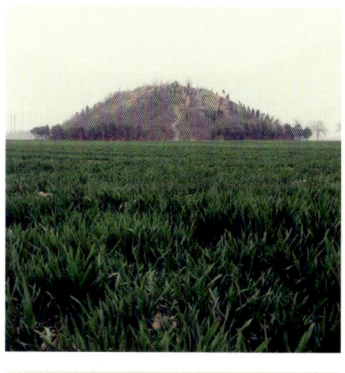
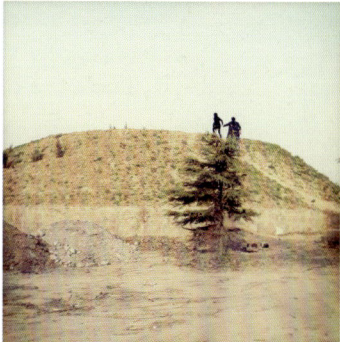
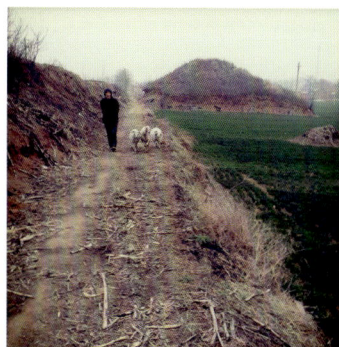
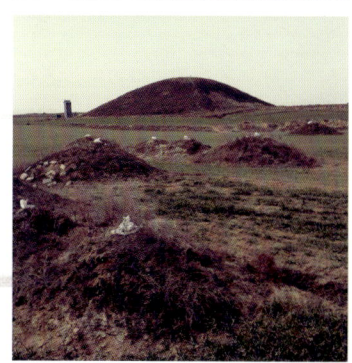
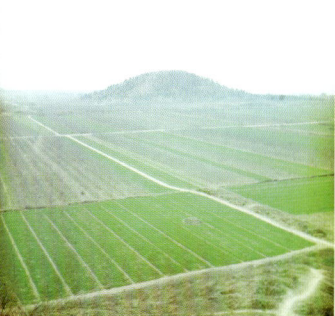
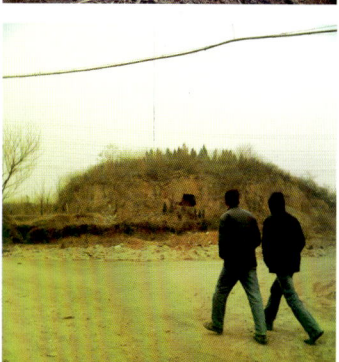

MILLET MOUNDS

2012, video installation composed of 171 videos, 171 sketches and texts,
dimensions variable, M+ museum, Hong Kong
Kan Xuan, born 1972, Xuancheng, China.

Having studied at the prestigious China Academy of Art in Hangzhou
from 1993 to 1997, Kan completed a residency at Amsterdam's
Rijksakademie Van Beeldende Kunsten from 2002 to 2003. Involved
in the evolution of Chinese video art, her early film and photography work focused on mundane moments of everyday life, with a mood
of exploration and self-effacement. Her 1999 video *Kanxuan! Ai!*
shows Kan hurrying through subway tunnels against the relentless
flow of people, calling her name in an existential quest for her individual identity. Taking a job at a movie production company, she learnt
to navigate digital video production and editing software. *Millet
Mounds*, included in 'The Encyclopedic Palace' exhibition at the
55th Venice Biennale in 2013, records Kan's 28,000-kilometre
(17,400-mile) journey across northern China, as she used an mobile
phone camera to document the traces of ancient imperial tombs,
colloquially named from their resemblance to heaps of grain. A series
of stop-motion videos, accompanied by a rock from each site and
a story about the once-revered figures buried there, represent nearly
2,000 years of dynastic rule, its vestiges of power gradually disappear-
ing and being incorporated into contemporary rural life.

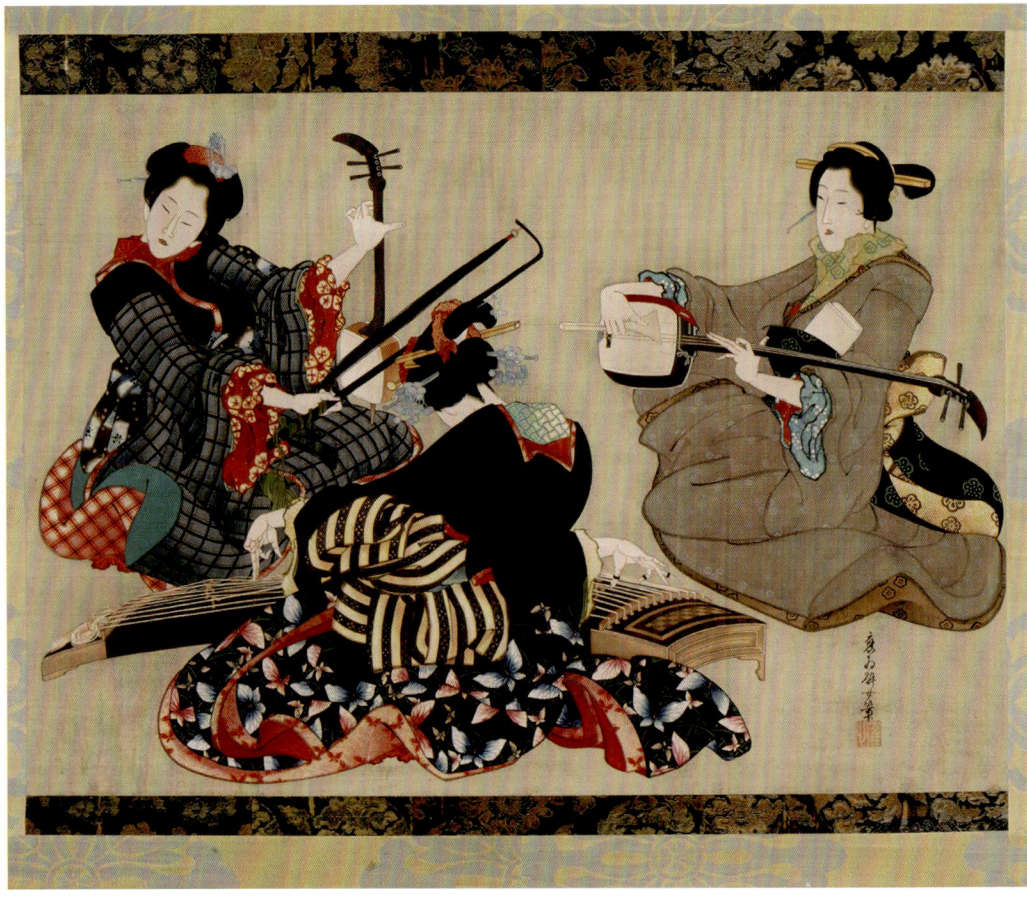

THREE WOMEN PLAYING MUSICAL INSTRUMENTS

*c.*1818–44, ink and colour on silk scroll, 46.5 × 67.5 cm (18 ½ × 26 ⅝ in),
Museum of Fine Arts, Boston
Katsushika Ōi, born *c.*1800, Edo (now Tokyo). Died *c.*1866, Edo (now Tokyo).

Working in the shadow of her father Katsushika Hokusai (1760–1849), Ōi was one of the very few successful female artists of the late Edo period. Like Hokusai, Ōi was a painter of *Ukiyo-e* ('pictures of the Floating World'), which depicted everyday scenes of contemporary life and leisure in her native city. Though she worked for much of her career as an assistant in her father's workshop, she was recognized as an accomplished artist in her own right. Hokusai himself noted that her *bijin-ga* portraits of beautiful women outshone his, and her style remains exemplary of Japanese art. While relatively few of Ōi's works can be identified today, among those attributed as hers is this undated painting. The musicians are a geisha troupe, employed to accompany traditional dances with music and singing. The depicted stringed instruments are the *koto*, *shamisen* and *kokyū*. In addition to painting, Ōi also illustrated books, though only two are known: the 1847 edition of Takai Ranzan's *Illustrated Handbook for Daily Life for Women*, and *A Concise Dictionary of Sencha* (1848), a guide to Japanese tea-drinking etiquette.

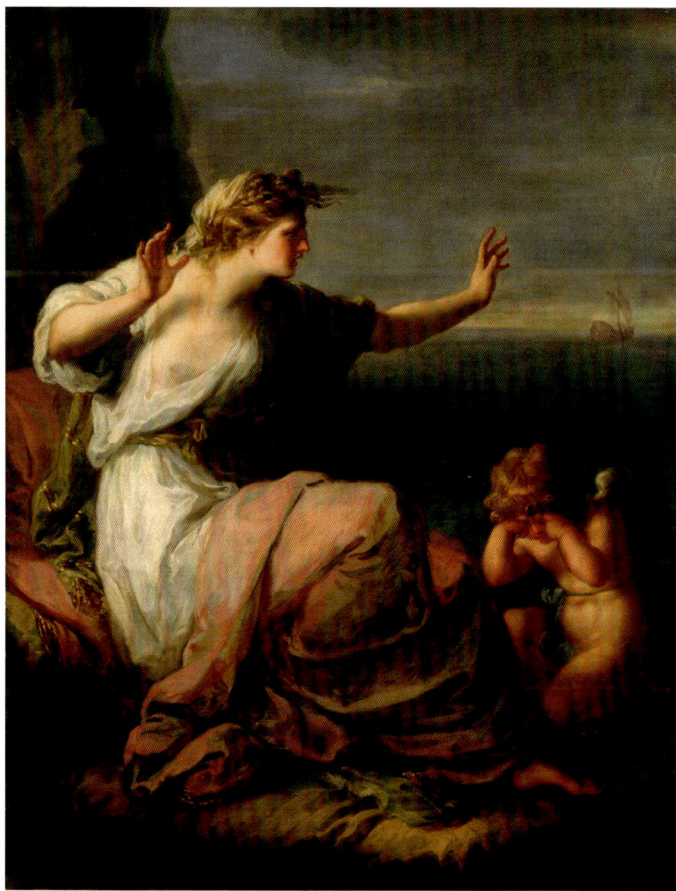

ARIADNE ABANDONED

before 1782, oil on canvas, 88 × 70.5 cm (34 ⅜ × 27 ¾ in), Gemäldegalerie Alte Meister, Staatliche Kunstsammlungen Dresden, Germany
Angelica Kauffman, born 1741, Chur, Switzerland. Died 1807, Rome.

Cosmopolitan, erudite and highly successful in her lifetime, Kauffman, together with Mary Moser (p.286), was a founder member of London's Royal Academy of Arts in 1768. Her artist-father had recognized her precocious talent and taught her from a young age. Familiar with the itinerant life of a working painter – as a child she moved between Austria, Switzerland and Italy – Kauffman arrived in London around 1765, before returning to Rome fifteen years later. A close friend of Sir Joshua Reynolds (1723–92), the first president of the Royal Academy, Kauffman was a portraitist,

landscapist and decorative painter, though, unusually for a woman at that time, saw herself primarily as a history painter, the most respected of the academic hierarchy of genres. A category that included mythological subjects, history painting required the artist to articulate morally edifying tales in a forceful and dramatic manner. Enthused by contemporaneous excavations of Pompeii in the late eighteenth century, which were revealing extensive Classical frescoes, in this work Kauffman depicts Ariadne's abandonment on Naxos by Theseus, despite having previously rescued him from the Minotaur's labyrinth.

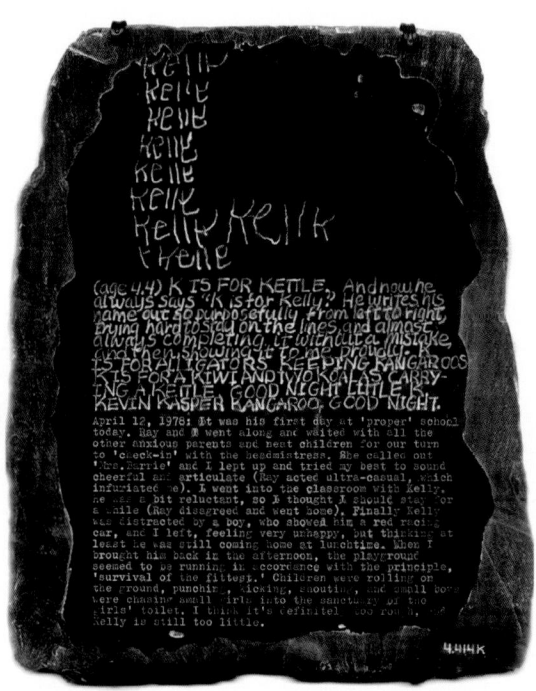

POST-PARTUM DOCUMENT: DOCUMENTATION VI, PREWRITING ALPHABET, EXERGUE AND DIARY

1978, (detail), Perspex unit, white card, resin and slate, 18 units, each 35.5 × 28 cm (14 × 11 in), Arts Council Collection, UK
Mary Kelly, born 1941, Fort Dodge, Iowa.

Sexuality, identity and the mother-child relationship comprise the core of Kelly's conceptual work, navigating her own experiences of becoming a parent in the mid-1970s. Making large-scale narrative installations and project-based pieces, her feminist practice has spanned five decades, starting from the women's movement in which she participated. Centred on female subjectivity, she has examined themes ranging from money to power, as mediated by the body. War became a focus in the 1990s, in response to the First Gulf War and Kosovo conflicts, with later explorations of collective memory. This piece is from the immense six-part project for which she is best known: *Post-Partum Document*, which began in 1973 when Kelly was pregnant with her son. This section, charting his verbal development, as well as the conditions in which Kelly was living at the time, resembles a latter-day Rosetta Stone, one domestic history standing for the whole of human communication. Other sections of the series include used nappy liners, children's drawings and philosophical writings, which are combined with the artist's own texts to meditate on this relationship. What society considers 'natural' – and, as such, imposes on mothers – is brought into question.

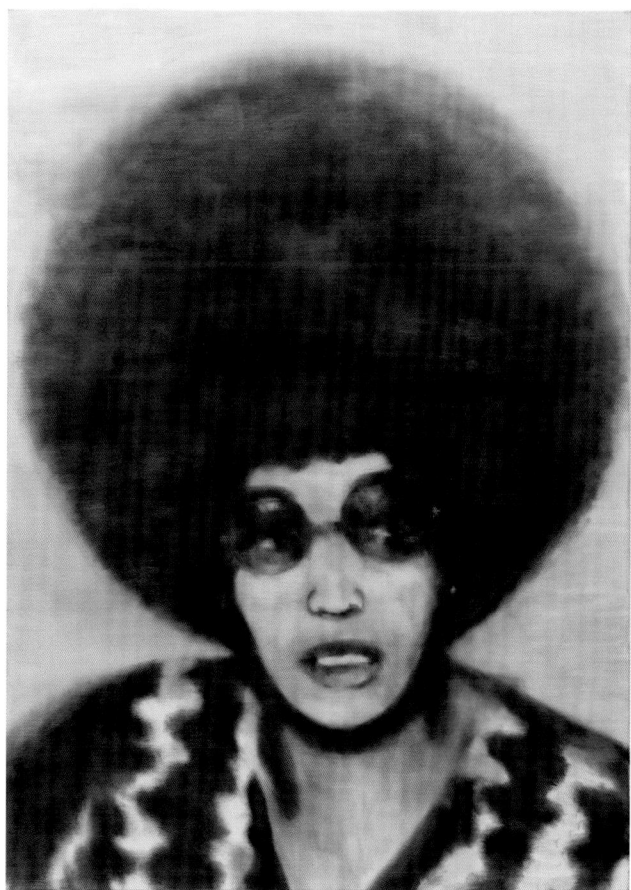

ANGELA DAVIS #2

2015, oil on canvas, 110.3 × 80.2 cm (43 ⅜ × 31 ⅝ in), Van Abbemuseum, Eindhoven, Netherlands

Iris Kensmil, born 1970, Amsterdam.

A Dutch artist of Surinamese descent, Kensmil represents black people and their life stories through drawing and painting, highlighting neglected narratives, particularly in art history, and showing reverence to the excluded. Since graduating from the Academie Minerva, Groningen, in 1996, she has explored themes relating to black emancipation and civil rights. In 2017, she presented 'Study in Black Modernity' at Van Abbemuseum, Eindhoven. This installation comprised graphic wall designs, drawings of black historical figures and a bookshelf of black, feminist reading material. Also

at the museum that year, *Angela Davis #2* was shown alongside her portrait of Jamaican political leader Marcus Garvey, set against a black-and-white mural inspired by the geometric art of Piet Mondrian (1872–1944), to form the installation 'Voices across the Ocean'. Davis rose to prominence in the 1960s as an outspoken counter-cultural activist of the Communist Party USA and feminist and civil rights movements. Seen in the light of new movements such as Black Lives Matter, Kensmil's work is a timely reminder of the power of black counterculture. Kensmil was selected to represent the Netherlands at the 58th Venice Biennale in 2019.

CORITA KENT

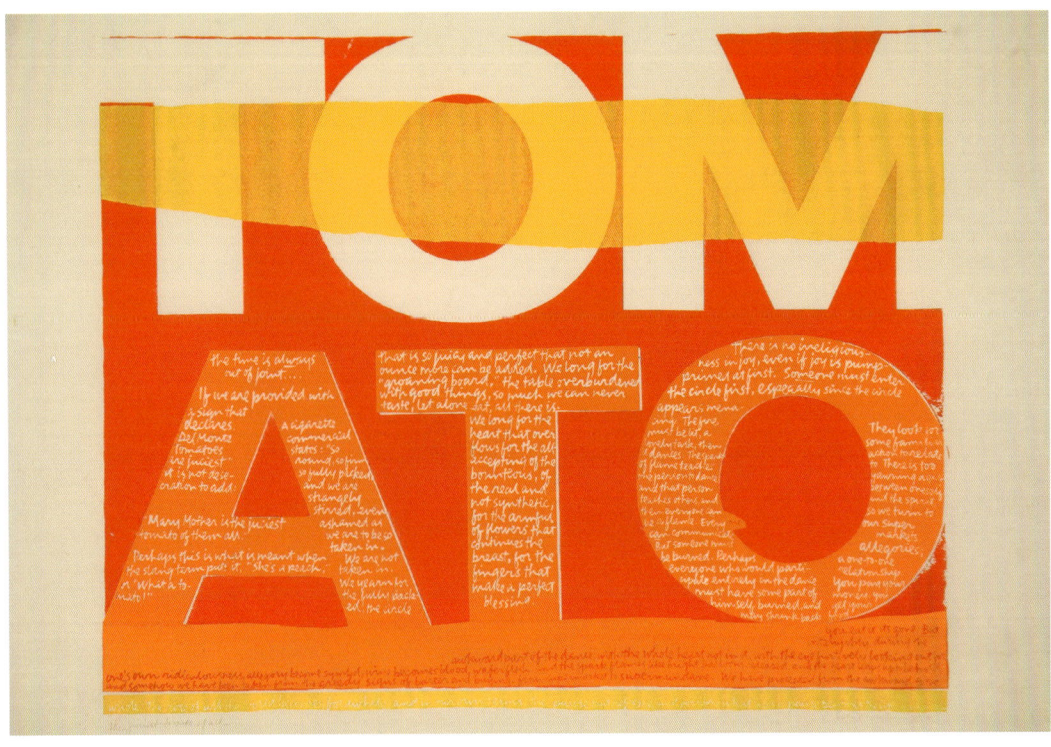

THE JUICIEST TOMATO OF ALL

1964, screen print, 75.6 × 91.4 cm (29 ¾ × 36 in), UCLA Grunwald Center for the
Graphic Arts, Hammer Museum, Los Angeles
Corita Kent, born Frances Elizabeth Kent, 1918, Fort Dodge, Iowa.
Died 1986, Boston.

Kent's vibrant screen prints reconfigured slogans from advertising
and vernacular culture into ardent spiritual messages. A Sister of the
Order of the Immaculate Heart of Mary, she became known as the
'Pop art nun', gaining attention at a time when the Roman Catholic
Church was attempting to embrace reform. Kent moved with her
family to Los Angeles when she was five and at eighteen entered the
Order, where she taught art. Seeing the 'soup cans' of Andy Warhol
(1928–87) in 1962 had a profound impact upon her and she began

making silkscreen prints that year, favouring the affordability and
boldness of the medium. These eye-catching, accessible text-based
works were likewise underpinned by Kent's strong social commitment and desire to connect with people. Although an apparently
innocent borrowing of a line used in advertisements for the
food manufacturer Del Monte, this print is in fact a subtle icon
of the Virgin Mary, and calling her 'the juiciest tomato of all'
brought Kent into conflict with the church's more conservative
factions. Following complaints from the Los Angeles archdiocese,
Kent took a sabbatical in 1968 and subsequently left her community to protect it from controversy.

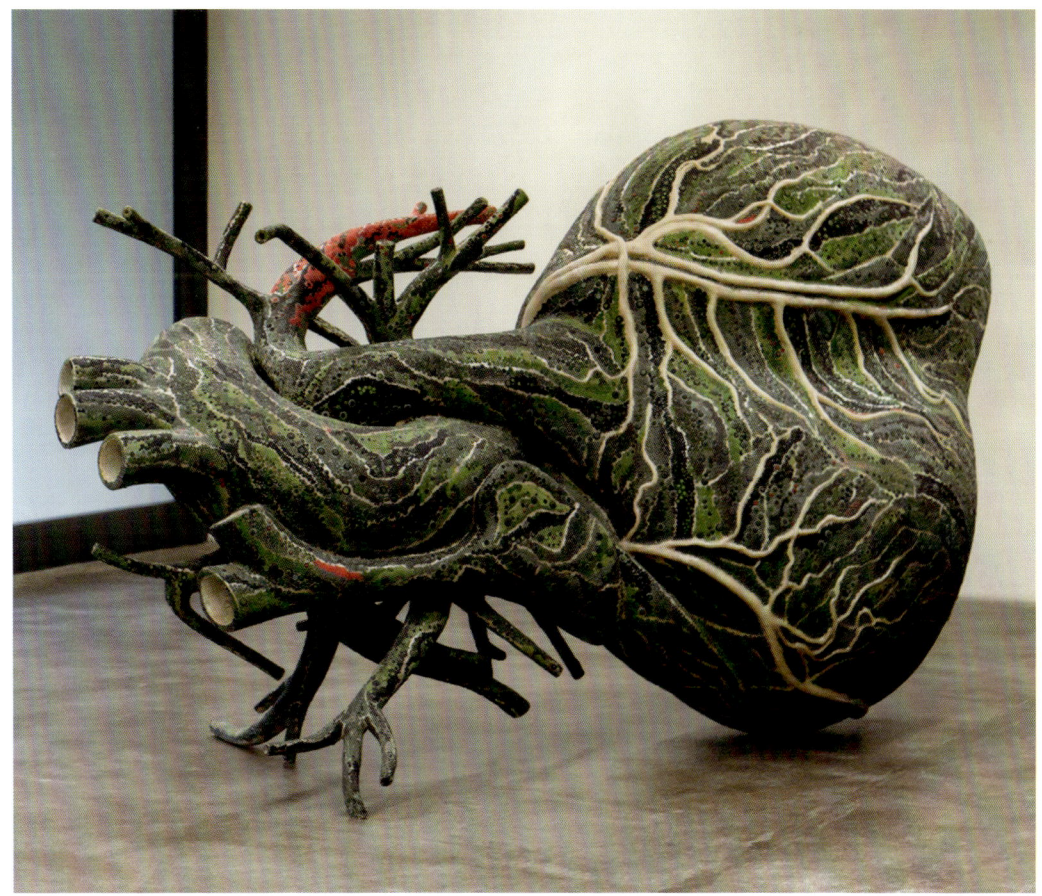

AN ABSENCE OF ASSIGNABLE CAUSE

2007, bindis on fibreglass, 173 × 300 × 116 cm (68 ⅛ × 118 ⅛ × 45 ⅝ in), private collection
Bharti Kher, born 1969, London.

Born in London to Indian parents and later studying painting at Newcastle Polytechnic, Kher moved to New Delhi at the age of twenty-three, where she continues to live. Her primary art material is the self-adhesive bindi, a decorative dot worn in the centre of the forehead by women of the Indian subcontinent. Traditionally painted on with pigment, it is now mass produced for faster, easier application. For Kher, this traditional Hindu symbol combines ideas of culture, religious practice, commodity, domesticity and beauty. She arranges and layers accumulations of bindis to make wall-based abstract works, or uses them to cover the surface of three-dimensional sculptures. Typically her works reference mythological stories, often depicting animal forms, as Kher integrates the magical into the every-day. *An Absence Of Assignable Cause* stems from her curiosity about the size and anatomy of the blue whale, specifically its heart. At the time, there was a lack of scientific documentation depicting the organ, so she imagined it as a huge form resting on its side, the aorta and pulmonary artery exposed. The surface is coated in a thin membrane of pink, green, blue and grey bindis to define a mottled surface of flesh and blood vessels.

KIMSOOJA

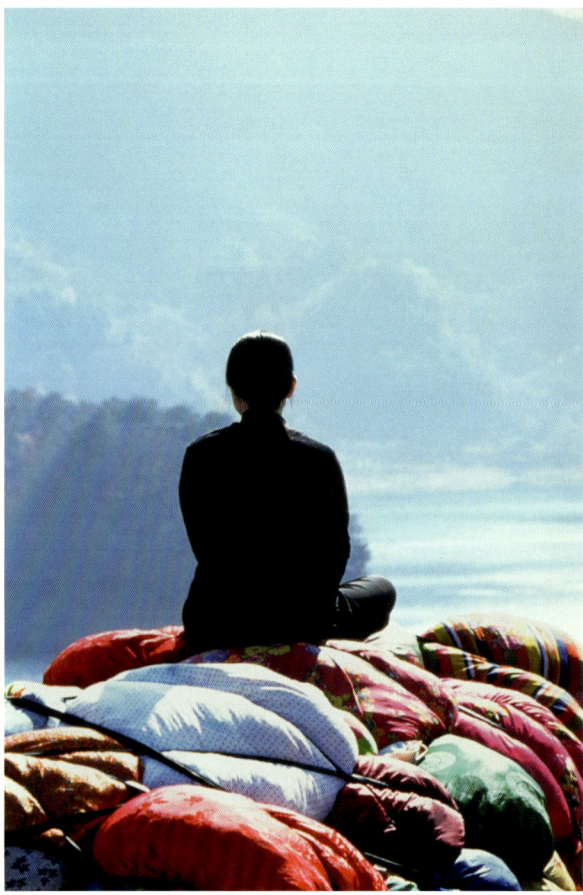

CITIES ON THE MOVE – 2727 KM BOTTARI TRUCK

1997, photograph, from eleven-day performance throughout South Korea
Kimsooja, born Kim Soo-ja, 1957, Daegu, South Korea.

Kimsooja's one-word name refuses gender identity, marital status, socio-political or cultural and geographical identity by not separating surname and first name. Her conceptual multimedia works evolve from her position as a painter and from her early sewn works to objects, performances, sculptures, videos and sitespecific installations. Focusing on existential questions and the human condition, Kimsooja conceptualizes women's domestic daily life activities in the context of contemporary art. She represented South Korea at the 24th São Paulo Biennial in 1998 and the 55th Venice Biennale in 2013. Her exploration of dislocation often makes use of *bottari*, traditional

Korean bedcovers tied into bundles to wrap and protect one's belongings during transit, originally made by women of all classes. Kimsooja's *bottari* works question universal issues of human destiny in this troubled era. In *Cities on the Move – 2727 km Bottari Truck*, Kimsooja sits atop a mound of *bottari* being transported across the country, documenting part of her eleven-day performance on her journey to places she resided before she made a cultural exile from Korea to New York at the end of the 1990s.

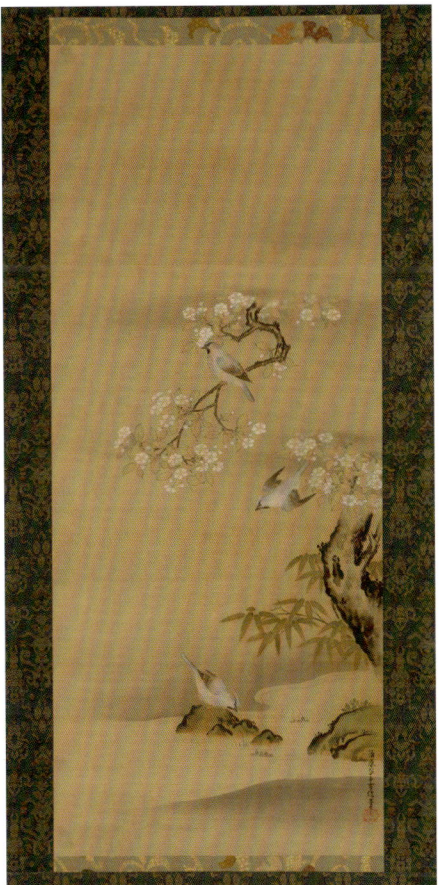

WAXWINGS, CHERRY BLOSSOMS AND BAMBOO

late 17th century, hanging scroll, ink and colour on silk, 99.4 × 41.6 cm
(39 ⅛ × 16 ⅜ in), Metropolitan Museum of Art, New York
Kiyohara Yukinobu, born 1643, Kyoto. Died 1682, Japan.

Kiyohara was one of the most notable female painters of Japan's
Edo period (1603–1868). It was an advantage for a budding woman
artist to have relatives who could offer training in the home, and
Kiyohara came from the Kanō family – the most influential artistic
dynasty of the age – which gave its name to the school of painting
that defined Japanese taste for centuries. She was the daughter
of Kusumi Morikage (c.1620–90) and the great-niece of the renowned
teacher Kanō Tan'yū (1602–74), with whom she probably studied.
Painting scrolls and screens, Kiyohara developed a reputation in her

own right, adding her personal style of fluid brushwork to existing
traditions. Flowers and birds are recurring subjects, though she also
completed works relating to classical Japanese literature. This work
features three birds posed around a cherry tree in bloom, which indicates that the scene is set in late spring. Cherry blossoms are
a symbol of new beginnings, and waxwings of family prosperity and
marital harmony; bamboo likewise carries auspicious meanings
relating to purity, flexibility and strength.

EMILY KAM KNGWARRAY

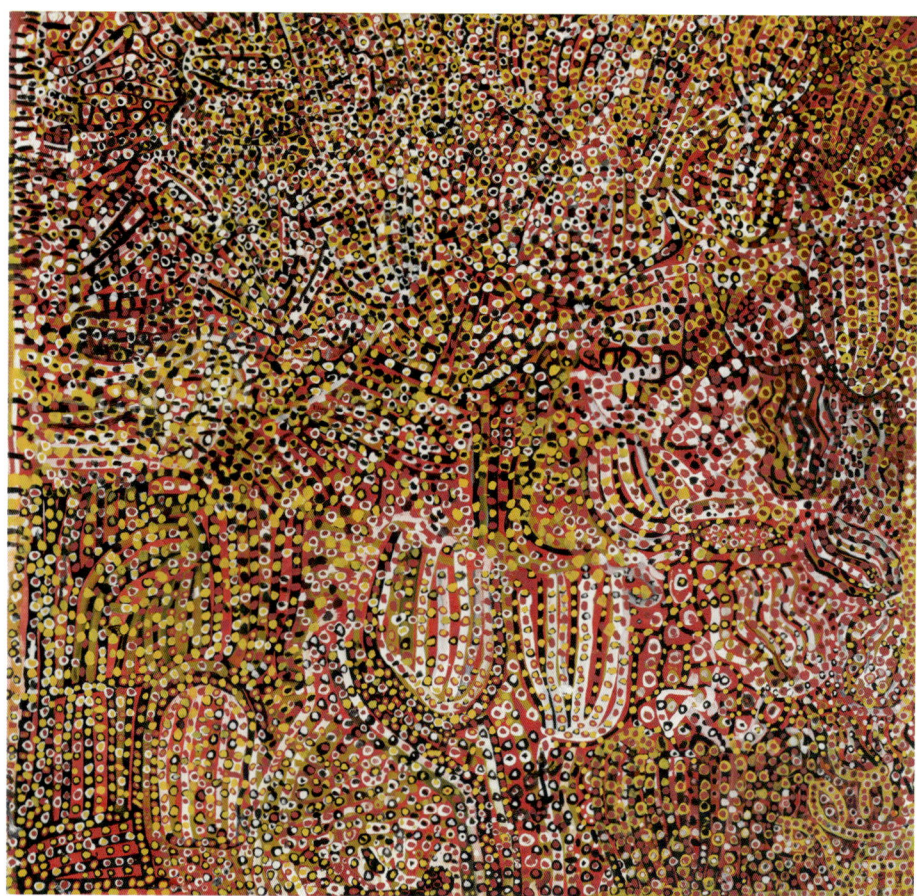

NTANGE DREAMING

1989, synthetic polymer paint on canvas, 135 × 122 cm (53 ¼ × 48 in),
National Gallery of Australia, Canberra
Emily Kam Kngwarray, born c.1910, Utopia, Northern Territory, Australia.
Died 1996, Alice Springs, Australia.

Kngwarray was born in an area known as Utopia, located northeast of Alice Springs in Australia's Northern Territory. Introduced to batik, then oils and finally acrylics, she is believed to have only begun painting in her seventies and it is estimated that she produced over 3,000 paintings during her eight-year career. The result of this extraordinary output was a deep and energetic expression of her life and knowledge as an Anmatyerre elder in her clan country, Alhalkere. Seen here, her country is depicted after the ancestral powers have fertilized the earth with rain, when women collect seeds from the native grasses (*ntange* in the Anmatyerr language) and use them to make a damper to eat following a ceremony. The marks symbolize the ancestral beings, or Dreamings, and are based on designs that are painted onto the upper body of women participating in the ceremony, a central aspect of the performance. With her fingers, Kngwarray transferred traditional methods of body decoration and applied them to canvas. In 2007, her 1994 painting *Earth's Creation* was the first work by an indigenous artist to sell at auction for over a million Australian dollars.

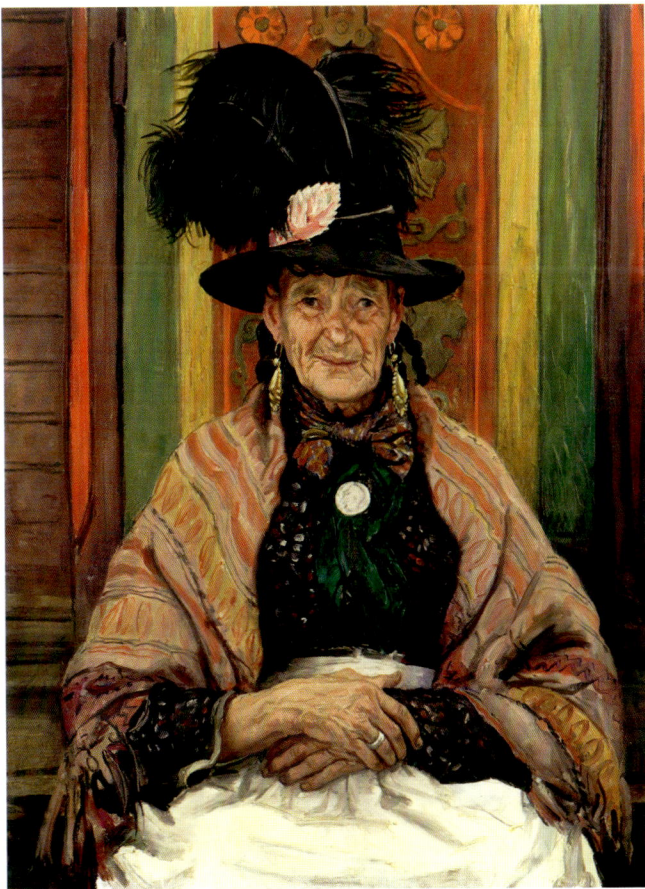

FINE FEATHERS

1939, oil on canvas, 101.6 × 76.2 cm (40 × 30 in), Nottingham Castle Museum and Art Gallery, UK
Laura Knight, born 1877, Long Eaton, Derbyshire, UK. Died 1970, London.

The first woman to be elected a full member of London's Royal Academy of Arts in 1936, Knight was one of the most successful artists in interwar Britain, with her work being exhibited and collected by museums across the country. Primarily using oils and watercolours, Knight's figurative painting was in the style of Impressionism, the movement's quick brushwork and focus on shifting light effects being characteristic of her practice. An official artist during both world wars, she produced memorable studies of the conflicts, particularly depicting women's roles in factories, the Land Army and the military. She later spent three months in Germany in 1946 observing the Nuremberg Trials, which resulted in her most ambitious work, a reinterpretation of the genre of history painting. Knight loved the stage, and alongside painting sets, she depicted ballet, theatre and circus performers. This work is a portrait of an elderly Romany woman in opulent fabrics and jewellery, and demonstrates Knight's empathy, in particular her affection for marginalized communities. Knight painted the sitter, Lilo Smith, and her daughter-in-law numerous times after befriending them at the Ascot races, after which she was invited to visit their gypsy encampment in Buckinghamshire.

BĚLA KOLÁŘOVÁ

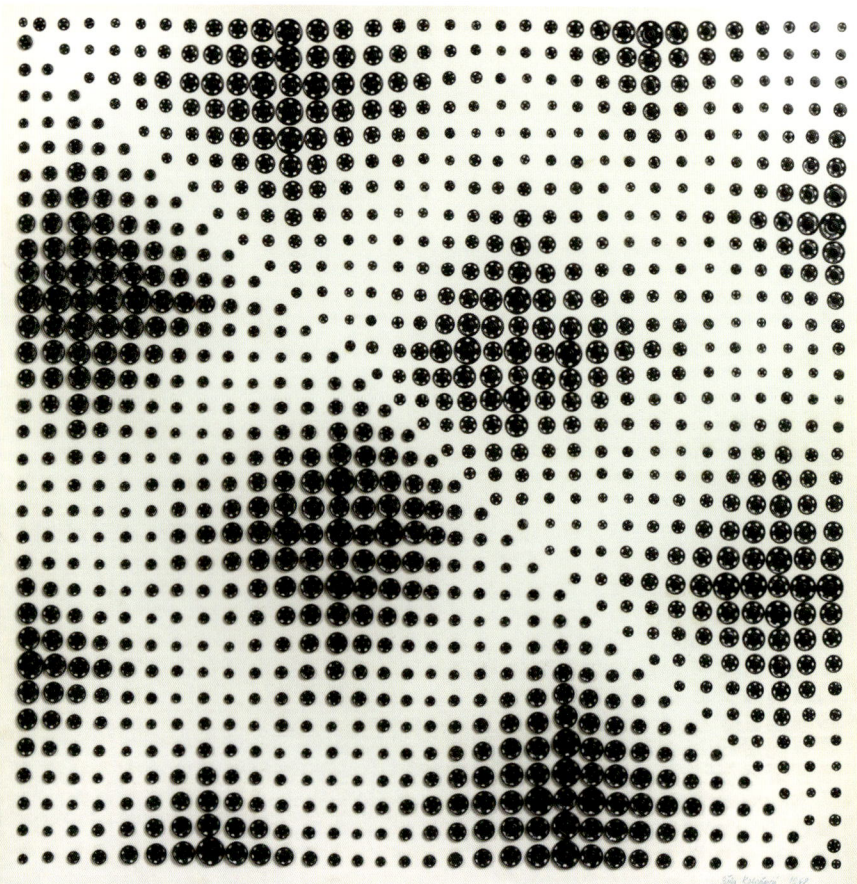

VARIATION: TWO TRIANGLES IV

1968, snap fasteners mounted on board, 58 × 58 cm (22 ⅞ × 22 ⅞ in)
Běla Kolářová, born Běla Helclová, 1923, Terezín, Czechoslavakia (now Czechia).
Died 2010, Prague.

Working with photography, collage and assemblage, Kolářová was interested in the agency of things, particularly small, overlooked objects used every day. In her early career she made photographs, photograms and works called 'traces', gathering household items that she imprinted into wax spread over a celluloid sheet. These were regarded as a form of secret writing – object poems. A persistent feeling of being limited by the camera and its ability to represent reality led Kolářová to advance this concept from the mid-1960s, making assemblages with utility objects like paperclips and matches. Kolářová and her husband artist Jiří Kolář (1914–2002) were key figures in Prague's intellectual scene in the 1960s, and their home was a gathering point for informal seminars to discuss political freedom and culture. Focusing on the avant-garde strategies of Fluxus and Conceptualism, they worked in a period of increasing optimism that culminated in the Prague Spring – and its violent aftermath of Soviet invasion and the repressive era of 'normalization'. Contemporary with that tumultuous year is this restrained Minimalist work, an assortment of tailor's snap fasteners mounted on card to create an insistent geometric rhythm.

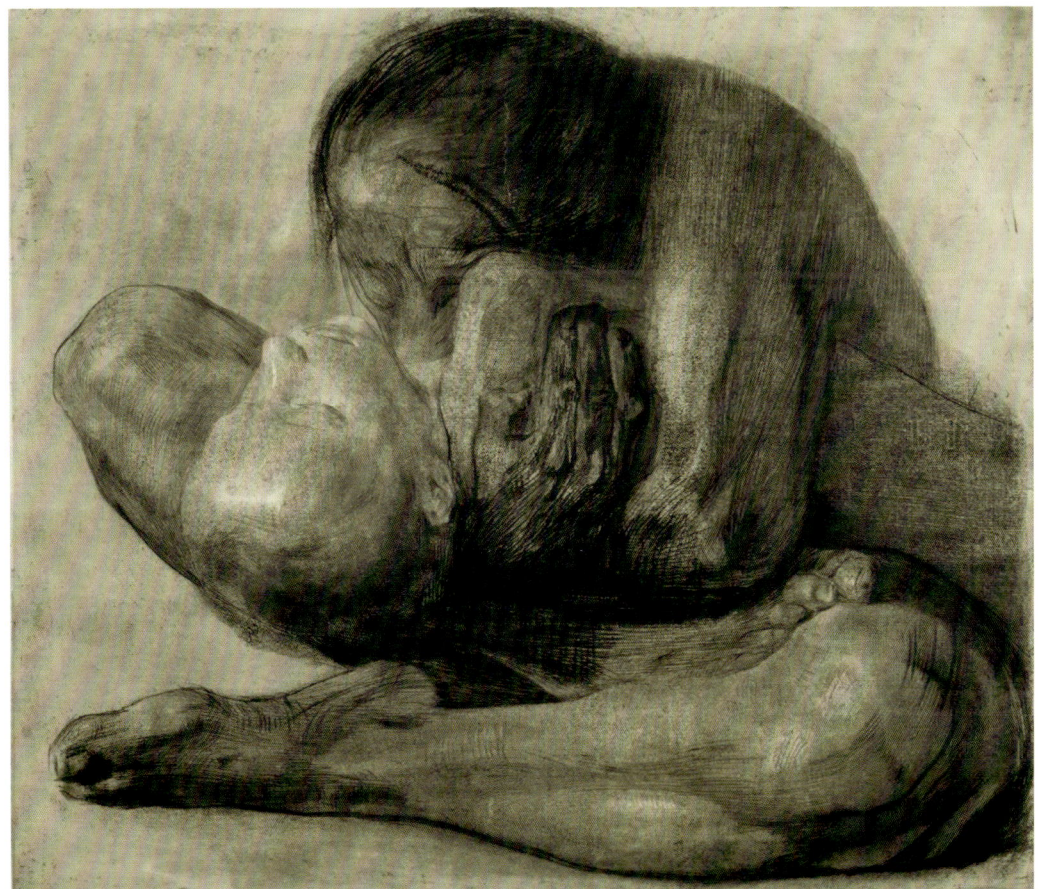

WOMAN WITH DEAD CHILD

1903, etching, 42.5 × 48.6 cm (16 ¾ × 19 ⅛ in), Kunsthalle, Bremen, Germany
Käthe Kollwitz, born Käthe Schmidt, 1867, Königsberg, Prussia (now Kaliningrad, Russia). Died 1945, Moritzburg, Germany.

Raised in a family of socialists and religious radicals, Kollwitz began lessons in drawing at the age of twelve, producing sketches of the sailors and peasants of her working-class milieu. In order to pursue her artistic studies further, she left provincial Prussia for the Academy of the Society of Women Artists in Berlin. Her breakthrough print series of 1897, 'A Weavers' Revolt', impressed the city's art establishment while incurring the personal disdain of the Kaiser, and her work became widely circulated, contributing to her international popularity. In 1919 she was the first woman elected to the Prussian

Academy of Arts, though the National Socialists removed her from this position in 1933, and in 1943 much of her work was destroyed in an air raid on Berlin. The suffering of marginalized, exploited and bereaved people remained Kollwitz's subject throughout her career, as in this reinterpretation of the Pietà subject of Christian art. A stark self-portrait with her seven-year-old son Peter, who was later killed in action early in the First World War, this composition – and its subsequent reimagining as a sculpture – was to become a profound symbol of collective grief in Germany.

EVA KOTÁTKOVÁ

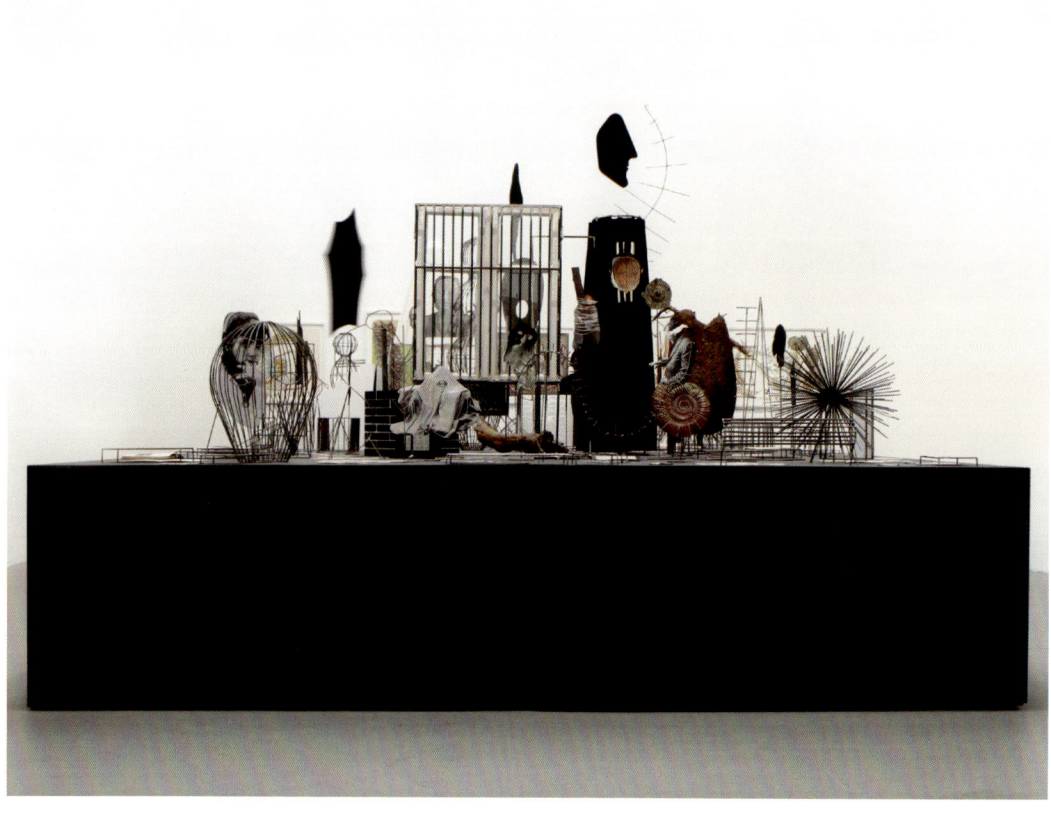

ASYLUM
2013, mixed media, dimensions variable, installation view, 'The Encyclopedic Palace',
55th Venice Biennale
Eva Kotátková, born 1982, Prague.

Kotátková is known for installations that explore how disciplinary institutions such as clinics and schools determine behaviour. A recurring theme in her work is confinement. After moving into her late grandmother's apartment in Prague, she emptied it entirely of its contents and built a restricted cave-like dwelling in one room. Four short films collectively entitled *Behind Between Over Under In (the Flat)* (2007) documented her actions, with their implication that identity is not shaped by the surroundings we choose but rather by imposed rules and conventions. She has worked with children, evincing candid descriptions of control in schools, and with psychiatric patients, as seen here in this large-scale, inchoate scene. Composed of various elements – metal structures, paper cut-out figures, texts and the glimpsed body parts of human performers – material symbols of imprisonment are juxtaposed with objects evoking inescapable nightmares, Kotátková's response to individual experiences of anxiety and powerlessness in a hospital. Her work echoes the emancipatory manifesto of the 'anti-psychiatry' movement of the 1960s and 1970s, yet her practice stems from fieldwork among patients living in institutions today and still subject to deep-rooted structures of domination.

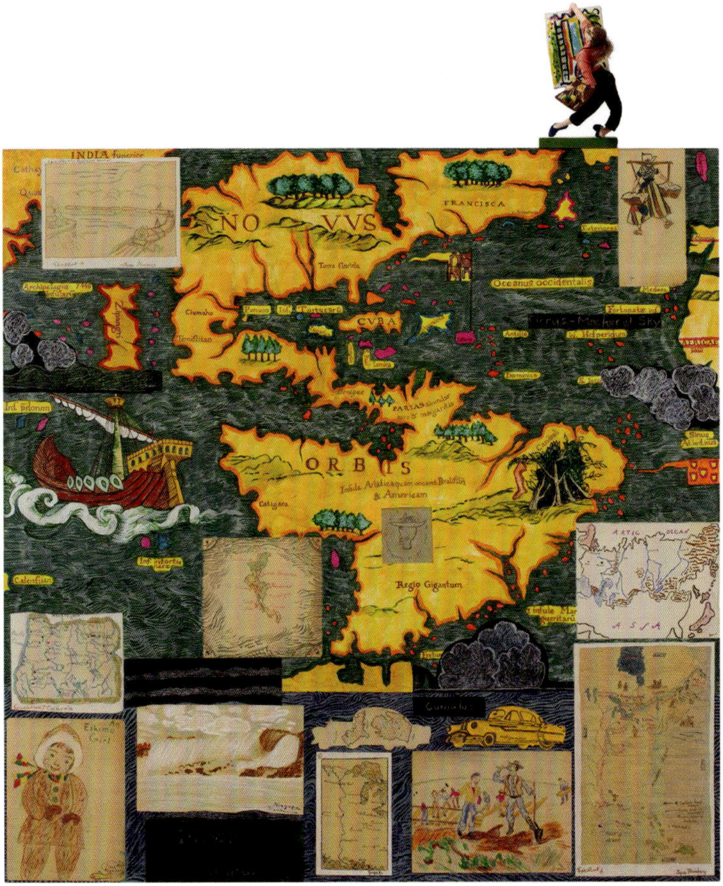

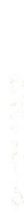

ART GIRL

2017, acrylic, collage and found object on canvas, painting: 137.2 × 137.2 cm (54 × 54 in); figure: 30.5 × 15.2 cm (12 × 6 in), Pennsylvania Academy of the Fine Arts, Philadelphia
Joyce Kozloff, born Joyce Blumberg, 1942, Somerville, New Jersey.

Having graduated with an MFA from Columbia University in 1967, by the early 1970s Kozloff had become involved in the burgeoning women's movement in America, co-founding the New York-based feminist collective and journal *Heresies* in 1977, alongside Dotty Attie (p.42) and Michelle Stuart (p.392). Two years earlier, she was also a founding member of the Pattern and Decoration movement, which sought to deconstruct the art/craft dichotomy through production of abstract canvases that drew eclectic inspiration from the decorative traditions of various non-Western cultures. Kozloff's political views have always been expressed through her artistic style, which seeks to break down hierarchies of 'high' art and 'low' craft. In the 1980s she moved away from painting to the more socially embedded realm of public art, her first work of this kind was a mural for Harvard Square subway station in Cambridge, Massachusetts. For the past three decades she has used cartographic imagery to consider the ways humans imagine and represent the world. From her recent series 'Girlhood', *Art Girl* brings together reproductions of historic maps with Kozloff's own childhood drawings and toys, exploring cultural fantasies about femininity and nationhood.

LEE KRASNER

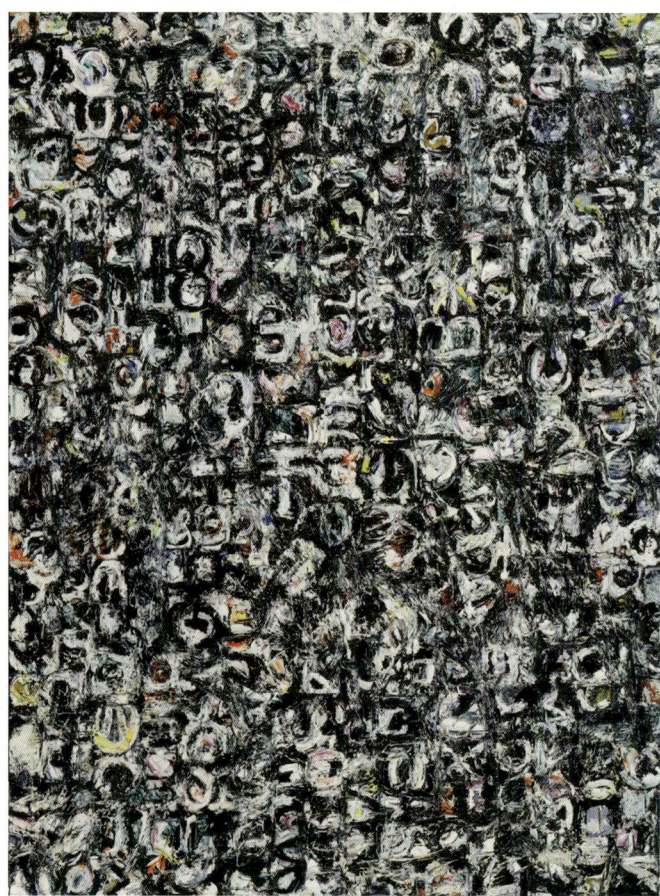

UNTITLED

1949, oil on composition board, 121.9 × 93.9 cm (48 × 37 in), Museum of Modern Art, New York
Lee Krasner, born Lenore Krassner, 1908, New York. Died 1984, New York.

A key member of the Abstract Expressionist movement, Krasner was known for her gestural, dynamic approach to painting. Learning art from an early age, including Old Master techniques, she became a skilled figurative painter and worked in that style as a muralist. The 1930s saw her explore technique, composition and theory – key tenets of modernism – and she began to make abstract gouaches later in the decade, hoping to develop their motifs further in mural form. She adopted a neo-Cubist style, abandoning it in 1942 after encountering the work of Jackson Pollock (1912–56), whom she significantly influenced and would later marry. Krasner was deeply self-deprecating and often scornful of her own practice, destroying whole series and leaving behind only 599 works. Seen here is one of nearly forty paintings from the series 'Little Image' of the late 1940s. These employed a thick build-up of paint using the drip technique and have a symbolic resonance, hinting at lost narratives or arcane traditions. The year after Krasner died, the Museum of Modern Art, New York, held a major retrospective of her work, releasing her from the shadow of her husband's reputation.

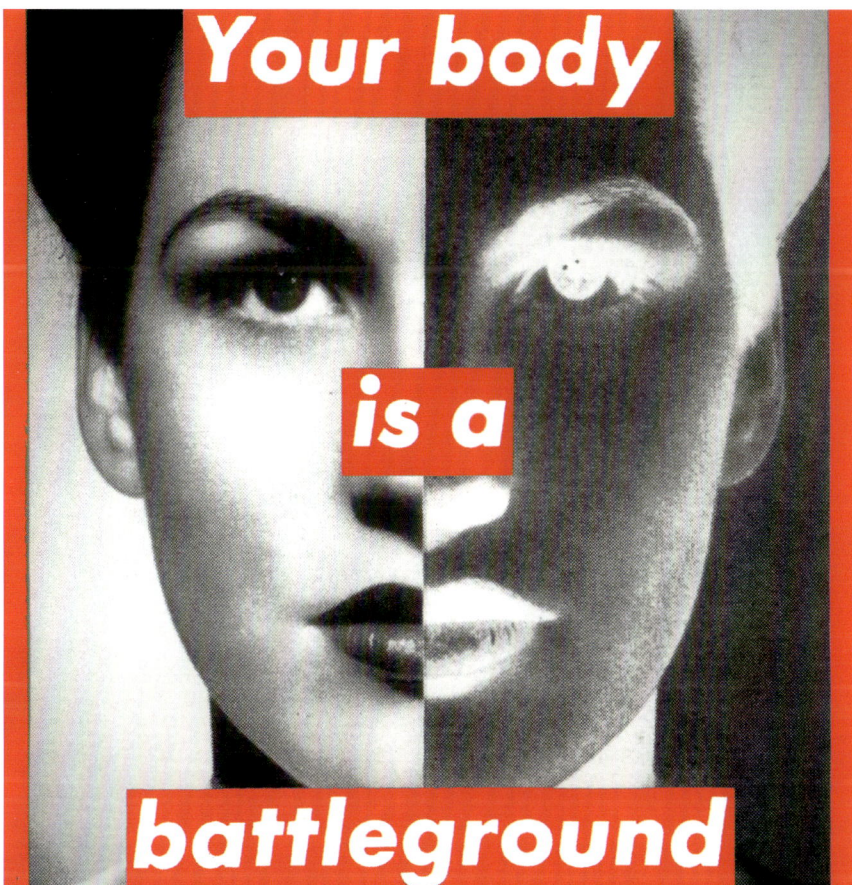

UNTITLED (YOUR BODY IS A BATTLEGROUND)

1989, photographic silkscreen on vinyl, 284.5 × 284.5 cm (112 × 112 in)
Barbara Kruger, born 1945, Newark, New Jersey.

A graphic designer for Condé Nast early in her career, Kruger's Conceptual art co-opts the arresting and bold techniques of advertising to explore gender and identity politics. Her work is often mounted in unusual spaces, on billboards, buildings and bus stops, as well as in museums. Typically set against a trademark red background, Kruger's work combines slogans with monochrome photographs of women in America from a post-Second World War period, with the use of the Helvetica and Futura Bold typefaces establishing a further recurring aesthetic or 'brand' for her practice. Her earlier work, from around 1969, already featured a strongly feminist intent, making wall hangings from 'craft' materials such as yarn and beads in order to question the distinction between traditionally 'female' pastimes and fine art. Seeking a new direction, Kruger stopped making art in the mid-1970s before publishing an artist book, *Picture/Readings* (1979) and initiating her now recognizable style, which exposes institutional oppression in order to provoke action in viewers. This example appeared in public spaces with the aim of recruiting protestors for rights to birth control and legalized abortion on the 1989 Women's March on Washington DC.

SHIGEKO KUBOTA

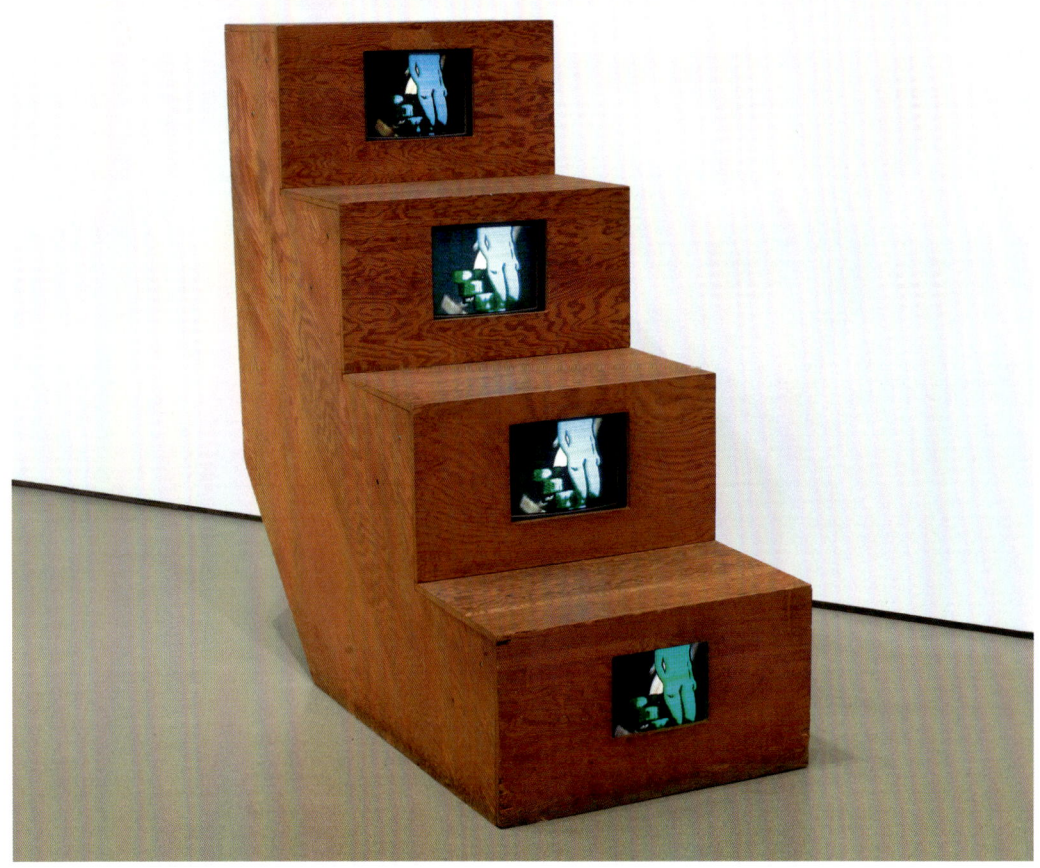

DUCHAMPIANA: NUDE DESCENDING A STAIRCASE

1976, Super 8mm film transferred to video and colour-synthesized video (colour, silent), monitors and plywood, 168.3 × 78.6 × 170.2 cm (66¼ × 30⅞ × 67 in), Museum of Modern Art, New York

Shigeko Kubota, born 1937, Niigata, Japan. Died 2015, New York.

After graduating from the Tokyo University of Education in 1960, Kubota became associated with avant-garde members of Group Ongaku, a collective of artists experimenting with music and perfor-mance. During this period she met John Cage (1912–92) and Yoko Ono (p.303), who inspired her on her arrival in New York to integrate into the experimental multimedia movement, Fluxus. Her first notable work was *Vagina Painting*, a 1965 performance piece in which crouched and made marks on sheets of paper with red pigment using a paint-brush attached to her underwear. She also began to work with video from the 1960s, and is considered a pioneer in its development as an artistic medium. The 'Duchampiana' series reflected her admiration for Marcel Duchamp (1887–1968), whom she met in 1968. This piece was the first video artwork to be acquired by New York's Museum of Modern Art. Referencing Duchamp's iconic 1912 painting of a nude figure walking down stairs – resembling a sequence of overlapping cinema stills to convey movement and time on a two-dimensional surface – Kubota effects a corresponding reinterpretation of video, at that time a still-nascent medium.

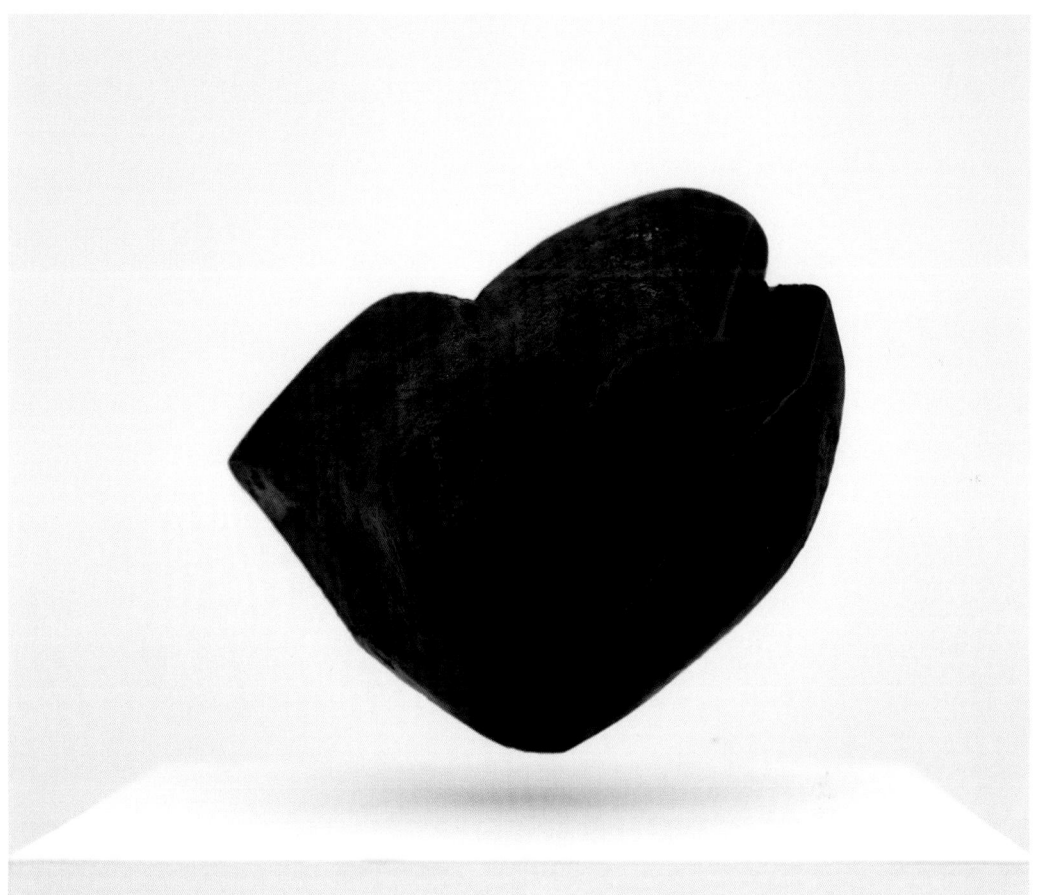

AIR RIGHTS 5

2016, powdered stone, foam, wood, electromagnets and custom pedestal,
meteorite: c.10.2 × 15.2 × 14 cm (c.4 × 6 × 5 ½ in), pedestal: 150.5 × 22.9 × 22.9 cm
(59 ¼ × 9 × 9 in), Collection of Kathleen Irvin Loughlin
Agnieszka Kurant, born 1978, Łódź, Poland.

Kurant's career as an artist began while studying for a master's
in curating at London's Goldsmiths College, her work exceeding the
traditional scope of this discipline by moving into actual making.
Investigating conceptual spaces with her sculpture and installations,
she examines how systems function, be they economic, social or cultural, and the degree to which they rely on blurring fact and fiction.
Invisibility and intangibility are her key artistic concerns, as she
brings imaginary territories, virtual capital and immaterial ideas into

concrete form. *Phantom Library* (2011–12) comprises a shelf of fictional titles that have appeared in *actual* books, and although
adorned with covers and barcodes, the blank pages reveal them
to be mere tokens of storytelling. *Air Rights 5* brings a similar ghostly
mystery to bear on the concept of real estate, a pressing concern
for many and with potentially drastic real-world effects. A black fake
rock levitates like a magical meteorite above a white plinth. Referring
to property rights, which extend to the empty space above buildings,
the work's title highlights the strange metaphysics that underlie
notions of ownership.

YAYOI KUSAMA

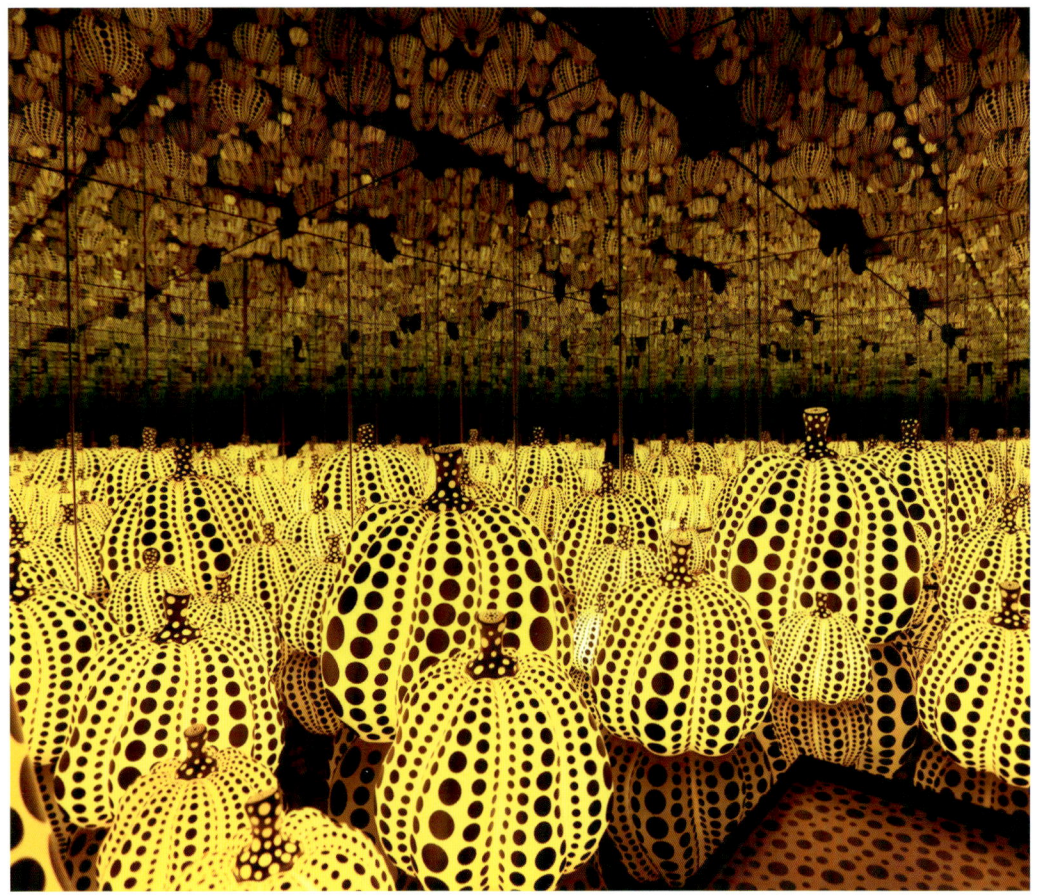

ALL THE ETERNAL LOVE I HAVE FOR THE PUMPKINS
2016, wood, mirror, plastic, acrylic, LEDs and metal, 292.4 × 415 × 415 cm
(115 ⅛ × 163 ⅜ × 163 ⅜ in), Dallas Museum of Art
Yayoi Kusama, born 1929, Matsumoto, Japan.

Reflecting on the origins of her practice, Kusama recalls lining up small pebbles from a riverbed behind her childhood home. She studied at the Kyoto School of Arts and Crafts and was trained in the conventions of the *nihonga* style of Japanese painting, but became disenchanted with this tradition. Upon moving to New York in 1958, she gained a reputation within the avant-garde community through her sculptures, installations, paintings and performances. While having connections with artists from the main movements of the time – Abstract Expressionism, Minimalism and the Fluxus group – Kusama firmly wanted to establish her own art. Her sustained exploration of repetition and hallucination characteristically uses simple forms such as polka dots or lights to address themes of self-obliteration and obsession. Surrounded by mirrored walls, these simple elements produce the overwhelming experience of the 'Infinity Rooms' that the artist has produced since 1965. The iteration seen here invites the viewer to enter a limitless field of glowing pumpkins, objects that have appeared throughout Kusama's career in both two- and three-dimensional works. For her, they convey humour, warmth and human-like qualities in size and shape.

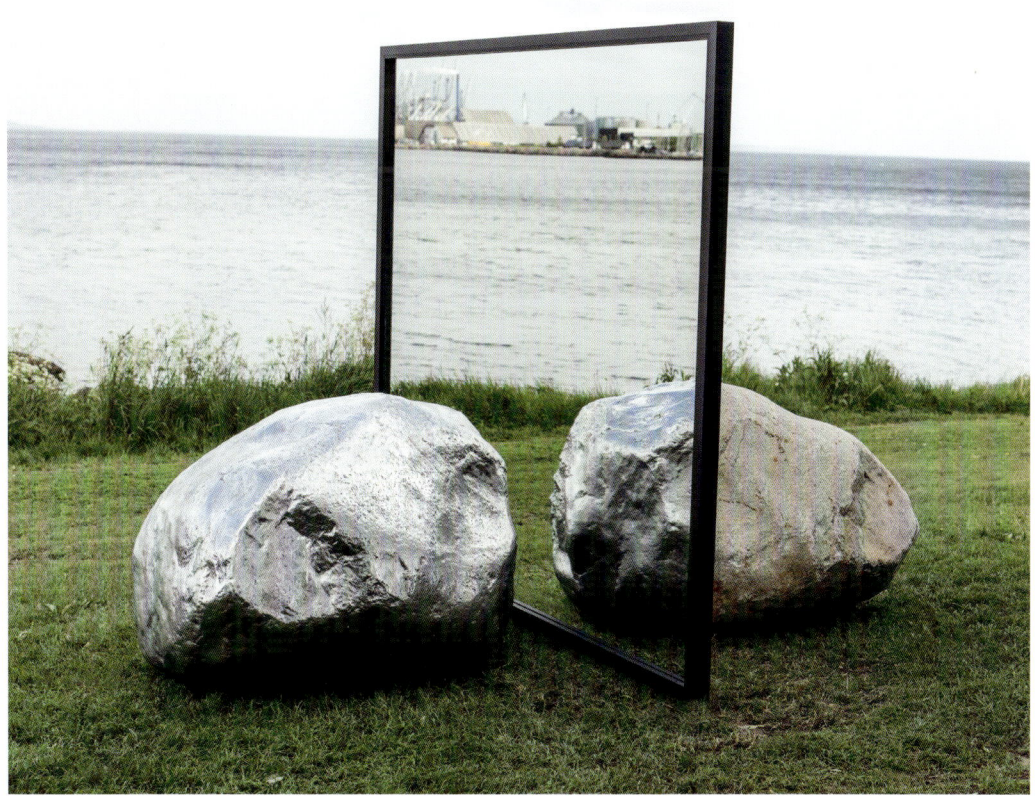

BIG BE-HIDE

2017, stone, aluminium, mirror and powder-coated stainless steel, 190 × 230 ×
272 cm (74¾ × 90½ × 107⅛ in), private collection
Alicja Kwade, born 1979, Katowice, Poland.

The 'big questions' of the universe are the catalysts for Kwade's ingenious conceptual works, which have been exhibited widely, including
two major installations in 'Viva Arte Viva' at the 57th Venice Biennale
(2017). She explores existential ideas with her practice, designing
situations that use materials such as mirrors, clocks and stone to
make philosophical conundrums manifest. Through their physicality
and artifice, her works expose the constructed nature of reality and
reveal how theories are often unequal to the task of accounting for
lived experience. For example, the piece *Against the Run* (2015)

reversed the mechanisms of familiar street clocks of Manhattan
so that time appeared to run backwards, destabilizing the everyday
experience of public time. In *Big Be-Hide*, two boulders are positioned
on either side of a freestanding double-faced mirror. They are similar but not identical – one is made of stone, while the other is an
aluminium cast of the first – and are installed exactly so that when
viewed from any angle, the reflection of one aligns with the other's
actual presence. A mirror image completes the real in a visual puzzle
that throws into question the difference between observed and
actual truth.

DOROTHEA LANGE

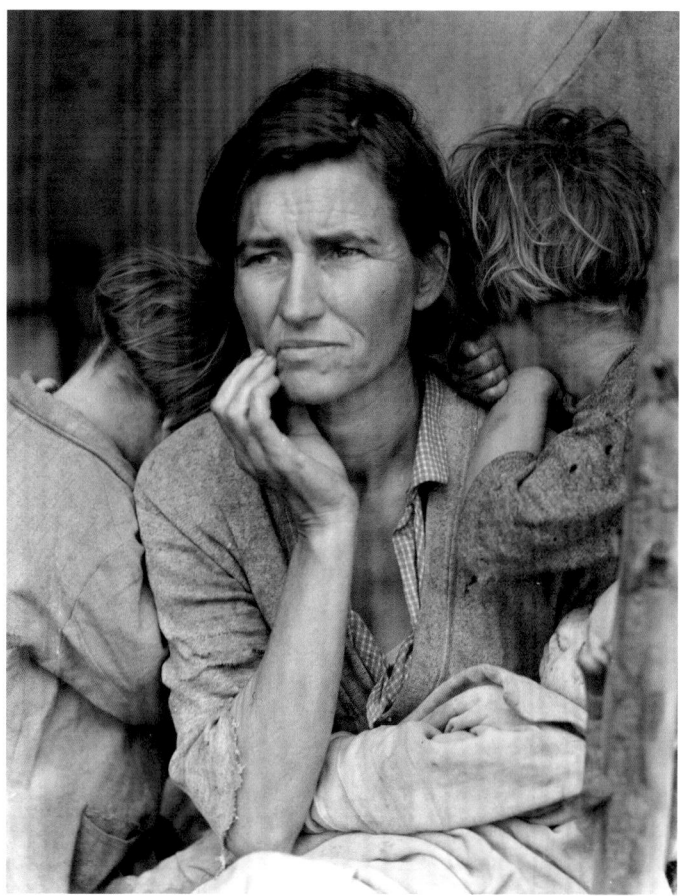

MIGRANT MOTHER, NIPOMO, CALIFORNIA

1936, gelatin silver print from original nitrate negative, 28.3 × 21.8 cm (11 ⅛ × 8 ⅞ in),
Library of Congress, Washington DC
Dorothea Lange, born Dorothea Nutzhorn, 1895, Hoboken, New Jersey.
Died 1965, San Francisco.

Lange's iconic photographs documented Depression-era America
and earned her a Guggenheim Fellowship and a place in the National
Women's Hall of Fame, among other accolades. Lange was
personally familiar with hardship, having contracted polio as a child,
which left her with a permanent limp, while her father abandoned
her family when she was twelve, hence her later adoption of her
mother's maiden name. She studied under Clarence H. White
(1871–1925), a pioneer of photography as a discipline of fine art, and
was later apprenticed to the famed Arnold Genthe (1869–1942).
She moved to San Francisco in the late 1910s initially to work at a
photography supply shop, then as a photographer to the city's social
elite, before focusing on poverty and exploitation from the 1930s.
Taken while on assignment with the Federal Resettlement
Administration and Farm Security Administration programmes,
this image depicts destitute sharecropper Florence Owens Thompson
with her children. Following the attack on Pearl Harbor, Lange
worked for the War Relocation Authority documenting the internment of Japanese Americans. Many such images were confiscated
by the authorities for their critical portrayal of the humanitarian
impact of US policy.

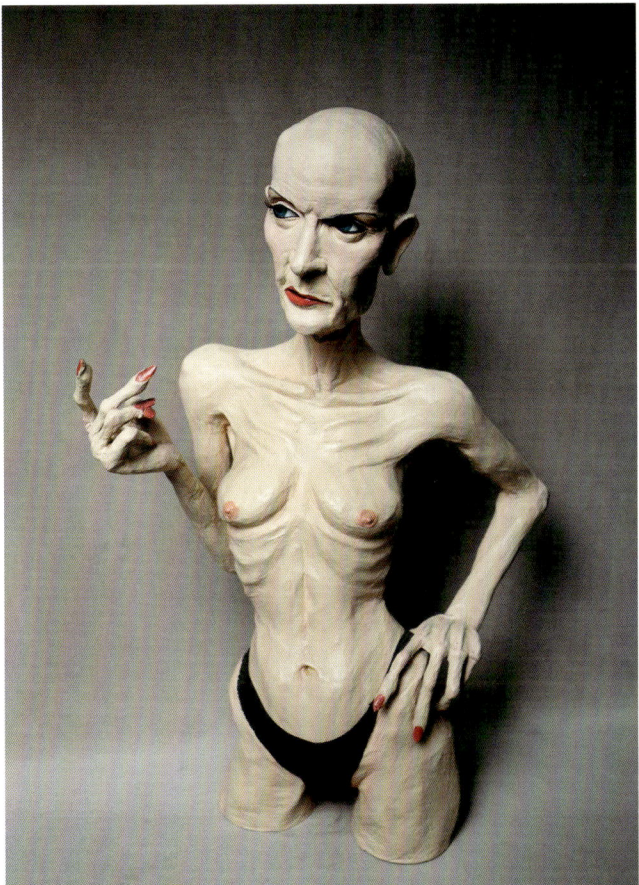

RACHEL

1986, papier-mâché, metal plates, wire, acrylic paint and matte medium,
71.1 × 53.3 × 27.9 cm (28 × 21 × 11 in), private collection, promised gift to the Art
Institute of Chicago
Greer Lankton, born Greg Robert Lankton, 1958, Flint, Michigan.
Died 1996, Chicago.

Dolls were the centre of Lankton's life and art. During a troubled childhood they were her companions and confidantes, and later became the focus of her adult exploration of identity, gender and sexuality. While studying sculpture at the Pratt Institute in New York, she began creating personalized figures – homages and send-ups of her alter egos, avatars and idols – using papier-mâché, recycled rubbish and soft materials. Much of her work reveals a fixation with her own body. Having undergone gender reassignment surgery at the age of twenty-one, she projected this traumatic experience onto her soft-sculpture effigies. One such example is *Rachel*, for which Lankton used a starting point, an image of the pioneering performance artist Rachel Rosenthal (1926–2015). Lankton was integral to the 1980s East Village art scene and a close friend of the photographer Nan Goldin (p.155). Her career was bookended by the Museum of Modern Art's legendary 'New York/New Wave' exhibition in 1981, a spectacular compendium of underground art and post-punk experimentation. Her final solo show, 'It's all about ME ... Not You' in 1996, is now a permanent installation at the Mattress Factory in Pittsburgh.

MARIA LASSNIG

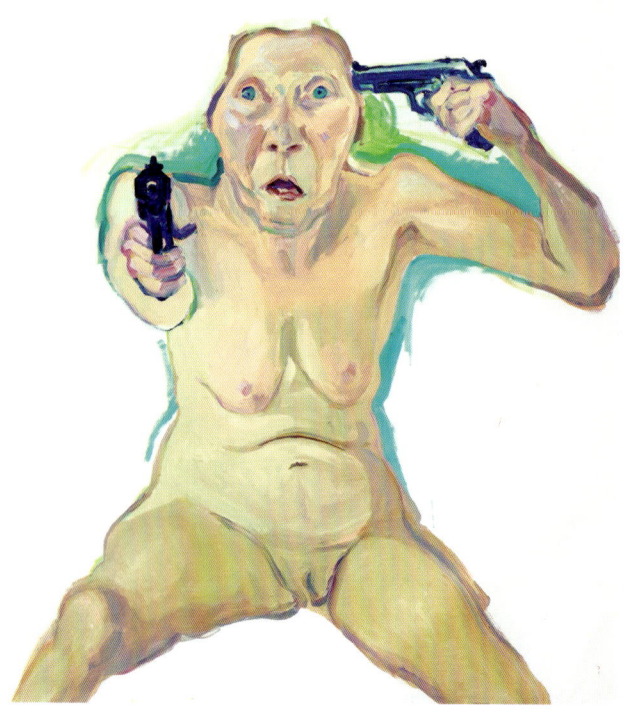

DU ODER ICH (YOU OR ME)

2005, oil on canvas, 203 × 155 cm (79 ⅛ × 61 in), private collection
Maria Lassnig, born 1919, Kappel am Krappfeld, Austria. Died 2014, Vienna.

Commercial and critical success came late in life to Lassnig: she had
her first retrospective in the UK aged eighty-nine and five years later
received the Golden Lion lifetime achievement award at the 55th
Venice Biennale (2013). By this time she had painted professionally for
over seventy years. Studying at the Academy of Fine Arts (1940–5)
in Nazi-occupied Vienna, she intially rejected state-approved realism,
and explored Abstract Expressionism and its European parallel,
Art Informel. She then found her place in the art-historical chain
of tradition of figurative self-portraiture, citing Diego Vélazquez
(1599–1660) and Edvard Munch (1863–1944) as influences among
others. After living in Paris (1961–8) and New York (1968–80) she
returned to Austria to take up a professorship at the University
of Applied Arts in Vienna. This striking selfportrait of the artist's
naked, hairless, elderly body demonstrates her method of 'body-
awareness painting', a term she coined to describe her efforts to
paint bodily sensations, which Lassnig at times combined with
external realities. Here, terror, violence and the absurd combine in
a larger-than-life figure that resists easy interpretation, yet powerfully challenges conventional representations of the female nude in
art history.

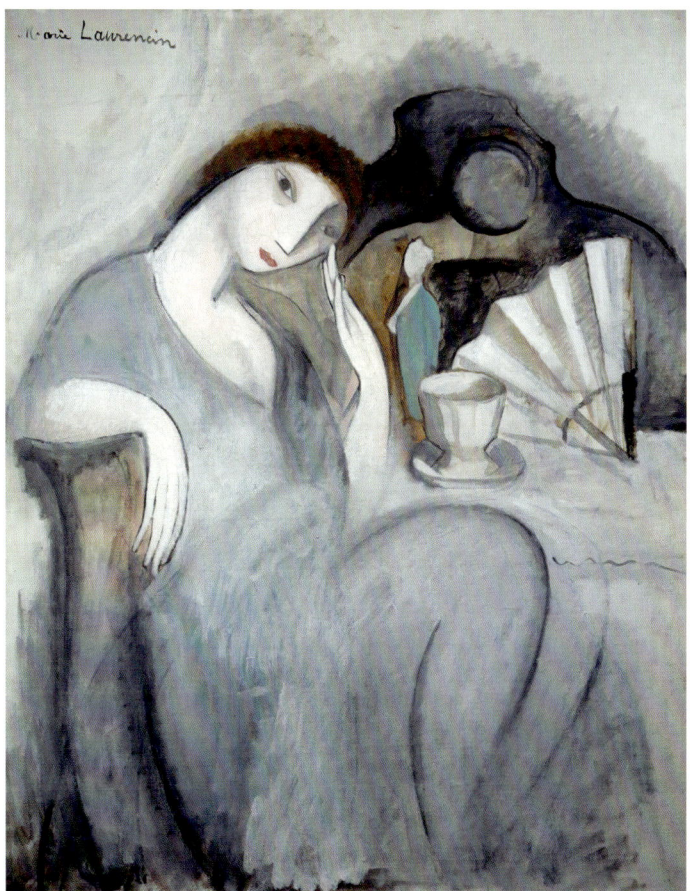

THE DREAMER

1910, oil on canvas, 91 × 73 cm (35 ⅞ × 28 ¾ in), Musée Picasso, Paris
Marie Laurencin, born 1883, Paris. Died 1956, Paris.

A sought-after portraitist of Parisian high society, whose clients included fashion designer Coco Chanel and cosmetics entrepreneur Helena Rubinstein, Laurencin had participated in modern art exhibitions of the early twentieth century including the Salon des Indépendants in Paris (1910–11), the first Cubist exhibition in Spain (1912) and the landmark 1913 Armory Show in New York. She was originally trained in the decorative arts, but soon entered Paris's avant-garde circles, becoming one of the few females, along with Gertrude Stein in the *Bateau-Lavoir* group, which also included Pablo Picasso (1881–1973) and the poet Guillaume Apollinaire, with whom she became romantically involved. She had relationships with both women and men, and her marriage to a German man led to exile in Spain during the First World War. Later she was recruited by the choreographer Serge Diaghilev to design costumes and sets for his Ballets Russes company. Although her work shares some of the techniques of flatness as employed by her avant-garde counterparts, Laurencin developed her own style. Here, a solitary woman – possibly the artist herself – sits deep in thought, her head resting upon elongated fingers, body dissolving into the meditative grey background.

LOUISE LAWLER

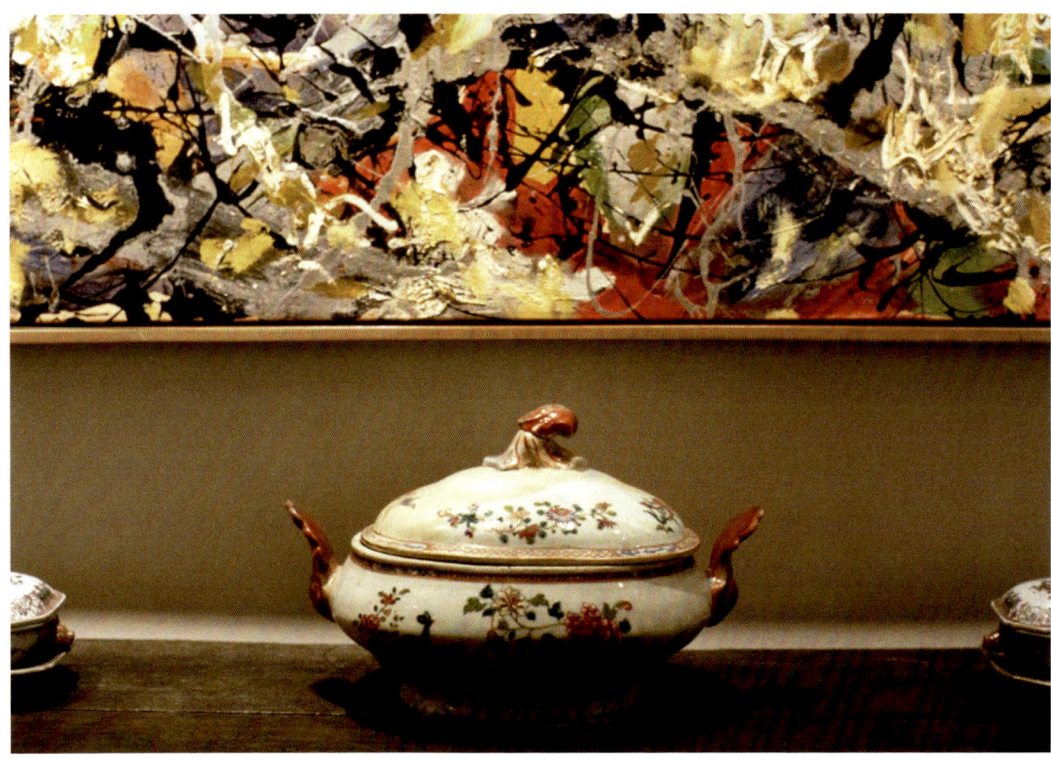

POLLOCK AND TUREEN

1984, Cibachrome print, 71.1 × 99.1 cm (28 × 39 in)
Louise Lawler, born 1947, Bronxville, New York.

Lawler was among a group of young artists in the 1970s, including
Cindy Sherman (p.371), Barbara Kruger (p.225) and Sherrie Levine
(p.241), who became known as the Pictures Generation. They
worked with appropriation, image and socio-political context, sig-
nalling a shift away from the modernist idea for art objects imbued
with inherent 'truth'. Lawler's art involves her taking photographs of
other artists' work but deliberately showing it in the context of how
it is owned and displayed. Moving to Manhattan in 1969, she initially
worked at Leo Castelli Gallery before taking pictures in galleries,
museums, auction houses and collectors' homes. In 1984, Lawler was
granted access to the New England home of the Tremaine family,
where she took this photograph, a voyeuristic glimpse of material
wealth. A painting by Jackson Pollock (1912–56) becomes the backdrop for eighteenth-century Chinese porcelain, emphasizing these
objects' positions within a wider collection of high culture. The teem-
ing lines of flower stems decorating the soup tureen resonate with
Pollock's gestural painting, a juxtaposition that reveals the refined
taste of the collectors and the coherence of their collection, which
in turn become signifiers of their class.

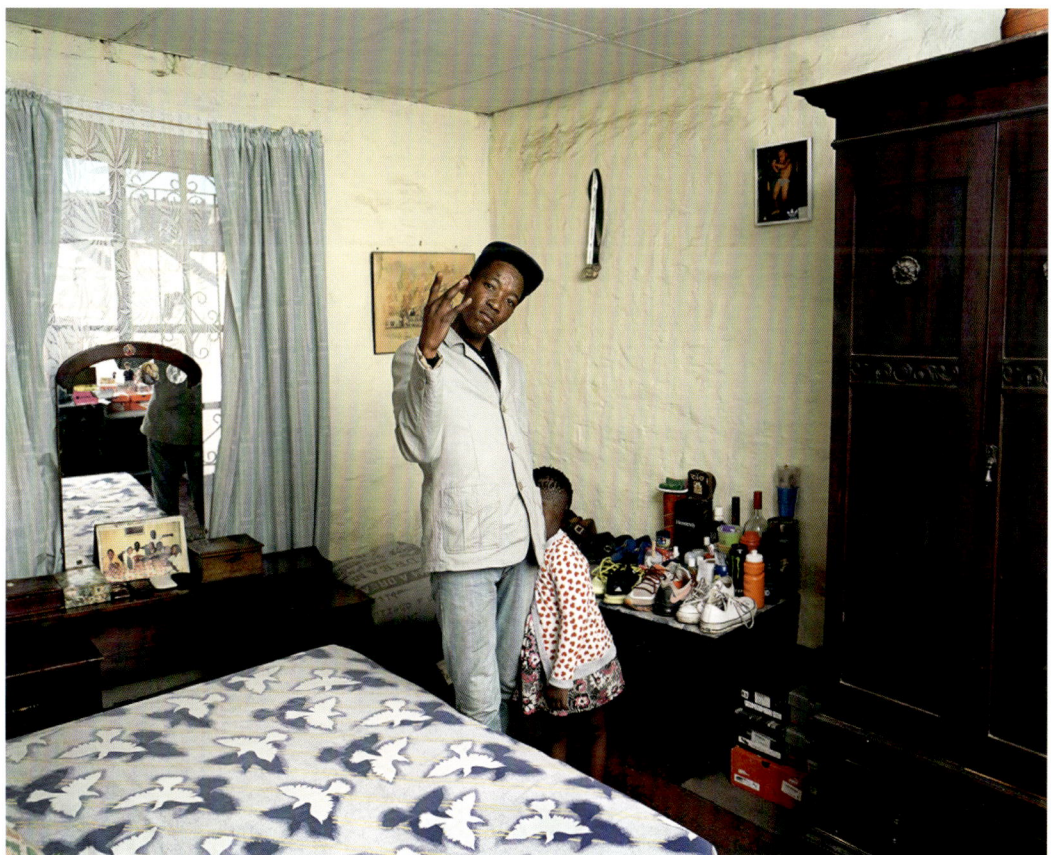

BROTHER AND SISTER SOWETO

2017, pigment print, 139.7 × 175.3 cm (55 × 69 in)
Deana Lawson, born 1979, Rochester, New York.

Predominantly taking photographs of black people in the United States, the Caribbean and Africa, Lawson conveys the nuances of individual lives throughout this diaspora, using carefully staged images that appear startlingly candid. Lawson was born into a working-class family in a town made by the camera – her grandmother and mother worked at Rochester's Eastman Kodak factory – while her father was a photographer. She was further inspired by artists such as Lorna Simpson (p.376), Carrie Mae Weems (p.427) and Renee Cox (p.108). While having photographed pop stars – for example Rihanna, whom she captured in 2018 for the magazine *Garage*

– Lawson mainly gives voice to the less wealthy in society. Printing her works on a monumental scale, her subjects often return a powerful gaze to the viewer; in the words of novelist Zadie Smith in a 2018 essay on Lawson for *The New Yorker* they are 'beautiful, creative, godlike', an idea reinforced by the artist's choice of gold ormolu frames. In this image, taken in Soweto, South Africa, Lawson asked the protagonist to 'claim his space' by holding up the 'West Side' hand symbol popularized in hip-hop culture, thereby 'collapsing the distance' between black men worldwide.

LEE BUL

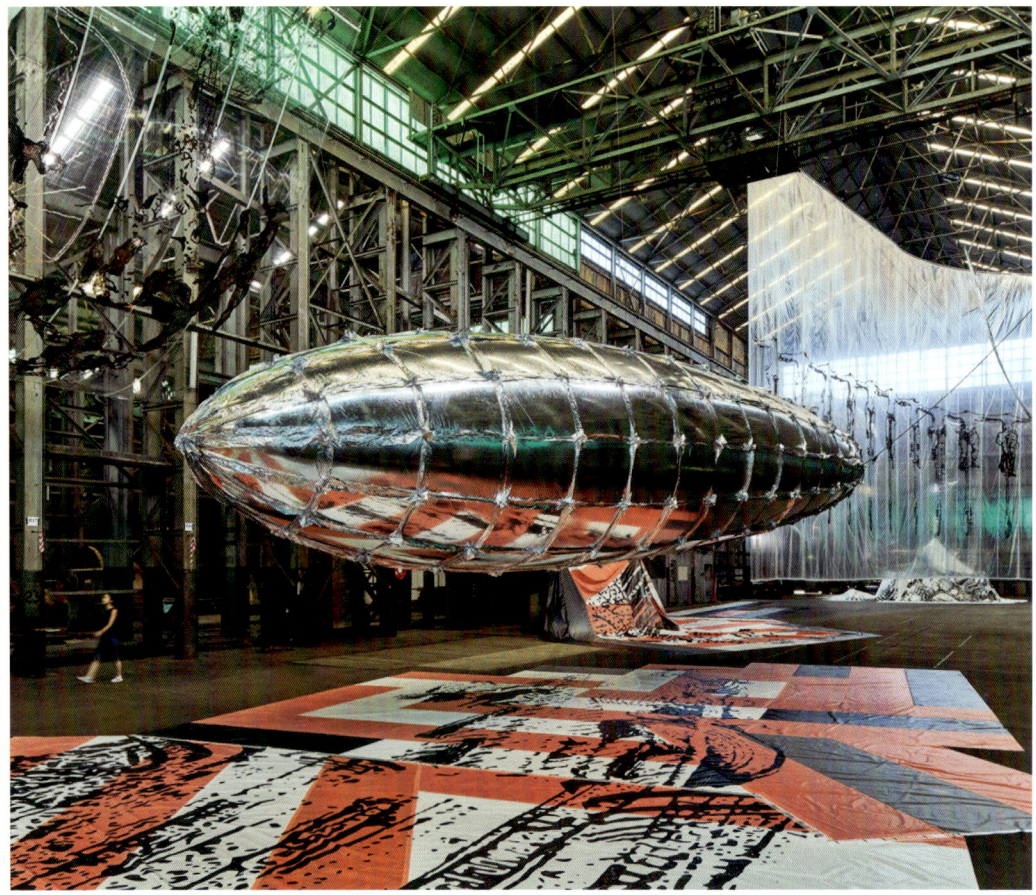

WILLING TO BE VULNERABLE

2015–16, heavy-duty fabric, metalized film, transparent film, polyurethane ink, fog machine, LED lighting and electronic wiring, dimensions variable, installation view, Cockatoo Island, 20th Biennale of Sydney, 2016
Lee Bul, born 1964, Yeongju, South Korea.

After completing a bachelor's degree in sculpture at Hongik University, Seoul, in 1987, Lee incorporated performance and installation into her art practice. Her earliest documented performance piece is *Abortion* (1989), in which she hung upside down while describing her experience of having an illegal termination of her pregnancy. Lee's sculptural installations frequently incorporate lights, mirrored surfaces and found objects; her first major exhibition in the United States was in 1997 at the Museum of Modern Art, New York, and included the work *Majestic Splendor*, composed from refrigerated, gradually decaying fish decorated with sequins. Lee's themes are often political, drawing on science fiction, the grotesque and sexual imagery to comment on patriarchal society and the pitfalls of modernity. It is through juxtaposing contemporary and historical references that Lee offers her thoughts on the future. *Willing To Be Vulnerable* includes the form of a Zeppelin – an airship regarded in the early twentieth century as the future of travel until the *Hindenburg* disaster of 1937 – perhaps suggesting the current risks of ever-growing reliance on emerging technologies, while the title emphasizes our enthusiastic consent to such potential dangers.

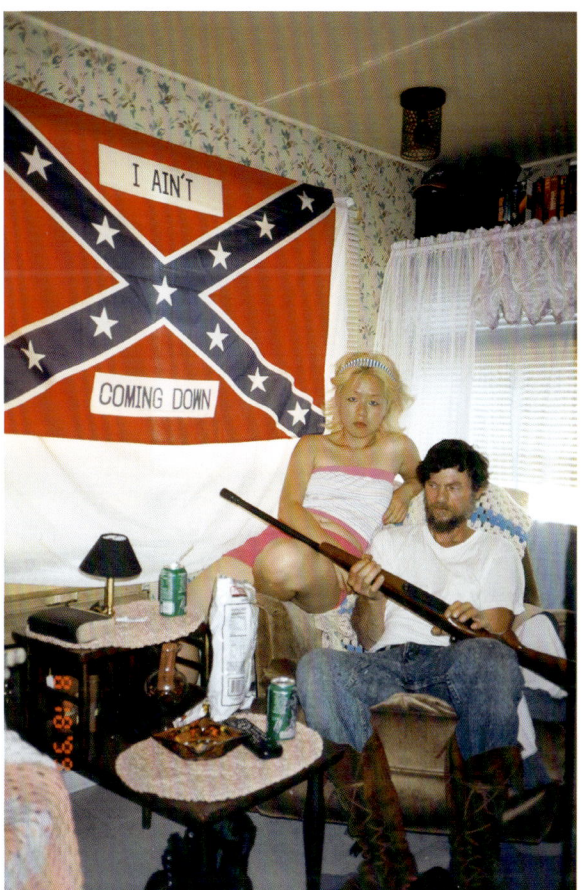

THE OHIO PROJECT (7)

1999, colour photograph, 101.6 × 76.2 cm (40 × 30 in)
Nikki S. Lee, born 1970, Kye-Chang, South Korea.

Lee examines how signs and codes are used in visual communication and can constitute group or individual identities. In her photographic practice, she flits between personas that embody social stereotypes to the point of satire, using stylized images that carry strong characterization. Moving from South Korea to New York in 1994, she attended the city's Fashion Institute of Technology and then worked as a commercial photographer in high fashion with David LaChapelle (b.1963). Seen here is an image from Lee's four-year 'Projects' series (1997–2001), in which she adopted and then performed quintessentially American characters, including 'the hispanic', 'the yuppie' and 'the drag queen'. By means of costume, make-up and physical actions, she here immersed herself in an Ohio trailer park community, making friends and getting another neighbour to record her interactions on a video camera – evidenced by the red date stamp to the bottom left of the image. Slumped next to a gun-wielding man, the flag on the wall offers an ambiguous commentary. Questioning the legitimacy of stereotypes and their undeniable power, this study continues to resonate both in its broad themes and specific content.

ANNIE LEIBOVITZ

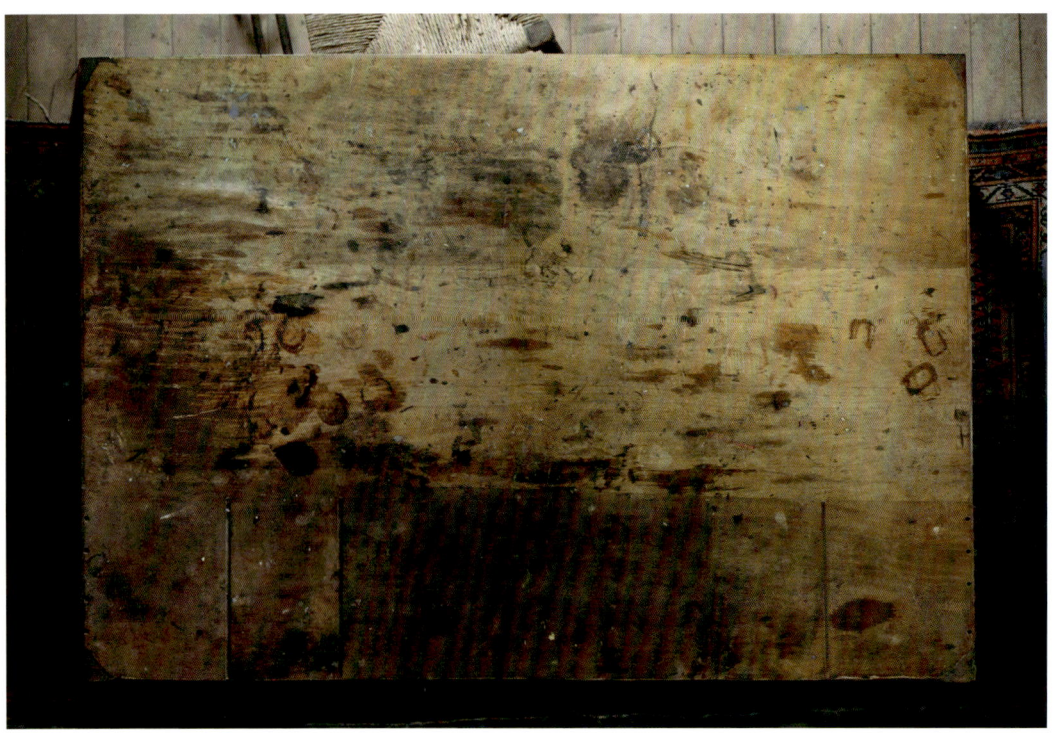

VIRGINIA WOOLF'S WRITING DESK, MONKS HOUSE, EAST SUSSEX, ENGLAND

2010
Annie Leibovitz, born 1949, Waterbury, Connecticut.

In 2019, over 4,000 images by Leibovitz were displayed on raw wood panels that cut across the exhibition space of Hauser & Wirth gallery, Los Angeles, to create a maze of archival material. 'Annie Leibovitz. The Early Years, 1970–1983: Archive Project No.1' presented her as both a commercial portrait photographer – albeit one who, in a career spanning more than four decades, has shot an unparalleled list of high-profile subjects – as well as a visual artist who uses photography as a medium. The experimental style of her early output reveals Leibovitz's merging of her formal training at the San Francisco Art Institute – where she switched from painting to photography – and a spontaneous and informal approach to photojournalism, honed during her time as staff photographer at *Rolling Stone* magazine from 1973 to 1983. While not as well known as the image of a nude John Lennon kissing Yoko Ono (1980) just hours before his murder, Leibovitz's *Virginia Woolf's writing desk* is no less powerful as a portrait. The straight-on and closely cropped image of Woolf's desk from her final home at Monk's House, East Sussex, becomes an evocative stand-in for the influential and celebrated modernist author.

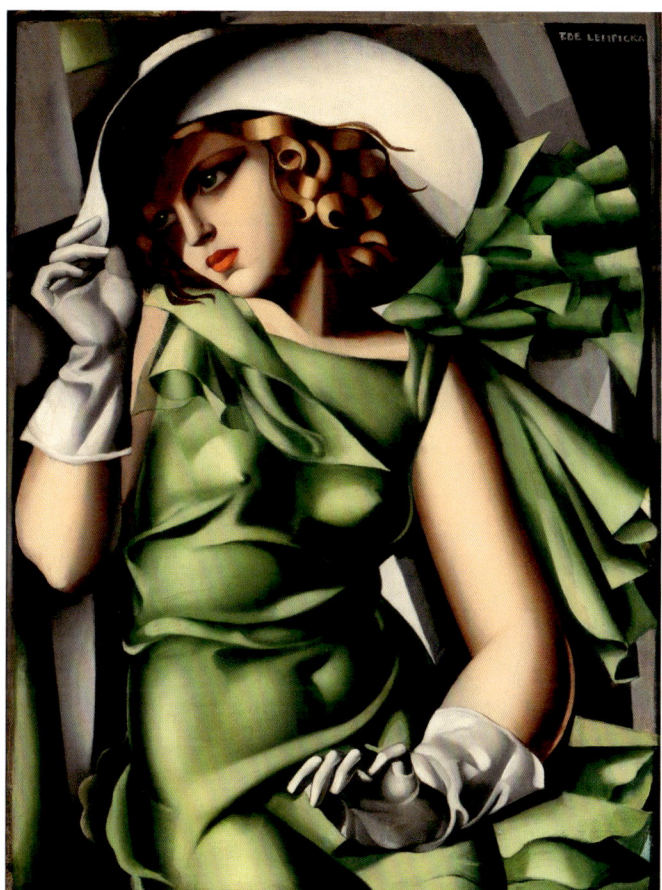

YOUNG WOMAN IN GREEN also called YOUNG WOMAN WITH GLOVES

1927–30, oil on plywood, 61.5 × 45.5 cm (24 ¼ × 17 ⅞ in), Musée National d'Art Moderne, Centre Georges Pompidou, Paris

Tamara de Lempicka, born Maria Górska, 1898, Warsaw. Died 1980, Cuernavaca, Mexico.

Immediately recognizable and enduringly popular, de Lempicka's paintings capture the essence of a glamorous age. Having studied in Paris with *Les Nabis* artist Maurice Denis (1870–1943) and French-Cubist André Lhote (1885–1962), and inspired by historical precedents such as Jean-Auguste-Dominique Ingres (1780–1867), de Lempicka developed a hybrid style that combined the facets of Cubism with a more fluid Neo-Classicism. After some small exhibitions and sales of work, her breakthrough came in 1925 as the

Art Deco style came to international attention at the *Exposition Internationale des Arts Décoratifs et Industriels Modernes*, held that year in Paris, and by 1929 she was travelling to the United States to undertake commissions. Consciously self-made as a highly successful artist, she moved among Europe's social elite, becoming mistress and later wife of the aristocratic art collector Raoul Kuffner, hence her nickname 'The Baroness with the Brush'. After the outbreak of the Second World War, she moved to America and painted society portraits in Los Angeles and New York. Typical of the period, but imbued with romanticism, de Lempicka's signature style is seen in this work's choice of palette, line and form, the woman's dress and hair a series of intersecting planes.

ZOE LEONARD

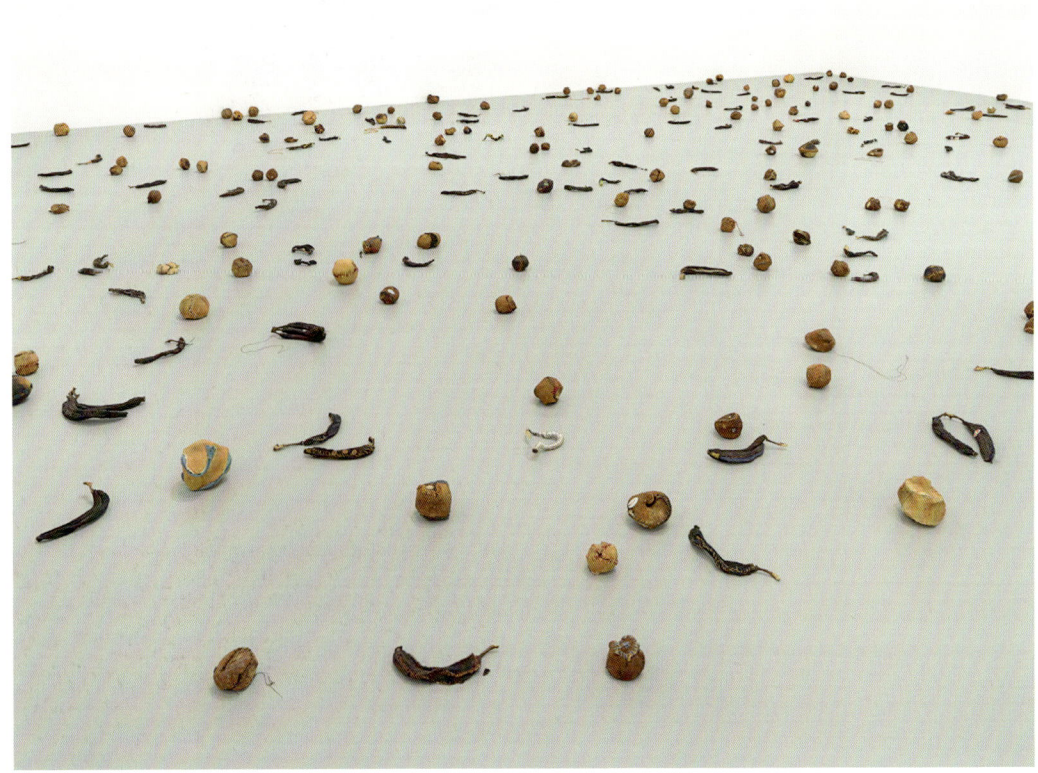

STRANGE FRUIT

1992–7, orange, banana, grapefruit and lemon skins; thread, buttons, zips, needles, wax, sinew, string, snaps and hooks, 297 parts, dimensions variable, Philadelphia Museum of Art
Zoe Leonard, born 1961, Liberty, New York.

Leonard has been a working artist since age sixteen, exploring socio-political themes relating to mortality, sexuality and urbanization through photography and sculpture. Her landmark photographic project 'Analogue' (1998–2009), documents New York's changing landscape in 412 images of the East Village, including shop windows, signage and graffiti. Presented in thematic grids, the work touches on themes of gentrification and globalization. Her earlier work, *Strange Fruit*, references the song famously performed by Billie

Holiday in 1939 that protested lynchings of African-Americans in the Southern states. Leonard employs this imagery to comment on the loss and alienation caused by the AIDS epidemic of the 1980s and 1990s. The installation consists of dried rinds from almost 300 pieces of fruit, which have been handsewn back together to make their hollow forms appear whole. Although the materials are novel, the work stands in long traditions of 'vanitas' still lifes, symbolic of the transience of life. What began as a self-healing project to cope with death became a powerful commentary on the finitude and preciousness of life and an homage to a community in mourning.

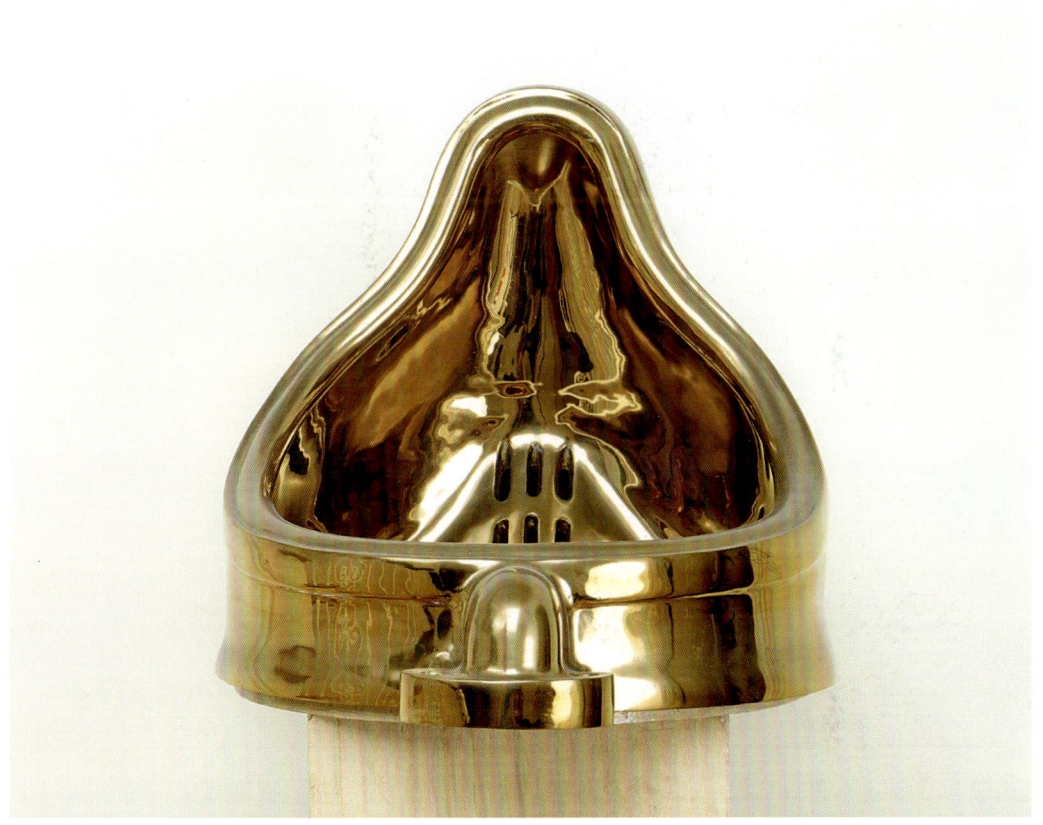

FOUNTAIN (AFTER MARCEL DUCHAMP)

1991, cast bronze, 157.5 × 36.8 × 63.5 cm (62 × 14 ½ × 25 in)
Sherrie Levine, born 1947, Hazleton, Pennsylvania.

Reflecting on the reproducibility of photography as source material, Levine was an early and prescient appropriator of mediated images – such as those published in art books – to challenge ideas about originality and authenticity, alongside other artists in the so-called Pictures Generation, which also included Cindy Sherman (p.371), Louise Lawler (p.234) and Richard Prince (b.1949). Since the 1970s Levine has appropriated the work of mostly male artists: for example, re-photographing images of Walker Evans (1903–75), Alfred Stieglitz (1864–1946) or Karl Blossfeldt (1865–1932) and presenting herself as the author. Levine directly quotes the godfather of Conceptual art,

Marcel Duchamp (1887–1968) and his quintessential 'ready-made', *Fountain* (1917), the infamous act of inserting a store-bought, factory-produced urinal into the art-historical canon by choosing and signing it 'R. Mutt'. Levine's cast-bronze version is lustrous, made from a classic sculptural material that contrasts with mass-produced porcelain. Scatological connotations are all but eliminated by the pristine shine of Levine's work and through its opulence, she reflects on the institutionalization of radical gestures like Duchamp's and questions art's reification in the luxury art market.

HELEN LEVITT

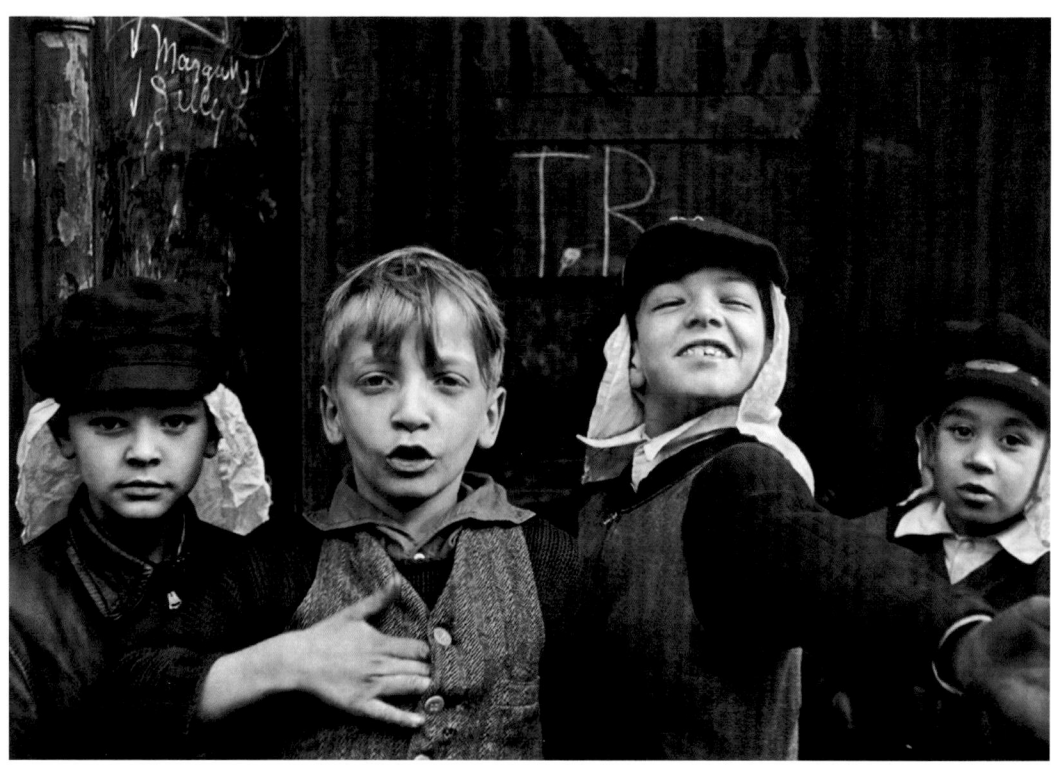

FOUR BOYS IN 'BEAU GESTE' HEADGEAR, NEW YORK CITY

*c.*1940, gelatin silver print, 16.4 × 24.4 cm (6 ½ × 9 ⅝ in), Metropolitan Museum of Art, New York
Helen Levitt, born 1913, New York. Died 2009, New York.

After dropping out of high school in Brooklyn, Levitt worked for a commercial photographer in the Bronx, learning to process film and develop photographs. In 1938, she studied with Walker Evans (1903–75), who would become a friend and admirer of her work. Levitt took to using a 35mm Leica camera after seeing the work of Henri Cartier-Bresson (1908–2004), although she wanted her work to contribute more to social movements. She photographed children, their games and their chalk graffiti. In 1939, the Museum of Modern Art, New York, included her work in its first photography show, 'Sixty Photographs: A Survey of Camera Esthetics'. Levitt worked in an era before the mass roll-out of television, when leisure time was mainly spent outdoors. She has created some of the most striking and enduring New York City scenes, capturing the dynamic movement of children and their inventiveness in play. This image is named after P.C. Wren's colonial-era novel and its film adaptation. Imagining themselves in the Algerian desert, boys emulate the protagonists of the adventure story by wearing handkerchiefs and caps on their heads like the kepis of French Foreign Legionnaires.

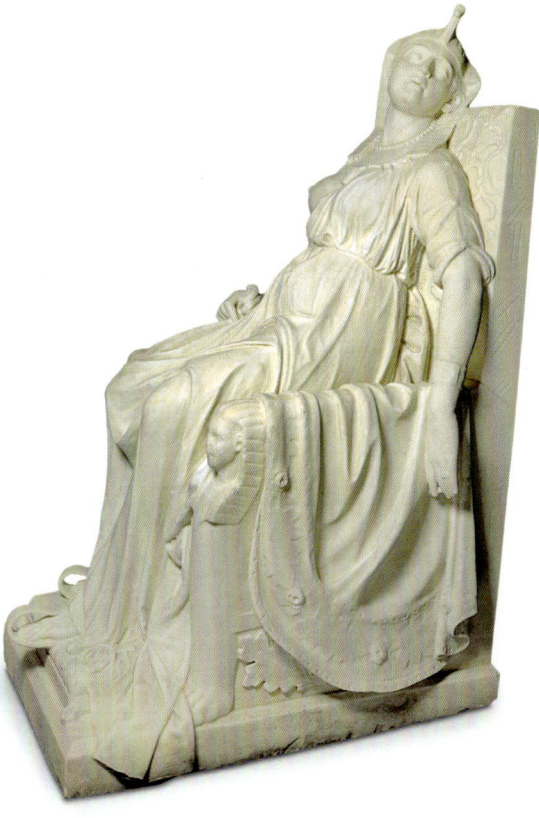

THE DEATH OF CLEOPATRA

1876, marble, 160 × 79.4 × 116.8 cm (63 × 31 ¼ × 46 in), Smithsonian American Art Museum, Washington DC
Edmonia Lewis, raised as Mary Wildfire, born 1843 or 1845, Ohio or New York. Died 1907, London.

Daughter of a free African-American father and Native American mother, Lewis was the first sculptor of her heritage to achieve an international career in the nineteenth century. Living with her mother's nomadic Chippewa tribe until the age of twelve, Lewis studied at Oberlin College, Ohio, with the financial support of her brother. She endured vigilantism and a highly publicized trial on questionable charges of poisoning two classmates, and was subsequently acquitted. The financial success of her medallion portraits

of well-known abolitionists enabled Lewis to travel across Europe before settling in Rome towards the end of 1865. Honing her practice by copying Classical and Renaissance marbles, Lewis worked in an artistic milieu defined by the Neo-Classical style and found ready subjects, materials and a profitable trade selling to American tourists in the city. The dramatic and much mythologized suicide of the last Egyptian queen Cleopatra (69–30 BC) was a popular subject among her peers, although Lewis's approach to it is unusual. Rather than an idealized queen calmly contemplating her demise, we see a lifeless, flaccid corpse, now considered a subversive statement about race and gender.

JUDITH LEYSTER

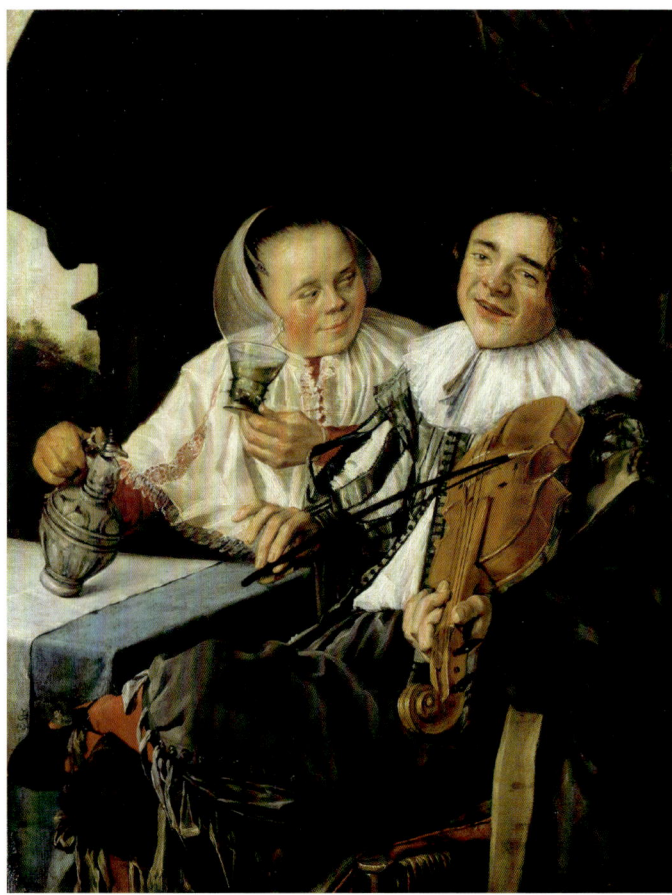

THE HAPPY COUPLE OR THE MERRY COMPANY

1630, oil on canvas, 68 × 57 cm (26 ¾ × 22 ½ in), Musée du Louvre, Paris
Judith Leyster, born 1609, Haarlem, Netherlands. Died 1660,
Heemstede, Netherlands.

Leyster trained during the Dutch Golden Age and was a contemporary of Frans Hals (1582–1666), whose earthy realism her work
shares. She carved out a career in the Haarlem art world of the 1620s,
producing portraits and genre scenes that reflected the rise of the
mercantile class. At the age of twenty-four, she was possibly the first
woman to earn membership of Haarlem's Guild of St Luke, which
allowed her to open her own workshop. After her marriage to the
painter Jan Miense Molenaer (1610–68) in 1636, she dedicated herself
to raising their five children and her artistic career ceased, although

the couple may have collaborated subsequently. For two centuries
following her death, much of her work was attributed to male contemporaries – notably Hals. In 1893, experts at the Louvre discovered Leyster's monogram under a crude forgery of Hals's signature
to this work. A court case ensued, with the plaintiff compensated
for having purchased a 'worthless' imitation. More recently, scholars have actively worked to reattribute her art. With its depiction
of a young couple, mellowed by wine and impromptu violin music,
the atmosphere of amorous leisure typifies the mood of many of
Leyster's paintings.

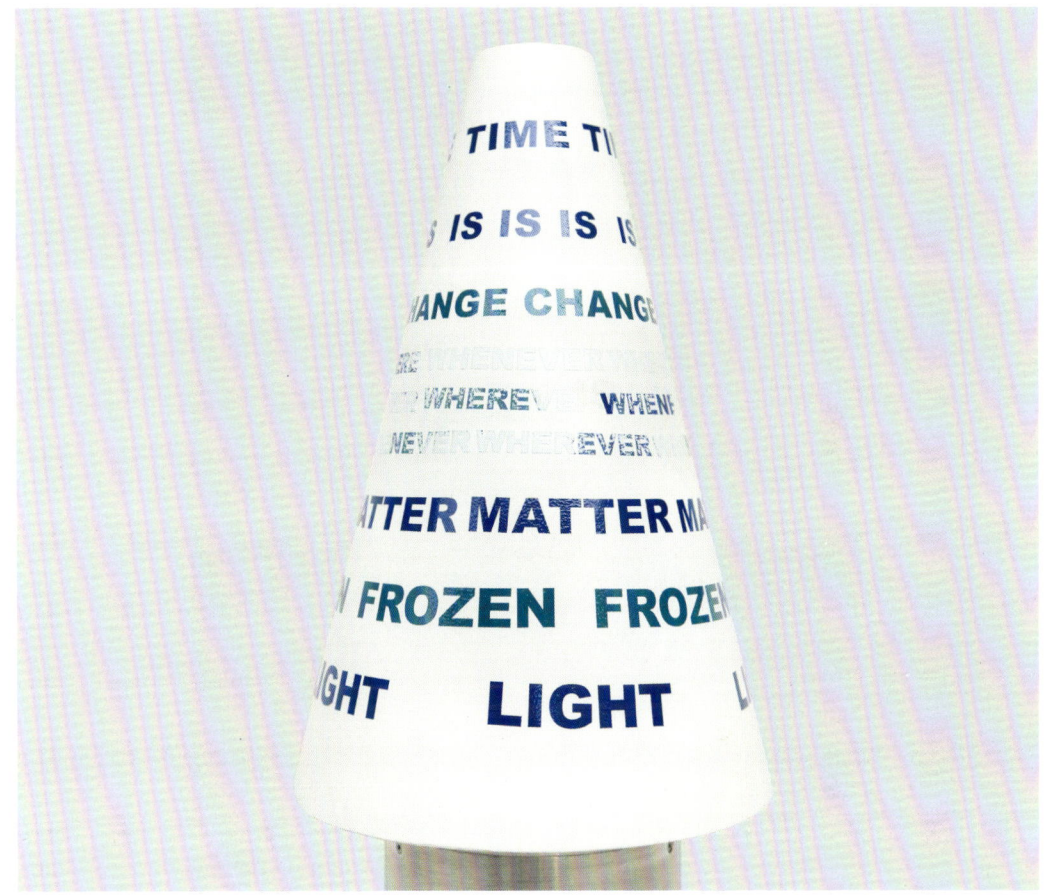

TIME IS CHANGE

1968, Letraset on painted truncated cork cone and motorized turntable, h: 54 cm (21 ¼ in), diam: 25 cm (9 ⅞ in), collection of the artist
Liliane Lijn, born 1939, New York.

From a Russian Jewish family who emigrated from Antwerp, Belgium, to New York just before the Second World War, Lijn was brought up speaking six languages and took up painting at a young age as another channel of communication. Studying archaeology and art history in Paris, she spent time living in Athens before settling in London in 1966. Her work investigates the interaction between light and language, and she was the first female artist to work with kinetic text. Her preoccupation with expression has converged with interests in science and technology as well as mythology and Buddhist philosophy, and she frequently works in collaboration with scientists – for example, at the Space Sciences Laboratory, in Berkeley, California, in 2005. The cone is a recurring motif in Lijn's work, its fundamental geometry also a visual wordplay on the Zen *koan*, a paradoxical story intended to test understanding. *Time is Change* is one of Lijn's many motorized rotating conical sculptures, which she called 'Poemcons'. Its hypnotic form is meditative, the Letraset text spins and blurs into light and sound. This form of experimentation is emblematic of her work, which has spanned more than forty years.

MAYA LIN

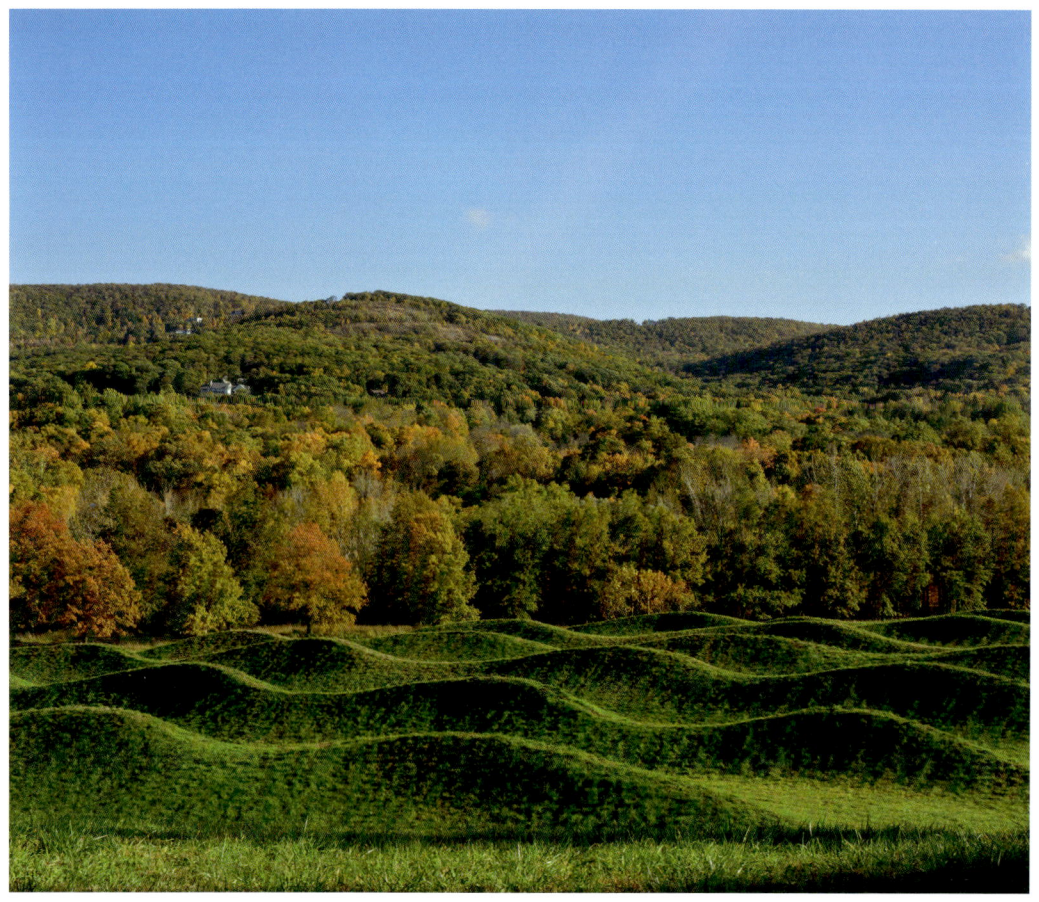

STORM KING WAVEFIELD

2007–8, earth and grass, 4.5 hectares (11 acres), Storm King Art Center,
Mountainville, New York
Maya Lin, born 1959, Athens, Ohio.

Lin is an environmentalist who makes Land art, focusing on humanity's relationship with the spaces we inhabit or behold. Her material
interventions in natural and urban landscapes transform the viewer's
experience of their surroundings. As an undergraduate at Yale
College in 1981, Lin's design for the Vietnam Veterans Memorial
in Washington DC was chosen in an open competition. Responding
to its site on the National Mall, the work transformed expectations
of public monuments by eschewing traditional figurative representation in favour of a sombre conceptual work that resembled an open

wound cutting into the earth. Lin has also created this field of seven
vast waves of earth, each nearing 122 metres (400 feet) in length and
whose peaks echo the surrounding mountains. Commissioned
by Storm King, an outdoor museum in upstate New York, the undu-
lating ground rises and falls rhythmically like the ocean, evoking
a sense of the sublime and the miraculous idea of walking on water.
Not only encouraging the viewer to become rooted in nature, the
work also provokes thought about our fragile planet, where climate
change and rising sea levels threaten to engulf the land and leave
many people rootless.

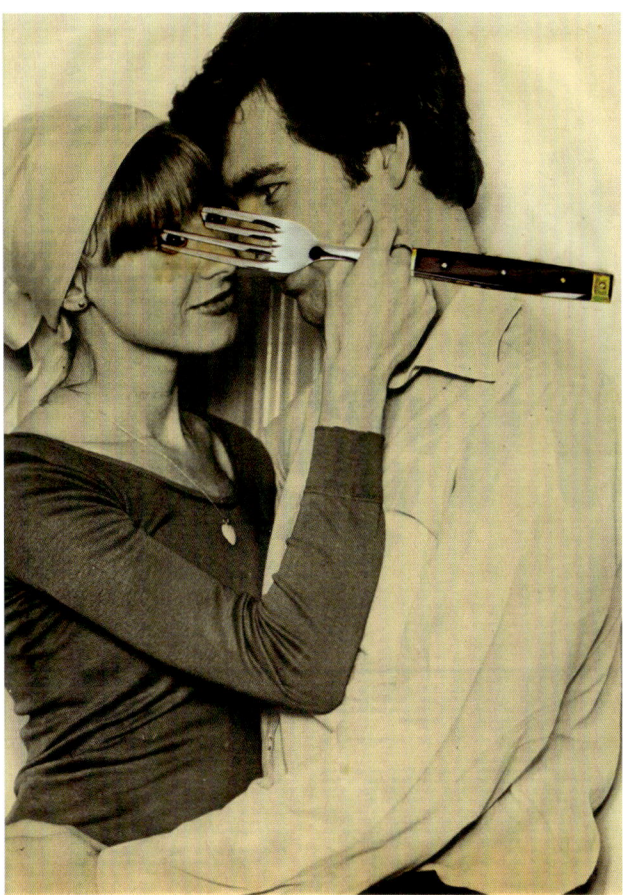

UNTITLED

1977, collage on card, 27.9 × 19.6 cm (11 × 7.7 in), Tate, London

Linder Sterling, born Linda Mulvey, 1954, Liverpool, UK.

Going by her first name only, Linder uses photography to make collages and photomontages. Studying graphic design from 1974 to 1977 at Manchester Polytechnic in the UK, her works combine pornography, fashion and interior design to make surreal and unnerving images, with her use of images from magazines being compared to that of Hannah Höch (p.189). Involved in Manchester's punk and post-punk scenes of the 1970s, the anarchist ethos of these subcultures combined with Linder's feminist politics to result in a practice that highlighted the expectations placed upon women in society, as well as the commodification and sexualization of their bodies. Often disseminating her work in magazines, some of her early photomontages featured in fanzines such as *The Secret Public*, and she made the cover art for The Buzzcocks's 1977 single 'Orgasm Addict'. Founding her own post-punk band, Ludus, Linder designed a number of its album covers and sleeves. This collage is typical of the artist's subversive aesthetic: inserting the image of a giant fork into a photograph of an amorous couple, the woman appears to gouge out her own eyes, symbolic of female subjugation to the blind pursuit of love.

HUNG LIU

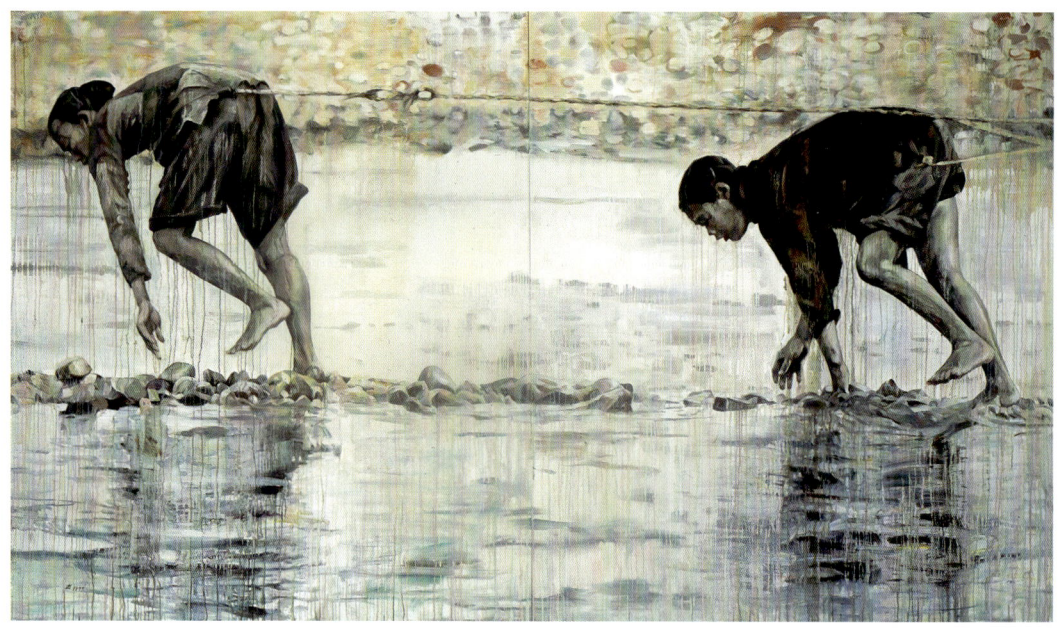

MOTHER AND DAUGHTER

1997, oil on canvas, diptych, 203.2 × 355.6 cm (80 × 140 in), Kemper Museum
of Contemporary Art, Kansas City, Missouri
Hung Liu, born 1948, Changchun, China. Died 2021, Oakland, California.

In 1984, when Liu arrived to attend graduate school at the University
of California, San Diego, she had only $20 and little English. Her life
in China had reflected a rapidly changing society. After high school,
she underwent four years of enforced proletarian 're-education',
working in the fields seven days a week. During that time, she took
photographs using a smuggled camera and made postcard-sized paintings. Later she presented a popular children's art programme on
Chinese television. Liu was one of the first artists from the People's
Republic to study in America, having previously been taught mural

painting at the Central Academy of Fine Arts, China's leading art
school, and became an American citizen in 1991. Making installations and large-scale figurative works inspired by Chinese revolutionary billboards, she later painted from historical photographs that she
had discovered in China. Typically veiling her images with washes and
drips of diluted paint and simultaneously preserving and obscuring
them, Liu's work evokes half-erased memories. In this work, two
women drag an unseen boat upstream, the effect like seeing history
through a rain-spattered window.

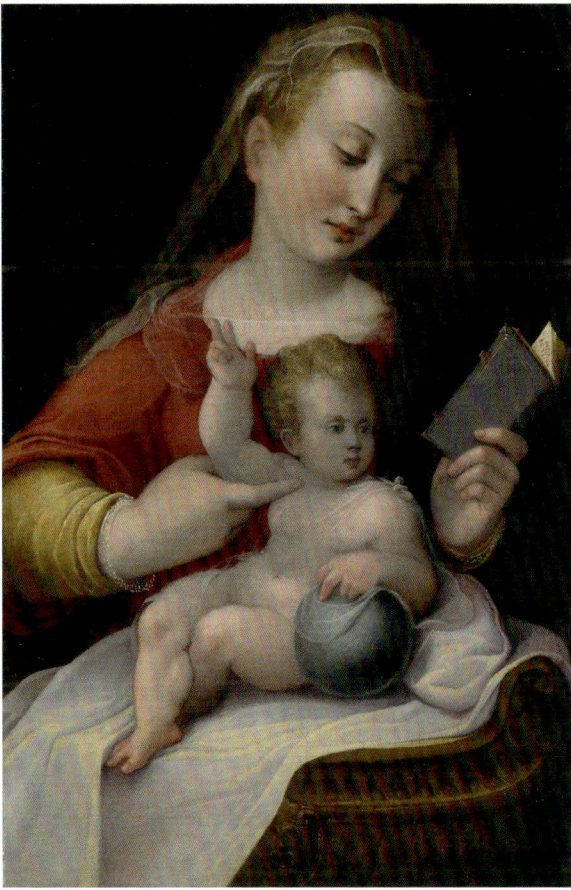

MADONNA AND CHILD

1580–5, oil on canvas, 43.8 × 28.9 cm (17 ¼ × 11 ⅜ in), Indianapolis Museum of Art
Barbara Longhi, born 1552, Ravenna, Italy. Died 1638, Ravenna, Italy.

Although Longhi did not achieve the international renown of her contemporary, Sofonisba Anguissola (p.35), she was well respected by her contemporaries in her native Ravenna, and secured the praise of painter and art historian Giorgio Vasari (1511–74) in the 1568 edition of his monumental survey of Renaissance artists, in which he applauded Longhi's 'purity of line and soft brilliance of colour'. Like many women artists of the period, she received training from her father, the artist Luca Longhi (1507–80), sometimes posing as a model for his compositions. Despite remaining close to the family studio after the completion of her artistic training

in 1570, her works' visual simplicity distinguishes her practice from her father's more Mannerist tendencies and the dramatic compositions typical of the period. During her life, she was praised as a portraitist, although of the fifteen works attributed to her today, twelve depict the Virgin and Child – including this example – a popular subject during the Counter-Reformation. Religious paintings were anonymized portraits, and it is believed that Longhi's *Saint Catherine of Alexandria* (1589) is a self-portrait of the artist.

SARAH LUCAS

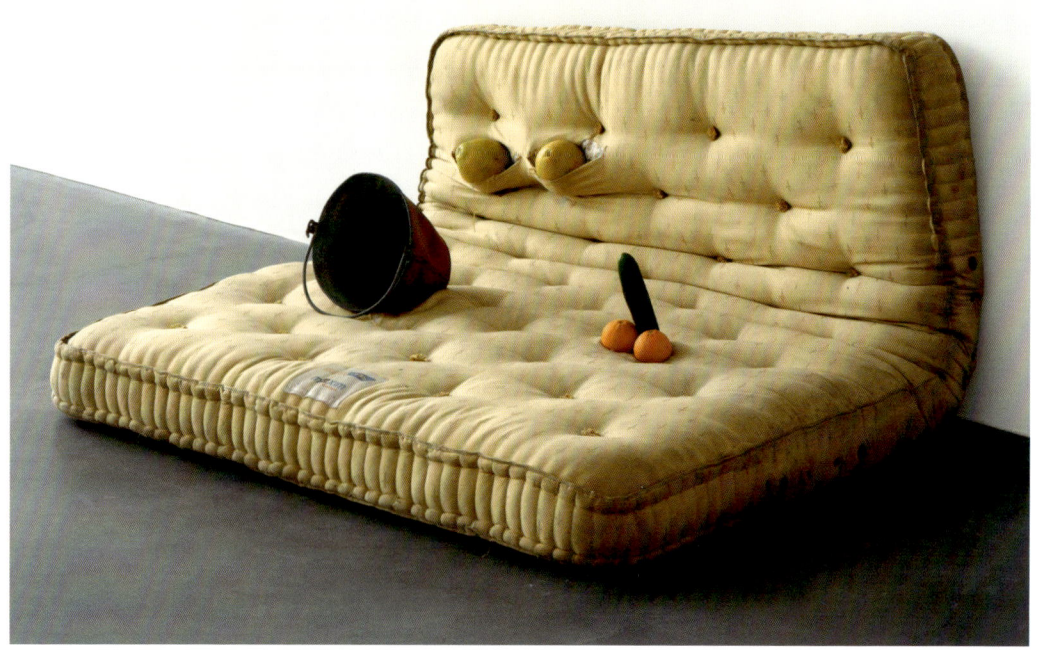

AU NATUREL

1994, mattress, water bucket, melons, oranges and a cucumber, 84 × 167.8 × 144.8 cm
(33 ⅛ × 66 ⅛ × 57 in), private collection
Sarah Lucas, born 1962, London.

Having studied at Goldsmiths College, London, alongside the cohort
who were to become the core of the Young British Artists (YBAs),
Lucas featured in the 1988 'Freeze' exhibition, organized by fellow
student, Damien Hirst (b.1965). In 1993, with Tracey Emin (p.132),
she founded The Shop in London's East End and sold customized
T-shirts, ashtrays, badges and other low-grade items. Primarily using
the assemblage of everyday objects in her sculptures and installations
– food, clothing, old furniture and found objects – Lucas addresses
sexuality and gender, through humour and visceral juxtapositions.

In this example, she uses crude symbols to evoke a sexual encounter
between a man and a woman, caricatured by fresh fruit and a bucket
on a stained mattress. The title, a euphemism for nakedness, translates literally as 'in the raw' or 'of nature' and plays on the essence
of these items and the starkness of their placement. Lucas's work is
often associated with the 'Ladette' culture of early-nineties Britain,
which took working-class identity as one of its vernacular references.
By using playfulness and innuendo, she satirizes overarching cultural norms and shifts them from the literal to the metaphorical.

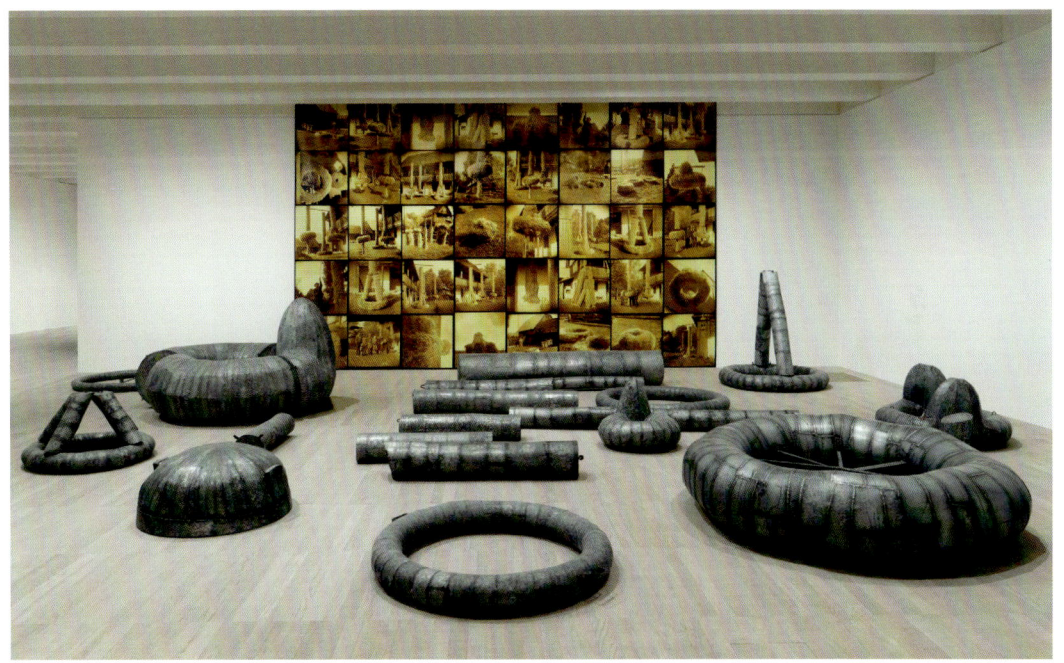

THE SOLEMN PROCESS

1964–74/76; 1980–5; 1985–2008, steel, straw, wire mesh and two digital prints on vinyl, *c*.600 × 600 cm (*c*.236 × 236 in), installation view, Tate Modern, 2017. Collection Tate, London
Ana Lupas, born 1940, Cluj-Napoca, Romania.

Lupas was an early practitioner of Land art and her work has evolved into a distinct durational practice that responds to failure and loss. From the early 1960s onwards, she enlisted rural communities from villages in Transylvania to create ambitious interventions in the surrounding countryside, often using using weaving techniques as a form of collective ritual, which she characterized as 'a bridge between the ancestral and the future'. In 1970, for *Humid Installation*, she mobilized villagers to transform a hill by covering it with dozens of laundry lines hung with wet white linen. In *The Solemn Process*, minimalist metal casings enclose woven straw wreaths and towers once made for harvest festivals. The artist's original aim in gathering these tactile organic structures was to celebrate vernacular traditions of crafts and farming, but with the urbanization of the countryside under the Communist Ceauşescu regime, these practices were steadily eroded. The title of the work implies a new meaning of salvage and reverent conservation. Lupas's focus shifted to preserving the straw forms, which were eventually sealed in mesh and steel sarcophagi, becoming relics of a vanishing agrarian culture.

DORA MAAR

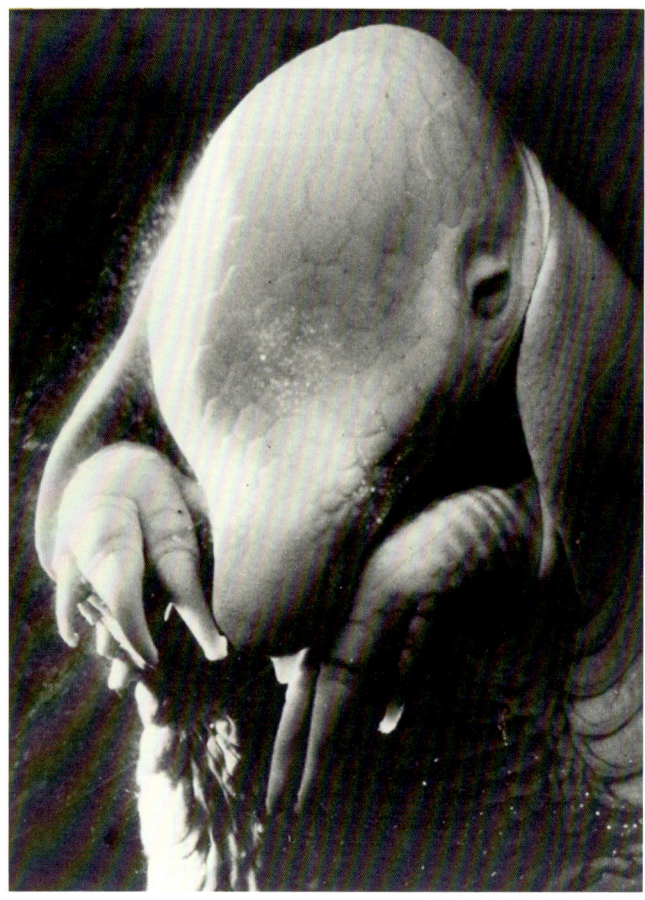

PÈRE UBU

1936, gelatin silver print, 39.7 × 29.2 cm (15 ⅝ × 11 ½ in), Metropolitan Museum of Art, New York

Dora Maar, born Theodora Markovitch, 1907, Paris. Died 1997, Paris.

An acclaimed photographer, painter and poet, Maar moved to Buenos Aires as a child, returning to Paris with her family in 1926 where she studied photography and attended the École des Beaux-Arts and Académie Julian. An intellectual and political activist, she became friends with the writers, painters and photographers of the Surrealist circle at the Café de la Place Blanche. In her own practice, she portrayed members of this movement, as well as depicting fashion and street life and creating ambiguous and strange photomontages. Travelling to Barcelona and London in the 1920s with a Rolleiflex camera, she recorded the effects of the period's economic depression before returning to Paris to open a workshop on rue d'Astorg. While working as a stills photographer for film director Jean Renoir in 1935, she was introduced to Pablo Picasso (1881–1973), becoming his lover and muse, and the model for his *Weeping Woman* (1937). This photograph depicts a mysterious creature, probably a preserved armadillo foetus. The cryptic title refers to the eponymous antihero of Alfred Jarry's absurdist play *Ubu Roi* (1896). An iconic Surrealist image, it is a grotesque acknowledgement of humanity's bestial nature.

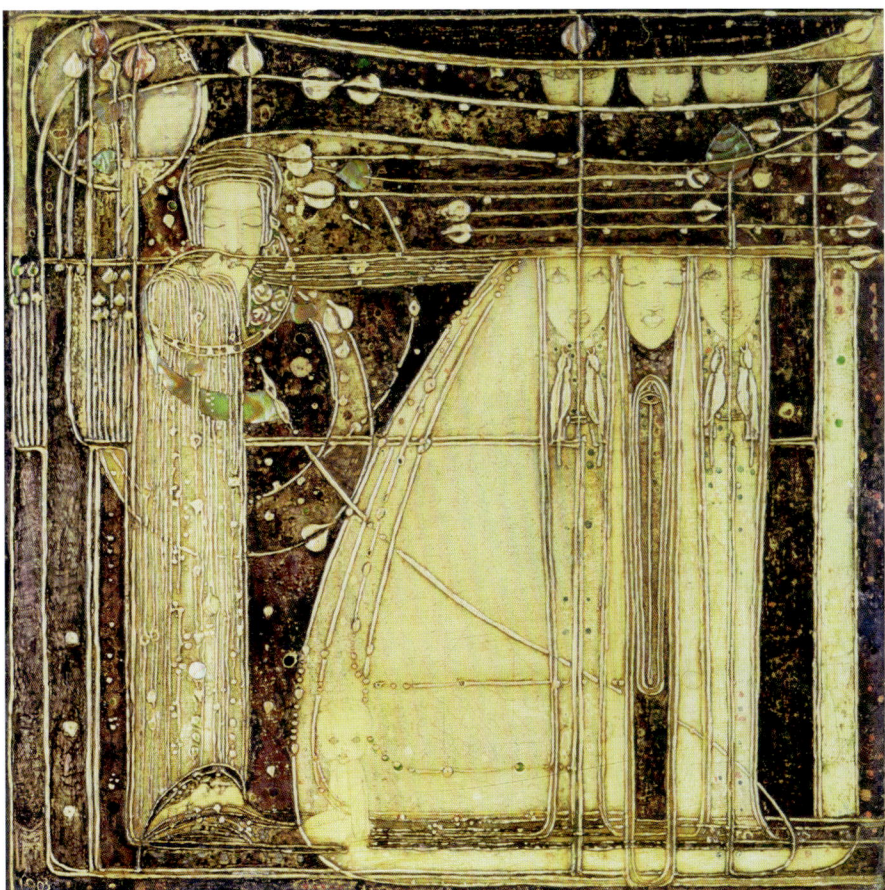

THE OPERA OF THE WIND

*c.*1902, gesso on panel, inlaid with abalone, set with string and glass beads,
20 × 20 cm (7 ⅞ × 7 ⅞ in), private collection
Margaret Macdonald Mackintosh, born Margaret Macdonald, 1864, Tipton,
Staffordshire, UK. Died 1933, London.

With her sister Frances (1873–1921), Mackintosh moved to Glasgow
around 1890 where they enrolled at the Glasgow School of Art.
There she met Charles Rennie Mackintosh (1868–1928) who became
her husband in 1900, her sister marrying their fellow student
Herbert McNair (1868–1955). Collectively known as 'The Four', they
constituted an informal artistic alliance central to the development
of the Glasgow Style. Mackintosh collaborated closely with her husband throughout his career on his most famous works of design,

and although her contribution is less well known, he fully acknowledged it. Influenced by the arabesque forms of Art Nouveau while
holding them in tension with severe geometrical frameworks, 'The
Four' passionately believed there should be no division between fine
and decorative art, and they found a staunch ally in Fritz Waerndorfer
(1868–1939), whose Viennese atelier, the Wiener Werkstätte, was
directly to influence much twentieth-century design. Seen here is the
precursor of a much larger commission for Waerndorfer, one of two
panels made to fit above a piano keyboard. Its sinuous lines emulate
the staves of a musical score, brought to flowing life.

ESTHER MAHLANGU

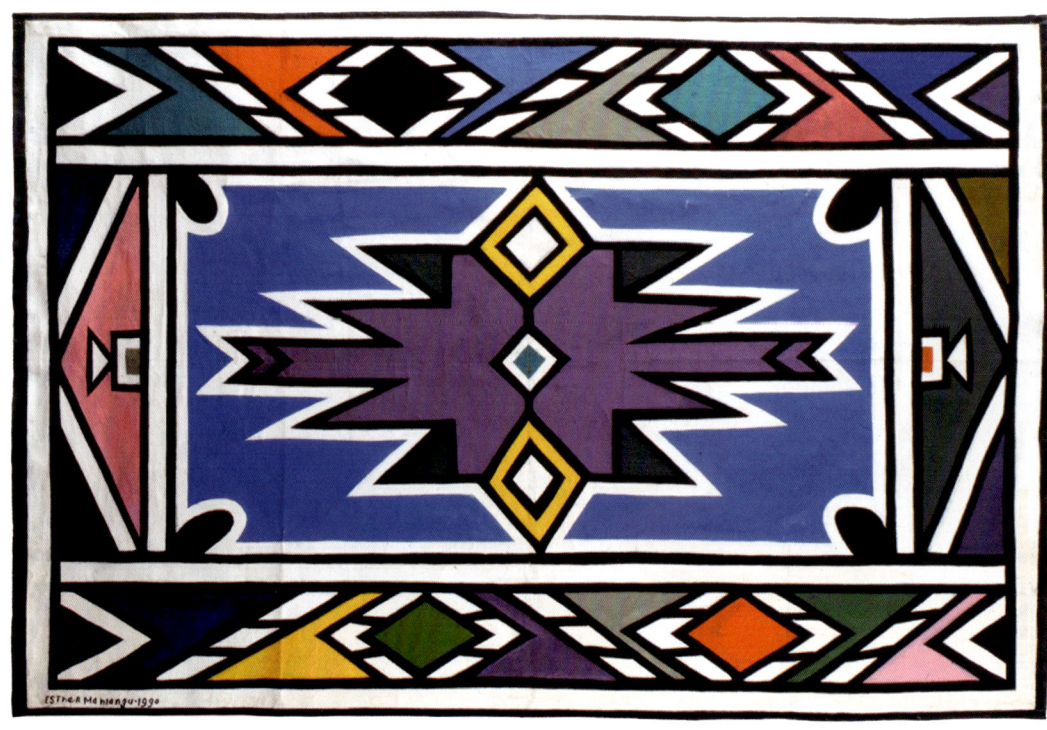

UNTITLED

1990, acrylic on canvas, 126 × 188 cm (49 ⅝ × 74 in), CAAC – The Pigozzi
Collection, Geneva

Esther Mahlangu, born 1935, near Middelburg, South Africa.

Painting is traditionally women's work in Ndebele culture – an ethnic
group native to South Africa. In the dry winter months, they paint the
exterior walls of their houses in bright colours and striking patterns.
Taught by her mother and grandmother, Mahlangu started painting
when she was ten years old, learning how to prepare pigments, imple-
ments and wall surfaces as well as the geometric designs themselves,
which despite their precision are rendered by eye, without rulers
or measuring devices. Her work was revealed to a wider audience
in 1989 when she painted a replica house for the now legendary

exhibition *'Magiciens de la Terre'* ('Magicians of the Earth') curated
by Jean-Hubert Martin at the Centre Georges Pompidou and the
Grande Halle at Parc de la Villette in Paris. Two years later, she
gained popular recognition as the first woman commissioned to
paint BMW's Art Car, and she now generally paints on canvas or
board, in order that her heritage may be seen more widely. The
central motif in this piece is inspired by the razorblade, an important
instrument in the daily lives of Ndebele people, used in ceremonies,
hair shaving and beadwork.

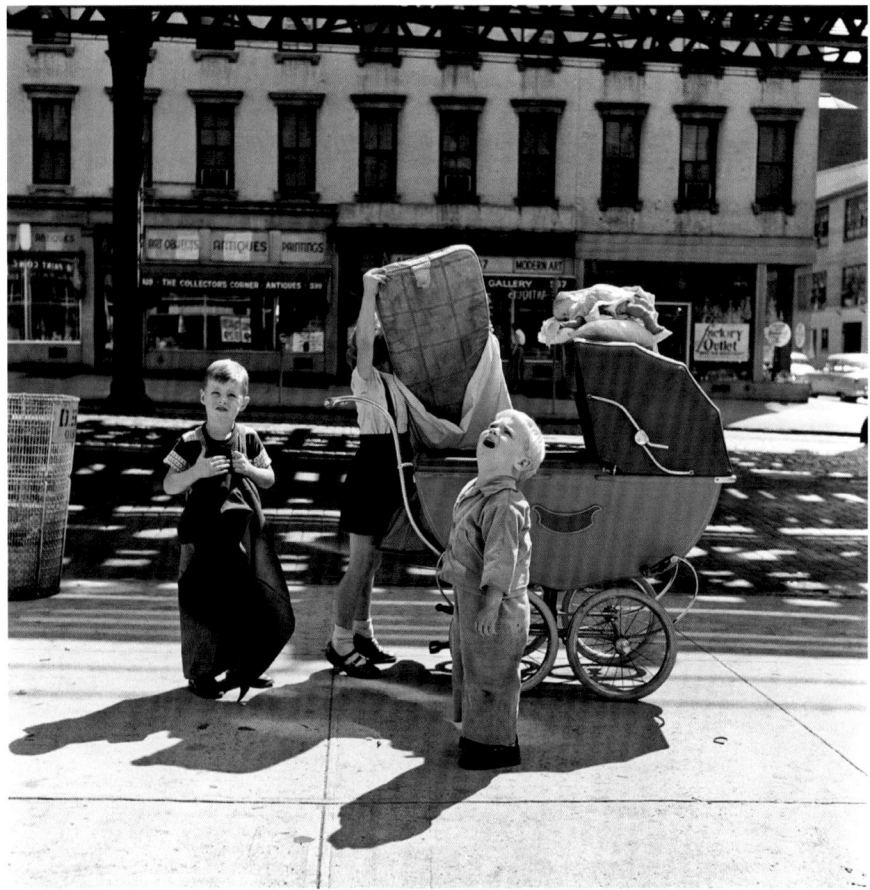

SEPTEMBER 1953, NEW YORK, NY

1953
Vivian Maier, born 1926, New York. Died 2009, Oak Park, Illinois.

For almost forty years of her adult life, Maier worked as a nanny in Chicago's North Shore, looking after the children of suburban households. She frequently photographed her wards at play, but was equally drawn to scenes of hardship and eccentricity, document-ing people in gritty urban surroundings. It is estimated that Maier took some 150,000 images, few of which were seen publicly in her lifetime. A reclusive character and self-proclaimed 'mystery woman', she was taciturn about her photography, apparently pur-suing it for herself only. Her Rolleiflex camera was held at the waist, which required Maier to look down to take a photograph. This

meant she usually passed her subjects unnoticed, allowing her to capture candid moments. Towards the end of her life, her prints, negatives and films were auctioned off from the storage facility in which she had stowed them, and have since reached a wider audience through publications, exhibitions and an Academy Award-nominated documentary film about her life. In contrast to Maier's enigmatic existence, images such as this study of childhood wonder demon-strate her worldliness, empathy and technical skill at conveying the joy of the everyday.

ANNA MARIA MAIOLINO

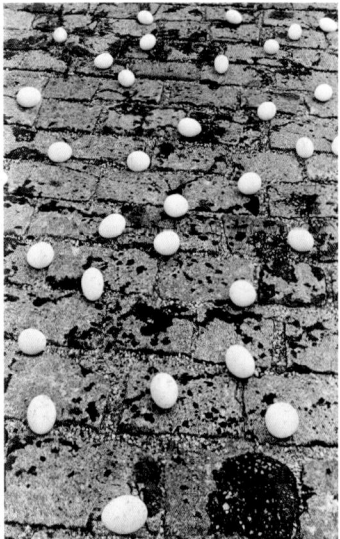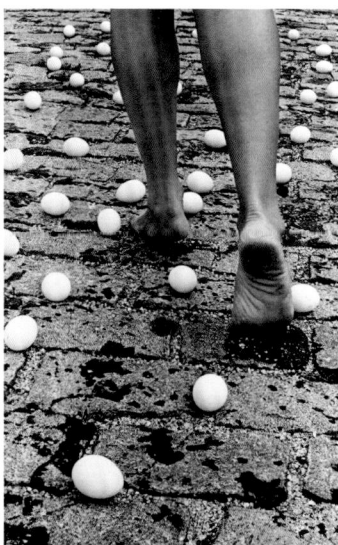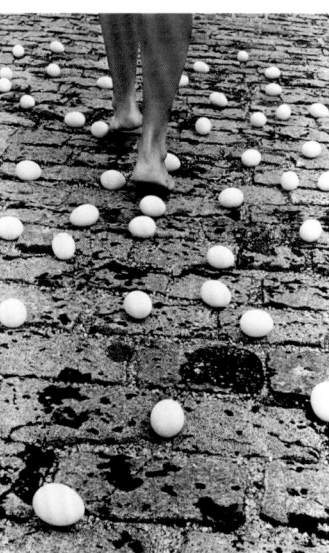

**ENTREVIDAS ('BETWEEN LIVES') from 'FOTOPOEMAÇÃO'
('PHOTOPOEMACTION') series**

1981, gelatin silver prints, each 144 × 92 cm (59 ¾ × 33 ¼ in)
Anna Maria Maiolino, born 1942, Scalea, Italy.

At the age of twelve Maiolino moved with her family from Italy to
Venezuela, before settling in Brazil in 1960. While studying at the
Escola de Belas Artes in Rio de Janeiro she became involved in the
Brazilian New Figuration movement, making woodcut prints and
mixed-media paintings that explored the country's repressive dictatorship and how this affected people's everyday experience. After
a period in New York from 1968 to 1971, Maiolino returned to Brazil
where she began experimenting with abstraction and language-
based work through action drawing. Her eclectic practice embraces

video and performance, considering themes of the body, daily life and
politics. This is exemplified in *Between Lives*, photographs that origi-
nated from a performance in which the artist walked barefoot across
Rua Cardoso Júnior, opposite the her studio in Rio de Janeiro, where
hundreds of chicken eggs had been scattered over the pebbled road
and pavement. The image recalls a minefield ready to explode. From
the late 1980s, her practice has shifted to clay installations with subtle
traces of her handprints. Essential to these traces of making are the
artist's touch and physical contact, restoring the desiring body to the
heart of the creative process.

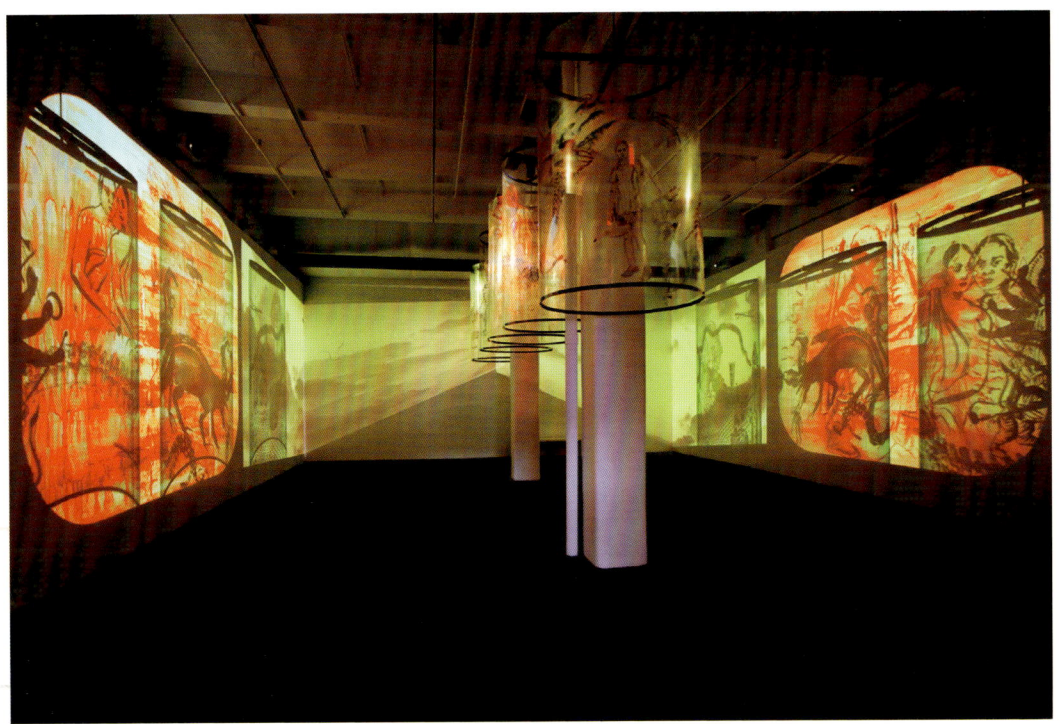

IN SEARCH OF VANISHED BLOOD

2012, six-channel video/shadow play with five rotating reverse-painted Mylar cylinders, sound, 11 mins, total dimensions variable, installation view at Galerie Lelong, New York, 2013
Nalini Malani, born 1946, Karachi, Pakistan (Indian national).

Malani has an interdisciplinary practice across painting, drawing and video installation, which addresses issues of inequality. Malani's family arrived in Calcutta (now Kolkata) during the 1947 partition of India and Pakistan, moving to Bombay (now Mumbai) later in her childhood. An activist and feminist, in 1985 she organized one of the first exhibitions of Indian women artists in Delhi. Since the 1990s, Malani has focused on creating experimental video works that look at marginalized individuals, drawing on her own personal experience of displacement and refugees portrayed in mythology, literature and history. First featured in Documenta 13 in Kassel, Germany, *In Search of Vanished Blood* is an immersive multimedia installation exploring violence. Uniting imagery from both Eastern and Western cultures, it consists of six video channels with five rotating reverse-painted Mylar cylinders, which together look at myth's regenerative power, the voices of women and the geopolitics of national identity. The work was influenced by *Cassandra* (1983), a portrait of a struggling female artist by the German novelist Christa Wolf (1929–2011), while its title derives from a poem by twentieth-century poet Faiz Ahmed Faiz.

JEANNE MAMMEN

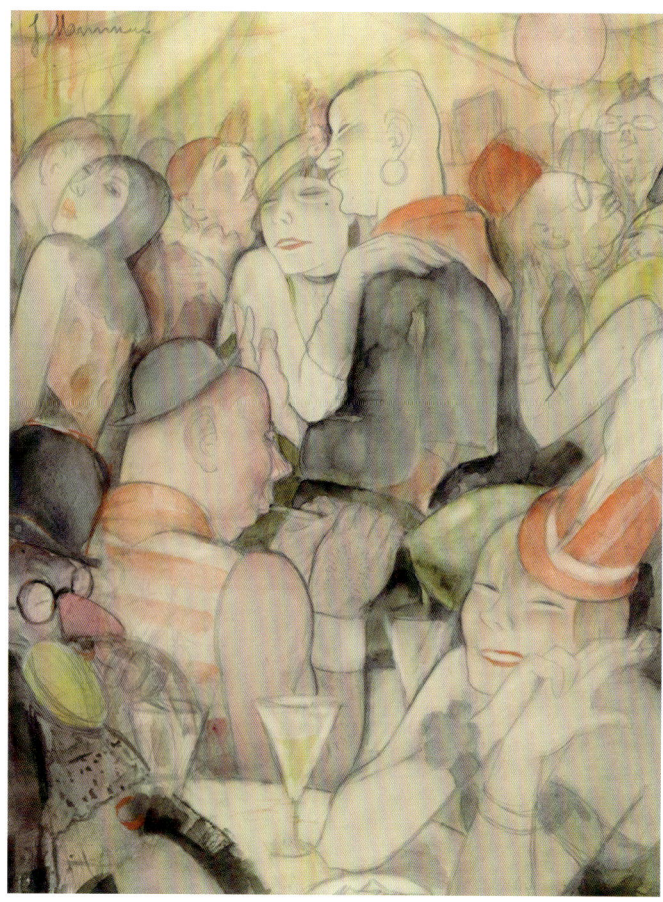

CARNIVAL IN BERLIN N III

*c.*1930, watercolour and pencil on paper, 60 × 47.3 cm (23 ⅝ × 18 ⅝ in),
Museum of Modern Art, New York
Jeanne Mammen, born 1890, Berlin. Died 1976, Berlin.

Mammen was a watercolour painter and printmaker known for her
illustrations of bustling city life in Berlin during the Weimar Republic.
Raised in Paris, and further educated in Brussels and Rome
between 1906 and 1911, her family fled France after the outbreak
of the First World War in order to avoid internment. While they
moved to Amsterdam, Mammen went alone to Berlin in 1916, losing
all of her possessions and then earning a living illustrating fashion
magazines. By 1924 she had gained a following for satirical drawings
in periodicals such as *Ulk* and *Simplicissimus*, and also become

noted for her distinctive depictions of empowered bohemian women
of this period. *Carnival in Berlin N III* has a stylistic likeness to the
Parisian avant-garde and portrays the louche atmosphere of a
crowded bar. When the Nazis came to power in 1933, they branded
her subjects 'Jewish' and 'decadent', banning her lithographs for
Pierre Louÿs's book of erotic lesbian poetry, *Les Chansons de Bilitis*
(1894). Mammen developed a love-hate relationship with Berlin, an
emotion that infiltrated into her painting style. After the war, she
largely abandoned drawing and painting, focusing instead on
sculpture and collage.

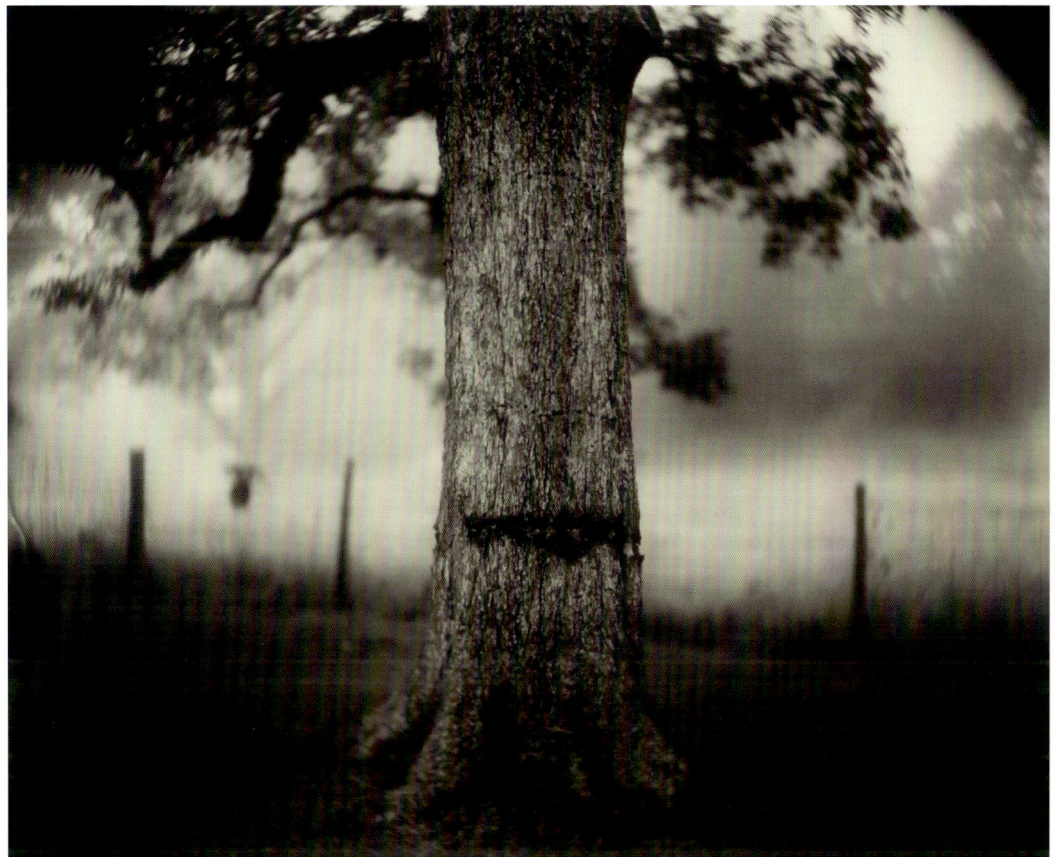

UNTITLED (SCARRED TREE) from the series 'DEEP SOUTH'
1998, gelatin silver print, 96.5 × 121.9 cm (38 × 48 in)
Sally Mann, born 1951, Lexington, Virginia.

Named 'America's Best Photographer' by *Time* magazine in 2001, Mann has devoted her career to photographing in and around the lush landscapes of southern Virginia, where she lives with her family. Shooting over the summer months on medium- and large-format cameras and printing during the winter, Mann is known for her technical precision and virtuosity in portrait and landscape genres. Her portrait series 'Immediate Family' (published 1992) chronicled the development of her three children, showing them playing, sleeping and dressing up. In the late 1990s, Mann began work on 'Deep South', a series that sought to capture 'the radical light of the American South', as Mann explained in a book devoted to it. Often using the collodion process, a nineteenth-century technique, Mann created hauntingly beautiful and seemingly timeless images of southern landscapes, including Civil War battlefields. *Scarred Tree* pays tribute to the iconic image *Beech Tree, Forest of Fontainebleau* (c.1856) by French photographer Gustave Le Gray (1820–84). Mann's tree, photographed in Mississippi, has healed its damaged bark, evidence of nature's resilience in the face of human violence.

BRITTA MARAKATT-LABBA

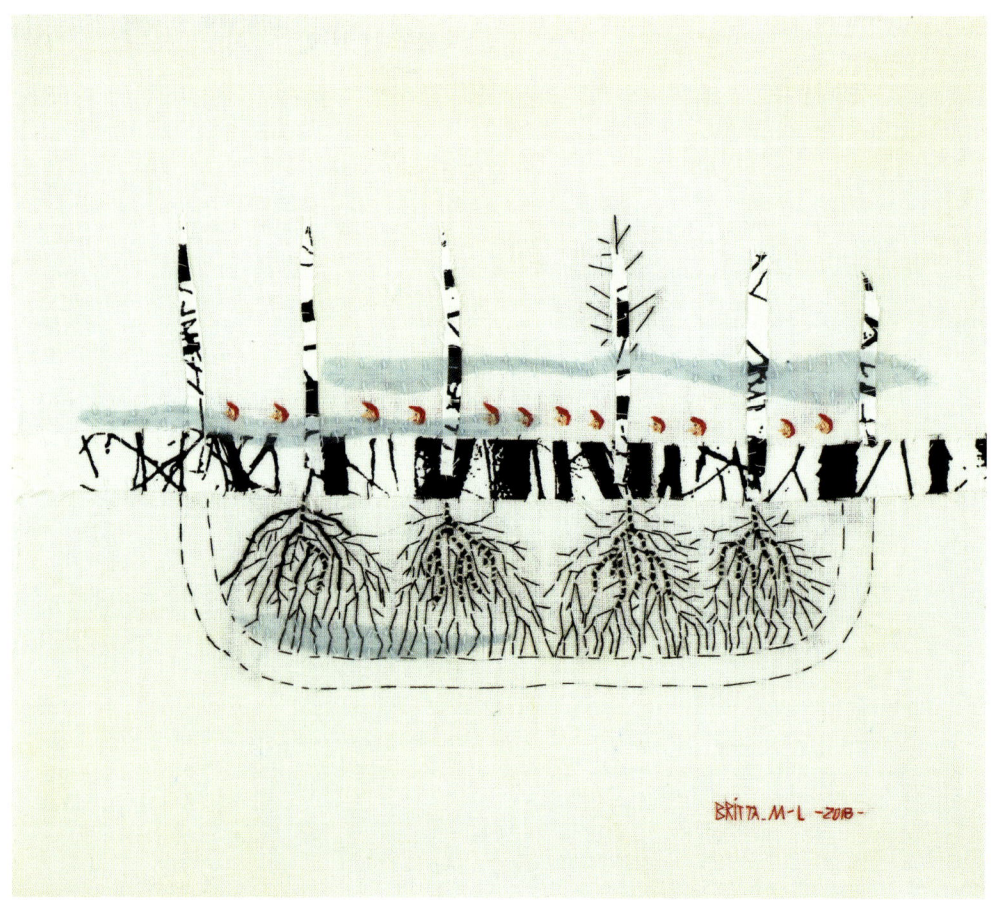

THE ROOTS

2018, embroidery and appliqué, 30 × 30 cm (11 ¾ × 11 ¾ in)
Britta Marakatt-Labba, born 1951, Idivuoma, Sweden.

Marakatt-Labba's art is imbued by her formative years in the
Scandinavian mountains where she was raised in a reindeer-herding
family of the Sámi community, one of the largest indigenous groups
of northern Europe. Embroidery has been her chosen medium since
the 1970s and she often portrays scenes of rural Sámi life. Everyday
activities including ice fishing and reindeer herding are shown alongside images from history and mythology, as demonstrated in her
epic 23.5-metre (77-foot) *Historjá* (2003–7), which introduced her
to a wider audience when it was exhibited at Documenta 14 in 2017.
Her works convey essential detail with just a few simple stitches,
and behind their sparseness, the images constitute the narratives of
a community whose voices have usually been silenced. Broader socio-
political reflections occur in works such as *The Roots*, a response
to the 2011 terrorist attacks in Norway, perpetrated by a far-right
extremist. Several Sámi youths were among the seventy-seven murder
victims. Six trees, with leaves dropped and roots severed, are a metaphor for those whose lives were tragically cut short and the twelve
figures represent their mourning mothers. 'Images are always stories,'
says the artist, in this case one of great sorrow.

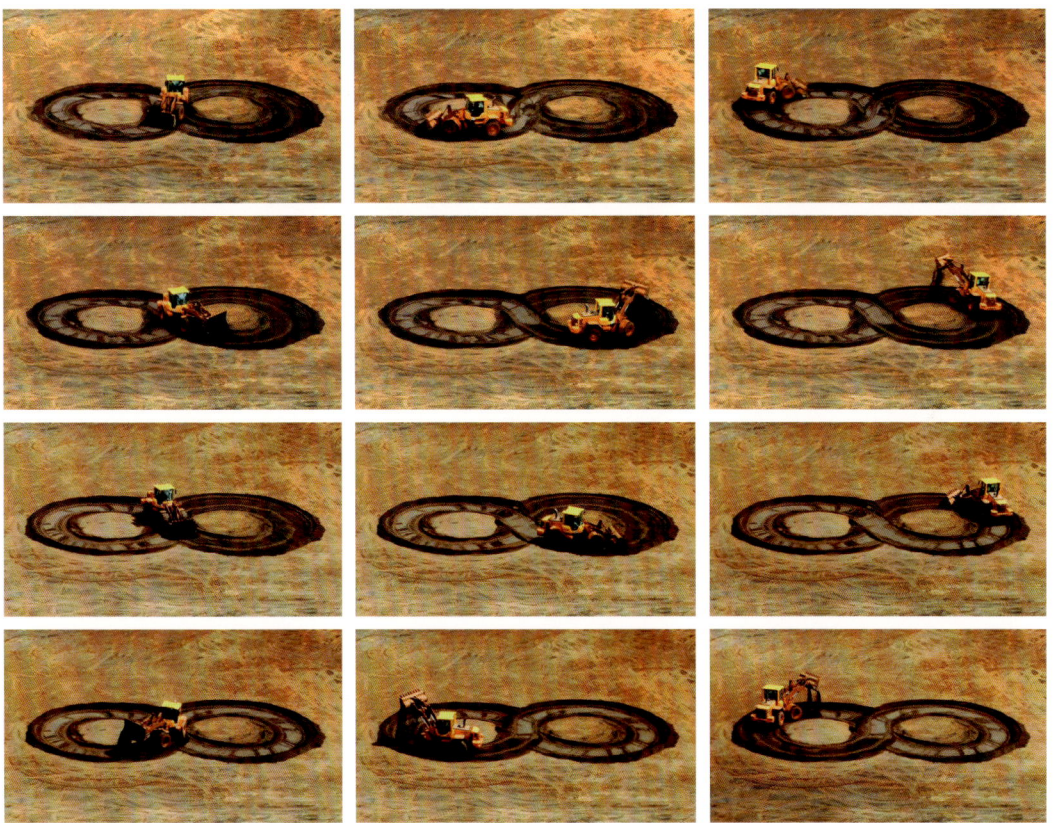

475 VOLVER (TO COME TO)

2009, stills from video, colour, sound, 8 mins 8 secs, looped
Cinthia Marcelle, born 1974, Belo Horizonte, Brazil.

Having studied in her native city at the Universidade Federal de Minas Gerais in the mid-1990s, Marcelle continued to develop her practice during an artist's residency in Cape Town in 2003. Coming to terms with disorientation of a new city and the different culture, she experienced a period of displacement and a fresh awareness of being embedded in a complex world, and these themes have continued to run through her work. Through large-scale installations, performances, video and photography, Marcelle stages interventions that challenge everyday conventions and behaviours by introducing chaos into otherwise familiar procedures or interactions. *For 475 Volver* *(to come to)*, Marcelle employed an earth-moving vehicle to stage her intervention, directing the driver to loop the machine along a path that resembled an hourglass or infinity symbol. The action was thereby rendered repetitive and pointless – a Sisyphean task – yet the routine nature of a manual job also effected an incessant transformation. With the artist's intent, a seemingly repetitive task became a creative accumulation. Like much of Marcelle's output, this process was documented from above using a video camera, revealing a geometric pattern and creating a bold earthwork within the landscape.

TERESA MARGOLLES

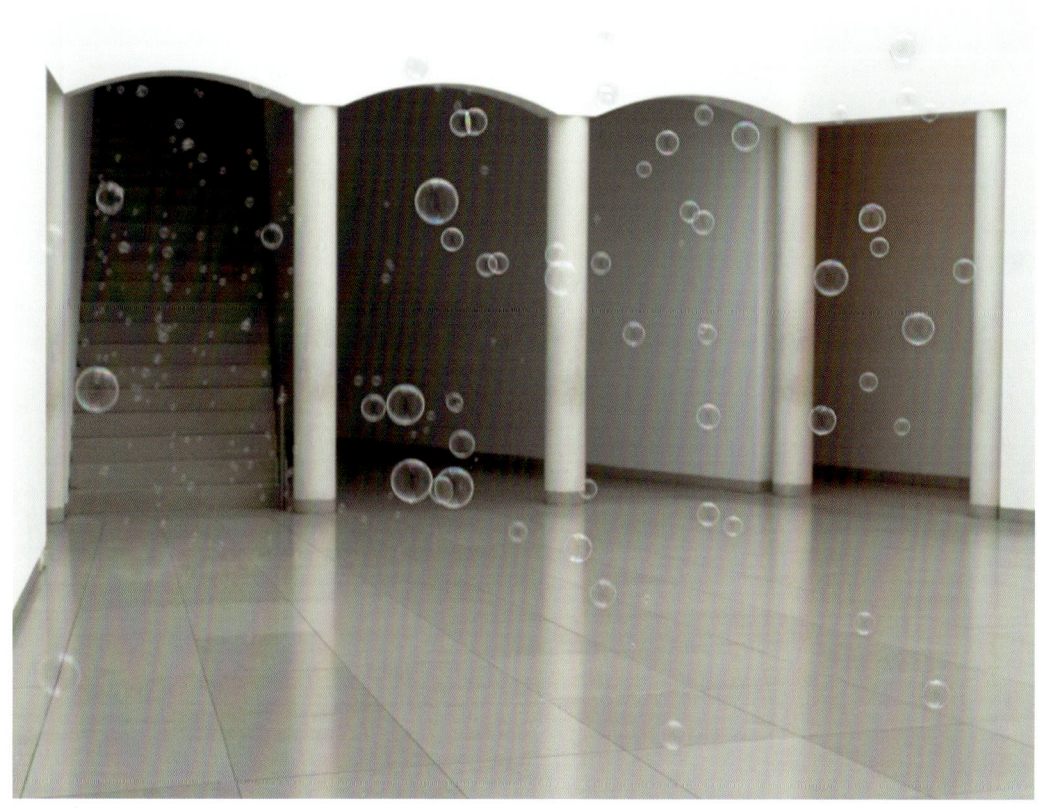

EN EL AIRE (IN THE AIR)

2003, installation with bubbles produced with a mix of water that was used to wash corpses of victims of violent deaths after their autopsy, dimensions variable, installation view, 'Muerte sin fin', Museum für Moderne Kunst, Frankfurt, 2004
Teresa Margolles, born 1963, Culiacán, Mexico.

Death plays a central role in Margolles's life and practice. After studying art and communication sciences, she trained as a pathologist and, since 1990, has worked and had her studio in Mexico City's morgue. At the 2006 Liverpool Biennial, she stated that she preferred 'not to exhibit the physical horror, but the silence' of autopsies, using the traces of death to reveal uncomfortable truths about inequality and social injustice. Mostly working with the bodies of victims of violent crime – casualties of Mexico's drug cartels in

particular – she focuses on what she calls 'the life of the corpse'. In the ethereal installation, *En El Aire (In The Air)* visitors are greeted with thousands of bubbles, inviting wonder, laughter and play. Only later does it sink in that these bubbles symbolize the transience of life: each one derives from soap and water used in the morgue and each represents a body. Since representing Mexico at the 53rd Venice Biennale in 2009, Margolles has increasingly worked outside the morgue and beyond her native country.

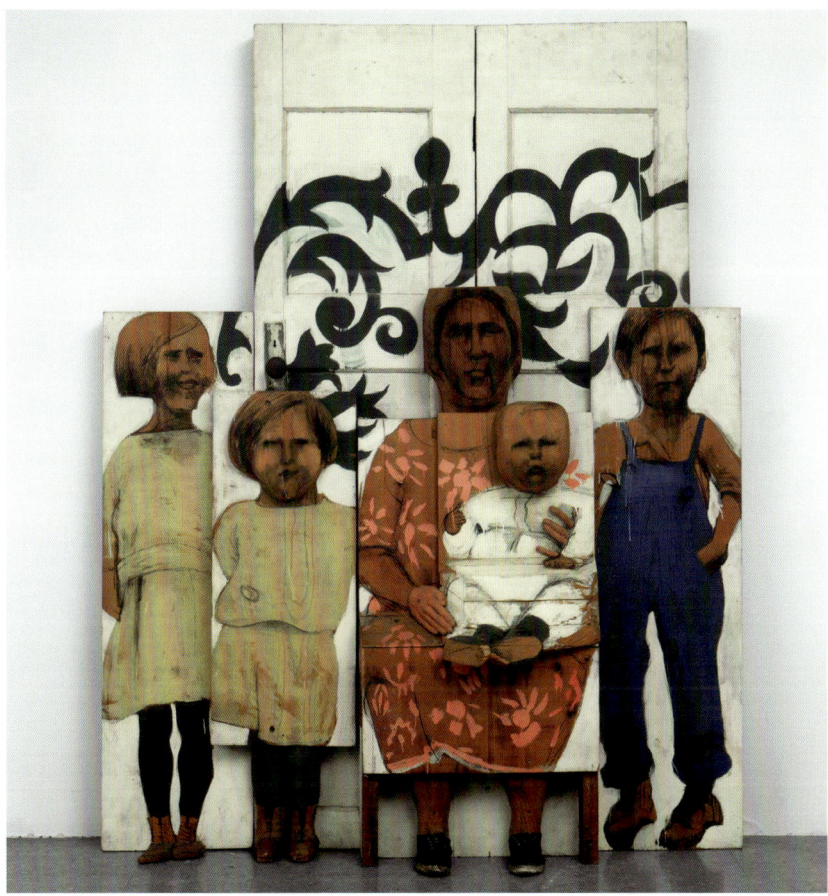

THE FAMILY

1962, painted wood, shoes, door knob and plate, 209.8 × 166.3 × 39.3 cm
(82 ⅝ × 65 ½ × 15 ½ in), Museum of Modern Art, New York
Marisol, born Maria Sol Escobar, 1930, Paris. Died 2016, New York.

During the early 1960s, Marisol is said to have been a bigger art star than Andy Warhol (1928–87), with whom she was friends, celebrated for her totemic sculptures that blended Pop and folk art. Born to Venezuelan parents in Europe before moving to study in America, Marisol ditched her surname to lose her patrilineal identity. After becoming interested in pre-Columbian art, she began making her signature tableaux, combining carved wooden figures – of her family, politicians and actors – with drawings and found objects. These works often questioned traditional female roles and

parodied the clichés of femininity. Despite early success, her lyrical art was overlooked in the heyday of Minimalism and Conceptualism, only attracting renewed interest towards the end of her life. The assemblage shown here, depicting a matriarch with her brood, revels in its artifice, comprising stiff figures painted on wooden boards that merge with a patterned door behind. The different-sized panels and sculptural elements, such as real shoes, create layers of movement, offering a more nuanced portrait than the 'happy families' shown in mainstream mass media of the period.

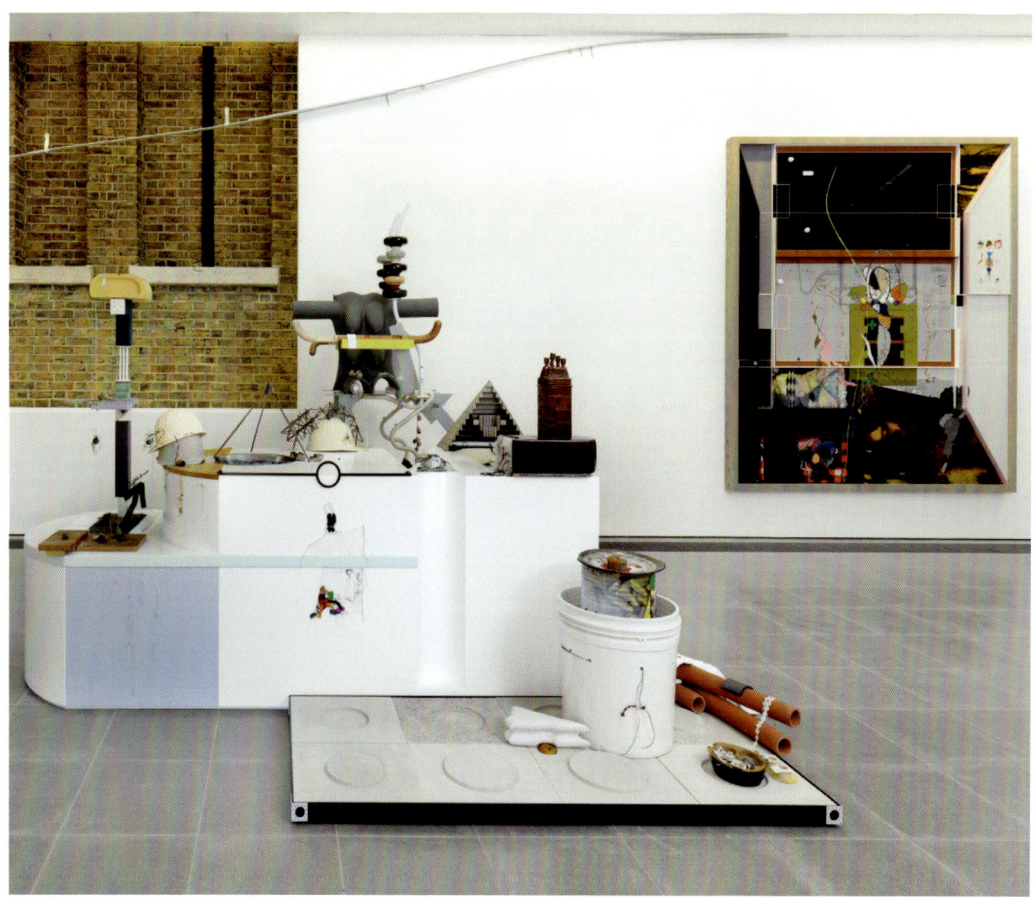

THE CAT FROM THE BACON

2015, steel, aluminium, hand-thrown glazed ceramic, terracotta, model board, ash, cherry, Valchromat, Sepili, chipboard, cardboard, sprayed MDF, fur, silk sequins, cast resin, cast Jesmonite, oil paint on paper, airbrushed steel, stitched and embroidered fabric, lace, stones, mother of pearl, rope, tin foil, brass bells, cast rubber, sand, bucket, microbeads, Formica, engraved brass, copper, matchbooks, beads, cotton and string, overall dimensions: 215.9 × 359.4 × 315 cm (85 × 141½ × 124 in), installation view, 'Drunk Brown House', Serpentine Sackler Gallery, London, 2016
Helen Marten, born 1985, Macclesfield, UK.

Two years after completing her bachelor's degree at Ruskin School of Drawing and Fine Art, Oxford, Marten's first solo show in 2010 at T293 gallery, Naples, established her international reputation. In 2016 she was awarded both the inaugural Hepworth Prize for Sculpture and Turner Prize. Influenced by the 'Combines' of Robert Rauschenberg (1925–2008), she integrates collections of found objects, made forms, screen prints, paint and text into complex sculptural compositions. Her destabilizing play with media and form invites the viewer to free-associate and reflect on the sensory overload of contemporary life. Her exhibition 'Drunk Brown House' incorporated fragments of the late Zaha Hadid's architectural plans for the Serpentine Gallery's extension, together with such diverse materials as ostrich eggs, wicker, feathers, sand, neoprene, construction timber, clay, fabric and embroidered text. A lyrical ribbon of white steel curling and winding through the entire exhibition from ceiling to floor fluidly drew together the disparate parts, yet the sheer incongruity is not resolved. Marten's practice has been described as archaeological, exposing the inchoate world of objects as artefacts of our culture.

THE TREE

1964, oil and pencil on canvas, 182.8 × 182.8 cm (72 × 72 in), Museum of Modern Art, New York

Agnes Martin, born 1912, Macklin, Saskatchewan, Canada. Died 2004, Taos, New Mexico.

Martin emigrated from Canada to New York in 1931 to study and to help her pregnant sister, and later lived alongside other artists, including Ellsworth Kelly (1923–2015) and Lenore Tawney (p.401) in the Coenties Slip area of Manhattan. From 1942 Martin spent substantial time living and working in New Mexico, often in remote circumstances, and she became an American citizen in 1950. It was not until 1958 that she had her debut solo exhibition at the Betty Parsons Gallery in New York, and only with works such as *The Tree*

did she finally discover a style with which she was happy. Its title conjures up the natural world, a favourite subject for the artist, although she destroyed her earlier figurative and biomorphic works with this change of direction. Continuing to make such 'Grid' paintings through the 1960s, Martin later developed these, producing 'Band' paintings – mostly in series form – which were composed of pale washes of soft-coloured paint scored with horizontal pencil lines. While often described as a Minimalist, Martin considered herself more of an Abstract Expressionist because her combinations of a geometric and abstract aesthetic awoke emotions, such as happiness, in viewers. Although she used titles sparingly, those she did select often alluded to such feelings.

MARY MARTIN

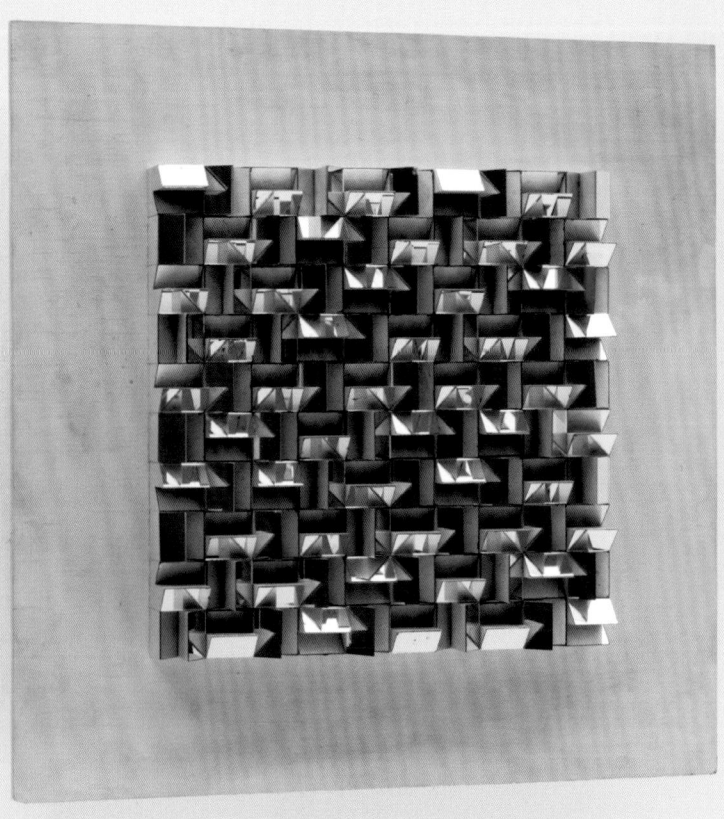

ROTATION 3

1969, injection-moulded polystyrene and mirrors on board, 50.5 × 50.5 × 10.5 cm (19 ⅞ × 19 ⅞ × 4 ⅛ in), private collection

Mary Martin, born Mary Balmford, 1907, Folkestone, UK. Died 1969, London.

Martin studied at London's Goldsmiths College and the Royal College of Art, and while still at the latter married fellow artist Kenneth Martin (1905–84). The couple often collaborated, perhaps most famously on the Whitechapel Gallery's 1956 exhibition of contemporary art, 'This is Tomorrow'. She produced her first abstract work in 1950, having painted landscapes and still lifes in the previous two decades, often under her maiden name, Balmford, as well as teaching applied arts. The following year she began making abstract reliefs with a pronounced sculptural quality. Martin is considered a significant exponent of 1950s Constructionism in Britain, a movement that, following in the footsteps of earlier British champions of modernist abstraction, dated back to Constructivism, itself a movement originating in Russia in 1913. Often working with a monochrome palette and using materials such as Perspex, plastic, wood, metal and mirrors, her works are explorations of geometry, shape, space and surface and convey a sense of mathematical precision. The way this work reflects light off its multifaceted surface demonstrates how qualities such as movement and dynamism as well as form were integral to her constructions.

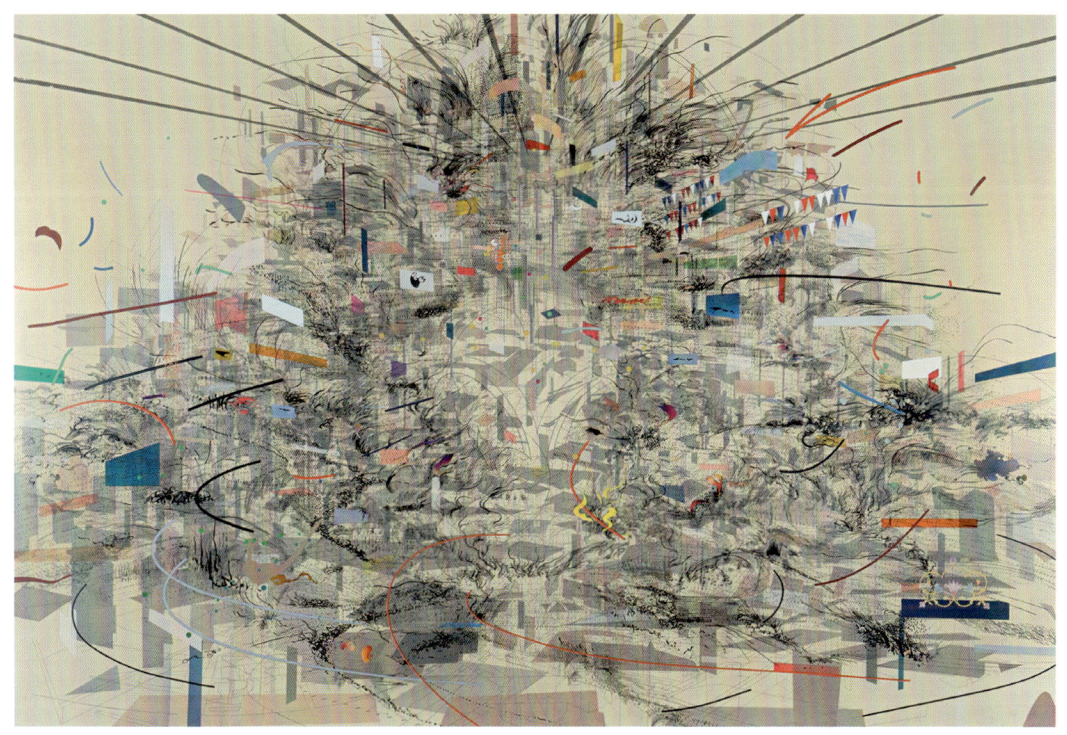

EMPIRICAL CONSTRUCTION, ISTANBUL

2003, ink and synthetic polymer paint on canvas, 304.8 × 457.2 cm (120 × 180 in), Museum of Modern Art, New York
Julie Mehretu, born 1970, Addis Ababa, Ethiopia.

How is a city felt? In this large-scale piece, Ethiopian-born, New York-based Mehretu layers fragmentary views of Istanbul, constituting the city as a mass of gestures, an organized explosion of geometric forms and intricate, swirling lines, that both advance outwards and recede. Similar to the seascapes of J.M.W. Turner's (1775–1851), an inspiration for Mehretu, her work speaks to the historical through the atmospheric. Yet instead of the sea and sky, her 'atmosphere' is architecture and the built environment. As the artist stated in an interview with *Art21 Magazine*, 'The buildings are so layered; the information can be so layered and disintegrated that it becomes a dust-like atmosphere.' Deciphering these layers is more or less impossible, which is intentional, despite the title's mention of 'empirical' implying an ordering of data. Her paintings and drawings hang between representation and abstraction, order and chaos, appearing simultaneously emergent and passing, as if we were somehow caught in a storm of illustration. Maybe this is what it means to feel a city, where fragments come together to form a whole that is never quite comprehensible.

ANA MENDIETA

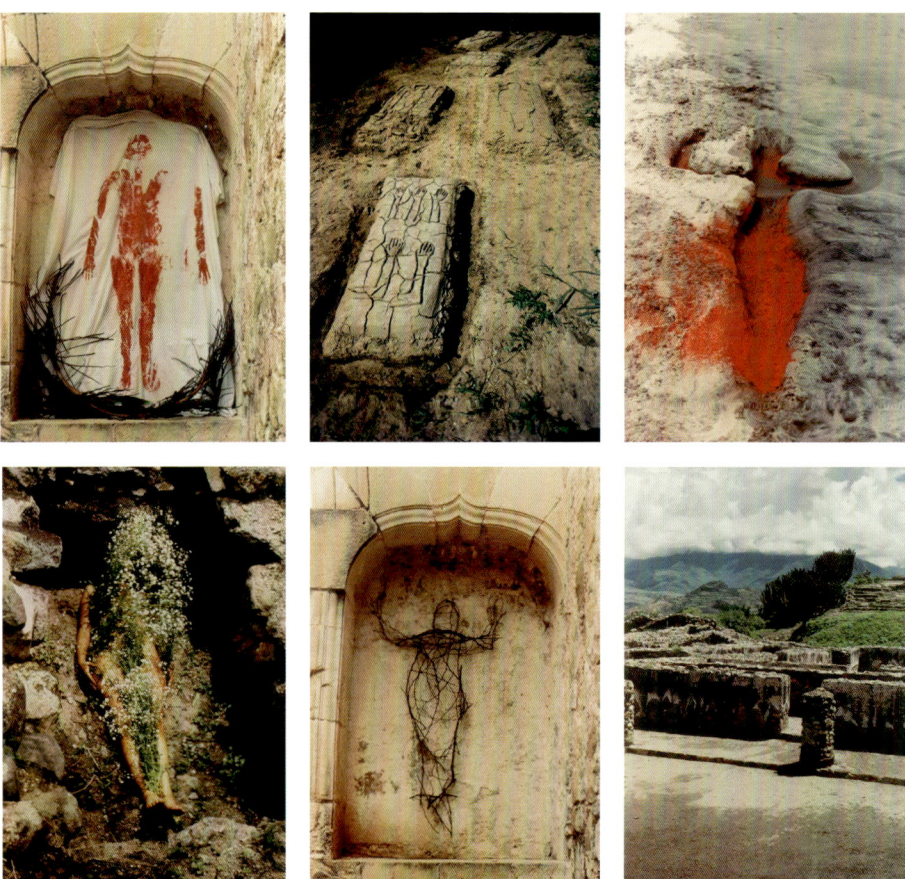

SILUETA WORKS IN MEXICO

1973–7/1991, pigmented inkjet prints, 4 parts: 33.7 × 50.8 cm (13 ¼ × 20 in),
eight parts: 50.8 × 33.7 cm (20 × 13 ¼ in), The Barbara Lee Collection of Art
by Women, Institute of Contemporary Art, Boston
Ana Mendieta, born 1948, Havana. Died 1985, New York.

In 1961, Mendieta and her sister Raquelin were sent to the United
States under Operation 'Pedro Pan' after her father joined anti-Castro
forces. Landing first in Miami, they then lived in Iowa orphanages
and foster homes, only being reunited with their mother and
brother five years later. Deeply affected by the experience of displacement, Mendieta developed a practice that she defined as 'earth-
body' sculpture, which in the early years of her career included
performing shamanistic rituals using her own body to reclaim her
roots and reconnect with the natural world. The long-running
'Silueta Series' comprises over a hundred films and photographs.
Referencing Afro-Cuban and Santería rituals specific to her birthplace, she left an ephemeral imprint of her body on the earth, covered her skin with blooms of white flowers or constructed her
silhouette using organic materials and fire. Moving to New York in
1978, she had a solo exhibition of her photographs at A.I.R. Gallery in
1979. During the 1980s, she was invited to participate in exhibitions
organized by the Cuban government, initiating a period of reconnec-
tion with her homeland.

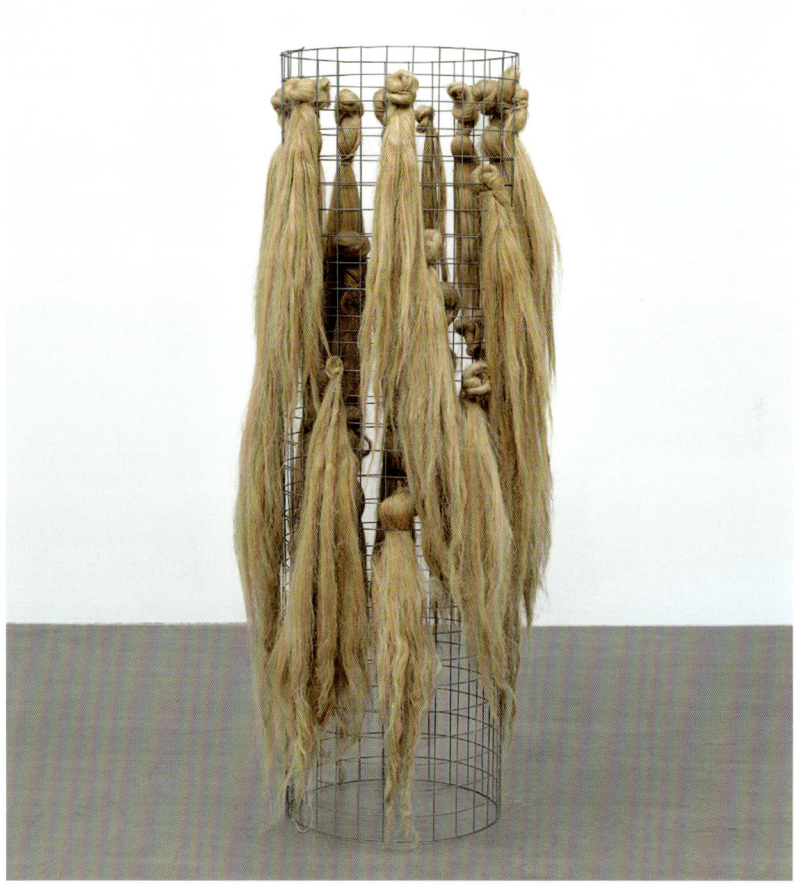

UNTITLED

1966, wire mesh and hemp, h: 152.4 cm (60 in), diam: 58.4 cm (23 in), Museum of Modern Art, New York

Marisa Merz, born 1926, Turin, Italy. Died 2019, Turin, Italy.

Merz was for many years the lone female member of the Italian Arte Povera movement, which espoused the use of cheap, anti-elitist materials to blur the line between art and life. Making works that often suggest organic forms, at various times she has used clay, copper, aluminium and waxed paper. Her first solo exhibition was held in 1967 at Gian Enzo Sperone Gallery in Turin, comprising an installation made from aluminium foil. A year later, she participated in 'Arte Povera + Azione Povera', a three-day event in Amalfi, Italy, which included other artists from the movement such as Michelangelo Pistoletto (b.1933) and her husband Mario Merz (1925–2003). Critic Peter Schjeldahl has called her 'the liveliest artist in a movement that was often marred by intellectual and poetic pretensions'. This work exemplifies the comedic and surrealistic undertones of her practice, with its tufts of blonde hemp fibres attached to a wire-mesh cylinder. Appearing like ponytails, they move bewitchingly between an animal and human presence. Merz was awarded the Golden Lion for Lifetime Achievement at the 55th Venice Biennale in 2013.

ANGELICA MESITI

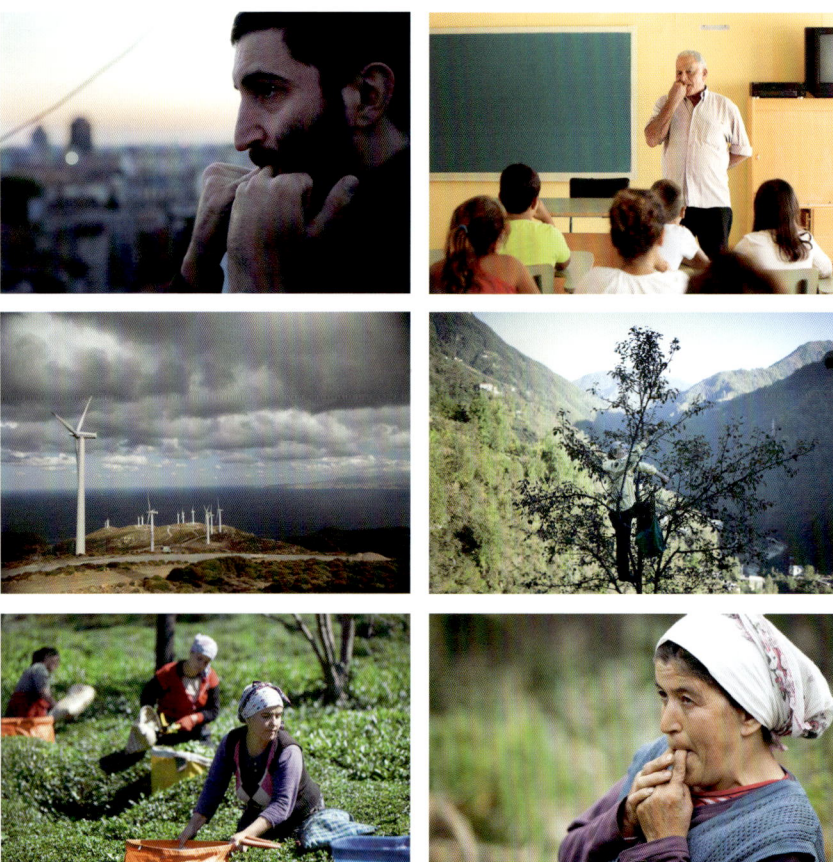

THE CALLING

2013–14, 3-channel HD video, colour, sound, 35 mins 36 secs
Angelica Mesiti, born 1976, Sydney.

Growing up in an Italian-speaking family in Australia, Mesiti's interests lie in non-verbal communication as signified by gesture, body language and the singing voice. Initially studying dance, the artist took bachelor's then master's degrees in time-based art at the University of New South Wales, with dance remaining her particular forte. She was influenced by the 'body weather' method of the Japanese dancer and actor Min Tanaka, which focuses on muscle and bone and its aesthetic potential. During her collaboration in 2008–9 with the all-female performance collective The Kingpins (of which she was a founding member), she made video art that appropriated the styles of mainstream culture. Primarily utilizing film and installation for her subsequent solo work, the artist uses movement and the body to 'speak', employing cinematic techniques to articulate heightened states of rapture and performance. In *The Calling* an expanded definition of language is presented: a woman farmer speaks to her goats, and a man whistles to his grandson, who responds in Spanish, creating a polyglot landscape of intuition. Now based in Paris, Mesiti was selected to represent Australia at the 58th Venice Biennale in 2019.

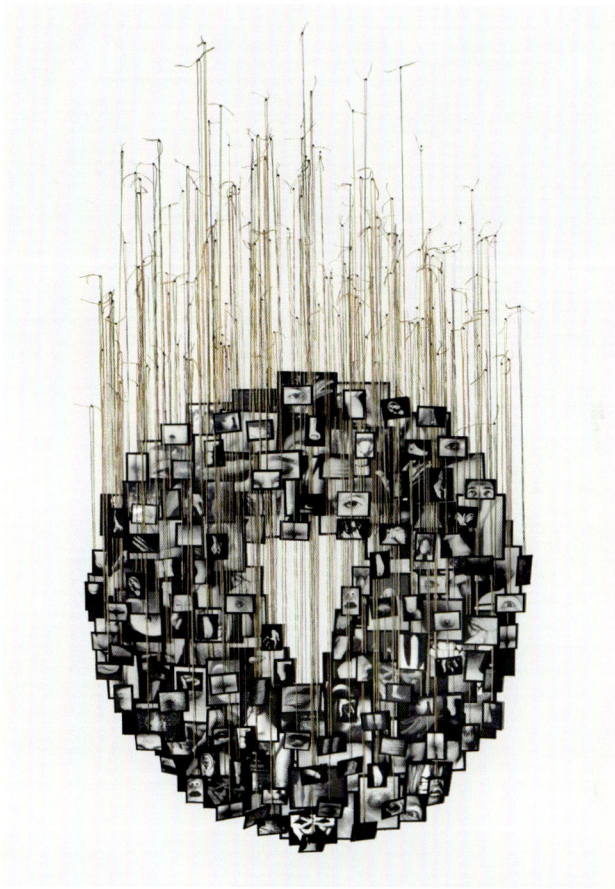

MY VOWS: CIRCLE – TRIANGLE

1990, framed black-and-white photographs and strings, h: 250 cm (98 ⅜ in) with strings, circle: 147 × 140 cm (57 ⅞ × 55 ⅛ in)
Annette Messager, born 1943, Berck, France.

Messager uses sewing, embroidery and taxidermy to make sculptures and installations. Although referencing the first person in titles, fact and fiction are often blurred in what the artist refers to as her 'false biography'. She adopts a role not only of artist, but of 'collector', 'peddler' and 'practical woman' to subvert and play with identity. Interested in the work of both Outsider artists and children, she shares their capacity for unpretentiousness and fantasy. Combined with text and inexpensive materials, photography features heavily in Messager's work, from the album collections produced in the 1970s to the series 'My Vows' (1988–91). In the example seen here, recurring motifs in her oeuvre – the body, portraiture and fragmentation – are synthesized to create a complex hanging form. A collective group portrait-cum-religious shrine, it evokes the *ex-voto* offerings seen in many Roman Catholic churches, while close-up images of buttocks, lips, nipples and open mouths suggest an unlikely coupling of the holy and profane. Having exhibited extensively internationally, Messager was awarded the Golden Lion at the 51st Venice Biennale (2005) for her presentation at the French Pavilion and the prestigious Praemium Imperiale global arts prize for Lifetime Achievement in Sculpture (2016).

BEATRIZ MILHAZES

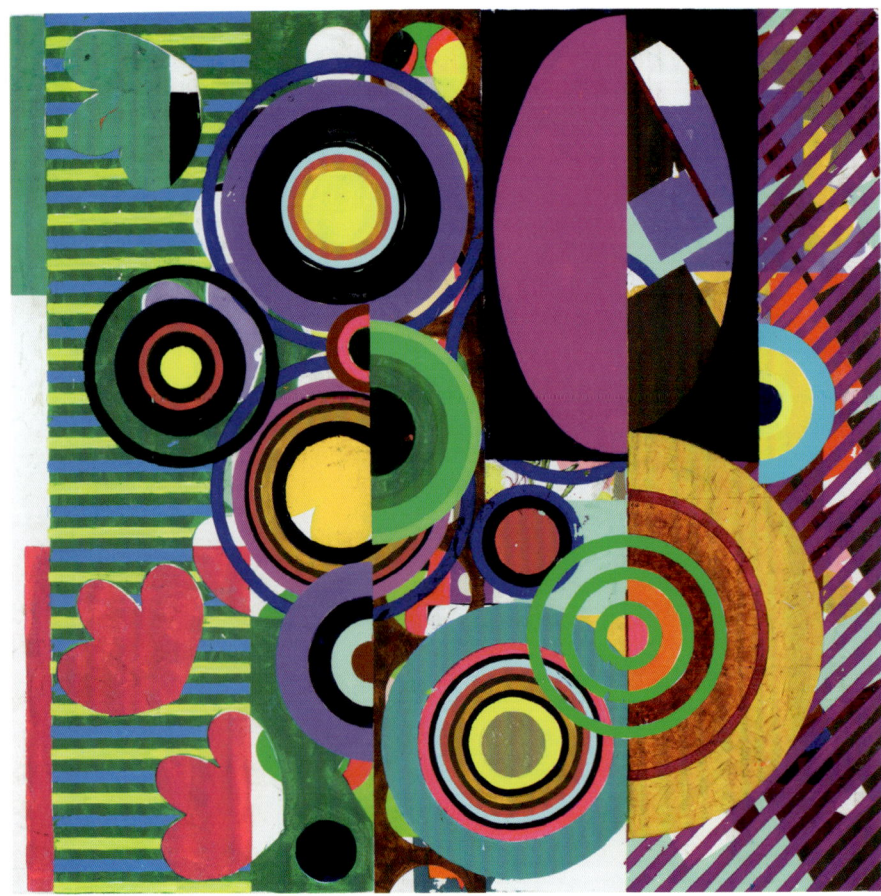

MAROTOLOCO
2014–15, acrylic on canvas, 79 × 79.5 cm (31 ⅛ × 32 ¼ in), Pérez Art Museum Miami
Beatriz Milhazes, born 1960, Rio de Janeiro.

After starting her artistic career during a heyday of Conceptual art in 1970s Brazil, Milhazes turned to painting in the 1980s. Her practice combines a Brazilian vernacular of heightened colour and hard-edged graphics with the plain geometric forms of early-twentieth-century European abstraction. In the following decade, she cultivated her signature technique of bringing different coloured elements directly together in a manner related to collage. Applying paint onto a transparent plastic sheet, she allowed the surface to dry before transferring the pigment to canvas using a method akin to monotype printing, with further prepared layers being applied on top. The resulting distressed quality to her paintings echoes the appearance of traditional artefacts. Initially interested in colonial-period motifs, Milhazes was later influenced by the Brazilian avant-garde 'happenings' of the 1960s – particularly those associated with the artistic and musical movements of Neo-Concretism and Tropicália. In the work seen here, Milhazes evokes shapes from the botanical gardens that sit just a few blocks away from her studio, with an exuberant flower-power aesthetic. The title of works in this series derives from the Portugese word *marola* ('rippling wave'), the edges of each concentric circle creating undulations in super-saturated colour.

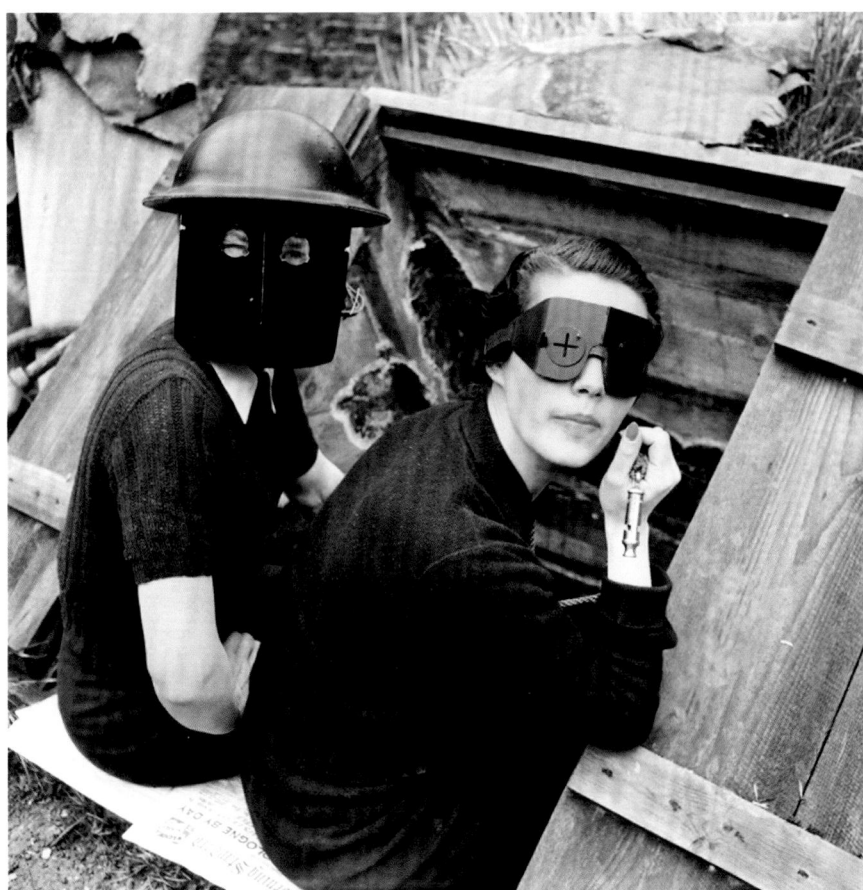

FIRE MASKS, DOWNSHIRE HILL, LONDON

1941, black-and-white photograph
Lee Miller, born 1907, Poughkeepsie New York. Died 1977, Chiddingly,
East Sussex, UK.

Initially a *Vogue* model, Miller learnt photographic techniques from Man Ray (1890–1976), to whom she became an apprentice, collaborator and lover. Together they rediscovered the process of solarization, where the image is reversed in tone. Part of the Surrealist movement, Miller captured startling images of female nudes and challenged the typical objectification of women in visual culture. For example, in her photograph of severed breasts that had been removed in a mastectomy, which she staged on a plate with a knife and fork. At the outbreak of the Second World War, Miller moved to London and started working for *Vogue* as a war correspondent. Applying her eye to the chaos of war, this image depicts women outside the air raid shelter in the garden of the home where she lived with her husband, the Surrealist artist Roland Penrose (1900–84). Wearing masks to protect them from incendiary bombs, the image reinforced how the conflict also offered women opportunities for empowerment. Taking on ambitious war assignments, sometimes under enemy fire, Miller photographed the Liberation of Paris in 1944 and of Dachau the following year, famously portraying herself later the same day in the bath of Hitler's Munich apartment.

MARILYN MINTER

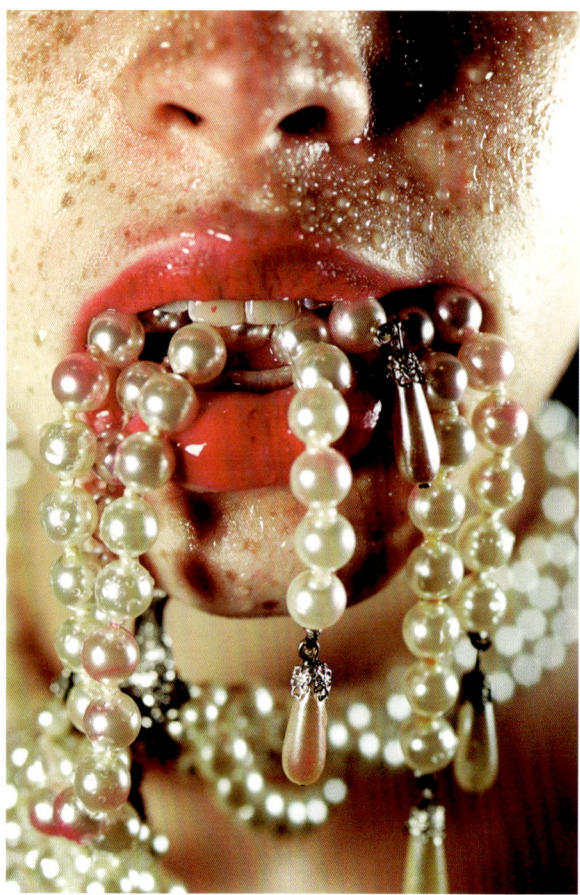

SATIATED

2003, chromogenic print, 218.4 × 152.4 cm (86 × 60 in)
Marilyn Minter, born 1948, Shreveport, Louisiana.

Since the late 1960s, Minter's paintings, photographs and videos
have centred on the depiction of women, particularly in the realms
of art, fashion and pornography. Raised in Florida, she graduated
from the state university in 1970 before completing her MFA in
Syracuse, upstate New York, and then moving to New York City,
where she continues to live and work. Her early creative output
ranged from black-and-white photographs of her mother to photore-
alist canvases depicting domestic scenes. In the 1980s she began to
attract attention and some controversy for her sensuous, colourful
renderings in paint of pornography imagery, as well as food and her

now-signature subject of women's bodies. Influenced by Pop artists such as Andy Warhol (1928–87), Minter initially based her
paintings on found imagery; from the 1990s, however, she has
staged her own photographs and used these as sources, as is the case
in this extreme close-up of a woman's mouth. The work is typical
of Minter's interest in deconstructing beauty: glossy, high-fashion
glamour is fused with visceral reality, beads of sweat adorning the
model's face and flecks of lipstick staining her teeth, as she bites
down upon lustrous pearls.

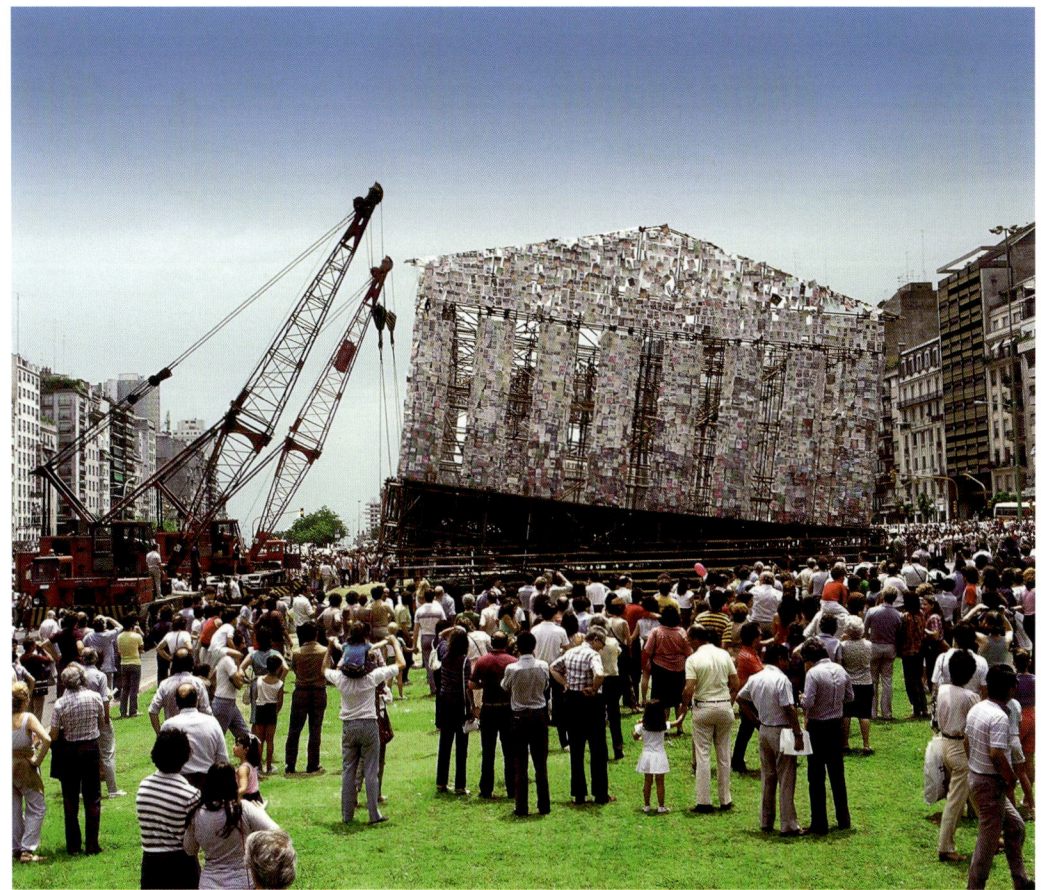

THE PARTHENON OF BOOKS

1983, metal scaffolding, books and wire, h: 12 m (39 ft 4 in), installation view, Buenos Aires

Marta Minujín, born 1941, Buenos Aires.

Arriving in Paris on an arts scholarship, Minujín developed 'living' sculptures, a form of social practice combining performance and community outreach. Exemplifying her interest in urban social space and its detritus, her 1963 *La Destrucción* saw artists including Christo (1935–2020) being invited to destroy an ephemeral installation of mattresses. After receiving a Guggenheim Fellowship, Minujín moved to New York in 1966 and began to practise 'psychedelic' art. An example of this that foreshadowed technologies still decades away was the interactive sculpture *Minuphone* (1967),

which encouraged people to make calls from a telephone booth only to see colours upon its window glass and their own image in a screen. By the time the Argentinian dictatorship fell in 1983, she was exploring themes of freedom of expression in her homeland. This work, part of the series 'The Fall of Universal Myths', is about cultural oppression. Minujín replicated Greece's Parthenon – the archetype of democracy – using 30,000 books formerly confiscated by military junta. Integrating them into an architectural framework, it is a monument to liberal egalitarianism, underlining how culture underpins and defends progressive societies. The epic work was restaged in 2017 for Documenta 14 in Kassel, Germany.

ALEKSANDRA MIR

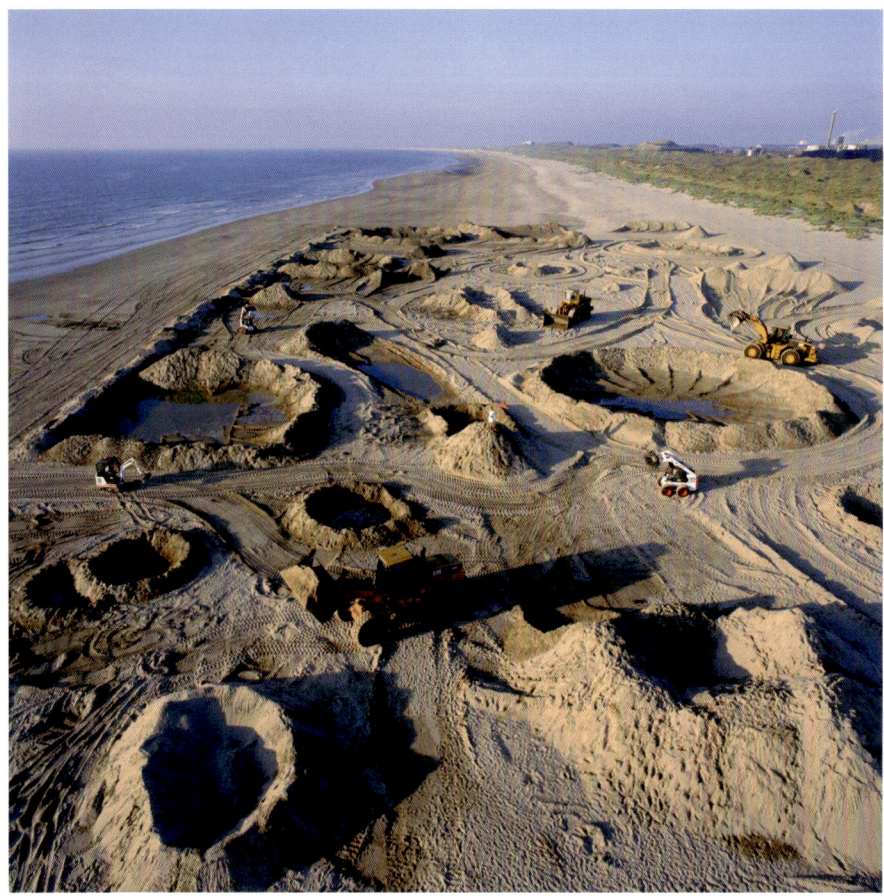

FIRST WOMAN ON THE MOON

1999, event produced by Casco Projects on location in Wijk aan Zee, Netherlands
Aleksandra Mir, born 1967, Lubin, Poland.

Mir's practice since the 1990s has counteracted the commodification of art, with subversive appropriation strategies and cryptically political gestures. Often asking people to participate in her work – friends, colleagues and strangers alike – she uses collaboration as a strategy to upend social norms and expose conditions of domestic and industrial labour. Widely travelled, Mir grew up in Sweden before attending university in New York and residence in Sicily and, finally, London. Her combination of darkly comedic playfulness and sharp political intent was exemplified in *Cinema for the Unemployed* (1998), a series of free disaster-movie screenings, held during daytime working hours in Moss, Norway. A similar sense of relentlessness was conveyed by *Newsroom 1986–2000* (2007), where regimented assistants drew copies of 240 American tabloid newspaper covers, the results presented in rotation as more images replaced them. *First Woman on the Moon* is a feminist and anti-imperialist critique on an absurdly ambitious scale. Mir instructed bulldozer drivers to transform 200 by 300 metres (650 by 980 feet) of beach into a moonscape, before sending several women to plant an American flag atop one sand-mound. The work was levelled the evening after it was created.

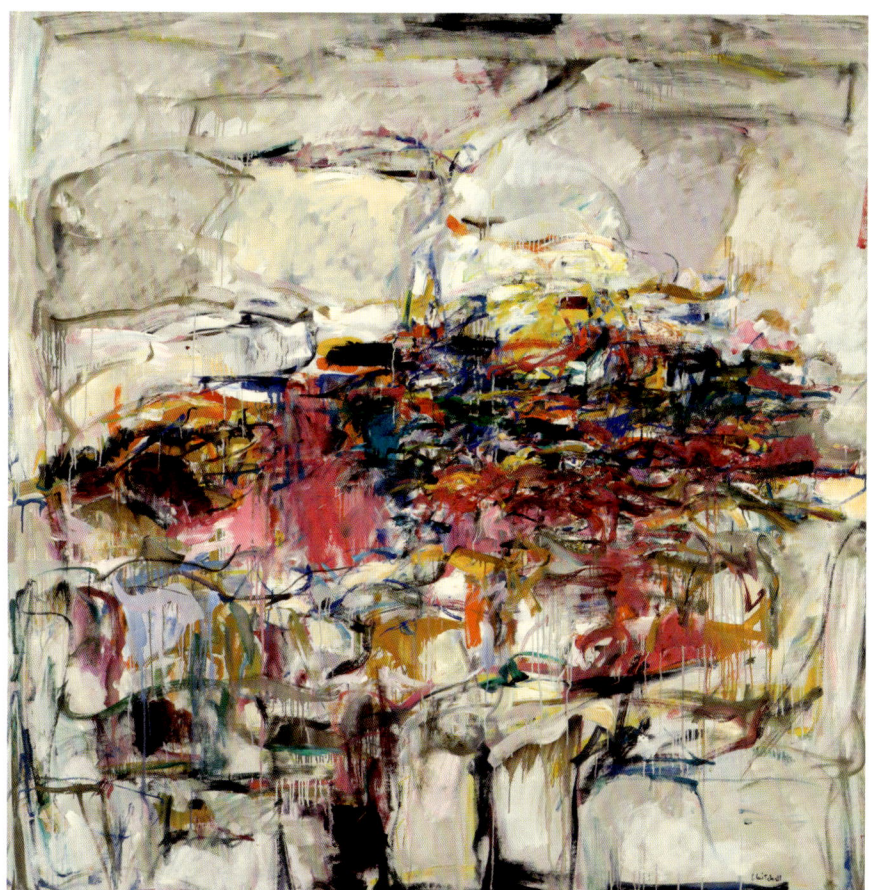

CITY LANDSCAPE

1955, oil on linen, 203.2 × 203.2 cm (80 × 80 in), Art Institute of Chicago
Joan Mitchell, born 1925, Chicago. Died 1992, Paris.

In her large-scale abstract paintings, Mitchell may have appeared to express her inner feelings upon the canvas, but explained that her works are actually about land- and cityscapes. Following an academic training in the late 1940s at the Art Institute of Chicago, Mitchell spent a year travelling in Europe where her painting moved towards abstraction in line with wider international trends in painting. Returning to the United States, she settled in New York in 1950 and became associated with Abstract Expressionists, holding her own in a movement dominated by male artists. From 1955 she divided her time between Paris and New York, moving to France permanently in 1959. Employing a deliberately slow, almost meditative technique of painting, Mitchell would lose awareness of the wider world when she worked, sometimes spending hours simply looking at the canvas. Her lyrical paintings are characterized by varied textures, vibrant colours and gestural brush marks, all of which are evident in *City Landscape*. Like most of her abstract pieces, it is a sustained recollection of landscape, created in the studio from her memories, becoming more about a sense of space, light and energy than a specific place.

LISETTE MODEL

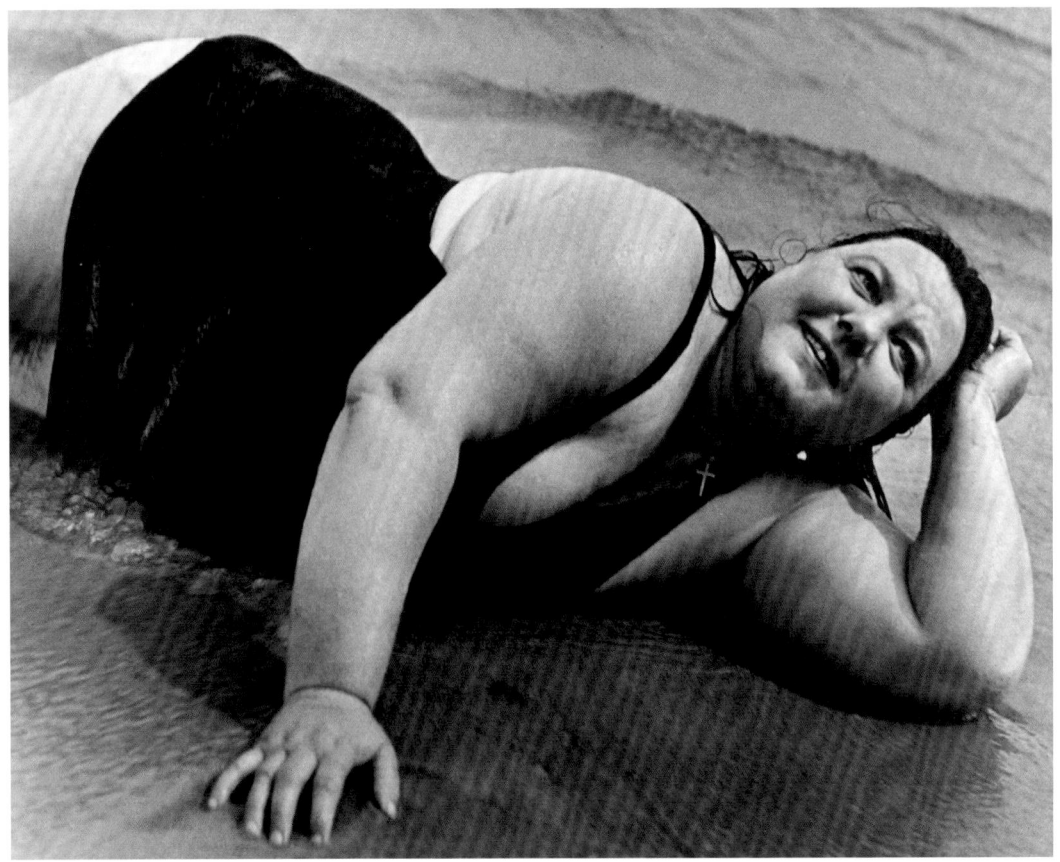

CONEY ISLAND

1941, gelatin silver print, 50.5 × 40.5 cm (19 ⅞ × 15 ⅞ in),
Museum of Modern Art, New York
Lisette Model, born Elise Stern, later Elise Seybert, 1901, Vienna.
Died 1983, New York.

Having previously studied singing and musical composition, Model
was introduced to the camera in the early 1930s by her sister Olga,
a scientific photographer, and her friend, the French-Hungarian
painter Rogi André (1905–70). In 1934, Model shot a series of candid portraits on the Promenade des Anglais in Nice, France, her
images capturing their subjects' character traits, foibles and aspirations. After moving to New York in 1938, she worked as a freelance
photographer for magazines including *Harper's Bazaar*, *Look* and

Ladies' Home Journal. In thrall to the energy of the city, Model photographed its busy thoroughfares from the ground up, often shooting
through the rapidly moving legs of passers-by. In neighbourhoods
including the Lower East Side she documented local life in a powerful realist style. For three decades, beginning in 1951, Model taught
at the New School for Social Research, imparting her expertise on
new generations of photographers, including Diane Arbus (p.39).
While some of Model's portraits suggest a wry view of life, this
image at the New York beach resort of Coney Island is warmly sym-
pathetic to its subject, who appears carefree, confident and thor-
oughly pleased with the glamour of the moment.

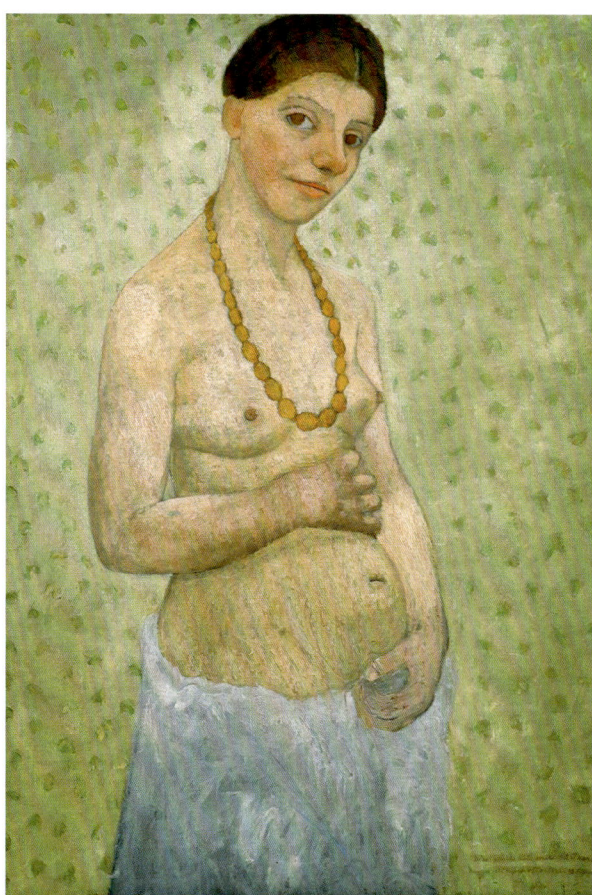

SELF-PORTRAIT ON SIXTH WEDDING ANNIVERSARY

1906, oil on card, 101.8 × 70.2 cm (40 ⅛ × 27 ⅝ in), Paula Modersohn-Becker
Museum, Bremen, Germany
Paula Modersohn-Becker, born 1876, Dresden, Germany. Died 1907,
Worpswede, Germany.

Modersohn-Becker was one of the first women artists to embrace
the emerging style of Expressionism at the turn of the twentieth
century. She is best known for her pioneering figure studies, painted
with thick oil pigments and distinctive textured surfaces, most notably producing portraits of children and farmers' wives while living
in the rural Worpswede artist colony in northern Germany. Her
canvases challenged traditional representations of femininity in art,
depicting mothers, children and the artist herself – often nude – in

studies of great honesty and tenderness. This self-portrait was
painted in Paris after she left her husband, the academic painter Otto
Modersohn (1865–1943). Despite appearing pregnant, she was not
expecting a child at the time. The image instead expresses her desire
to break free from what she saw as the shackles of matrimony: she
is not about to birth a baby but a new life as a liberated modern artist.
However, Modersohn-Becker's dream of creative freedom was not
to materialize; returning to her husband the following year, she fell
pregnant and died prematurely following the birth of her daughter.

TINA MODOTTI

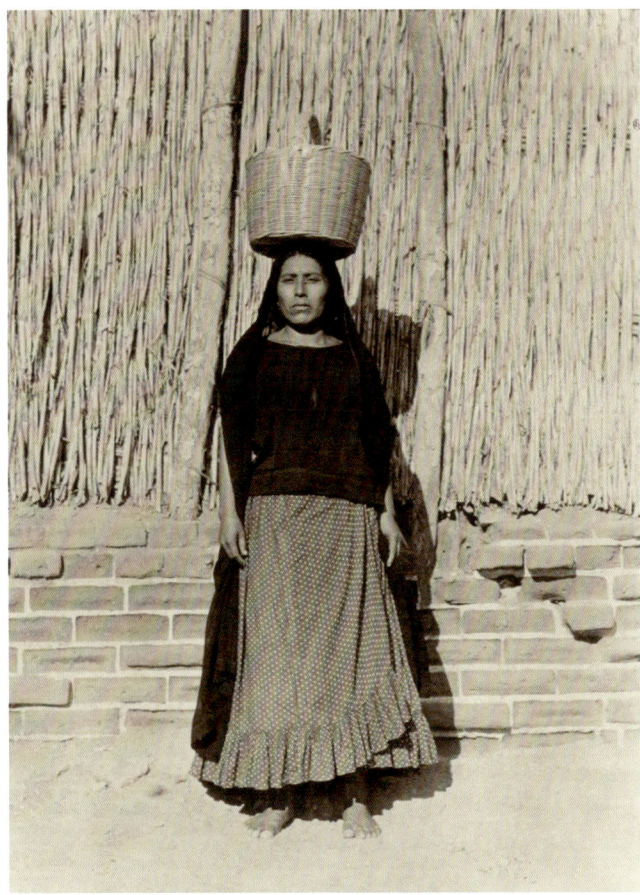

UNTITLED (WOMAN WITH BASKET)
1923–30, palladium print, 25 × 17.5 cm (9 ⅞ × 6 ⅞ in)
Tina Modotti, born Assunta Modotti Mondini, 1896, Udine, Italy.
Died 1942, Mexico City.

A model and minor star of silent-era Hollywood in her youth, Modotti turned to photography after meeting Edward Weston (1886–1958), who became her mentor and lover. In 1923, the couple moved to Mexico City and set up a portrait studio. They were later commissioned to travel the country, recording landscapes, folk art and people from indigenous backgrounds and different social classes. Her images display formal precision and great attention to texture: in this work, a reed fence, brick wall and sandy ground create a powerful graphic backdrop. She depicted her sitters with dignity, while her images of urban architecture and infra-structure celebrated progress and technology. Modotti considered photography a democratic art and used it to document social change. She mixed with international intellectuals and political exiles, as well as the Mexican avant-garde, including Frida Kahlo (p.207). After Weston left Mexico in 1926, Modotti developed Communist sympathies and joined the party in 1927, when her photography took an explicitly political turn. Exiled for a decade, in the aftermath of the assassination of her then lover, the Cuban revolutionary Julio Antonio Mella, in 1929, Modotti abandoned her camera in order to devote herself to political work.

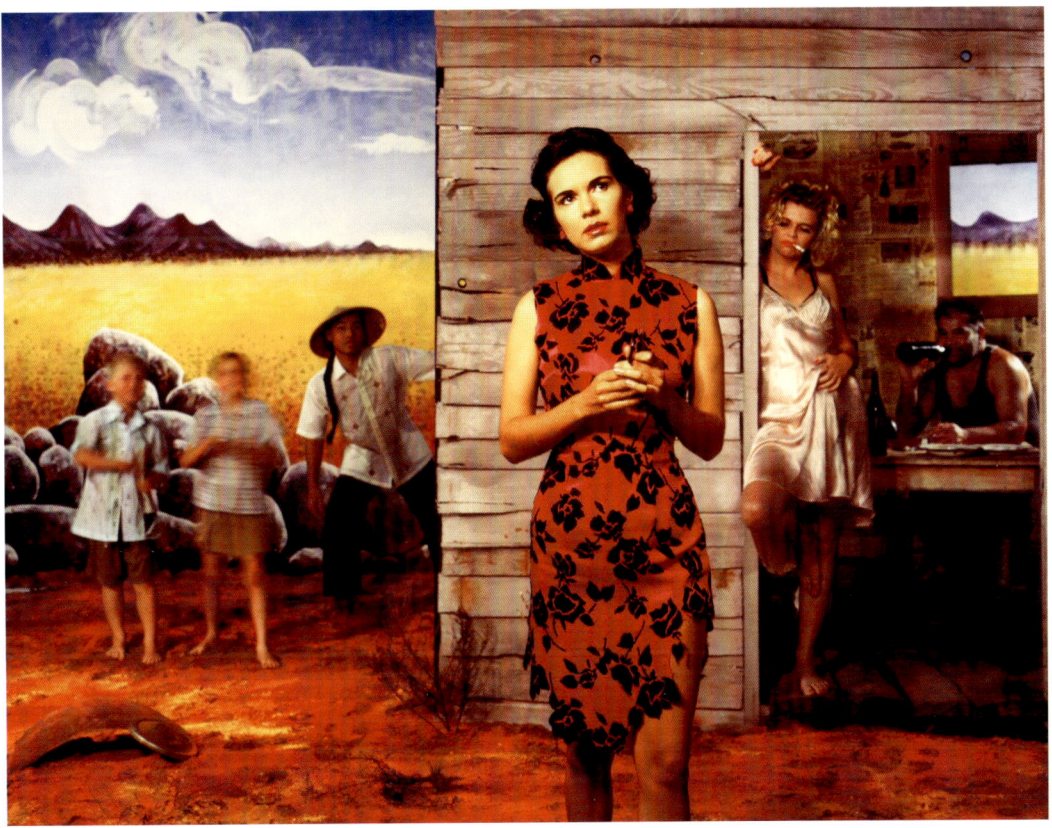

SOMETHING MORE #4

1989, Cibachrome print, 98 × 125 cm (38 ⅝ × 49 ¼ in)
Tracey Moffatt, born 1960, Brisbane, Australia.

Since the mid-1980s Moffatt has used photography and film to probe issues of personal and national identity, trauma, gender and race in her native Australia. Eschewing easy interpretation, fiction infringes on fact through a careful staging of images, which often juxtapose official histories with her own indigenous perspective. She playfully appropriates mass media, from sensational fashion photography to mawkish Hollywood motifs. Blurring the distinction between the still and moving image, her film *Night Cries: A Rural Tragedy* (1989) and her photographic series 'Something More' brought the artist international recognition, the latter work consisting of theatrical black-and-white and colour photographs presented as film stills. The protagonist (played by Moffatt) is represented in rural Australia, though wears a ripped Asian-style dress. She looks longingly into the distance, away from the melodrama that takes place behind her and inviting the viewer to speculate on her ensuing predicament. In the context of Australia's ongoing reckoning with its colonial history, Moffatt's work continues to offer non-didactic and evocative entry points into the past and its effects on the present.

LOUISE MOILLON

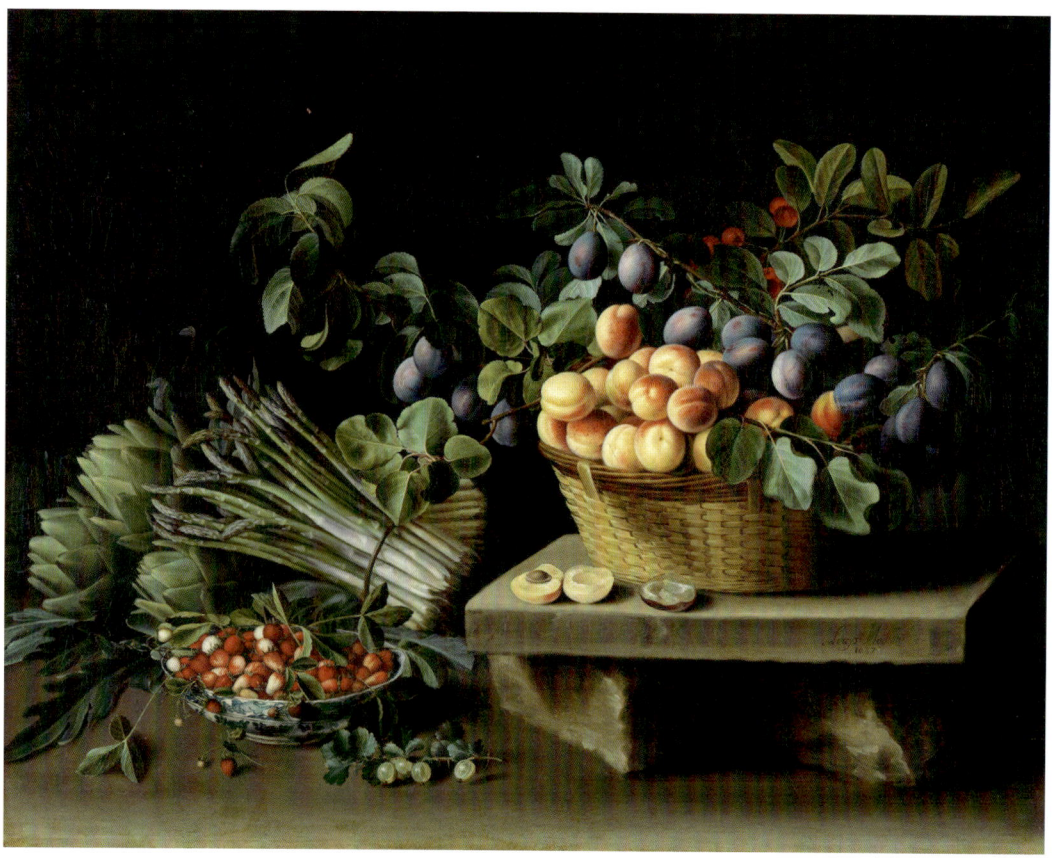

STILL LIFE WITH FRUIT

*c.*1637, oil on canvas, 87.5 × 112 cm (34 ½ × 44 ⅛ in), Museo Nacional
Thyssen-Bornemisza, Madrid
Louise Moillon, born 1610, Paris. Died 1696, Paris.

From a family of painters – including her brother Isaac (1614–73),
one of the earliest members of the Académie Royale de Peinture et de
Sculpture in Paris – Moillon was esteemed as equal in talent to her
male peers, despite being shut out of the artistic institutions because
of her gender. Her oeuvre consists exclusively of still lifes, a genre
associated at the time with artists from the Netherlands, a number
of whom had settled in Moillon's neighbourhood of Saint-Germain-
des-Prés. They were enthusiastically received and widely collected,
including by Charles I of England. Many of her still lifes have a similar

format and content, presumably created speculatively for the open
market rather than as commissions. At over a metre (almost four foot)
in width, meticulously rendered and more compositionally complex
than other works, this painting would have been intended as a show-
case of Moillon's talents in reproducing such scenes. Using complex
effects of light and shade and a rich colour palette to create a sense of
depth and harmony, this is nevertheless a work of artifice, its bounty
of fruit and vegetables unlikely to be in season at the same time.

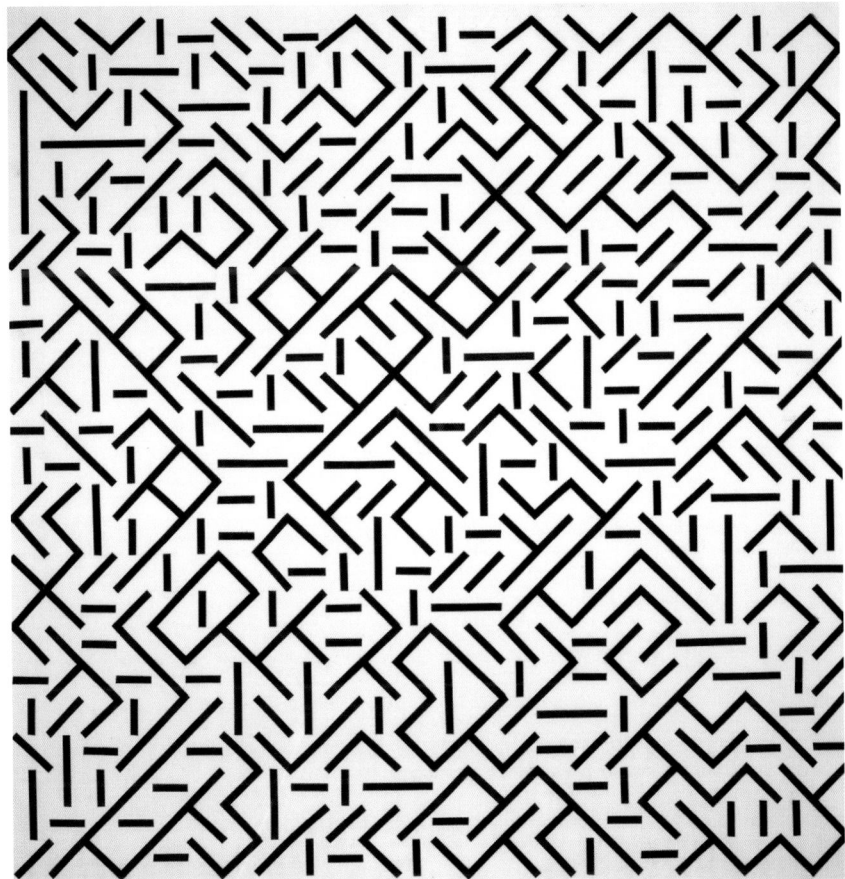

FOUR ITEMS DISTRIBUTED AT RANDOM

1959, adhesive tape on card, 75 × 75 cm (29 ½ × 29 ½ in), Musée National d'Art Moderne, Centre Georges Pompidou, Paris
Véra Molnar, born Gacs Vera, 1924, Budapest. Died 2023, Paris.

Moving to Paris in 1947, Molnar began her career there as an innovative geometric abstractionist and has since been celebrated for her contribution to computer art. First inspired by Constructivism and the gridded abstractions of Piet Mondrian (1872–1944), she became one of the pioneers of the 'Algorism' movement, defined by its program-based abstraction. Teaching herself the early coding languages FORTRAN and BASIC, she began to produce computer-based drawings in 1968, at a time when hardware was mainly confined to research laboratories. Prior to adopting software as her medium, the artist used a strategy she called *machine imaginaire*, whereby her own imagination became a quasi-mathematical instrument. Shown here is a result of this method, the piece somehow transcending its schematic coldness, evolving with a strange and inscrutable rhythm. Despite their apparently rigid determinism, all of her works contain at least one per cent of randomness. In a world increasingly governed by algorithms yet with life still subject to chance, Molnar's approach has gained in resonance, as her works ask us to reconsider the relationship between the human agency and the technologies on which we depend.

MARIKO MORI

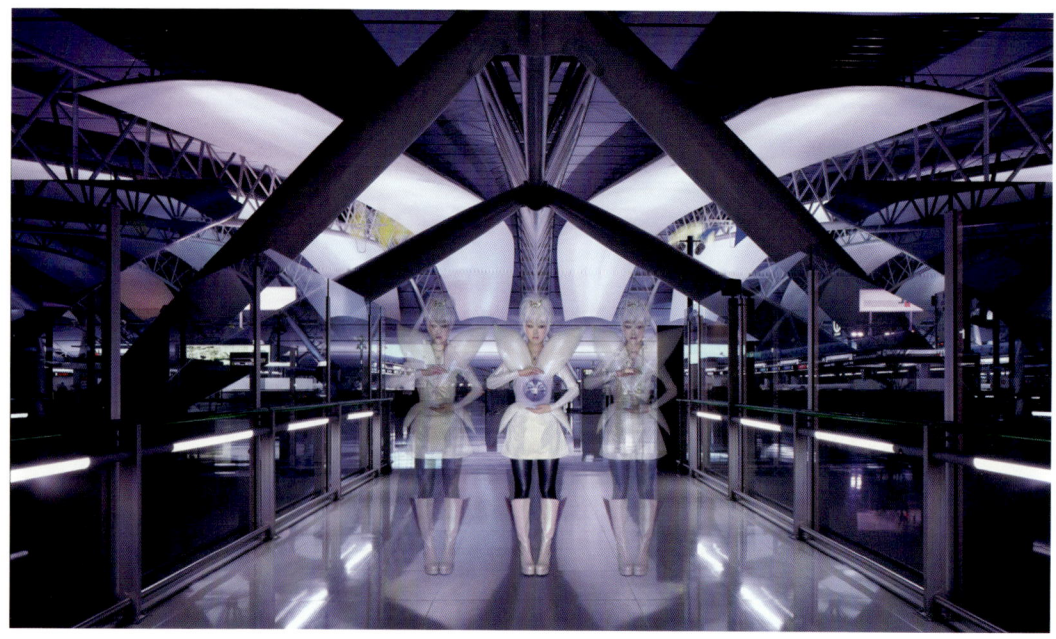

LAST DEPARTURE
1996, Cibachrome print, wood, aluminium and smoked aluminium frame,
3 panels, each 213 × 122 × 7.6 cm (83 ⅞ × 48 × 3 in)
Mariko Mori, born 1967, Tokyo.

Long fascinated with themes of life and death, progress and recurrence, technology and the cosmos, Mori produces videos, installations and prints that propose new roles for spirituality and ritual in our contemporary world. In works such as *Transcircle 1.1* (2004), a reimagining of an ancient stone circle out of modern materials, she suggests that technology can take on magical properties. One of her most celebrated sculptures, *Enlightenment Capsule* (1998), is a memorial to her father and contains a plastic lotus flower, the Buddhist symbol of purity. It is illuminated by sunlight transmitted by a fibre-optic cable that filters out ultraviolet rays, a system invented by her father and used to illuminate underground offices in Japanese cities. The work seen here was made in the early days of computer-generated imagery. Using aesthetics of manga and cosplay, the artist portrays herself as the Shaman-Girl, a character recurring from an earlier work, who seems to have replicated herself in a futuristic setting. Mori, who studied fashion at Tokyo's Bunka Fashion College in the 1980s and worked as a model, embodies a refined and glamorous ideal of hypermodernity.

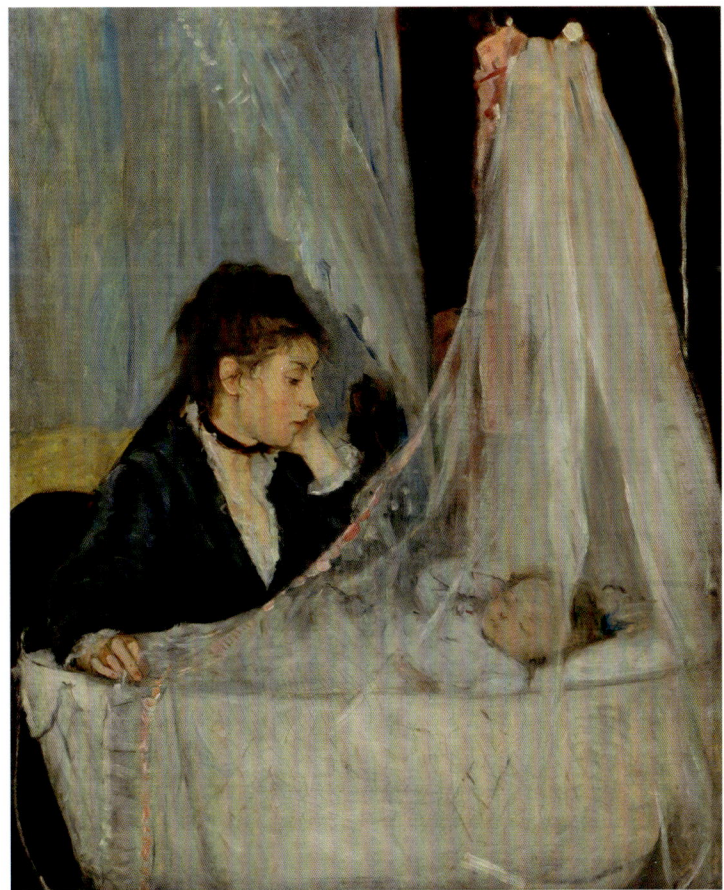

THE CRADLE

1872, oil on canvas, 56 × 46.5 cm (22 × 18 ¼ in), Musée d'Orsay, Paris
Berthe Morisot, born 1841, Bourges, France. Died 1895, Paris.

Although her work was for a long time considered only in relation to her brother-in-law, Édouard Manet (1832–83), Morisot is now rightly regarded as a pivotal figure of the Impressionist movement, described in 1894 by critic Gustave Geffroy as one of its 'trois grandes dames', along with Mary Cassatt (p.91) and Marie Bracquemond (1840–1916). One of the movement's founder members, Morisot helped to finance the group and to organize its first exhibition, held in 1874 at 35 Boulevard des Capucines. Morisot's critical reception at the time was largely positive, although this was partly because of sexist attitudes that considered Impressionism unworthy of men.

Herself a member of the *haute bourgeoisie*, many of her paintings examined the spaces inhabited by women of the wealthy elite. This work depicts Morisot's sister, Edma (1839–1921), a fellow painter who abandoned her promising professional career when she married in 1867 and became a mother. The painting's composition is defined by two enclosing drapes that echo Edma's body language, suggesting confinement and exhaustion as well as tenderness and introspection, and offer an honest portrayal of the pressures of motherhood and marriage in any social class.

MARY MOSER

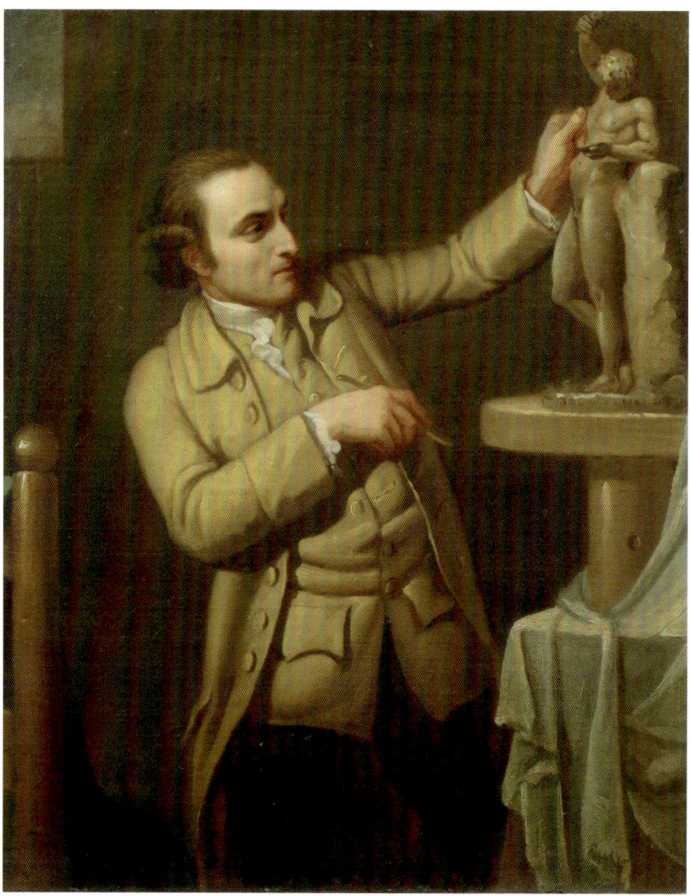

JOSEPH NOLLEKENS

1770–1, oil on canvas, 63.5 × 48.3 cm (25 × 19 in), Yale Center for British Art,
New Haven, Connecticut
Mary Moser, born 1744, London. Died 1819, London.

Aged twenty-four, Moser was the youngest founding member of
London's Royal Academy of Arts, alongside only one other woman,
Angelica Kauffman (p.211). Another founder member was her father,
the Swiss-born enamellist George Michael Moser (1706–83) who
became the first Keeper of the Royal Academy Schools. A group portrait of the first Academicians included Moser and Kauffman only
by their portraits on the wall, and despite no official ruling on the
matter, women were subsequently excluded from the Academy
until the election of Laura Knight (p.219) in 1936. Moser is most
celebrated for her flower paintings, a metier that led to a position as
drawing mistress to Princess Elizabeth and a commission from her
mother Queen Charlotte, wife of King George III, to create a *trompe-
l'oeil* ensemble of murals depicting an open-air arbour at Frogmore
House, Windsor. Joseph Nollekens (1737–1823), painted shortly
before his election to the Royal Academy in 1772, was a leading
light of English portrait sculpture in the classical style. Depicted
in harmony with his mythological subject, Moser's portrait implies
a professional intimacy, equality and fellowship between the two artists.

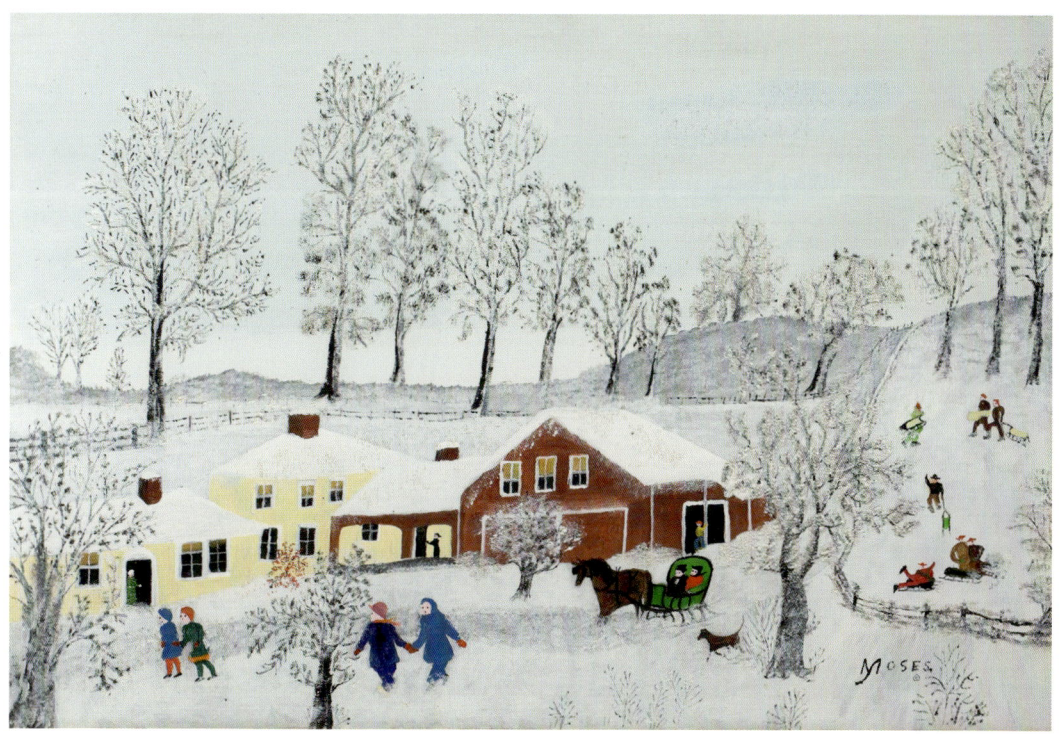

YELLOW HOUSE

1955, oil on board, 30.5 × 45.4 cm (12 × 17 ⅞ in), Davis Museum,
Wellesley College, Massachusetts
Anna Mary Robertson ('Grandma') Moses, 1860, Greenwich, New York.
Died 1961, Hoosick Falls, New York.

Anna Mary Robertson Moses, popularly known as 'Grandma Moses', was an American folk artist who only began to work prolifically in her seventies. Her scenes of traditional rural life, painted from memory and rendered in a naïve, picturesque style, resonated with her public image of an all-American grandmother. Moses had left home as a girl of twelve to work as a servant for a wealthy family, and later worked on a series of farms. In old age, she began making embroidered pictures for friends and family, until arthritis prevented her from continuing. She then took up painting at the suggestion of her sister, resurrecting a long-deferred passion – as a child she had painted landscapes using pigments made from whatever natural materials were to hand, such as lemon and grape juice. In *Yellow House*, tiny figures trudge across a blanket of white snow, past toy-like houses. Moses became a national treasure in her last three decades of life. President Truman presented her with the Women's National Press Club Trophy for outstanding accomplishment in art in 1949, the same year she published her autobiography.

MARLOW MOSS

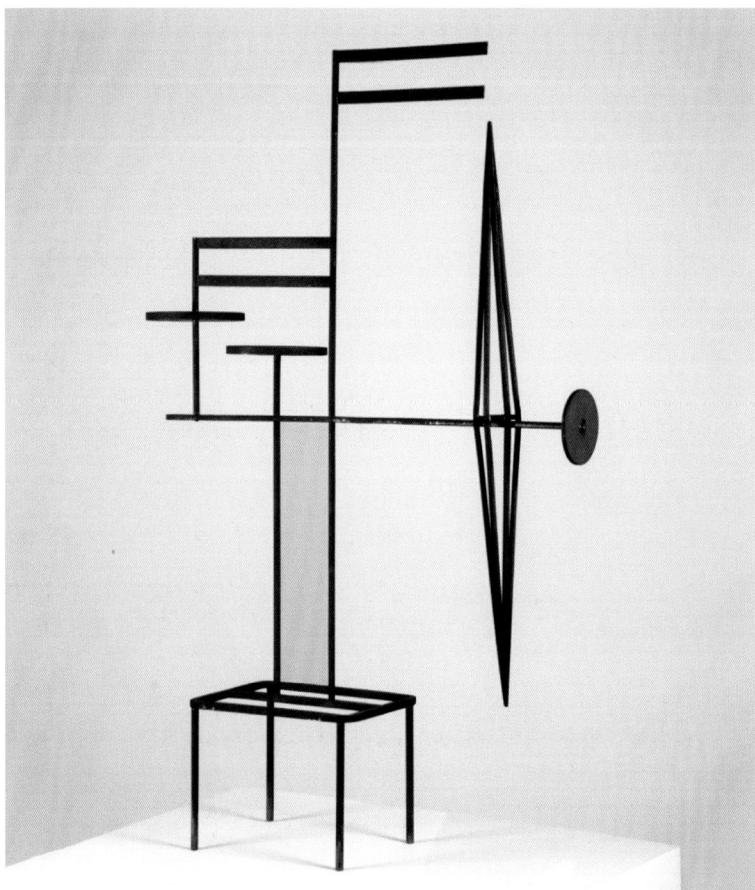

SPATIAL CONSTRUCTION

1956–7, steel, 130 × 81.2 × 22.8 cm (51 ⅛ × 32 × 9 in), Leeds Art Gallery, UK
Marlow Moss, born Marjorie Jewel Moss, 1889, London. Died 1958, Penzance, UK.

In 1919, having abandoned her art-school course in London, Moss
reinvented herself, moving to Cornwall, changing her name and
dressing as a man. In the late 1920s, she relocated to Paris where she
studied with Fernand Léger (1881–1955) and met her life partner,
the Dutch writer Nettie Nijhoff. Moss's early paintings explored austere geometric abstraction and bear a superficial resemblance to those
of her friend and interlocutor Piet Mondrian (1872–1944), whose
work she influenced, although her approach was far more mathematical.
In 1931 she became a founder member of Abstraction-Création, the
Paris-based association of abstract artists and the centre of the
Constructivist avant-garde. Forced to return to England during
the Second World War, she left all her work in France; it was later
destroyed in a bombing raid. She settled in Cornwall and studied
architecture while continuing to paint and create reliefs and sculptures. Moss was concerned above all with space, movement and
light, three elements that characterize this static sculpture – the
largest of her known works – where space is animated through
shadows cast by its vanes, struts and wheel-like parts.

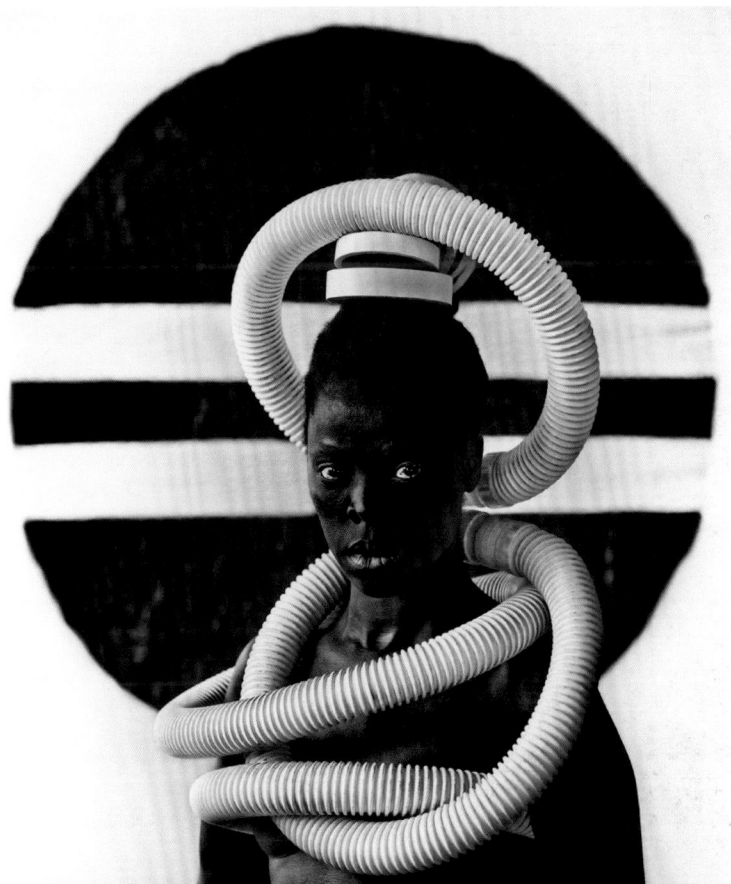

SEBENZILE, PARKTOWN

2016, gelatin silver print, 70 × 61 cm (27 ½ × 24 in), edition of 8
Zanele Muholi, born 1972, Umlazi, South Africa.

Describing herself as a 'visual activist', Muholi sees the image as a political tool. Having taken up photography at a time when she was suicidal, Muholi credits it with saving her life and considers it a healing practice. In 2007 she initiated 'Faces and Phases', a unique and growing archive of portraits of women from South Africa's black lesbian community. Her year-long series of black-and-white self-portraits 'Somnyama Ngonyama' ('Hail the Dark Lioness') began in the aftermath of an unpleasant encounter with staff at a New York hotel, when she sensed their suspicion and contempt. Shooting one image a day, Muholi mapped moments of oppression,

homophobia and hate crime that she witnessed, experienced or heard about. She playfully reclaims visual motifs from colonial representations of African women, revelling in the textures and tones of her dark skin, something mainstream media often avoids by making black women appear lighter than they are. In *Sebenzile, Parktown*, flexible plastic tubing wrapped around Muholi's head and body evokes halos in Christian religious icons and traditional headdresses depicted in ethnographic illustrations.

MRINALINI MUKHERJEE

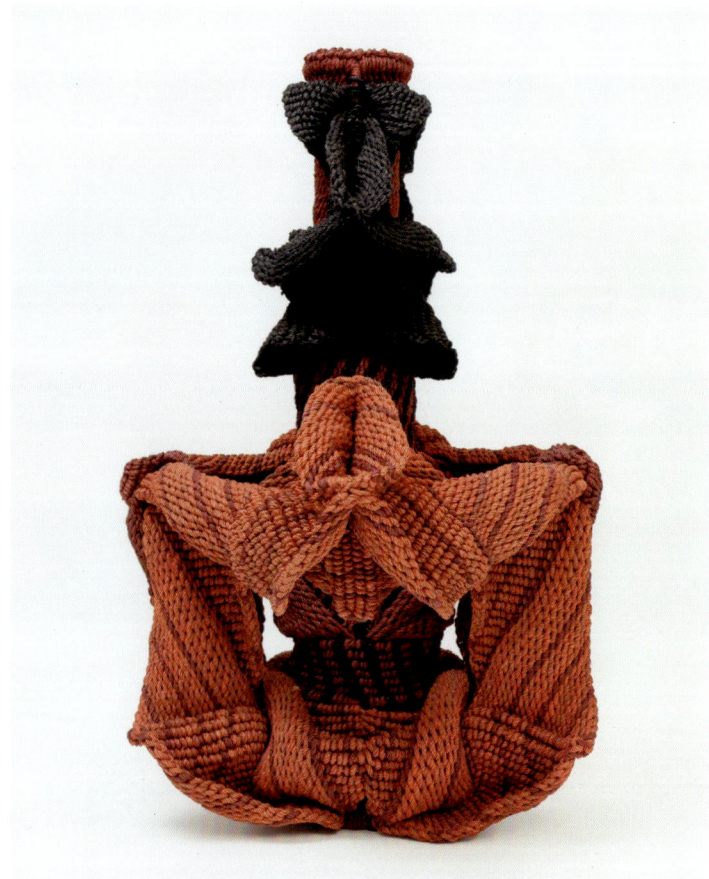

ADI PUSHP II

1998–9, hemp, 140 × 112 × 94 cm (55 ⅛ × 44 × 37 in), collection of Amrita Jhaveri
Mrinalini Mukherjee, born 1949, Mumbai (then Bombay). Died 2015, New Delhi.

After specializing in mural painting at the Maharaja Sayajirao
University in Baroda, India, in the early 1970s, Mukherjee eschewed
the figurative painting of her predominantly male peers, in contrast
using natural fibres to create three-dimensional biomorphic forms,
hung or set directly on the floor. Reflecting her training with K.G.
Subramanyan (1924–2016), himself a student of Mukherjee's father
Benode Behari (1904–80), she engaged with twentieth-century
debates concerning legitimate mediums in art, transposing craft
materials into complex totemic structures by weaving, knotting
and twisting hand-dyed hemp and jute. In *Adi Pushp II*, whose title
alludes to flowers in bloom, cavernous folds seductively cascade into
each other evoking an ambiguous sacred figure. Her genderless
deities were intended to have universal appeal: as she stated, 'my
mythology is de-conventionalized and personal … the sacred is
not rooted in any specific culture'. Although her work has been exhibited internationally, it was not until 2015 that she was critically
acknowledged in India with a major retrospective at the National
Gallery of Modern Art in New Delhi. Sadly, she was never to see
the show; being hospitalized two days before the opening and dying
a week later.

VERA MUKHINA

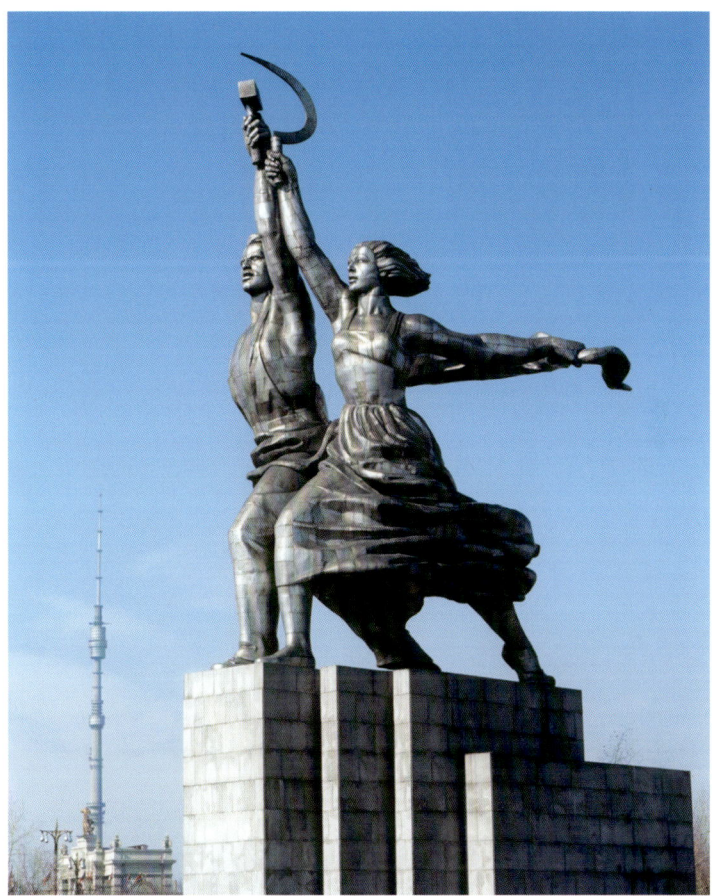

WORKER AND COLLECTIVE FARM GIRL

1937, stainless steel, h: 24.5 m (78 ft), Exhibition of Achievements of National
Economy (VDNKH), Moscow
Vera Mukhina, born 1889, Riga, Latvia (then Russian Empire). Died 1953, Moscow.

Remembered for monumental sculptures that helped forge the
national visual identity of the Soviet Union, Mukhina had trained
in Moscow, Italy and France, receiving instruction in Paris from
the Neo-Classical sculptor Antoine Bourdelle (1861–1929). Returning
to Russia, she was briefly an assistant to artist and set-designer
Alexandra Exter (p.133). After brief involvement with the post-
revolutionary avant-garde, she turned to the Socialist Realism style
that became the hallmark of the Soviet epoch. Seen here is her colossal
emblem of male and female workers from a *kolkhoz* (collective farm),

holding aloft the hammer and sickle. It was created for the 1937 World's
Fair in Paris, crowning the Soviet Pavilion, directly opposite Albert
Speer's equally imposing architectural representation of Nazi Germany.
Mukhina's sculpture was subsequently installed in Moscow. Adopting
radically modern materials and techniques and a streamlined aesthetic, Mukhina's striding figures also evoke classical statues, such as
the Winged Victory of Samothrace or the Tyrannicides. Alongside
her sculptural work, Mukhina was a designer, responsible for a style
of bevelled glass that is still to be found throughout Russia. Her many
essays on art were published posthumously in 1960.

GABRIELE MÜNTER

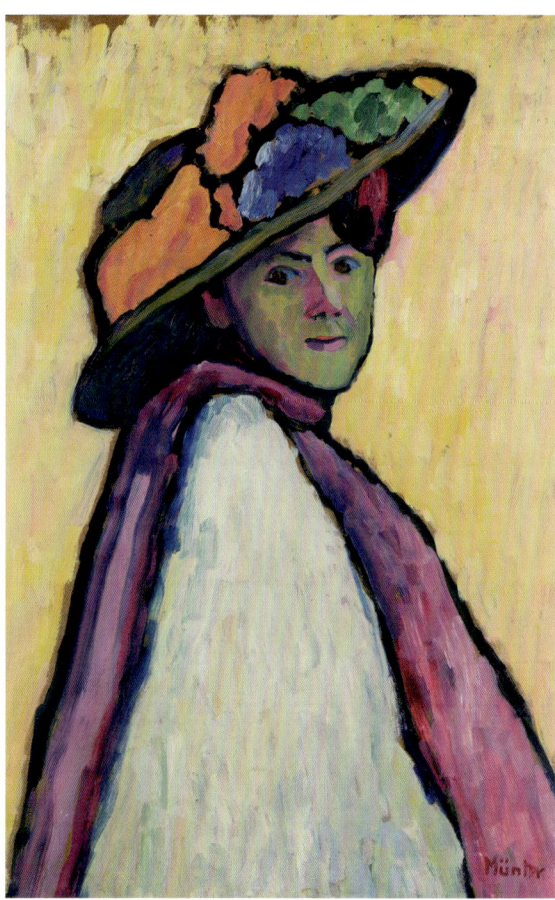

PORTRAIT OF MARIANNE VON WEREFKIN

1909, oil on card, 81 × 55 cm (31 ⅞ × 21 ⅝ in), Städtische Galerie im Lenbachhaus und Kunstbau München, Munich

Gabriele Münter, born 1877, Berlin. Died 1962, Murnau, Germany.

A founder member of Munich's New Artists' Society and later of the movement the Blaue Reiter ('Blue Rider'), Münter was at the forefront of German Expressionism. She grew up in comfortable circumstances but developed a distinct self-reliance following her father's early death. Trained at a private academy in Düsseldorf (women being barred from state art schools at that time), she visited America around the turn of the century, drawing people and land-scapes. Returning to Europe, she enrolled in 1902 at the Phalanx school in Munich where she was taught by Wassily Kandinsky

(1866–1944), the two subsequently becoming lovers, travelling widely, then basing themselves for a number of years in Murnau, rural Bavaria. Using colour to suggest spiritual essence rather than objective experience, Münter's parallel practice in woocut- and linocut-printing, alongside a penchant for stained glass, influenced her use of bold outline and simple shapes. Both features are evident in this portrait of Russian painter Marianne von Werefkin (p.428), another key figure in Munich's Expressionist avant-garde. Favouring spontaneity, Münter often completed a work in one session, here capturing the mood of a specific moment.

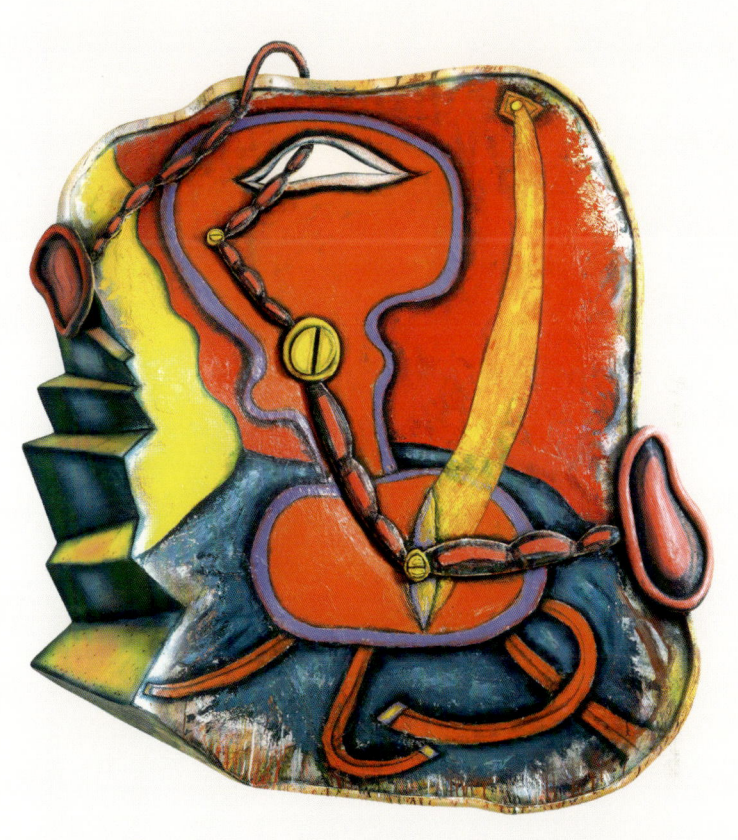

ARM-EAR

1993, oil on canvas mounted on shaped and bent wood, 198.1 × 172.7 × 38.1 cm (78 × 68 × 15 in), Newark Museum, New Jersey

Elizabeth Murray, born 1940, Chicago. Died 2007, New York.

Initially training in Chicago as a commercial artist, encounters with the work of Paul Cézanne (1839–1906) led Murray to painting instead. She was also influenced by the strident tones and offbeat shapes of the city's Imagist school, a loose association that included several women artists. At a time when painting was seen by many art critics as being in crisis, or even dead, Murray reacted by fully embracing the medium on an ambitious scale. However, she rejected its conventional rectangular limits, becoming known for canvases with complex geometries and eccentric forms. By eschewing the illusionistic space induced by the traditional 'frame', her canvases are often three-dimensional structures that dynamically jut out from the wall, the artwork present in the room rather than pictures 'seen through a window'. Her work was first seen in New York at the Whitney Museum's Annual Exhibition in 1971. Unlike her contemporary Frank Stella (1936–2024), who also used shaped canvases to investigate space and colour, Murray was interested in the figure and representation. This work, directly referencing body parts and possibly a staircase, merges the aims of abstraction and figuration.

WANGECHI MUTU

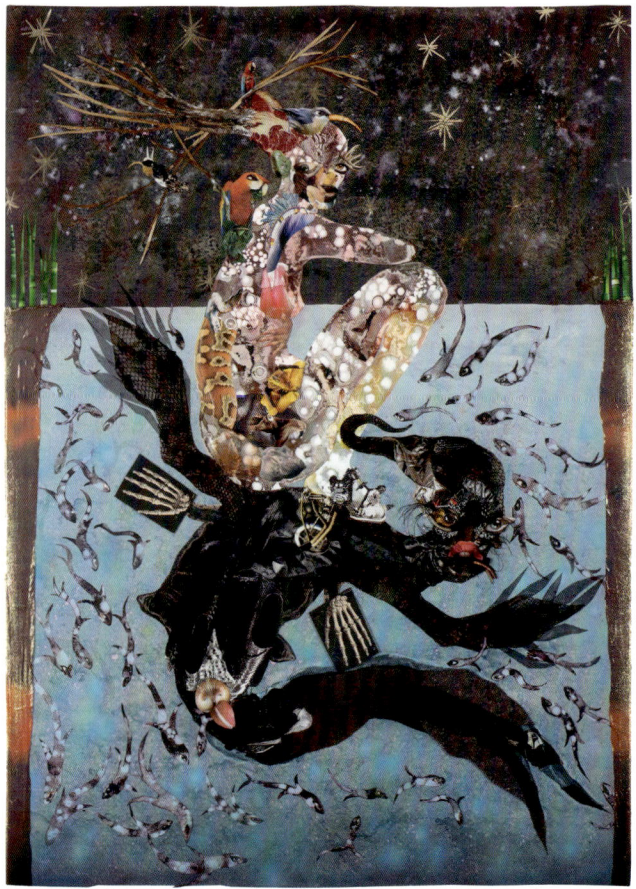

BENEATH LIES THE POWER

2014, collage painting on vinyl, 231 × 175 cm (91 × 69 in)
Wangechi Mutu, born 1972, Nairobi, Kenya.

Cutting up printed matter and repurposing it via collage is a creative strategy used by Mutu, juxtaposing images to startling effect. For Mutu, the outcome is both grotesque and seductive, surpassing the sum of its individual parts. As with artists who used techniques of photomontage before her – such as Hannah Höch's (p.189) dismantling of female stereotypes and Romare Bearden's (1911–88) portrayal of the black body – Mutu renegotiates representations of black women. Cutting, blending and grafting, she creates intricately elaborate collages that explicitly connect to sexuality, femininity and politics. Her practice addresses issues of black peoples'

invisibility in the media, challenging power hierarchies that define who is and is not 'seen'. Inspired by aquatic animals known as *nguva* – manatee-type sea cows that are believed to be the reality behind the myth of mermaids – the dark serpent-like creature in *Beneath lies the Power* supports a colourful crouching figure. Made using Mutu's signature collage/painting in combination with watercolour, this fantastical scene reflects on metamorphosis and the fear evoked by liminal spaces, such as those between the land and the sea, and between life and death.

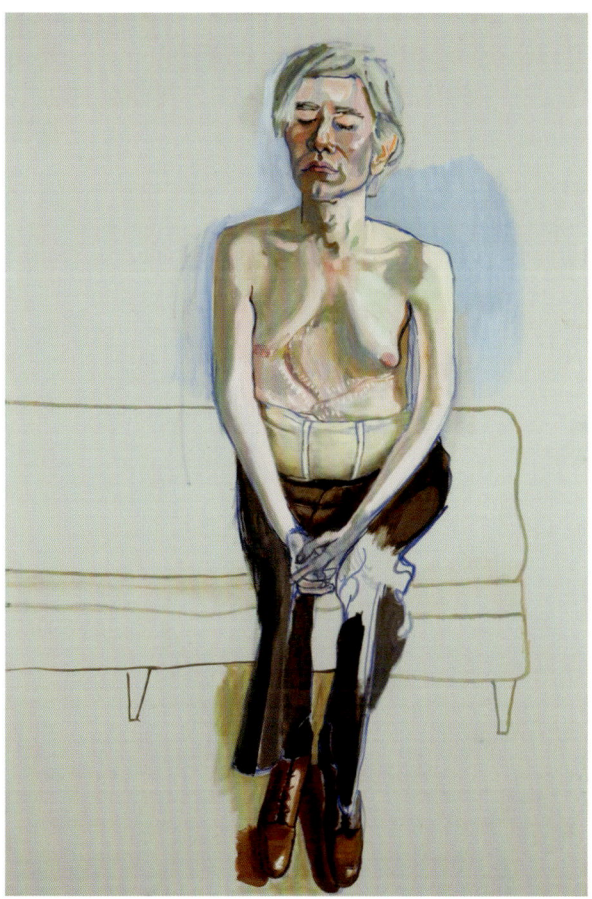

ANDY WARHOL
1970, oil and acrylic on linen, 152.4 × 101.6 cm (60 × 40 in), Whitney Museum of American Art, New York
Alice Neel, born 1900, Gladwyne, Pennsylvania. Died 1984, New York.

With her humane and psychologically penetrating portraits being out of step with mid-twentieth-century art movements, American figurative painter Neel gained acclaim only later in life. It was not until 1971, a year after creating this portrait, that she was given her first major exhibition at Moore College of Art and Design and, three years later, a retrospective at the Whitney Museum. Born into a middle-class family in the suburbs of Philadelphia, she moved in 1927 to New York and chronicled the city's diverse cast of characters over the next five decades. Her own tragic circumstances

doubtless heightened her empathetic sensibility – her first daughter died in infancy and her second was kidnapped by her estranged Cuban husband. This searing, candid portrait depicts Andy Warhol (1928–87) two years after his near fatal shooting by writer Valerie Solanas. Neel sees through the sitter's celebrity veneer to expose a vulnerable figure with sagging breasts and scar-ravaged torso, wearing a protective surgical corset to protect his incisisions. Warhol, a master at constructing his own image, shuts his eyes, perhaps symbolically against the pain of confronting his defaced, ageing body.

PLAUTILLA NELLI

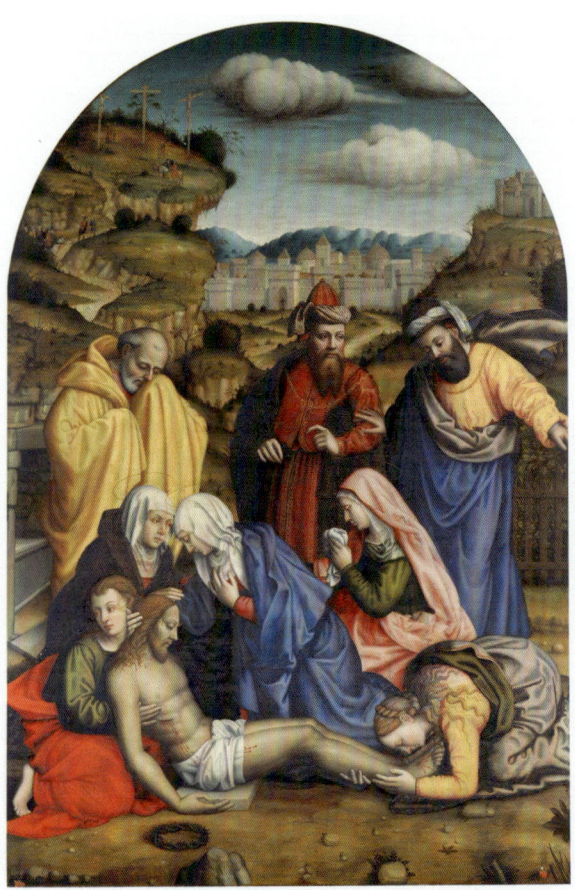

LAMENTATION WITH SAINTS

1550, oil on canvas, 288 × 192 cm (113 ⅜ × 75 ⅝ in), Museo di San Marco, Florence
Plautilla Nelli, born Pulisena Nelli, 1524, Florence. Died 1588, Florence.

A nun, and later prioress, of the Santa Caterina da Siena convent in Florence, Giorgio Vasari noted in the second edition of *The Lives of the Most Excellent Painters, Sculptors, and Architects* (1568) that there were so many of Nelli's paintings 'in the houses of gentlemen in Florence, that it would be tedious to mention them all'. Today, only four works are securely attributed to her, but Vasari's comment reveals that she was prolific and able to take advantage of the expanding art market of Renaissance Italy. Although Nelli received no formal training, she attentively studied the work of Andrea del Sarto (1486–1530) and Fra Bartolomeo (1472–1517). *Lamentation With Saints* – the

first work to be restored by the Advancing Women Artists Foundation in 2005 – features mourners with highly emotional expressions. This suggests Nelli's familiarity with northern European artists, who were known for their raw depictions of grief in religious art. Such exposure to other artworks and styles, as well as her broad network of patrons, reveal the extent to which sixteenth-century convents were active centres of artistic production. In 2017, Nelli was the first in a new series of exhibitions by female artists, aiming to address the historic gender imbalance, at the Galleria degli Uffizi, Florence.

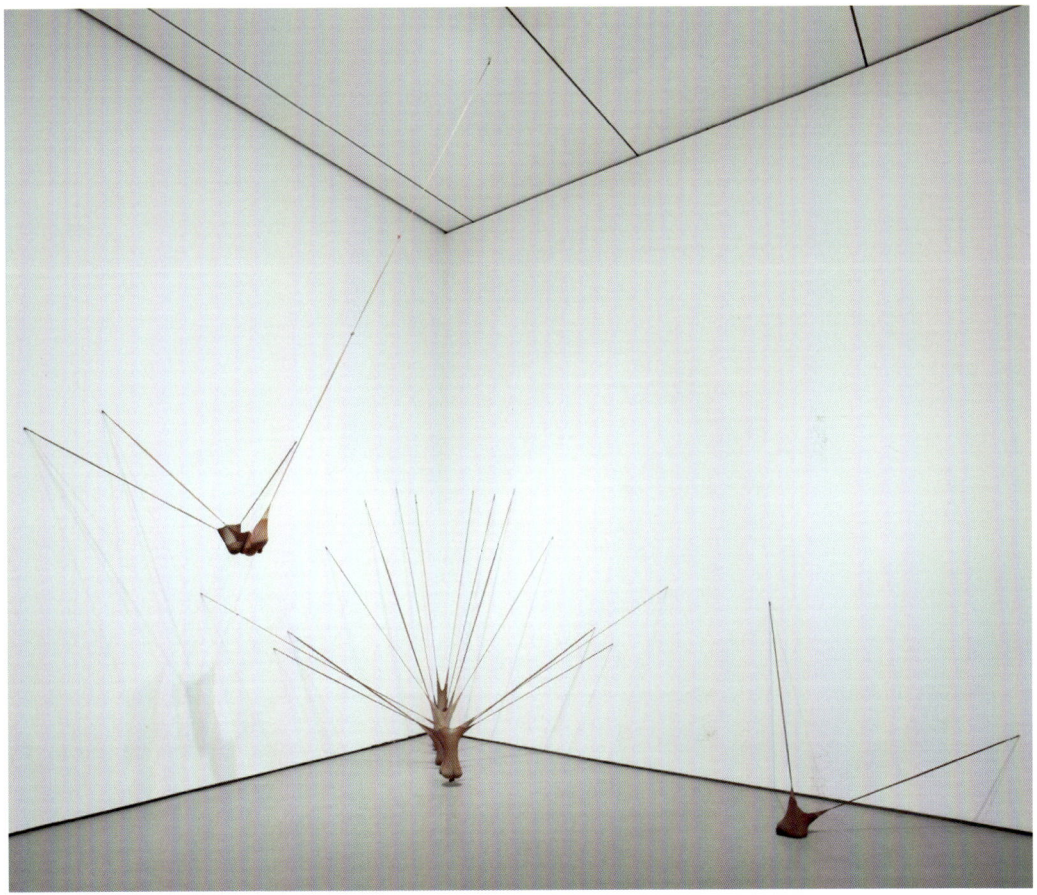

R.S.V.P. 1

1977–2003, tights and sand, 10 pieces, dimensions variable, installation view, 'Contemporary Galleries: 1980–Now', Museum of Modern Art, New York, 2011 Senga Nengudi, born Sue Irons, 1943, Chicago.

Growing up in Los Angeles, Nengudi studied art and dance at the city's California State University in the 1960s, followed by a year studying in Tokyo. Subsequently, she gravitated towards radical black art scenes in New York and Los Angeles, and was among the African-American founders of the experimental Studio Z collective (also known as 'LA Rebellion'). Nengudi's work explores the black experience both in society and in their own bodies. She is particularly known for abstract sculptures made using nylon tights that evoke the body. She modifies the usual form of these garments by stretching, knotting or filling them with sand, or letting their fabric blow in a breeze. Tights represent issues of race and gender, and the resilience of the female body during pregnancy and childbirth, which came to preoccupy the artist when she was pregnant in 1974. The long-running series 'R.S.V.P.' references the French phrase *répondez s'il vous plaît*, inviting the viewer to respond. With tights tacked to and extending from the walls, it represets the artist's experience of skin being stretched, recalling elastic, corporeal forms. The tights are also 'activated' with live performers, choreographed by Nengudi, tangling their bodies in the work.

SHIRIN NESHAT

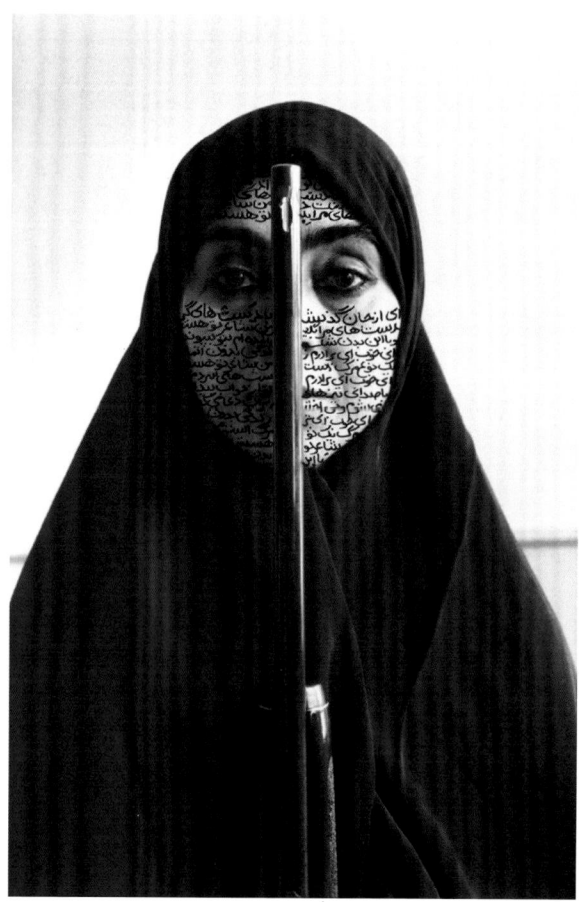

REBELLIOUS SILENCE

1994, black-and-white resin-coated print and ink (photograph taken by Cynthia Preston), 27.9 × 35.6 cm (11 × 14 in)
Shirin Neshat, born 1957, Qazvin, Iran.

Neshat moved to the United States aged seventeen, three years before the Iranian Revolution of 1979. Having completed a master's in fine art at the University of California, Berkeley, she moved to New York in 1983. She abandoned her own art at this time, instead devoting many years to an independent gallery, Storefront for Art and Architecture, with her former husband, Kyong Park. On visiting Iran in 1990, she found the country unrecognizable from that of her childhood after a decade of social upheaval and war. This initiated an artistic practice in photography and moving image. *Rebellious*

Silence is from 'Women of Allah', a series of portraits where faces and bodies are inscribed with calligraphic Farsi texts by female authors of the revolutionary period, in this case of the poet Tahereh Saffarzadeh (1936–2008). The subject wears a chador to cover her body, reflecting the dress codes that were an aspect of the culture-shock Neshat felt when visiting her homeland. The series addresses religious fervour and female militancy in post-revolutionary Iran.

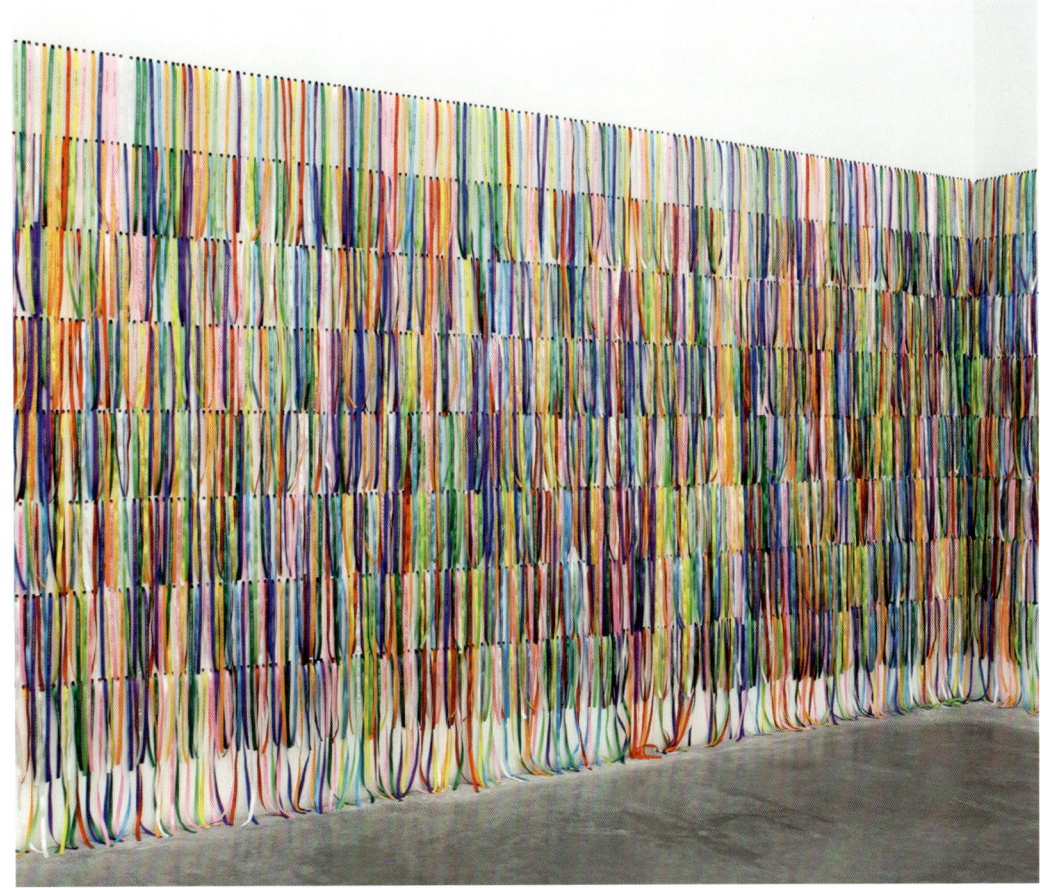

I WISH YOUR WISH

2003, printed fabric and wishes, dimensions variable, installation view, 'Rivane Neuenschwander: A Day Like Any Other', New Museum, New York, 2010. Collection Francesca von Habsburg, Thyssen-Bornemisza Art Contemporary, Vienna

Rivane Neuenschwander, born 1967, Belo Horizonte, Brazil.

Having moved to London to study at the Royal College of Art in the mid-1990s, Neuenschwander subsequently spent time in Italy, Germany, Spain and Sweden before returning to her native country. Working in the traditions of Conceptual art, she uses simple objects to convey complex ideas in a strategy she has referred to as 'ethereal materialism'. Language, nature and geography, among other themes, are explored in her often participatory works. *I wish*

your wish is one of her best-known works, in which she draws on a Brazilian folk tradition observed by Catholic pilgrims to the Church of Nosso Senhor do Bonfim in Salvador, Brazil. Binding ribbons to their wrists, or to the church's front gate, they believe that when the ties fall off or disintegrate, their wishes will be granted. In Neuenschwander's version, colourful silk ribbons are each stamped with one of sixty wishes that were left by previous visitors. Neuenschwander invites viewers to take a ribbon from one of 10, 296 small holes in the wall; in exchange they must scribble a new wish on a slip of paper and then insert this into the hole, replacing what has been taken.

LOUISE NEVELSON

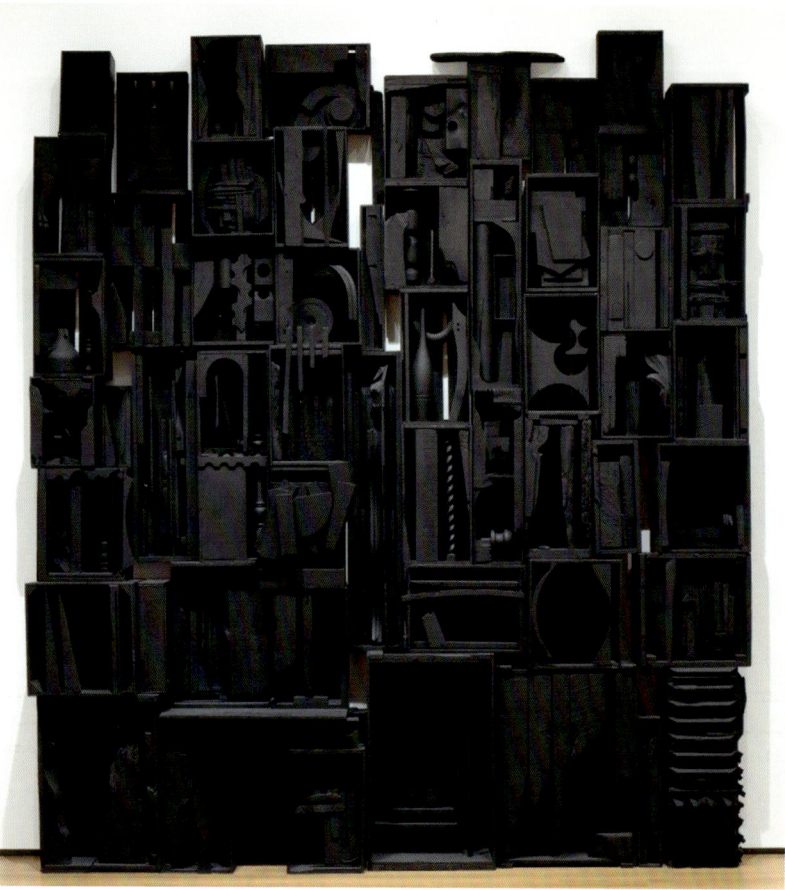

SKY CATHEDRAL

1958, painted wood, 343.9 × 305.4 × 45.7 cm (135 ½ × 120 ¼ × 216 in),
Museum of Modern Art, New York
Louise Nevelson, born Leah Berliawsky, 1899, Pereiaslav, Ukraine (then Russian
Empire). Died 1988, New York.

Emigrating to the United States in 1905, Nevelson became inspired
to study art at the age of nine upon seeing a sculpture of Joan of Arc
at the public library in Rockland, Maine. Having worked as an assistant to Diego Rivera (1886–1957) in the early 1930s, by the mid-
twentieth century she was known for her monumental sculptures
in wood, aluminium and steel. These were partly inspired by visits
to Guatemala, where she saw Mayan ruins and steles – elaborately
carved sacred pillars. One of the few women acknowledged as being

associated with the Abstract Expressionist movement, Nevelson
nevertheless struggled to make money from her art and taught
sculpture in adult education programmes in New York. In periods
of extreme poverty, she foraged for firewood in the city. *Sky Cathedral*
is an early, puzzle-like sculpture, likewise comprising wood salvaged
from old buildings; the architectural mouldings, spindles and balus-
ters are nailed together and painted black. Nevelson was fascinated
by art's potential for spiritual transcendence and the shrine-like
form of this piece suggests a place of devotion, a theme that would
become increasingly explicit in her later works.

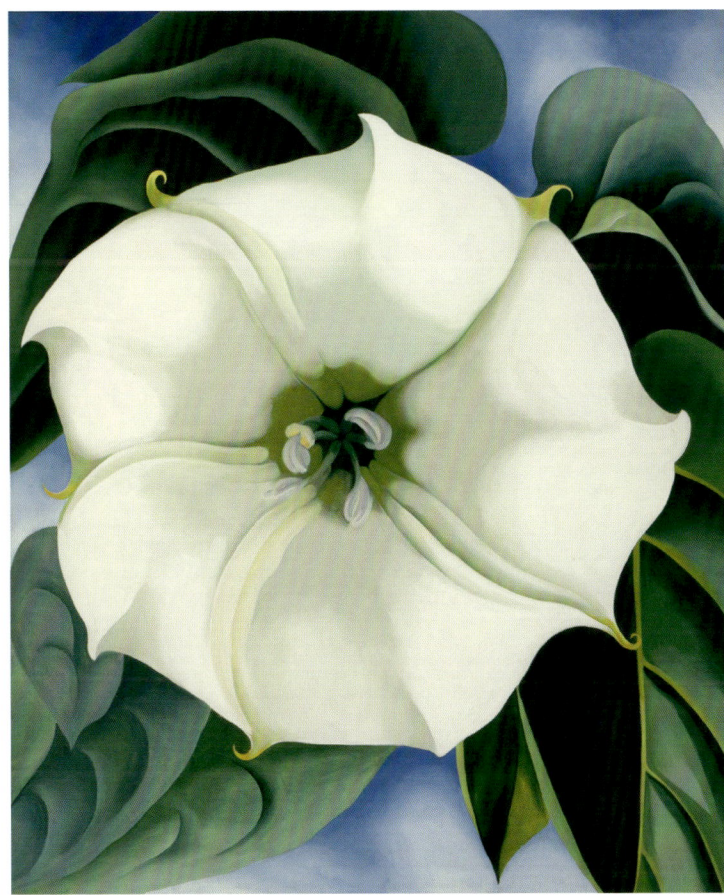

JIMSON WEED/WHITE FLOWER NO. 1

1932, oil on canvas, 121.9 × 101.6 cm (48 × 40 in), Crystal Bridges Museum of American Art, Bentonville, Arkansas
Georgia O'Keeffe, born 1887, Sun Prairie, Wisconsin. Died 1986, Santa Fe, New Mexico.

In 1946 O'Keeffe, a pioneer of American modernism, was the first woman to be given a retrospective at New York's Museum of Modern Art. Twenty years earlier, she had developed her unique, meticulous and detailed painting style from close observation and personal experience. She had also absorbed the formal techniques of modernist photography, emulating such close-up views and cropped images from friends in the circle around her husband, the photographer and art promoter Alfred Stieglitz (1864–1946). He encouraged O'Keeffe's highly personal vision, which found its early expression in paintings of New York, as seen from their thirtieth-floor apartment. However, O'Keeffe's greatest inspiration was nature, especially in the faraway desert regions of New Mexico, where they also had property. It was there that she produced many of the flower paintings for which she is most celebrated worldwide. They were quite unlike any that had been painted before, as demonstrated by this large-scale, magnified and simplified image of a Jimson weed bloom demonstrates. When it came up for auction in 2014, the work was sold for $44.4 million, a record price for an artwork made by a woman.

LYDIA OKUMURA

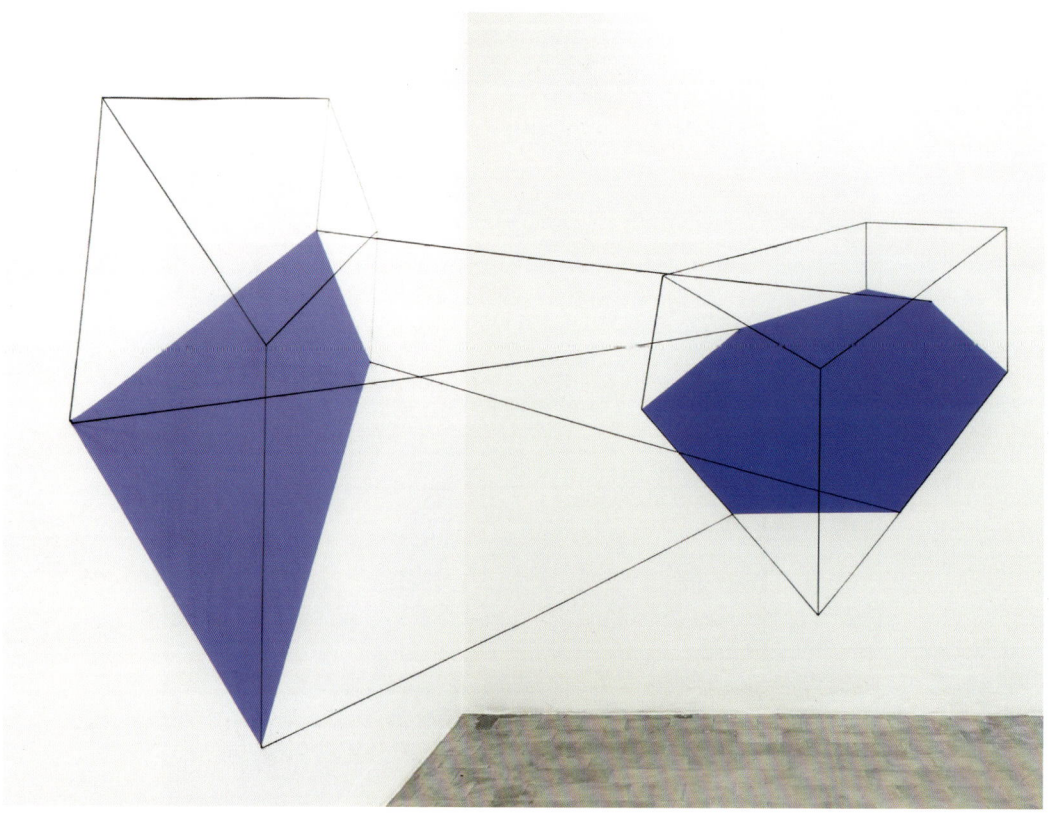

UNTITLED I, ORIGINAL INSTALLATION AT PRATT INSTITUTE, NEW YORK 1980

1980, cord and acrylic on wall, 235 × 440 × 180 cm (92 ½ × 173 ¼ × 70 ⅞ in), Galeria Jaqueline Martins, São Paulo
Lydia Okumura, born 1948, Oswaldo Cruz, São Paulo.

Okumura's practice focuses on the simplicity of line, form and the interstices between two- and three-dimensional space. Of Japanese heritage, she became interested in art through her calligrapher father and she studied ceramics and painting in São Paulo during Brazil's military dictatorship. As co-founder of Equipe 3, an experimental art collective that participated in the 12th São Paulo Biennial in 1973, she met a number of artists who piqued her interest in New York, and she moved there the following year to take up a scholarship at the Pratt Graphics Center. Although Okumura's work eludes easy art-historical categorization, her practice of appropriating print ephemera showed the influence of Conceptual and Minimalist art movements of the period, while later work echoes Brazilian Neo-Concretism. Using materials including wire and paint, her site-specific installations extend the tradition of Op art, using walls and floors to create illusionary sculptural effects. Seen here is a geometric construction comprised of cords stretched across the corner of a room. Selected panels of the resulting wall shapes are painted in ultramarine, flattening the form and challenging the viewer's spatial perceptions, probing the boundaries of the three-dimensional physical realm.

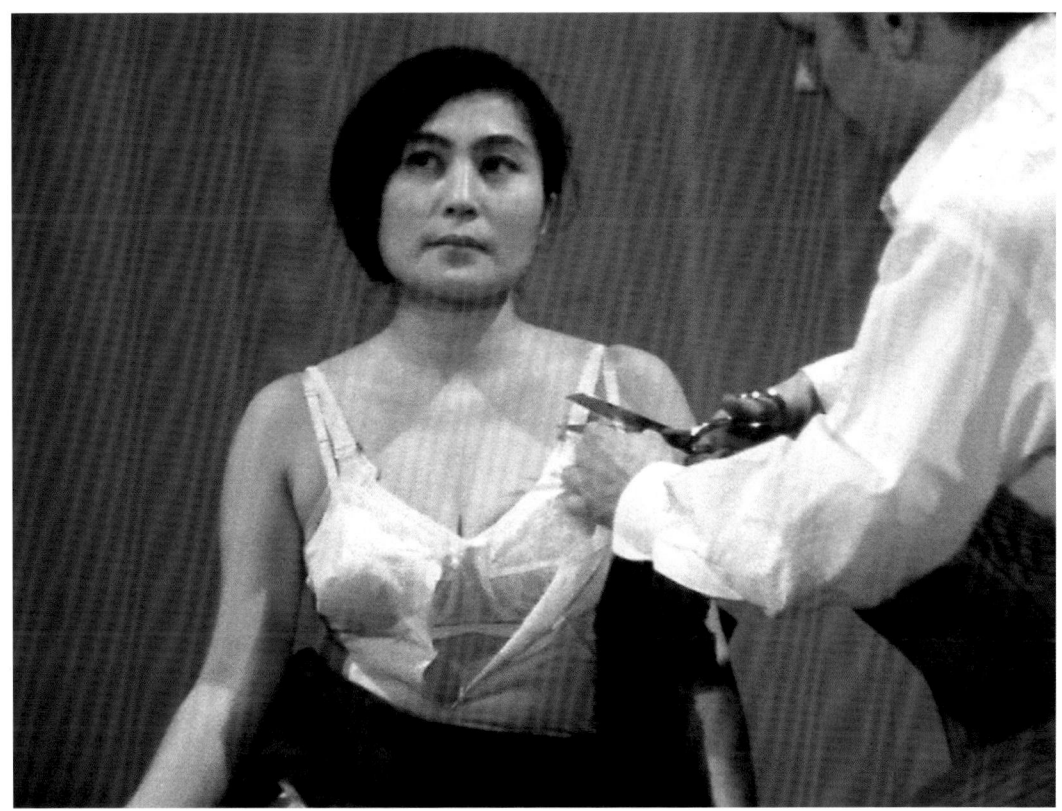

CUT PIECE

1964, film still from *Cut Piece* (1966) by Albert Maysles and David Maysles, documenting Yoko Ono's performance at Carnegie Recital Hall, New York, 21 March 1965
Yoko Ono, born 1933, Tokyo.

After a childhood in Japan and direct experience of wartime, Ono was the first woman accepted to read philosophy at Gakushuin University, Tokyo. Moving in 1953 to New York where her family were residing, she studied at Sarah Lawrence College and associated with avant-garde musicians, composers and artists, many of whom became part of the Fluxus movement – a group of artists who gave priority to impermanence and spontaneity over commodifiable object-based art. Her lifelong practice involves performance, music

and political activism and, over past decades, growing interest in her work has begun to remediate the many years during which it was overshadowed by her relationship with John Lennon. One of her most well-known early works, *Cut Piece* (first performed in 1964 at the Yamaichi Concert Hall, Kyoto), finds Ono wearing a suit, sitting motionless and expressionless, while viewers are invited to use scissors to slowly cut her clothing away. Challenging the idea that the relationship between viewer and art object is neutral, and reinforcing the vulnerability of the human form, the viewer became an active participant in creating the work, implicated in the act of unveiling the female body.

MARIA VAN OOSTERWIJCK

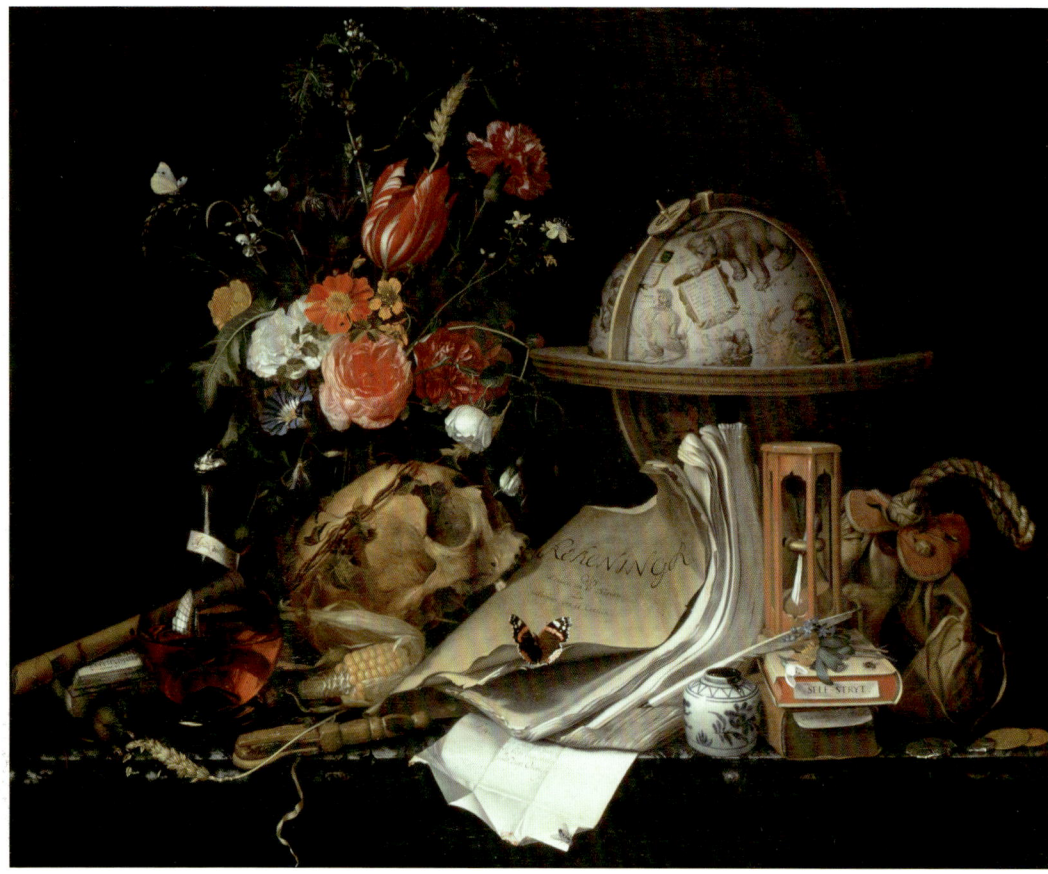

VANITAS STILL LIFE

1668, oil on canvas, 73 × 88.5 cm (28 ¾ × 34 ⅞ in), Kunsthistorisches Museum, Vienna

Maria van Oosterwijck, born 1630, Nootdorp, Netherlands. Died 1693, Uitdam, Netherlands.

The daughter of a church minister, van Oosterwijck became fascinated by art after being taken by her father to the studio of Dutch still-life painter Jan Davidszoon de Heem (1606–84), who subsequently became her teacher. She pursued her career with single-minded determination, turning down a marriage proposal from her professional associate, the painter Willem van Aelst (1627–83). Her depictions of flowers are sumptuous examples of the Dutch 'vanitas' genre – fecund studies of vegetation underscored by a sense of

nature's inevitable transience. Realized with *trompe l'oeil* precision, these small-scale pictures serve as religious allegories of the vanity of human desires and ephemerality of material things, in visible contrast to the implied immortality of the soul. All these themes are encapsulated within the work seen here. A profusion of brilliant blooms emerges from behind a skull, alongside a celestial globe, a mouse eating an ear of corn and other casually strewn symbols of time and fleeting leisure. Van Oosterwijck's servant Geertgen Wyntges (1636–1712), also known as Geertje Pieters, was taught to mix her paints, eventually becoming an artist in her own right.

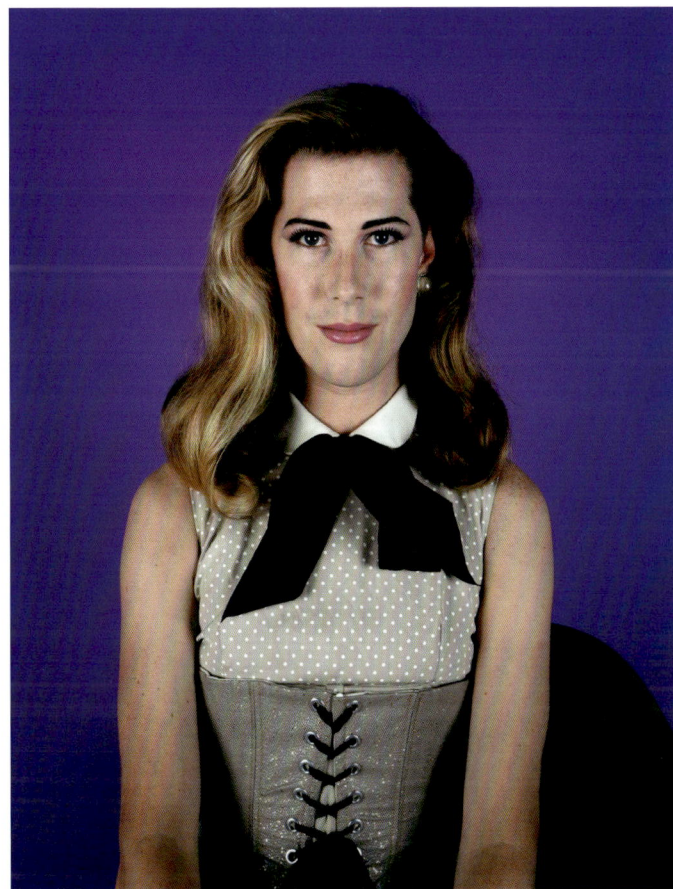

JUSTIN BOND

1993, chromogenic print, 50.8 × 40.6 cm (20 × 16 in)
Catherine Opie, born 1961, Sandusky, Ohio.

Having graduated from the California Institute of the Arts (CalArts) in 1988, Opie came to international attention in the 1990s with her 'Portraits' series, comprising over fifty photographs taken between 1993 and 1997 that documented her friends in the gay, lesbian, bisexual and transgender communities around San Francisco. Even in this early series, her influences from the history of both photography and painting are apparent, blending aspects of early-twentieth-century studio portraiture and more recent traditions of street photography with the aesthetics of the Renaissance, and are deployed to record the people and fashions of a subculture that was rarely acknowledged in mainstream American society at the time. In this portrait, the nightclub performer Justin Bond (b.1963), sometimes known under his drag persona of Kiki, is depicted wearing a vinyl corset, offsetting an otherwise prim appearance. Opie articulates Bond's challenge to the conventional notions of the housewife, expressed via his stated obsession with Samantha Stephens, the subversive lead character endowed with magical powers in the 1960s American fantasy sitcom *Bewitched*.

MERET OPPENHEIM

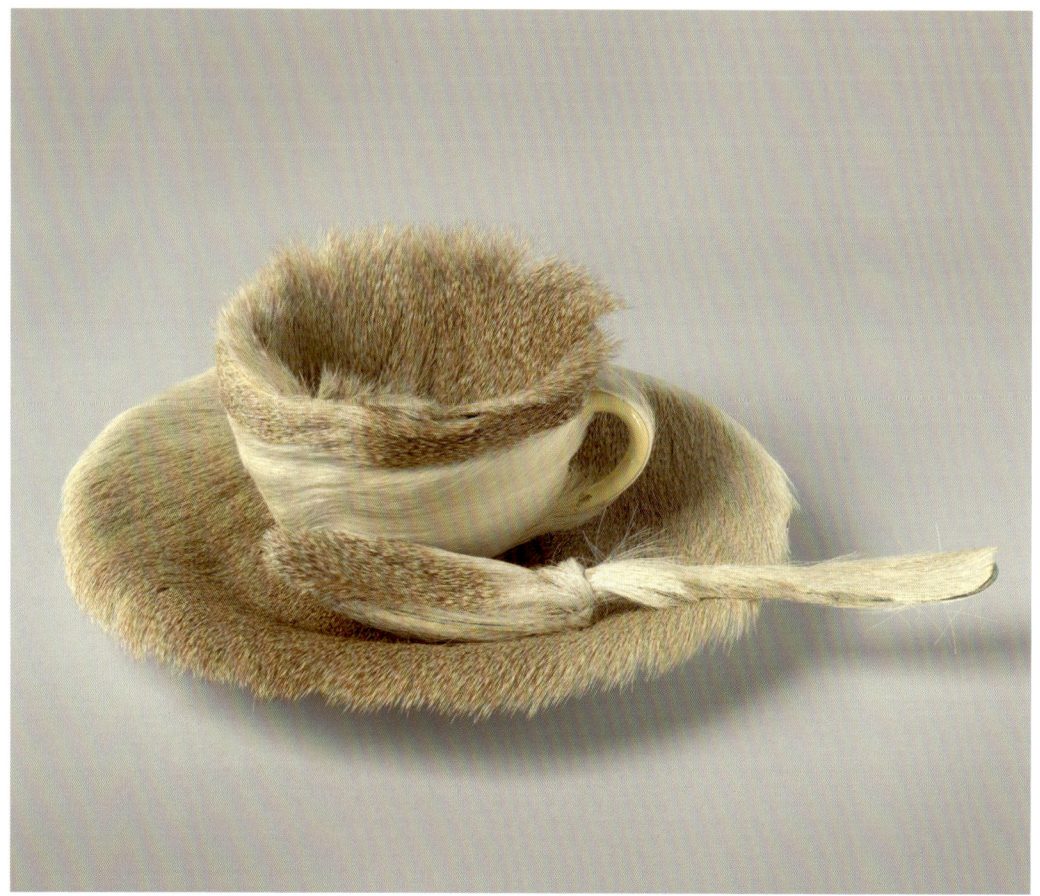

OBJECT

1936, fur-covered cup, saucer and spoon, cup diam: 10.9 cm (4 ⅜ in); saucer diam: 23.7 cm (9 ⅜ in); spoon length: 20.2 cm (8 in); overall h: 7.3 cm (2 ⅞ in), Museum of Modern Art, New York

Meret Oppenheim, born 1913, Berlin. Died 1985, Basel.

Aged eighteen, the German-born Swiss Oppenheim moved to Paris to study at the Académie de la Grande Chaumière, Montparnasse, and there befriended the artists and writers associated with Surrealism, including André Breton (1896–1966), Marcel Duchamp (1887–1968) and Man Ray (1890–1976), who also photographed her. She was one of the only women in the Surrealist circle whose role went beyond that of muse or wife. Her work, akin to the Conceptual approach of Duchamp and Francis Picabia (1879–1953), often involved using household objects as 'ready-mades', which, as artworks, became stripped of their use value. *Object* (called 'Luncheon in Fur' by Breton) was inspired by a conversation in a café with Pablo Picasso (1881–1973) and Dora Maar (p.252) about a fur bracelet Oppenheim had designed. She responded to Picasso's challenge that anything could be covered in fur, saying, 'Even this cup and saucer'. *Object* can be read as a critique of the ideals of womanhood in the early twentieth century – combining and subverting hallmarks of refined femininity. This strange, haunting object, which evokes both attraction and repulsion, has become iconic.

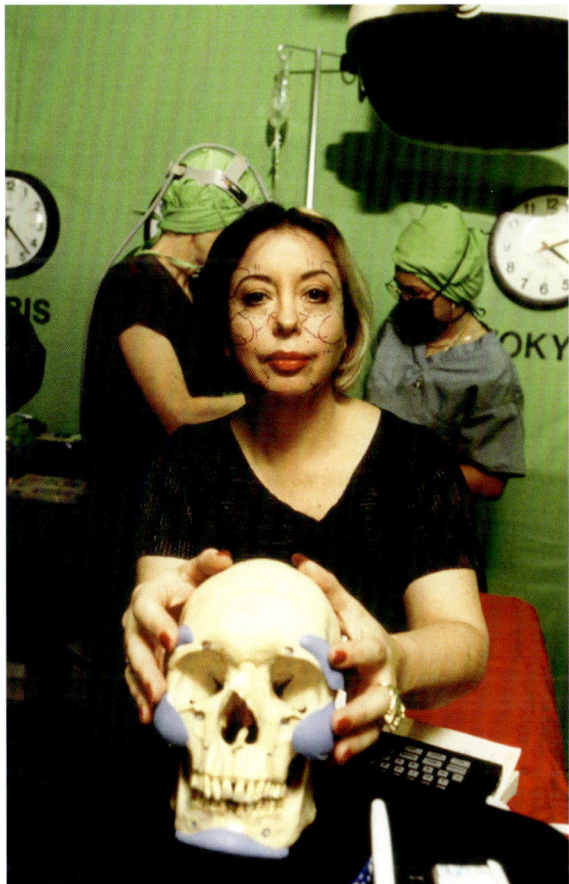

OMNIPRESENCE 7TH SURGERY PERFORMANCE. NOVEMBER 21ST 1993

1993, Cibachrome print in Diasec mount, 165.1 × 109.2 cm (65 × 43 in),
National Museum of Art, Osaka, Japan
Orlan, born Mireille Porte, 1947, Saint-Étienne, France.

Orlan uses her flesh as a sculptural medium, surgically changing
her appearance to explore constructs of sexuality as well as perceptions of beauty and selfhood. She became interested in surgery after
an operation for an ectopic pregnancy. Even prior to altering her body,
she was exploring its creative potential: in the 1960s she enacted
slow-motion walks in her home town, used her limbs as a measuring
instrument and photographed herself naked in athletic poses. She
also baptized herself and kissed viewers for money outside the Grand
Palais in Paris in the 1970s. From the early 1990s she began the
series 'The Reincarnation of Saint Orlan'. Her lips, nose, eyes, chin
and forehead were modelled into female prototypes from art history
and classical mythology, including the *Mona Lisa* as well as Venus,
Diana, Europa and Psyche. This photograph documents a moment
in Orlan's seventh surgery: a performance she staged live for international media broadcast. Her work invites viewers to consider
the status of the body in society, the pressure for women to conform
to idealized visions of perfection and the drastic measures available
to achieve this vision.

LUCY ORTA

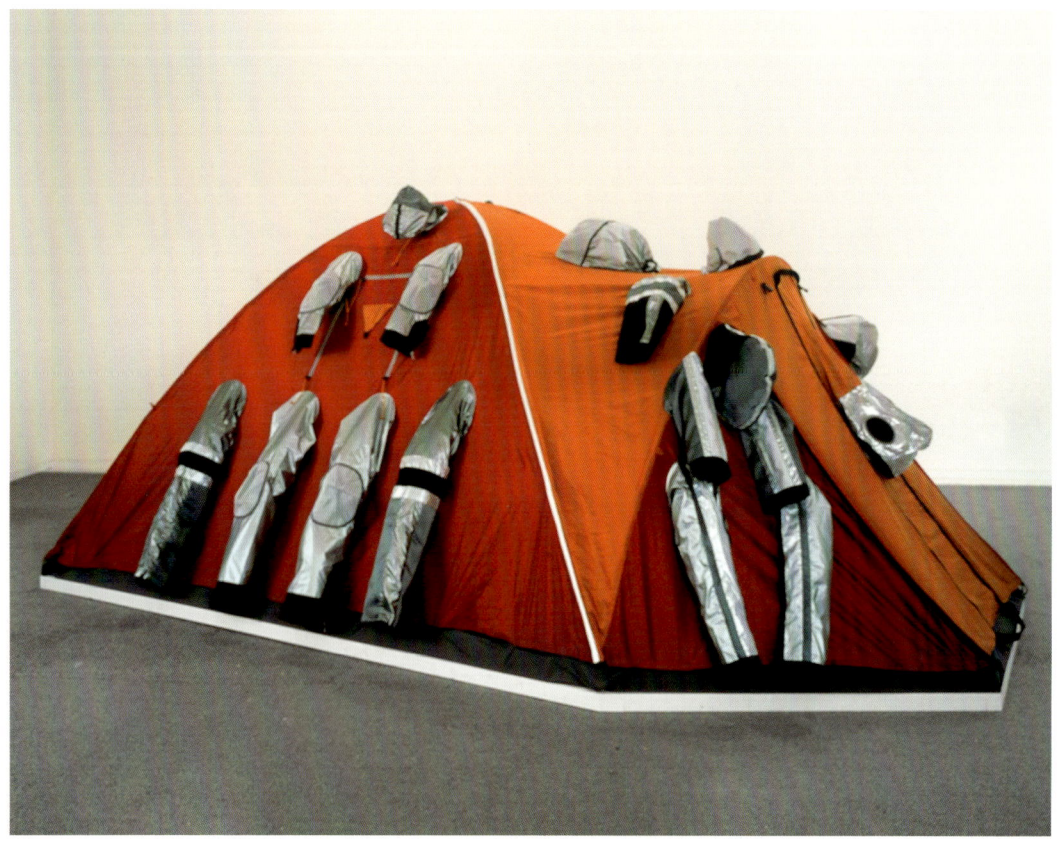

BODY ARCHITECTURE – COLLECTIVE WEAR X 8

1998, polyamide tent, aluminium-coated polyamide, various textiles, 3 telescopic
aluminium armatures and zippers, 400 × 260 × 120 cm (157 × 102 × 47 in)
Lucy Orta, born 1966, Sutton Coldfield, UK.

Orta studied Fashion Knitwear Design in Nottingham, UK, before
moving to Paris in 1991. She first gained recognition in the art world
for her series 'Refuge Wear' and 'Body Architecture' (1992–8), which
featured structures that modified and fused clothing and survival
equipment. Together with her partner Jorge (b.1953), she founded
Studio Orta in 1992, and since 2005 they have co-authored work
under the name of Lucy + Jorge Orta. With a focus on the body
and its environment, their artworks range from modified vehicles
to public sculptures and large-scale installations, and in 2007

they received the Green Leaf Award for Sculpture, in recognition
of the environmental aspect of their practice. Orta created this work,
one of the final 'Body Architecture' pieces, for the exhibition
'Visions of the Body' at the National Art Museum in Kyoto, Japan.
She added sleeve-like garments to the outside of a tent, to which
people could join themselves using zips. A metaphor for the social
fabric of existence through which everyone is related, the sculpture
highlights our inescapable, indispensable interconnectivity, something especially evident in times of crisis and adversity.

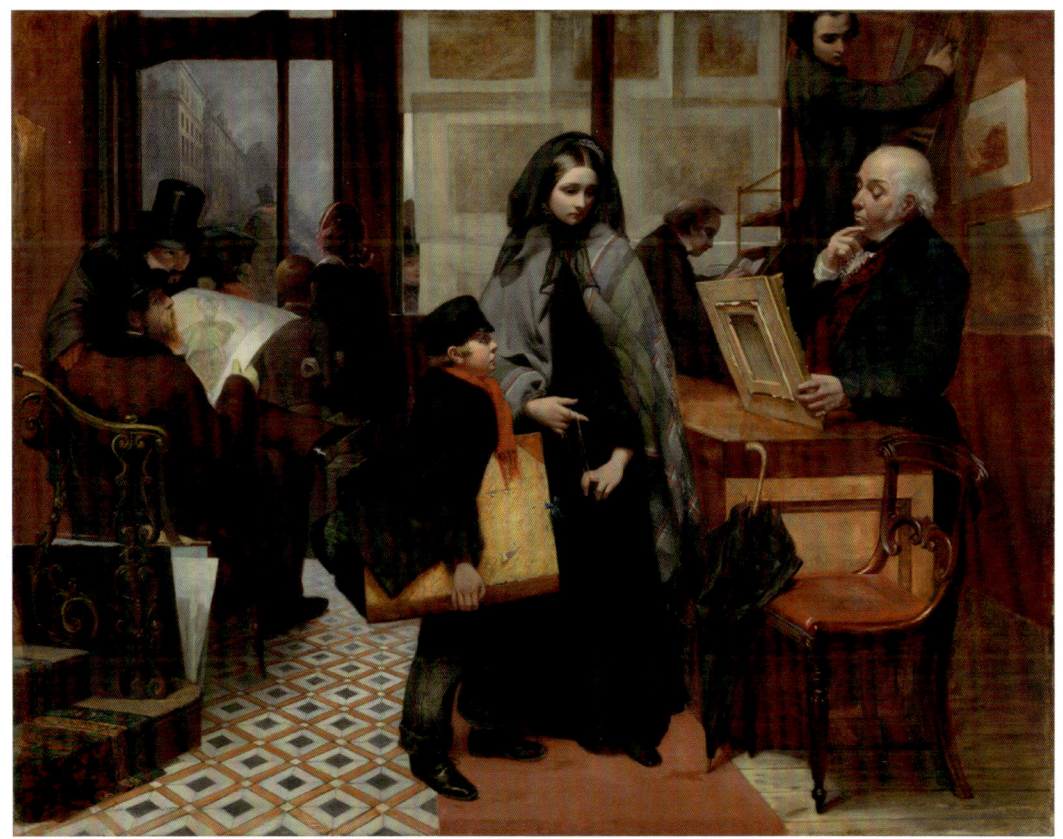

NAMELESS AND FRIENDLESS. 'THE RICH MAN'S WEALTH IS HIS STRONG CITY, ETC.' – PROVERBS, X, 15

1857, oil on canvas, 82.5 × 103.8 cm (32 ½ × 40 ⅞ in), Tate, London
Emily Mary Osborn, born 1828, London. Died 1925, London.

One of the most successful female artists of the nineteenth century, Osborn actively campaigned for women's rights in Victorian England. She is best known for paintings depicting women and children in difficult circumstances. In this, her most famous work, a diffident young woman attempts to sell a painting. Accompanied by a small boy, she gazes at the floor while the portly art dealer assesses her picture; behind, two top-hatted men ogle her, emphasizing the woman's vulnerability in a male-dominated arena. The subtitle, a biblical quotation, ironically highlights both the economic injustice faced by women and the moralizing hypocrisy that oppressed them. The painting was likely intended as a political statement since its exhibition at London's Royal Academy of Arts in 1857 coincided with the formation of the Society of Female Artists, which aimed to give women opportunities to exhibit and sell their work publicly. Osborn also campaigned for women to be admitted to the Royal Academy and was a signatory of the 1889 Declaration in Favour of Women's Suffrage. Unlike the women she painted, she had a long and successful career, enjoying the support of wealthy patrons, including Queen Victoria.

PAN YULIANG

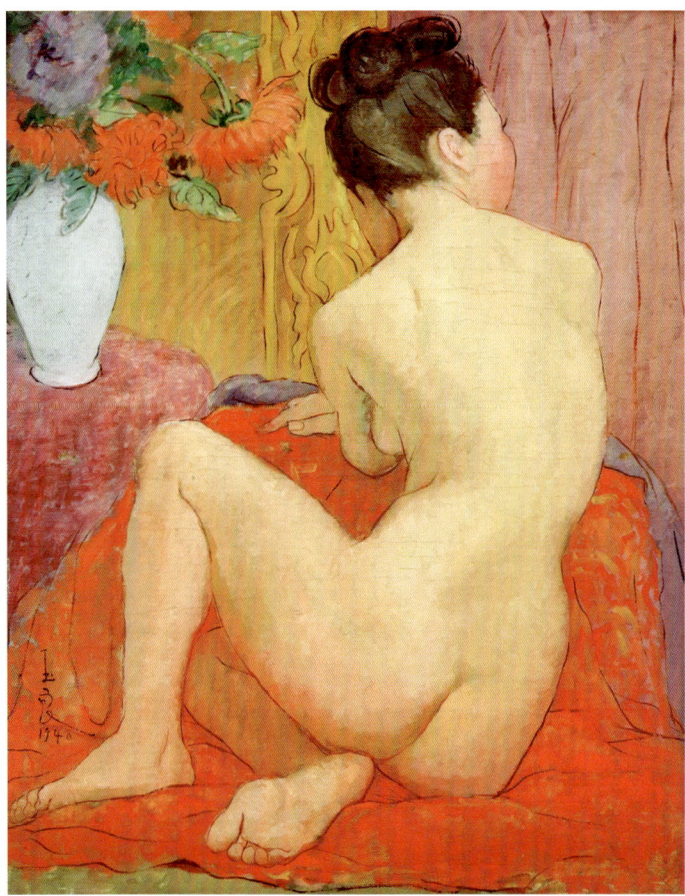

CHRYSANTHEMUM AND FEMALE NUDE

1948, oil on canvas, 90 × 72.5 cm (35⅜ × 28½ in), National Art Museum of China, Beijing

Pan Yuliang, born Chen Xiuqing 1895, Yangzhou, China. Died 1977, Paris.

At the age of fourteen, Pan was forced to work in a brothel after the death of her parents. After living for a period as the concubine of a wealthy patron who had purchased her freedom, she passed exams to study Western-style painting at the Shanghai Art Academy, and in 1922 went to Europe, first to the École Nationale Supérieure des Beaux-Arts, Paris, then to Italy as recipient of the Prix de Rome. Her oil paintings are characterized by the juxtaposition of East and West, modern and traditional, using elements of Chinese ink painting. Though she was respected in Europe, her hybrid work was subject to heavy criticism in socially conservative China, with some of her paintings being defaced. A prolific artist producing over 4,000 works in her lifetime, Pan is best known for her portraits and nude studies of Chinese women, often using herself as the model. This work shows a figure with arms crossed and her back turned to the viewer – a recurring motif in her paintings. This strategy of limiting and controlling the viewer's gaze asserts the priority of the subject over her own body.

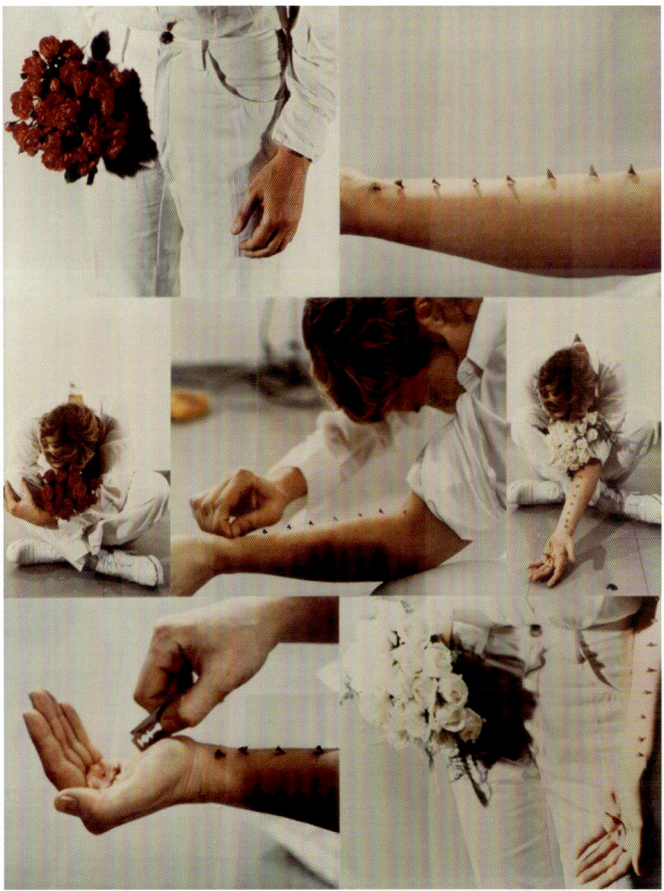

SENTIMENTAL ACTION, 9 NOVEMBER 1973, DOCUMENTATION
OF AN ACTION REALIZED AT GALERIE DIAGRAMMA, MILAN

1973, 7 chromogenic colour prints arranged on a panel, 122.5 × 102 cm
(48 ¼ × 40 ⅛ in), Museum of Modern Art, New York
Gina Pane, born 1939, Biarritz, France. Died 1990, Paris.

While her practice encompassed photography and sculpture, it was Pane's performance work connected with the body art movement in the 1970s for which she is most celebrated. Born to Italian parents, she grew up in Italy and southern France before moving to Paris to study and then working from a studio in Paris's recently opened arts complex, Centre Georges Pompidou. Her early works included Minimalist metal sculptures painted in primary colours, but her practice gradually assumed a ritual dimension, looking at the relationship between the body and nature. Influenced by the political protests of May 1968, Pane became interested in humanity's potential for empathy and cruelty. Inflicting injuries upon her own body, she sought to arouse the viewer's discomfort, compassion and their own lived experience. Such 'actions' included smothering fires by hand and making her skin bleed. In the public performance documented by this series of photographs, Pane explored the mother-child relationship and what she termed an 'intra space'. She pressed thorns from roses into her arms, also cutting her palm with a razor blade while moving from a standing to foetal position. The action was performed twice, once with red roses and once with white.

LYGIA PAPE

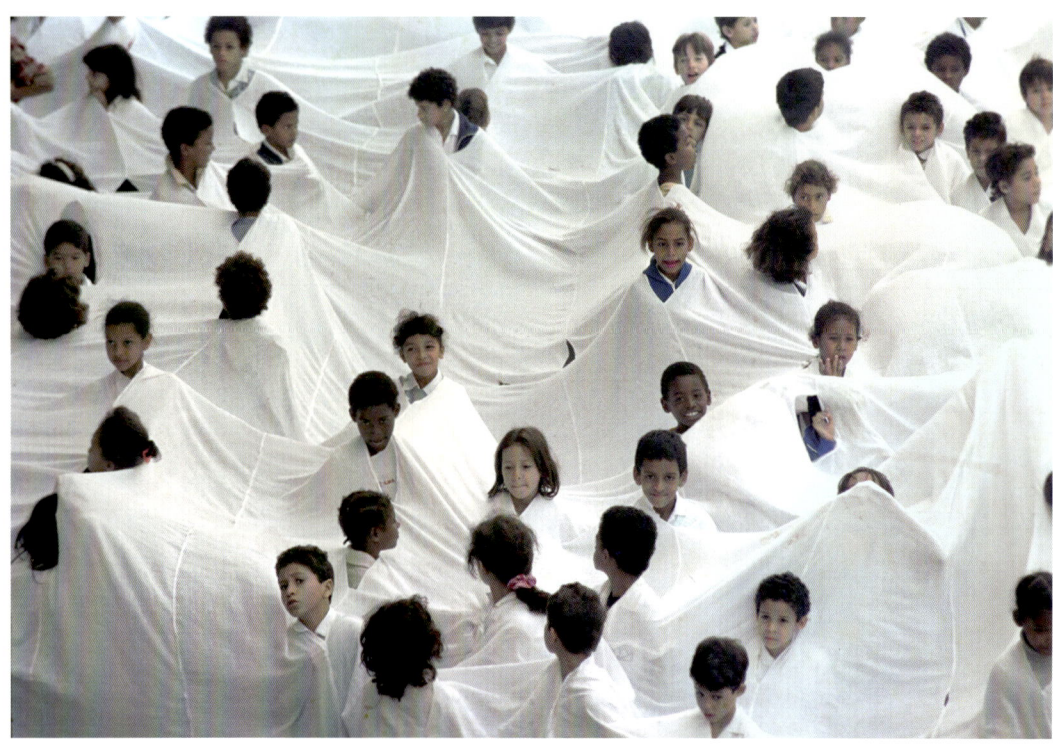

DIVISOR (DIVIDER)

1968, image of performance at Museu de Arte Moderna, Rio de Janeiro, 1990.
Lygia Pape, born 1927, Nova Friburgo, Brazil. Died 2004, Rio de Janeiro.

Along with peers Hélio Oiticica (1937–80) and Lygia Clark (p.101), Pape was a member of Brazil's *Grupo Frente* ('Front Group'), which formed in Rio de Janeiro in 1954, inspired by the early-twentieth-century movements of European Concretism and Soviet Constructivism. Recognized equally for her engagement with abstract geometric forms as for her performance work, Pape's multi-disciplinary practice was tirelessly experimental, as she made innovative art that required the viewer's participation. During the 1950s she produced her 'Weaving' series of woodcuts on paper, composed of deceptively simple arrangements of geometric forms.

In 1959, disenchanted with the constraints of rationalism, Pape and others co-founded the Neo-Concrete movement, which aimed at inventing an artistic language that involved the viewer in a sensorial experience with objects. Her iconic performance *Divisor (Divider)* presented a subtly subversive response to the brutal dictatorship that followed the 1964 military coup in Brazil. Comprising a forty-square-metre (430-square-foot) expanse of white material punctured with holes, participants were invited to poke their heads through the sheet and join together in a glorious collective action intended to refashion symbolically an alternative social fabric.

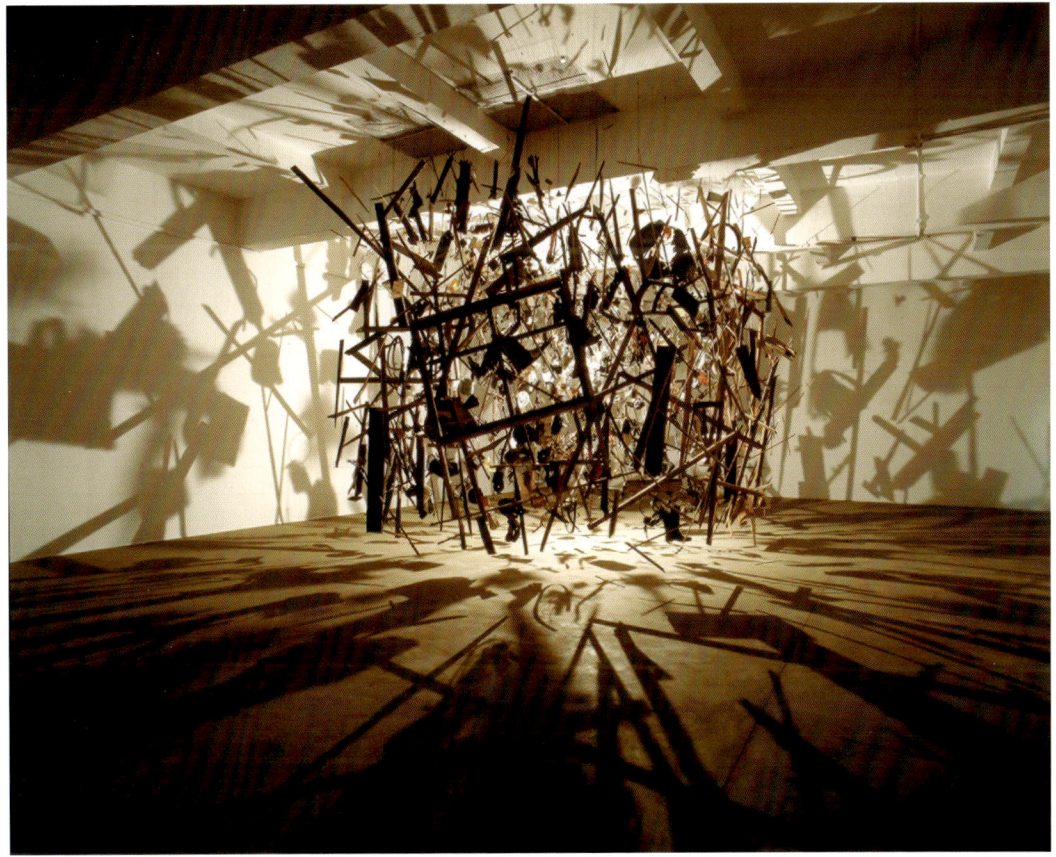

COLD DARK MATTER: AN EXPLODED VIEW

1991, garden shed and contents blown up for the artist by the British Army, the fragments suspended around a light bulb, dimensions variable, Tate, London
Cornelia Parker, born 1956, Cheshire, UK.

Parker is a British conceptual artist who primarily works in sculpture and installation. In recognition of her distinguished career, she was elected as Academician at London's Royal Academy of Arts in 2010. Familiar domestic objects are often incorporated into her works to question the collective instincts that guide us as humans and the elements that define our everyday existence. She focused on the human experience in *The Maybe* (1995) at the Serpentine Gallery, which included presenting the actor Tilda Swinton asleep inside a vitrine, her vulnerability exposed for all to see. Two years later,

her work *Mass (Colder Darker Matter)* used the remains of a Texan church that had been struck by lightning. The work's name alluded to a hypothetical substance postulated as the invisible constituent of most of the universe. In this earlier work, *Cold Dark Matter: An Exploded View, Parker* arranged for the British Army to destroy a garden shed with military explosives. The shed had been filled with second-hand bric-a-brac items and their charred and deformed remains were suspended within the installation's ceiling, allowing the audience to traverse a frozen instant in space, as if caught within the exploding moment itself.

KATIE PATERSON

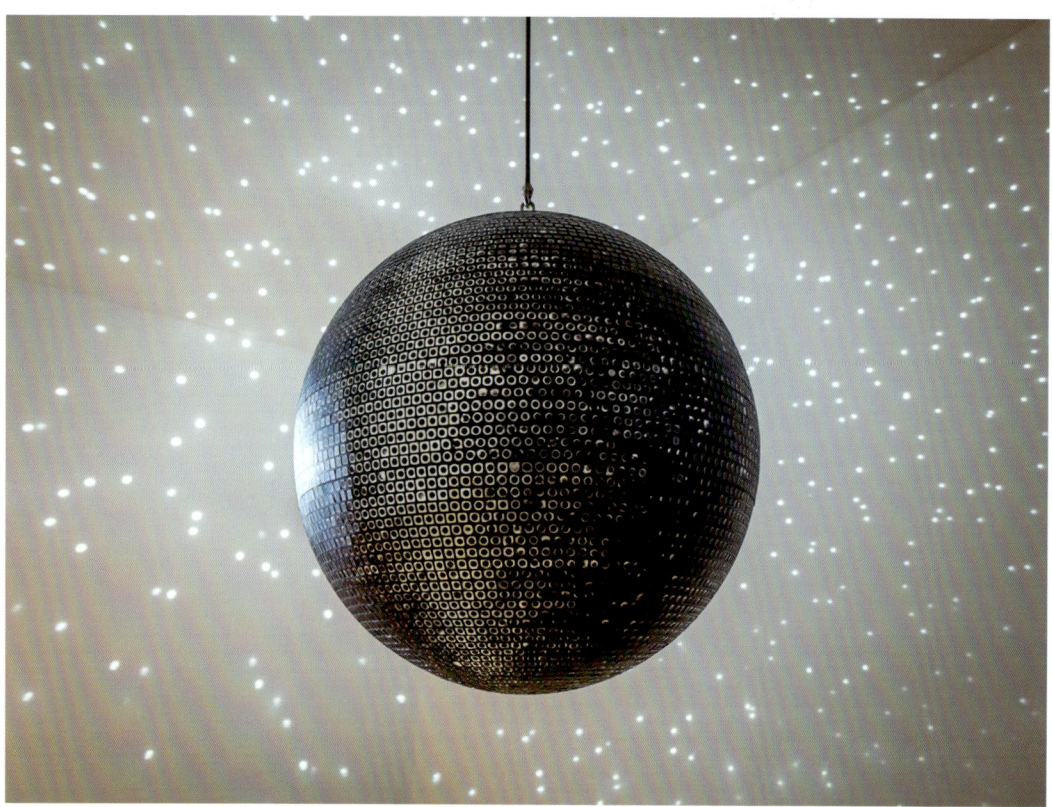

TOTALITY
2016, printed mirror-ball, motor and lights, diam: 83 cm (32 ⅝ in),
Art Council Collection, UK/James Zang Collection
Katie Paterson, born 1981, Glasgow.

Working across multiple mediums, Paterson engages with ecology, geology, cosmology and time to create poetic encounters with our place in the universe. Having completed a BA at Edinburgh College of Art in 2004 and a MFA at the Slade School of Art, London, in 2007, Paterson has frequently collaborated with leading scientists and researchers to realize her technologically ambitious artworks. One of her earliest pieces, *Vatnajökull (the sound of)* (2007–8), featured a phone number rendered in neon that, when dialled, connected the caller to the live sound of an eroding glacier in Iceland.

In *Earth–Moon–Earth* (2007), a pianola played a fragmentary version of Beethoven's *Moonlight Sonata* (1801) that the artist had transmitted to the moon and back using Morse Code. The work seen here demonstrates the meticulous research typically involved in Paterson's art-making. A slowly rotating mirror-ball is covered with thousands of images gathered by the artist that depict nearly every solar eclipse documented in the past two centuries. Ranging from an eighteenth-century drawing to present-day digital images, they are arranged in sequence from partial to total eclipse, and immerse the viewer in the reflections that they cast around the room.

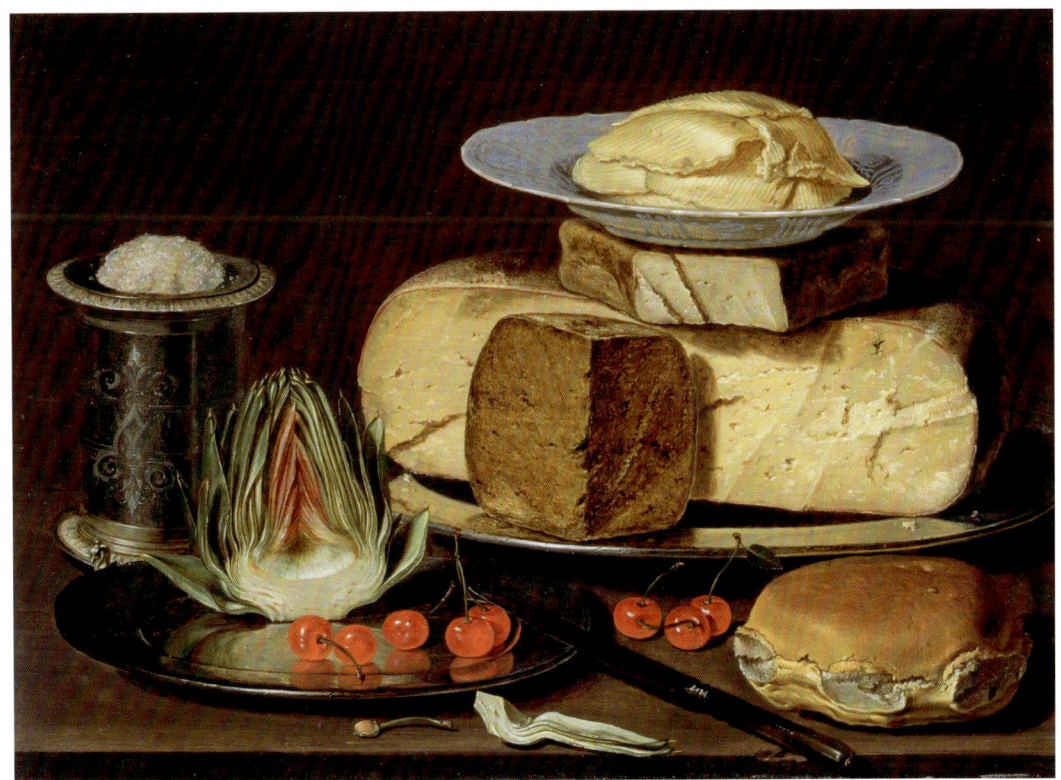

STILL LIFE WITH CHEESES, ARTICHOKE AND CHERRIES

c.1625, oil on wood, 33.3 × 46.7 cm (13 ⅛ × 18 ⅜ in), Los Angeles County Museum of Art

Clara Peeters, born *c*.1590, Antwerp, Belgium (then Duchy of Brabant). Died *c*.1659, probably in Antwerp.

Peeters is the only Flemish woman known with certainty to have been active in the genre of still life, which was the dominant painting style of the Low Countries at the turn of the seventeenth century. Innovative as a painter of food, she was integral to the development of 'breakfast pieces', depicting more simple meals and vessels, and 'banquet pieces', which showed off choice cuisine and costly tableware. Her skill in rendering texture and surfaces have led some to speculate that she was trained by the influential Flemish painter Osias Beert

(*c*.1580–1623); however, there is scant information available about her life, and others believe her technical innovation made her a leader, not a follower. Religious symbolism is prevalent in her paintings; this work, for example, represents two ways of life: the spiritual and the carnal. Bread references the Eucharist, while the dairy products denote motherhood. The reference to Christ is reinforced by the cherries, indicating the Passion. On the left, the artichoke (once considered an aphrodisiac) symbolizes lust, while the mirrored plate refers to vanity. In 2016, Peeters was the first female artist to be given a solo exhibition at the Museo del Prado, Madrid.

BEVERLY PEPPER

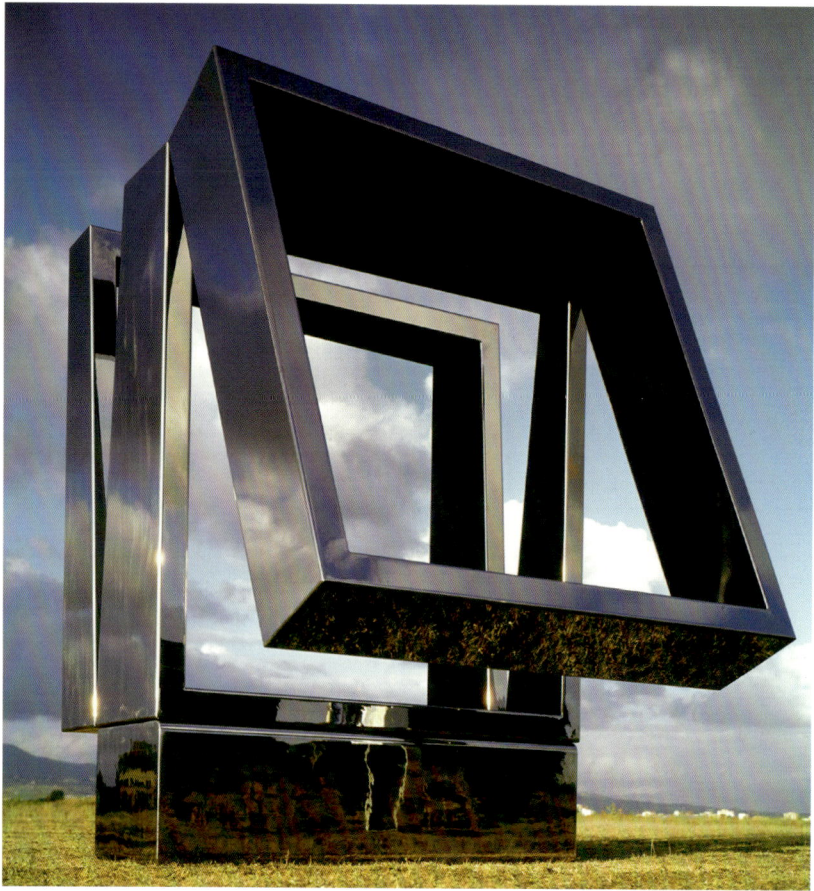

ZIG-ZAG

1967, stainless steel and baked enamel, overall: 189.9 × 149.9 × 165.1 cm
(74 ¾ × 59 × 65 in), Albright-Knox Art Gallery, Buffalo, New York.
Beverly Pepper, born 1922, New York. Died 2020, Todi, Italy.

Celebrated in the United States in particular for her large-scale
public sculptures and site-specific works, Pepper uses a vocabulary of geometric abstraction. Having studied in Paris and
encountered artists such as Fernand Léger (1881–1955), she initially worked as a painter during the 1950s. Pepper began considering spatial forms in relation to the landscape following a 1960
trip to Angkor Wat, Cambodia, where she was inspired by the
magnificent temple ruins. The only woman among ten sculptors
included in the 1962 Spoleto Festival, she made a series of works,

including *The Gift of Icarus*. In preparation for the exhibition, she
was invited by the festival's sponsor to fabricate her work in a local
factory, giving her an introduction to industrial techniques of cutting and welding, and she continued to prepare for exhibitions in
this way. Expressive and contemplative, her sculptures appear
pliable and dynamic, the artist manipulating solid materials such
as cast iron, steel, bronze and stone to contradict their unyielding
state. This work's highly polished form expands into its environment, its geometry seeming to dissect and open itself, angling into
the surrounding space and framing the vast void of sky.

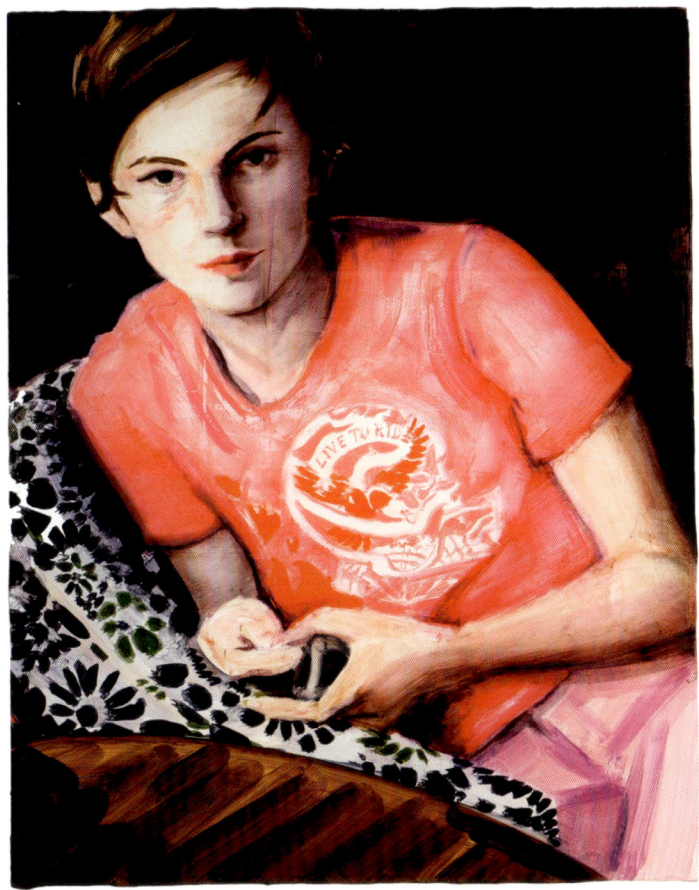

LIVE TO RIDE (E.P.)

2003, oil on board, 38.1 × 30.5 cm (15 × 12 in), Whitney Museum of American Art, New York
Elizabeth Peyton, born 1965, Danbury, Connecticut.

Peyton achieved recognition in the art world in the mid-1990s for her small-scale portraits depicting people from her own life as well as those beyond it. Working alternately from life and from photographic sources, her paintings and works on paper have portrayed subjects as diverse as Barack Obama, David Bowie and the performers of Wagnerian opera. In *Live to Ride (E.P.)* she turns the gaze onto herself. The self-portrait is characteristic of her oil paintings, employing shades of brown and pink in a combination of precise and expressive gestures – at once stylized and highly intimate.

The surface textures – whether the pattern of the blanket she rests against or her T-shirt proclaiming 'live to ride' – bear witness to the power of small-scale, incidental details in Peyton's work. In recent years, this interest has been reflected in a series of still-life compositions. The alternation between defined and impressionistic marks is another recurring trait; the shifting focus invests her work with a dual air of softness and seclusion. The observer observed, Peyton looks directly at the viewer, yet, like many of her sitters, does not give all of herself away.

SUSAN PHILIPSZ

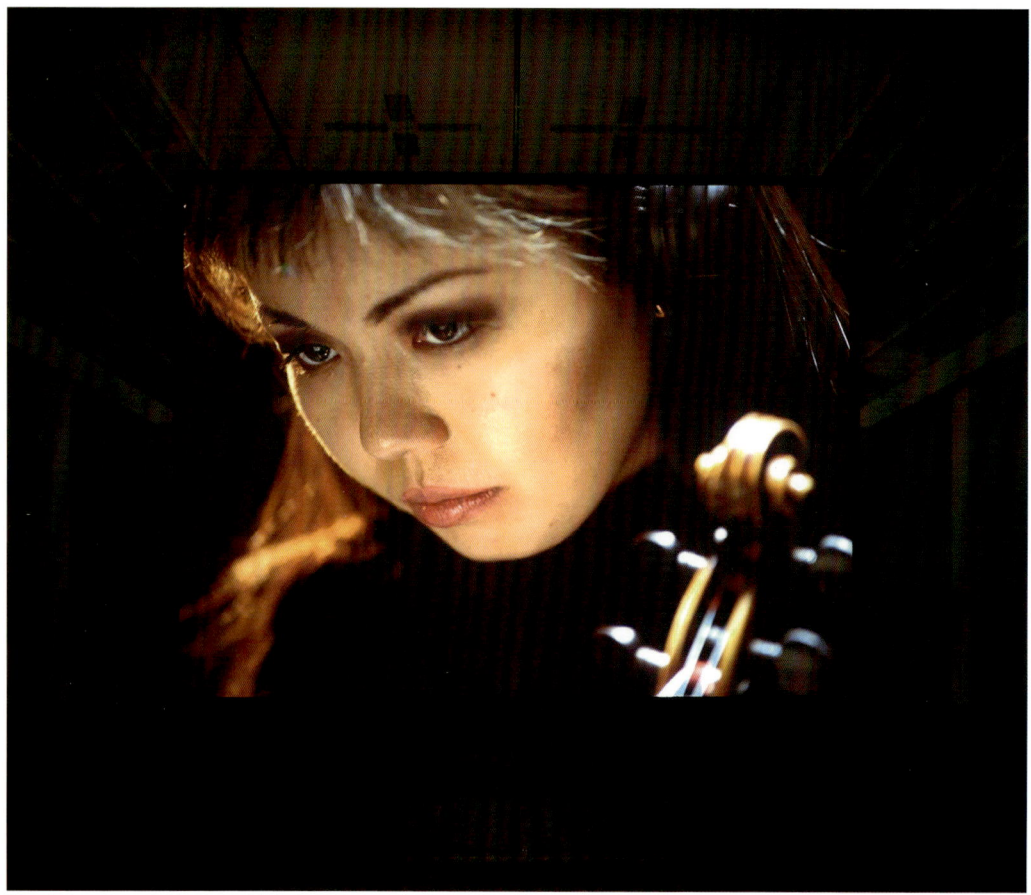

A SINGLE VOICE

2017, (detail), single-channel HD film and 12-channel sound installation, 56 mins 7 secs, looped, installation view, 'Susan Philipsz: A Single Voice', BALTIC Centre for Contemporary Art, Gateshead, UK
Susan Philipsz, born 1965, Glasgow.

Philipsz's sound works could be encountered in a museum or by chance while walking around a city, the haunting sounds of some of her pieces emanating from buildings, bridges and train stations. Her installations emphasize the emotional and psychological qualities of sound, and are usually site-specific. Philipsz uses oral histories and narratives of longing, loss and hope to explore how sound can affect our consciousness by arousing memories and emotions, or by defining particular spaces. Her works often feature recordings of her own untrained singing voice, looped and layered into choruses and song cycles. She recapitulates and transforms compositions ranging from sixteenth-century ballads to the songs of David Bowie, whose 1972 album *Ziggy Stardust* she sang a cappella for her eponymous work of 2001. Seen here is a still from Philipsz's first major film work, a large-scale projection with twelve speakers arranged in a sculptural formation. Each plays single tones adapted from the first violin line of the twentieth-century opera *Aniara* by Karl-Birger Blomdahl, the story of a spaceship bound for Mars that veers off course, condemning its human passengers to drift through the cosmos, in solitude forever.

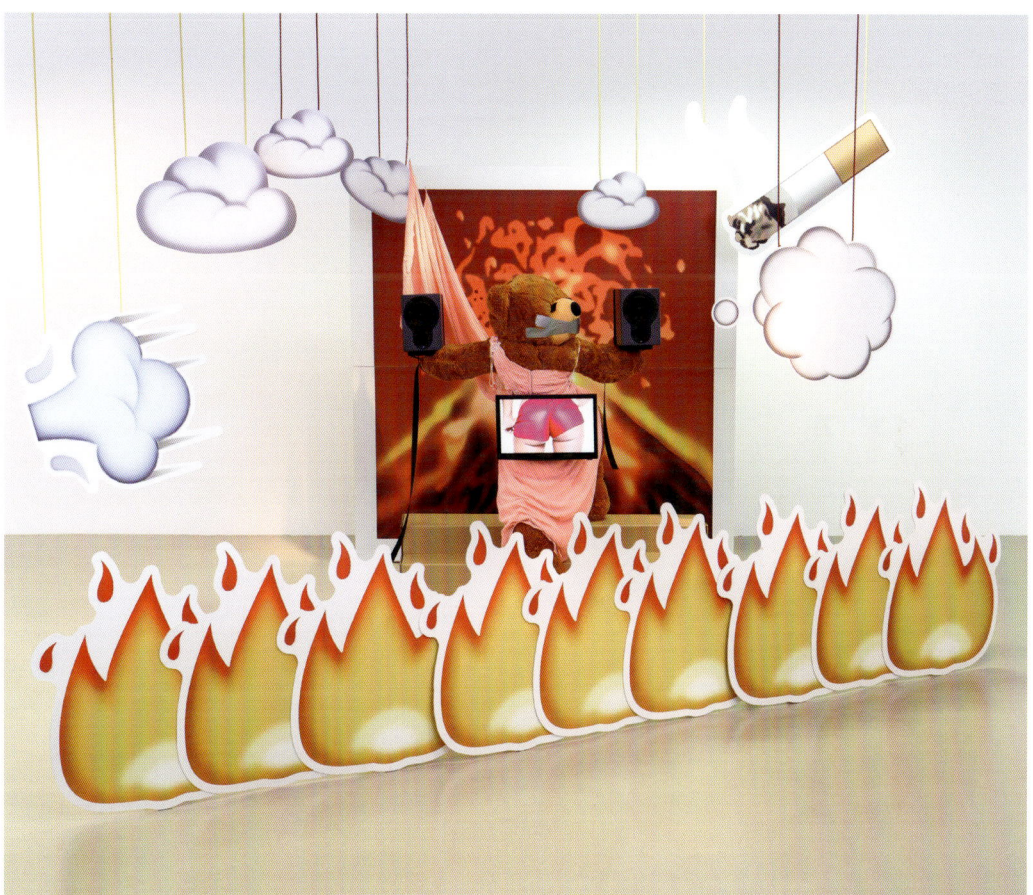

TRUE TO SIZE

2016, (detail), HD video, LCD monitor, active monitor speakers, digital print on display board, stuffed toy bear, wedding dress, steel timber, ratchet straps, bungee cord and gaffer tape, dimensions variable, installation view, 'Heather Phillipson: TRUE TO SIZE', Plymouth Arts Centre, UK. Arts Council Collection, UK
Heather Phillipson, born 1978, London.

Phillipson creates multilayered environments that seem to operate according to their own logic. She often uses found images and phrases in ways that release them from prior meanings. Winner of The Jarman Award for artists using moving image in 2016, her videos are presented in colourful, resonant sculptural theatres, in which architectural elements, furniture, cardboard cut-outs and video screens vie for attention. Musically trained and an active DJ, Phillipson is also

an acclaimed poet, having had her first public success in this field at the age of nine. Her installations could be considered poems in time and space, which examine the physical and affective aspects of human subjectivity. She assembles materials to provoke wry dislocations between word and image, all the while affirming a deep suspicion of stock phrases and pictorial clichés. Editing and techniques of looping, repetition and layering are all-important in her practice, which values precise structure and rhythm. In *TRUE TO SIZE*, flamboyant teddy bears perform in sexualized poses and outfits and run into troublesome situations. A seam of dark humour runs through Phillipson's work, and she conveys with bathetic enthusiasm the sense that humanity might similarly be doomed by its own actions.

PATRICIA PICCININI

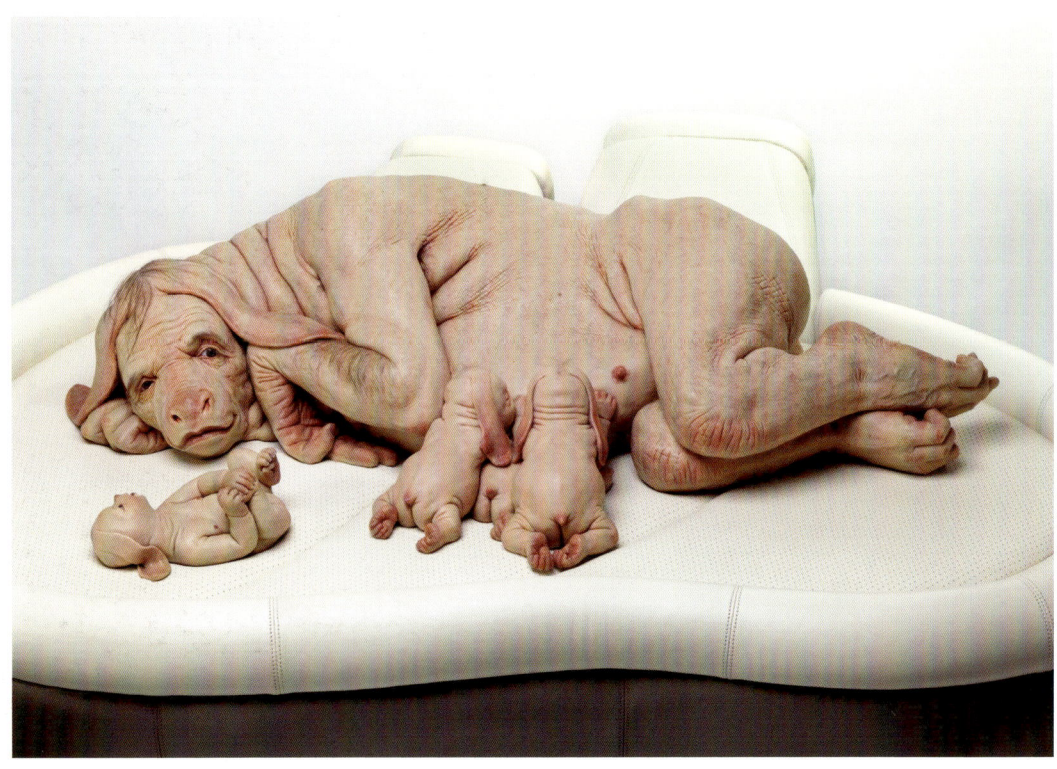

THE YOUNG FAMILY

2002, silicone, polyurethane, leather, plywood and human hair, 80 × 150 × 110 cm
(31 ½ × 59 × 43 ¼ in), Bendigo Art Gallery, Victoria, Australia
Patricia Piccinini, born 1965, Freetown, Sierra Leone (Australian national).

Piccinini investigates emergent themes in technology and science, speculating about biological futures on the verge of becoming present realities. Her hybrid creatures suggest complex ethical questions concerning genetic engineering and synthetic biology, although Piccinini leaves these questions open. She also touches on wider social issues around difference, prejudice and human vulnerability, suggesting possibilities of transformation that are both hopeful and disturbing. Using techniques akin to those of fellow Australian artist Ron Mueck (b.1958), her creations are rendered with a hyperreal

attention to detail, inviting the viewer to relate to them emotionally. Her 2016 solo show in Rio de Janeiro was top of *The Art Newspaper*'s rankings for exhibition visitor numbers worldwide that year. In *The Young Family*, a mother feeds her offspring, a motif that recurred in her gigantic balloon piece, *Skywhale* (2013). The creatures appear to be part-human, but crossed with pig, wombat or ape. In interviews, the artist has said that she imagines these creatures being bred for organ transplantation – a technique already being attempted with pigs. The caring and concerned expression of the mother as she looks at her children complicates the viewer's response, evincing empathy as well as disgust.

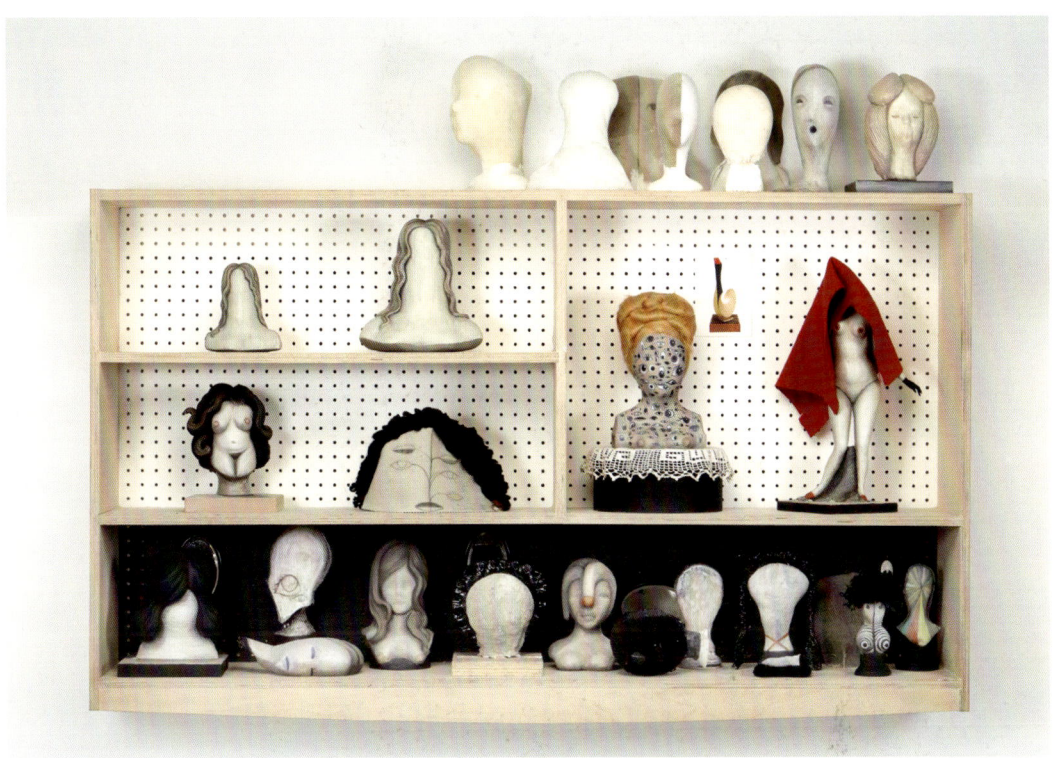

HEAD CASE

2016, plaster, clay, fabric, leather, wood, paint, synthetic hair and pegboard,
155 × 112 × 27 cm (61 × 44 × 10 ⅝ in), collection of the artist
Cathie Pilkington, born 1968, Manchester, UK.

Pilkington studied silversmithing at Edinburgh College of Art, later moving to London to focus on sculpture at the Royal College of Art. With a notable career in making and teaching, Pilkington was elected a member of London's Royal Academy of Arts in 2014. Her work defies categorization, encompassing different media and moods, and often incorporating ready-made objects like clothing. This combination of fine art with traditionally craft materials intentionally confronts hierarchical and gendered notions of artistic value. Pilkington's work is by turns humorous, tender and disturbing. Her

first public sculpture, *Bill and Bob* (1999), featured two bronzes of small dogs frolicking in a pool-like expanse of blue rubber paving in Bristol, UK. *Head Case* is a work typical of Pilkington's frequent use of dolls as a motif. She considers these as well-loved children's toys, often imbued with vivid personalities, but also as contested territories of gendered play. Dolls have also been implicated in unsettling examples of female representation in art, sometimes verging on complete objectification, especially in the twentieth century. In this assemblage, the multiple heads and mannequin-like forms recall Surrealist depictions of hyper-stylized women.

HOWARDENA PINDELL

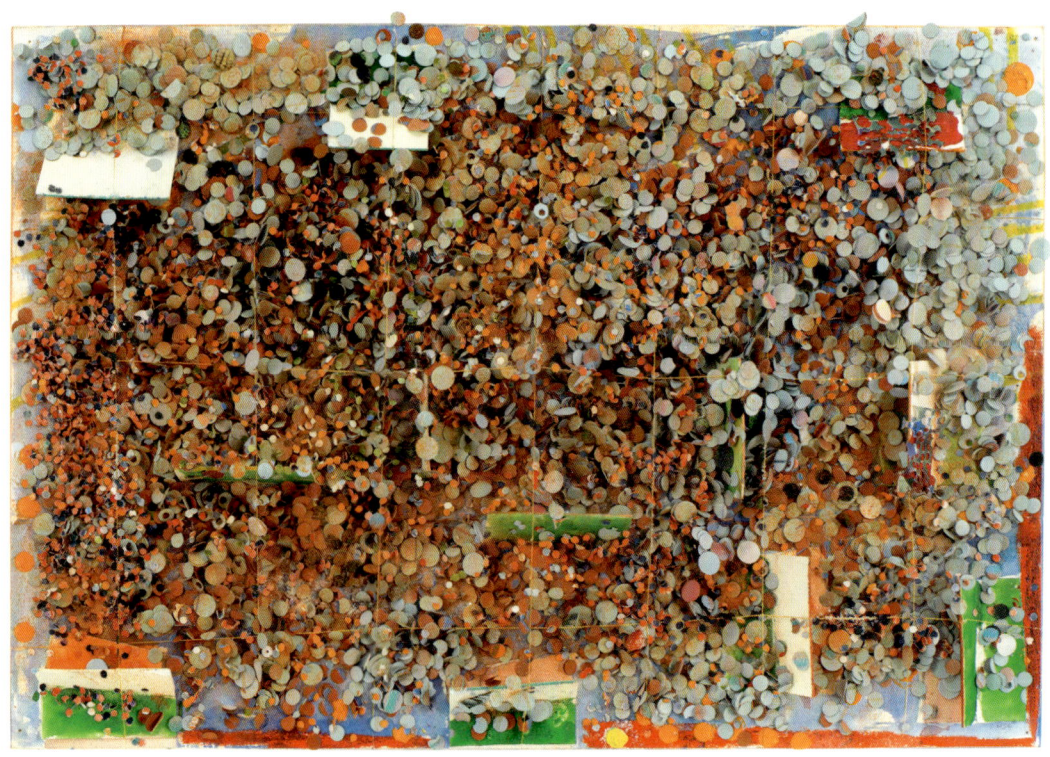

UNTITLED #84

1977, mixed-media collage on board, 31.8 × 45.7 cm (12 ½ × 18 in), private collection
Howardena Pindell, born 1943, Philadelphia.

Acts of destruction and reconstruction are central to Pindell's
mixed-media paintings and collages. Her art takes inspiration from
the loose, fluid forms and irregular shapes associated with African
textiles, which she encountered during a trip to the continent in 1973
and also shortly beforehand, when New York's Museum of Modern
Art exhibited its collection of Akan batakari tunics. At this time, she
was a founding member of A.I.R., the first American gallery to
be dedicated to women artists. A car accident in 1979 caused Pindell
severe memory loss, after which her work took an autobiographical turn. In the 1980s, she tackled political themes, creating collages
about social injustice, war, racism, AIDS and sexism. However,
abstraction is the mainstay of her practice. Spray-painting different
colours onto sheets of paper, Pindell then punches holes in them using
an office hole punch. The confetti-like dots are scattered onto
painted boards, creating richly textured yet delicate abstract surfaces,
as seen in the dense layers of this collage. As with many of her
works from this period, a fragile grid of thread overlays the sculptural
mass of circles, hinting at order amid chaos.

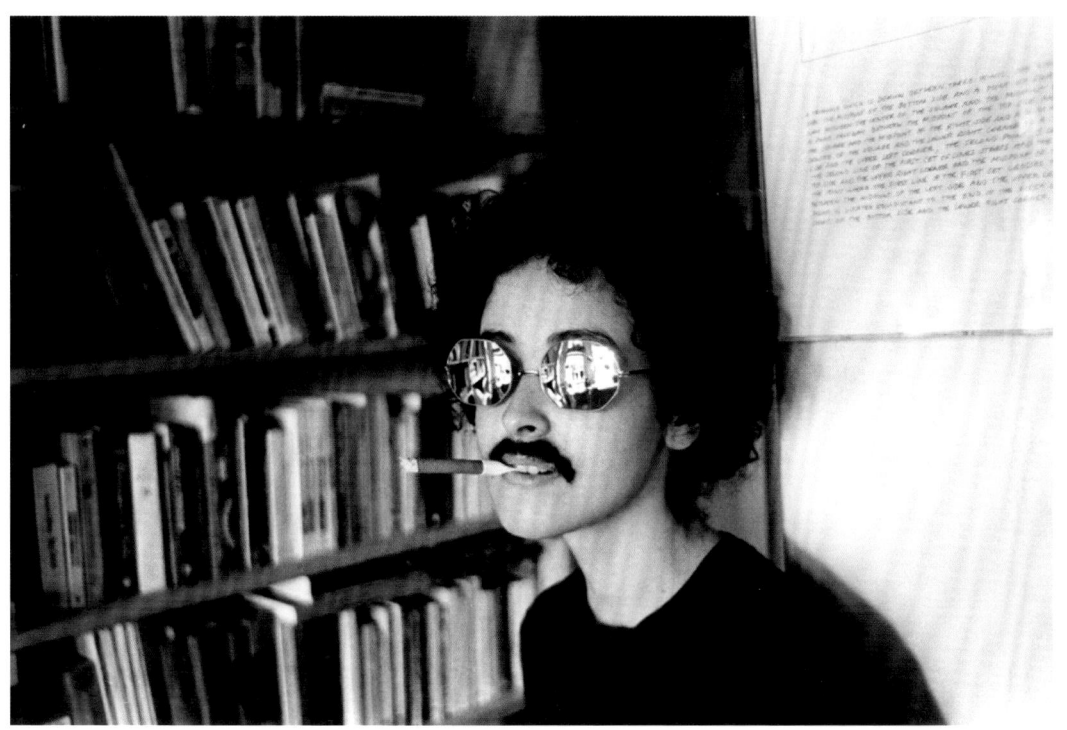

THE MYTHIC BEING: SOL'S DRAWING

1974, series of 5 gelatin silver prints (vintage photographs), 25.4 × 20.3 cm
(10 × 8 in), photograph #2 of 5
Adrian Piper, born 1948, New York.

As well as being an acclaimed artist, Piper is a philosopher with a doctorate from Harvard University. She has described her philosophical work as the 'theory' that her artworks – which span a range of media, from early figurative self-portraits and Minimalist grid drawings to later video and performance – put into 'practice'. In 1967 she met conceptual artist Sol LeWitt (1928–2007), whose serial sculptures were a profound influence. Since the 1970s, Piper has herself pioneered a form of Conceptualism that confronts social and political realities – as in text works, street performances and installations that bring up questions of race and gender identity, and notions of the 'outsider'. This is seen in her 'Mythic Being' performance series (1973–5), in which Piper, who is mixed race, dressed up as an African-American man, evoking issues and stereotypes around black, masculine aggression. Since 2005, Piper has lived in self-imposed exile from the United States in Berlin, and when in 2018 she was the subject of a major retrospective at the Museum of Modern Art in New York, she chose not to attend.

LIUBOV POPOVA

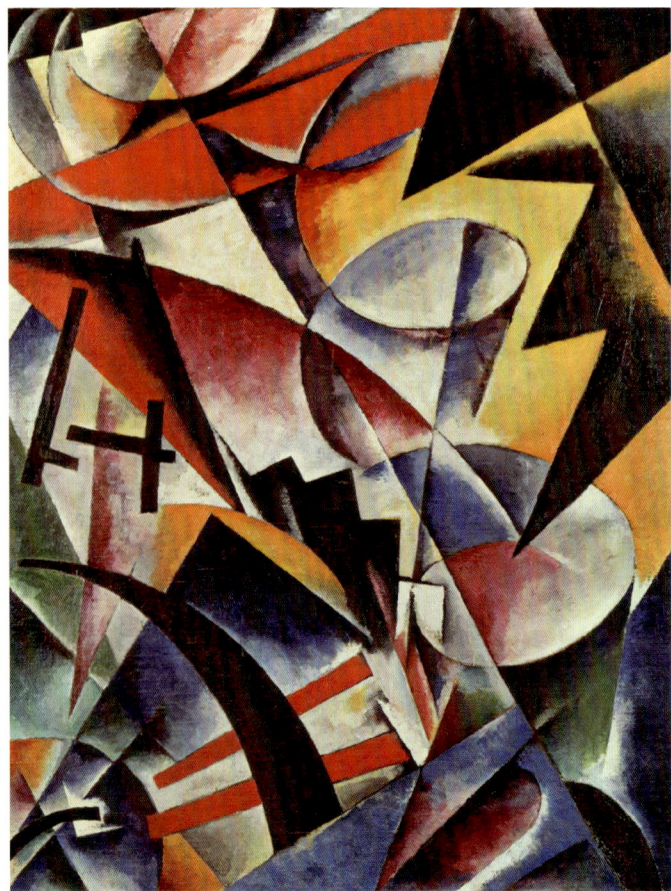

PAINTERLY CONSTRUCTION
1920, oil on canvas, 159 × 125 cm (62 ⅝ × 49 ¼ in), State Tretyakov Gallery, Moscow
Liubov Popova, born 1889, Moscow. Died 1924, Moscow.

Born into a wealthy family, Popova was surrounded by patrons of the arts. Aged eighteen, she studied with members of the romantic and revivalist Mir Iskusstva art movement. Although her work appeared quintessentially modern, it always revealed a rich complexity, drawing on the eclectic, even contradictory, styles that shaped the artist, from the Italian Renaissance to Russian icon painting together with the influence of the burgeoning Russian avant-garde. In the last years before the First World War, she worked alongside Vladimir Tatlin (1885–1953), and then travelled to Paris and Italy, where she was influenced by Futurism, a movement inspired by the

era's headlong rush into a new and uncertain mechanized state of being. This style is expressed in the work seen here in its angular, raucously overlapping shapes. Equally, it reflects the desire to free art from the material world, the manifesto of the Suprematist group to which Popova belonged with Alexandra Exter (p.133) and Kazimir Malevich (1879–1935). However the singular resonance of Popova's canvas derives from its hybrid nature, and the artist's reluctance to subscribe wholly to any one ethos.

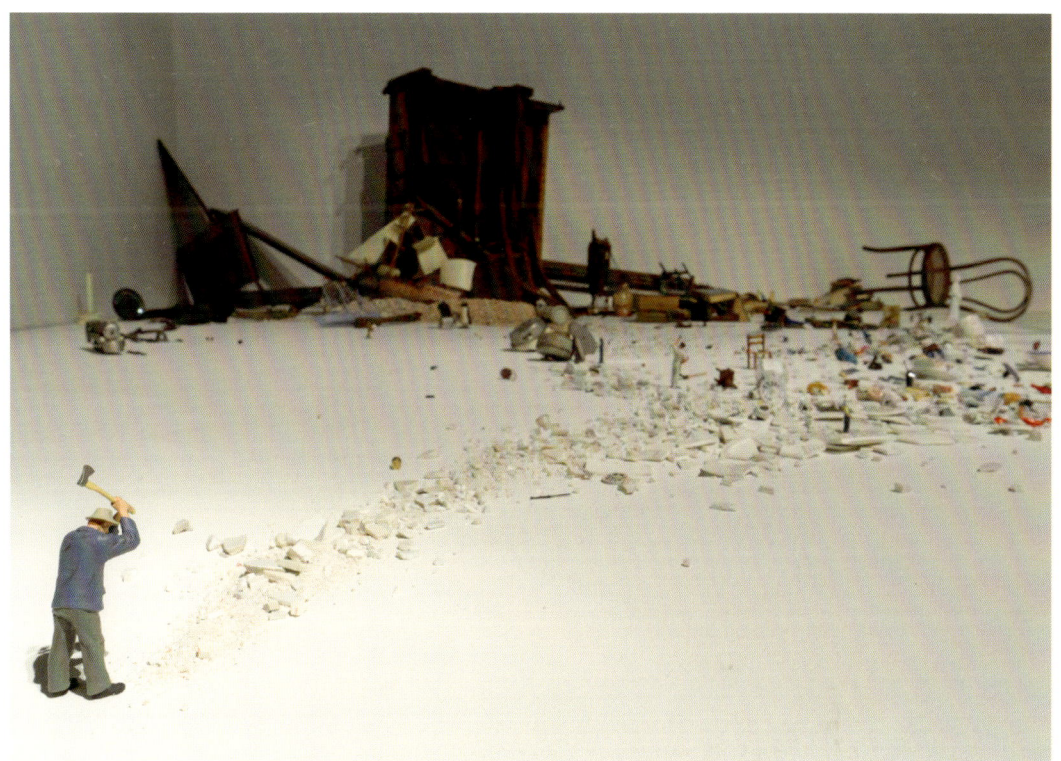

MAN WITH AXE

2017, figurines, objects and wooden base, 10 × 7 m (33 × 23 ft), installation view, 'Viva Arte Viva', 57th Venice Biennale. Collection Pérez Art Museum Miami
Liliana Porter, born 1941, Buenos Aires.

After attending the Universidad Iberoamericana in Mexico City, Porter moved to New York in 1964, where she co-founded the New York Graphic Workshop, a place that fostered a conceptually invested and culturally resonant approach to printmaking. In 2018, Porter's retrospective 'Other Situations', at El Museo del Barrio in New York, celebrated her wider contributions to sculpture, photography and public art. An example of the latter is *Alice: The Way Out* (1994), a mural in a Manhattan subway station that depicts characters from Lewis Carroll's *Alice in Wonderland* (1865). Its silhouettes have a graphic quality that evokes the fantastical narrative. This sense of playfulness is also evident in this installation, part of Porter's 'Trabajo Forzado' ('Forced Labour') series, begun in the 1990s, of tiny figurines placed on wooden shelves. *Man with Axe* finds a miniscule protagonist seemingly hell-bent on destruction, leaving in his wake a trail of dramatically demolished furniture, plates, trinkets and even a piano. With nods to Pop art and Arte Povera, a classical sculptural concern of scale is combined with a cryptic but humorous reflection on the individual's capacity for struggle and revolt.

HARRIET POWERS

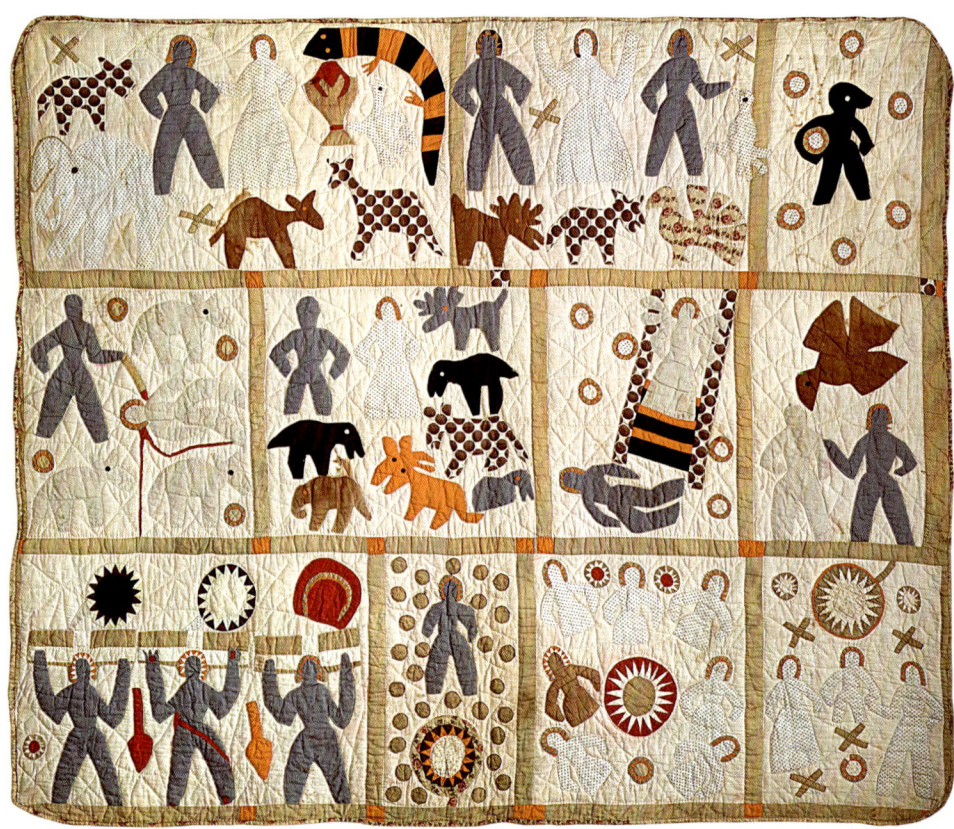

BIBLE QUILT

1885–6, cotton, 191 × 227 cm (75 × 89 in), The National Museum of American History, Washington DC

Harriet Powers, born 1837, Clarke County, Georgia. Died 1910, Clarke County, Georgia.

Born into slavery, Powers used appliqué methods to depict a range of themes, from biblical stories to astronomical phenomena. She spent her early life on a plantation, learning her craft either from other slaves or her mistress. Marrying at the age of eighteen, Powers had nine children and in the 1870 census is listed as 'keeping house'. Only two quilts made by her are known to have survived: this example, and the later *Pictorial Quilt* (1898), though it is not uncommon for quilts – long considered as craft rather than art – to have lost the name of their maker. *Bible Quilt* was first shown at the 1886 Athens Cotton Fair in Georgia, where it was seen by Jennie Smith, a local artist and teacher, who was drawn to the bold design and naivete of expression. She offered to buy it, but it was told it was not for sale. A few years later, when faced with financial difficulties, Powers agreed to sell it for five dollars. Smith was able to record the artist's explanation of its iconography, its eleven panels including Adam and Eve in the Garden of Eden, Cain killing Abel, Jacob's ladder, Christ's crucifixion, and the Last Supper. Some scholars have connected its designs with those found in Dahomey in West Africa, thus making it a symbol of cultural endurance.

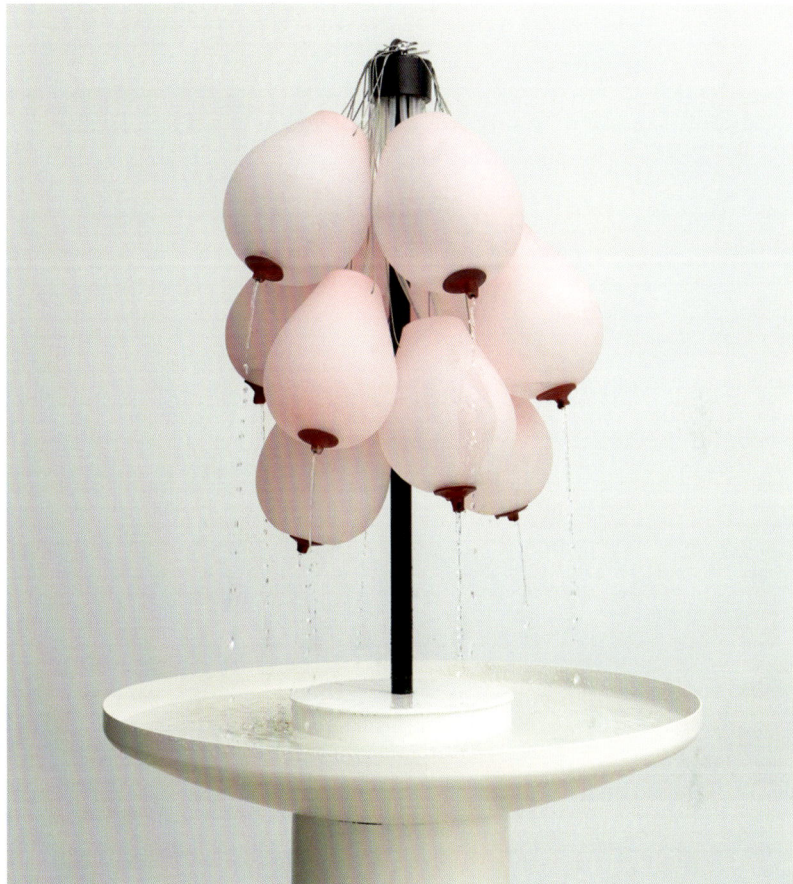

WE WILL FEED YOU, COOLING FOUNTAIN (FOR GLOBAL WARMING)
2018, painted metal, pump, blown glass, plastic tubes, aircraft cable, water,
183 × 75.8 × 75.8 cm (72 × 29 ⅞ × 29 ⅞ in)
Laure Prouvost, born 1978, Croix, France.

After growing up in France, Prouvost moved to London to continue her education, studying film at Central Saint Martins and
towards an MFA at Goldsmiths College. During this time, she was
studio assistant to the artist John Latham (1921–2006), who she
described as being like a conceptual grandfather. Her film *The Artist*
(2010) is, in part, a homage to him. Unsettling the connection
between language and understanding, Prouvost's multimedia practice integrates real and imagined memories, as well as making
reference to different artistic and literary modes, in order to merge
fiction and reality. She has gained major awards, first winning the
Max Mara Art Prize for Women (2011), and then the Turner Prize
(2013) for *Wantee*, an install-ation and film dedicated to her own
grandfather, who was a friend of Dadaist artist Kurt Schwitters (1887–
1948). The work shown here is a functional fountain that delivers
water into a basin. When it was first exhibited, the water contained
live goldfish and two submerged mobile phones. The piece relates
to a similar fountain she later created for her 2018 solo exhibition
'Ring, Sing and Drink for Trespassing' at Palais de Tokyo, Paris.
Prouvost was selected to represent France at the 58th Venice Biennale
in 2019.

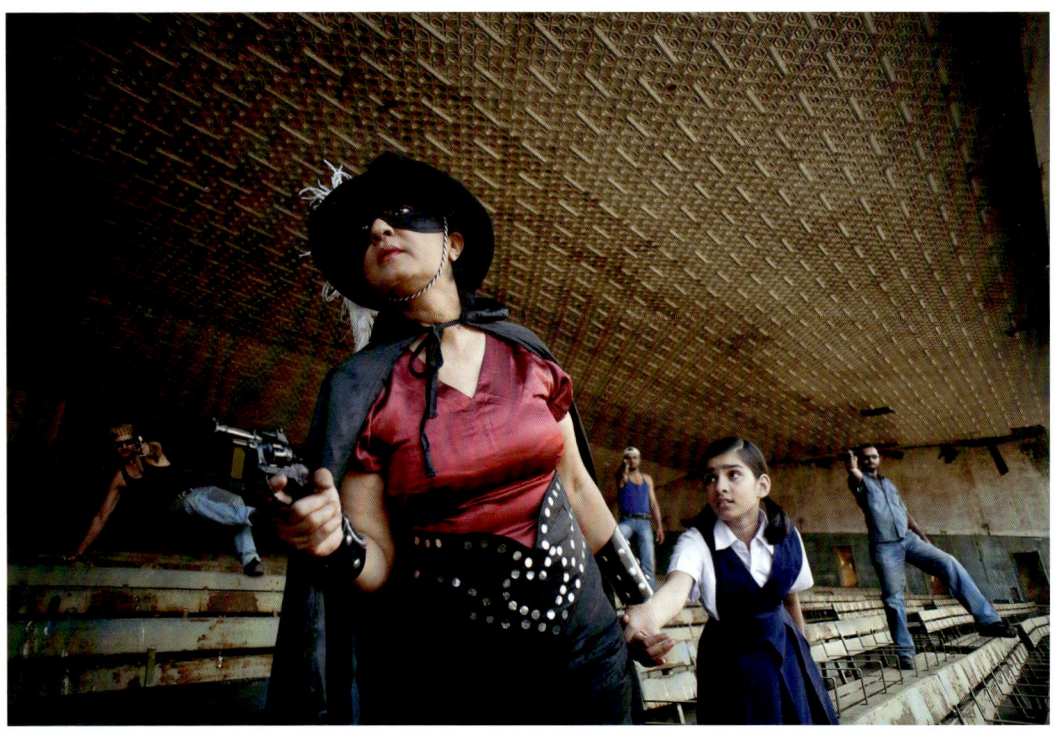

RETURN OF THE PHANTOM LADY (SINFUL CITY)

2012, 1 of 21 colour photographs, archival inkjet prints, each 50.8 × 76.2 cm
(20 × 30 in)
Pushpamala N, born 1956, Bangalore (now Bengaluru), India.

With wit, humour and theatricality, Pushpamala N's photographic
work presents a feminist critique of contemporary India. Taking
the visual representation of women as a central theme, she mixes elements of popular culture with film history, Hindu mythology and
aspects of India's colonial past. Beginning her career as a sculptor, she
addressed her heritage using simple materials such as terracotta
and papier-mâché. Moving away from figurative sculpture to narrative-led photography and video, she has since become one of India's
foremost female artists. Pushpamala N regularly casts herself
as archetypal female characters drawn from modern and historical
sources, including heroines, mothers, femme fatales and sages,
among others, her practice sometimes compared to that of Cindy
Sherman (p.371). In the twenty-one-part photo-romance 'Return
of the Phantom Lady (Sinful City)', she plays the titular masked hero
based on Indian actress and stunt-woman 'Fearless Nadia', the star
of *Hunterwali* (1935), one of the earliest Indian female-led films. Set
amid the historic buildings and markets of Mumbai, Pushpamala
N's upbeat work celebrates the notion of the female hero, following
the protagonist's daring mission to rescue an orphaned girl from
armed gangsters.

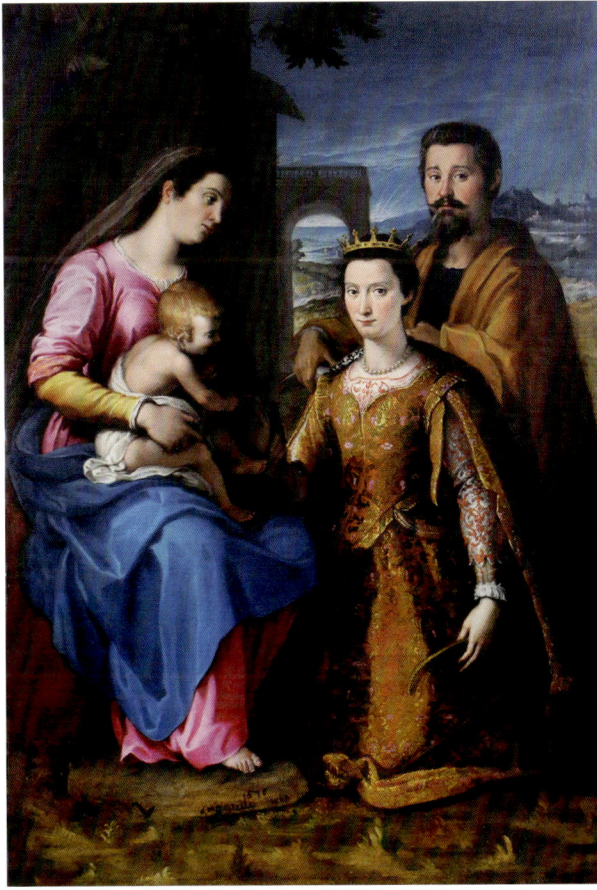

THE MYSTICAL MARRIAGE OF SAINT CATHERINE

1576, oil on canvas, 180 × 122 cm (70 ⅞ × 48 in), Church of Santa Maria e
San Pietro, Silvano Pietra, Italy
Lucrezia Quistelli della Mirandola, born 1541, Florence. Died 1594,
probably in Florence.

While many sixteenth-century women artists were trained by their
fathers, Quistelli's noble parents sent her, to complement her education in the liberal arts, to the studio of Alessandro Allori (1535–1607),
a former student of the Mannerist painter Bronzino (1503–72).
Plautilla Nelli (p.296) had earlier trained a number of women painters in Florence, which set a precedent for Quistelli's artistic development outside the family home. Her endeavours were further
supported by her husband, Count Clemente Pietra, with whom she

circulated in Florence's upper social circles including at the Medici
court. This painting, made for an altarpiece in her husband's home
town, depicts Saint Catherine kneeling before the Christ-child and
his mother while staring resolutely at the viewer. According to thir-
teenth-century accounts, Catherine was martyred by the Roman
Emperor Maxentius, having refused his hand in marriage owing to
her singular devotion to Jesus. This scene illustrates a vision that the
saint was said to have received, in which a wedding ring is placed onto
her finger by the infant Christ. The apostle and saint are thought to
be portraits of Count Alfonso Pietra and his wife Fausta Visconti.

CAROL RAMA

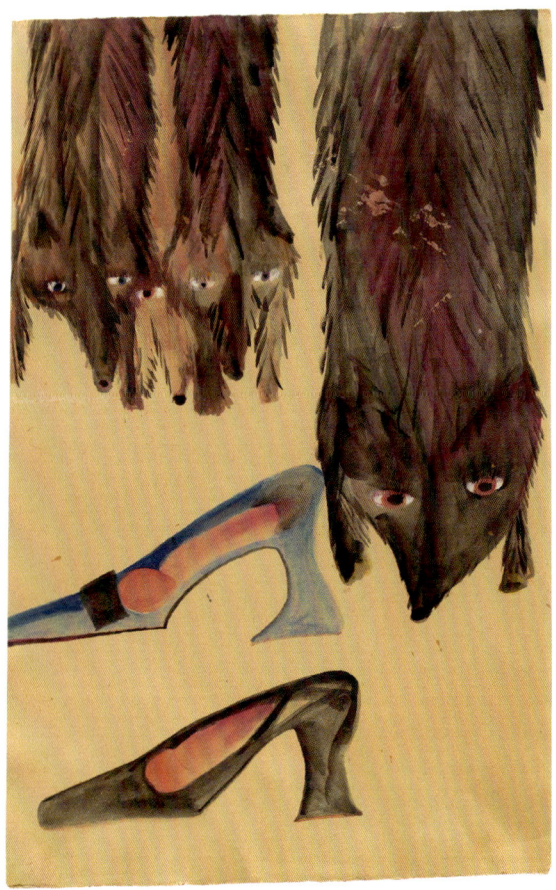

WORK NO.11 (FOXES)

1938, watercolour on paper, 71.8 × 46.7 cm (28 ¼ × 18 ⅜ in), Museum of Modern Art, New York

Carol Rama, born 1918, Turin, Italy. Died 2015, Turin, Italy.

Growing up in Fascist-era Italy, Rama lost her father, a bicycle maker, to suicide, while her mother was institutionalized in a psychiatric clinic when she was fifteen. Self-taught, Rama described art as her cure: 'We all have our own tropical disease within us … My remedy is painting.' Her major series 'Appassionata' is partly based on her mother's experience. Unnerving imagery characterizes her work – for example, figures with distinctive pointed tongues – together with an unsettling eroticism hinted at in this early painting. Rama first exhibited her watercolours at Turin's Galleria Faber in 1945; with its depiction of disembodied limbs, exposed genitals and scatological motifs, the show was closed by police on grounds of indecency. Sidestepping figuration in favour of geometric abstraction in the following decade, she gradually turned to bricolage, incorporating unusual materials such as rice, seeds, claws, medical equipment and, in particular, bicycle inner tubes. From the 1980s, Rama returned to her love of figuration, her erotic watercolours and pen-and-ink drawings drawing on mythology. In 2003, she was recognized with the Golden Lion for Lifetime Achievement at the 50th Venice Biennale.

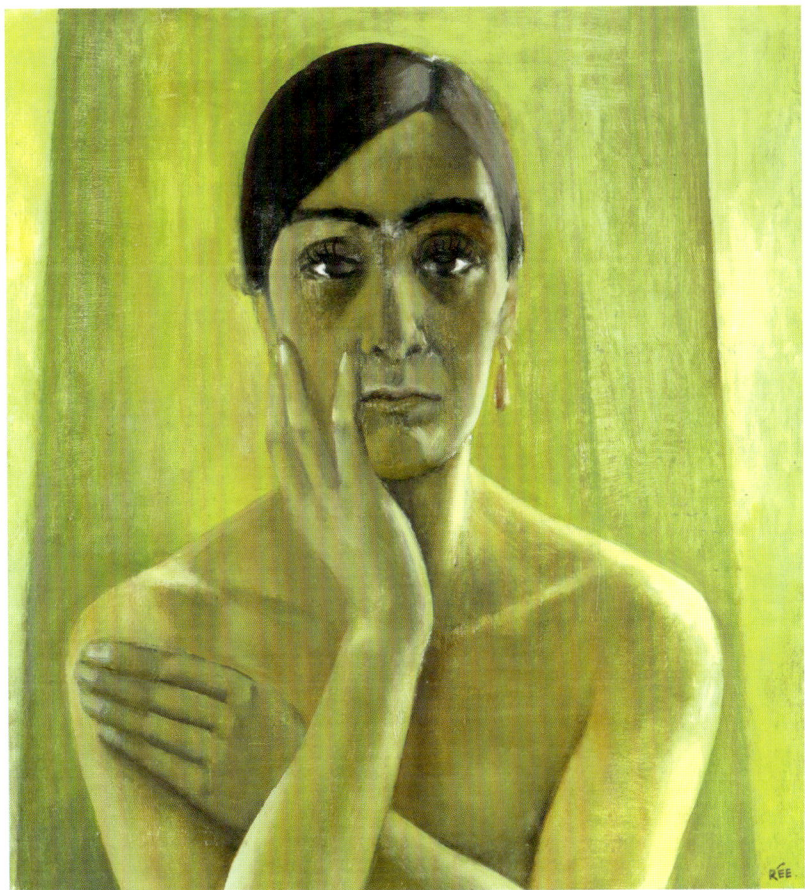

SELF-PORTRAIT

1930, oil on canvas, 66 × 60.8 cm (26 × 23 ⅞ in), Hamburger Kunsthalle, Hamburg, Germany

Anita Rée, born 1885, Hamburg, Germany. Died 1933, Kampen (Sylt), Germany.

A leading artist in Hamburg during the Weimar period (1919–33), Rée had trained privately from 1904 as women were not admitted to art academies in the Hanseatic city. Doubting her own abilities, she received encouragement from Germany's leading Impressionist painter, Max Liebermann (1847–1935). Rée spent the winter of 1912–13 in Paris, acquainting herself with both historical and contemporary art. On her return to Germany, she experimented with different styles, chiefly inspired by Paul Cézanne (1839–1906) and Paula Modersohn-Becker (p.279). Living on Italy's Amalfi coast in the 1920s, her style shifted to *Neue Sachlichkeit* ('New Objectivity'). In 1926, back in Hamburg, she helped found GEDOK, an association of women artists. As with much of Rée's art, this self-portrait questions her own identity – Lutheran by upbringing, Jewish by birth and of German and Venezuelan heritage. In 1932 a commission for a church altarpiece was withdrawn when she was denounced as a Jew by local Nazis, factors that contributed to her suicide. Later, her work was declared 'degenerate', but a number of her paintings were saved by a caretaker at the Hamburg Kunsthalle.

PAULA REGO

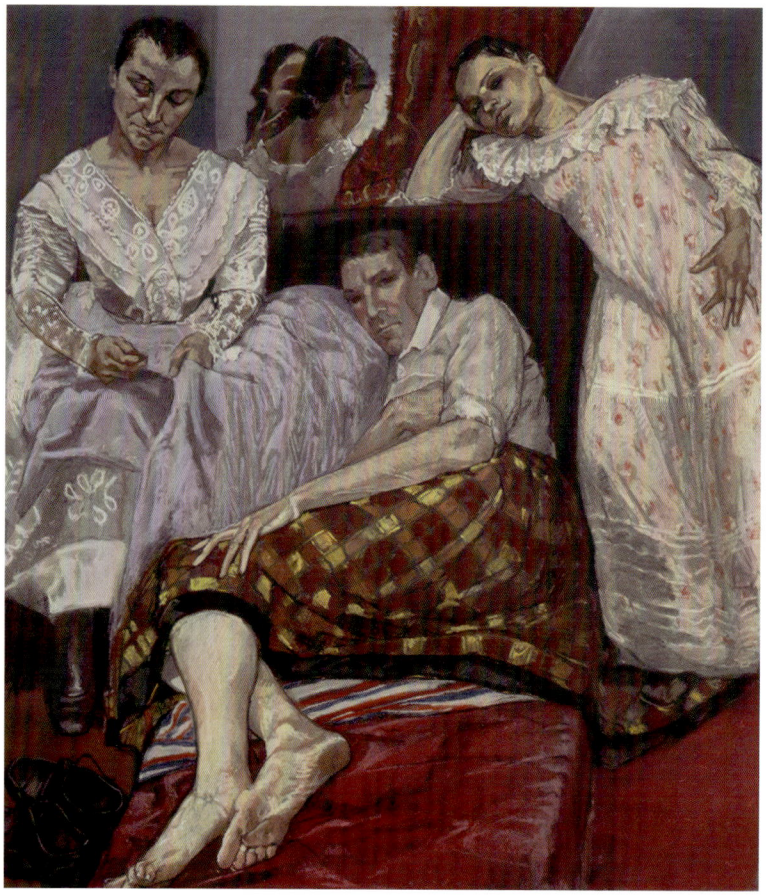

THE COMPANY OF WOMEN

1997, pastel on paper mounted on aluminium, 170 × 130 cm (66 ⅞ × 51 ⅛ in),
Casa das Histórias Paula Rego, Cascais, Portugal
Paula Rego, born 1935, Lisbon. Died 2022, London.

Rego's art focuses on what she has frequently referred to as 'the beautiful grotesque'. As a child she was enthralled by the thrilling and ferocious Portuguese folk tales told by her grandmother, and countless other stories have fed her imagination and art ever since. Women are the subjects of many of her paintings, drawings and prints, and often concern traumatic themes such as illegal abortion, female circumcision and sex trafficking. Studying at London's Slade School of Art alongside David Hockney (b.1937) and Frank Auerbach (1931–2024), she was one of the few females associated with the London Group. Continuing to live in London, in 1990 she became the first Associate Artist at the National Gallery. In her native Portugal she was honoured with a museum dedicated to her work, the 'House of Stories'. This large-scale pastel reimagines an episode from *The Sin of Father Amaro* (1875), a novel by the nineteenth-century Portuguese writer José Maria de Eça de Queirós. Here, in a scene that prefigures a clandestine and ultimately tragic affair between a young priest and his landlady's daughter, the nine-year-old Amaro is pictured as a man-child: pampered, dolled-up and indulged by doting nursery maids.

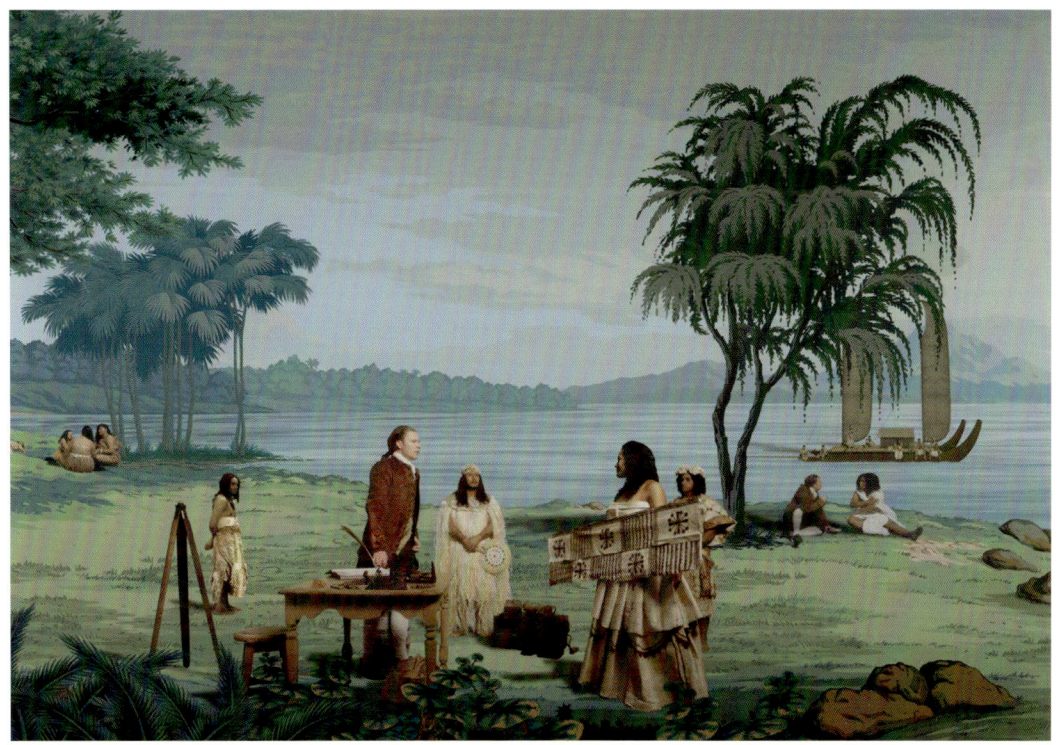

IN PURSUIT OF VENUS [INFECTED]

2015–17, (detail/video still), single-channel video, Ultra HD, colour, 7.1 sound, 64 mins, Auckland Art Gallery/Toi o Tāmaki, New Zealand/Aotearoa Lisa Reihana, born 1964, Auckland/Tāmaki, New Zealand/Aotearoa.

Reihana is a multidisciplinary artist of Māori (Ngā Puhi) descent, based in Auckland. She is known for creating digital animations that explore indigenous and colonial histories, gender and representation. Earlier works draw on Māori designs, considering their presentation in museum collections for instance, and using them to question stereotypes past and present. Presented when Reihana represented New Zealand at the 57th Venice Biennale in 2017, *In Pursuit of Venus* is an epic panoramic video many years in the making. It restages and animates a Western design – the multi-panel scenic wallpaper

Les Sauvages de la Mer Pacifique, manufactured in early-nineteenth-century France by Joseph Dufour as decoration for wealthy European homes. Inspired by Captain Cook's voyages to the Pacific, the wallpaper was a fictionalized and exoticized interpretation of his encounters. Reihana complicates the wallpaper both formally and conceptually, bringing static images to life and doing so from an indigenous perspective. The title refers to Cook's mission to reach Tahiti in order to record the transit of Venus, a rare astronomical phenomenon. It also alludes to the selfish desires that fuelled the colonial enterprise, as well as to a frequent mythological theme in historical art.

LILI REYNAUD-DEWAR

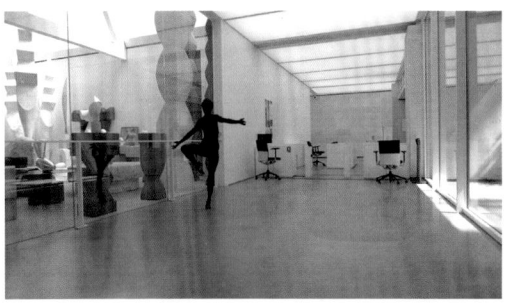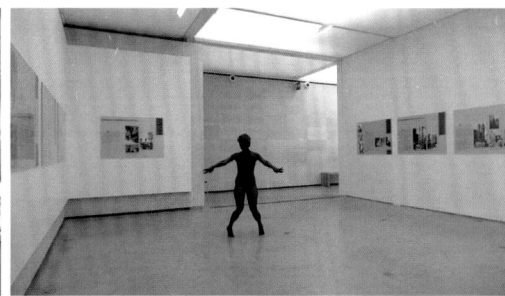
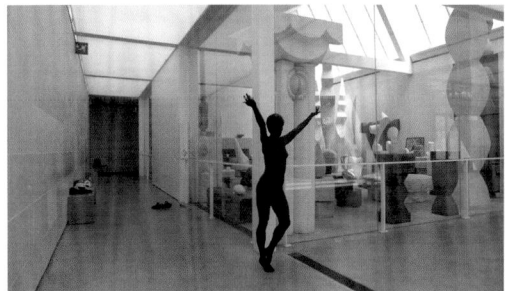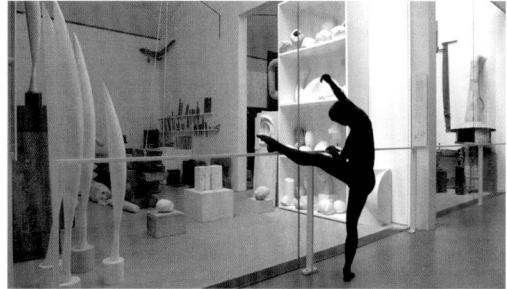
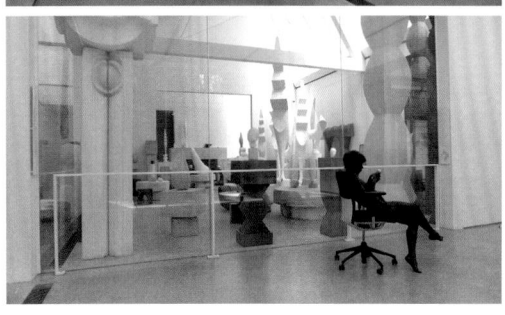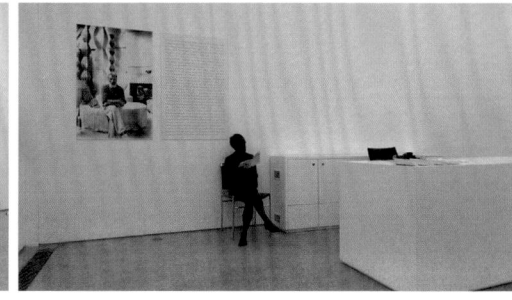

LIVE THROUGH THAT?! (ATELIER BRANCUSI)

2014, black-and-white video, silent, 7 mins 35 secs
Lili Reynaud-Dewar, born 1975, La Rochelle, France.

Reynaud-Dewar creates installations and performances that explore transgression and the blurring of boundaries between biography and fiction. Previously a law student and trained as a classical dancer, she studied art criticism at Glasgow School of Art, graduating in 2003. Her work has been included in major international exhibitions including the 12th Lyon Biennale (2013) and 56th Venice Biennale (2015). Inspired by novelist Jean Genet, film director Rainer Werner Fassbinder and writer/filmmaker Marguerite Duras, Reynaud-Dewar mixes text, film and sculpture to examine the possibilities of mediation across different art forms. *Live Through That?!* is the title

of multiple videos shot in museums after hours. In this example, she is in the reconstructed studio of Constantin Brancusi (1876–1957) at Centre Georges Pompidou, Paris. Appearing naked and in black body paint – a deliberately provocative strategy – Reynaud-Dewar performs choreography by the 1920s African-American French cabaret star Josephine Baker, then enacts everyday actions such as smoking and reading. Taking its title from an essay by contemporary American poet and writer Eileen Myles, the video focuses attention on how institutions control public access to art, and suggests how one might revolt in such spaces.

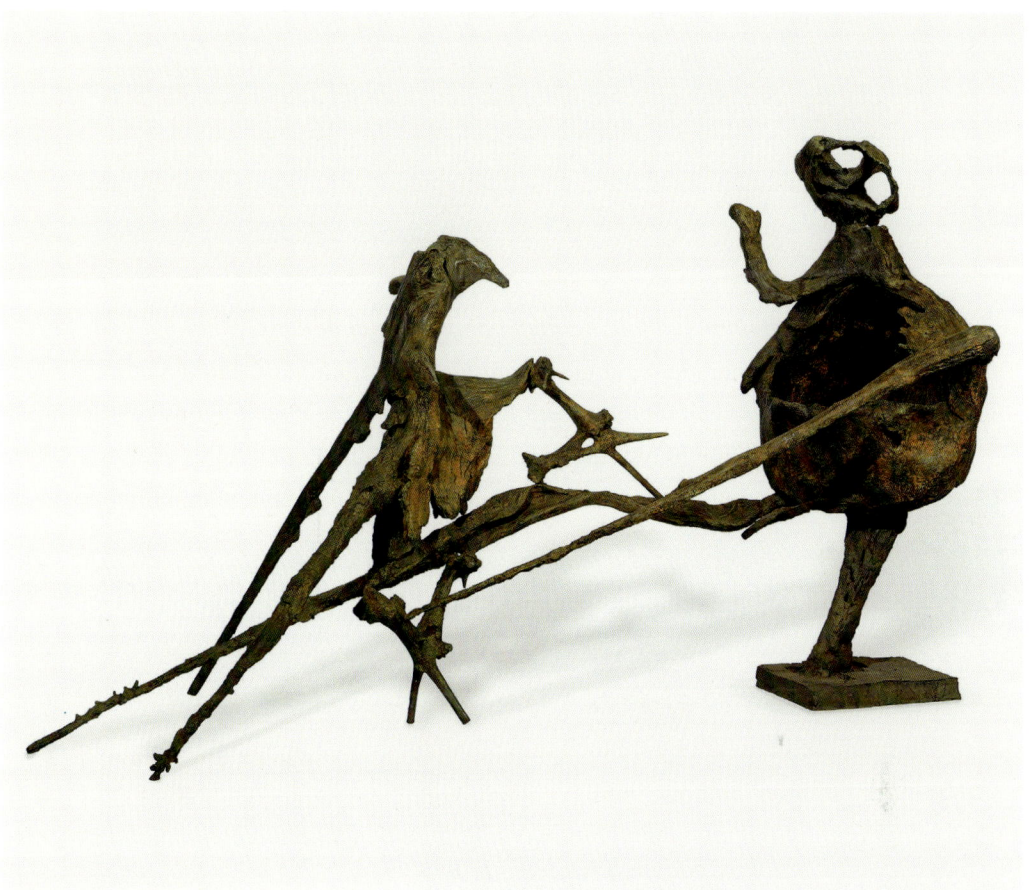

THE MOUNTAIN

1955–6, patinated bronze, 185 × 330 × 130 cm (72 ¾ × 129 ⅞ × 51 ⅛ in),
private collection

Germaine Richier, born 1902, Grans, France. Died 1959, Montpellier, France.

Richier was taught by the Neo-Classical French sculptor Antoine Bourdelle (1861–1929). This prolific teacher, who had earlier trained Vera Mukhina (p.291) and Maria Helena Vieira da Silva (p.417), influenced a diverse generation of sculptors, a student contemporary of Richier's being the Swiss artist Alberto Giacometti (1901–66). Active in interwar Paris, she was documented in her studio by the photographer Brassaï (1899–1984) and exhibited alongside some of the most recognizable names of twentieth-century art, including Georges Braque (1882–1963), Marc Chagall (1887–1985)

and Jean (Hans) Arp (1886–1966). Unlike her male contemporaries, her name fell into obscurity following her death. Sometimes compared to Giacometti, with whom she was acquainted but not close, Richier's bronzes bear the marks of an intense, heavily worked process. Yet she was more interested in the hybrid than the human, with animal, insect and vegetal forms lending her sculptures fantastical and mythological traits. In this her final work, a fragmented figure bears signs of multiple injury while a bird-like creature comes at it with what could be a spear. There is possibly also humour to this violence, the fight between these characters almost cartoon-like.

BRIDGET RILEY

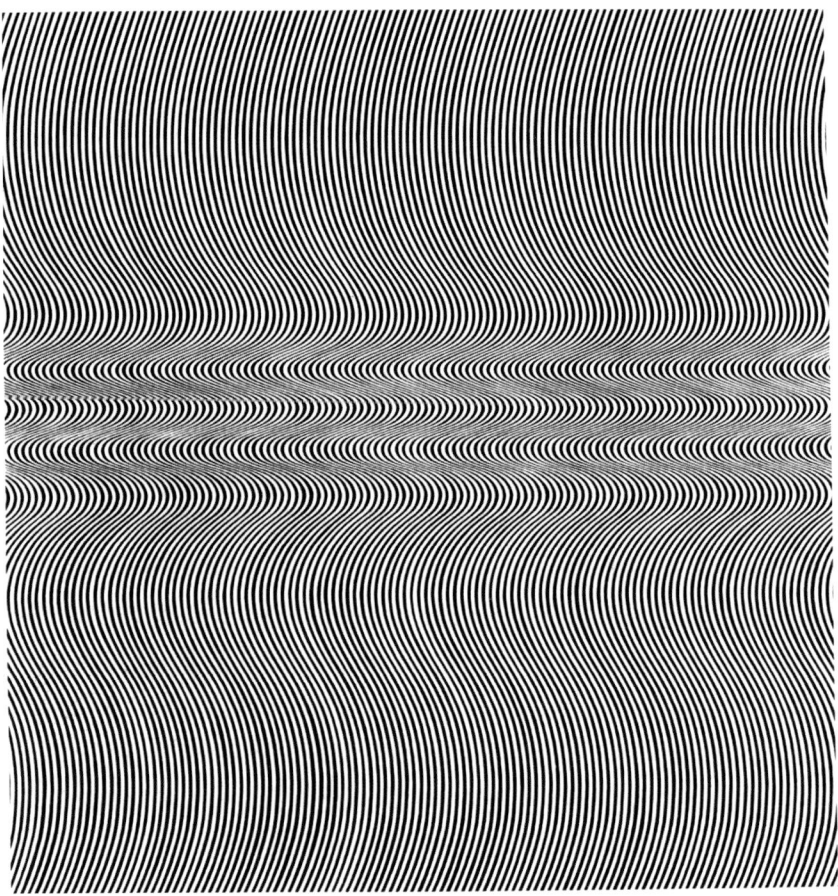

CURRENT

1964, emulsion on hardboard, 148.1 × 149.1 cm (58 ⅜ × 58 ¾ in),
Museum of Modern Art, New York
Bridget Riley, born 1931, London.

Living in Cornwall as a child during the Second World War, Riley's
family included an aunt who had studied art at Goldsmiths College
in London. Riley went to study drawing at the same institution,
followed by a further period at the Royal College of Art from 1952
to 1955. By the following decade, Riley had become one of the most
prominent members of the international Op art movement of the
early 1960s – using squares, circles and lines as units, in such a way
that they seem to be jumping, flashing and curving. Although some
critics at the time described vertigo, migraine and general uneasi-

ness in response to her images, others saw this disturbing element
to symbolize an interplay between feelings of anxiety and composure.
Riley initially worked in black and white, introducing colour to her
practice in 1966. In this iconic painting, *Current*, the influence of her
time spent on the Cornish coast is evident, the curves appearing
to respond to the force of the sea, emulating the tides. Although the
artist only uses black and white, various shades of colour seem
to appear by looking attentively at the painting for some time.

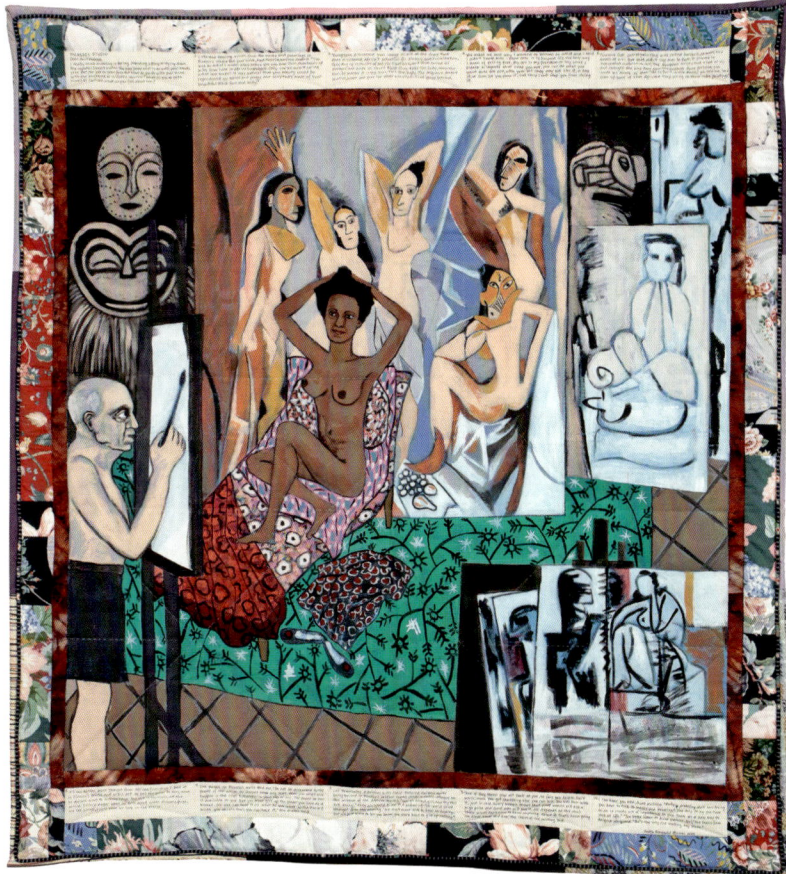

PICASSO'S STUDIO

1991, acrylic on canvas, printed and tie-dyed fabric, 185.4 × 172.7 cm (73 × 68 in),
Worcester Art Museum, Massachusetts
Faith Ringgold, born Faith Jones, 1930, New York. Died 2024,
Englewood, New Jersey.

As a young woman, Ringgold experienced the vibrancy of the recent Harlem Renaissance, a confident blooming of African-American culture. Sexism hampered her education: the City College School of Liberal Arts refused to admit women to major in fine art so she studied art education instead. Her work encompasses paintings, murals and picture books and particularly textiles. She addressed overtly political themes with subjects ranging from Martin Luther King Jr. to gay-rights activist Marlon Riggs as well as scenes of a racially divided society. Her own activism saw her protest US militarism and male dominance of the art world in the 1960s. Open to a wide range of traditions, she first saw Tibetan *thangkas* – paintings on cloth with silk brocade frames – in 1972. Captivated by this ancient medium she incorporated it into her work, fabric narratives enclosing painted worlds. From 1980 she worked with appliqué – when she made her first 'story quilt', *Echoes of Harlem*, with her mother – she patched brightly coloured blankets as a ground for her figurative paintings and these often reflect her own history. In *Picasso's Studio* she employed imagery relating to one of modern art history's most famous paintings, emphasizing the often overlooked place of African culture within that story.

PIPILOTTI RIST

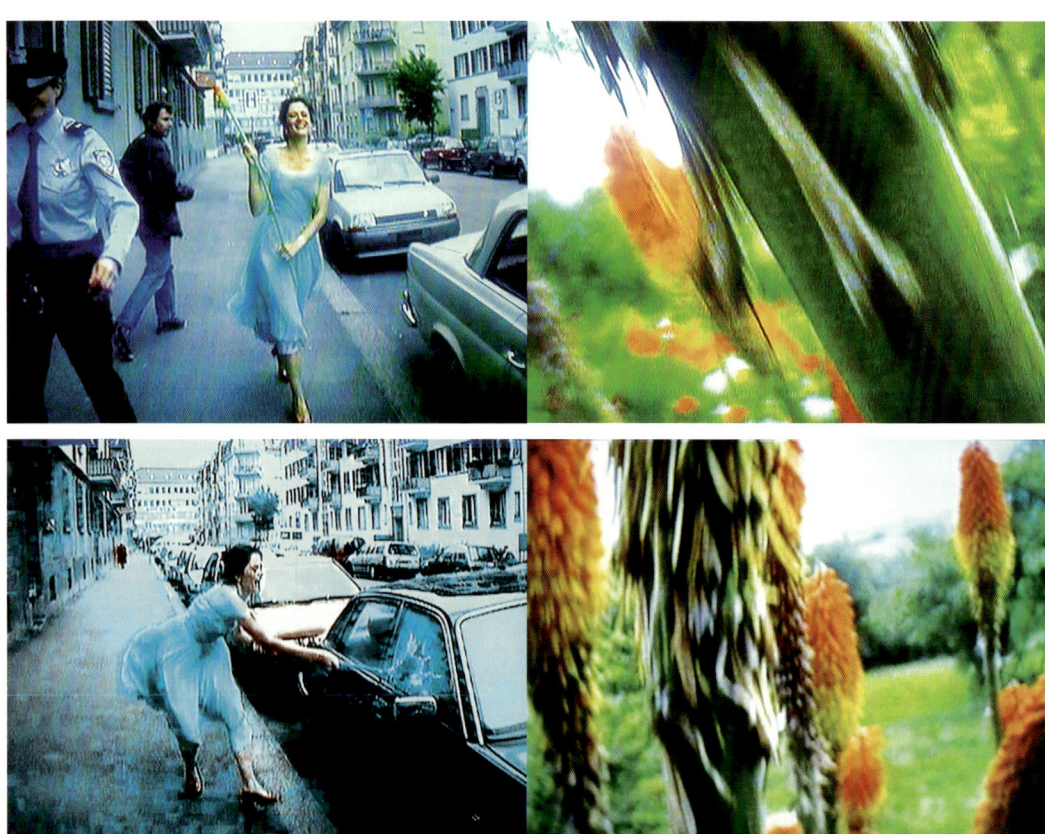

EVER IS OVER ALL

1997, 2-channel video with overlapping projections, colour, sound,
(with Anders Guggisberg), 4 mins 7 secs, looped
Pipilotti Rist, born Elizabeth Rist, 1962, Grabs, Switzerland.

Rist is a pioneer of video art and a leading figure making audio-visual
installations. A combination of playfulness, irreverence and social
commentary characterizes her work. Her first video work, *I'm Not the
Girl Who Misses Much*, was produced in 1987 while she was studying
at the School of Design in Basel. Referencing pop music videos, she
filmed herself blurred, dancing in a black dress with her breasts
exposed, repeatedly singing the opening line from the 1968 Beatles
track *Happiness is a Warm Gun*. Typically of her work, soundtrack
and footage intermittently speed up and slow down, complemented
with glitches and lo-fi visual effects. In *Ever is Over All*, two channels
of video are presented at right angles: the right-hand projection
immerses the viewer in a field of red-hot-poker plants, while on the
adjacent wall, a young woman wearing a light blue dress walks in slow
motion down an urban street, holding what appears to be one of the
long-stemmed flowers. As she passes parked cars, she occasionally
smashes in their windows with what is actually a concealed weapon,
smiling as she goes while nature is enabled by anarchy to exact its
revenge on the industrialized world.

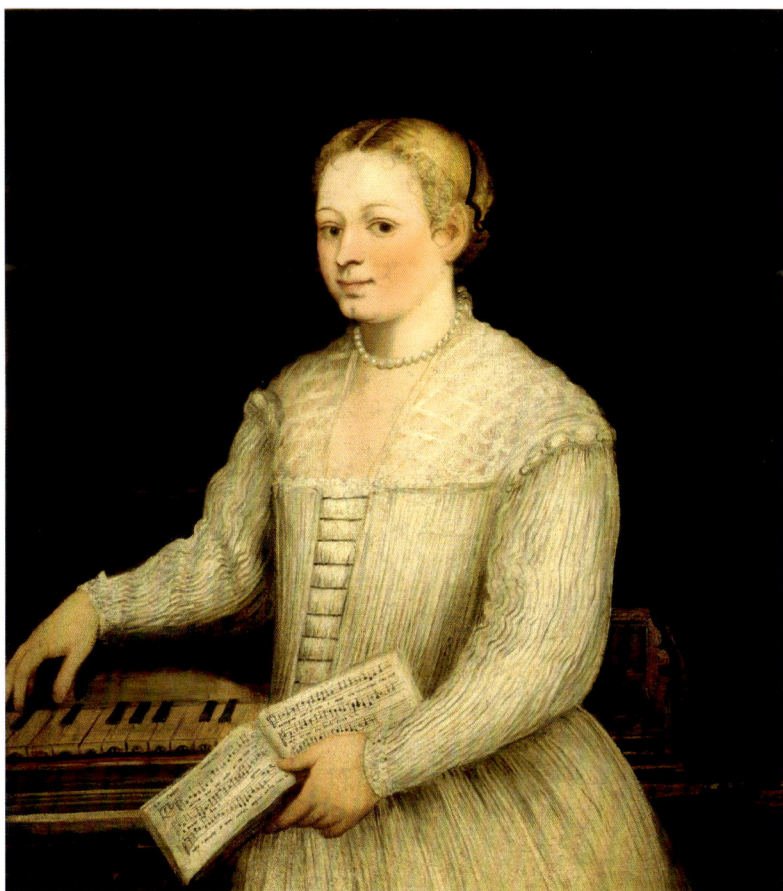

SELF-PORTRAIT

*c.*1580, oil on canvas, 93.5 × 91.5 cm (36 ¾ × 36 in), Galleria degli Uffizi, Florence
Marietta Robusti, born 1550–60, Venice. Died 1590, Venice.

The daughter of the Venetian Old Master Tintoretto (Jacopo Robusti, 1518–94), Robusti had her own nickname – 'La Tintoretta' – a sign of comparable esteem in which she was held by contemporaries. Her father had taught her to paint, dressing her as a boy so that she could accompany and assist on site with his monumental public commissions. Robusti was also an accomplished portraitist, sought after as a court painter by both Emperor Maximilian II and Philip II of Spain. However, her father denied her these opportunities in order to keep her home, eventually marrying her to a local jeweller with the provision in their wedding contract that she 'remain under the

paternal roof'. The artist died in childbirth, around the age of thirty. Her story is indicative of how few legal rights women had in sixteenth-century Venice – even those respected as professionals. Many paintings from her father's studio formerly regarded as his are now thought to be Marietta's, although this self-portrait is the only painting definitively attributed to her. In it, she stands before the keyboard of an instrument (probably a harpsichord) and holds sheet music of a madrigal, testifying to her additional musical as well as artistic talents.

LUISA ROLDÁN

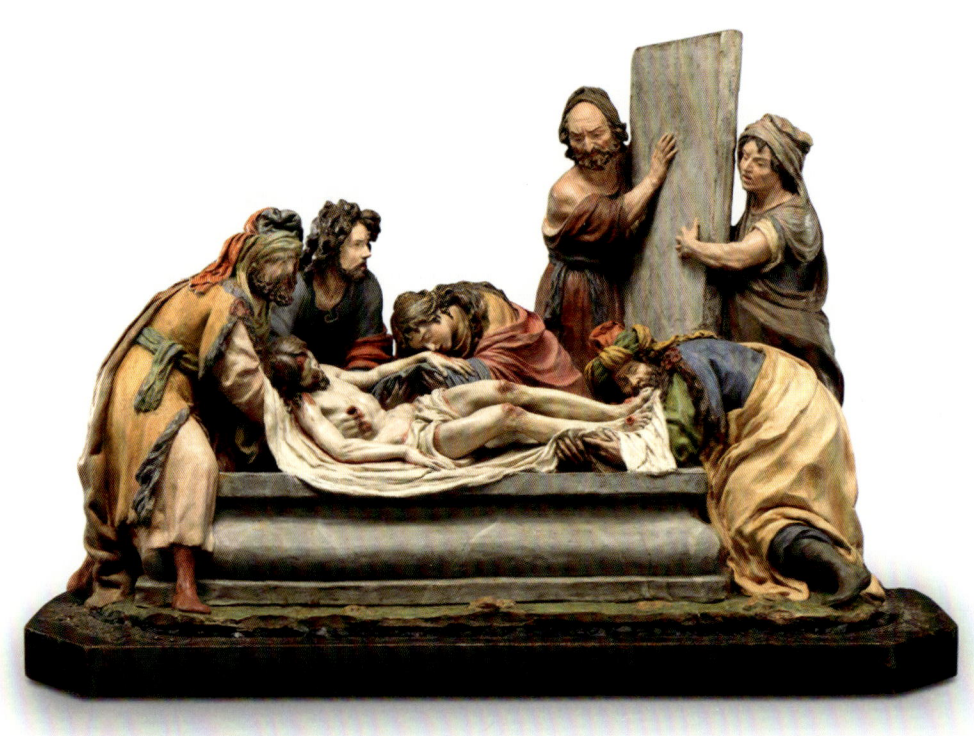

THE ENTOMBMENT OF CHRIST

1700–1, polychrome terracotta, 49.5 × 66 × 43.2 cm (19 ½ × 26 × 17 in),
Metropolitan Museum of Art, New York
Luisa Ignacia Roldán, born 1652, Seville, Spain. Died 1706, Madrid.

The first documented female sculptor in Spain, Roldán – also known as 'La Roldana' – was the daughter of the Sevillian Baroque sculptor Pedro Roldán (1624–99), who trained her before she married, against his will, and set up her own studio in Cádiz, southern Spain, with her husband Luis Antonio de los Arcos (1652–1711). Here she created painted wooden statues for the city's cathedral. After moving north to Madrid in 1688, she served the courts of Charles II and Philip V as 'sculptor of the bedchamber', although economic straits during Charles's reign forced her to appeal for adequate wages – she

was afflicted by poverty throughout her life. Roldán was also known for small-scale terracotta sculptures, this devotional work being one such object. Originally one of a pair of 'jewel-like sculptures' that the artist gave to Philip in 1701 as part of a petition for the renewal of her role at court, the tableau represents the dead, maimed Christ being lowered into his tomb, attended by five mourners. The figures retain the theatrical poses and staging of a painting, yet their intense expressions epitomize Roldán's grasp of psychological realism.

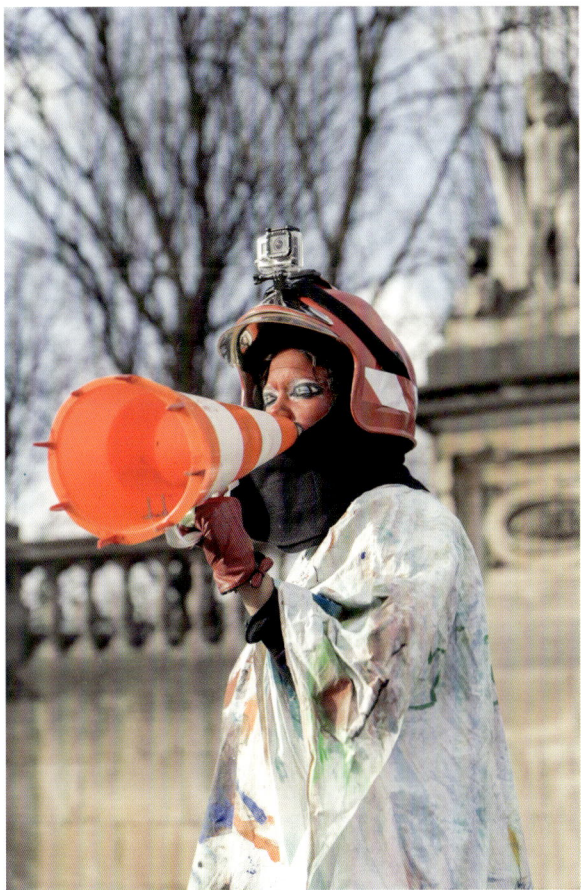

DIE WIT MAN (THE WHITE MAN)
2015, single-channel colour HD projection, stereo surround sound, 42 mins 40 secs
Tracey Rose, born 1974, Durban, South Africa.

Growing up in South Africa, Rose graduated from the University of the Witwatersrand, Johannesburg, in 1996. Making work relating to themes of gender and race, her prolific practice encompasses performance, video, photography and installations that are typically confrontational of difficult issues. After a period in early 2001 as artist-in-residence at the South African National Gallery, Cape Town, Rose's work was included later that year in Harald Szeemann's 'Plateau of Humankind' exhibition at the 49th Venice Biennale. The artist has used her own body in her work to investigate aspects of identity and stereotypes; performances have involved her completely shaving her body or plaiting her cut hair in ways evocative of contemplation or productive labour, but also of how hair was used as a racial marker in apartheid-era South Africa. The impact of colonialism in Africa is a recurrent theme, seen in this performance and video piece, staged by Rose in Brussels to highlight Belgium's brutal colonialist past in the Congo. Dressed like a shaman, with a painted face and robe, she repeatedly chanted the names of victims of Leopold II's genocidal project, before symbolically raising his ghost in order for him to face justice.

MARTHA ROSLER

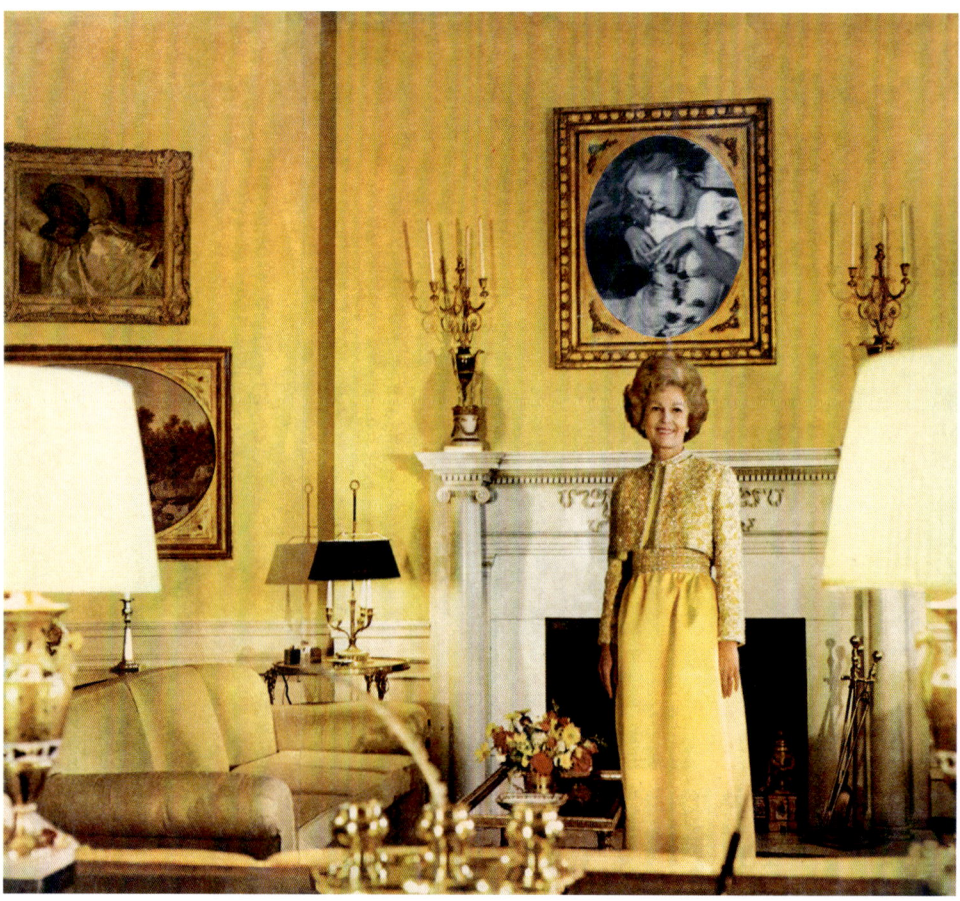

FIRST LADY (PAT NIXON) from the series 'HOUSE BEAUTIFUL: BRINGING THE WAR HOME'

*c.*1967–72, photomontage
Martha Rosler, born 1943, Brooklyn, New York.

After moving to California in 1968, Rosler formed her artistic approach in the politically charged America of the late 1960s. Her innovative work in montage, video, performance and writing has dealt with feminist and anti-war struggles, alongside issues of housing, homelessness and the urban environment. In 1967, she began the series 'House Beautiful: Bringing the War Home' to demonstrate how ideals of female domesticity were inextricable from American militarism. In *First Lady (Pat Nixon)*, the President's wife stands in an ornate White House reception room, an icon of feminine poise, while behind her a violent image – the slain outlaw Bonnie Parker, as played by Faye Dunaway in the iconic film *Bonnie and Clyde* (1967) – has been inserted into an ornate frame. Reducing the graphic image to background information, the montage emphasizes the way that scenes of violence, particularly those relating to women, are played in the mass media. In the following decades, Rosler laid bare the inadequacy of 'factual' documentary to fully capture socio-urban complexity, and critiqued how popular TV cookery shows served patriarchal values about women's domestic roles. She returned to New York in the 1980s, where she still lives.

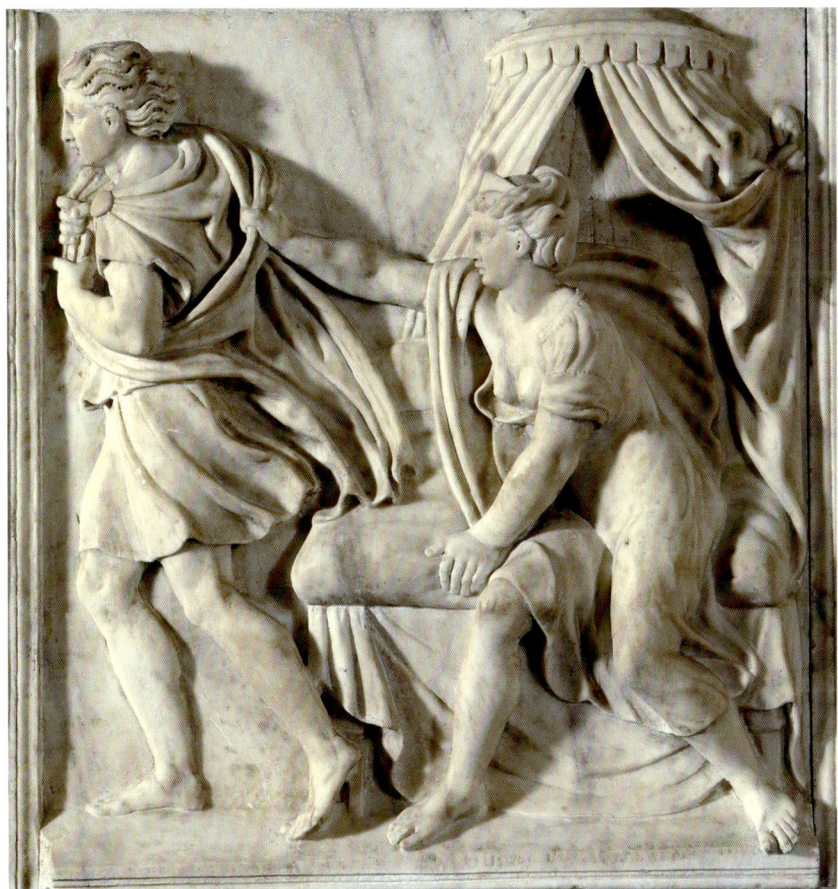

JOSEPH AND POTIPHAR'S WIFE

*c.*1526, marble panel, 54.5 × 59 cm (21 ½ × 23 ¼ in), Museo di San Petronio, Bologna, Italy
Properzia de' Rossi, born *c.*1490, Bologna, Italy. Died 1530, Bologna, Italy.

The only woman to be included in the first edition of Giorgio Vasari's foundational art history book *The Lives of the Most Excellent Painters, Sculptors, and Architects* (1550), de' Rossi overcame additional barriers in coming from a non-artistic household – women artists were usually apprenticed to their fathers – and in choosing the 'masculine' discipline of sculpture. She was known for her practice of carving stones of peaches and other fruits into tiny sculptures that were 'marvellous to behold', according to Vasari, 'not only for the subtlety of the work, but also for the liveliness of the little figures'. She later

carved in marble, and this relief – one of the few works attributed to her to have survived – was originally commissioned as part of a scheme for the facade of the Basilica di San Petronio in Bologna. The panel (or *quadro*) tells the story of Joseph fleeing from the advances of his master's wife. Vasari claimed that this biblical tale echoed de' Rossi's own experience of rejection by a young man. A forceful character, de' Rossi is known to have appeared twice before a tribunal in the city – first for damaging a neighbour's garden and later for assaulting another artist.

SUSAN ROTHENBERG

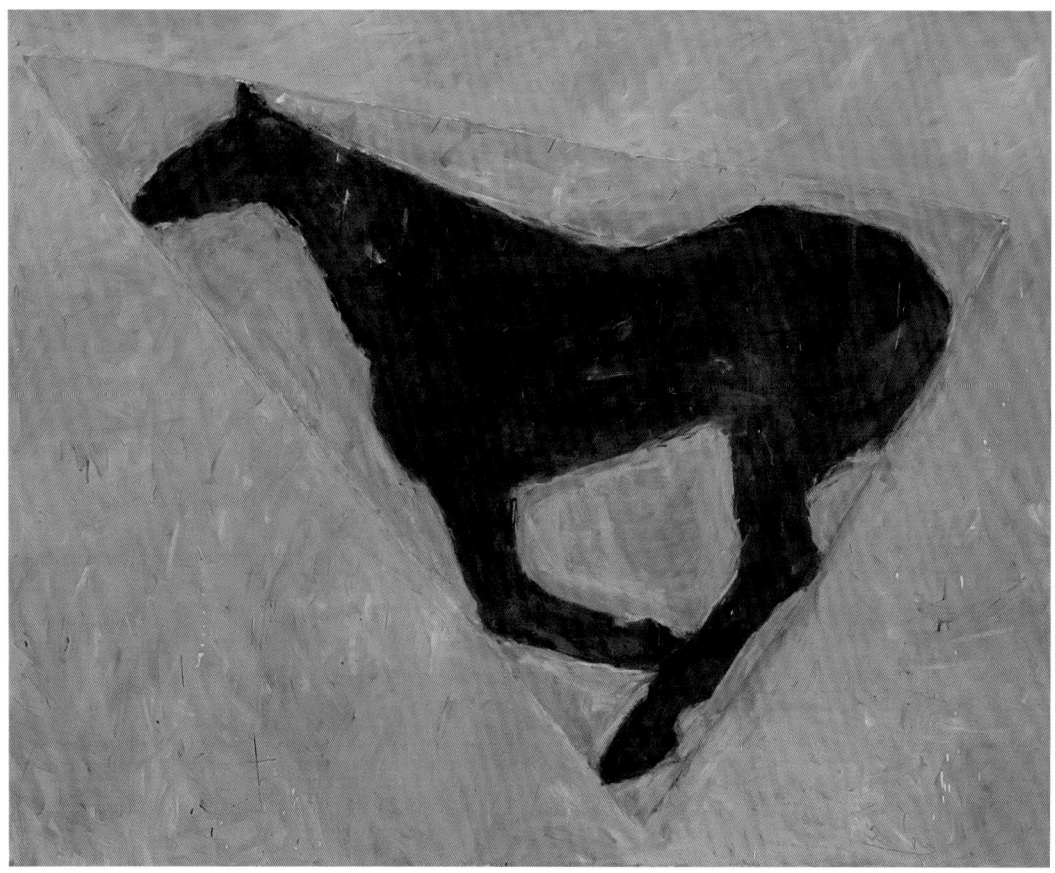

BLACK IN PLACE

1976, synthetic polymer paint and tempera on canvas, 174 × 217.2 cm
(68 ¼ × 85 ½ in), Museum of Modern Art, New York

Susan Rothenberg, born 1945, Buffalo, New York. Died 2020, Galisteo, New Mexico.

Following decades in which abstraction dominated the visual arts, Rothenberg emerged at the forefront of a turn to more figurative art in 1970s New York, gaining success with her iconic and powerful paintings of horses. She focused on this animal because of its universally recognized form and significance as a subject throughout art history. Monochromatic and lacking detail, these pared-down compositions were a synthesis of abstraction with representation, not a rejection of it, and her repetitive practice of painting this subject connects with the Minimalist strategies of the previous decade. She also recognized the horse as a symbol of dynamism and energy, which she was able to capture via an expressionist painting style characterized by thick, brash brushstrokes. From the 1980s, she began to work in oils, depicting a wider range of animals, including birds and dogs, as well as parts of the human body. Her work often suggests the violence of the natural world or alludes to personal mishaps and health concerns. In 1988 she married fellow artist, Bruce Nauman (b.1941), and lived for many years in New Mexico.

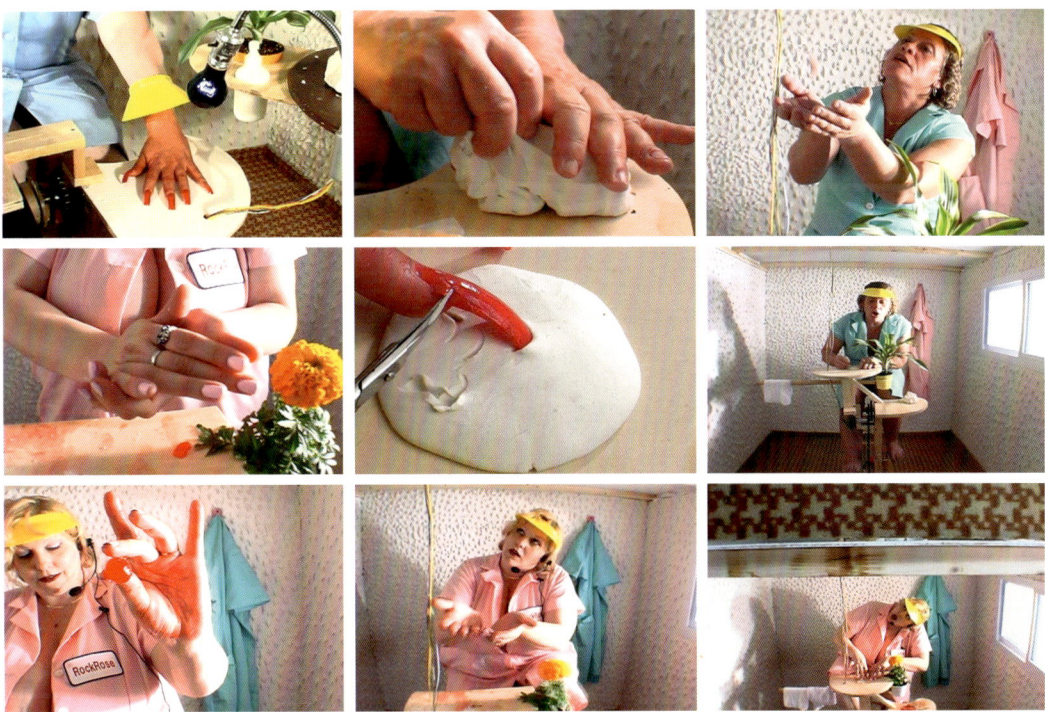

MARY'S CHERRIES

2004, video, colour, sound, 5 mins 50 secs, and digital C-prints,
Museum of Modern Art, New York
Mika Rottenberg, born 1976, Buenos Aires.

Rottenberg's sculptures and video works scrutinize fictionalized women subjects in order to examine actual conditions of female labour. Her works are often shown within immersive environments that reproduce the architectural interiors and moods of the videos. While superficially humorous and light-hearted, her surreal scenarios can also be read as allegories reflecting more disturbing ironies of the modern human condition. She is interested in the lengths women go to establish their subjectivities, or simply to find paid work. The characters in her films often exhibit physical singularities, being particularly tall or muscular, for example, echoing the experiences of women led to marketing unusual personal attributes online. Seen here are stills from Rottenberg's reinterpretation of a story she heard about a woman with a rare blood type who resigned from her job to make a living selling it instead. Two women cycle on an exercise machine to make their ruby red nails grow, which are then clipped and turned into maraschino cherries. Becoming increasingly grotesque and bizarre, the action is not supposed to make sense or be realistic, but rather to represent endless cycles of exhaustive labour.

NANCY RUBINS

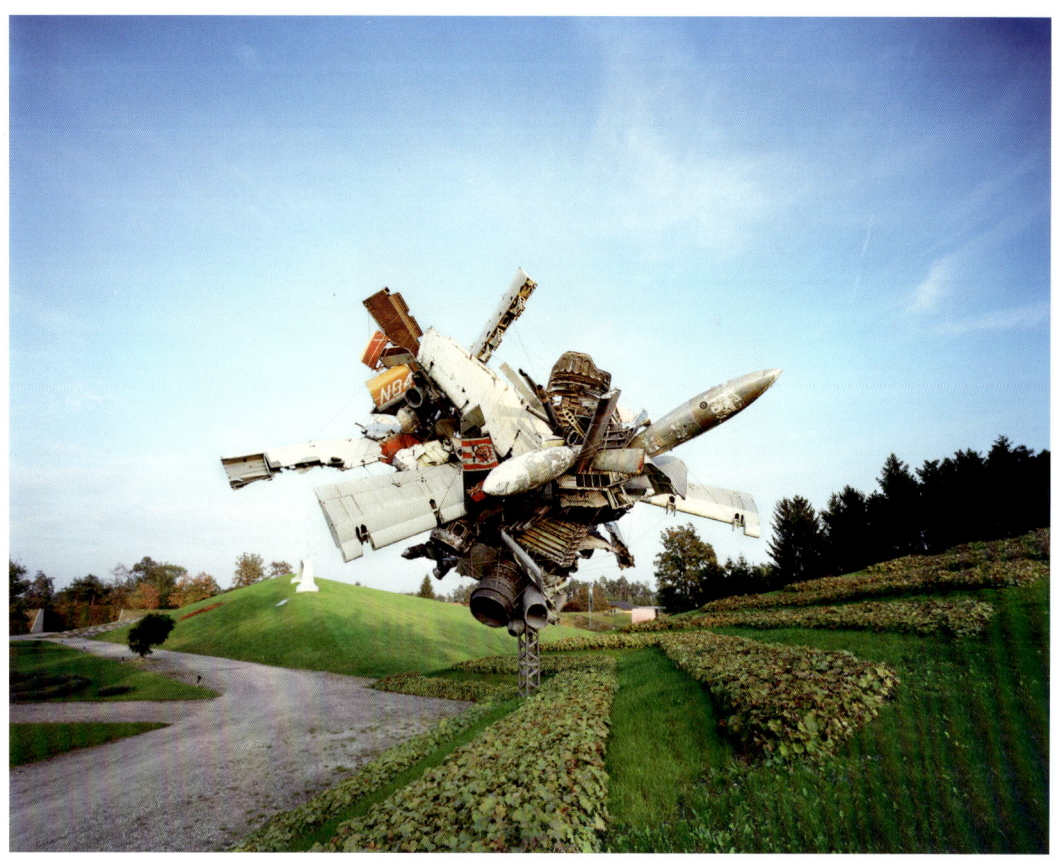

AIRPLANE PARTS & HILLS

2003, airplane parts, stainless steel armature and stainless steel wire cable,
*c.*11 × 15 × 17 m (*c.*36 × 49 × 56 ft), Austrian Sculpture Park, Premstätten
Nancy Rubins, born 1952, Naples, Texas.

As a student in the 1970s, Rubins made igloo-like structures out
of mud, concrete and straw, a contrast to the industrial objects she
became known for appropriating into large-scale sculptures. Her
practice consistently reflects a fascination with found objects, which
have included mobile homes, aircraft and boats. Rubins initially scav-
enged for domestic appliances at charity shops around San Francisco,
collecting nearly 300 television sets for one piece. Her first public
work, the controversial *Big Bil-Bored*, stood from 1980 in Berwyn,
Illinois, but was eventually removed following a poll of local residents.

A precarious tower of discarded objects bursting up from a tiny base,
it exemplified not only Rubins's choice of abject materials but also
her skill in balancing them. Many of her sculptures appear to defy
gravity, objects blooming and spiralling outwards in feats of
engineering. Her arrangements of aeroplane parts (a material she
has used since the 1980s) include *Airplane Parts & Hills*. It conveys
notions of disaster and wreckage, but also of poise and beauty, in its
reorganization of disused components, which challenge the typically
ordered forms of twentieth-century modernist sculpture.

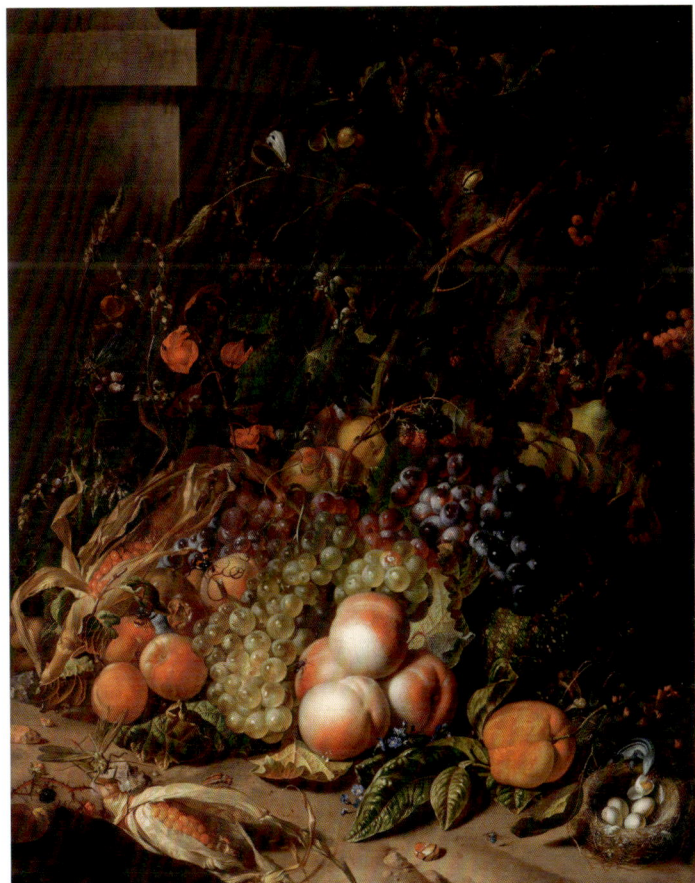

STILL LIFE WITH FRUIT, BIRD'S NEST AND INSECTS

1710 or 1716, oil on canvas, 76.2 × 57.1 cm (30 × 22 ½ in), National Trust,
Dudmaston, Shropshire, UK
Rachel Ruysch, born 1664, The Hague. Died 1750, Amsterdam.

One of the most widely admired and highly paid painters of the
early eighteenth century, Ruysch's background and training were
unusual. Her father Frederik Ruysch was a botanist and anatomist
celebrated for his uncannily lifelike anatomical preparations, which
his daughter helped to arrange and display. Aged fifteen, Ruysch
showed extraordinary skill in drawing from nature and was apprenticed to the still-life painter Willem van Aelst (1627–83); five years
later she was an independent painter, producing virtuoso still lifes
of flowers and fruit. In 1699 she became the first woman elected

to The Hague artists' society, the Confrerie Pictura, and in 1708 was
named court painter to Johann Wilhelm, Elector Palatine. The
mother of ten children, she continued to paint until her early eighties.
When this outdoor still life was created she was at the height of her
powers and it is typical in her use of dramatic lighting and a diagonal
composition. In a mix of exotic fruits interwoven with woodland
plants and punctuated by insects and other wildlife, each element
is carefully placed and depicted with meticulous attention to the
details of texture and rhythm.

HANNAH RYGGEN

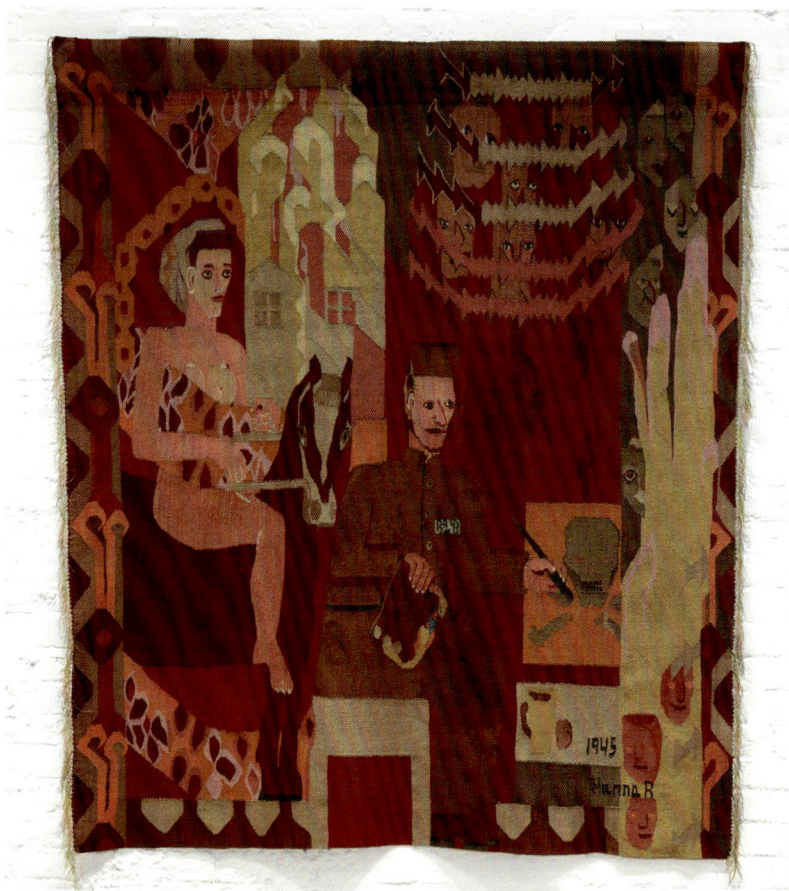

GRINI

1945, tapestry weave in wool and linen, 189 × 166 cm (74 ½ × 65 ⅜ in),
Trondheim Kunstmuseum, Norway
Hannah Ryggen, born Hannah Jönsson, 1894, Malmö, Sweden. Died 1970,
Trondheim, Norway.

Swedish-born Ryggen and her artist-husband Hans (1894–1956) lived from subsistence farming in a remote coastal district in northern Norway. By the time of the Nazi occupation, she had been recording their brutality for several years using folk art. Self-taught as a weaver, she composed her tapestries directly at a standing loom, using homespun yarn dyed with foraged plant materials. In her lifetime she was widely recognized as one of Scandinavia's most important artists, and in 1964 became the first woman artist to represent Norway at the Venice Biennale. A leftist, pacifist and member of the Norwegian Communist Party, Ryggen was renowned for monumental works that weave tumultuous political events into highly personal narratives, combining fantastical elements with fact. During the war, the nearest town, Trondheim, became a major German military base and she defiantly hung her tapestries on her washing line as a protest. Hans was arrested as a dissident and sent to Grini prison camp near Oslo, though he survived the war. This piece represents his experience, its vibrant palette belying the subject's fear. He is shown painting skulls, fellow inmates peering from behind barbed wire and his daughter depicted as a dreamy apparition on horseback.

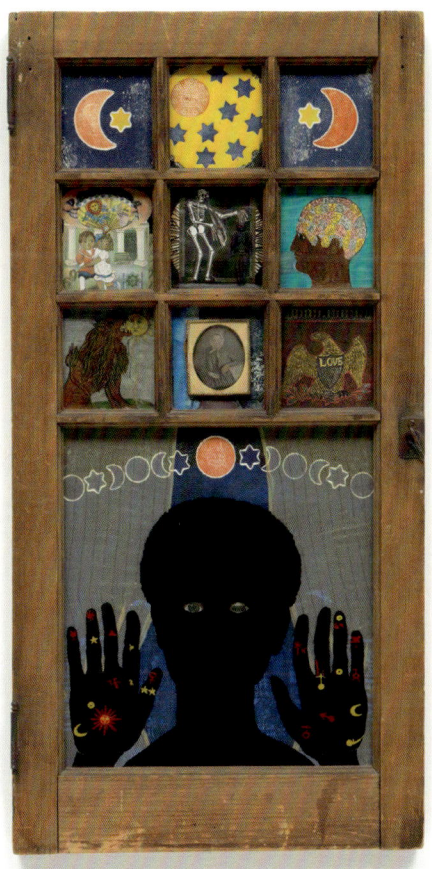

BLACK GIRL'S WINDOW

1969, wooden window frame, painted wood, painted pasted paper, lenticular print, daguerreotype and plastic figurine, 90.8 × 45.7 × 3.8 cm (35 ¾ × 18 × 1 ½ in), Museum of Modern Art, New York

Betye Saar, born Betye Irene Brown, 1926, Los Angeles.

A poem by Saar written in 1998, now published on the homepage of her website, introduces her practice by giving centre-stage to 'curiosity about the unknown' and 'the mystical'. Saar is best known for her assemblages, made since the 1960s, which became explicitly political after the assassination of Martin Luther King Jr. in 1968. She is especially interested in the lives of recycled objects: the stories they carry into the present and the cleansing processes that can be activated by putting them to new uses. *Black Girl's Window*

is an iconic and autobiographical work. A figure is surrounded by stars, moons and symbols – on the palms of her hands and in the window frames that float above her. Inside these, images include a white skeleton that bounces X-rays at a black one, and the Great Seal of the United States, emblazoned with the word 'LOVE'. The girl's facial features are erased except for the eyes, which open and close when the viewer shifts back and forth in front of the work, materializing a further 'window' or connection path – to the figure's soul, as well as to the symbolic objects employed to represent her.

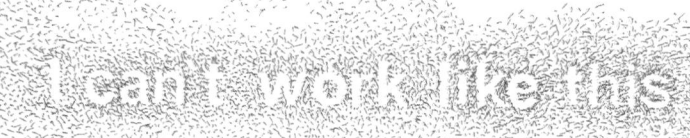

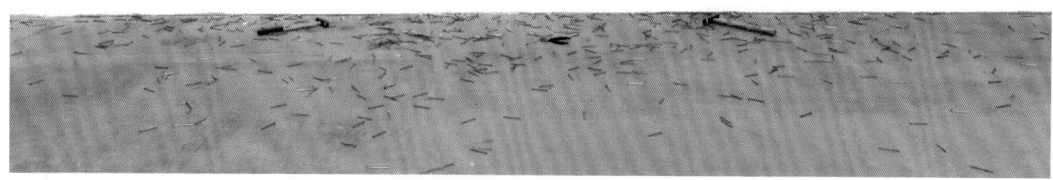

I CAN'T WORK LIKE THIS

2007, wall installation, nails and 2 hammers, 220 × 450 cm (86 ⅝ × 177 ¼ in)
Natascha Sadr Haghighian, date and birthplace withheld.

Sadr Haghighian's biographical information is deliberately in flux. Her website bioswop.net is a 'CV-exchange platform' and seeks to undermine the notion of CVs altogether. For each of her shows she provides a different biography to subvert imposed narratives that consider work in the context of career development. She has also collaborated with an art production company to produce a show by a fictional artist, 'Robbie Williams'. Such projects are driven by the need to question existing social relations and conditions, 'to avoid accepting them as naturally given', as she stated in a 2008 interview. Her piece *I Can't Work Like This* came about after Sadr Haghighian was invited by her gallery to make work for their booth at a commercial art fair. She created an installation that literally spelled out her response, with nails hammered into the wall – the common tools used for art installation and indicative of labour more generally. As such, the work drew attention to exploitative labour conditions that have been normalized or rendered invisible, including those on the periphery of the art world, as well as making a comment about the nature of creativity. Sadr Haghighian was selected to represent Germany at the 58th Venice Biennale in 2019.

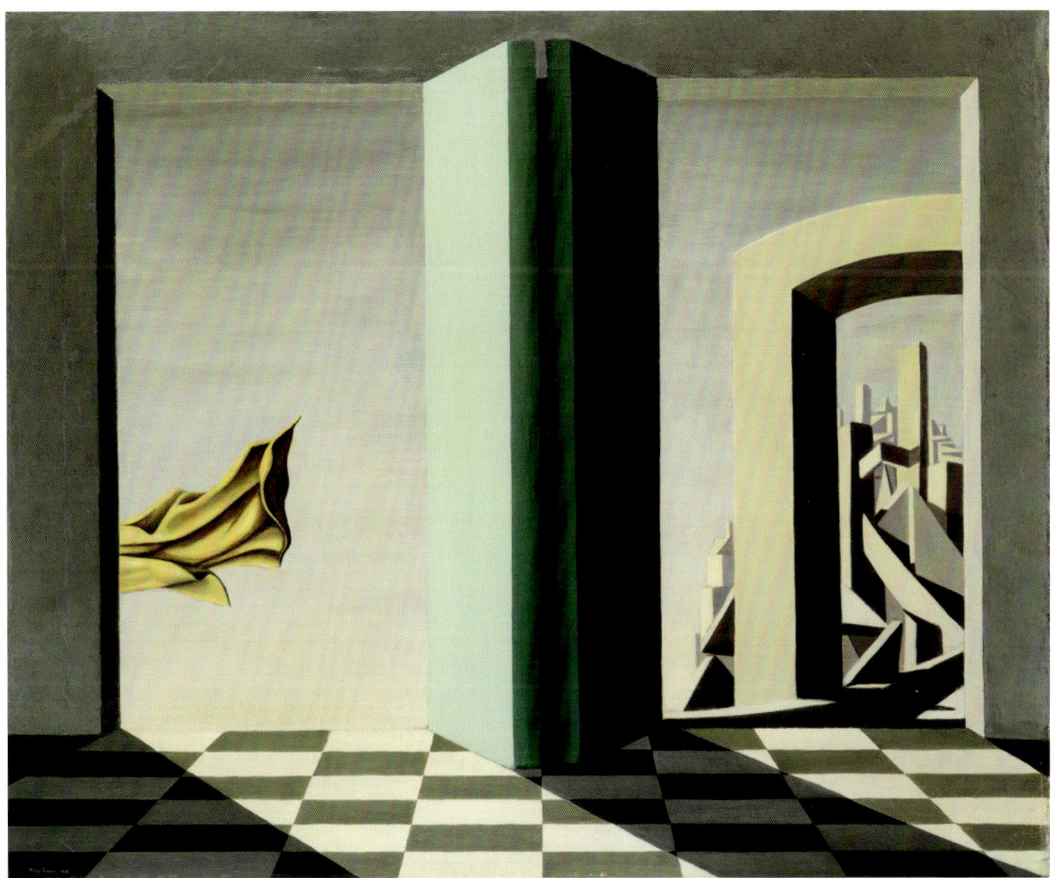

THE UPPER SIDE OF THE SKY

1944, oil on canvas, 58.4 × 71.4 cm (23 × 28 ⅛ in), Israel Museum, Jerusalem
Kay (Katherine) Sage, 1898, Albany, New York. Died 1963, Woodbury, Connecticut.

Following her parents' separation, Sage lived with her mother in Italy and became connected to wealthy European society. She studied art in Washington DC and Rome, although later claimed to be self-taught. Her first solo exhibition was in Milan in 1936 and the following year she moved to Paris, where she encountered Surrealist painting, notably that of Giorgio de Chirico (1888–1978), and mixed with members of the movement, including her second husband, the painter Yves Tanguy (1900–55). She returned to America at the outbreak of the Second World War, Tanguy joining her, and moved to rural Connecticut. Theirs was a complicated and abusive relationship, despite Sage's feeling uniquely understood by her partner. Sage's mature work developed in the 1940s, her paintings marked by sparse iconography and psychological depictions of architecture – sombre skies, blank walls and bold structures – as seen in *The Upper Side of the Sky*. Her work was included in Peggy Guggenheim's 1943 'Exhibition by 31 Women' at New York's Art of This Century gallery. Depressed after Tanguy's death, she made small sculptures of wire, stones and bullets from 1960 to 1961, and took her own life with a gun in 1963.

NIKI DE SAINT PHALLE

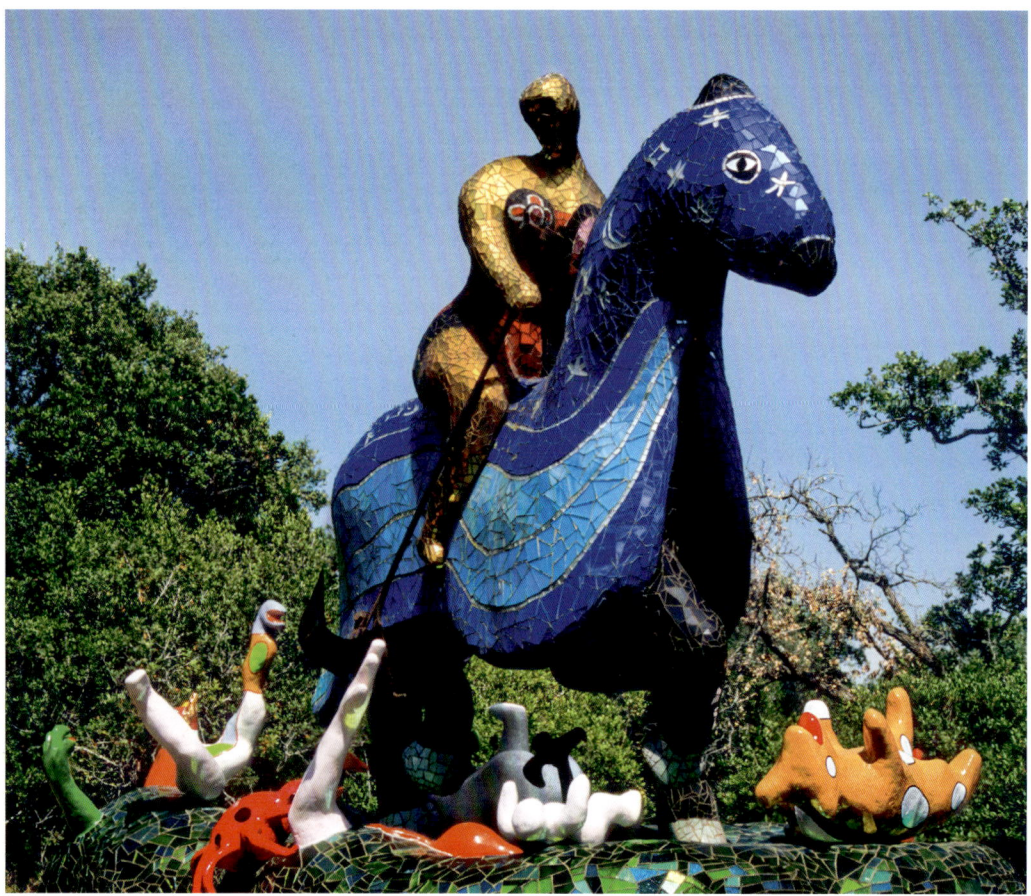

DEATH

1978–2002, reinforced concrete, mirrors and ceramic mosaic, Giardino dei Tarocchi, Capalbio, Italy

Niki de Saint Phalle, born Catherine Marie-Agnès Fal de Saint Phalle, 1930, Neuilly-sur-Seine, France. Died 2002, La Jolla, California.

With no formal training, Saint Phalle's first forays into making art occurred during a period in a psychiatric clinic in 1953, the culmination of an unhappy childhood and marriage. She gained recognition in the art world for a series of works in which guns were fired at bags of coloured paint, an approach reflecting the experimental 'happenings' of the time and also parodying the Abstract Expressionist 'drip paintings' of Jackson Pollock (1912–56). She became associated with an avant-garde circle as the only woman member of *Nouveau Réalisme*, a group that included the Swiss sculptor Jean Tinguely (1925–91), who was to be her partner for many years. Saint Phalle is best known for her whimsical 'Nanas', depictions of voluptuous women decorated with vibrantly coloured designs, one of which, decorated with a mosaic of mirrors and ceramic tiles, rides a blue armoured warhorse in the equestrian work seen here. It is one of twenty-two statues that populate Saint Phalle's monumental 'Tarot Garden' in Tuscany. Inspired by Antoni Gaudí's Parc Güell in Barcelona and the sixteenth-century grotesque tradition of landscape gardening, each of her sculptures represents a different card of the esoteric Tarot.

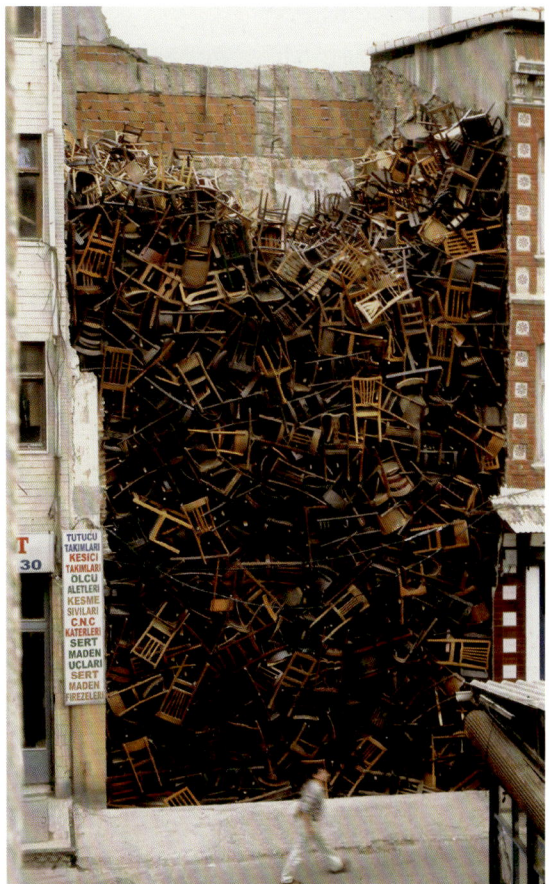

UNTITLED INSTALLATION FOR THE 8TH INTERNATIONAL ISTANBUL BIENNIAL

2003, 1,550 wooden chairs, *c*.10.1 × 6.1 × 6.1 m (*c*.33 × 20 × 20 ft)
Doris Salcedo, born 1958, Bogotá, Colombia.

Growing up during the decades-long Colombian civil war, in which some of her own family members disappeared, Salcedo's sculptures and installations embody a sense of loss and mourning, conveying absence through sheer materiality. Having studied in New York, she returned to teach at Colombia's national university in Bogotá in the 1980s. Since then she has interviewed people whose relatives were also among the disappeared as a basis for works that often commemorate specific political events and atrocities. *Noviembre 6 y 7* (2002) refers to the brutal storming of Colombia's Supreme Court on those days

in 1985, while *Flor de Piel* (2016) is a tapestry of rose petals intended to shroud a nurse who was tortured to death. Other works are more generalized memorials. In 2007, Salcedo made *Shibboleth*, her Tate Modern Turbine Hall commission, in which a vast, deep fissure traversed the floor for the length of the building, segregation made concrete. Seen here is Salcedo's epic 2003 site-specific installation, which comprised 1,550 wooden chairs crammed in a vacant lot between two buildings in Istanbul. Suggesting a mass grave or blitzed neighbourhood, everyday objects are transformed into a contorted suffocating mass.

CHARLOTTE SALOMON

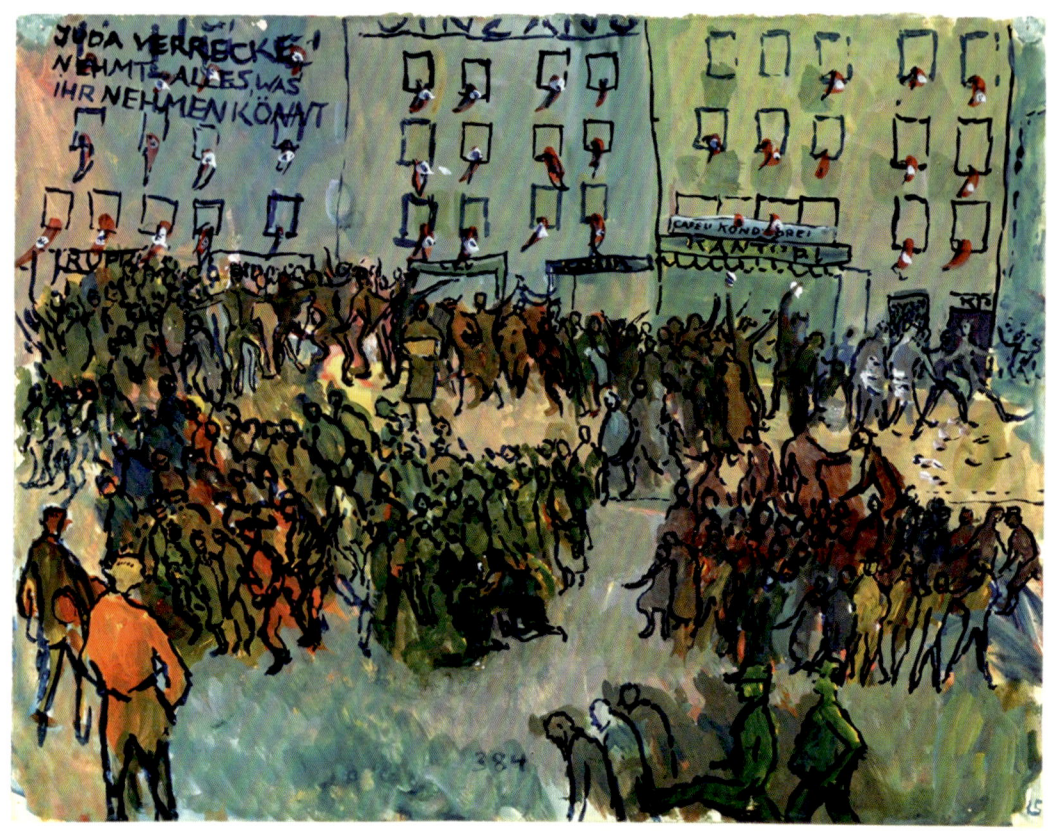

KRISTALLNACHT from 'LIFE? OR THEATRE? A SONG-CYCLE'

*c.*1940–2, gouache on paper, 25 × 32.5 cm (9 ⅞ × 12 ¾ in), Joods Historisch
Museum, Amsterdam
Charlotte Salomon, born 1917, Berlin. Died 1943, Auschwitz, Poland.

After studying applied arts in Berlin followed by training in illustration and drawing under Ludwig Bartning (1876–1956), Salomon
fled Nazi Germany in 1939 and settled in Villefranche-sur-Mer,
near Nice, France. While in exile and later in hiding, she created
an epic body of work. Notable for its highly individual and expressionist style, it comprises almost 800 pictures, divided into scenes and
acts like a play, and conceived as a *Gesamtkunstwerk* (a holistic work
of visual and literary art). Accompanied by texts on parchment paper
that overlaid the images or were incorporated directly into the

paintings, Salomon often quoted poetry and musical lyrics to convey her thoughts and feelings. Her subjects ranged from incidents
in her traumatic autobiography to representations of wider historic
events, as seen here in this depiction of Kristallnacht. The chaos
and drama of the coordinated night of attacks against Jews in
November 1938 is represented in vivid detail: the dense throng of
Brownshirts and the abundant red flashes of Nazi flags. Deported
to Auschwitz in 1943 where it is thought she was killed on arrival,
Salomon had left a collection of some 1,325 gouache paintings with
a doctor in France, saying, 'Keep it safe, it is my whole life.'

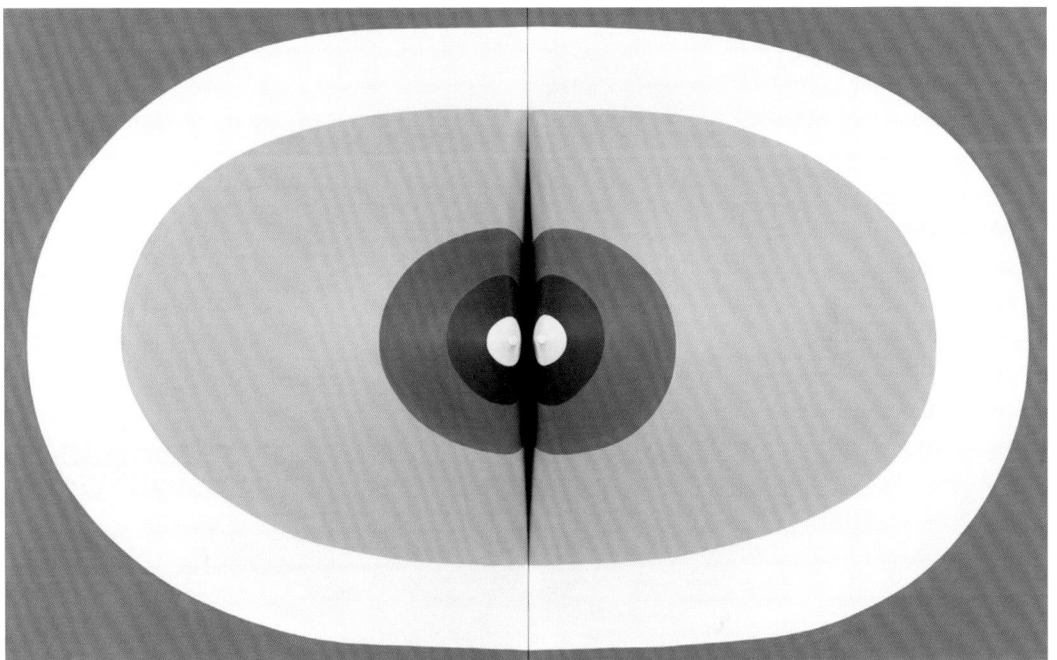

UNTITLED

1978, acrylic on stretched canvas, 182.9 × 298.5 × 26.7 cm (72 × 117 ½ × 10 ½ in)
Zilia Sánchez, born 1926, Havana. Died 2024, San Juan, Puerto Rico.

Sánchez's signature contoured paintings have their origin in a precise moment in her life: standing on a Havana rooftop in the 1950s, she witnessed a hanging sheet – the very bedsheet on which her father had died – blowing against a tubular pipe. The swelling fabric inspired her to abandon flat canvases in favour of relief works. Combining an austere palette with curved outlines and protuberant surfaces created by pulling canvas tautly over handmade wooden armatures, her paintings inflect Minimalist abstraction with a sense of the corporeal: 'I always thought about feminine, erotic forms,' she remarked in a 2016 interview. The example shown here is typical of her work, straddling painting and sculpture. Smooth lozenges of grey and white contain a 'splitting nucleus' of darker concentric shades and the symmetrical halves fold into a suggestive crease. After being the only woman connected with (although not formally a member of) the 1950s Los Once ('The Eleven') artists' group, who pioneered gestural abstraction in Cuba, Sánchez left the country in 1960 and moved to New York with a growing community of émigré artists, poets, writers and performers escaping Castro's regime. In 1971, she permanently settled in San Juan, Puerto Rico.

AUGUSTA SAVAGE

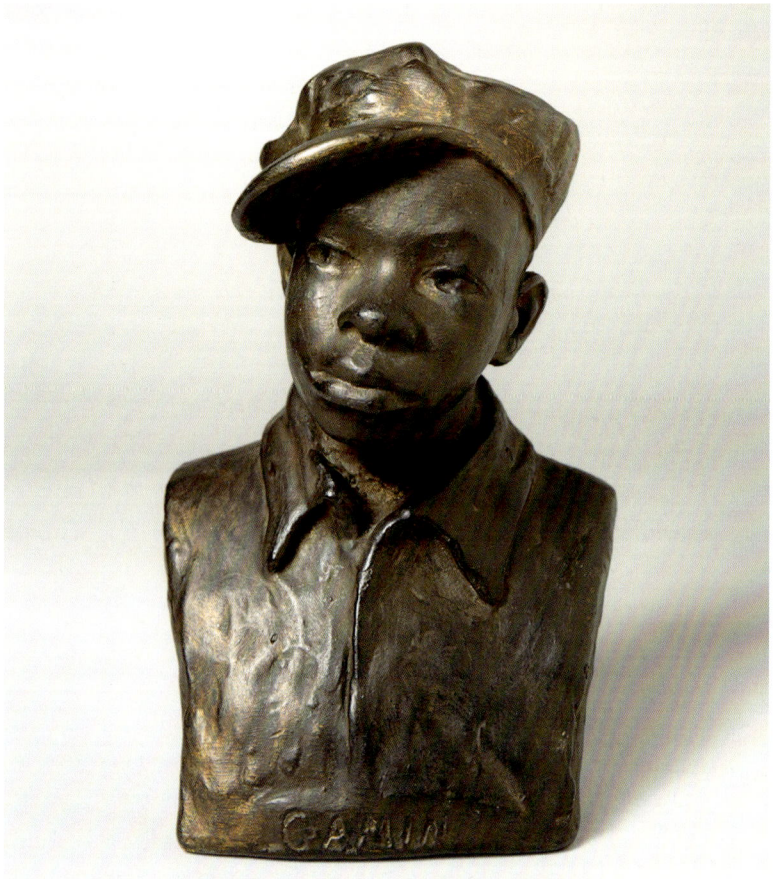

GAMIN
*c.*1929, painted plaster, 22.9 × 14.7 × 11.2 cm (9 × 5 ¾ × 4 ⅜ in),
Smithsonian American Art Museum, Washington DC
Augusta Savage, born 1892, Green Cove Springs, Florida. Died 1962, New York.

Savage's talent was recognized by her high-school principal, who also inspired her commitment to teaching. After winning first prize at a state fair, she moved to New York in the early 1920s, and attended Cooper Union, being chosen for the course ahead of 142 men. An outstanding student, she was nevertheless turned down for a summer scholarship in France in 1923 because she was black. Her response was to become a fighter for racial equality. As a member of the Harlem Renaissance, the African-American nexus of arts and culture, she made highly regarded public sculptures of leading figures of the civil rights movement, including busts of W.E.B. Du Bois and Marcus Garvey. A grant finally enabled her to study in Paris and in 1934 she was the first African-American elected to the National Association of Women Painters and Sculptors. She later launched the Savage Studio of Arts and Crafts in a Harlem basement with an open-door policy to prospective students. Conveying the innate dignity that had sometimes been denied her, this sculpture depicts an unnamed Harlem youth (*'gamin'*, an old French word meaning 'street urchin').

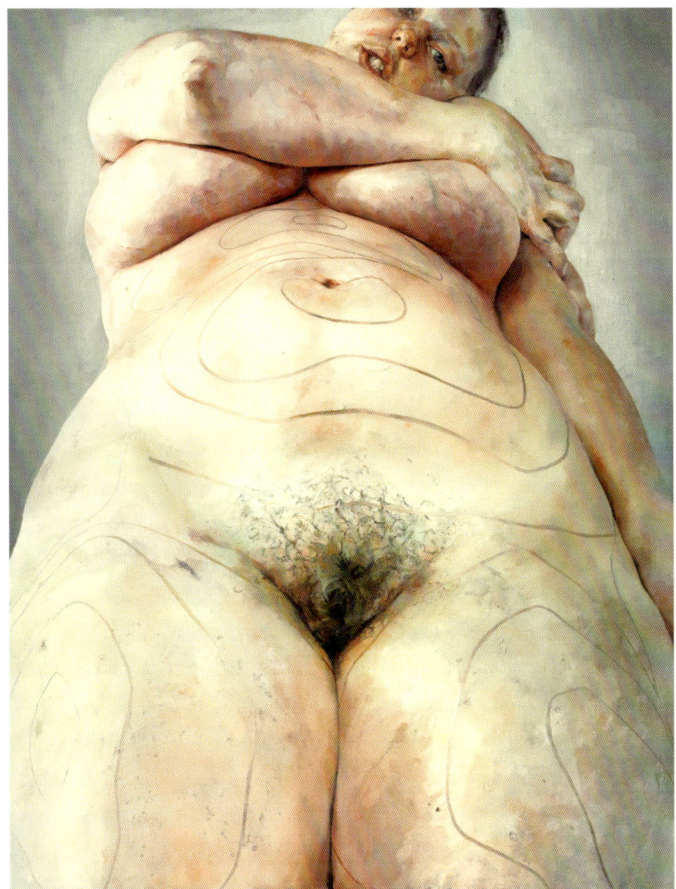

PLAN

1993, oil on canvas, 274.3 × 213.4 cm (108 × 84 in)
Jenny Saville, born 1970, Cambridge, UK.

Having studied painting at Glasgow School of Art, Saville came to public attention when her work was included in the third 'Young British Artists' exhibition at the Saatchi Gallery in 1994. In 2018, her painting *Propped* (1992) set a record for the highest price paid at auction for a work by a living woman artist. Saville's work deals almost exclusively with the naked female body, depicted large-scale, up-close and in stark contrast to the idealization of the classical nude in art history. She uses the physical qualities of paint to convey the tactility of the flesh in ways that have drawn comparison to British figurative painter Lucian Freud (1922–2011). *Plan* is typical of her early self-portraits, which were often painted from below so that the fore-shortened lower body appears enlarged. The lines drawn across her body suggest that liposuction is to be performed, but also evoke the contour lines on a map. Presenting larger female bodies that do not conform to traditional notions of beauty, Saville has commented that, while a lot of women look this way, they have come to 'fear their own excess'.

MIRIAM SCHAPIRO

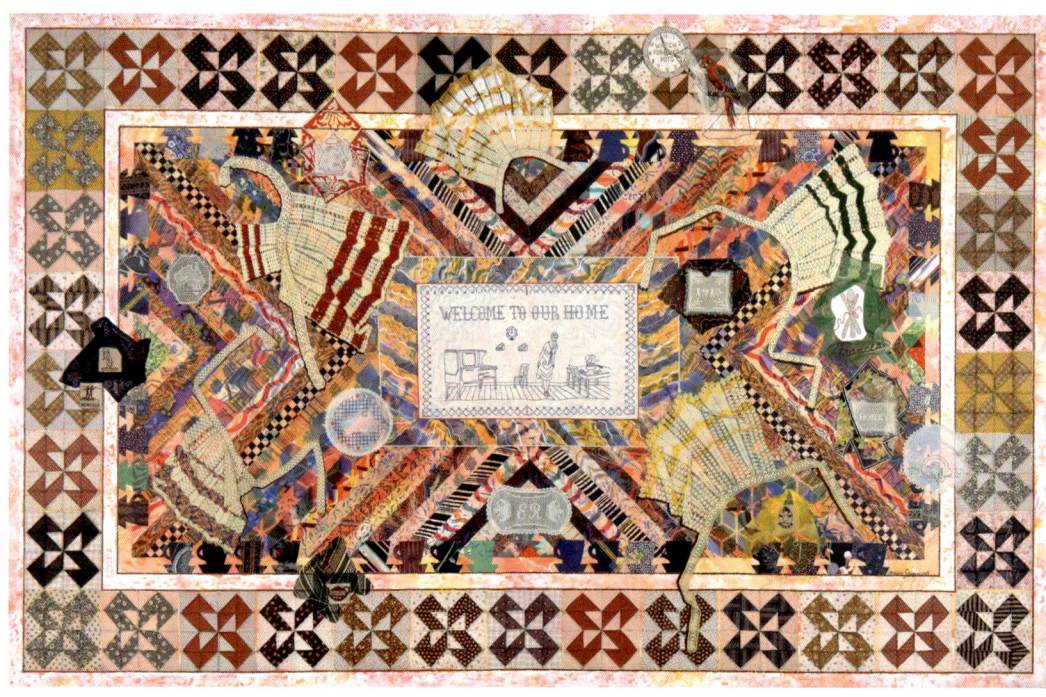

WONDERLAND

1983, acrylic, fabric and plastic beads on canvas, 228.6 × 367 cm (90 × 144 ½ in),
Smithsonian American Art Museum, Washington DC
Miriam Schapiro, born 1923, Toronto. Died 2015, Hampton Bays, New York.

A pioneer of feminist art, Schapiro fused techniques of craft into
fine art to subvert the idea that the former was 'women's work' – so
why not painting, too? Schapiro was a founder of the Pattern and
Decoration movement, which focused on blurring the boundary
between the applied and 'pure' arts. She grouped together practices
including assemblage, collage and photomontage as 'femmage',
seeing in them the possibility that from throwaway things something new can be made. In her work she paid homage to historical
women artists, making paintings and collages with photographic
reproductions of Mary Cassatt (p.91), Frida Kahlo (p.207) and
women of the Russian avant-garde. As the child of Russian-Jewish
parents, her own identity became the focus of her work in the 1990s.
Having pursued the Abstract Expressionist style of the 1950s,
followed by more restrained geometric language, her later work is
exuberant in comparison. Consciously appropriating symbols and
images considered feminine, Schapiro often used stereotypically
saccharine forms such as hearts and butterflies rendered in shades
of pink. *Wonderland* is one such example: a semi-abstract, large-
scale needlework that incorporates plastic beads on canvas.

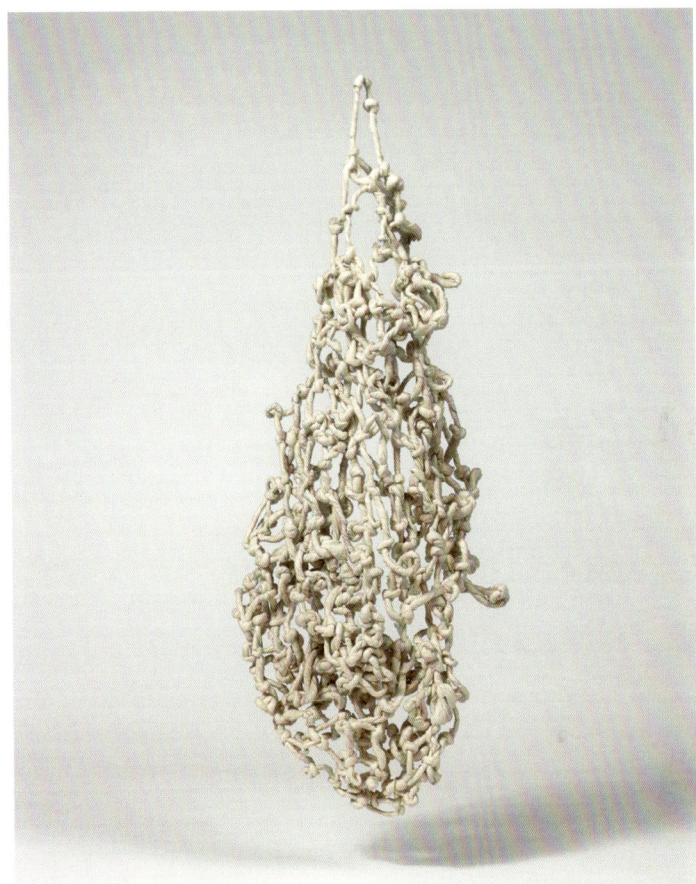

UNTITLED from the series 'DROGUINHAS' ('LITTLE NOTHINGS')

*c.*1964–6, Japanese paper, 90 × 70 cm (35 ½ × 27 ½ in), Museum of Modern Art, New York

Mira Schendel, born Myrrha Dagmar Dub, 1919, Zürich. Died 1988, São Paulo.

Schendel was raised in Milan, where she pursued studies in art and philosophy. Beginning in 1941, she was forced to move between Bulgaria, Austria and Yugoslavia to avoid persecution, finally settling in Brazil in 1953. Arriving in her new country at a moment of social and artistic revolution, Schendel immersed herself in São Paulo's vibrant cultural and intellectual milieu and integrated into a thriving artistic community that included Lygia Clark (p.101) and Hélio Oiticica (1937–80). Schendel developed a signature style as a painter and sculptor, her themes touching on the idea of being, nothingness and mysticism. Her preferred material was Japanese rice paper and she used it to make precise line drawings and sculptures. *Untitled* from the series 'Droguinhas' ('Little Nothings') is a tangle of knots made from textured paper that Schendel brought together to create a biomorphic form reminiscent of a fishing net or a beehive. The delicate sculpture is soft and its shape undefined – a reflection of Schendel's interest in philosophy and Zen Buddhism as well as in the yielding qualities of paper, in contrast with traditional hard, sculptural materials.

HÉLÈNE SCHJERFBECK

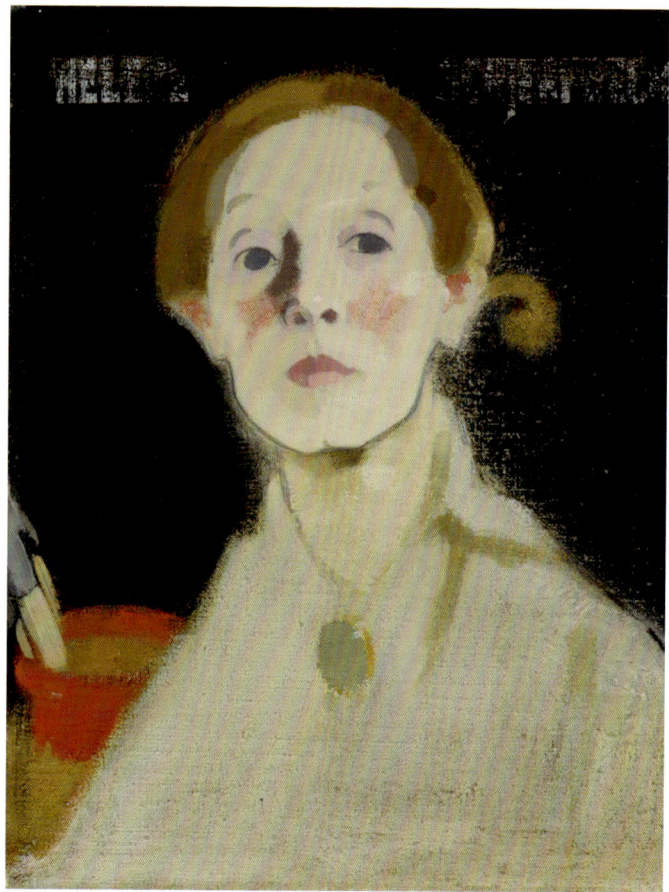

SELF-PORTRAIT WITH BLACK BACKGROUND

1915, oil on canvas, 45.5 × 36 cm (17 ⅞ × 14 ⅛ in), Ateneum Art Museum, Finnish National Gallery, Helsinki
Hélène Schjerfbeck, born 1862, Helsinki. Died 1946, Saltsjöbaden, Sweden.

Long revered in her native country, Schjerfbeck was little known outside of Finland during her lifetime. Poverty and illness marked her childhood, but she began studying art at the age of eleven thanks to free drawing classes at the Finnish Art Society, Helsinki. In 1880 she received a government grant that allowed her to study in Paris, where she travelled with fellow Finnish artist Helena Westermarck (1857–1938) and developed skills in painting scenes of everyday life in the prevalent mode of French Realism. Throughout the 1880s Schjerfbeck visited artists' colonies in Brittany and

Cornwall, adopting the Impressionist's plein air tradition of working outdoors. She returned to Finland the following decade, teaching at first before moving with her mother to the isolated town of Hyvinkää in 1902. Here, she began exploring a new aesthetic, creating increasingly expressive figurative studies, as seen in *Self-Portrait with Black Background*. The subject's jaw is outlined, giving the composition a strongly graphic quality, while the body is barely mapped in, reduced to little more than a flat white mass. In her final years, her style dissolved into almost pure abstraction.

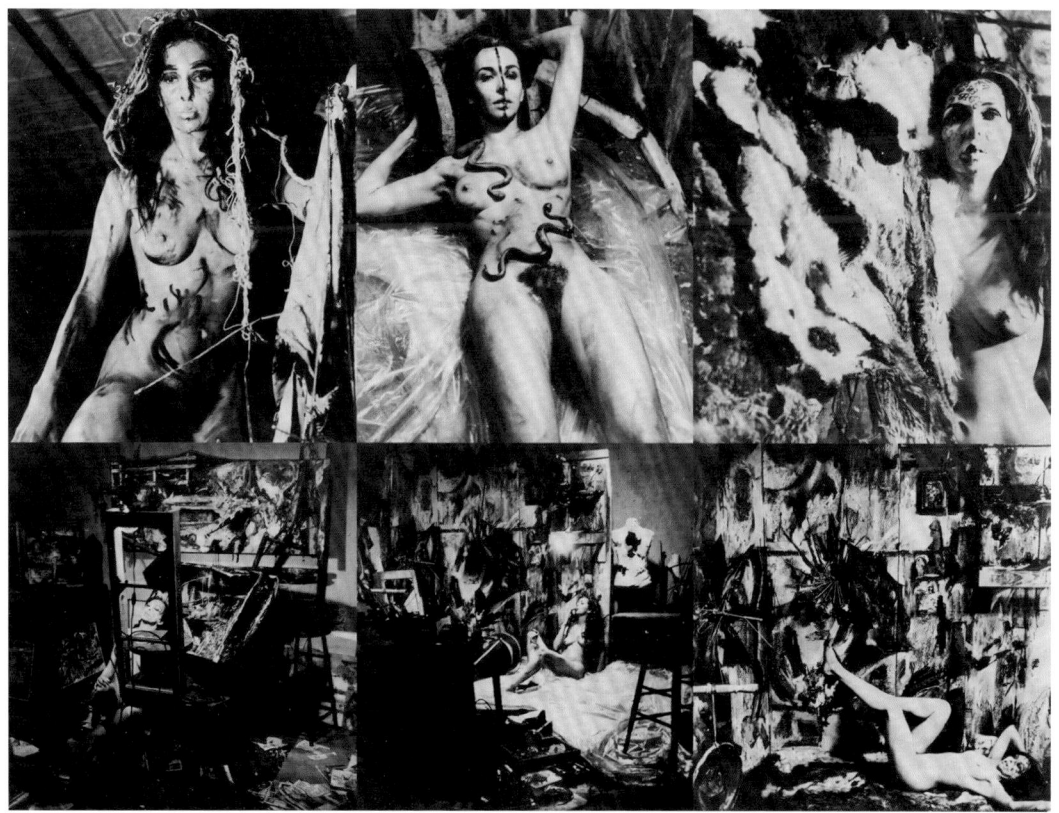

EYE BODY: 36 TRANSFORMATIVE ACTIONS FOR CAMERA

1963, performance with paint, glue, fur, feathers, garden snakes, glass and plastic with the studio installation 'Big Boards', photographed by Erró on 35mm black-and-white film

Carolee Schneemann, born 1939, Fox Chase, Pennsylvania. Died 2019, New Paltz, New York.

Throughout her career, Schneemann challenged patriarchal structures, making work that focuses on sexuality and gender. As a painter, she began to use both her own body and those of other women as sites for mark making and, by extension, for the mapping of social relations. In the shadow of the dominant Abstract Expressionism scene of the 1950s, often characterized in terms of priapic egos, Schneemann retorted by emphasizing the expressiveness of women artists and their connection to embodied experience. Her response made her a leading figure of the feminist art movement. Seeing herself as critically engaged with the masculinist heritage of Western art, her book *Cezanne: She was a Great Painter* (1975) suggests a reworking, not simple iconoclasm, of this tradition. Although not part of any group, was been influenced by the Fluxus and 'happenings' movements as seen in her iconic 1975 performance *Interior Scroll*, which involved her reading from a text that she unravelled from her vagina. *Eye Body* comprises thirty-six photographs taken by the Icelandic artist Erró (b.1932) of an elaborate series of interventions that Schneemann made on herself to be captured by the camera.

ANNA MARIA VAN SCHURMAN

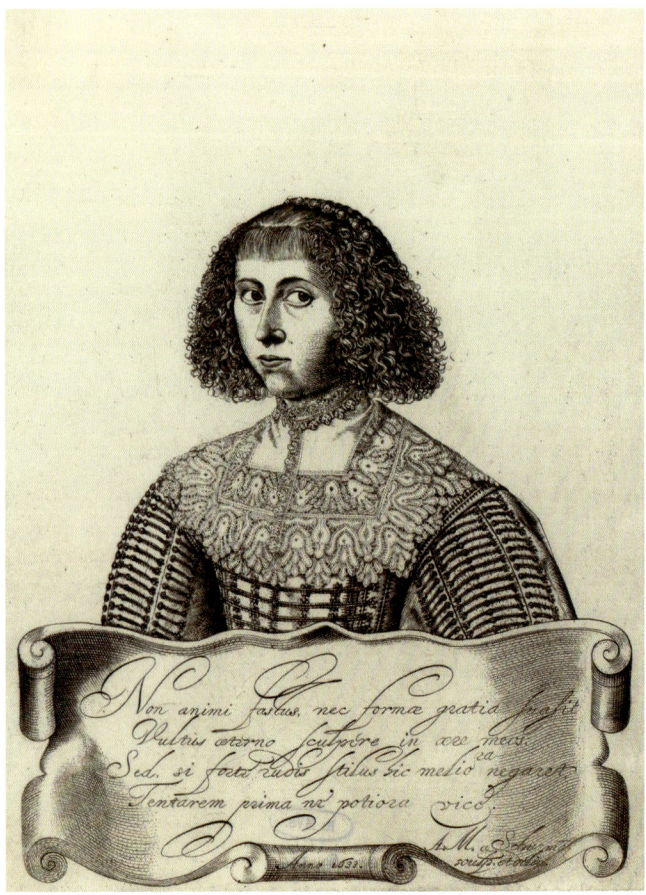

SELF-PORTRAIT

1633, etching on paper, 19.8 × 15.2 cm (7¾ × 6 in), Rijksmuseum, Amsterdam
Anna Maria van Schurman, born 1607, Cologne, Germany. Died 1678,
Wieuwerd, Netherlands.

A prodigy and polymath born into a prosperous Flemish family
in the Dutch Golden Age, van Schurman gained a reputation as one
of the most educated women of her day. Speaking fourteen languages, she was invited in 1634 to compose a Latin ode celebrating
the new university in Utrecht and in it challenged the institution's
exclusion of female students. After this she was allowed to attend,
becoming probably the first female European university student,
though she had to attend lectures behind a curtain. She graduated
in humanities, medicine and theology, then in 1638 she wrote

a treatise on women's education (translated into English as *The Learned
Maid* in 1657). Skilled in engraving and carving, van Schurman also
pioneered the use of pastel in portraiture, and was recognized by
Utrecht's society of painters, the Guild of St Luke, in 1643. In this
self-portrait, one of several she made, she confidently meets the
viewer's gaze. Largely devoting her creative efforts to writing and
campaigning, her denunciations of corruption in the Dutch Reformed
Church led to a split in 1669 and she became a leading figure
of the Labadists, a radical Protestant sect with whom she then
lived and travelled.

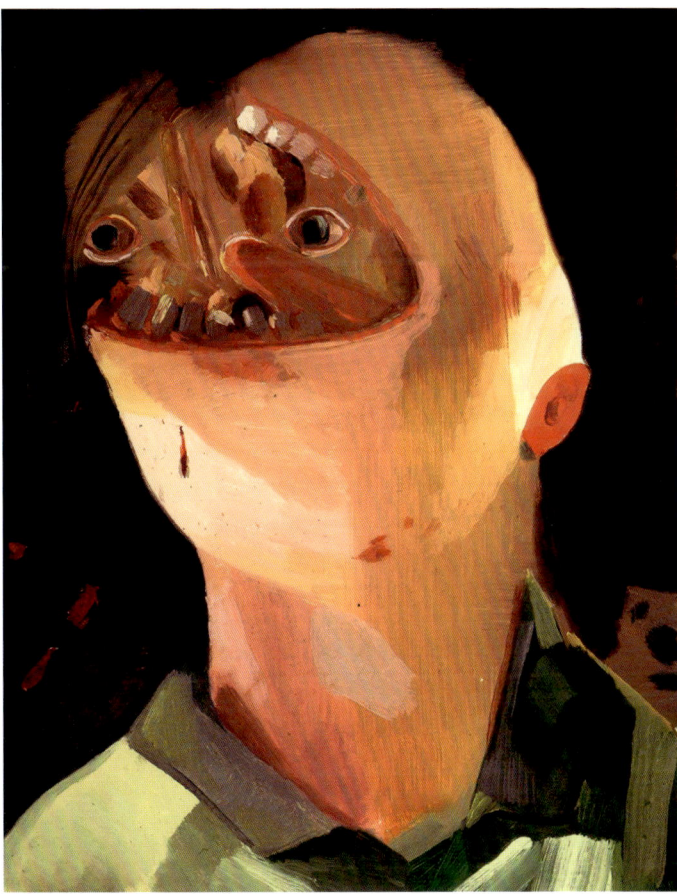

FACE EATER

2004, oil on canvas, 58.4 × 45.7 cm (23 × 18 in)
Dana Schutz, born 1976, Livonia, Michigan.

Having graduated from the Cleveland Institute of Art in 2000, Schutz undertook an MFA at Columbia in New York, where she produced the 'Sneeze' paintings that first brought attention to her work. Her first gallerist Zach Feuer invited the artist to hold her debut solo exhibition soon after completing her studies in 2002. Entitled 'Frank from Observation', it played on the idea of Schutz being the last painter on the planet. She depicted her fellow remaining human, Frank, on his quest for survival, which seemingly caused evolution to slide into reverse. A curious blend of playful, colourful humour and dark, morbid abjection, Schutz's oeuvre references modernist styles such as Expressionism and Cubism alongside the language of cartoons and the distortion of images in the digital era. Atrocious, ridiculous or impossible acts are often rendered with energetic painterly glee, such as the man seen here consuming his own features. A more challenging approach to the human condition permeates her increasingly existential mid-career works, exploring the boundaries between real life, the imagination and paint, in ways that have, on occasion, proved uncomfortable, emotive and controversial.

BERNI SEARLE

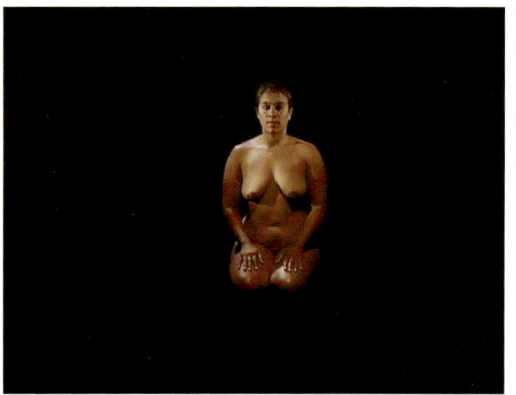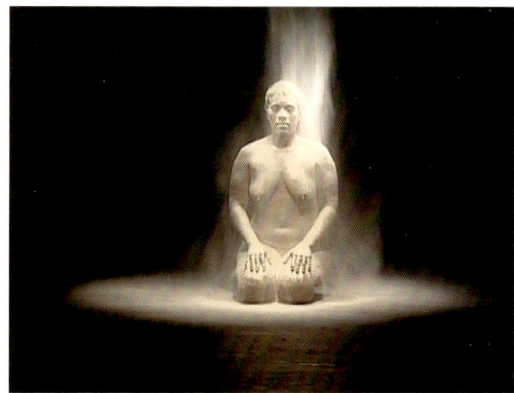

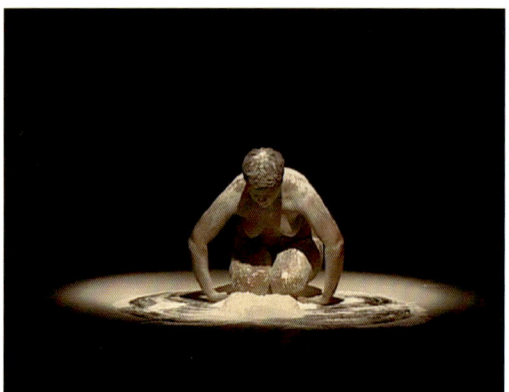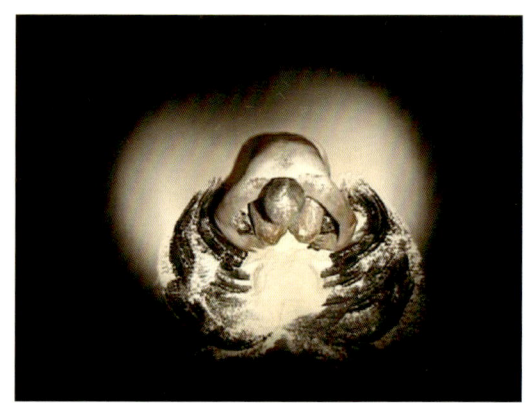

SNOW WHITE

2001, 2-channel video projection with sound, shot on DVCAM, 9 mins
Berni Searle, born 1964, Cape Town.

Raised and based in Cape Town, where she is currently Associate Professor and Director of the Michaelis School of Fine Art, Searle's art responds to the socio-political climate that led up to and followed the 1994 democratic elections in South Africa. She predominantly uses her own body in photographs and videos that interrogate identity and race in relation to history and place. This work, commissioned for the 49th Venice Biennale, was exhibited as a synchronized double projection viewed on opposite walls, one with a frontal viewpoint and the other aerial. The artist kneels, as a figure in meditation, bathed in dramatic light, and remains motionless as white flour falls on her nude body, creating ghost-like clouds around her. Her body is gradually transformed and covered in flour, which she then shakes off as drops of water fall from above, beginning to knead it into dough. The work can be read simultaneously as a homage to traditional ritual and cultural practices as well as a performative act of decolonization. It can be seen to embody the ambivalence and instability of identities in a postcolonial context.

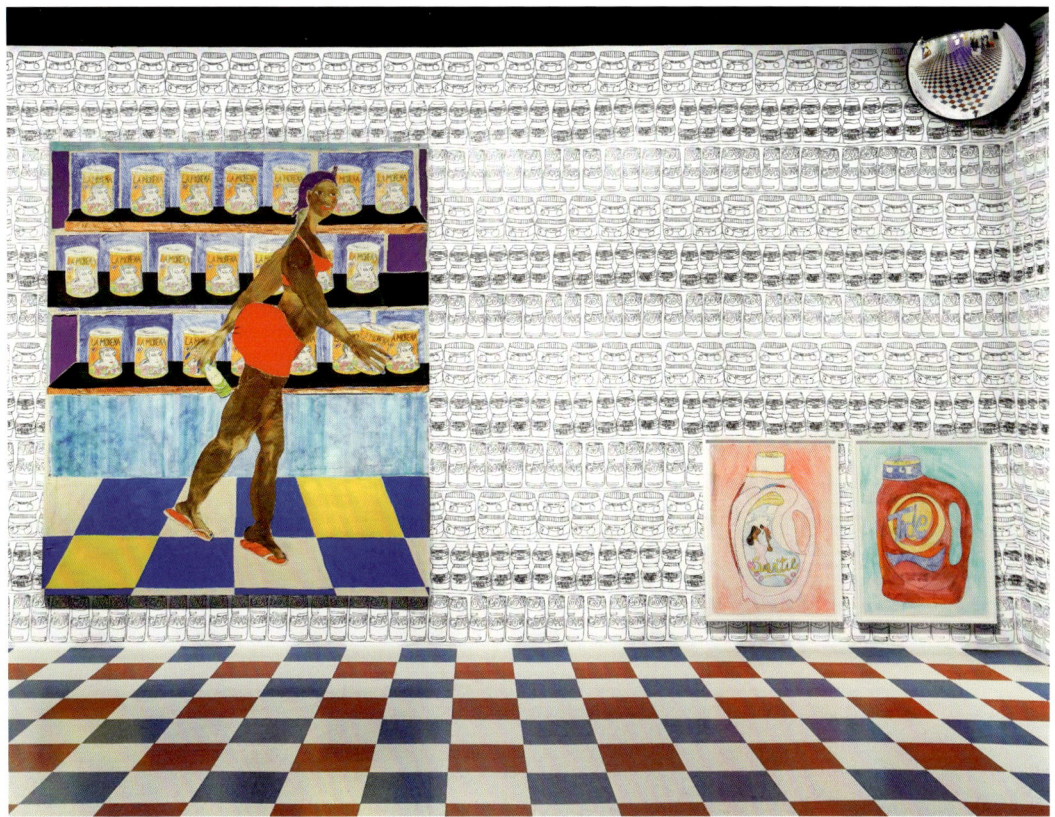

BAYO / PINK SOAP / RED SOAP

2017, acrylic, watercolour, flashe, crayon, coloured pencil, hand-coloured photocopy, coloured photocopy, hand-coloured canvas on canvas, 243.8 × 213.4 cm (96 × 84 in) / 2018, coloured pencil, gouache, acrylic and silkscreen on paper, 88.9 × 66 cm (35 × 26 in) / 2018, coloured pencil, gouache, acrylic and silkscreen on paper, 88.9 × 66 cm (35 × 26 in), installation view, 'Tschabalala Self: Bodega Run', Yuz Museum, Shanghai, 2018)

Tschabalala Self, born 1990, New York.

Self's work celebrates the female form through depictions of black women's bodies. Using a wide range of materials, her works combine print, paint and fabrics to give life to a range of characters who represent different registers of what it means to be a black woman today. Graduating from Yale School of Art's MFA programme in 2015, Self was quickly embraced by the art establishment, with international solo exhibitions at London's Parasol Unit in 2017 and at Shanghai's Yuz Museum in 2018, where this installation was seen. Its immersive environment included her playful painting, *Bayo*, of a woman shopping for pickled jalapeño peppers in a supermarket, as well as the stylized portraits *Pink Soap* and *Red Soap*, referencing detergent bottles. Dealing with emotions and ideas, Self defines her work as assemblage, repurposing found debris and 'accumulating' it to reflect how the body is one form comprised of numerous elements. She encourages people to look at each piece as a joyful exercise, an exploration of the female figure that, beyond stereotype or stigmatization, is the vessel by which we have all come into this world.

JOAN SEMMEL

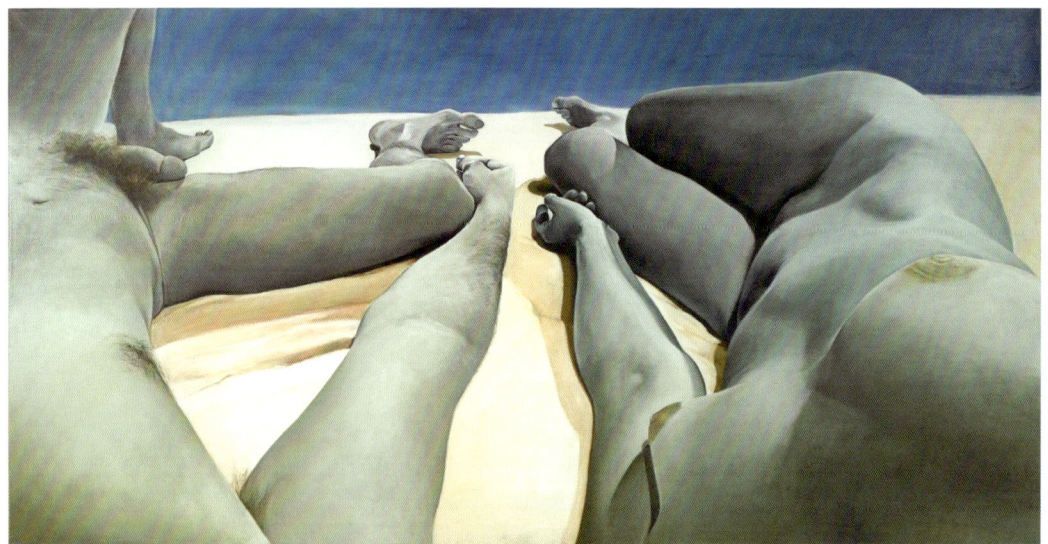

INTIMACY–AUTONOMY

1974, oil on canvas, 127 × 248.9 cm (50 × 98 in), Brooklyn Museum, New York
Joan Semmel, born 1932, New York.

Semmel's nude paintings of women and heterosexual couples are seen from angles that subvert the male gaze and reclaim female subjectivity. Having painted in an abstract style while living in Europe, she returned to New York in 1970 at the height of the feminist movement, also a time when uncensored and highly objectified images of women proliferated in commercial media. Both these cultural shifts prompted a figurative turn in her work in order to assert a specific woman's viewpoint. Semmel usually takes her own body as the model, painting from a photograph of what she sees through the camera. To the viewer, being more used to art that involves gazing at other people's bodies, these images seem strange and distorted. Semmel thus reminds us of exactly how we look to ourselves – from the head downwards, unable to see our own faces. Portrayed with her partner, this work from the 'Self-Images' series reclaims depictions of others, too, the artist acknowledging the full reality of another person while equally exposed to them. With uncompromising honesty, Semmel continues to explore the human figure, celebrating the ageing body and challenging obsessions with youthful femininity.

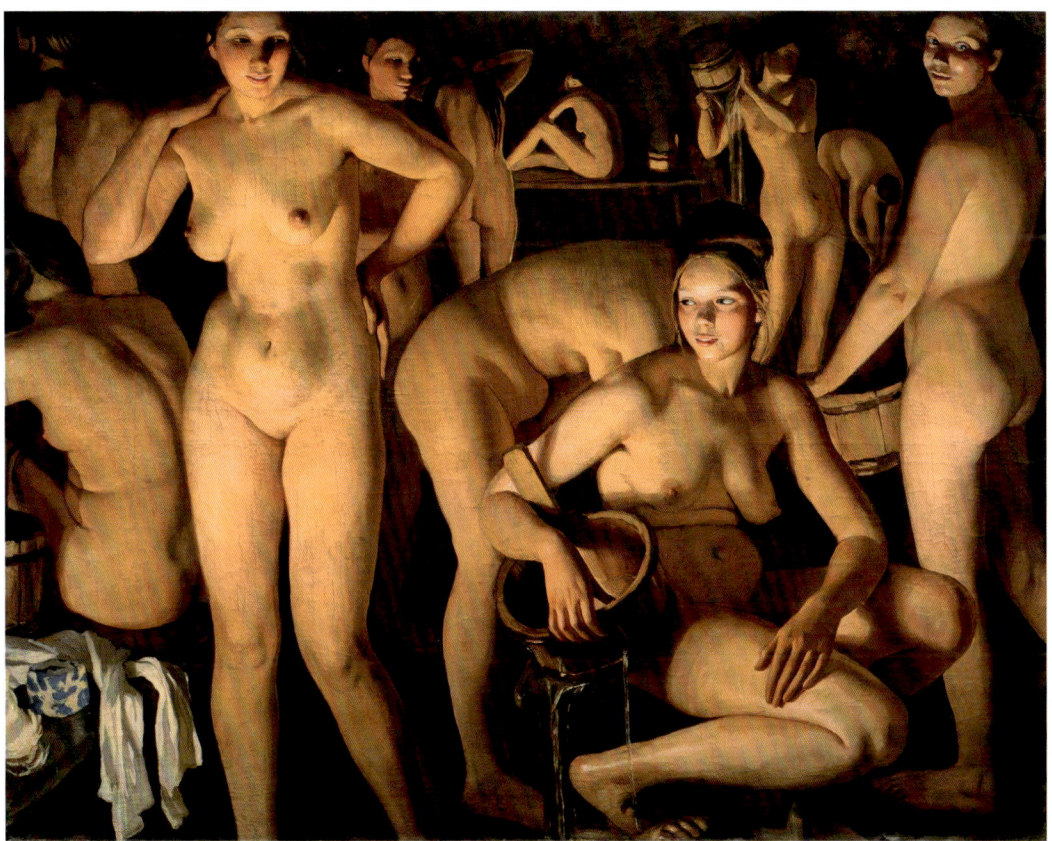

BATHHOUSE

1913, oil on canvas, 135 × 174 cm (53 ⅛ × 68 ½ in), State Russian Museum, St Petersburg

Zinaida Serebriakova, born Zinaida Lanceray, 1884, Neskuchnoye, near Kharkov, Ukraine (then Russian Empire). Died 1967, Paris.

In the years before the Russian Revolution, Serebriakova became known for heroic nudes and idealized scenes of peasant life. Often monumental in scale, these anticipated the Socialist Realism art of the Soviet era, albeit without the same propagandistic intent. Serebriakova had studied in France, Italy and her native Russia – her sketches from Paris in 1905 reveal an early fascination with artists including Titian (1488–1576), Jean-Antoine Watteau (1684–1721) and Edgar Degas (1834–1917). The Revolution had a devastating impact on her life: her husband was imprisoned by the Bolsheviks and died of typhus, and she lost her livelihood. Serebriakova went to Paris in 1924 to undertake a mural commission, leaving behind her four children (only two of whom subsequently joined her). Based in France for the remainder of her life, her works were not exhibited in the Soviet Union until the 1960s. *Bathhouse* dates from her pre-revolutionary phase. Nude female figures stand and crouch in multiple poses, their dramatically lit skin glowing, evoking the vigour of the Russian peasantry and the robust bodies of a classical Golden Age. The work is a refreshing alternative to more typical depictions of sexualized, reclining nudes in such settings, most famously *The Turkish Bath* (1852–9) by Jean-Auguste-Dominique Ingres.

SHEN YUAN

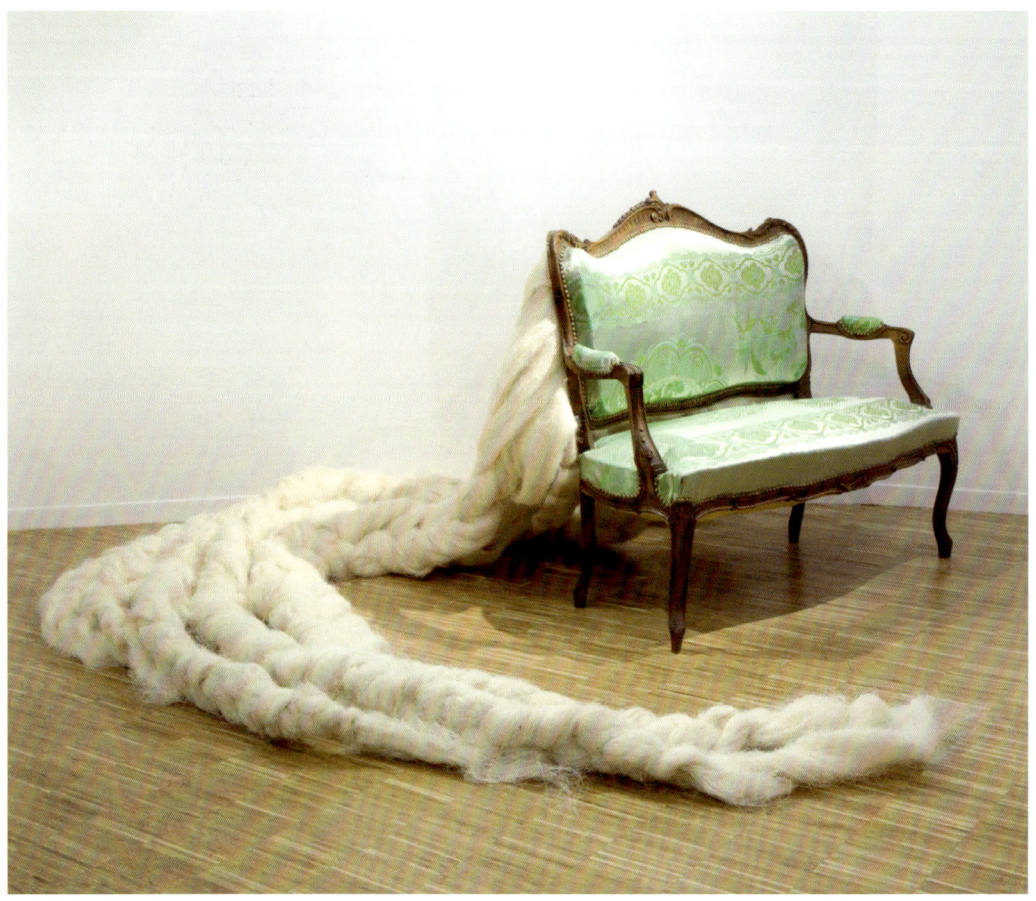

UNTITLED

2009, sofa and sisal, dimensions variable
Shen Yuan, born 1959, Xianyou, China.

Born into a family of artists, Shen studied traditional painting at the China Academy of Art, Hangzhou, in the early 1980s. Subsequently part of the avant-garde Xiamen Dada group, she married its founding member, Huang Yong Ping (1954–2019). In 1990, the couple moved permanently to Paris, where Shen still lives and works. Shen addresses contemporary issues faced by women, particularly around poverty and low-status female employment, and references traditional Chinese culture fused with elements drawn from elsewhere. Her early experiences as an immigrant in France – unable to speak the language – forged themes of communication in her sculpture and installations, and her strategy of immersion in local communities. Tongues and hair are recurring motifs, parts of the body that express identity but which can also bind people to it. Hairstyles have great historic significance for both women and men in China and the artist was struck by a 1930s photograph of male prisoners tied to each other by their traditional queue hairstyles. This installation alludes to that image, a French Regency-style sofa with long, thick braids emanating from the back.

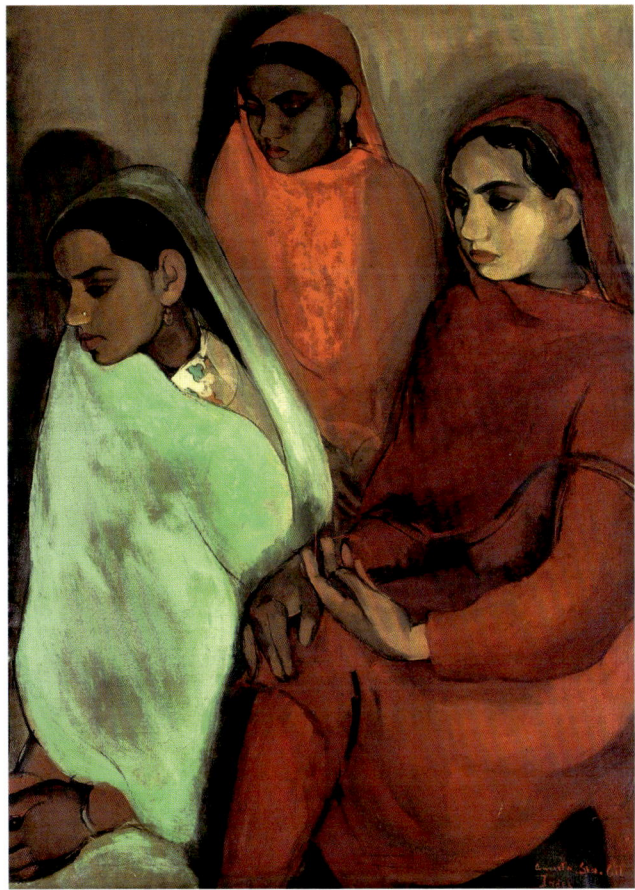

THREE GIRLS

1935, oil on canvas, 92.8 × 66.5 cm (36½ × 26⅛ in), National Gallery of Modern Art, New Delhi

Amrita Sher-Gil, born 1913, Budapest. Died 1941, Lahore, India (now Pakistan).

Following studies at the École des Beaux-Arts, Paris, and a five-year period in the city's artistic milieu, Sher-Gil became adamant that her future career would be in India, moving there in 1934. Of Sikh-Hungarian heritage, her father's ancestral home was in the foothills of Shimla, Himachal Pradesh. With a mastery of European painterly traditions, Sher-Gil was confident in her experimentation and positioned her work against the romantic nationalism of the concurrent Bengal school. She travelled the country painting from observation, focusing on the representation of women and their inner emotional lives. Her style developed as her European realism became assimilated with the aesthetics of her surroundings. With a growing appreciation of classical Indian art, she drew inspiration from the compositional structure of the Ajanta cave paintings and Mughal miniatures. In this work, which won a Gold Medal at the Bombay Art Society in 1937, a solemn stillness pervades the scene, the women averting their eyes from the artist's gaze. Whether in reverie or sorrow, they appear to be adrift from the space they inhabit but are nevertheless contained in the artist's empathy.

AMY SHERALD

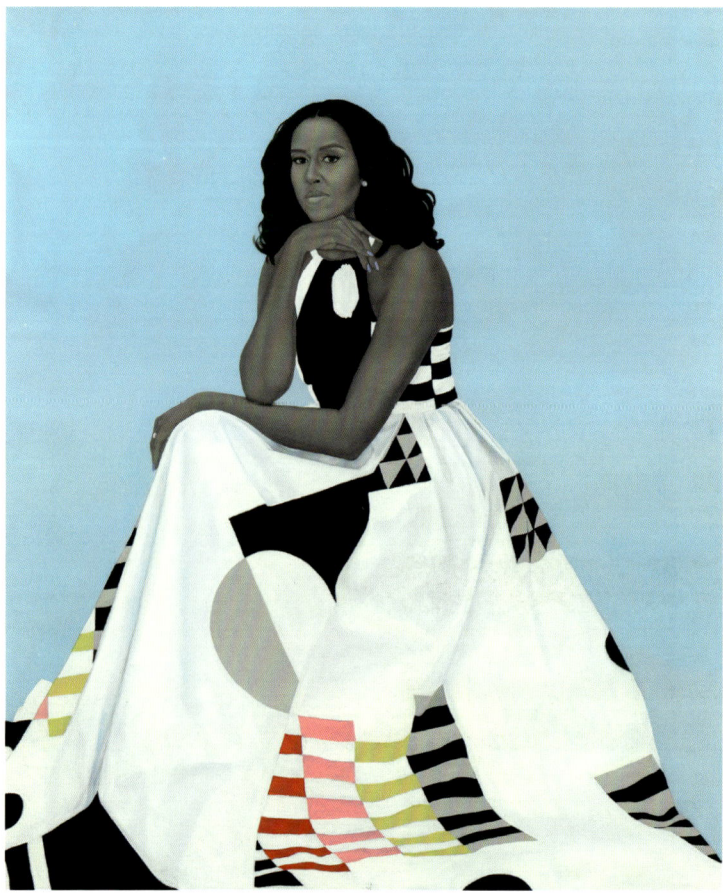

MICHELLE LAVAUGHN ROBINSON OBAMA
2018, oil on linen, 183.2 × 152.7 cm (72 ⅛ × 60 ⅛ in), National Portrait Gallery,
Smithsonian Institution, Washington DC
Amy Sherald, born 1973, Columbus, Georgia.

Sherald shot to fame in 2018 with this portrait of Michelle Obama, depicted as confident and amiable, and wearing a flowing dress. Sherald chose the garment, designed by Michelle Smith for her label MILLY, for its formal affinity to both abstract painting and the celebrated Gee's Bend quilts made by African-American women in rural Alabama. Despite painting for years, Sherald only gained wider attention in 2016 when she was the first woman to win the prestigious Outwin Boochever Portrait Competition, before becoming the first black woman to receive the official commission to portray America's First Lady. While her early works were autobiographical, later paintings address issues of race and identity, focusing exclusively on African-American subjects. Challenging perceptions of black identity, she renders skin tones in shades of grey. Her figures assertively confront the viewer's gaze, while colourful patterned clothing and blotchy monochrome backgrounds offset their grisaille complexions. Whether painting anonymous faces or one of the best known in America, Sherald's work emphasizes the intrinsic worth of her subjects as human beings.

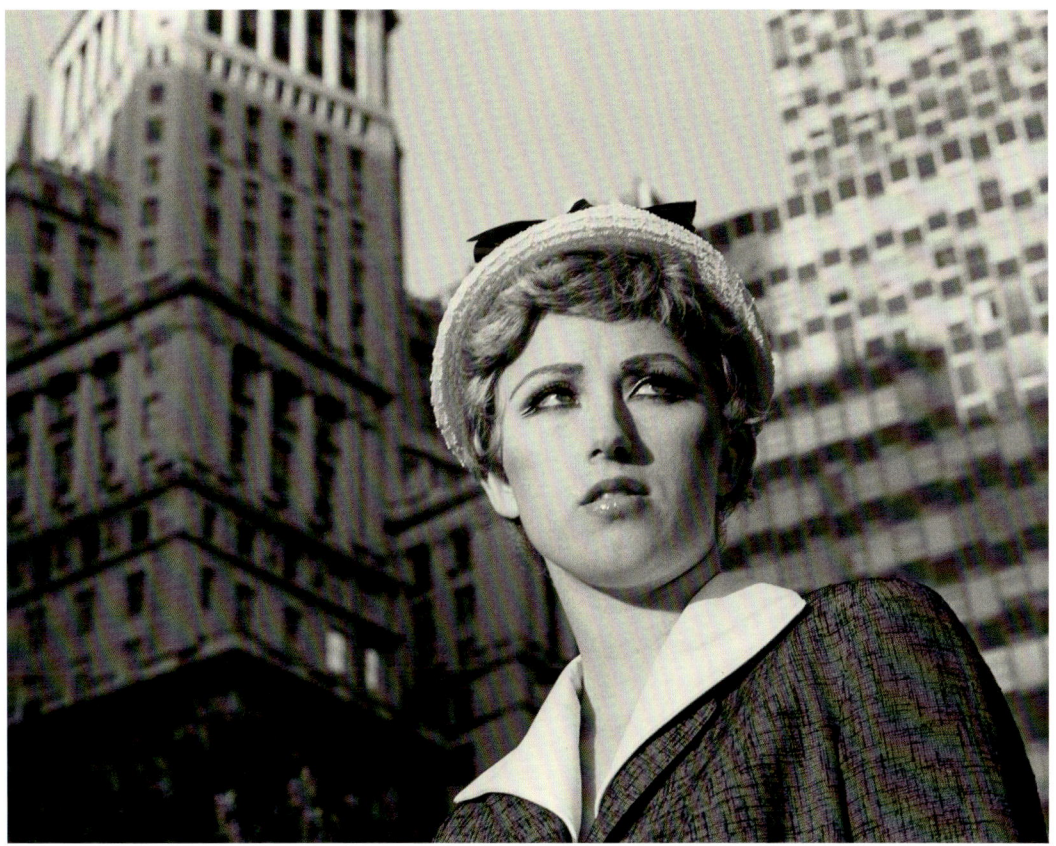

UNTITLED FILM STILL #21

1978, gelatin silver print, 19.1 × 24.1 cm (7½ × 9½ in)
Cindy Sherman, born 1954, Glen Ridge, New Jersey.

Sherman has used herself as a model in her photographic works since her student days at Buffalo State College. Early works involved headshots and photobooth images of the artist dressed up as different types of person, especially – but not exclusively – female, and issues of identity and metamorphosis have prevailed throughout her work. Transforming herself across sequences of images, with props ranging from her own belongings to elaborate prostheses and masks, she questions the role, image and spectacle of being a woman. Her practice for more than forty years has evolved from this underlying interest in appearances and the complicity between camera and stagecraft, and what this implies about both a person's inner life and existence in society at large. Soon after graduating, Sherman started her 'Untitled Film Stills' series (1977–80). In the black-and-white aesthetic of Hollywood noir and European art cinema, she depicted herself as different characters in staged 'publicity shots' for imaginary movies. One of the world's leading art photographers, her subsequent series were devoted to themes including fairy tales, pornography, disasters and historical portraits, with more recent works addressing topics such as ageing and social status.

MARY SIBANDE

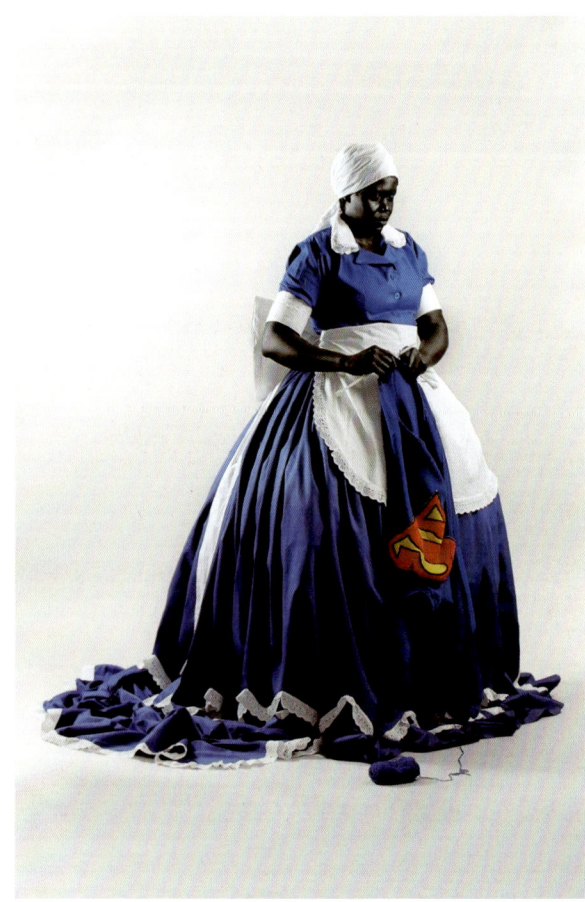

THEY DON'T MAKE THEM LIKE THEY USED TO

2008, archival digital print, 90 × 60 cm (35 ⅜ × 23 ⅝ in), UNISA Art Gallery,
Pretoria, South Africa and Johannesburg Art Gallery
Mary Sibande, born 1982, Barberton, South Africa.

Born twelve years before the end of apartheid, Sibande's practice of
painting, sculpture and photography examines the socio-political
effects of her context on race, gender and class. The first woman in
her family to attend university – she graduated from the University
of Johannesburg in 2007 – she went on to represent South Africa at
the 54th Venice Biennale (2011). Her work looks at female identity
in the postcolonial context and how women are often excluded from
the leading roles in society. Sibande has created an alter ego called
Sophie, who appears in many of the human-scale sculptures she makes
based on her own body. In *They Don't Make Them Like They Used To*,
Sophie wears the Victorian-style outfit typically worn by women –
including Sibande's ancestors – when forced into conditions of racial-
ized domestic servitude. The use of modern fabrics and a familiar
motif reminds the viewer that female subjugation continues to this day.
However, the choice of a Superman costume for Sophie to stitch
symbolizes the potency of these women and the possibility of transcendence, with the title alluding to both labour and fortitude.

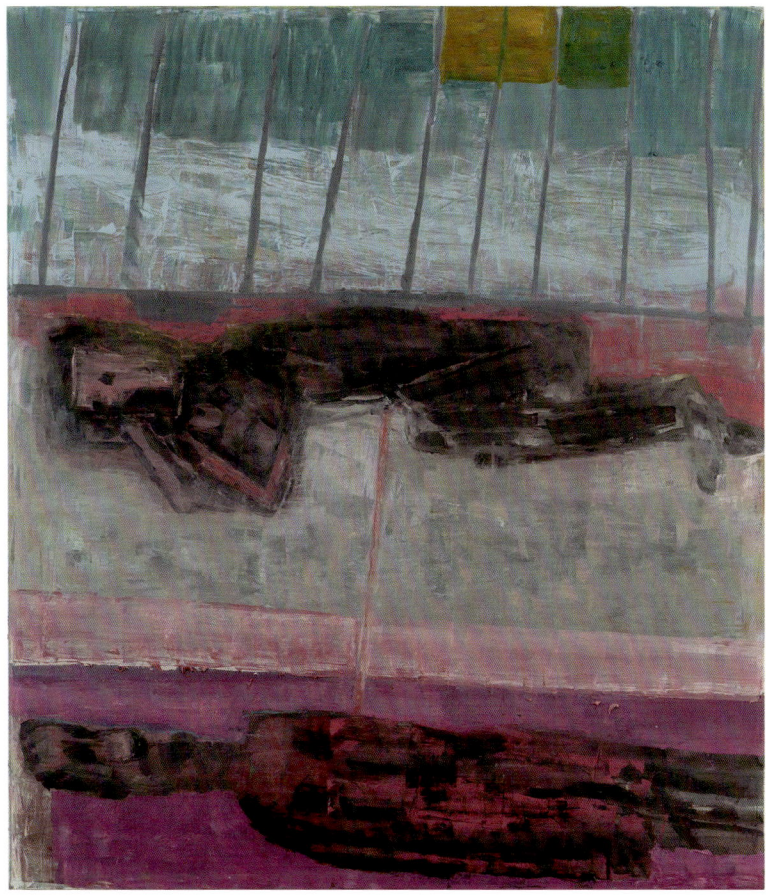

IN ILLINOIS

2017–18, oil on canvas, 190.5 × 167.6 cm (75 × 66 in)
Amy Sillman, born 1955, Detroit, Michigan.

In a practice that is based in drawing and informed by sources outside of painting, Sillman invites a reconsideration of the limits of the painted canvas. She has experimented with abstraction and figuration, line and brushstroke, form and colour, and also recently with digital processes. The diptych *Duel* (2013), for example, features a canvas alongside an animation of thousands of hand-drawn frames presented on an iPad. She explains that the animation proposes a new set of possible endings for the painting and 'takes up where the painting leaves off'. An influential educator, Sillman held the position of co-chair of the Painting Department at Bard College's MFA Program (2002–13) – where she completed her master's in 1995. Her process of making can be immediate or extensively prolonged – she digs, scrapes back and reworks canvases repeatedly, reorienting them along the way. This commitment to the temporal element of the process of painting testifies to Sillman's relationship with the medium, open to both irreverence and humour, but always deeply embodied and materialist. Such qualities are in evidence in *In Illinois*, where fine lines and figurative forms interrupt the pace of the otherwise abstract, chunky and layered painted surface.

LAURIE SIMMONS

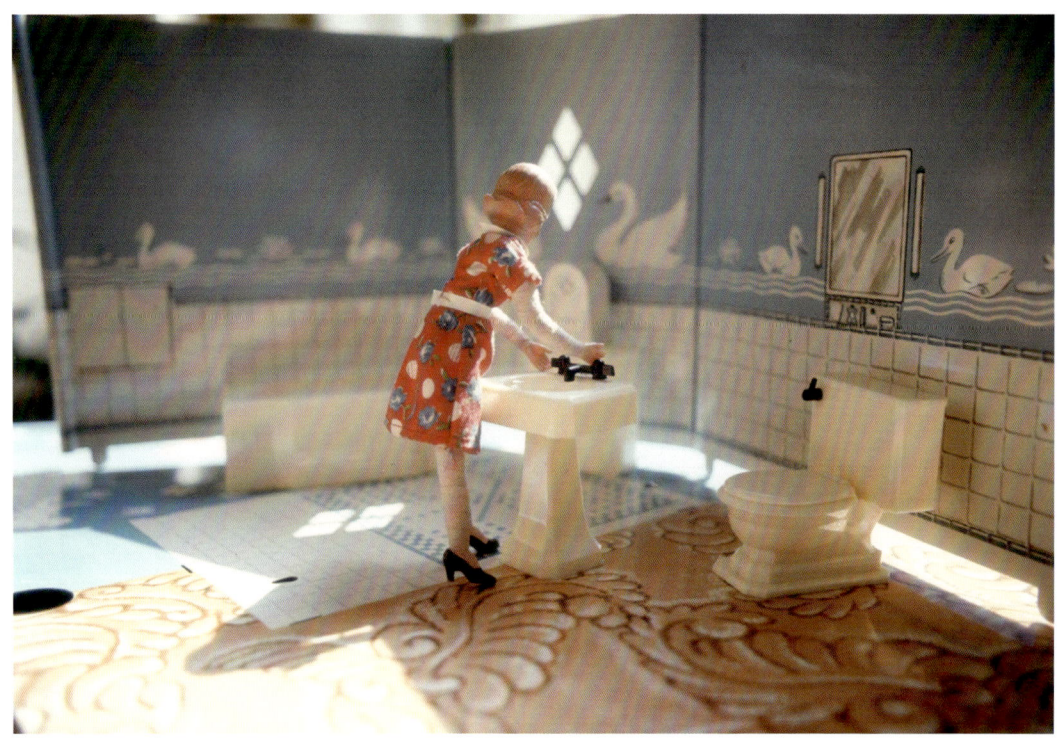

FIRST BATHROOM / WOMAN STANDING

1978, Cibachrome print, 8.9 × 12.7 cm (3 ½ × 5 in)
Laurie Simmons, born 1949, New York.

Simmons's work exposes the constructed nature of femininity. Since the early 1970s, she has used photography and film to stage scenes that are populated by people or various dolls – from shop dummies to objects on legs and, more recently, a 'love doll', a highly realistic mannequin intended for sex and companionship. Her art considers the role that images play in creating desire and the value judgements women face in society. In 1972 Simmons found a doll's house similar to the one she had played with as a child and began creating photographs of it featuring a tiny housewife, and – using hobbyist techniques – made small-format prints in keeping with the miniaturization of their subject matter. At the time, feminists decried children's toys that reinforced the patriarchal ideas of a woman's place being in the home, that sexualized women's bodies or that emphasized their role as mothers. The gendered environment of a doll's house was an ideal space for Simmons's critique of the oppressive demands on femininity in contemporary society. To exacerbate the uncanny effect of the project in this work, Simmons photographed the doll's house in sunlight, introducing natural lighting into a wholly artificial environment.

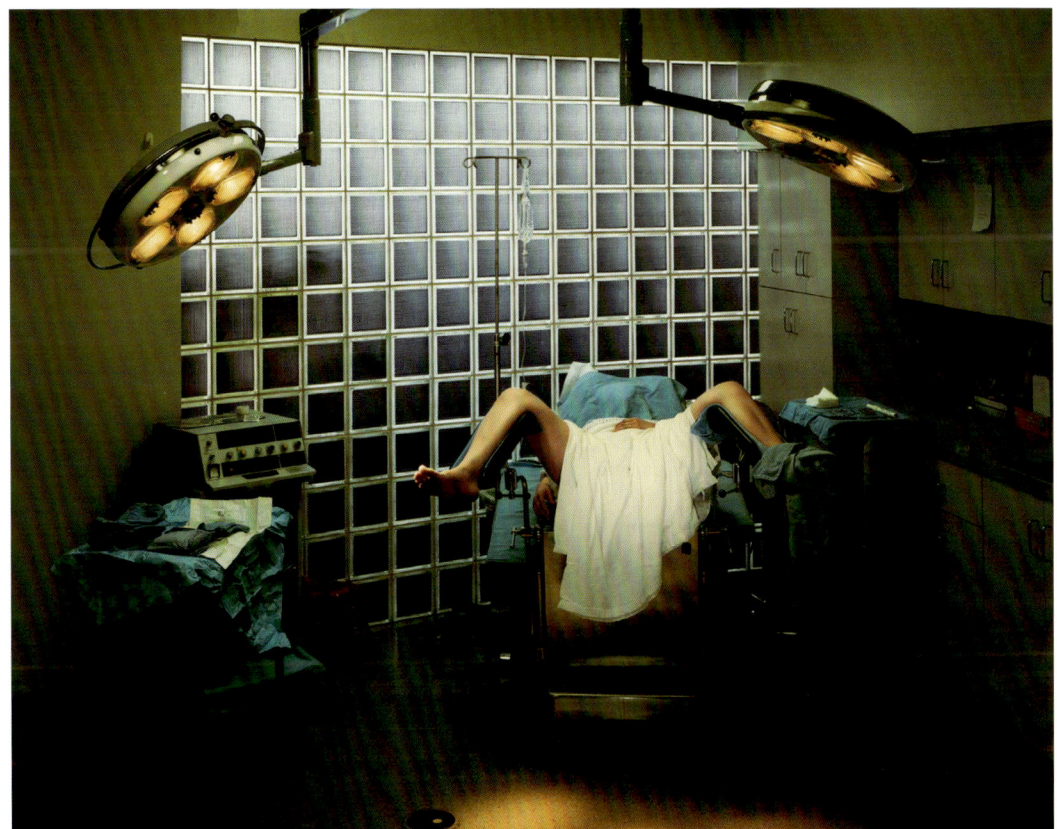

HYMENOPLASTY, COSMETIC SURGERY, P.A., FORT LAUDERDALE, FLORIDA from the series 'AN AMERICAN INDEX OF THE HIDDEN AND UNFAMILIAR'

2007, framed archival inkjet print and letraset on wall, 94.6 × 113.7 cm (37¼ × 44¾ in)
Taryn Simon, born 1975, New York.

After graduating in 1997 with a degree in semiotics, Simon's first major photographic project, for which she received a Guggenheim Fellowship in 2001, was 'The Innocents'. The series documents cases of wrongful conviction and interrogates the role of photography and the eyewitness memory in the criminal justice system. Exploring structures of power and authority, and the organizational systems behind everyday life, each of Simon's projects involves years of intensive research and planning, including obtaining access to normally off-limits institutions such as the CIA and the Department of Homeland Security. Simon has worked extensively in photography, text and graphic design and her recent projects have also featured sound, sculpture and performance, including her major work, *An Occupation of Loss* (2018). For 'An American Index of the Hidden and Unfamiliar', Simon photographed objects and places central to the American way of life, but which are inaccessible or unknown, so rarely seen. This image depicts a twenty-one-year-old of Palestinian descent living in the United States undergoing surgical reconstruction of her hymen to meet cultural and familial expectations about virginity before marriage.

LORNA SIMPSON

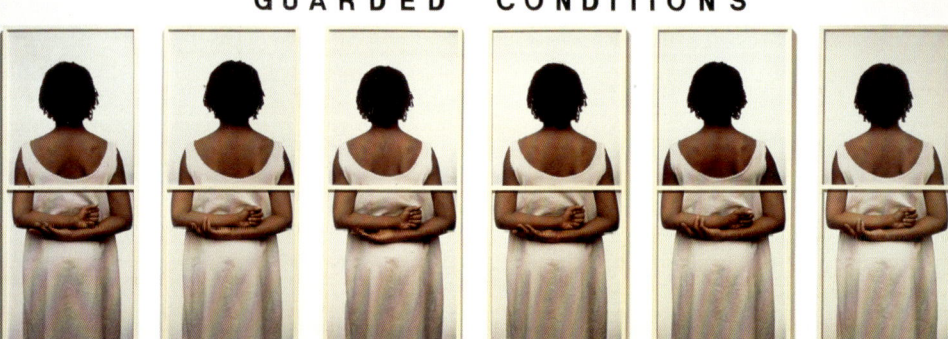

GUARDED CONDITIONS

1989, 18 dye diffusion colour Polaroid prints, 6 frames total (3 prints in each), 21 engraved plastic plaques, 17 plastic letters, 214 × 376.6 × 4.1 cm (84 ¼ × 148 ¼ × 1 ⅝ in), Museum of Contemporary Art, San Diego
Lorna Simpson, born 1960, New York.

Simpson combines pictures and text to destabilize viewers' expectations of the truthfulness of photography. Addressing the experience of African-American people and black women in particular, her collages use images from vintage magazines such as *Ebony* and *Jet* to consider issues of representation, identity and difference. Travelling in Europe and Africa in the 1980s, her early works used documentary photography, which later shifted to incorporate text and objects, using the photographic image as a component in a wider conceptual practice. For example, her recent series 'Earth & Sky' (2016) shows glamorous women with gemstones collaged in place of their hair. In this earlier work, *Guarded Conditions*, her signature use of 'photo-text' combines words and graphics in a form of an unusual portrait. The image of a woman, fractured into three parts, is repeated six times with only minor variations, but unlike traditional portraits that show a face, here the subject has no individual identity. Her simple white dress has echoes of living with oppression – under 'guarded conditions'. The recurrent phrases beneath evoke cycles of power and violence, their rhythms mirroring relentless patterns of abuse.

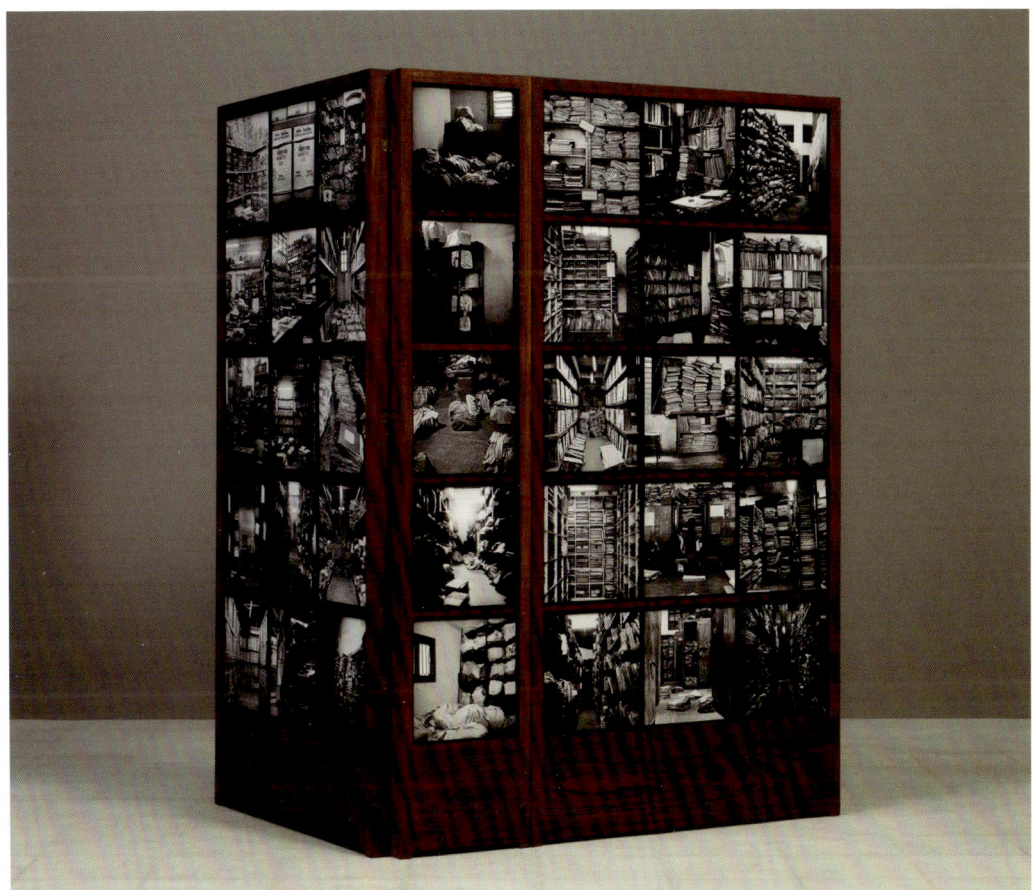

FILE MUSEUM

2012, (detail), 1 large and 3 small structures, 140 archival pigment prints, large structure: 188 × 109 × 48 cm (74 × 42 ⅞ × 18 ⅞ in), each small structure: 32.5 × 32.5 × 10.5 cm (12 ¾ × 12 ¾ × 4 ⅛ in), each print: 30 × 30 cm (11 ¾ × 11 ¾ in) Dayanita Singh, born 1961, New Delhi.

Observations of daily life in India are central to Singh's practice as a photographer and publisher. Graduating from the National Institute of Design, Ahmedabad, and the International Center of Photography School, New York, she began her career as a photo-journalist, a viewpoint that made her aware of the malleability of images and their potential for transformation, dependent on context. Using a vast stock of archive images, she experiments with modes of display, often adopting the book as a medium: for example, in her groundbreaking 2008 work, *Sent a Letter*. Singh edits her work through a process of engaging with her emotional responses to the pictures. Primarily working in black and white and often recording depopulated scenes, thus divesting India of its stereotypical vibrancy, her photos are at once elusive and intimate. In this work, 140 such prints are stored in single compartments as framed panels within four teak cuboids. These can be folded in on themselves or opened out. Constructed to allow the photographs to be shuffled and resequenced, Singh sets up seemingly endless potential narratives and connections in her moveable museum, a recursive archive of archives.

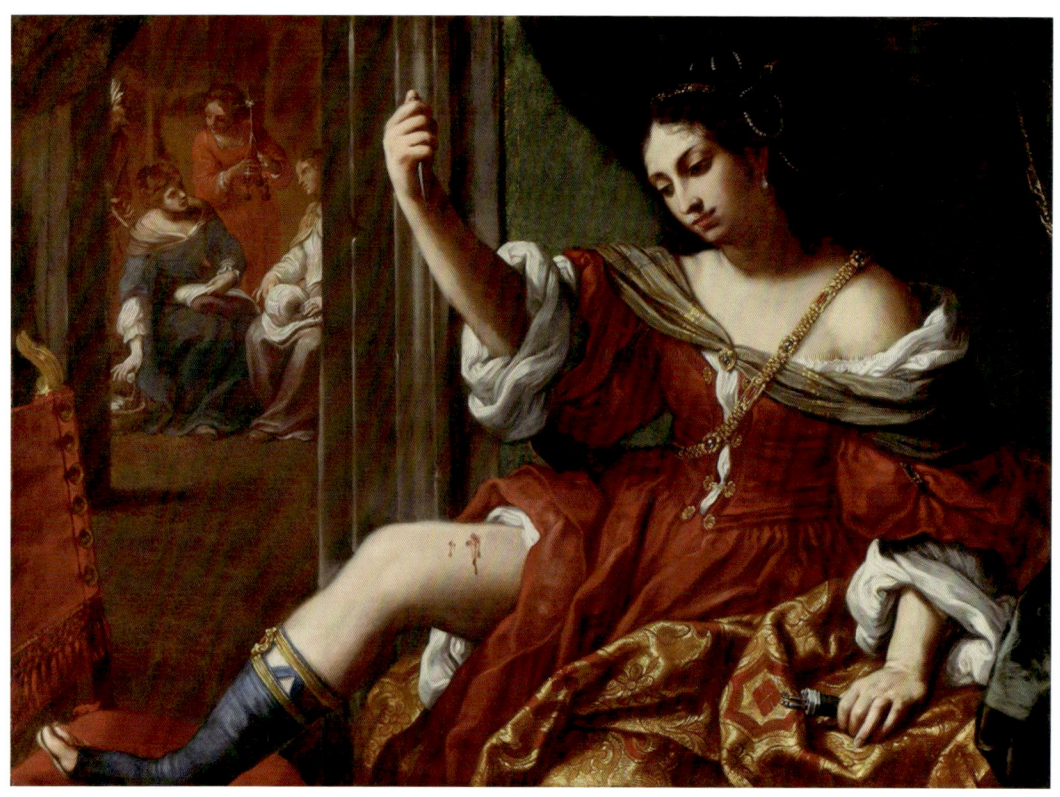

PORTIA WOUNDING HER THIGH

1664, oil on canvas, 101 × 138 cm (39 ¾ × 54 ⅜ in), Fondazione Carisbo, Bologna, Italy
Elisabetta Sirani, born 1638, Bologna, Italy. Died 1665, Bologna, Italy.

Sirani was the eldest child of Bolognese artist Giovanni Andrea Sirani (1610–70) though her artistic reputation quickly surpassed his. At age sixteen she took over her father's studio and became the family's principle breadwinner. She trained her two sisters – Anna Maria (1645–1715) and Barbara (1649–92) – and also opened her own school for female painters, the first such academy established outside a convent during the Renaissance. When depicting *femmes fortes* – heroic women – Sirani emphasized virtue and idealization rather than the violent drama of Artemisia Gentileschi (p.150). Commissioned by a silk merchant, this work depicts a first-century BC Roman woman dressed in luxurious fabrics. Portia was the wife of Brutus and is shown wounding her own thigh to prove to her husband that she is impervious to pain and can be trusted to share his secrets: the conspiracy to assassinate Julius Caesar. This is the only known depiction to omit Brutus's image, foregrounding feminine courage. Producing nearly 200 canvases in the ten years before her untimely death, Sirani was highly esteemed in Bologna and granted a public funeral with architecture, music, oratory and poetry commissioned in her honour.

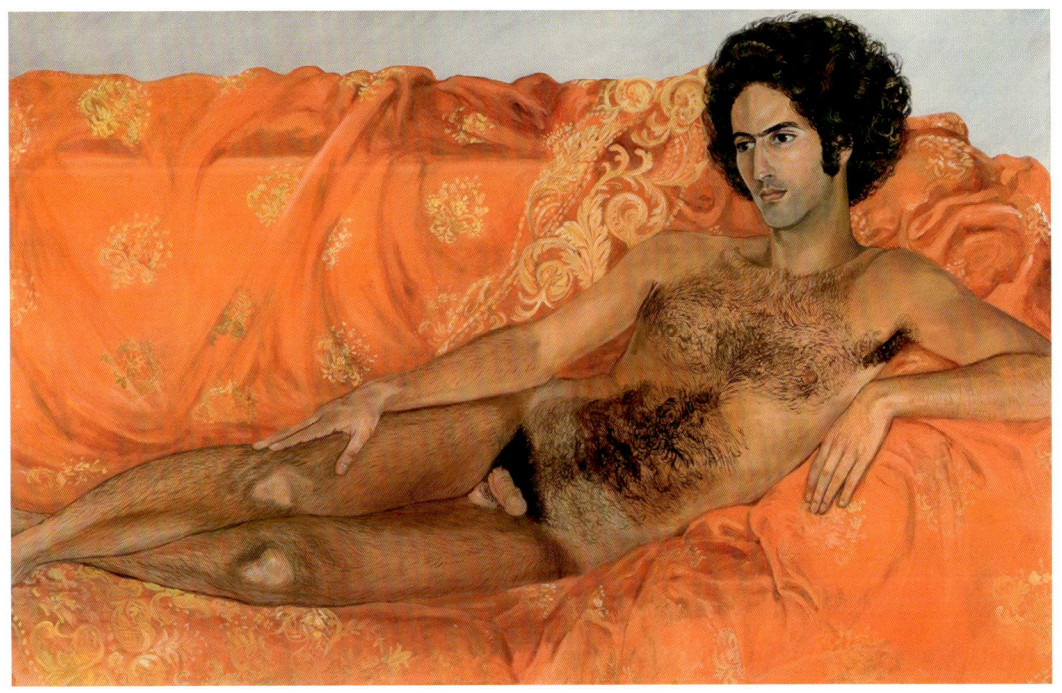

IMPERIAL NUDE: PAUL ROSANO

1977, oil on canvas, 107 × 168 cm (42 ⅛ × 66 ⅛ in), private collection
Sylvia Sleigh, born 1916, Llandudno, UK. Died 2010, New York.

Welsh-born Sleigh was a realist painter known for her ground-
breaking paintings of nudes. Having gained little recognition in
London in her early career, Sleigh moved to New York in the 1960s,
where she met and married the art critic and Guggenheim curator
Lawrence Alloway. She became an important part of the city's
feminist art scene, mixing with culturally significant writers and
artists, some of whom would later become subjects for Sleigh's
paintings. Adopting a unique style of portraiture that portrayed
the humanizing traits and imperfections of her sitters, including
details such as body hair and tan lines, Sleigh challenged art-historical
traditions that objectified and idealized the body, particularly
female. In some works, Sleigh deliberately subverted gender roles,
such as in *Turkish Bath* (1973), which echoed the composition of
JeanAuguste-Dominique Ingres's painting of 1852–9, but cast
lounging naked men as subjects. Despite such political undertones,
she also made a point of highlighting beauty in every sitter, regard-
less of their gender. She often painted the same people multiple
times, including her friend Paul Rosano, who, in this work, adopts
a classical Venus-like pose, often performed by female models and
suggested in the title.

KIKI SMITH

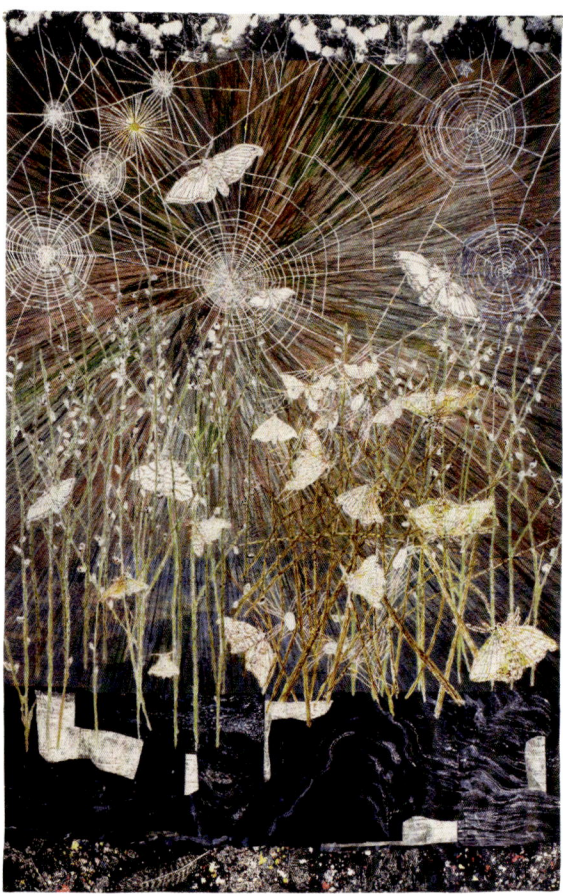

SPINNERS (MOTHS AND SPIDERS WEBS)
2014, cotton Jacquard tapestry, hand-painting and gold leaf, 294.6 × 193 cm
(116 × 76 in). Published by Magnolia Editions
Kiki Smith, born Chiara Smith, 1954, Nuremberg, Germany.

A German-born American artist, Smith is known for her anatomi-
cal-based works that address the human condition in relation
to nature. Having begun to gain critical recognition in the 1980s
in the aftermath of the second-wave feminist movement in New York,
Smith forged a unique figurative path in the midst of an abstract-
dominated era. Prompted by the AIDS epidemic, in which she was
personally affected by the loss of friends and family members, Smith
focused her earlier works on organs and cellular forms, which gave
her a deep understanding of the internal body. Breaking away from
her abject and bodily work in recent years, Smith has drawn on her
interests in Norse mythology, folk art and fairy tales, and medieval
signs and symbols in her sculptures and tapestries. Smith's woven
pieces are devised by collaging lifesize cartoons from her drawings
and prints, to which she adds glimmers of gold leaf to emphasize
their enchanted qualities. Typical of her recent explorations,
Spinners connects transient natural forms with themes of life, death
and resurrection.

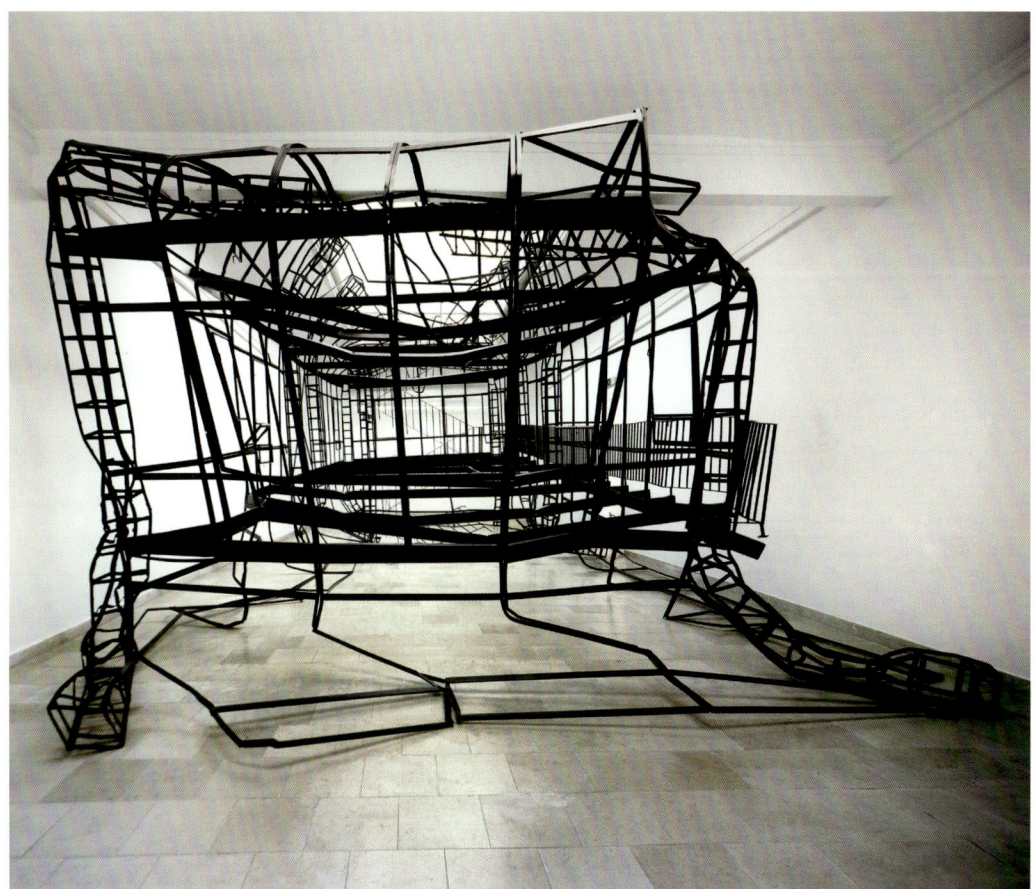

1:1

2007, steel construction, 700 × 1,400 × 600 cm (275 × 550 × 235 in), installation view,
Polish Pavilion, 52nd Venice Biennale
Monika Sosnowska, born 1972, Ryki, Poland.

Since the Second World War, cities in Poland, including Warsaw, Sosnowska's current home, have undergone considerable redevelopment. During the 1980s in particular, several Soviet-era housing blocks and civic spaces were destroyed or refurbished, while rashly planned new developments were neglected as quickly as they sprang up. Sosnowska was deeply affected by these changes, carefully documenting and responding to their impact on the urban fabric through photographs, sculptures and large-scale installations. Often using illusion and subverting the structural logic of architecture, she has stated that her work is about creating 'surrealist, impossible situations' that emphasize architecture's vulnerability as much as its power. This is evident in her installation for the 52nd Venice Biennale (2007), where she created a lifesize steel copy of the frame of a postwar apartment block, which she then crushed to fit into the Polish Pavilion. Appearing at once like a frail creature and a monstrous parasite threatening its host environment, *1:1* exemplifies Sosnowska's interest in structures that seem to feed off one another, introducing 'chaos and uncertainty' into architecture's supposed rationality and order.

MARIE SPARTALI STILLMAN

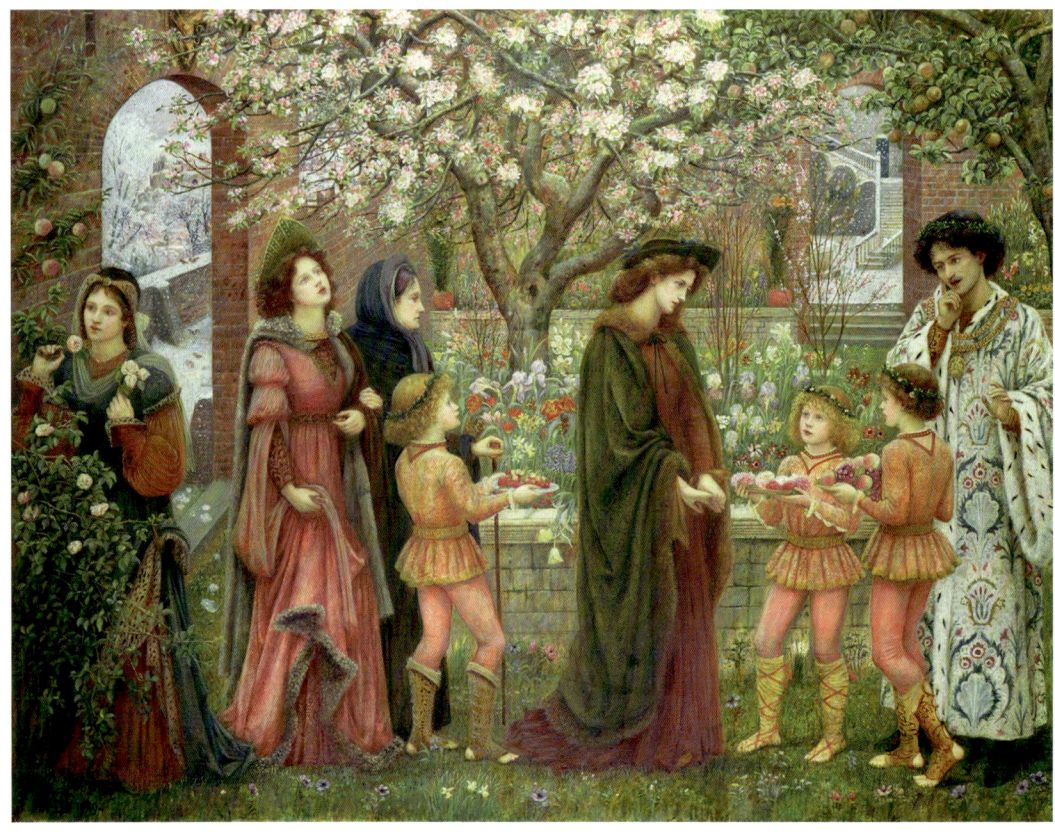

THE ENCHANTED GARDEN OF MESSER ANSALDO

1899, watercolour on mounted paper, 76.2 × 101.6 cm (30 × 40 in), private collection
Marie Spartali Stillman, born Marie Euphrosyne Spartali, 1844, London.
Died 1927, London.

The daughter of the Greek consul-general in London, Spartali
Stillman was well known as a model for many of the Pre-Raphaelite
painters, also posing for the photographer Julia Margaret Cameron
(p.84). Though long overlooked, several women associated with the
Pre-Raphaelite Brotherhood were significant artists in their own
right. Spartali Stillman painted watercolours with layers of luminous
colour, producing over 150 works throughout her sixty-year career.
She exhibited and sold work internationally: in 1870 at London's
Royal Academy of Arts; in 1873 in Boston, becoming involved in

that city's intellectual circles alongside her American-born journalist
husband; and at the *Exposition Universelle* in Paris in 1878. In this
painting, the idealized protagonist Dianora (from Boccaccio's
Decameron, a collection of novellas first published in 1353 – a suitable
subject for an artist looking to the period prior to Raphael for inspiration) has rejected the incessant advances of her suitor Ansaldo. She
promises to leave her husband for him only if his garden blooms
in January – a seemingly impossible task, which he accomplishes with
the help of a necromancer. Spartali Stillman captures Dianora's look
of astonishment and despair as she's presented fresh fruit.

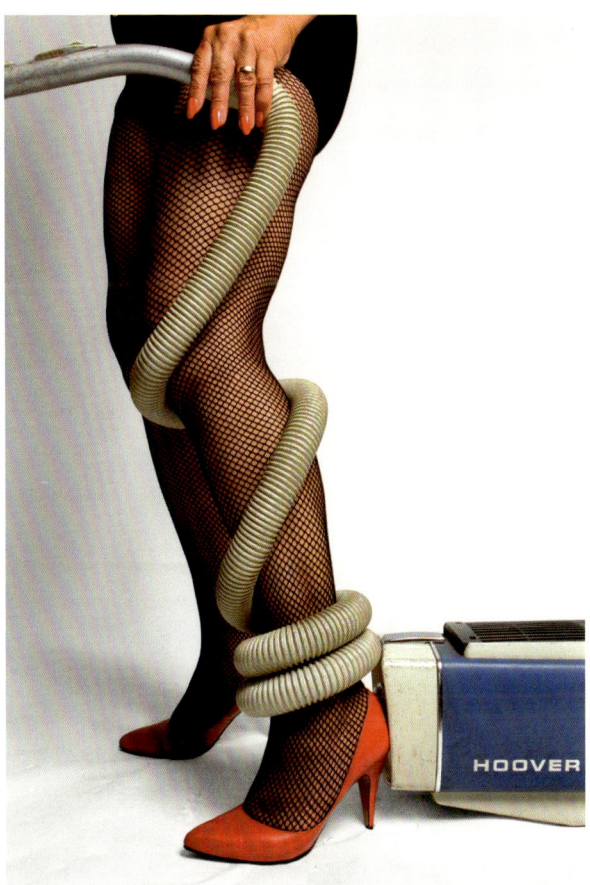

LIBIDO UPRISING PART I

1989, collaboration with Rosy Martin, pigment print, 105 × 70 cm (41 ³⁄₈ × 27 ½ in), edition of 3, printed 2018
Jo Spence, born 1934, London. Died 1992, London.

From a working-class family, Spence was an active socialist and feminist from the early 1970s, producing agitprop images while working as a secretary and high-street photographer to fund her artistic practices. She attended university in 1979 as a mature student at the Polytechnic of Central London, engaging with theories of communication, psychoanalysis and identity. In 1982, she was diagnosed with cancer, an event that triggered a new approach to her art as she researched the disease and its treatments and looked for ways of conceptualizing them. Eventually, Spence used cancer as a

metaphor for all forms of struggle against oppression, including feminism's struggles against the patriarchy and consumerism. For her series 'Libido Uprising', Spence appropriated and subverted symbols of femininity, including the wedding band, high heels and the instruments of housekeeping. She made the series in collaboration with Rosy Martin (b.1946), whom she met at a co-counselling session, and with whom she developed the practice of 'phototherapy', a turning of the camera on oneself and one's therapeutic partner in a process that combined feeling and acting and brought together Spence's interests in sexuality, identity and collaboration.

NANCY SPERO

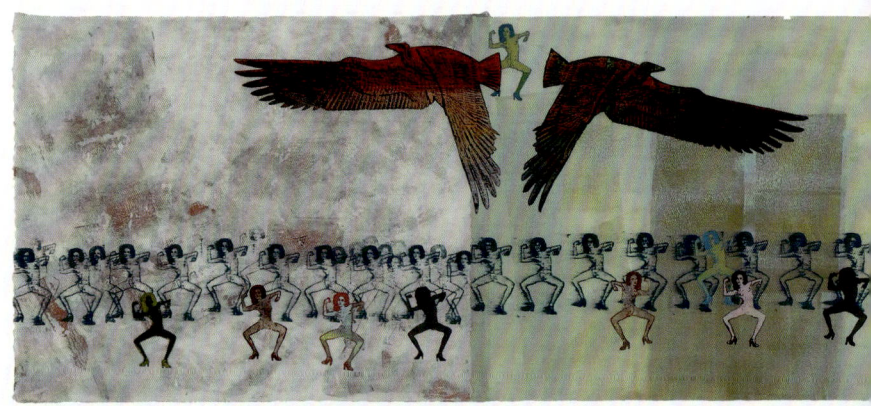

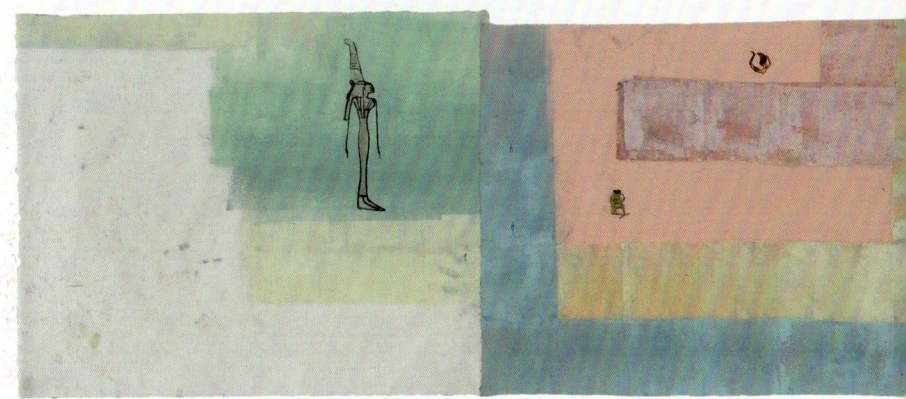

AZUR

2002, panels 19 and 20 from 39 total, silkscreen, linocut and synthetic paint on oriental paper, 50 × 244 cm (19 ¾ × 96 in)and 49 × 250 cm (19 ⅓ × 98 ½ in), Musée National d'Art Moderne, Centre Georges Pompidou, Paris
Nancy Spero, born 1926, Cleveland, Ohio. Died 2009, New York.

A pillar of the feminist art movement in New York through the 1960s and 1970s, Spero was an activist for women's rights. She participated in the actions of WAR (Women Artists in Revolution, 1969–72) and was one of twenty founding members of A.I.R. Gallery, America's first women's cooperative gallery in 1972. Through art and campaigning, she represented the position and subjectivity of women, producing a body of work that spoke truth to power about the struggles of marginalized communities around the world. Spero regarded many of her works as anti-war manifestos, her subjects ranging from the Algerian struggle for independence to the Vietnam War; her 'War' series (1966–70) uses familiar imagery of bombs and helicopters in drawings and paintings that angrily condemned the violence and destruction of the American-backed campaign. In 1966, Spero abandoned working on canvas, considering the medium too masculine, and employed collage, printing, drawing and painting on paper as her primary media. Her epic 82-metre (270-foot) frieze, *Azur*, took five years to complete and presents a cast of female characters drawn from throughout history, including ancient Egyptian and Greek figures, Romanesque 'Sheela na gigs' and modern-day dancers.

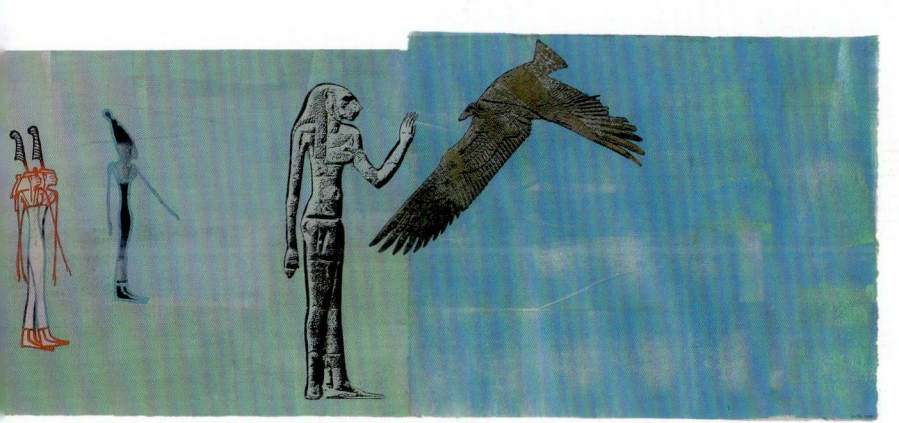

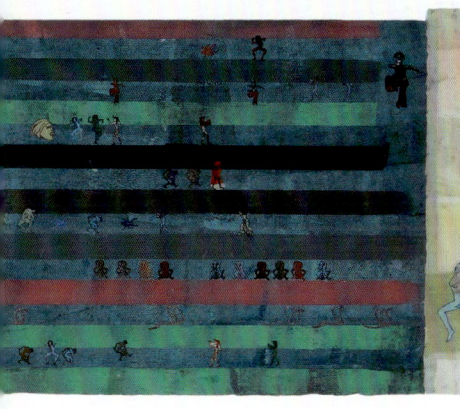

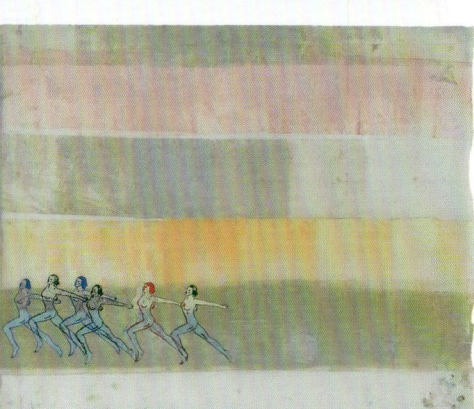

385

FRANCES STARK

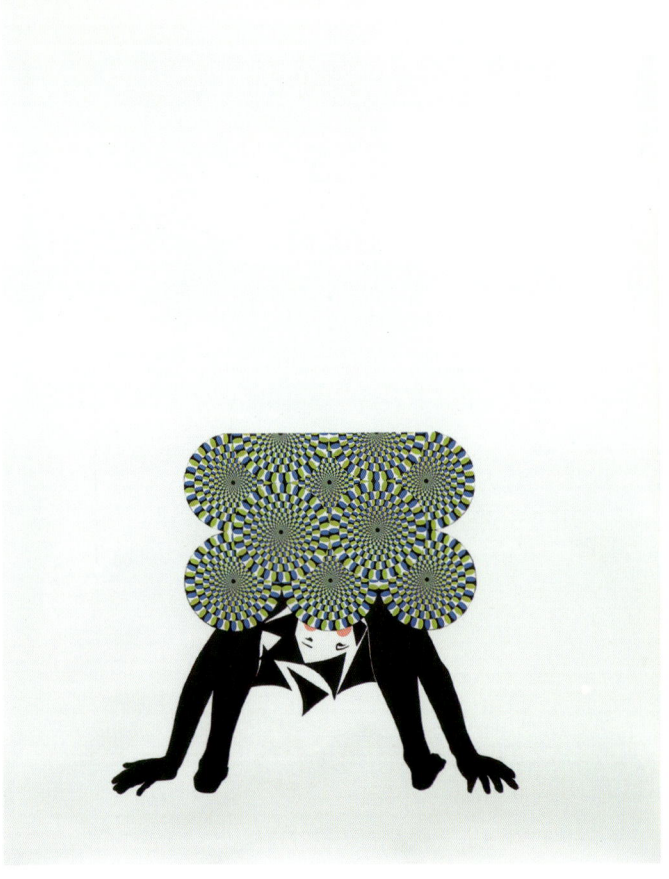

CHORUS GIRL FOLDING SELF IN HALF

2008, collage and graphite pencil on paper, 181.3 × 134.9 cm (71 ⅜ × 53 ⅛ in),
Whitney Museum of American Art, New York
Frances Stark, born 1967, Huntington Beach, California.

Formerly an associate professor at the USC Roski School of Fine
Arts, Stark is a key figure in the Los Angeles art scene. The meaning
of language and especially the written word sit at the core of her
work, as she explores everything from pride to self-doubt, procrasti-
nation and parenthood. Working with writing and images, she considers some of the largest questions – how personal communication
shapes human existence – and also examines smaller moments of
beauty where words transform the mundane into the poetic. She
often works in printing and reproduction – including hand-tracing

letters by famous writers – and digital animations. Her video
My Best Thing was premiered to great acclaim at the 54th Venice
Biennale (2011), placing two Lego-like avatars against a green
screen as they shared intimate and sexual details. Stark often combines references to philosophy and literature with sexually explicit
imagery, deploying deliberately stylized typefaces. This collage and
pencil drawing depicts a pink-cheeked girl bent over, with an Op
art-inspired, oscillating moiré pinwheel pattern emanating from her
behind. Almost reduced to a silhouette, she is simultaneously performing, revealing and concealing, shaking her derrière yet careful
of what remains hidden.

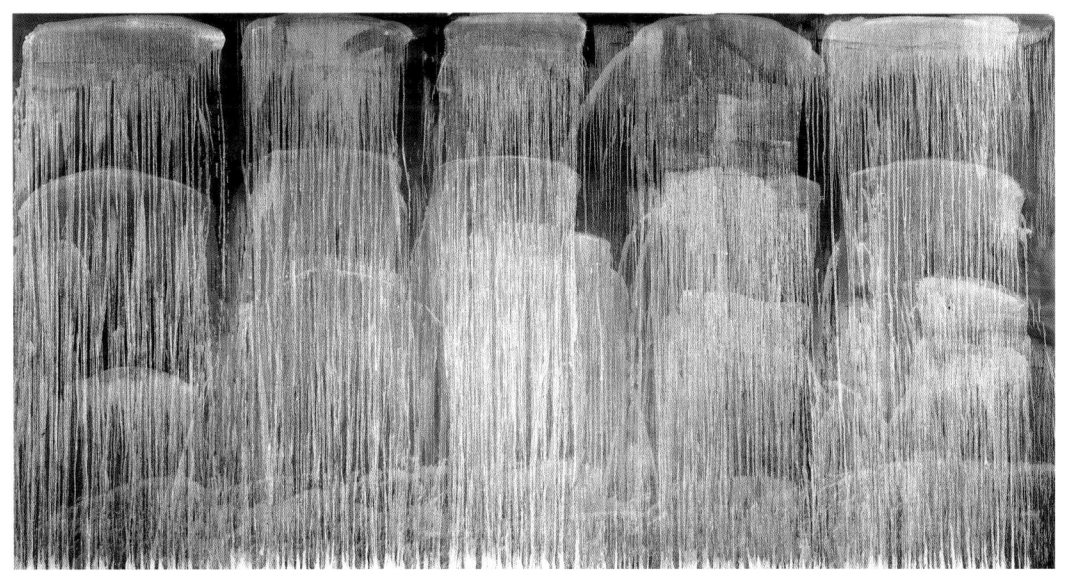

SIXTEEN WATERFALLS OF DREAMS, MEMORIES, AND SENTIMENT
1990, oil on canvas, 199.3 × 383.9 cm (78 ½ × 151 ⅛ in), Metropolitan Museum of Art, New York
Pat Steir, born 1940, Newark, New Jersey.

In the 1970s, Steir grappled with representational art, her paintings depicting crossed-out roses and other symbols. The late 1980s heralded a shift in approach, influenced by her individual friendships with the Minimalist artists John Cage (1912–92), Sol LeWitt (1928–2007) and Agnes Martin (p.265). Embracing Cage's reliance on chance, LeWitt's interest in systems and Martin's insistence on inspiration, Steir began making her signature 'Waterfall' paintings. Climbing a ladder, throwing paint onto the canvas and then allowing gravity to take its course, her practice superficially resembles that of Jackson Pollock's (1912–56), yet Steir's gestural paintings are not rapidly executed. Profoundly inspired by Taoist philosophy and Asian painting traditions, the dynamic and lyrical qualities of her paintings derive from precise rituals and respect for process as much as from accident and serendipity. Delicate curtains of spray descend from horizontal bands of white over a dark ground, embodying an elemental sense of time's passing, yet they are ultimately frozen and suspended, the luminous cascades and filigree-like drizzles transformed into objects of contemplation. These harmonious compositions suggest an internal, meditative state of mind in which the viewer is invited to partake.

IRMA STERN

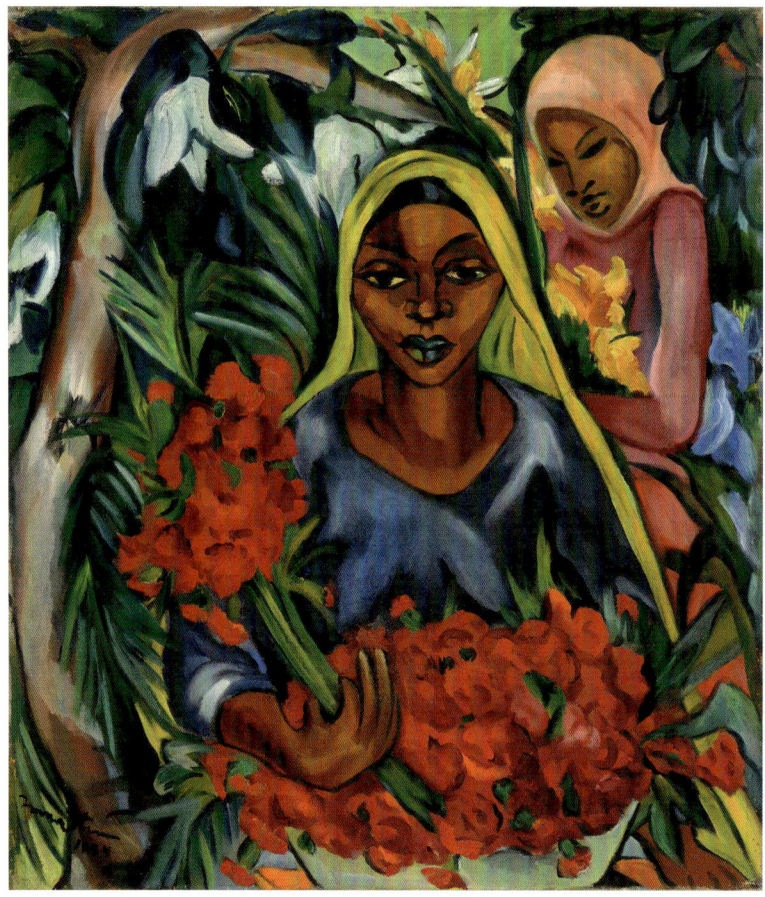

THE FLOWER MARKET, CAPE TOWN

1924, oil on canvas, 93.9 × 80 cm (37 × 31 ½ in), private collection
Irma Stern, born 1894, Schweizer-Reneke, South Africa. Died 1966, Cape Town.

The child of German-Jewish immigrants to South Africa, Stern's
formative years involved frequent visits to Germany. She enrolled
at the Weimar Academy in 1913, and then transferred to the
Levin-Funcke studio in Berlin. In the capital, she was mentored
by the painter Max Pechstein (1881–1955), previously a member
of Die Brücke ('The Bridge') – a group of German Expressionist
artists (1905–13) – and in 1918 Pechstein and Stern founded the
Novembergruppe of radical artists and architects. The saturated
colours and vigorous brushwork of Expressionism remained
hallmarks of her work throughout her fifty-year career. After the
Nazi rise to power, and following an unsuccessful marriage, she
ceased contact with Germany. Increasingly drawn to the sights,
colours and cultural heritage of Africa, she travelled through
Senegal, Zanzibar and Congo. Reactions to her work in South
Africa were hostile for a long time (one critic characterizing her
style as 'ugliness as a cult'), although she later became recognized as the country's foremost modernist painter. Her travels
and her extensive collection of artefacts inspired her subject matter. This painting employs heightened pigments to depict two
market sellers – shawled women embedded in a brilliant, flat-
tened scheme of flowers and shrubbery.

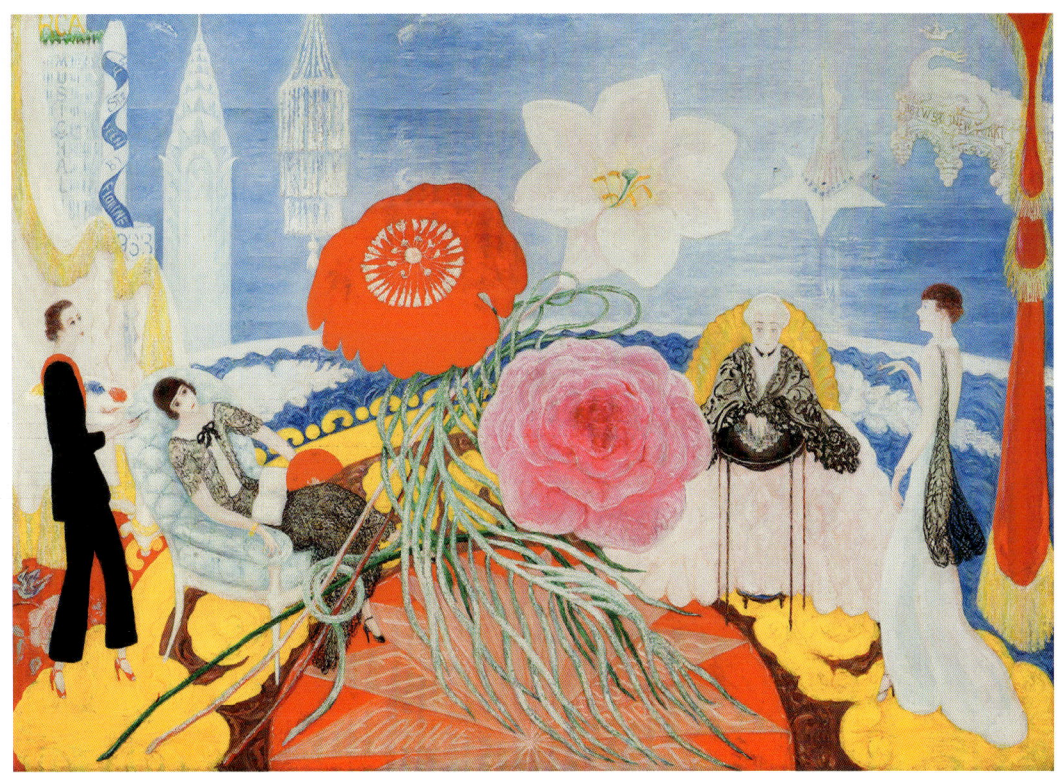

FAMILY PORTRAIT II

1933, oil on canvas, 117.4 × 164 cm (46 ¼ × 64 ⅝ in), Museum of Modern Art, New York

Florine Stettheimer, born 1871, Rochester, New York. Died 1944, New York.

Born into a wealthy New York banking family, Stettheimer moved in 1906 to Europe where she studied art and saw the Ballets Russes productions that would later inspire many of her paintings. Between 1915 and 1935, she hosted a Manhattan salon with her sisters, the 'Stetties', which became the haunt of avant-garde artists including Georgia O'Keeffe (p.301) and Marcel Duchamp (1887–1968). A sense of theatrical space and blithe unreality pervades her work. Her paintings appeared in over forty-six important exhibitions in New York and Paris, though she preferred to show her works privately to close circles of friends, her sole commercial gallery exhibition in Manhattan proving to be a financial failure. Also writing poems, she circulated these on scraps of paper. In 1938, Stettheimer and O'Keeffe were the only two women artists to be selected by the Museum of Modern Art for inclusion in the first exhibition of American art to tour to Europe. In *Family Portrait II*, Stettheimer created an allegory of her family: the 'Stetties' and their mother appear within a dreamlike pageant of giant roses, alongside their city's landmark buildings.

HITO STEYERL

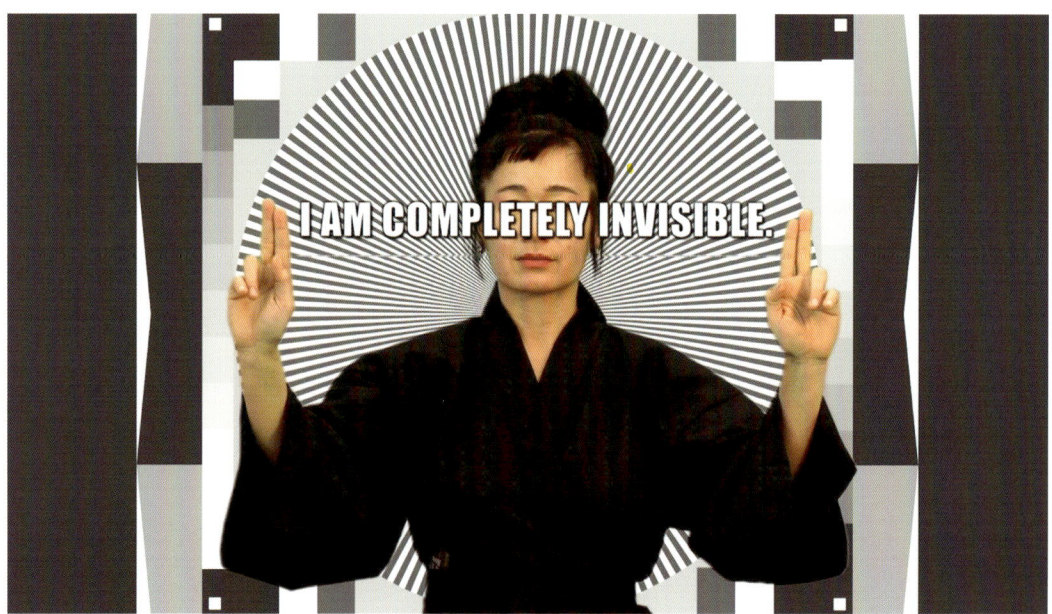

HOW NOT TO BE SEEN: A FUCKING DIDACTIC EDUCATIONAL .MOV FILE
2013, HD video, single screen in architectural environment, 15 mins 52 secs
Hito Steyerl, born 1966, Munich.

With wit and profundity, Steyerl's work investigates what images are and what they do. Studying at institutions in Toyko, Munich and Vienna, she holds a PhD in philosophy, an honorary doctorate from the Royal College of Art, London, and a professorship in experimental film and video in Berlin. Influenced by German filmmaker Harun Farocki (1944–2014) and film writer Helmut Färber (b.1937), her films, visual art and writings address the changing essence of images and their global circulation as mediated by technology. Her installation *Factory of the Sun* was presented in the basement of the German Pavilion at the 56th Venice Biennale in 2015. Drawing on the writing of feminist philosopher Donna Haraway, Steyerl invited viewers to enter a surreal, dystopian scenario where human motion is captured and harnessed as an energy source. Leisure, entertainment and labour are underpinned by subtle threats of institutional violence. Her wry humour and satirical strategies are also evident in *How Not To Be Seen*. With a title derived from a spoof public information film by the surreal British comedy group Monty Python, Steyerl offers five lessons in how to be invisible: a position loaded with irony when considering female artists' frequent invisibility in art history.

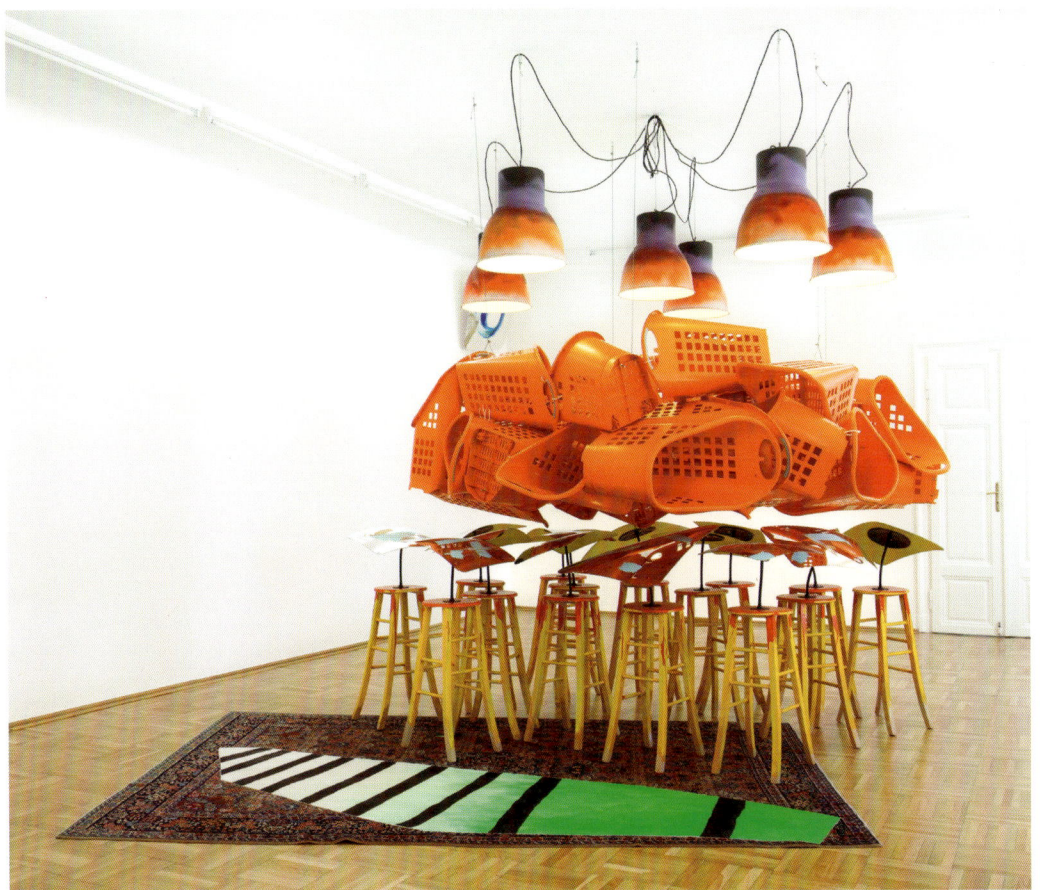

LAY OF THE LAND

2014, orange plastic shopping baskets, drive-way mirrors, oriental carpet,
15 wooden stools, acrylic paint, pendant lights and bulbs and hardware,
275 × 345 × 350 cm (108¼ × 135¾ × 137¾ in), installation view, 'Snug Parting',
Galerie Nächst St. Stephan, Vienna, 2016
Jessica Stockholder, born 1959, Seattle.

Now chair of the Department of Visual Art, University of Chicago,
Stockholder was a professor at Yale School of Art from 1999 to 2011,
where she herself received an MFA in 1985. As an artist, she is best
known for the sculptural installations she has made since the mid-
1980s. Yet it was painting that was the starting point for Stockholder's
practice and it remains an underlying tenet in her work. Driven
by formal, visual interests over narrative per se, she uses colour, space,
light, form, material and architecture in ways that resonate with the
site in which her art is displayed. Stockholder looks at how things
are organized and, equally, how these systems of order can disintegrate. *Lay of the Land* was originally inspired by the traditional Italian
bowling game of *bocce*. Disparate elements come together: wooden
stools are arranged on a rug, a disorderly cluster of orange plastic baskets above, and warm synthetic light shining over these, reflected
in mirrors below. Painting, sculpture and environment coalesce
in a strange amalgam that suggests an alchemical reordering of the
elements and activities of everyday life.

MICHELLE STUART

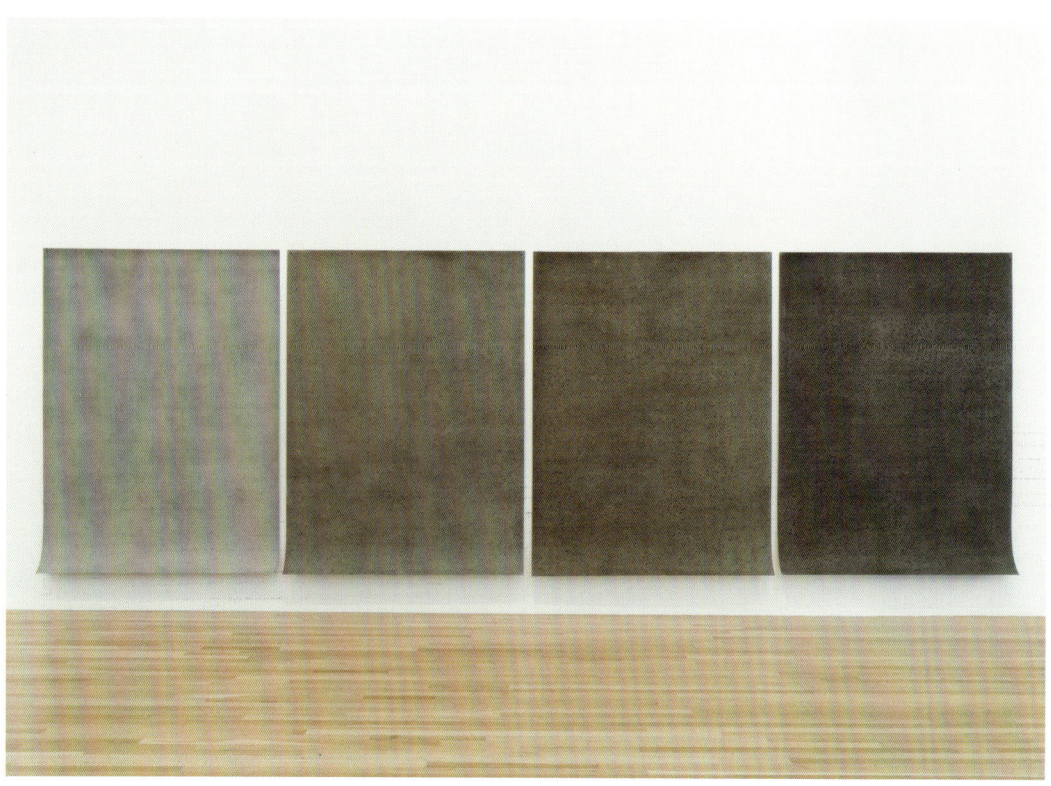

SERPENT MOUND, OHIO

1978–9, earth on muslin-mounted rag paper, overall (4 units): 203.2 × 635 cm
(80 × 250 in), Glenstone Museum, Potomac, Maryland
Michelle Stuart, born 1933, Los Angeles.

Part archaeologist, part alchemist, Stuart has spent five decades
making sculptures and paintings with unconventional art materials,
including soil, rocks, beeswax, shells and plant material. She occupies a unique intersection between the traditions of Land art,
Conceptualism and Minimalism. Having worked as a topographic
draughtsperson, her interest in pre-Columbian culture took her
to Mexico where she worked as a mural assistant to Diego Rivera
(1886–1957). Moving to New York in 1957, Stuart experimented with
impressing crushed and atomized natural materials into sheets

of rectangular paper. The example shown here features four hues
of soil, each taken from a different strata of earth at one location – the
place named in its title. Worked into sheets of muslin-mounted paper
to create large monochromatic blocks, it indicates the mythic force
that humble earth can assume, investigated further in her 'Rock Book'
series: records of her experiences from specific sites. One of many
artists associated with 1960s feminism, she made contributions to this
cause by co-founding the feminist journal *Heresies* and the Women's
Art Registry in New York, which provided important visibility to overlooked women artists.

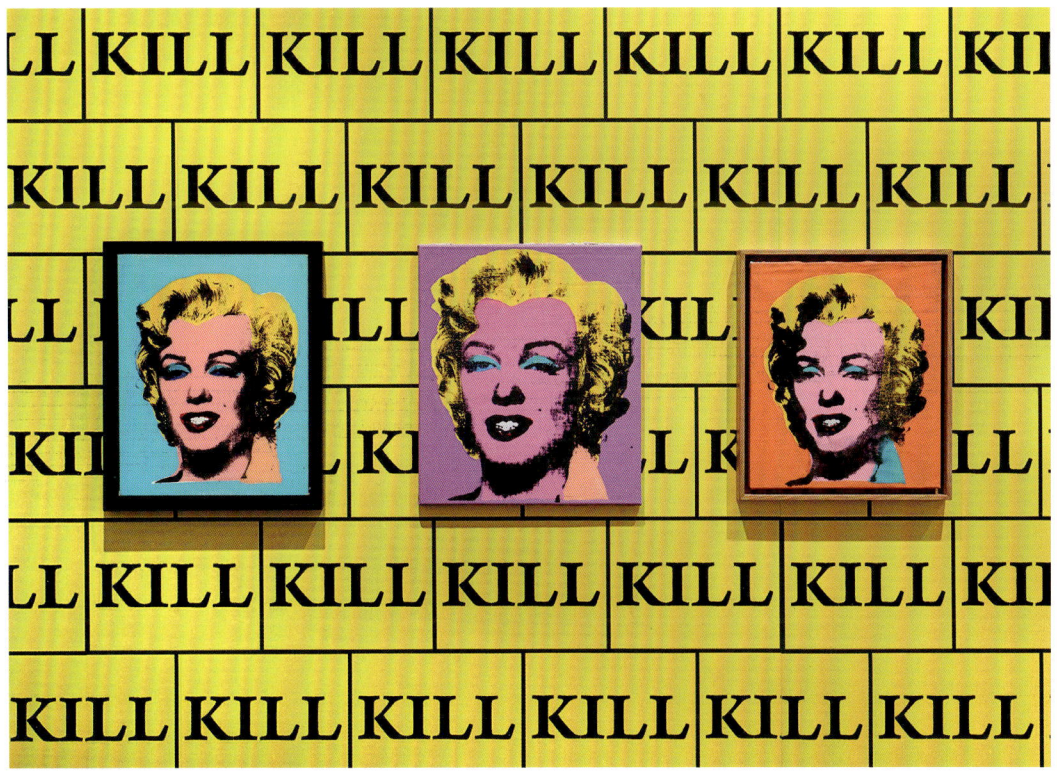

WARHOL MARILYNS

1973, synthetic polymer silkscreen and acrylic on canvas, each c.45 × 39.5 × 4 cm (17 ¾ × 15 ½ × 1 ½ in), installation view, 'Vice Versa', Galerie Thaddaeus Ropac, London, 2018

Sturtevant, born Elaine Horan, 1924, Lakewood, Ohio. Died 2014, Paris.

Sturtevant became notorious in the 1960s for her copies of emblematic works by male Pop artists, including Jasper Johns (b.1930), Roy Lichtenstein (1923–97), Tom Wesselmann (1931–2004) and Andy Warhol (1928–87). However, while her canvases and sculptures closely resemble those of others, they are neither forgeries nor replicas; made predominantly from memory and using the same techniques, they are approximations of each respective artist's individual style. Often called the 'mother of appropriation art',

she referred to her practice more simply as 'repetition'. In the works shown, she appropriates the famous series of silkscreened canvases of the actress Marilyn Monroe. Sturtevant even employed Warhol's own studio assistant to produce the stencil using the same press image. The results were so close to the originals that when Warhol was asked how he produced his silkscreened canvases, he simply replied: 'Ask Elaine.' Sturtevant's approach challenged notions of authorship, authenticity and originality, anticipating issues that would characterize a generation of artists working in the 1970s and 1980s, including Sherrie Levine (p.241). From 2000 Sturtevant produced moving-image works and installations addressing the image-saturated nature of early-twenty-first-century life.

MAUD SULTER

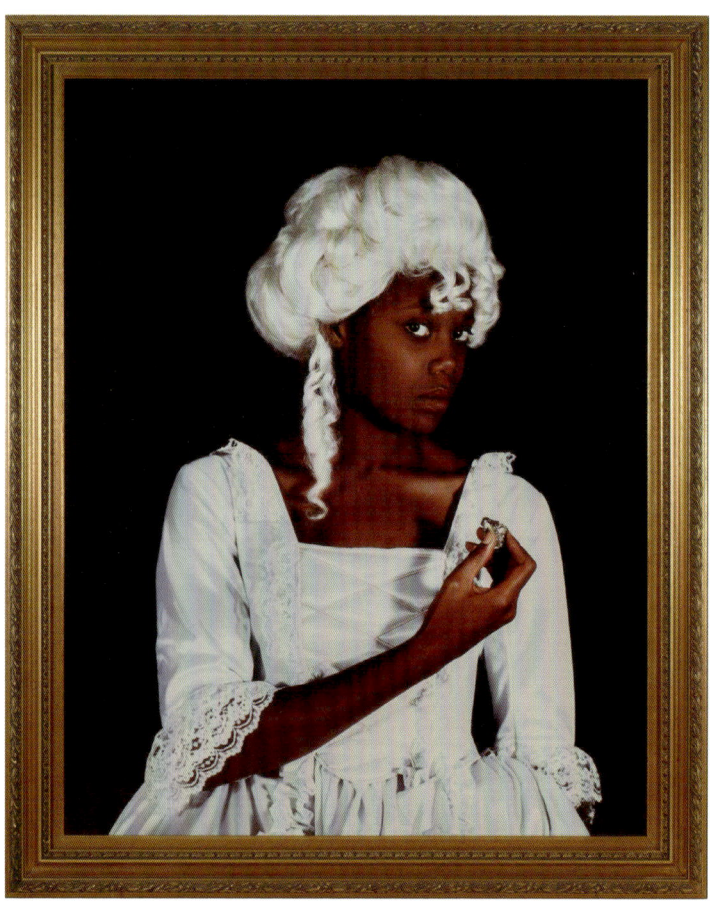

TERPSICHORE from the series 'ZABAT'

1989, framed Cibachrome print, 152 × 122 cm (59 ⅞ × 48 in),
City Art Centre, Edinburgh
Maud Sulter, born 1960, Glasgow. Died 2008, Dumfries, UK.

A Scottish artist of Ghanaian heritage and active in the black feminist and lesbian movements of the 1980s and 1990s, Sulter was a polymath, working as an artist, curator, poet, publisher and playwright. Often reworking historical and mythological subjects into intricate, multivalent narratives, her photographic portraits and photomontages celebrated black women and challenged racist cultural exclusion. Sulter made the photomontage series 'Syrcas' during the early 1990s. Combining images of African art objects with vintage postcards of alpine landscapes, she drew attention to the murder and victimization of black Europeans during the Holocaust, an aspect often excluded from accounts of the Nazi atrocities. For her earlier series 'Zabat', Sulter portrayed contemporary black women artists, musicians and writers as the nine muses of ancient Greek mythology. Sulter herself assumed the character of Calliope, the muse of epic poetry, in an imagined staging by Jeanne Duval (1820–62), mistress of the French Romantic poet Charles Baudelaire. *Terpsichore*, the muse of dance, was incarnated by Delta Streete, a performance artist who wore the costume she had made for a work exploring relationships between women, in particular those complicated by race.

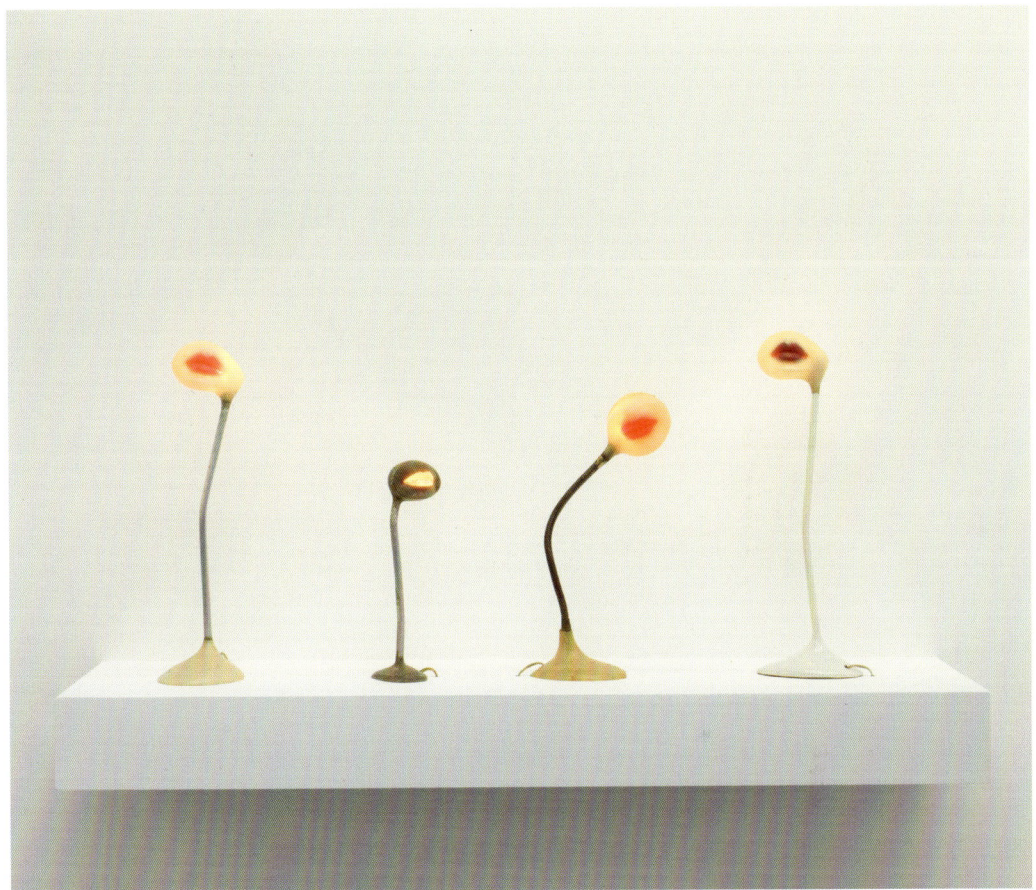

LAMPE-BOUCHE (ILLUMINATED LIPS)

1966, coloured polyester resin, electrical wiring and metal, 45 × 11 × 15 cm (17 ¾ × 4 ⅜ × 5 ⅞ in); 29 × 12 × 11 cm (11 ⅜ × 4 ¾ × 4 ⅜ in); 43 × 15 × 11 cm (16 ⅞ × 5 ⅞ × 4 ⅜ in); 48 × 16 × 13 cm (18 ⅞ × 6 ¼ × 5 ⅛ in), installation view, 'Luminous Works', Galerie Loevenbruck, Paris, 2013
Alina Szapocznikow, born 1926, Kalisz, Poland. Died 1973, Passy, France.

Szapocznikow's practice is often seen through the lens of her biography as a Holocaust survivor. Afflicted by tuberculosis in mid-life, her later works were a response to having breast cancer, but her work goes beyond an investigation of her own suffering. Szapocznikow's corporeal sculptures oscillate between abstraction and figuration, challenging reductive perceptions of gender, in particular womanhood, through an exploration of the body. Living in Prague after the war, she adopted a Socialist Realism style in line with her political commitments. Later in Paris, she was exposed to wider modernist influences, her work taking a radical turn in 1963 when she began to take casts of her own body and pushed the boundaries of sculptural media, using new materials such as polyurethane. From this point onwards, she depicted anthropomorphic forms in flux, the body revealed as a site of celebration and degradation, desire and cruelty. The symbolism of the fragmented corpus is evident in these works, where illuminated lips appear as severed, organic forms, their plump sensuality and seductive lightness accentuated in candy-coloured shades of red and pink.

SARAH SZE

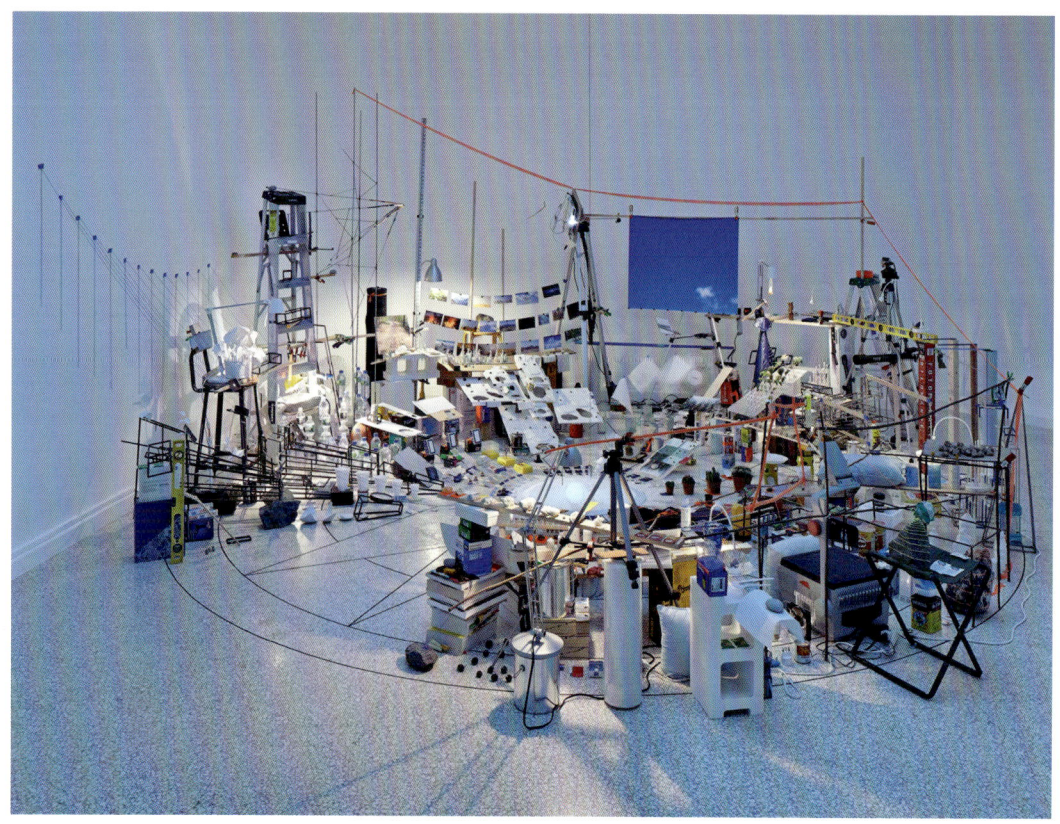

TRIPLE POINT (PENDULUM)

2013, salt, water, stone, string, projector, video, pendulum and mixed media,
*c.*381 × 533.4 × 508 cm (*c.*150 × 210 × 200 in), installation view, United States
Pavilion, 55th Venice Biennale. Collection Museum of Modern Art, New York
Sarah Sze, born 1969, Boston.

Sze gained a BA at Yale University in 1991 and later attended the
School of Visual Arts, New York, where she was taught by Post-
Minimalist sculptor Jackie Winsor (1941–2024). Often colossal in
scale, her multimedia installations span architectural spaces and
appear to be in a state of becoming or falling apart. She brings
together everyday materials and found objects to make constellations
of meticulous intricacy, some of which have the appearance of a scientific laboratory. The title of this work, conceived for the United
States Pavilion at the 55th Venice Biennale in 2013, refers to the ther-
modynamic conditions in which a substance exists simultaneously as
a solid, liquid and gas. With its bewildering composition of ladders,
clamps and makeshift scaffolding, it resembles a building under construction, a work in progress. Inside, recurring concentric circular
motifs that recall instruments like orreries and compasses point to
the impulse to measure, model and stabilize our surrounding universe. The organized chaos and dynamic elements of Sze's installations suggest that such attempts are at best provisional, with the true
complexity of the world something that can only ever be appre-
hended in part.

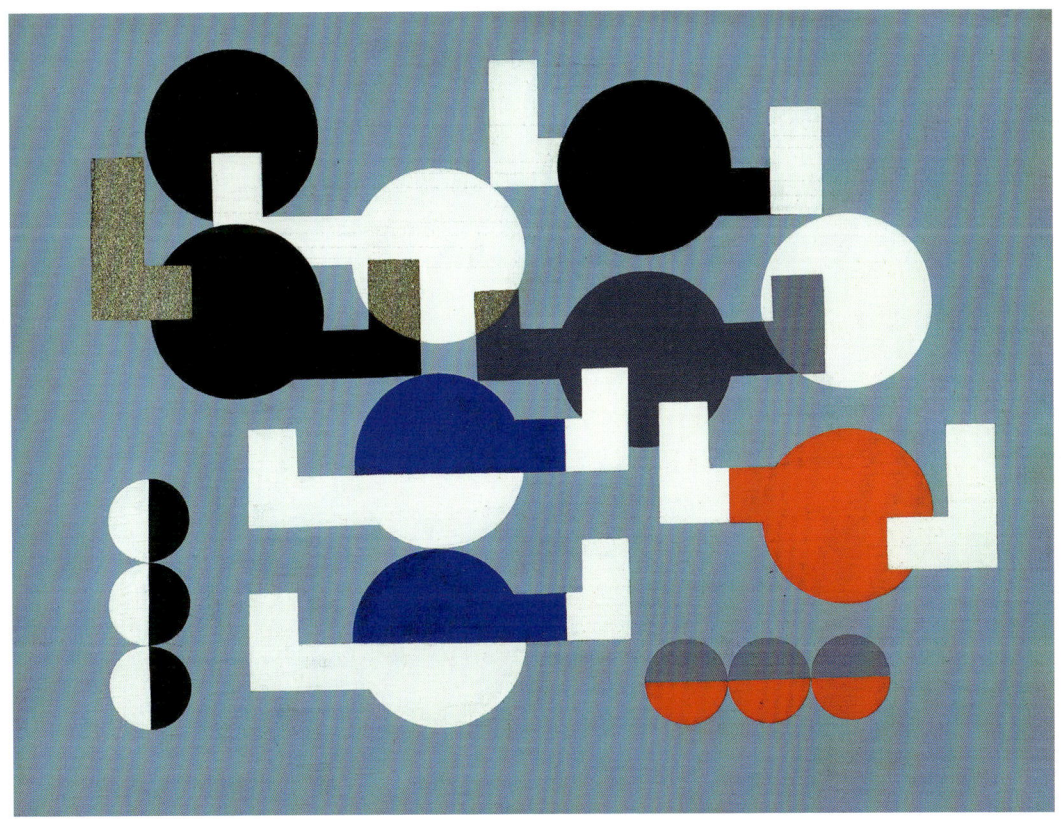

COMPOSITION OF CIRCLES AND OVERLAPPING ANGLES

1930, oil on canvas, 49.5 × 64.1 cm (19 ½ × 25 ¼ in), The Riklis Collection of McCrory Corporation, Museum of Modern Art, New York
Sophie Taeuber-Arp, born 1889, Davos, Switzerland. Died 1943, Zürich.

With a desire to break down boundaries between creative disciplines, Taeuber-Arp worked as a painter, sculptor, dancer, choreographer and puppeteer, as well as designing textiles, furniture and theatre sets. Married to artist Jean (Hans) Arp (1886–1966), Taeuber-Arp was a prominent figure in Zürich's radical Dada movement, which sought to challenge traditional notions of art alongside conceptions of gender, class and national identity. She performed regularly at Cabaret Voltaire, the raucous nightclub of the Dada artists, over a few months in 1916 as well as making Dadaist artworks, such as *Dada Head* (1920), a sculpture of a pear-shaped head, created from a wooden hatstand, which undermined the conventions of typical portrait busts of the time. Celebrated for her sophisticated geometric abstractions, Taeuber-Arp was also one of the earliest proponents of Constructivism outside Russia. After moving to France in 1926, she became a member of the Parisian abstract artists' group *Cercle et Carré* and its successor, *Abstraction-Création* (1931–4) and founded the Constructivist review *Plastique* in 1937. This composition is one of numerous abstract paintings and drawings she made using geometric forms throughout her career, before she died in her sleep from accidental carbon monoxide poisoning.

ATSUKO TANAKA

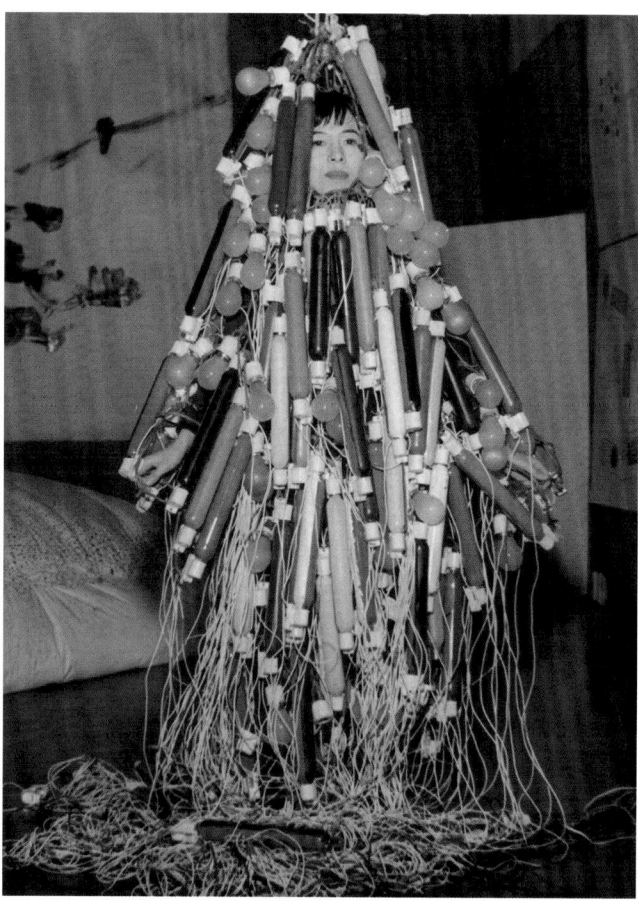

ELECTRIC DRESS

1956, artist wearing dress made of enamel paint on light bulbs, electric cords and control console, performance at Gutai Art Exhibition, Ohara Kaikan Hall, Tokyo
Atsuko Tanaka, born 1932, Osaka, Japan. Died 2005, Nara Prefecture, Japan.

Among the pioneers of media art and sound art, Tanaka joined the Gutai Art Association in 1955 – Japan's first significant post-war avant-garde art movement and a key organization in the international development of both Conceptual and performance art. She was to remain a member of the group for ten years. Working in media ranging from textiles to painting, and using innovative materials including sound and electricity, a notable piece was the interactive sound installation *Work (Bell)* (1955) for the first Gutai Art Exhibition at Ohara Kaikan Hall in Tokyo, which featured twenty electric

bells ringing at various intervals. The following year at the same venue, the movement held its second exhibition and Tanaka presented what was to become her most famous work, a garment made up of electrical cables powering small light bulbs painted in primary colours. Designed either to be worn or to exist as a sculptural installation, the illuminated, flickering dress referenced both the traditional Japanese kimono and the rapid industrialization of the country in the 1950s, representing an uncertain state of being to inhabit as well as to behold.

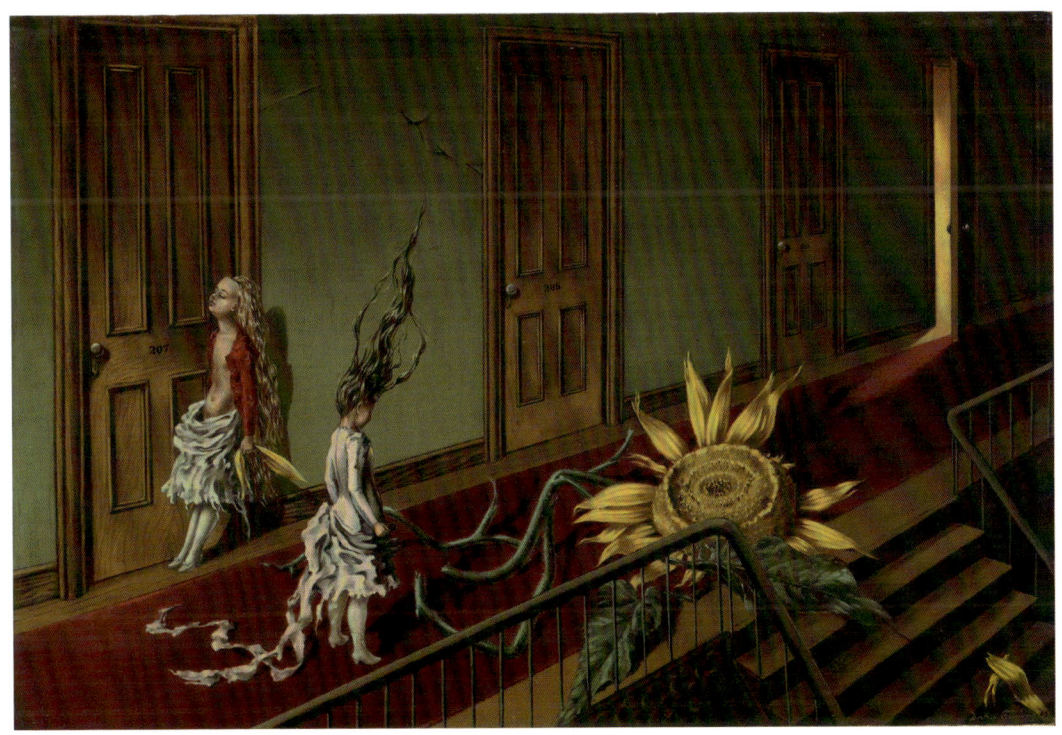

EINE KLEINE NACHTMUSIK

1943, oil on canvas, 40.7 × 61 cm (16 × 24 in), Tate, London
Dorothea Tanning, born 1910, Galesburg, Illinois. Died 2012, New York.

During a career spanning eight decades, Tanning created fantastical scenes in the mediums of painting, sculpture, collage and prints. A self-taught artist who attended art school in Chicago for just three weeks in 1930, Tanning's early work demonstrates a fascination with Gothic novels, Surrealism, dreams and sexuality. Throughout the 1940s and 1950s, she plumbed the depths of the unconscious to produce imagery of strange yet familiar realms. While her 1960s work neared abstraction, she became a pioneer of soft sculpture in the early 1970s, combining fabric forms with furniture to create uncanny hybrids. She also had a lifelong devotion to writing, which flourished

in her eighties and nineties, publishing poetry, memoirs and a short novel. Tanning believed that a woman's art should be assessed according to the same criteria as a man's, and was quoted in *BOMB Magazine* in 1990 as saying: 'Women artists. There is no such thing.' Her paintings often delineate interiors, as is the case in *Eine Kleine Nachtmusik*. Two girls appear to sleepwalk, eyes closed as though lulled by the night music alluded to in the work's title. Their tattered clothing and long hair wafts in an eerie hotel corridor, which is dominated by a gigantic sunflower, its petals semi-plucked.

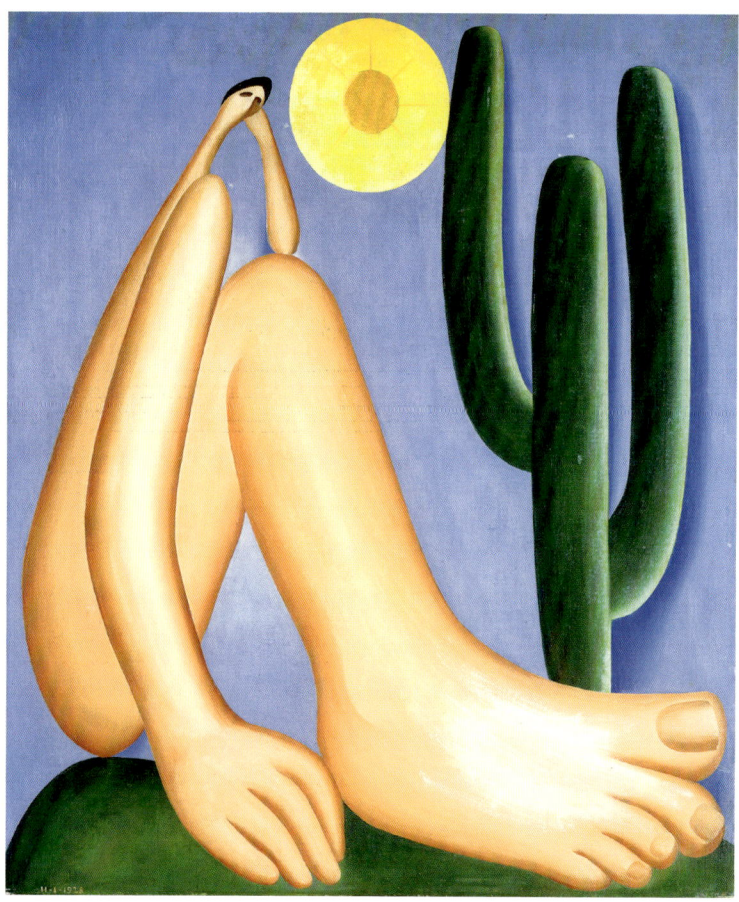

ABAPORÚ

1928, oil on canvas, 85 × 72.5 cm (33 ½ × 28 ½ in), Museo de Arte
Latinoamericano de Buenos Aires
Tarsila do Amaral, born 1886, Capivari, Brazil. Died 1973, São Paulo.

A driving force and founder of the 1920s Brazilian avant-garde movement, the Grupo dos Cinco ('Group of Five'), Tarsila, who is known
simply by her first name, had previously left her artistically conservative homeland to study at the Académie Julian in Paris and, later, with
Fernand Léger (1881–1955). It was here, during what she referred to
as her 'military service in Cubism', she absorbed the tenets that seem
to shape this nude's enlarged limbs and pronounced curves. A birth-
day gift from Tarsila to her husband at the time, fellow artist and
Grupo member Oswald de Andrade (1890–1954), *Abaporú* translates

from Tupi-Guarani as 'the man that eats people'. Andrade used the
image to illustrate the cover of his *Manifesto of Anthropophagy* (1928),
which advocated subordinating and subsuming European culture
to forge a national aesthetic, and it became a symbol of modernity,
combining French Surrealism with a Brazilian perspective. From the
1930s onwards, Tarsila's work reflected the agenda of Socialist
Realism and became narrative in subject matter. Renowned in her
native country, she represented Brazil in the 32nd Venice Biennale
(1964), although her work received international attention only after
her death.

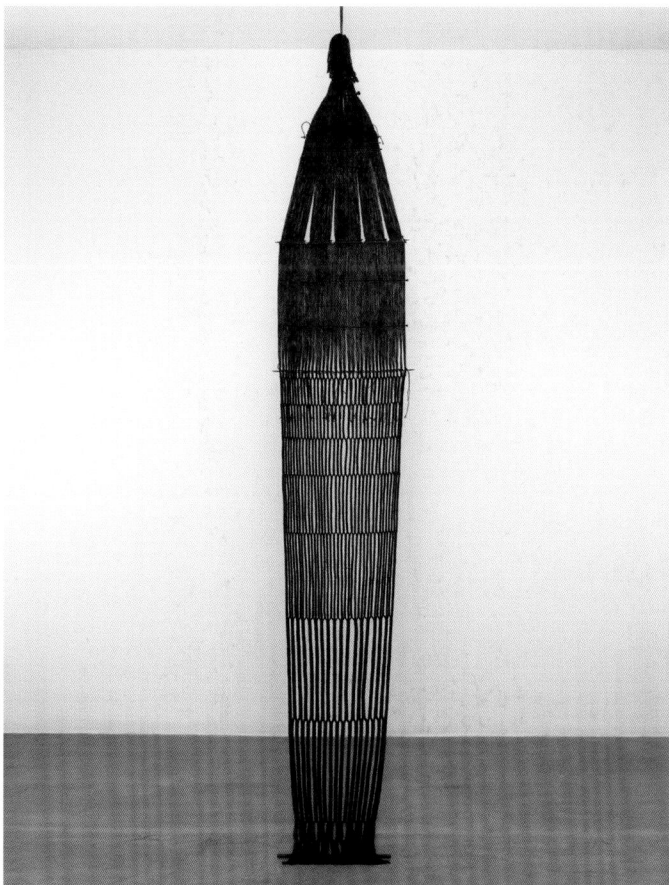

DARK RIVER WALL HANGING

1962, linen and wool, 416.6 × 57.2 cm (164 × 22 ½ in), Museum of Modern Art, New York

Lenore Tawney, born Leonora Gallagher, 1907, Lorain, Ohio. Died 2007, New York.

Tawney trained in sculpture in the early 1940s. Exposed to the Bauhaus tradition at the School of the Art Institute of Chicago, she studied the rudiments of weaving with Marli Ehrman (1904–82). In her late forties, her work changed decisively: at the 1954 Penland School of Crafts workshop she was taught by Finnish weaver Martta Taipale (1893–1966), and in the same year learnt ancient Peruvian gauze techniques of weaving. Over the next decades Tawney became a pioneer of fibre art, in which radical experimentation and rediscovery blurred the distinction between fine art and

craft, freeing textiles from being utilitarian. In 1957 Tawney moved to Coenties Slip, Manhattan, then a home to artists such as Chryssa (p.100), Robert Indiana (1928–2018) and Agnes Martin (p.265). Like the latter, Tawney explored the spirituality of nature through abstract geometry. This slender yet colossal minimalist design, belonging to her 'Woven Forms' series, used boat knotting to investigate shape and structure in a palette of dark natural colours. The series turned away from traditionally rectilinear woven grids, made possible by Tawney's modification of the reed of her loom and emphasized the sculptural potential of textiles as three-dimensional objects.

ANNA DOROTHEA THERBUSCH

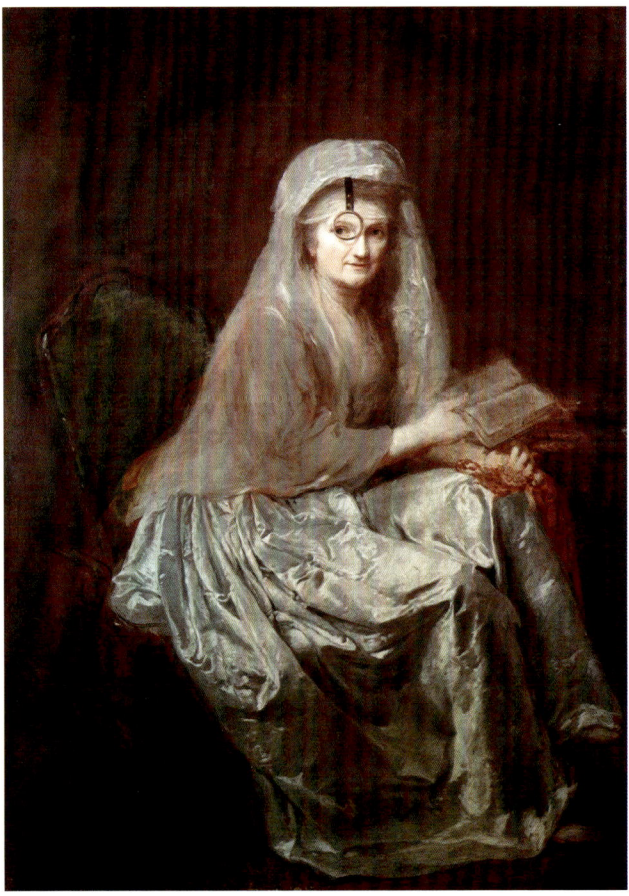

SELF-PORTRAIT

*c.*1782, oil on canvas, 153.5 × 118 cm (60 ⅛ × 46 ½ in), Gemäldegalerie, Berlin
Anna Dorothea Therbusch, born Anna Dorothea Lisiewski, 1721, Berlin
(then Kingdom of Prussia). Died 1782, Berlin.

A member of art academies in Stuttgart, Paris and Vienna, Therbusch
was a fashionable artist who achieved notable success in the last two
decades of her life. The daughter of celebrated Baroque portrait
painter Georg Lisiewski (1674–1750), both her sister and brother
were also painters. Despite learning painting from childhood and
demonstrating significant talent, her marriage to a Berlin innkeeper
required her to abandon her easel and help run her husband's business. In her early forties she returned to art at the invitation of
a string of courtly German patrons before being elected to become
a member of the Académie Royale de Peinture et de Sculpture, Paris,
in 1767. Later, she returned to her native city, where she ran a successful studio from 1773, painting portraits on commission including
eight Prussian royals for Catherine II of Russia (Catherine the Great).
Therbusch also produced several self-portraits in later life, all
of which are frank, honest portrayals marked by a vivid intensity.
In this work, a large monocle attests to the artist's failing eyesight
while also demarcating her countenance and highlighting her gaze.
Loosely classical, it presents her as a priestess of Vesta, the Roman
goddess of the domestic hearth, an appropriate allusion to past years
of drudgery.

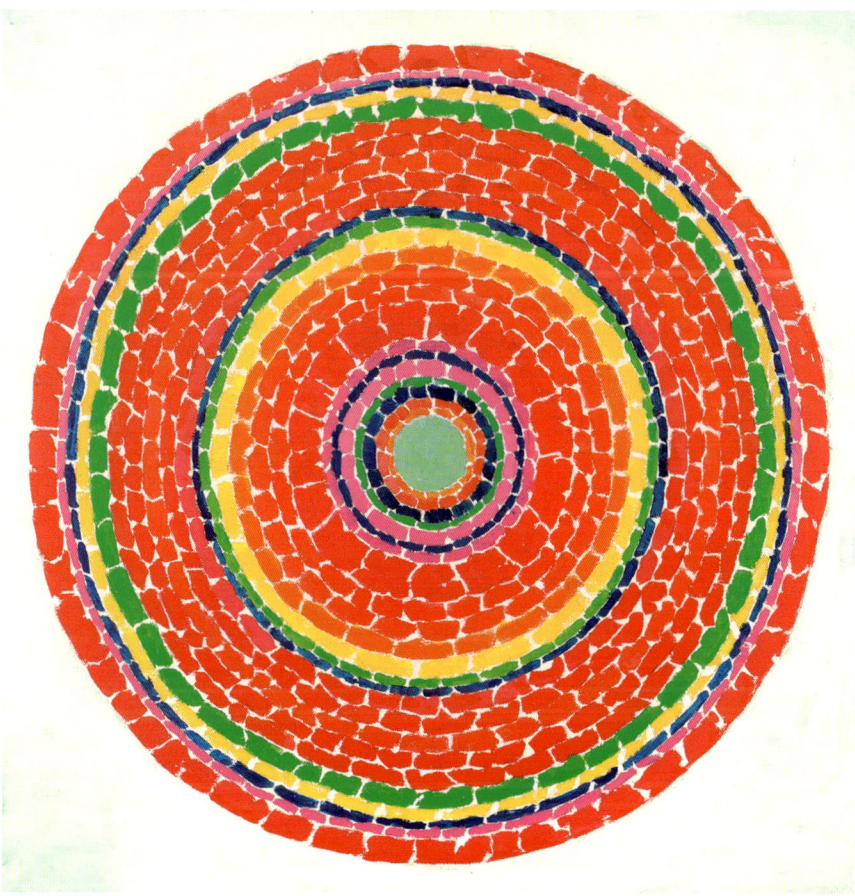

SPRINGTIME IN WASHINGTON

1971, acrylic on canvas, 121.9 × 121.9 cm (48 × 48 in), private collection
Alma Thomas, born Alma Woodsey Thomas, 1891, Columbus, Georgia.
Died 1978, Washington DC.

In 1924 Thomas became the first graduate of the new fine art course at Howard University, Washington DC. Thomas subsequently began a teaching career in child and community education in the capital and, while her artistic talent was not publicly recognized until she retired, she continued to develop over her lifetime with the encouragement of Loïs Mailou Jones (p.204). Thomas's watercolours were first shown in 1960 at the Dupont Theatre Art Gallery, with a retrospective at Howard in 1966 identifying her with the colour field movement. In 1972 she became the first African-American woman to have a solo exhibition at the Whitney Museum of American Art, New York. Her investigations into abstraction often involved a bold pointillist-like method, which linked her practice to the vigour of the Abstract Expressionists, although Thomas declined to be restricted to any category that would limit her practice or subjectivity as a black woman artist. *Springtime in Washington* highlights her appreciation of nature, a frequent source of inspiration. Typical of Thomas's approach, the vibrant colour palette and confident mosaic style of this circular composition project a sense of seasonal energy and rebirth.

MICKALENE THOMAS

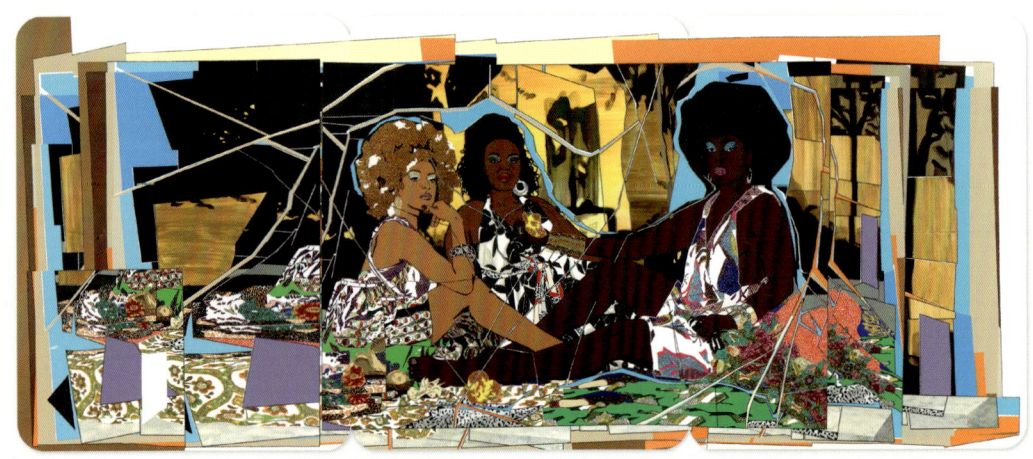

LE DÉJEUNER SUR L'HERBE: LES TROIS FEMMES NOIRES

2010, rhinestone, acrylic and enamel on panel, 304.8 × 731.5 × 5.1 cm
(120 × 288 × 2 in), Seattle Art Museum
Mickalene Thomas, born 1971, Camden, New Jersey.

Thomas's mother worked as a model in the 1970s, and issues around depicting the female body both in fashion and painting's figurative tradition are central to the artist's practice. Her works suggest the obviously stylized poses of the former, but also the attitudes towards women in the canon of French painting, exemplified by Gustave Courbet (1819–77), Édouard Manet (1832–83) and Henri Matisse (1869–1954). Thomas's compositional and chromatic techniques draw on this legacy, while also subverting it – she employs a radical 'blaxploitation' aesthetic of her childhood years and

is powerfully influenced by African-American artists, including Romare Bearden (1911–88) and Carrie Mae Weems (p.427). Thomas represents females in ways that redress their long exclusion from positions of power, with queer African-American women in particular taking centre-stage. Working in photography or painting on wood panels with acrylic and enamel, often adorned with rhinestones, her sitters communicate autonomous subjectivity amid luxuriant scenes of colour and sparkle. This large-scale painting is a repurposing of Manet's famous work of 1862, but with the two male figures replaced by women and all three shown clothed, staring confidently and directly into the eyes of the viewer.

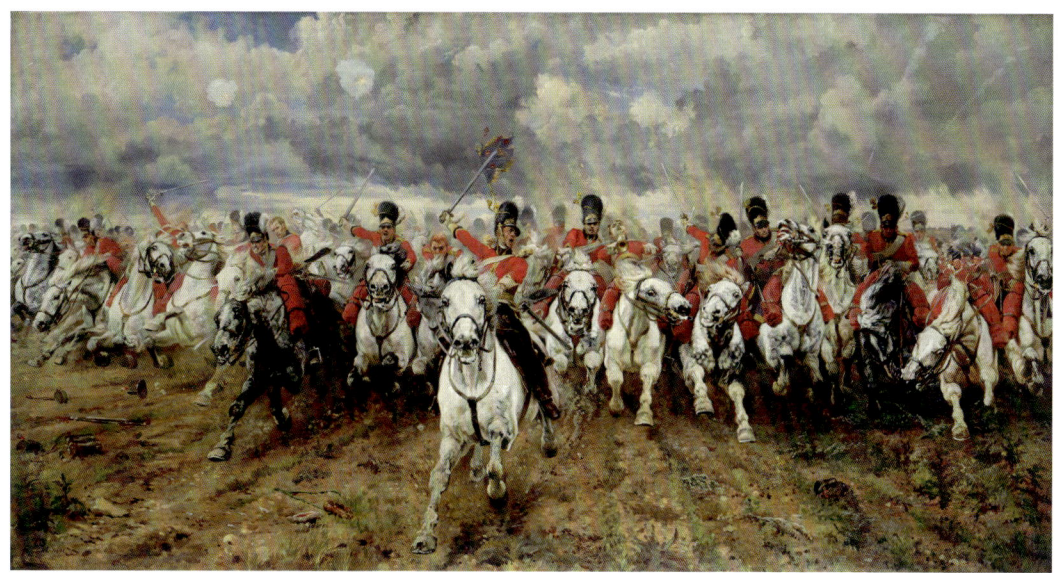

SCOTLAND FOREVER!

1881, oil on canvas, 101.6 × 194.3 cm (40 × 76 ½ in), Leeds Art Gallery, UK
Elizabeth Thompson, Lady Butler, born 1846, Lausanne, Switzerland. Died 1933,
Gormanston, County Meath, Ireland.

As one of the few British women history painters, Thompson found
fame in the nineteenth century with her depictions of military cam-
paigns. She is particularly remembered for her epic studies of the
Napoleonic Wars, though she also painted battle scenes from later
conflicts such as the Crimean War and First World War. She was
first tutored in art in 1862 while growing up in Italy, and four years
later moved to London, studying at the Royal Female School of Art
(founded 1842) before further training in Florence. Painted with
exacting detail, the work shown depicts the energetic charge of the

Royal Scots Greys, a regiment of British cavalry that fought at the
decisive Battle of Waterloo (1815). The work's title reflects the soldiers' purported battle cry: 'Now, my boys, Scotland forever!'
Despite its realism, it is an imagined scene, Thompson never wit-
nessing an actual battle and creating her compositions from observational sketches of soldiers and horses as they trained. In her
autobiography of 1922, she stated that it was never her intention to
glorify war, but rather 'to portray its pathos and heroism'.

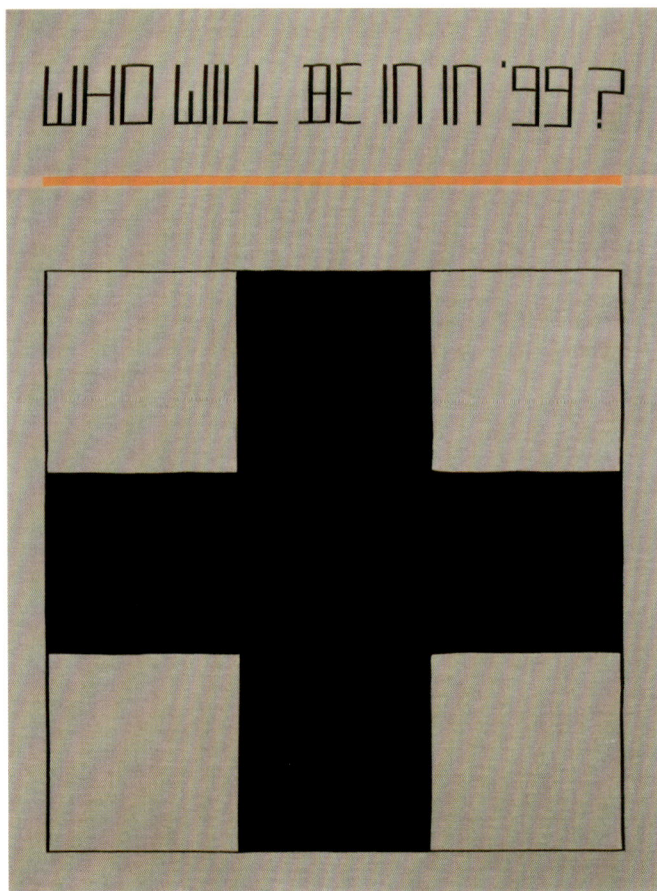

WHO WILL BE IN IN '99?

1988, beige and black wool, 210 × 160 cm (82 ¾ × 63 in), Städel Museum, Frankfurt
Rosemarie Trockel, born 1952, Schwerte, Germany.

Alongside a long career as a professor at Kunstakademie Düsseldorf until 2015, Trockel has exhibited her work extensively, starting in 1983 with solo exhibitions at Monika Sprüth Galerie, Cologne, and Galerie Philomene Magers in Bonn. Using diverse media – including clay and fabric – she explores gender as a social construct. *Who Will Be In In '99?* is part of the '*Strickbilder*' or 'Knitting Pictures' series, which began in the early 1980s and features symbols with cultural and political connotations, including the hammer and sickle, swastika, Playboy bunny and Woolmark. Her use of wool creates associations of domesticity and femininity, yet she counteracts these by using a computerized knitting machine so that her large-scale images are closer to products of consumer society than handicraft. In this piece, the black squares evoke the aesthetics of Minimalism and the formal legacy of early modernism, while the text reveals artists' archetypal anxieties about career longevity. Her question pokes fun at the legacy of male artists who were celebrated ahead of their female contemporaries while also knowingly answering it: Trockel herself is firmly part of the art establishment.

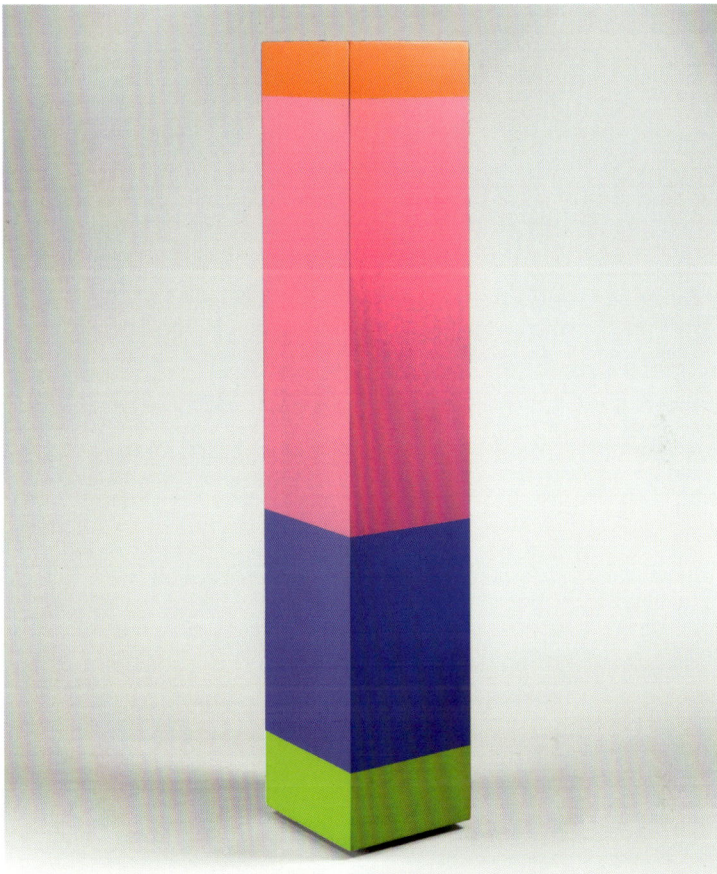

MORNING CHOICE

1968, acrylic on marine mahogany plywood, 182.9 × 35.6 × 35.6 cm (72 × 14 × 14 in),
Saint Louis Art Museum, Missouri
Anne Truitt, born Anne Dean, 1921, Baltimore. Died 2004, Washington DC.

Truitt practised as a psychologist for a few years before studying sculpture at the Institute of Contemporary Art in Washington DC, deciding around 1950 to pursue art full time. After her first solo exhibition in 1963 at André Emmerich Gallery, New York, Truitt's work was included in the seminal exhibitions 'Black, White and Gray' at the Wadsworth Atheneum Museum of Art (1964) and 'Primary Structures: Younger American and British Sculpture' at New York's Jewish Museum (1966). The development of her signature style had been inspired, in part, by seeing Abstract Expressionist paintings by Barnett Newman (1905–70) and Ad Reinhardt (1913–67) in 1961. These she admired for their simplicity of form in straight lines and blocks of colour, aesthetics she brought to her three-dimensional works. Formally aligned with Minimalism, Truitt made art that functioned simultaneously as painting and sculpture. The monolithic work *Morning Choice*, for example, is a wooden construction covered with a highly finished surface of sanded-down paint in layers that Truitt described as 'skins' and 'membranes'. Also a writer, Truitt published two biographies: *Daybook: The Journal of an Artist* (1982) and *Turn: The Journal of an Artist* (1986).

UEMURA SHŌEN

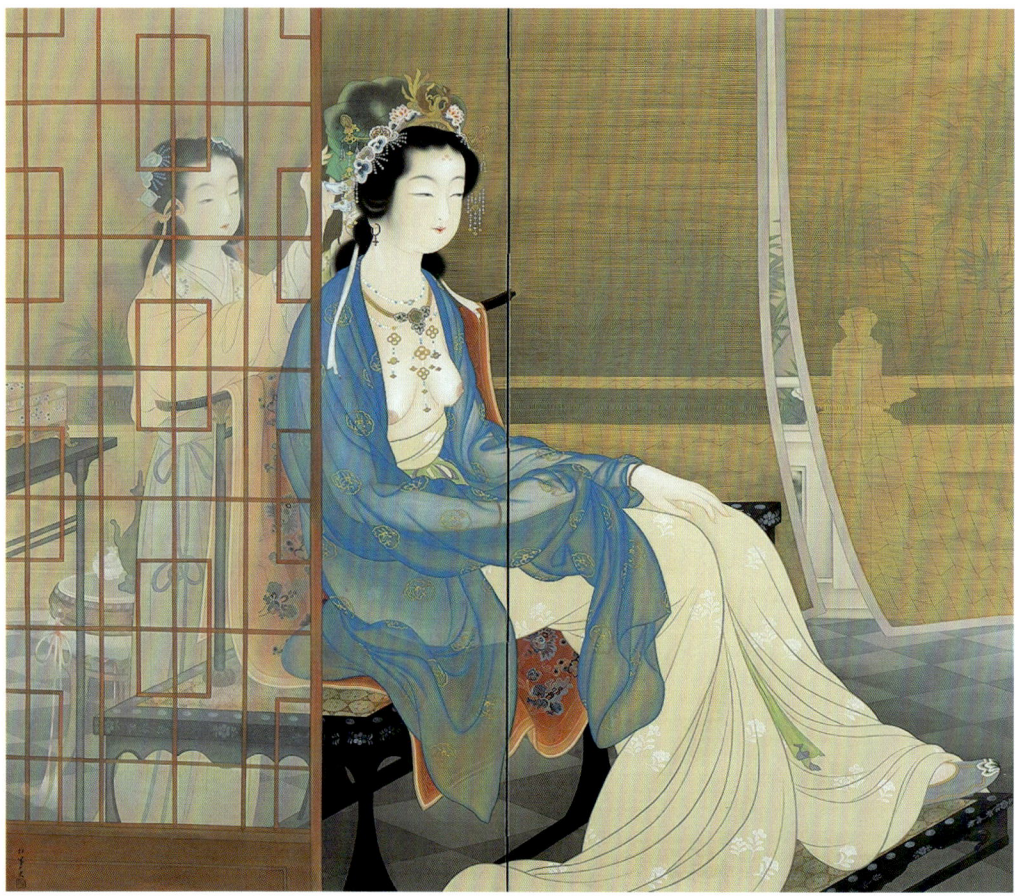

YANG GUIFEI

1922, pigment on silk, 189 × 161 cm (74 ⅜ × 63 ⅜ in), Shohaku Museum
of Arts, Nara, Japan
Uemura Shōen, born Uemura Tsune, 1875, Kyoto. Died 1949,
Nara Prefecture, Japan.

As a girl, Uemura drew pictures in the back of her mother's teashop
in Japan, and honed skills that would see her exhibiting and taking
commissions by the age of fifteen. Formally trained in the Sesshū
and Kanō schools of painting at Kyoto Prefectural Painting School,
she was encouraged to pursue figurative themes by her tutor Suzuki
Shōnen (1849–1918): her adopted name was derived from his
as a mark of esteem. She later became a painter to the Imperial Court.
Best known for *bijin-ga* – paintings and woodblock prints of beautiful

women in an apparently traditional style – her portraits were subtly
subversive: for example, portraying the subjects as the female characters from *Noh* plays: roles usually performed by men. In 1941,
Uemura became the first woman to join the Imperial Art Academy,
and in 1948 was the first to be awarded Japan's Order of Culture.
This work depicts a consort of a Chinese Tang emperor known as one
of China's legendary 'Four Great Beauties'. Yang was a popular
figure in Japan as well, and is referenced in the classic story *The Tale
of Genji*, written by the twelfth-century novelist and noblewoman
Murasaki Shikibu.

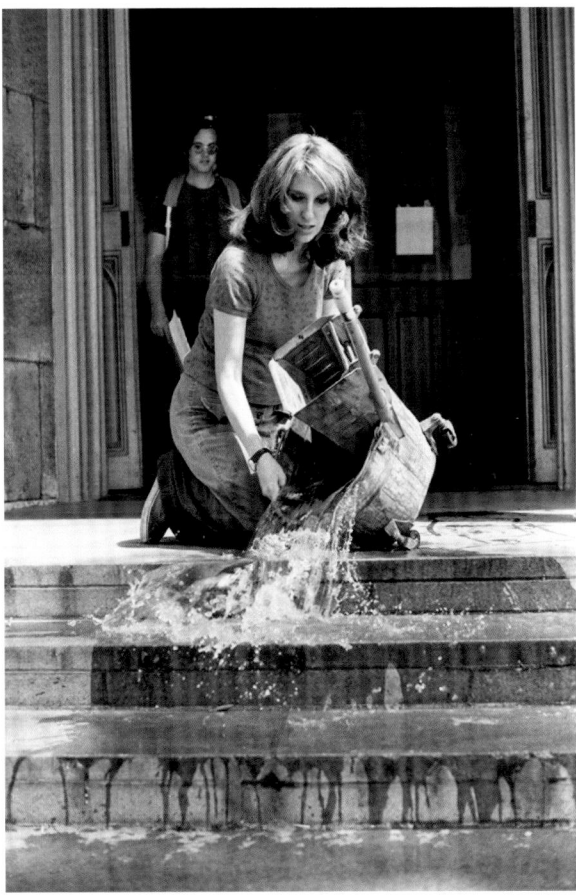

**WASHING/TRACKS/MAINTENANCE: OUTSIDE, JULY 23, 1973 part of
'MAINTENANCE ART PERFORMANCE' series**

1973–4, performance at Wadsworth Atheneum, Hartford, Connecticut;
1 photograph: 40.6 × 60.8 cm (16 × 20 in); 11 photographs: 60.8 × 40.6 cm
(20 × 16 in); one handwritten text: 28 × 21.6 cm (11 × 8 ½ in)
Mierle Laderman Ukeles, born 1939, Denver, Colorado.

A feminist, Ukeles challenges societal values and norms regarding
gendered work. Writing her seminal *Manifesto for Maintenance Art
1969!* soon after she had become a mother, Ukeles acknowledged the
difficulty in negotiating life as an artist with everyday domestic and
service-sector work, which was usually carried out by women or people of colour. She had recently left the Pratt Institute, where the
male-dominated faculty had largely dismissed her early efforts

in painting and sculpture and casually scorned her aspiration
to be an artist and mother. In 1973, Ukeles created an all-woman
group show at the Wadsworth Atheneum, where she engaged
in a series of actions involving cleaning and securing the building
while working closely with the maintenance staff. Throughout her
practice, Ukeles has emphasized the importance of care work and
interdependence, rather than individualism and competition. To this
day, she is the official, unsalaried artist-in-residence for New York's
department of Sanitation, a position she has held since 1979, introducing herself to the Department's 8,500 workers with the words,
'Thank you for keeping New York City alive.'

AMALIA ULMAN

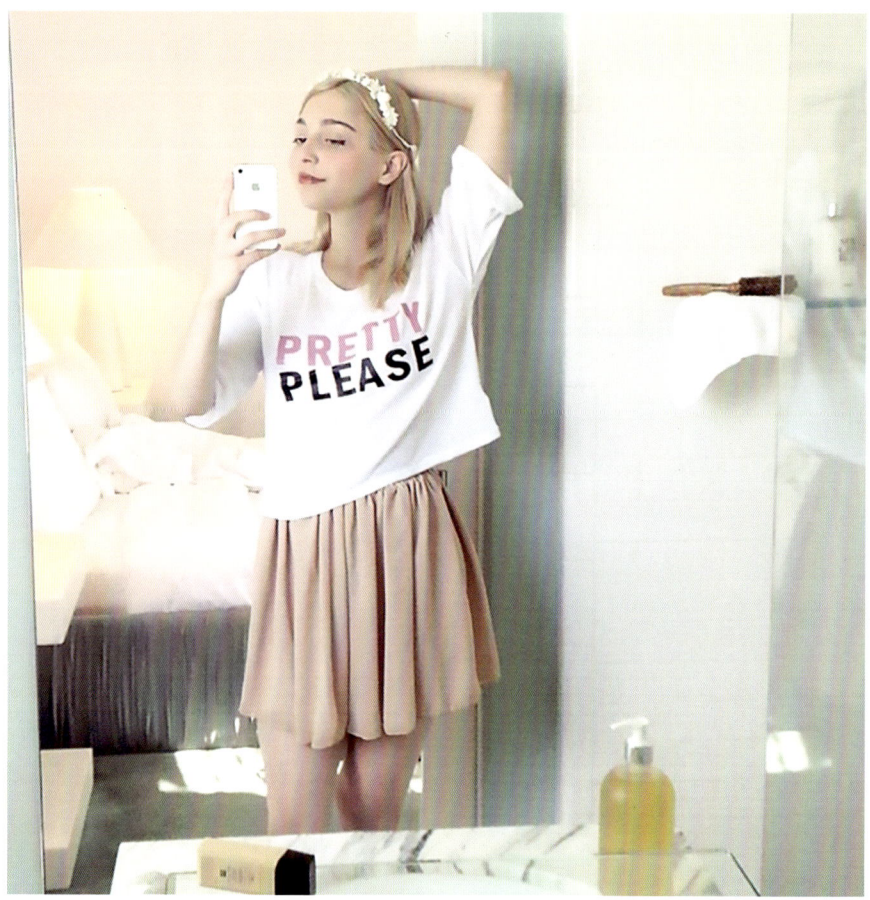

EXCELLENCES & PERFECTIONS, EPISODE 1
2014, performance, Instagram
Amalia Ulman, born 1989, Buenos Aires.

As a child Ulman moved with her family from Buenos Aires to the Spanish province of Gijón, and later studied at Central Saint Martins in London. She graduated in 2011 and in 2014 relocated to Los Angeles. Her art practice explores how identity and power are constructed and circulated. While she makes physical objects, including sculptures and paintings, she also gives lectures on Skype and uses social-media platforms to disseminate her work, revealing the power of immateriality. Much of this involves adopting semi-fictional personas to highlight how social media has exploited the blurred distinctions between fantasy and reality to promote ideologies of success and beauty, while upholding and reinforcing existing power relations in gender, class, race and sexuality. In *Excellences & Perfections*, a four-month Instagram and Facebook performance, Ulman presented images from the lives of three different online characters – 'cute girl', 'sugar babe' and 'life goddess' – all documented in luxurious surroundings. During the course of the performance, Ulman began actually participating in aspects of her characters' lifestyles (such as taking up pole dancing). This confusion between real life and art ultimately became a factor in her decision to end the project.

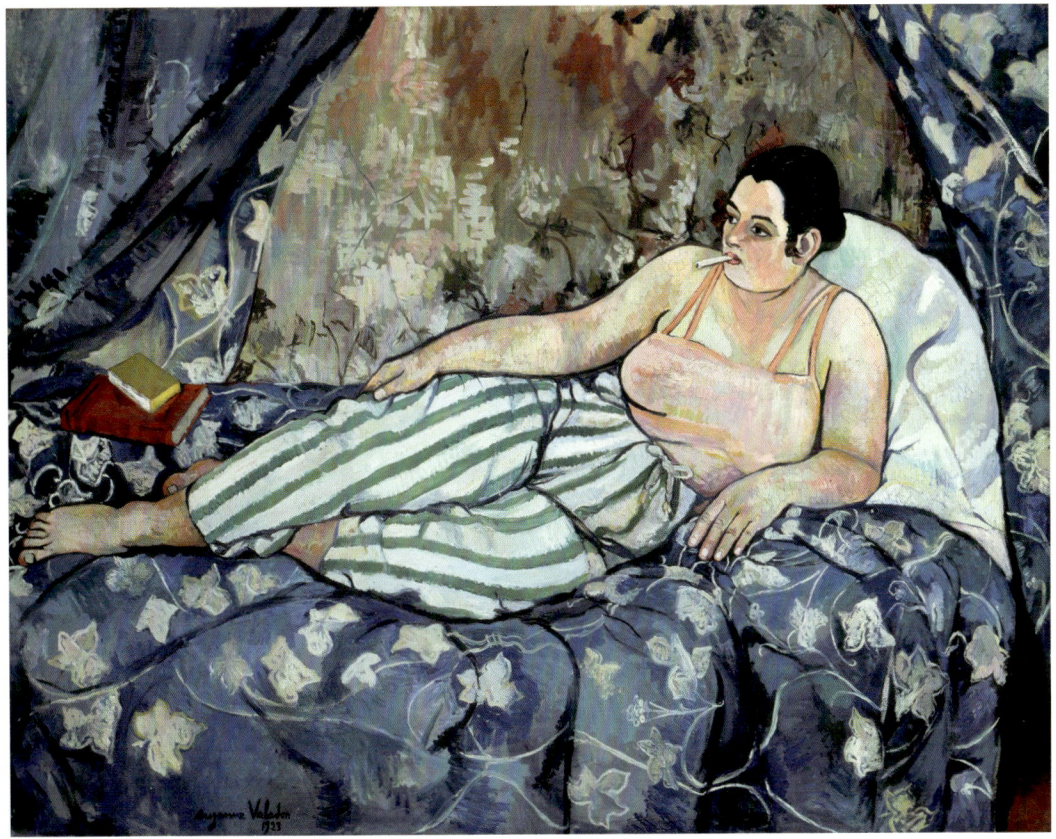

THE BLUE ROOM

1923, oil on canvas, 90 × 116 cm (33 ½ × 45 ¾ in), Musée National d'Art Moderne, Centre Georges Pompidou, Paris

Suzanne Valadon, born Marie-Clémentine Valadon, 1865, Bessines-sur-Gartempe, France. Died 1938, Paris.

Having taught herself to draw as a child, from the age of fifteen Valadon modelled for artists, including Edgar Degas (1834–1917), Henri de Toulouse-Lautrec (1864–1901) and Auguste Renoir (1841–1919). Her first sale of an artwork, in the early 1890s, was to Degas, who became a lifelong supporter of her artistic career. In 1894, Valadon was the first female painter to be admitted to the Société Nationale des Beaux-Arts, Paris. A painter of all figurative genres, including landscapes, still life and portraits, Valadon is most celebrated for her anonymous female figures that challenge the idealizing conventions of art history, and (unusually for their time) include a number of nude self-portraits. Stylistically aligned to Post-Impressionism and Symbolism in her use of strong line and bold colours, yet rooted in everyday settings, her figures are notable for their honest physiques and awkward poses. *The Blue Room* – one of her most celebrated paintings – subverts the classic reclining nude, such as Titian's *Venus and the Lute Player* (*c.*1565). A cigarette-smoking, book-reading woman relaxes in comfortable clothing and is neither seductive nor submissive: she exists as an individual, not solely as the subject for a voyeuristic male gaze.

VALIE EXPORT

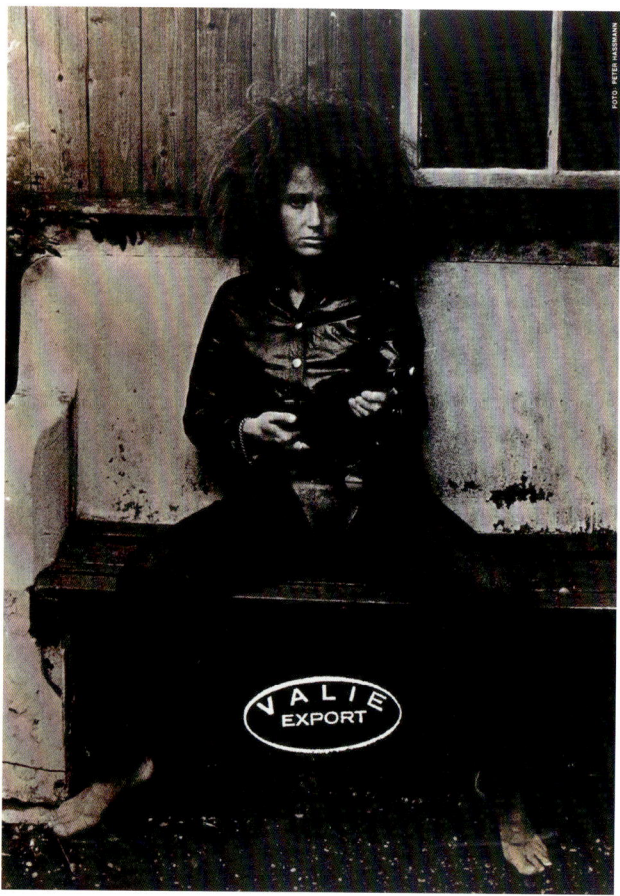

FOTO: PETER HASSMANN

ACTION PANTS: GENITAL PANIC

1969, from a set of 6 identical silkscreen posters, 69.8 × 49.8 cm (27 ½ × 19 ⅝ in), Musée National d'Art Moderne, Centre Georges Pompidou, Paris
VALIE EXPORT, born Waltraud Lehner, later Waltraud Höllinger, 1940, Linz, Austria.

VALIE EXPORT's radical ethos was informed by feminist critique. She was educated up to the age of fourteen at a convent and, later, at vocational colleges in Linz and Vienna, studying textiles, before working in film production. In response to masculinist ideology in Austria she abandoned the names relating to her father and ex-husband, changing hers to VALIE EXPORT, borrowed from a popular cigarette brand and emphasizing her self-determined openness to the outside world. Her art practice, which was influenced by the Viennese Actionist movement of the 1960s, involved her putting her body in extreme situations to examine power relations in society. One street performance involved her wearing a box-like costume resembling a theatre, complete with curtains, through which spectators were invited to touch her bare breasts and body while looking her in the eyes. In the performance documented here, VALIE EXPORT strolled through a cinema in Munich, dressed in crotchless trousers. This gesture was intended to expose the hypocrisy between the sexist tropes in cinema and conservative social taboos around female genitalia. The work's militancy is emphasized in this image, showing the artist sitting with her legs spread, brandishing a gun.

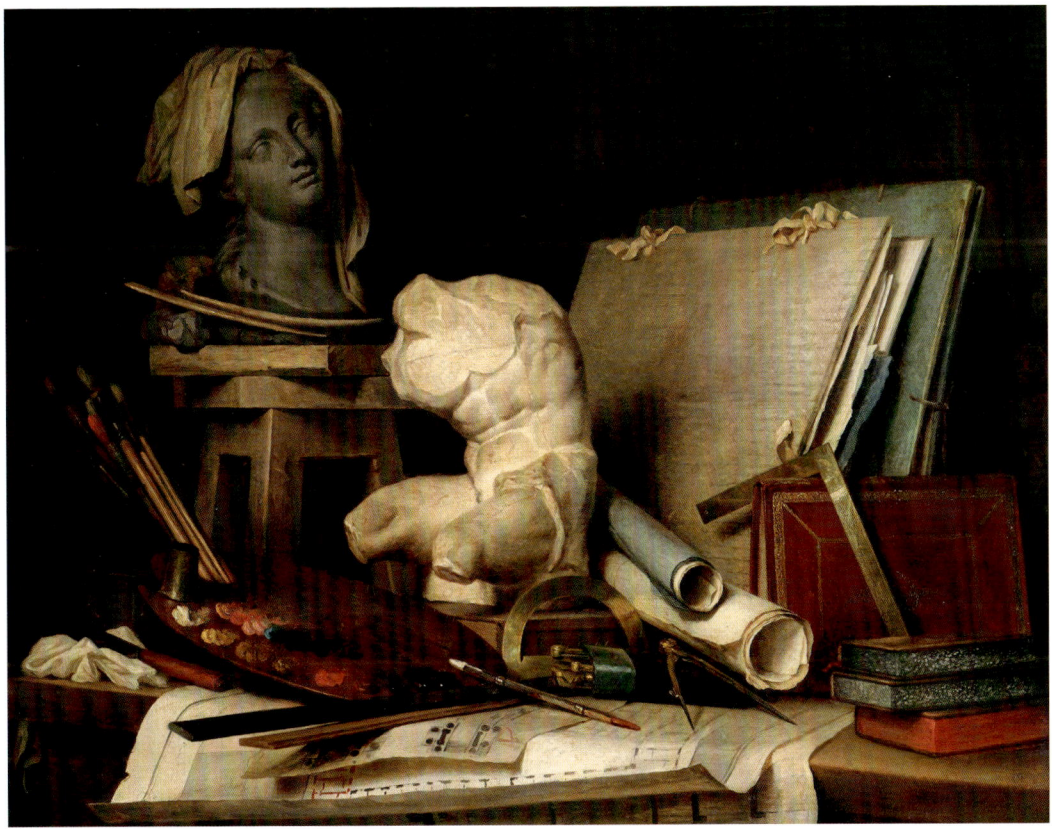

THE ATTRIBUTES OF THE ARTS

1769, oil on canvas, 90 × 121 cm (35 ⅜ × 47 ⅝ in), Musée du Louvre, Paris
Anne Vallayer-Coster, born Anne Vallayer, 1744, Paris. Died 1818, Paris.

Vallayer-Coster was born into an elite social milieu in France, her circle of aristocratic patrons including Marie Antoinette. The queen named her painter to the court in 1780 and her skill afforded her regular patronage. In 1770 she had been unanimously elected to the Académie Royale de Peinture et de Sculpture, one of only four women members before the Revolution. Aged twenty-six, she began regular, well-received participation at the Academy's Salons, where she showed her still-life paintings. While considered an inferior genre in the canonical hierarchy of painting subjects, Vallayer-Coster garnered praise for her detailed technique, complex compositions and scholarly references. This is clear in this painting, where she demonstrated her knowledge of the *paragone* debate, a theoretical discussion from the Italian Renaissance about the relative merits of painting and sculpture. She firmly lays claim to painting's triumph over the other arts through her skilful composition depicting the fruits of sculpture, architecture and literature, painting itself represented by its tools. Ingenious, multilayered and many decades ahead of debates about representation, her recursive study encompasses all of art within the overlooked genre of still life.

REMEDIOS VARO

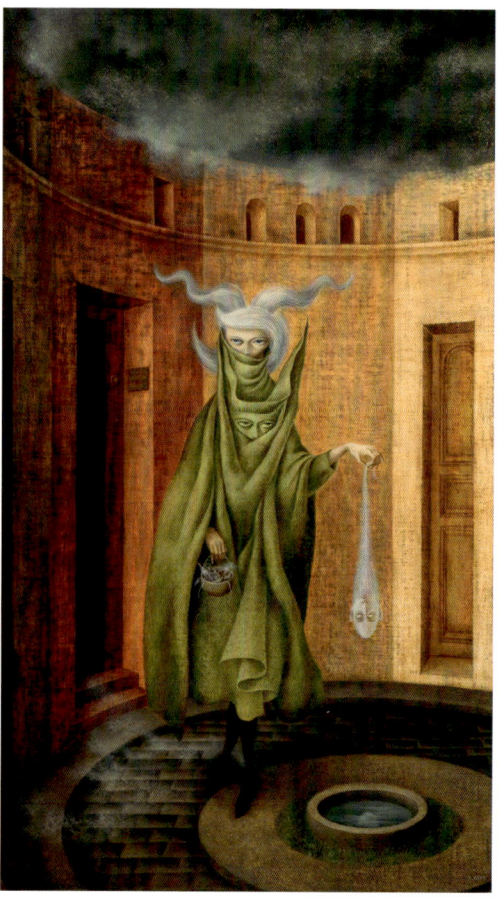

WOMAN LEAVING THE PSYCHOANALYST

1960, 71 × 41 cm (28 × 16⅛ in), Museo de Arte Moderno, Mexico City
Remedios Varo, born María de los Remedios Alicia Rodriga Varo y Uranga, 1908,
Anglès, Girona, Spain. Died 1963, Mexico City.

Raised in a devout Catholic family and introduced to the Gothic
imagination as a girl, Varo enrolled aged fifteen at the Real Academia
de Bellas Artes de San Fernando in Madrid. In the 1930s she lived in
Paris and then Barcelona, becoming actively involved in the Surrealist
movement and wider avant-garde there before returning to France
during the Spanish Civil War. After the German invasion of 1940,
she fled to Mexico, where she would spend the rest of her life. Alongside collaborator, friend and fellow European Surrealist Leonora
Carrington (p.90), Varo found stability in Mexico, and although not

influenced by Central American motifs, she enjoyed a culture that
was permeable to myth and narrative. From the early 1950s until her
death, she was prolific, making work that explored her mystical and
esoteric preoccupations. After her first solo exhibition in 1955, Varo
found considerable acclaim and commercial success. This late work
contains numerous characters – a woman with wavy hair, a face buried in her cloak, the ghostly decapitated head of an old man – bringing
the twentieth-century's psychological turn into collision with brooding, hermetic mysteries.

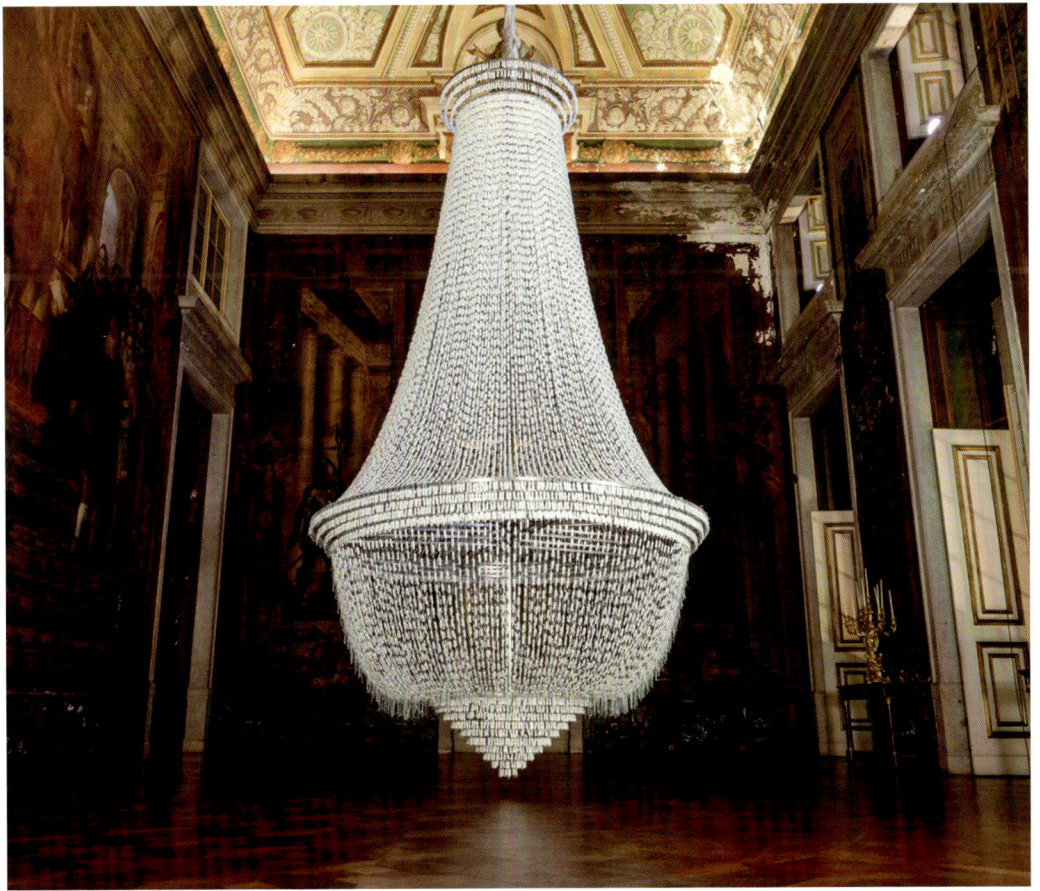

A NOIVA [THE BRIDE]

2001–5, OB tampons, stainless steel, cotton thread and steel cables [work produced and restored with the support of Johnson & Johnson Ltd], h: 600 × diam: 300 cm (h: 236 ¼ × diam: 118 ⅛ in), installation view, Palácio da Ajuda, Lisbon, 2013. António Cachola Collection, Elvas, Portugal
Joana Vasconcelos, born 1971, Paris.

Born in France, where her parents lived in temporary exile from Portugal's Salazar dictatorship, Vasconcelos returned with her family to Lisbon after the Carnation Revolution in 1974. These experiences taught her that everyday life is socially and politically loaded, an outlook that has influenced her art. Her monumental, touring public artwork *Pop Galo* (2016) takes a traditional Portuguese emblem – the Rooster of Barcelos – and transforms it into a dynamic architectural intervention in urban space and has travelled internationally. Vasconcelos uses non-traditional materials for her sculptural practice, exemplified by *The Bride*, a chandelier made of tampons. The piece is so large that when hung in most interiors, it occupies space from floor to ceiling. When light hits the plastic-covered cotton products, they shimmer, like the prisms of a real chandelier, yet these are objects that women are taught to keep private. Presented for the first time in the Arsenale at the 51st Venice Biennale (2005), it was shown again at the Centquatre in Paris after being censored by the Palace of Versailles from Vasconcelos's major exhibition there, which was also its first show by a living female artist.

CECILIA VICUÑA

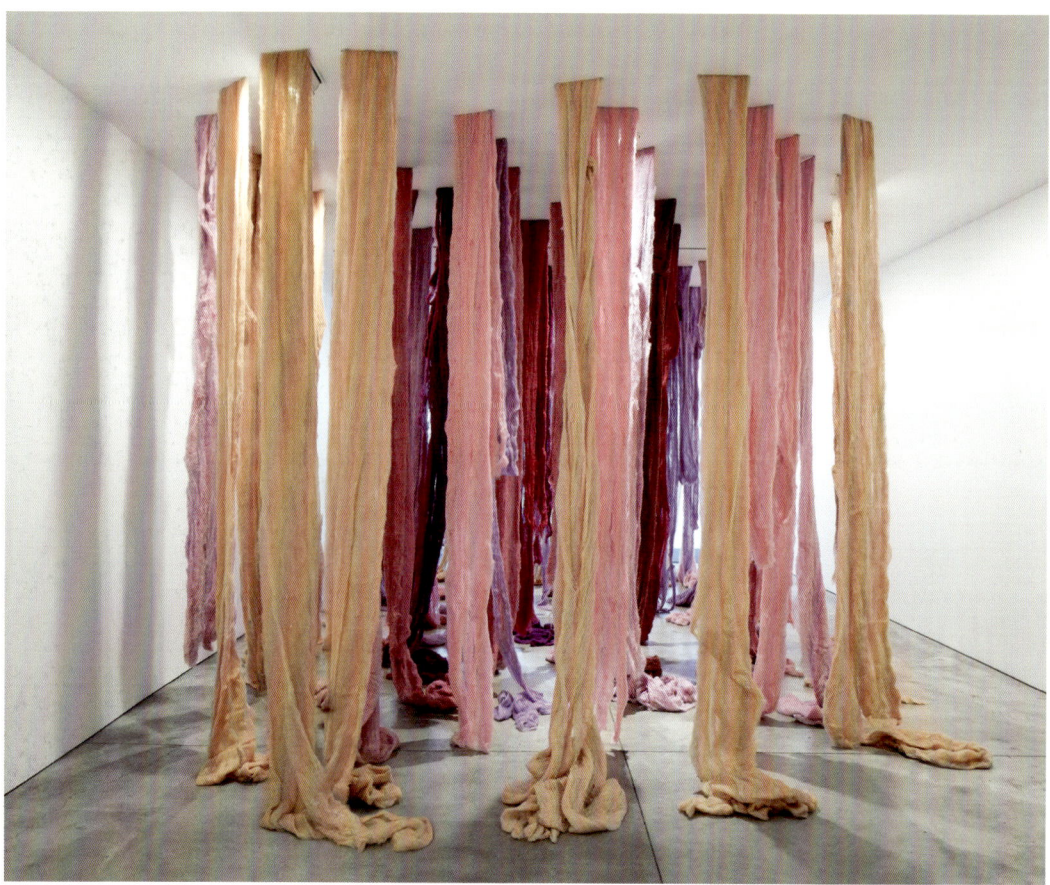

Vicuña's artworks speak of both the ancient traditions of her native
Latin America and current affairs, including ecology, human rights
and cultural identity. An activist as well as artist working with performance, video, poetry and sculpture, her practice ranges from
ephemeral small groupings of natural and man-made objects, which
she left to nature at the ocean's edge – the 'Precarios' series (1972–3)
– to political paintings made in the 1970s in which she depicted social
unrest and her own exile from Chile in 1973. Living first in London,
then Bogotá, in 1980 she moved to New York where she has resided

ever since. Since the mid-1960s, Vicuña has worked with *Quipus* –
a recording method used by the Inca civilization to keep track
of commercial and social activities, and possibly other things.
In *Quipu Visceral* the artist employs raw wool dyed colours reminiscent of bodily organs and fluids to create an immersive installation.
Viewers are invited to enter the soft, protective structure and appreciate the power of the ancestral form, becoming themselves part
of the mysterious network it weaves. Vicuña's art continues to raise
social awareness, as issues of climate change and multiculturalism
gain traction in the twenty-first century.

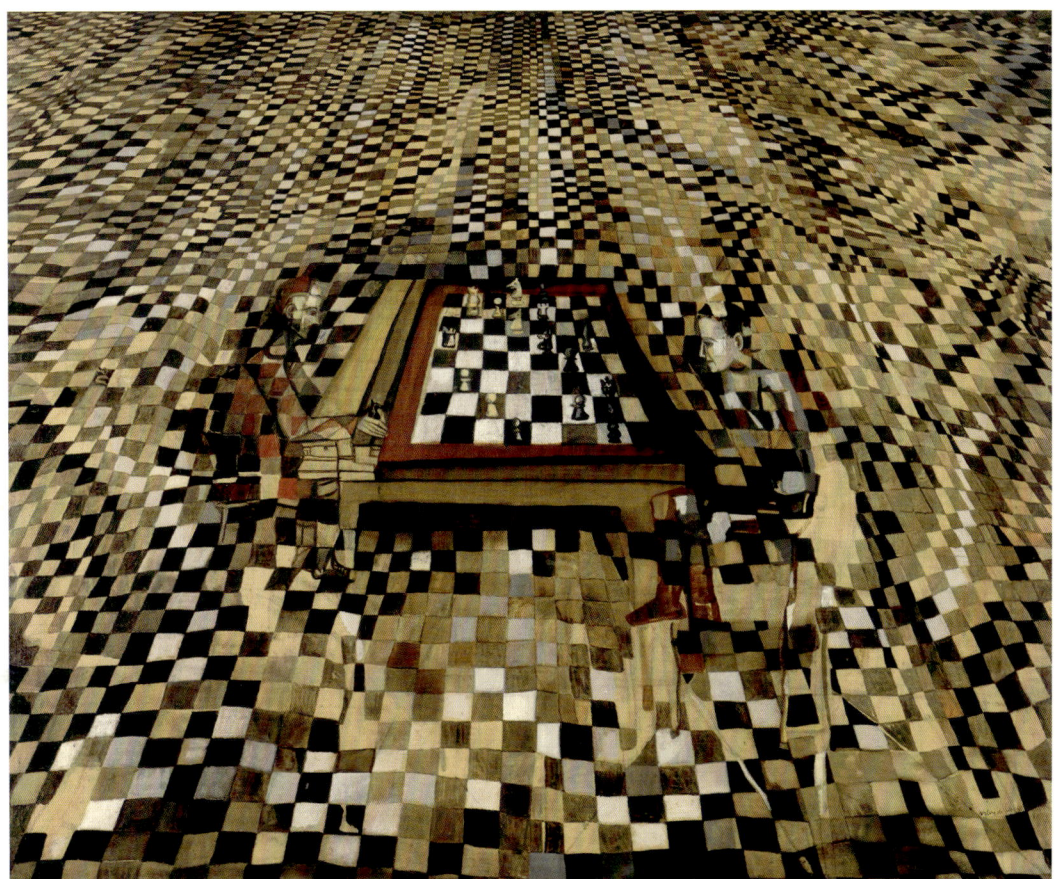

THE CHESS GAME

1943, oil on canvas, 81 × 100 cm (31 ⅞ × 39 ⅜ in), Musée National d'Art Moderne, Centre Georges Pompidou, Paris

Maria Helena Vieira da Silva, born 1908, Lisbon. Died 1992, Paris.

A child prodigy and encouraged by her family, Vieira da Silva attended Lisbon's Academia Nacional de Belas-Artes from the age of eleven. In 1928 she went to Paris to attend the Académie de la Grande Chaumière, studying sculpture with Antoine Bourdelle (1861–1929) and meeting her future husband, Hungarian painter Árpád Szenes (1897–1985). After 1929, she prioritized painting, receiving further instruction from Fernand Léger (1881–1955). Exhibitions in Paris from the early 1930s were the start of a career in which she became known and acclaimed internationally. Aside from a period of exile

during the Second World War, Vieira da Silva lived in Paris for most of her life and a mark of the esteem in which she was held was the award of the Légion d'Honneur in 1979. With Paul Cézanne (1839–1906) a strong influence, her paintings also fuse the later modernist styles of Cubism, Surrealism and Expressionism. This work depicts two chess players in the midst of play against a distorted chequerboard background. So absorbed in the game that they melt into it, they are enveloped in a contest that seems to have neither beginning nor end.

ÉLISABETH VIGÉE-LEBRUN

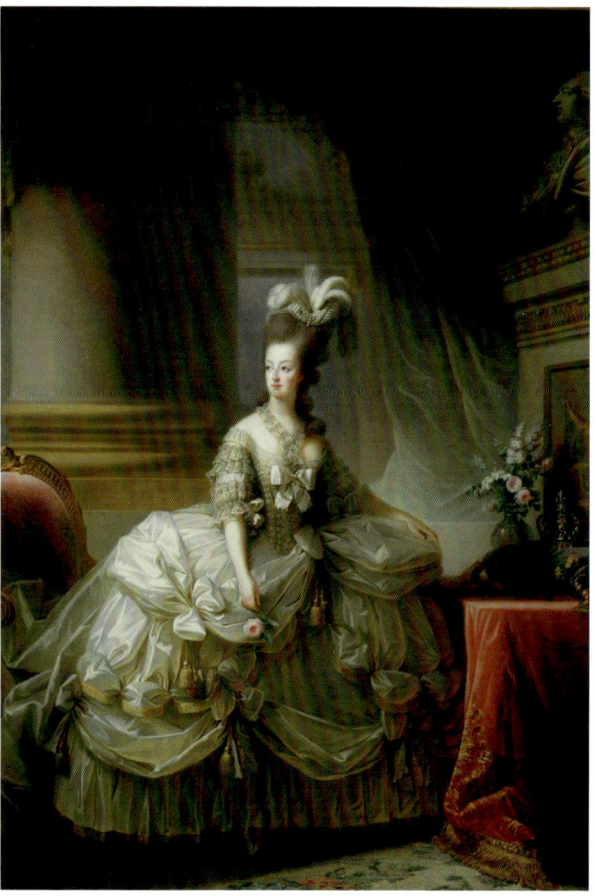

MARIE ANTOINETTE IN COURT DRESS

1778, oil on canvas, 273 × 193.5 cm (107 ½ × 76 ⅛ in), Gemäldegalerie, Kunsthistorisches Museum, Vienna

Élisabeth Vigée-Lebrun, born Marie-Louise-Élisabeth Vigée, 1755, Paris. Died 1842, Paris.

An established portraitist of Europe's social elite – she completed some 660 portraits – Vigée-Lebrun had a profitable and highly respected career from a young age. Closely associated with the court of Louis XVI and Marie Antoinette, in the Paris Salon of 1783, she scandalized viewers of her portrait of the queen in a simple muslin dress. By contrast, this earlier work depicts her in majesty, her attire and surroundings proverbially lavish. In her memoirs, Vigée-Lebrun noted the warm companionship between herself and the queen. Indeed, this association was so close that during the French Revolution in October 1789 she was forced to flee with her daughter. With no money, just her unparalleled reputation, she travelled to Naples, where she painted Marie Antoinette's sister, then later to Vienna, and eventually to the court of Catherine the Great in St Petersburg. During this time she was elected to the academies of ten cities and despite her twelve-year exile from Paris, she continued to exhibit in its Salons. Her return to the city in 1802 was finally made possible thanks to the efforts of her family, who had her name removed from the list of anti-revolutionary émigrés.

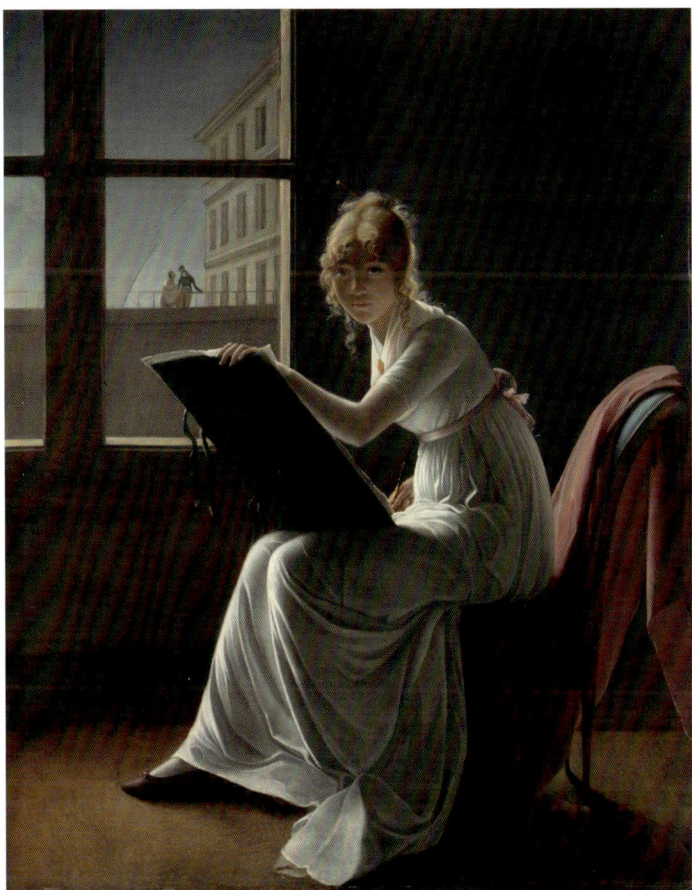

MARIE JOSÉPHINE CHARLOTTE DU VAL D'OGNES

1801, oil on canvas, 161.3 × 128.6 cm (63 ½ × 50 ⅝ in), Metropolitan Museum of Art, New York

Marie-Denise Villers, born Marie-Denise Lemoine, 1774, Paris. Died 1821, Paris.

Little is known of Villers's biography, but her celebrated painting of fellow aspiring artist Charlotte du Val d'Ognes (d.1868) provides insight into the life of women artists in Paris at the turn of the nineteenth century. Acquired by the Metropolitan Museum of Art in 1922, it was first attributed to Jacques-Louis David (1748–1825), then to Constance Marie Charpentier (p.97). In 1996 art historian Margaret Oppenheimer published evidence to suggest that it was painted by Villers. The spartan setting is likely to represent a studio in the Louvre where a few women artists, such as Anne Vallayer-Coster

(p.413) and Élisabeth Vigée-Lebrun (p.418) led professional careers, albeit for the most part unofficially, in studios formally assigned to their male relatives. With the complex foreshortening of the drawing board and the dramatic difference in scale between the sitter and the figures seen through the broken window, it is a confident demonstration of perspective, fundamental to artistic study at the time. Noting this, art historian Anne Higonnet has suggested that it may be an allegory of painting, which would have lifted its status from portraiture, a minor genre, to a more elevated work at the Paris Salon of the time.

URSULA VON RYDINGSVARD

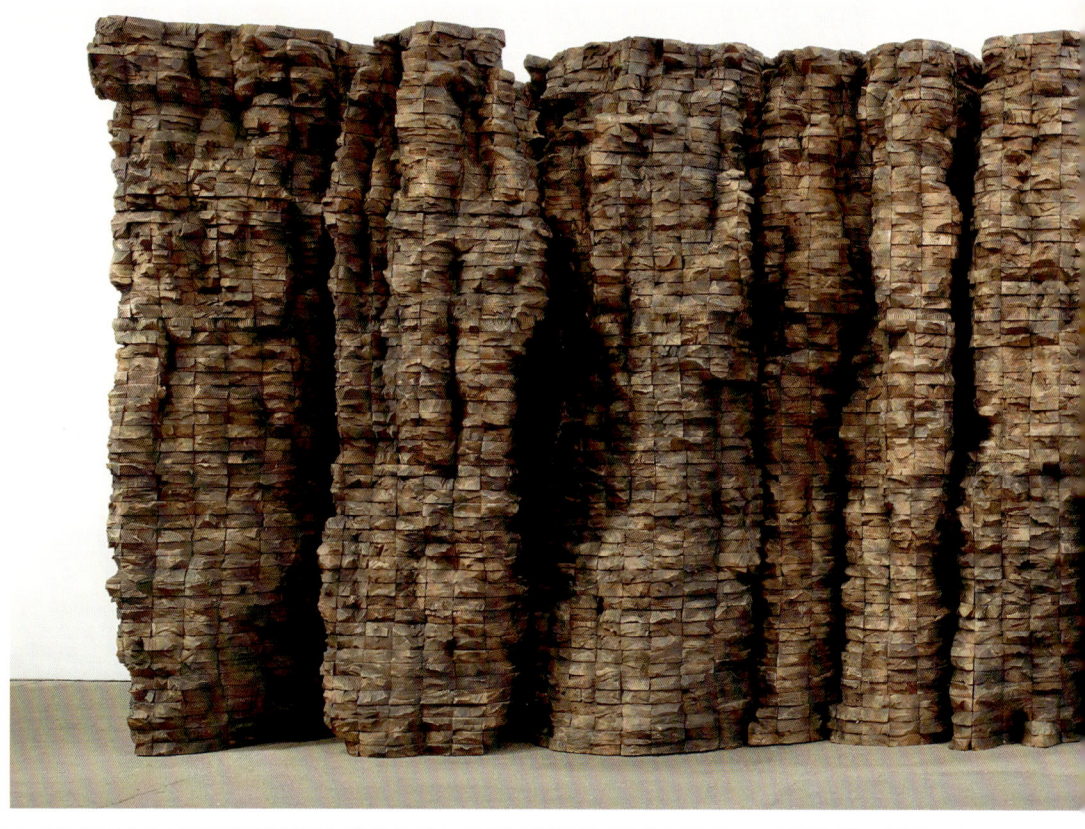

BLACKENED WORD

2008, cedar and graphite, 205.8 × 629.9 × 198.2 cm (81 × 248 × 78 in),
Albright-Knox Art Gallery, Buffalo, New York
Ursula von Rydingsvard, born Ursula Karoliszyn, 1942, Deensen, Germany.

Inspired by 1970s Land art, as well as by Classical Greek statuary and medieval effigies, von Rydingsvard is best known for large-scale abstract wood sculptures. Born in Germany to displaced Ukrainian-Polish parents, she emigrated to the United States as a child in 1950 and has lived and worked in New York for over forty years. As a single parent, von Rydingsvard completed an MFA in sculpture at Columbia University in 1975 but regards 1988 as the turning point in her career, when the Metropolitan Museum of Art and Brooklyn Museum each purchased her work. Consisting of 8,000

parts, the shape of the monumental piece *Blackened Word* is determined by a floor outline of the enlarged handwritten text that gives the work its title. The wood is cut, assembled and laminated together, its textured surface then rubbed with graphite and oil to achieve a dark patina. Forms taken from objects both ubiquitous and ancient – such as bowls, spoons and walls – recur throughout her creations. The intertwining of contemporary ideas and techniques with tradition and memory results in powerful and emotionally charged work.

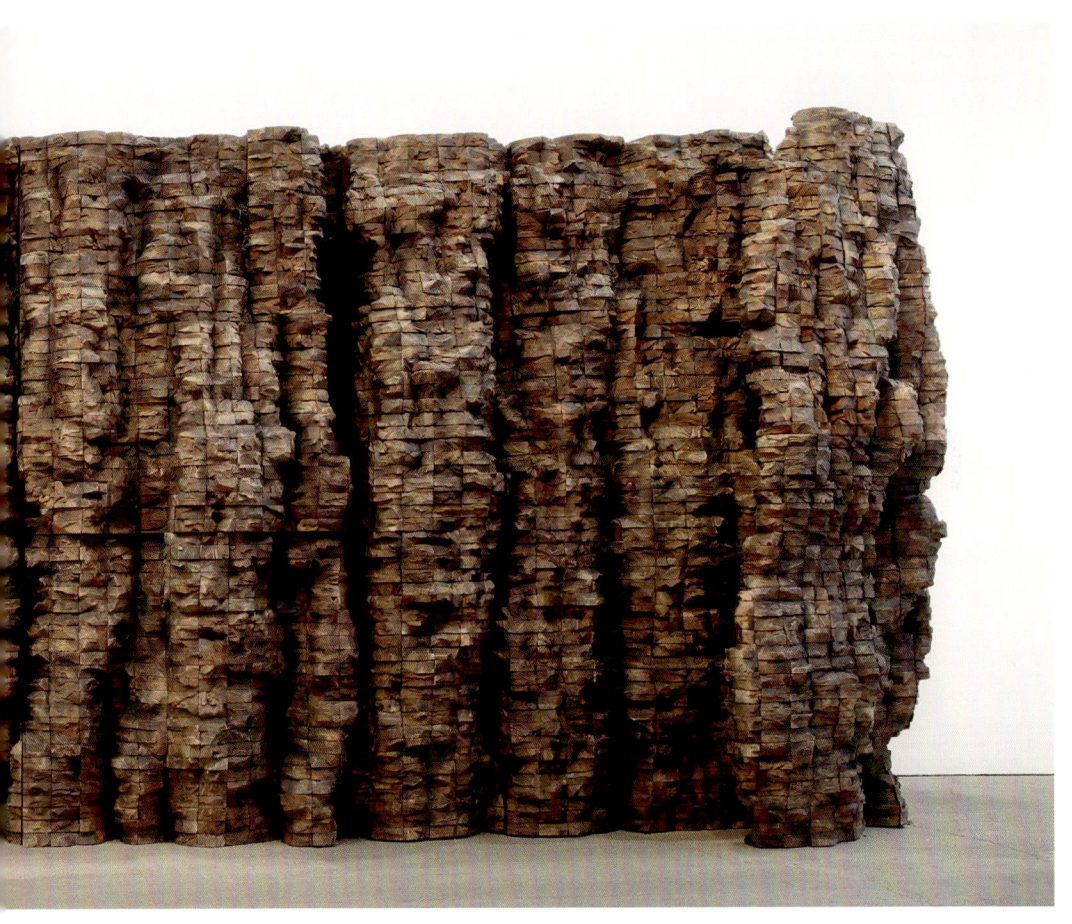

KARA WALKER

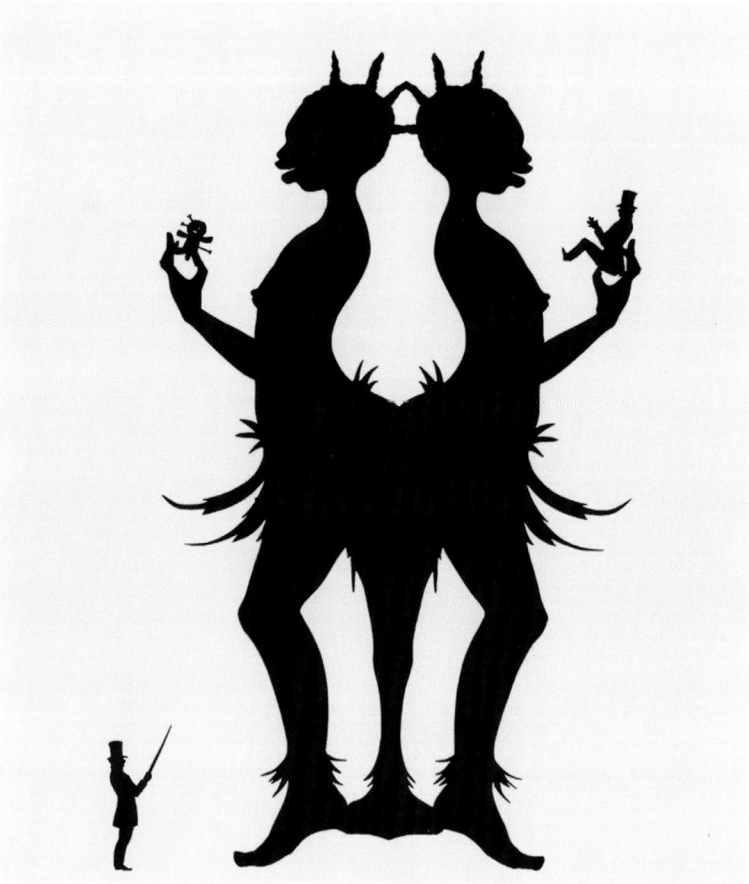

YOU DO

1993/4, cut paper on canvas, 139.7 × 124.5 cm (55 × 49 in), private collection
Kara Walker, born 1969, Stockton, California.

Walker's art addresses issues of race, gender and identity, although
having grown up in a middle-class, multicultural environment,
she has stated that she was 'protected from considerations of race'
as a child, only discovering the realities of the legacy of racial segregation when moving to Atlanta, as a teenager. During her MFA
studies at Rhode Island School of Design in the early 1990s, she
began to produce works that explored these themes, experimenting
with the art form for which she would become best known: the
silhouette. A style of portraiture popular in the eighteenth and nineteenth centuries as an alternative to the more expensive miniatures

tradition, Walker's paper cut-out figures wear old-fashioned clothing in a nod to the craft's history, while also representing a terrible
legacy of the same era. Depicting the testimonies of slaves in the
American South, Walker portrays them with their 'owners', remind-
ing viewers of the country's violent racial past and its continued
resonance today. *You Do* is an example of how unnerving these silhouettes can be; while the women in the image are huge compared
to the men, the history of subjugation remains visible, especially
that of the black woman at the hands of their 'master'.

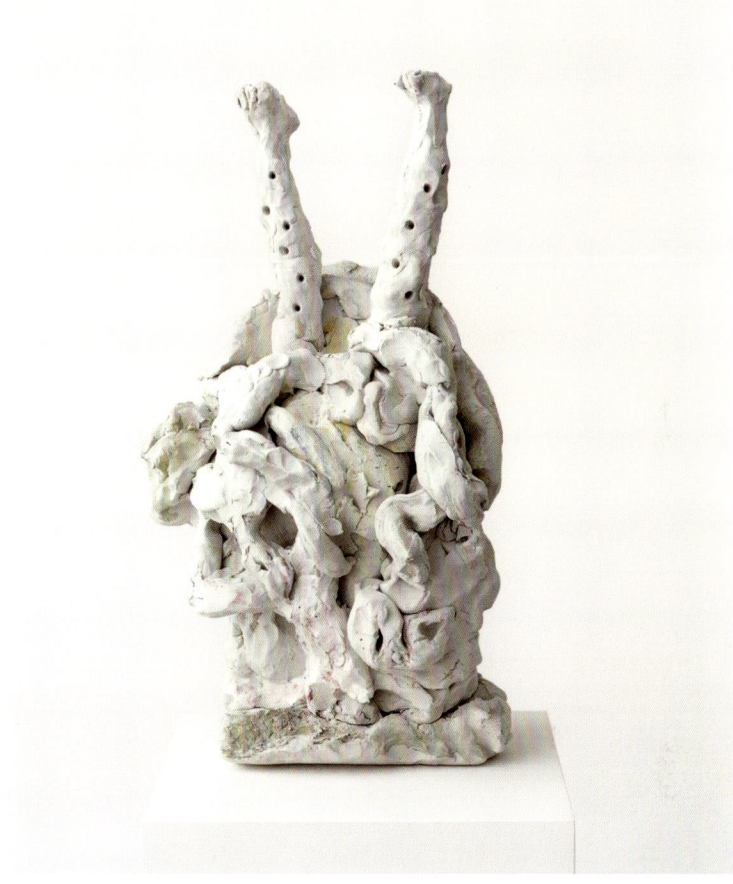

HUNDEMEISTER

2004, hand-painted clay on painted MDF plinth, 49 × 23 × 21 cm (19¼ × 9 × 8¼ in), private collection

Rebecca Warren, born 1965, Pinhoe, UK.

Warren is a London-based artist known for her corporeal sculptures in raw clay and bronze, which she has been making since the early 1990s. Often playing with a cartoonish eroticism, she works within a historical lineage of intense interest in human – especially female – bodily forms and their potential for anatomical improbability. Her work, with its lavish convexities of breasts, buttocks, thighs, calves and ambivalent or absent heads and faces, particularly draws on that of Auguste Rodin (1840–1917) and Alberto Giacometti (1901–66), as well as fusing elements derived from the satirical and prurient cartoons of Robert Crumb (b.1943). *Hundemeister* – the Germanic title might loosely translate as 'Master of Hounds' – is an agglomeration of forms, some more identifiable than others. Protruding vertically from an arrangement of limbs, rocks and skulls is a pair of upturned legs riddled with holes. Viewed as a whole, the sculpture takes on the shape of a horned skull or a long-eared animal head, monstrous and deathly in its effect. Warren's works hold themselves in confident untidiness, simultaneously seeming overwrought and provisional, coming apart and reassembling, like contending forces in search of an uneasy harmony.

ANNA WASER

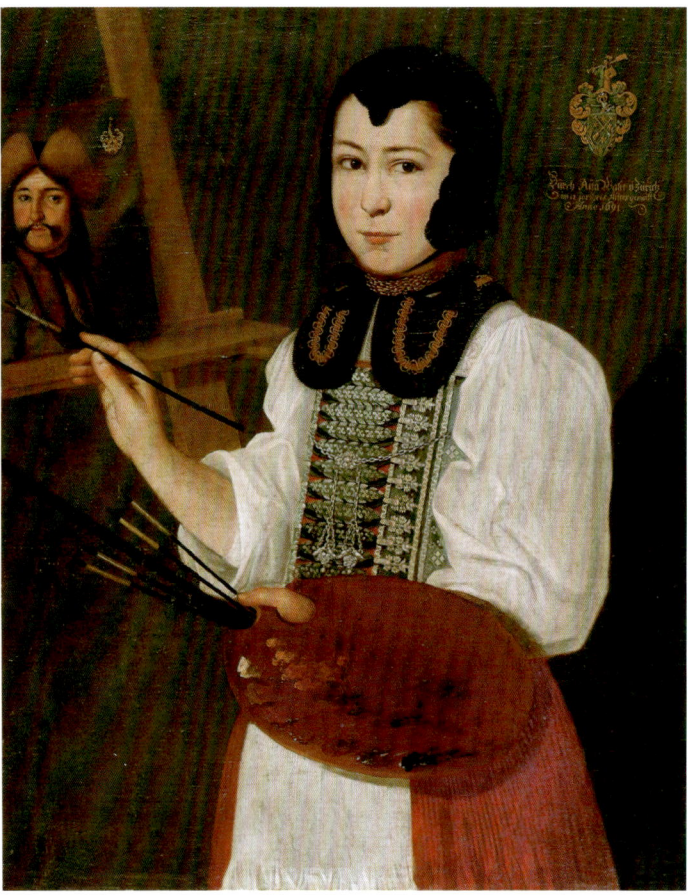

SELF-PORTRAIT AT TWELVE YEARS OF AGE

1691, oil on canvas, 83 × 68 cm (32 ⅝ × 26 ¾ in), Kunsthaus Zürich
Anna Waser, born 1678, Zürich. Died 1714, Zürich.

Waser was the first female painter from Switzerland to achieve inter-national fame, as a painter of miniatures and an engraver whose work was sought by courts and private collectors across Europe. Receiving what at the time was considered an extraordinary education for a girl, she painted this assured self-portrait, her best-known surviving work, when she was only twelve. The child artist stands alongside one of her own portraits, easel in hand and holding a brush to an unfinished picture, with a look out at towards the viewer of disarming poise and candour. The following year, Waser made a copy of one of the paint-ings of Swiss master Joseph Werner (1637–1710), convincing those

around her that she was destined for an artistic career – although the same sense of destiny seems evident in the earlier self-portrait. Waser trained under Werner for three years. Accounts of her later career are incomplete – her autobiography was lost – but suggest that her success was a burden, with her father pressurizing her into undertaking more commissions than she could finish. After long periods of depression, she died aged thirty-four after suffering a fall.

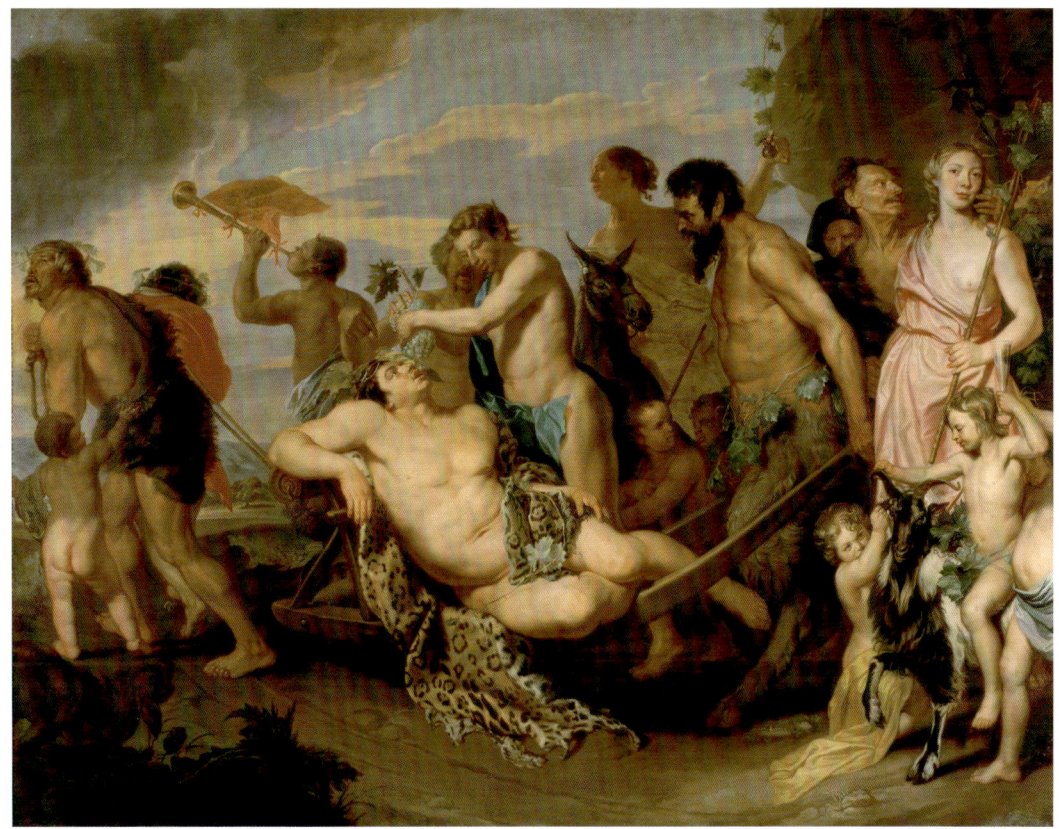

THE TRIUMPH OF BACCHUS

before 1659, oil on canvas, 270 × 354 cm (106 ¼ × 139 ⅜ in), Kunsthistorisches Museum, Vienna

Michaelina Wautier (or Woutiers), born 1617/18, Mons, Belgium (then County of Hainaut). Died 1689, Brussels.

Wautier achieved recognition and success in her lifetime but much of her work was later misattributed to her brother, Charles (1609–1703), and other Flemish Baroque painters including Jacob van Oost (1603–71). Only recently has her name been reclaimed from obscurity, the Museum aan de Stroom in Antwerp, Belgium, presenting an exhibition of her work in 2018. The breadth of her oeuvre included portraiture as well as both still lifes and large-format history painting and she was also celebrated for her command of

ambitiously expansive scales. Seen here is her depiction of the Greco-Roman god of wine, slumped and voluptuous amid a rabble of followers. To the right, a young woman confronts the viewer, one breast bared and ignoring the attentions of an older male reveller: this is in fact an unashamed self-portrait, perhaps a sign of self-confidence from one of the first female painters to depict a naked man. Making a living from sales to high-profile clients also marked her out from other women artists of her day. Four paintings were sold to Archduke Leopold Wilhelm of Austria, as noted in his gallery's 1659 inventory. Only fifteen paintings signed by her are now known to have survived.

GILLIAN WEARING

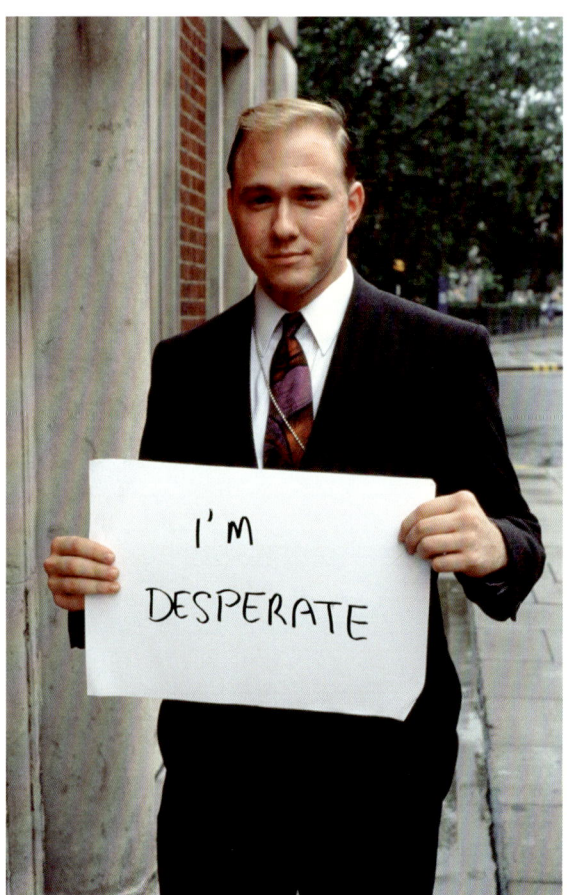

**I'M DESPERATE from 'SIGNS THAT SAY WHAT YOU WANT THEM TO SAY
AND NOT SIGNS THAT SAY WHAT SOMEONE ELSE WANTS YOU TO SAY'**

1992–3, C-type print mounted on aluminium, 44.5 × 29.7 cm (17 ½ × 11 ⅝ in)
Gillian Wearing, born 1963, Birmingham, UK.

Wearing studied at Goldsmiths College, London, and graduated
in 1990. Her first solo exhibition was at the influential artist-run City
Racing gallery in Vauxhall, in 1993. Four years later, Wearing
became the second woman to win the Turner Prize, and in 2018, her
sculpture of the suffragist Millicent Fawcett was the first statue
of a woman in London's Parliament Square, as well as the only one
designed by a female artist. Primarily using video and photography,
her work addresses issues of the individual and society, public and
private, fact and fiction. She has often featured her own image, most

recently with her identity altered by use of masks or, in the case of
Rock 'n' Roll 70 (2015) using age progression software to make possible versions of her future self. In the series 'Signs that say what you
want them to say and not signs that say what someone else wants you
to say', in contrast, she depicted over 200 anonymous subjects.
Stopping strangers on the street, she asked them to write a word
or phrase of their choosing, then photographed them holding it.
The images range from a uniformed police officer saying simply,
'HELP', to a man who asks, 'Will Britain get through this reces-
sion?' and reveal the hidden and often unexpected nature of the
thoughts of others.

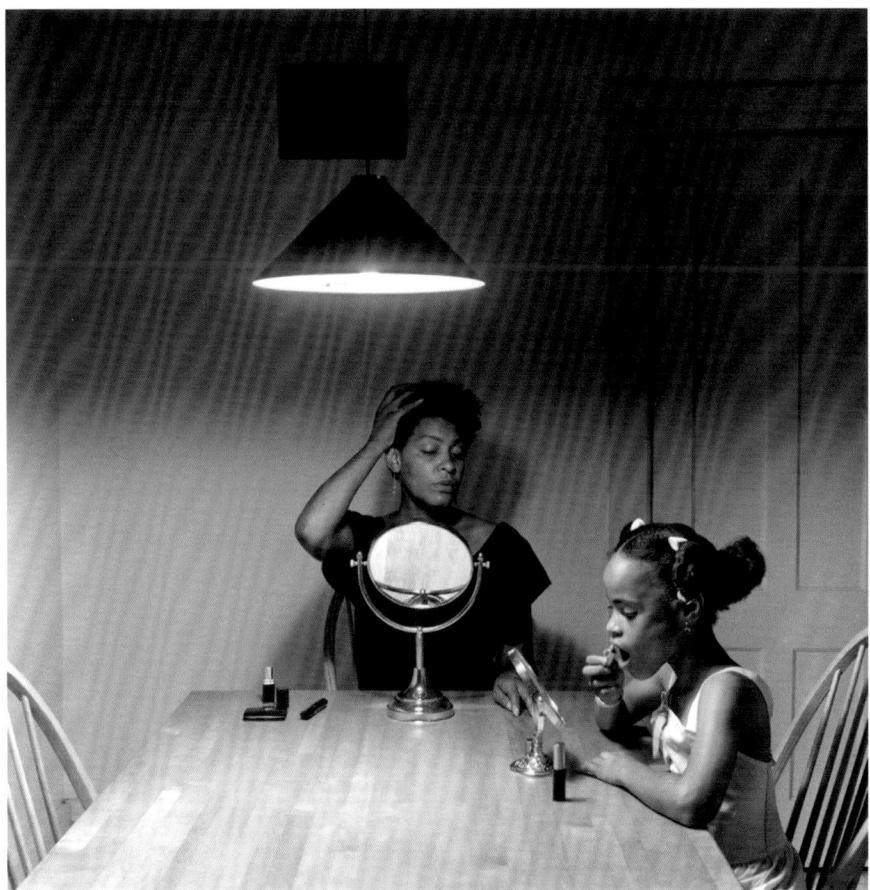

UNTITLED (WOMAN AND DAUGHTER WITH MAKEUP)
1990, gelatin silver print, 69.2 × 69.2 cm (27¼ × 27¼ in), edition of 5 + 2 aps
Carrie Mae Weems, born 1953, Portland, Oregon.

Having moved to California as a teenager to study with the pioneering dancer and choreographer, Anna Halprin (1920–2021) at the San Francisco Dancer's Workshop, Weems turned to photography and became known for her black-and-white works that evoke the lives and experiences of black Americans. Combining both documentary and fictional registers, her portraits address modes of recollection, from storytelling to the construction of history and the workings of memory. Her subjects, who include the artist herself as well as people she knows personally, often pose to ironic or enigmatic effect. Take, for example, the series 'The Kitchen Table' (1989–90), where Weems photographed herself and her friends on a daily basis over many months – always at her kitchen table from the same angle, but engaged in different day-to-day activities. *Untitled (Woman and Daughter with Makeup)* depicts the artist and her child each looking at themselves in small table-top mirrors, seemingly oblivious to the lens. Weems is fixing her hair and her daughter applies lipstick. Weems uses her body to explore the complex realities of women's lives and, here, also includes her child to represents young girls likely grow up encountering these same realities.

MARIANNE VON WEREFKIN

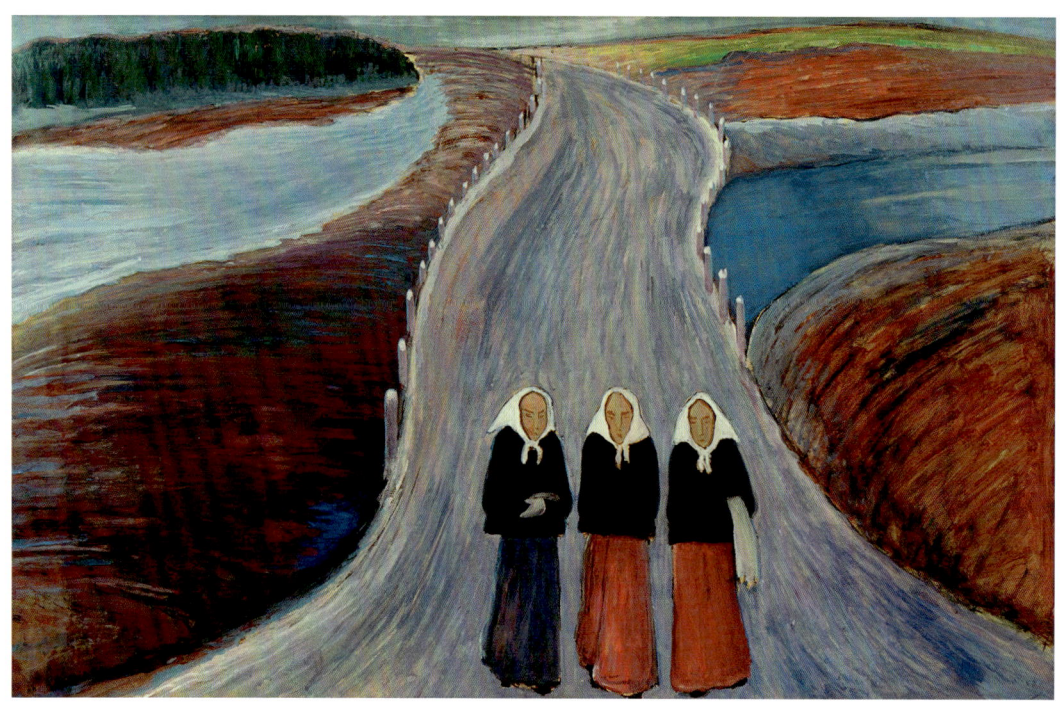

THE COUNTRY ROAD

1907, tempera on paper, 69 × 105 cm (27 ⅛ × 41 ⅜ in), Museo Communale d'Arte
Moderna, Ascona, Switzerland
Marianne von Werefkin, born Marianna Werefkina, 1860, Tula, Russia.
Died 1938, Ascona, Switzerland.

Born to an aristocratic Russian family, von Werefkin began painting
in the 1870s, moving between studios in St Petersburg and Lithuania.
She studied with Ilya Repin (1844–1930), chief exponent of the
Russian Realist style, who portrayed her in 1888. The same year,
she shot her right hand in a hunting accident. Following a lengthy
recuperation, von Werefkin embarked on her first major artistic phase
as a Realist, earning her the soubriquet of the 'Russian Rembrandt'.
However, she then abandoned her career for nearly a decade to support

her then-partner, the painter Alexei Jawlensky (1864–1941). The couple moved to Munich where she established a salon that became
a focus of the artistic community and the eventual core of the Blaue
Reiter ('Blue Rider') group of artists, one of whom, Gabriele Münter
(p.292) painted von Werefkin in 1909. She had resumed painting in
1906 and quickly galvanized her circle towards Expressionism,
the movement with which she is now most associated. *The Country
Road*, one of her first in the new style, is typical in its intense, striated
colours, its elevated viewpoint suggesting a ghostly weightlessness.

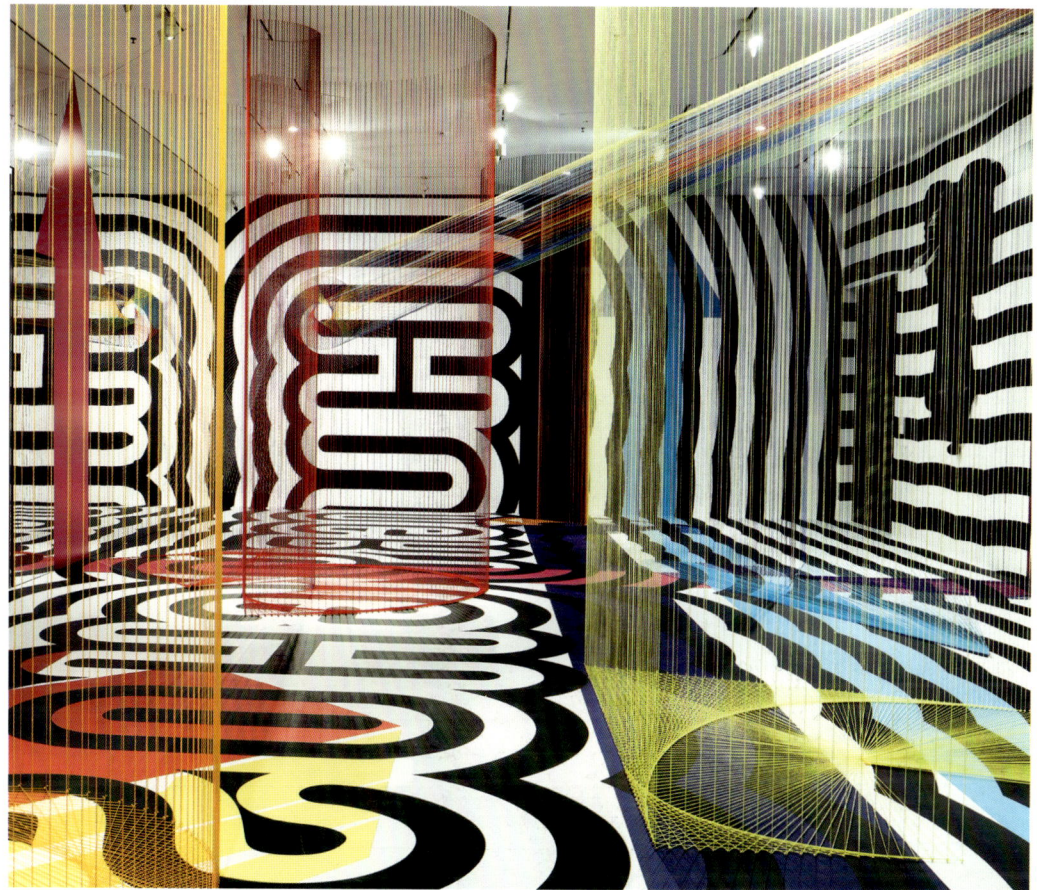

UNTITLED

2017, acrylic yarn, vinyl, wall paint and mirrored Dibond; mask: foam and Cinefoil, dimensions variable, site-specific installation for the NGV Triennial at the National Gallery of Victoria, Melbourne, Australia
Pae White, born 1963, Pasadena, California.

White explores the neglected and forgotten, the temporary and transient, and the space between things, subverting the viewer's expectations of the everyday. Her multimedia practice often manifests itself in immersive installations and aims to break down the barriers that categorize creativity, considering design, craft, architecture and fine art to be as one. The materials White works with are diverse, ranging from textile and paper to thread and paint. She combines these in large-scale installations that respond directly to the spaces in which they are displayed. Although she also paints and makes smaller-scale sculptures, it is for her huge architectural works that White is best known. This is one such example, drawing inspiration from two long-standing interests of the artist: the swirling black-and-white graphic identity of the 1968 Summer Olympics in Mexico City and a colourful utopian community founded around the same time in Northern California called Sea Ranch. Op art effects and delicate threads are interwoven in a bold experiment, the marriage of these two aesthetics resulting in an environment where surprise is genuine, not contrived, and shared by artist and viewer alike.

RACHEL WHITEREAD

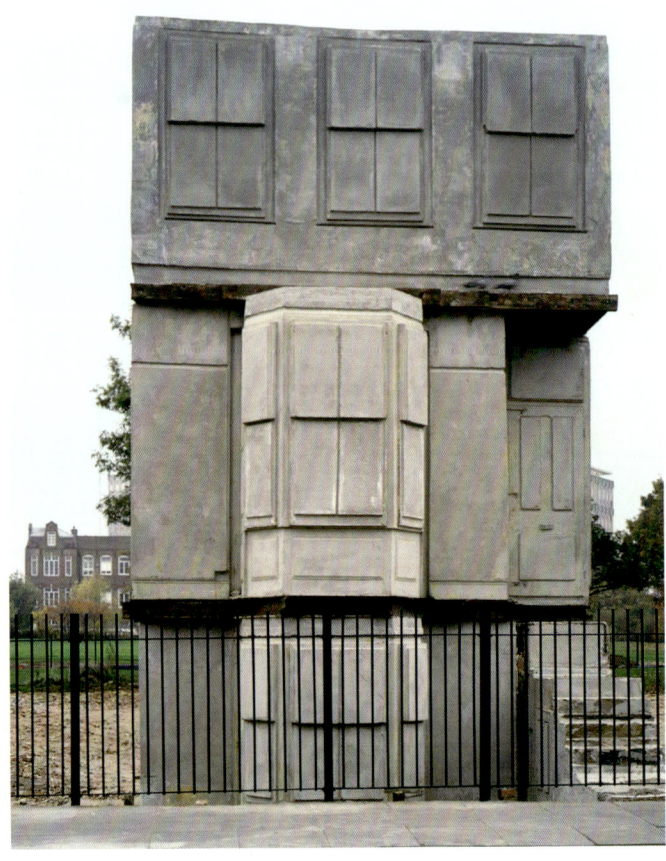

HOUSE

1993, 193 Grove Road, London E3. Destroyed 1993
Rachel Whiteread, born 1963, London.

After studying in the mid-1980s at London's Slade School of Art, where she took a course in casting with the sculptor Richard Wilson (b.1953), Whiteread became known for making positive casts of common domestic objects – such as tables, chairs and hot water bottles – and also of their negative space. *House* earned her the Turner Prize in 1993; she was the first woman and youngest person to be awarded this honour for British artists. Commissioned and produced by the arts organization Artangel, Whiteread cast in concrete a recently vacated terraced house, due for demolition, at 193 Grove Road in east London. It was a monument to the marginalized working-class communities of London's East End, as well as a public sculpture. Following the inside contours of the entire building, its windows, stairs and door became ghost-like duals. Existing for only eighty days, it was itself demolished early the following year. Whiteread rejected offers to relocate the work, emphasizing its location and ephemerality. As a sculpture engaged with the idea of memory, the work itself became exactly that, and now exists only in photographs.

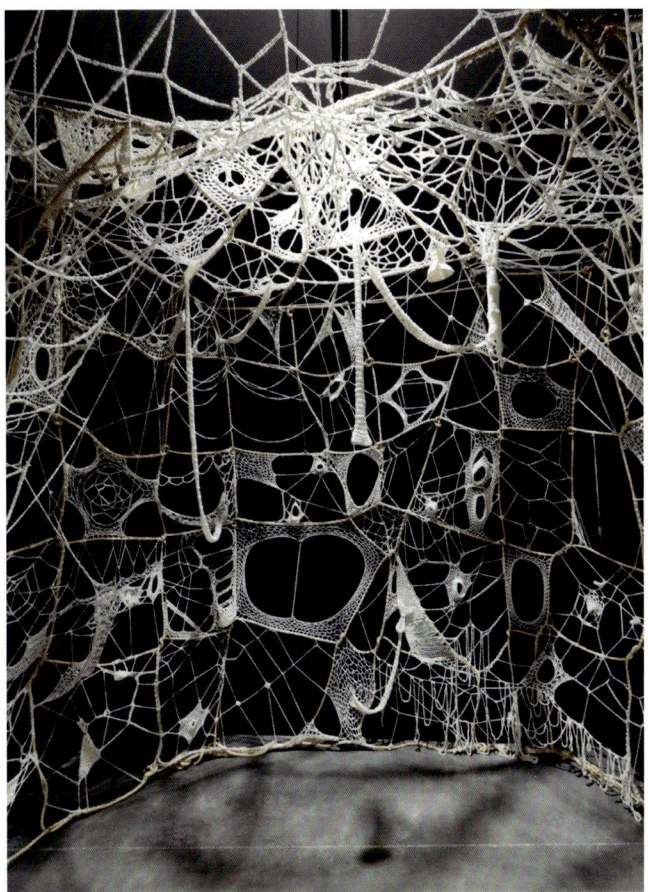

CROCHETED ENVIRONMENT

1972/1995, Woolworth's Sweetheart acrylic yarn and sisal rope, c.274.3 × 274.3 × 274.3 cm (c.108 × 108 × 108 in), Institute of Contemporary Art, Boston
Faith Wilding, born 1943, Colonia Primavera, Paraguay (British national).

After moving to the United States in 1961, Wilding studied English literature in Iowa and a master's degree in fine art at California Institute of the Arts. Together with Judy Chicago (p.98), she became central to creating the Feminist Art Program at California State University, Fresno, and participated in *Womanhouse* (1972), a ground-breaking, month-long feminist collaboration and performance space, where this large sculptural installation was first seen. With strong links to the tradition of women making fibre art in many different cultures, *Crocheted Environment* was initially conceived as a dwelling for visitors to the event. Also known as *Womb Room*, it suggested both the female body and the private sphere, and was intended to raise contradictory impressions of security and entrapment in those who entered. In doing so, the sculpture offered a feminist perspective crucial to Wilding's diverse and extensive body of work about the complex experience of being a woman. Her 1977 book *By Our Own Hands* is a key text of feminist art, and having co-founded cyberfeminist art collective subRosa in the late 1990s, her continued exploration of issues from social justice to biotechnology remains influential.

HANNAH WILKE

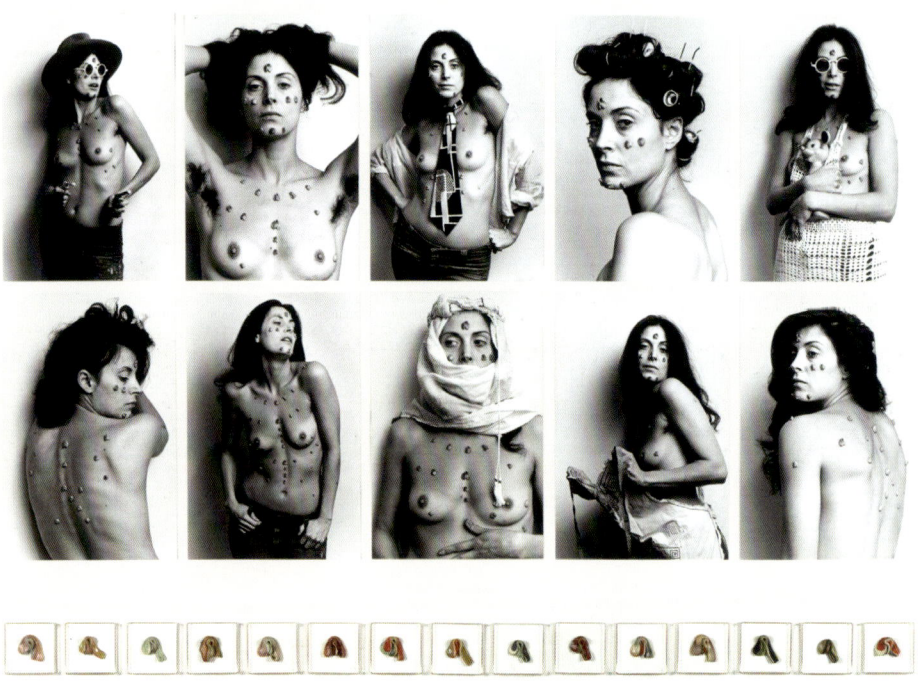

S.O.S. – STARIFICATION OBJECT SERIES

1974–82, gelatin silver prints with chewing gum sculptures, 101.6 × 148.6 × 5.7 cm (40 × 58 ½ × 2 ¼ in), Museum of Modern Art, New York
Hannah Wilke, born Arlene Hannah Butter, 1940, New York. Died 1993, Houston.

During the 1960s and 1970s women's liberation movement, Wilke used sculpture, photography and performance to surreptitiously critique commercialized representations of the female body. In the 1960s specifically, she made vulva-shaped terracotta sculptures, which under the guise of appearing abstract were in fact raw and explicit. In 1974, she began her 'Starification Object Series', which comprised numerous black-and-white photographic self-portraits in which she posed like a model. She dotted her body and face with tiny representations of vulvas made from chewing gum, and the series'

title likens this gesture to tribal scarification rituals while also parodying the inherently sexist Freudian interpretation of the vagina as a symbolic wound. Wilke exposed such institutional subjugation of women as it combined with the American cultural reverence for idealized femininity. The minute sculptures covering her body also suggest disease and take on a sense of tragic premonitions in light of her later self-portrait series 'Intra-Venus', which documented her battle with lymphoma. Wilke's eschewal of analytical distance in favour of the discomfortingly personal made her a lasting exemplar of the feminist ethos in art-making.

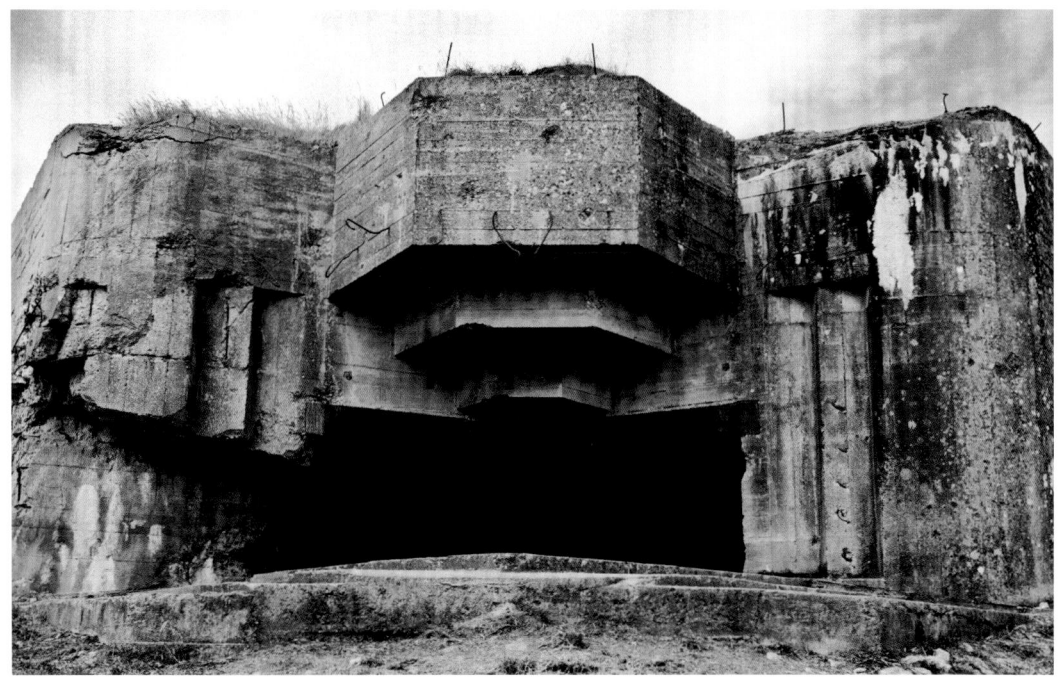

AZEVILLE

2006, gelatin silver print on paper mounted onto aluminium, 180 × 290 cm
(70 ⅞ × 114 ⅛ in)
Jane and Louise Wilson, born 1967, Newcastle upon Tyne, UK.

Twin sisters Jane and Louise Wilson first made work together while
studying art at different colleges in the late 1980s. Since then, their
collaboration has seen them use photography, film, video and digital
technologies to explore architectural spaces and places that bear the
traces of history, politics and personal narratives. They filmed the
four-channel video installation *Stasi City* (1997) in the former head-
quarters of the East German secret police in Berlin. As in many
of their works, it explores the psychological residues associated with
particular events, summoning up memories associated with a site
to convey a lingering sense of unsettling forces. *Azeville*, from their
'Sealander' series, is one of three large-format photographs of derelict Second World War concrete bunkers situated on the coast
of Normandy, France, the so-called Atlantic Wall. The ruined structure, a monumental relic of German occupation and ultimately
unsuccessful defence, now appears untethered from its original function, its previously sharp edges frayed by time and nature, yet not
quite at rest. The bunker seems to stand as a testament to both the
persistence and futility of war.

BETTY WOODMAN

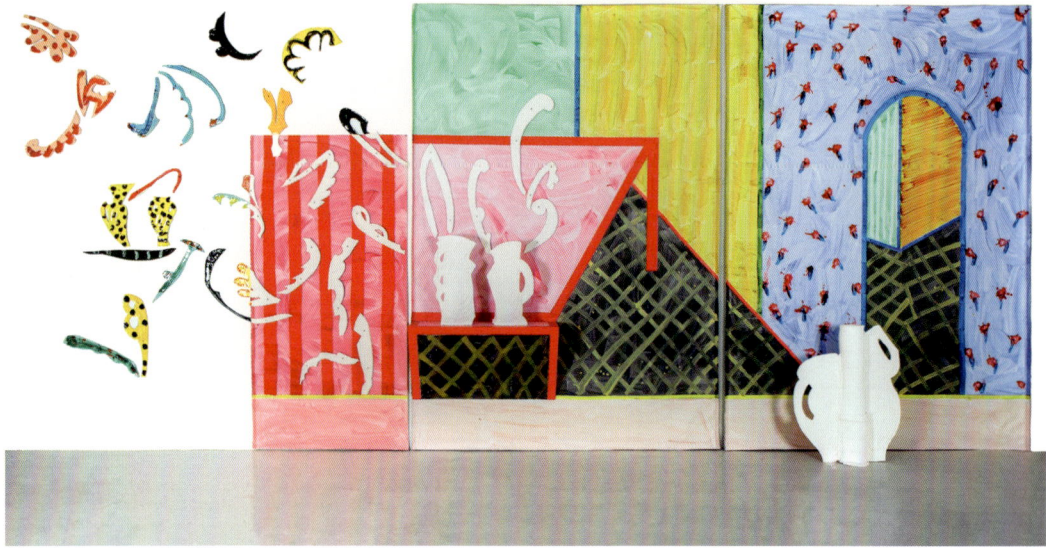

A SINGLE JOY OF SONG

2017, glazed earthenware, epoxy resin, lacquer, acrylic paint, canvas and wood,
304.8 × 711.2 × 30.5 cm (120 × 280 × 12 in)
Betty Woodman, born Elizabeth Abrahams, 1930, Norwalk, Connecticut.
Died 2018, New York.

Woodman's practice combined the flat medium of painting with three-dimensional ceramics. She took her first pottery class at the age of sixteen and trained as a functional potter at the School for American Craftsmen in Alfred, New York. In 1952, she visited Florence and, surrounded by what she described as piles of rubble and hope, was inspired to pursue art. Her avowed eclecticism and blurring of the distinction between fine art and craft made the art world slow to appreciate her creative talent. The influence of Italian Renaissance colours are evident, presented via methods of far-ranging periods and cultures including tin-glazed Majolica ware, Japanese Oribe ware, Chinese Tang dynasty ceramics and eighteenth-century European porcelain, and with the form of the Classical vase a recurrent motif. Collaboration with other artists, including Joyce Kozloff (p.223), encouraged Woodman to adopt a vibrant, witty style, in which she challenged the idea that ceramics are synonymous with functionality, existing merely to carry matter, as demonstrated by works such as *A Single Joy of Song*, made the year before her death. The large-scale installation combines canvas with glazed earthenware shapes to depict a theatrical domestic interior where ceramic forms enter the realm of painting.

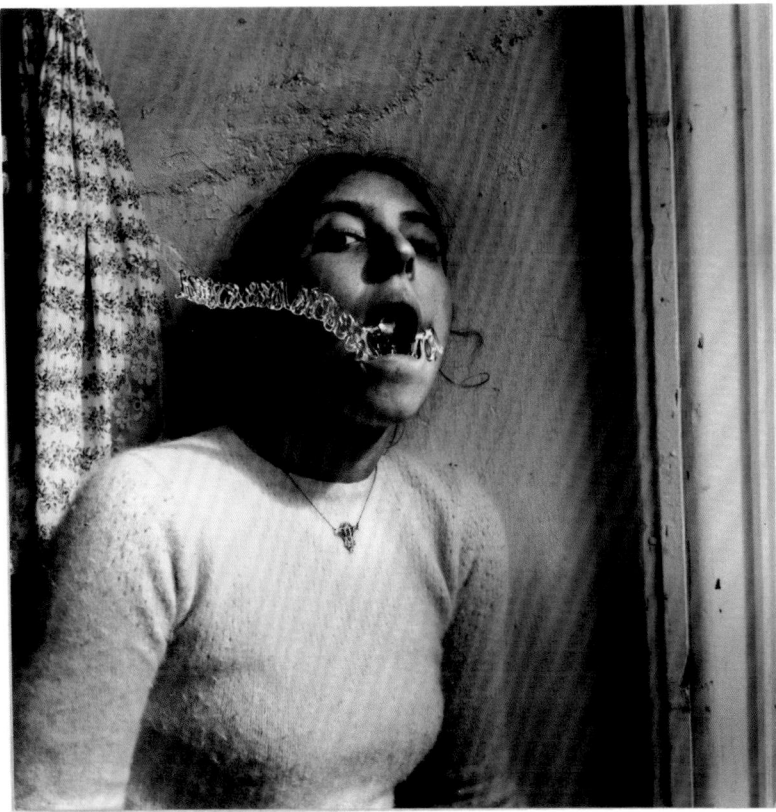

self portrait talking to vince

SELF-PORTRAIT TALKING TO VINCE, PROVIDENCE, RHODE ISLAND
1977, vintage gelatin print, 13.2 × 13.1 cm (5¼ × 5⅛ in)
Francesca Woodman, born 1958, Denver, Colorado. Died 1981, New York.

The daughter of artists Betty Woodman (p.434) and George Woodman (1932–2017), Woodman expanded the family's artistic tradition through her black-and-white photography. Growing up in Colorado, she spent the summers in Tuscany, becoming fluent in Italian, and studied in Rome in 1977–8 as part of the Rhode Island School of Design honours programme, in which she was enrolled. Often turning the camera on herself, Woodman's self-portraits are numerous, yet she also photographed other subjects in sparse domestic spaces or desolate landscapes, suggesting psychological anguish. This image was taken during her time as a student in Providence.

She gazes at the camera with what appears to be smoke spiralling from her open mouth. Woodman used movement combined with long-exposure periods to create images that are often strange, obscured and haunting. Upon graduating, she moved to New York in 1979 and had a fellowship at the prestigious MacDowell Colony. Moving back to her parents after a failed suicide attempt in 1980, she took her own life the following year aged just twenty-two, leaving behind a prolific body of work and at least 10,000 negatives.

ROSE WYLIE

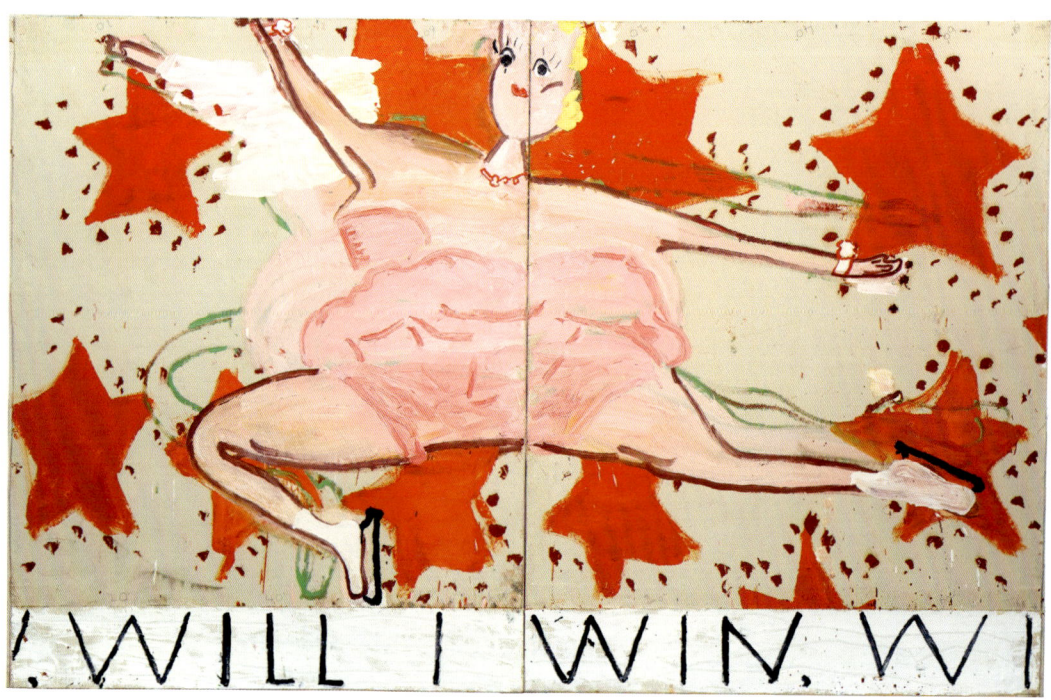

PINK SKATER (WILL I WIN, WILL I WIN…)
2015, oil on canvas, 208 × 329 cm (88 ⅞ × 129 ½ in)
Rose Wylie, born 1934, Hythe, Kent, UK.

Trained at Dover School of Art in Kent in the early 1950s and, twenty-five years later at London's Royal College of Art, Wylie works in her house in Kent where she lived with her husband, the painter Roy Oxlade (1929–2014). Success came to Wylie later in life, including a number of solo exhibitions when she was in her eighties. In 2014, she won the John Moores Painting Prize, and in 2018 she was awarded an OBE. She has emphasized the importance of not identifying her work with her age or gender, stressing that the quality of the painting itself is most important, rather than the biography of its maker. Current affairs and diverse art-historical sources, from ancient wall paintings to films, inform her unstretched and unprimed canvases. Wylie engages with several paintings at once using a loose technique where parts are continuously reworked yet not hidden. This painting style, comprising textural gestures and urgent brushstrokes, is exemplified in *Pink Skater (Will I Win, Will I Win…)*, where – across two conjoined canvases – a cartoonish ice skater joyously leaps into the air, the banner beneath stating her intent and reading like a television newsflash.

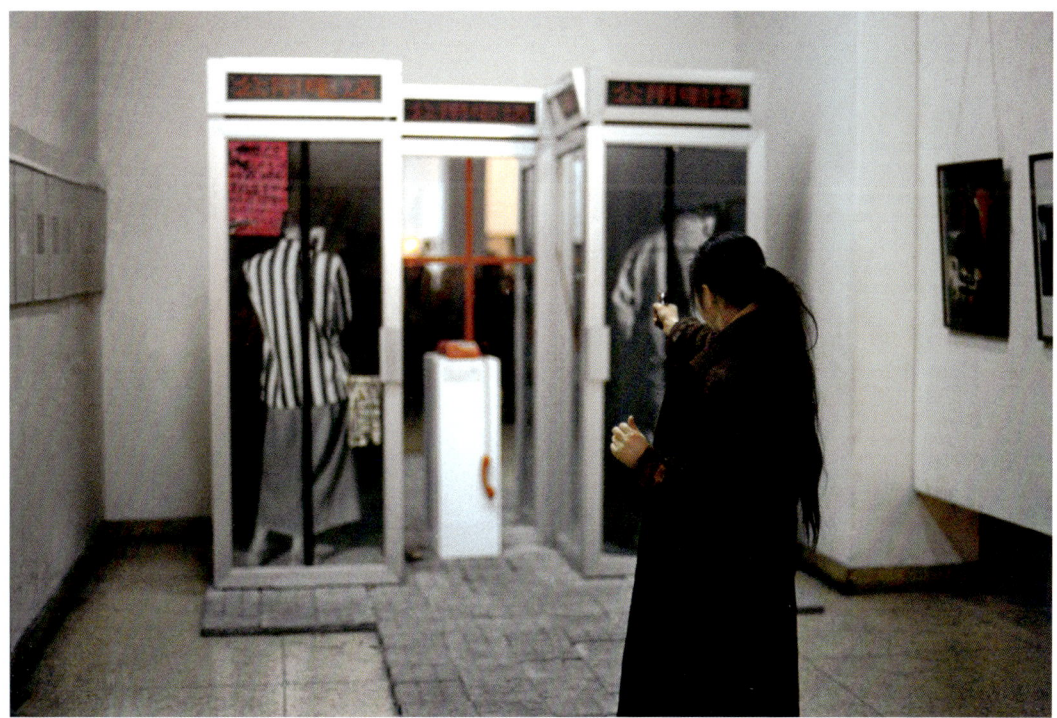

DIALOGUE

1989, installation and performance at 'China/Avant-Garde' exhibition, China National Art Gallery, Beijing, 5 February 1989

Xiao Lu, born 1962, Hangzhou, China.

Born to two Socialist Realism painters shortly before China's Cultural Revolution (1966–76), Xiao was exposed to art and politics from a young age. She attended the Zhejiang Academy of Fine Arts, Hangzhou, with the work shown in this image serving as her graduation piece. A study of distance and alienation between the sexes, it consists of lifesize images of a woman and man in respective phone booths with backs turned away from the viewer, and a phone, off its hook, on a plinth between them. The installation was then included in the landmark 'China/Avant-Garde' exhibition at

China National Art Gallery in Beijing, 1989. On the opening day, Xiao shot the piece twice with a gun, which led to the Chinese authorities immediately closing the exhibit. She has stated that the piece related to her inability to communicate with her boyfriend at the time, though it was adopted as a symbol of the country's simmering political unrest, which came to a head later that year. After a break from art that lasted until 2003, she returned to her practice, working in media of video, performance and installation and exploring themes related to personal identity, sexuality and relationships.

XING DANWEN

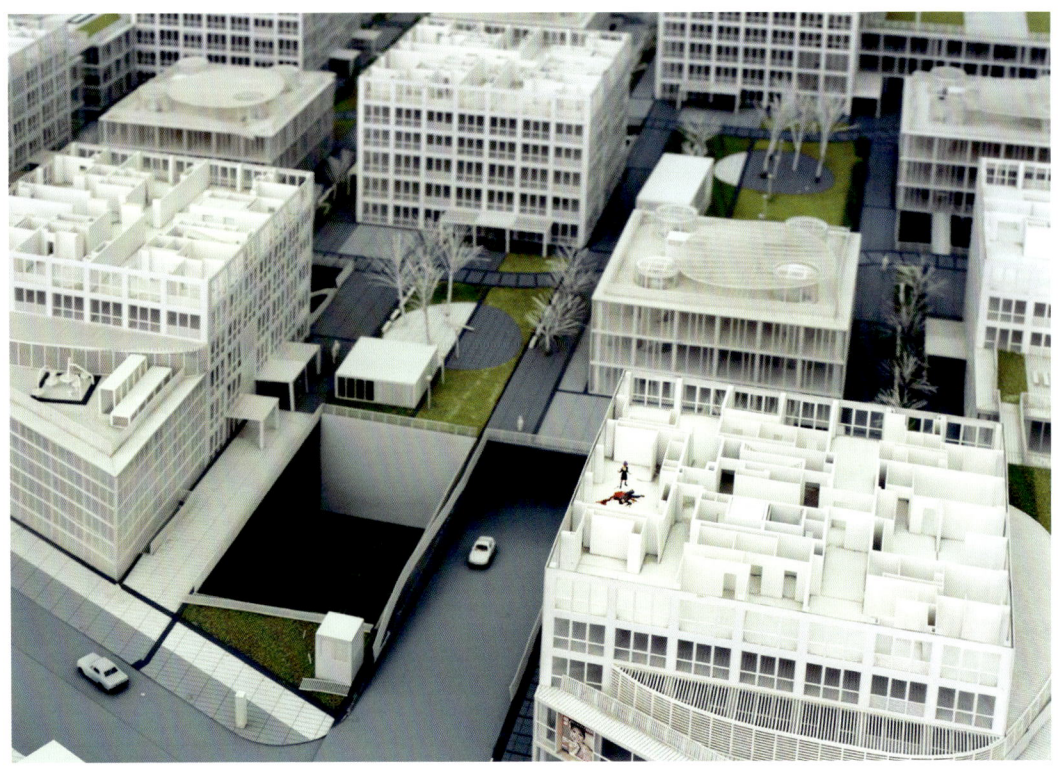

URBAN FICTION, IMAGE 0
2004, photograph with digital manipulation, 241.8 × 140 cm (95 × 67 in)
Xing Danwen, born 1967, Xi'an, China.

Xing took up painting as a teenager before formal training in Xi'an, Shaanxi province, and, from 1989 to 1992, at the Central Academy of Fine Arts, Beijing, with a mid-career return to study at the School of Visual Arts in New York. Early on, she taught herself photography and used the medium to explore themes relating to gender and to her generation's experiences within Chinese society during a period of profound change. Xing became a pioneer of photography as a fine art medium in China, though she has since expanded her practice to include mixed media, video and installation. In the early 1990s, she documented events in Beijing's 'East Village' scene, where politically concerned artists used body and performance art as a means of evading official restrictions on cultural output. In the series 'Urban Fiction' (2004–), Xing alters promotional architects' models by inserting small cut-out characters – including of herself – to create small-scale fictional encounters within deserted environments, dramatic focal points within otherwise sterile cityscapes. Her photographs juxtapose ideas of urbanization and luxury with a strange emptiness, commenting on the isolation that can accompany growing city environments.

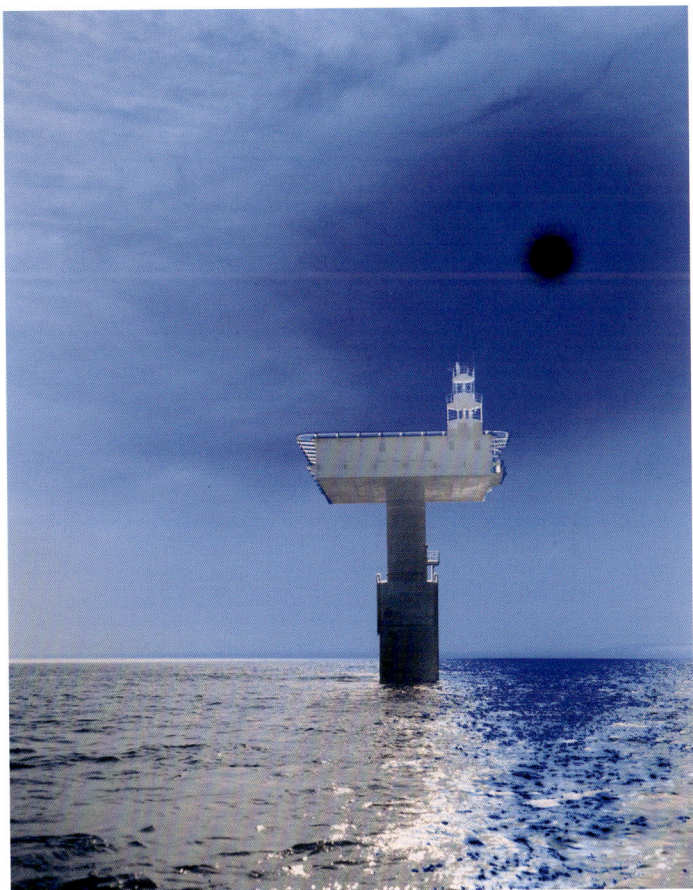

LIGHTHOUSE (EAST)

2011, Duratrans transparency and lightbox, 129 × 103.5 × 16.5 cm
(50 ¾ × 40 ¾ × 6 ½ in)
Catherine Yass, born 1963, London.

Yass studied in London and Berlin, completing her MFA at
Goldsmiths College in 1990. A series of photographs taken inside
a nineteenth-century psychiatric hospital in London, 'Corridors'
(1994), demonstrates the approach for which she became best
known: wall-mounted lightboxes illuminate positive and negative
transparencies, which are overlaid so that light appears dark
blue, colours become distorted, the everyday becomes otherworldly.
Also working with moving image, *Descent* (2002) was made the
same year as Yass was nominated for the Turner Prize. Shot from

a camera being slowly lowered from a crane on a skyscraper's construction site, the footage is presented upside down, adding to the
vertiginous impact. In 2011, Yass was commissioned by De La Warr
Pavilion, in the English town of Bexhill-on-Sea, to produce a new
body of work relating to the Royal Sovereign lighthouse, located
eleven kilometres (seven miles) offshore. Accompanying a twelve-
minute film shot from a helicopter that explored the architecture
of the structure from above and below, this image was taken from
a boat. Yass described it as 'ambiguous' – visually seductive while
simultaneously containing 'a deathly darkness about being pulled
into the water and going under'.

LYNETTE YIADOM-BOAKYE

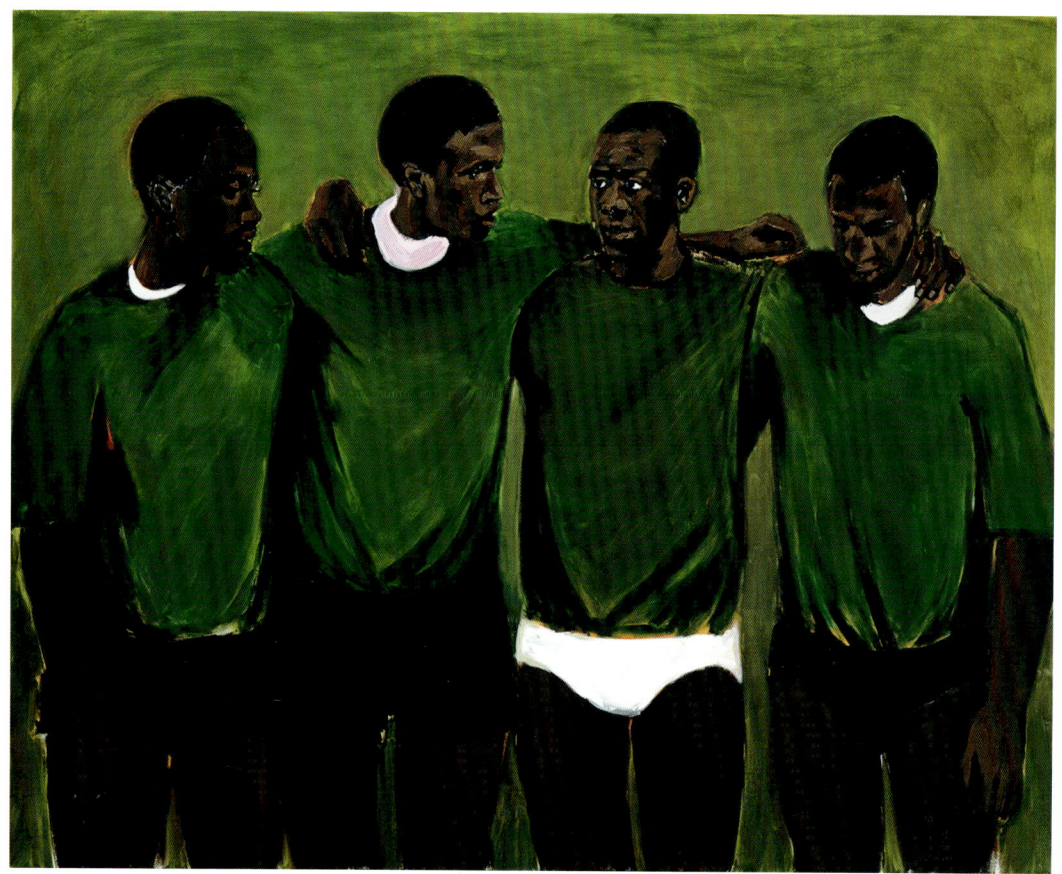

COMPLICATION

2013, oil on canvas, 200 × 250 cm (78 ¾ × 98 ⅜ in), private collection
Lynette Yiadom-Boakye, born 1977, London.

Yiadom-Boakye's figurative paintings depict individuals and groups with apparent realism, yet her characters are entirely invented. Of Ghanaian heritage, the artist – who completed an MFA at London's Royal Academy Schools in 2003 – predominantly portrays black people, painted with loose, dynamic brushstrokes. Some are seated in the manner of formal portraiture, while others are captured in a moment of action: gesticulating mid-conversation, laughing at a shared joke or dancing. The images are imbued with relaxed, everyday ordinariness and the subjects are mostly depicted against backgrounds devoid of details that would situate them in a specific place or time. Deprived of a narrative setting, these works invite myriad interpretations. In this example, which features four young men with matching green (a recurrent colour in her palette) jerseys, the viewer can only speculate on the wider circumstances that brought the group together in this moment. The work's title perhaps relates to the character wearing gleaming white underpants, at whom another figure looks with concern – though the nature of the complication remains ambiguous. Winner of the 2012 Pinchuk Foundation Future Generation Art Prize, Yiadom-Boakye was shortlisted for the Turner Prize in 2013.

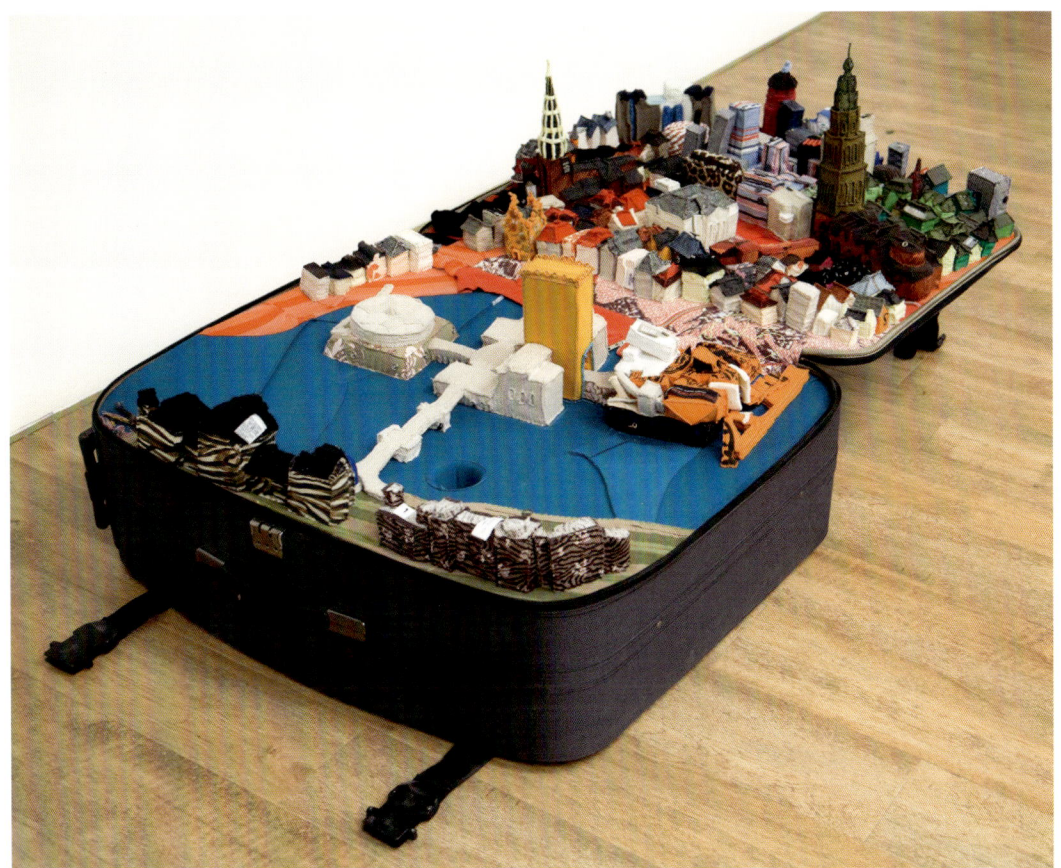

PORTABLE CITIES (GRONINGEN)

2012, suitcase, used clothes, light, map and sound, 148 × 88 × 30 cm
(58 ⅛ × 34 ⅔ × 11 ¾ in), installation view, Groninger Museum, Netherlands
Yin Xiuzhen, born 1963, Beijing.

Initially trained in the Socialist Realism style of oil painting at the Capital Normal University in Beijing, Yin now works in installation and sculpture, exploring themes relating to urbanization and collectivity. Her interest in the dual identity of group versus individual is informed by her experiences growing up during China's Cultural Revolution, a period of politically enforced 'oneness'. During this time, she picked up skills in sewing from watching her mother, which she has utilized when constructing her textile-based works, including the 'Portable Cities' series, of which this example is based on the Dutch city of Groningen. The series comprises colourful soft sculptures of cities contained within open suitcases, the fabric used being sourced from her family's old clothes. Yin's practice has been inspired in part from her international travels, experiences that have deepened her interest in globalization, but also hark back to memories of the women in her family making garments from second-hand materials. These sculptural landscapes offer a loose sketch of the cities as one might remember them, identified by a few selected landmarks. Mixing specificity with general trends in urban design, Yin addresses simultaneous feelings of individuality and sameness.

LISA YUSKAVAGE

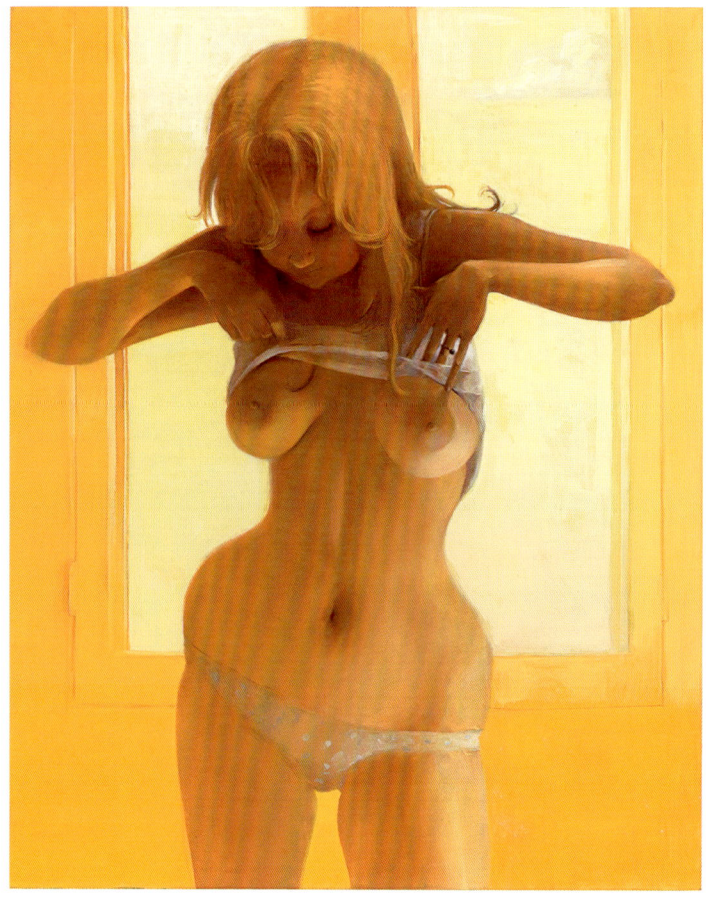

DAY

1999–2000, oil on linen, 195.6 × 157.5 cm (77 × 62 in), private collection
Lisa Yuskavage, born 1962, Philadelphia.

Coming to prominence in New York in the 1990s after studying
at Tyler School of Art's programme in Rome and Yale School
of Art, Yuskavage is credited with the re-emergence of figuration
in American contemporary painting. Her work divides opinion
between those who argue that it extends the nude tradition in art,
challenging taboos and pushing at the boundaries of conventional
genres, and others who see it as soft-porn voyeurism perpetuating
the objectification of women. Yuskavage intentionally provokes
this debate and discomfort, with women (and occasionally men)
appearing in fantastical landscapes or domestic interiors. As with

many of Yuskavage's paintings, *Day* explicitly depicts female sexuality: a woman styled as if she might have been in a 1970s 'glamour'
photoshoot, lifts up her top and stares down at her navel in front
of a window. Hazy orange backlighting accentuates her breasts and
suggests a staged undressing or performance. The exaggerated waist–
hip ratio emphasizes its cartoonish feel, and as the viewer follows the
figure's own gaze to look at her body, a mixed mood of sexual awaken-
ing, empowerment and subjugation is simultaneously conveyed.

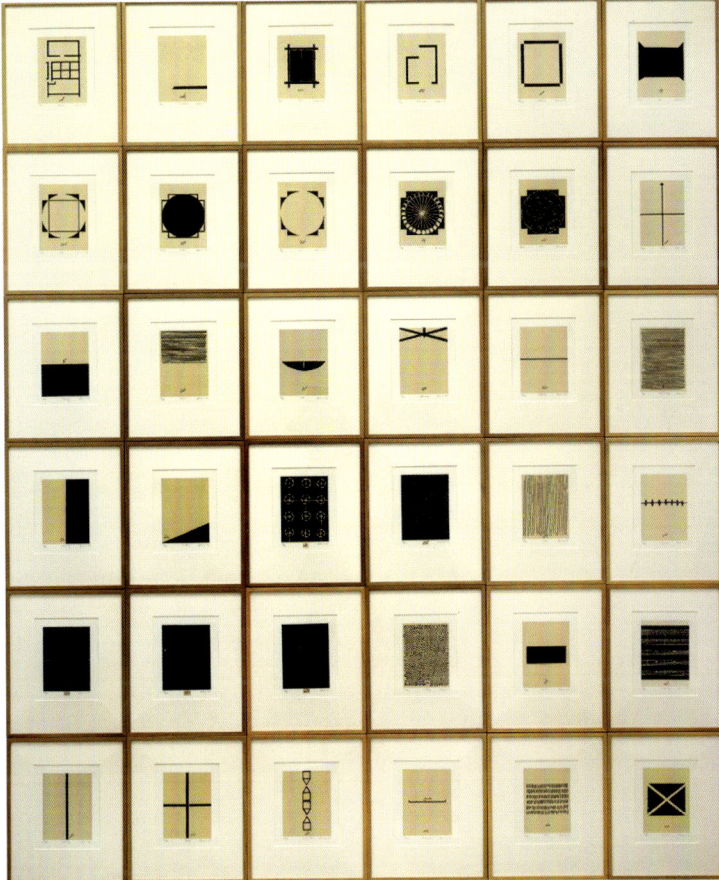

HOME IS A FOREIGN PLACE

1999, portfolio of 36 woodcuts with Urdu text printed in black on Kozo paper and mounted on Somerset paper, each 20.3 × 15.2 cm (8 × 6 in), edition of 25 + 5 Roman Numeral sets
Zarina, born Zarina Hashmi, 1937, Aligarh, India. Died 2020, London.

The work of Indian artist Zarina (who preferred to be known by her first name only) is focused on the notion of home, especially as it is experienced during displacement and in our memories, with *Home is a Foreign Place* being her most sustained exploration of this theme. In thirty-six wood-block prints, she drew on her experience of living in many homes from her and her family's early experiences of exile after the 1947 partition of India and Pakistan, and from a peripatetic life following her marriage to an Indian diplomat in 1958.

She made a list of words related to different recollections of home, which were transcribed by a calligrapher into the traditional *nastaliq* Urdu script. From these, Zarina created images using a spare language of geometric abstraction that derives both from her study of mathematics and from an enduring interest in architecture. The work is conceived as a piece of poetry intended to be read from left to right, starting from the top. In an artistic career that spanned almost six decades, Zarina received numerous awards and accolades, including the grand prize at the International Biennial of Prints in Bhopal, India (1989).

FAHRELNISSA ZEID

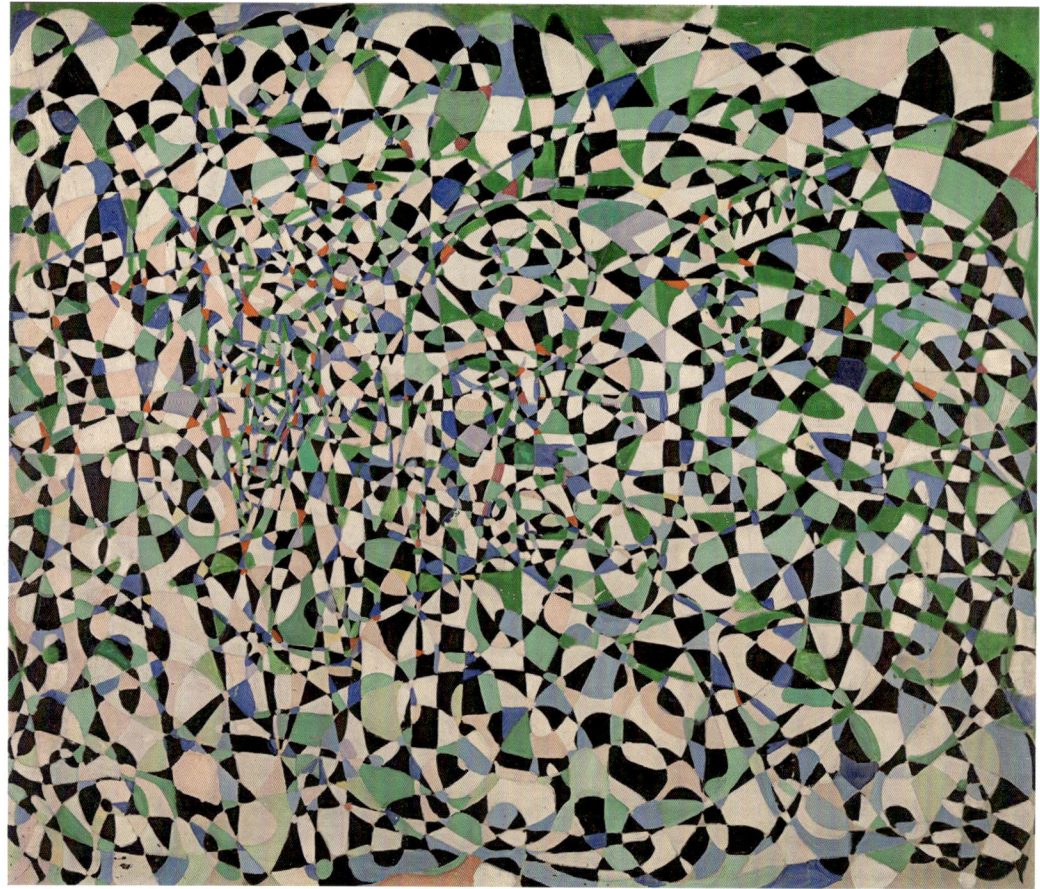

UNTITLED

*c.*1950, oil on canvas, 182 × 222 cm (71 ⅝ × 87 ⅜ in), Tate, London
Fahrelnissa Zeid, born Fahrünissa Şakir, 1901, Istanbul (then Constantinople,
Ottoman Empire). Died 1991, Amman, Jordan.

Growing up in the multicultural Ottoman Empire, Zeid's work
drew on this diversity and on experiences of turbulent politics of the
Near East, including personal tragedy – her elder brother assassi-
nated her diplomat father when she was thirteen and in 1958 her
husband's entire family were killed during the Iraqi *coup d'état*. Zeid
was one of the first women to study at the Academy of Fine Arts
in Istanbul and to have a solo show at the ICA, London, in 1954.
Arriving in London in 1946 with her husband, the first Iraqi ambas-
sador to Britain, she ran art salons from the embassy, and travelled
frequently to Paris, evolving her modernist style. Associating with
Sonia Delaunay (p.118) and Marc Chagall (1887–1985) among others,
Zeid took European influences such as Orphism and made them her
own. This painting featured in her first major retrospective, held
at Tate Modern in 2017, its expressive aesthetic combining Zeid's
wide-ranging influences. Persian and Byzantine geometries are
twisted to form a simultaneously coherent and chaotic kaleidoscopic
vision. The work compels the viewer to become a part of the artist's
fervent world, which in later years she shared with young women
artists through the informal school she established at her home.

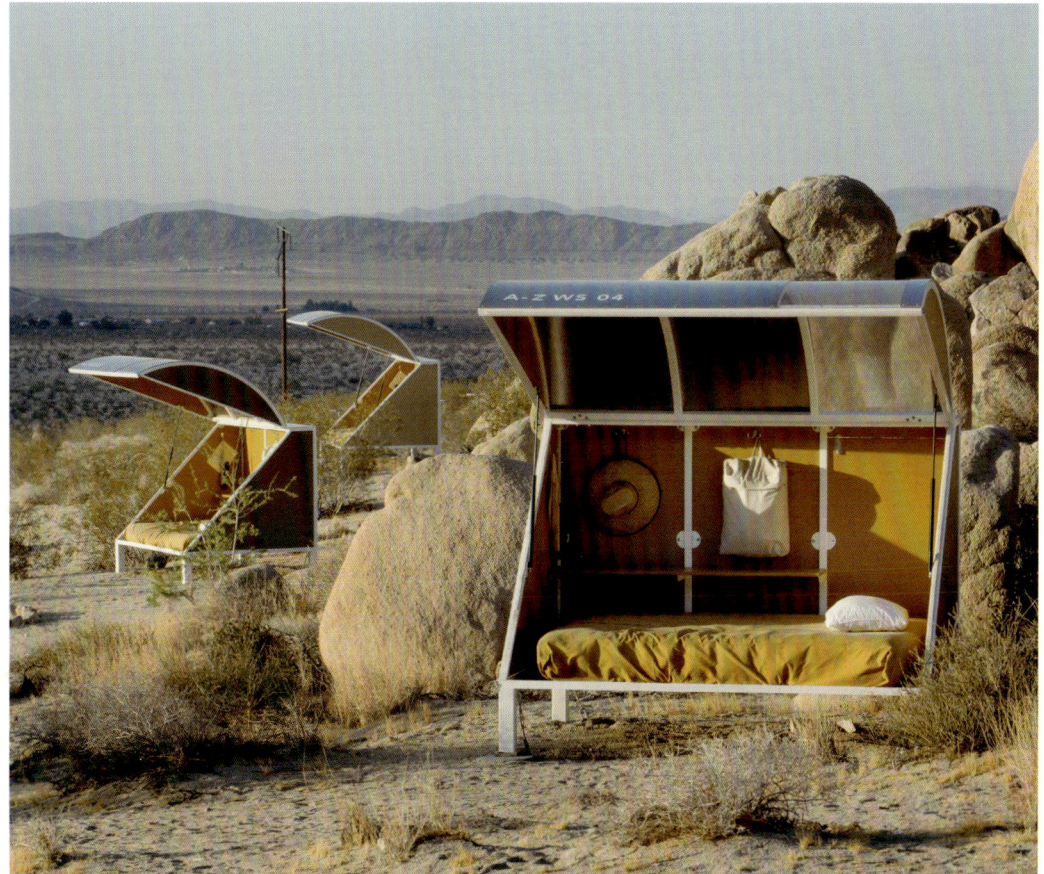

WAGON STATION ENCAMPMENT AT A–Z WEST, JOSHUA TREE, CA
2012–present, powder-coated steel, MDF, aluminium and Lexan, closed
dimensions: 154.9 × 208.3 × 144.8 cm (61 × 82 × 57 in)
Andrea Zittel, born 1965, Escondido, California.

Soon after completing an MFA in sculpture at Rhode Island School
of Design, Zittel established 'A–Z', an enterprise dedicated to investigating different ways of living in the world. Blurring the boundaries
between the disciplines of architecture, design and philosophy, since
the early 1990s A–Z's projects have explored various human practices,
from how we eat and dress ourselves to how we furnish our homes.
Interested in querying how and why we attribute significance to chosen structures or ways of life, the artist experiments in situations
from everyday life, constructing prototypes and living structures that
challenge concepts such as 'freedom', 'security' or 'authorship'.
In 2000, Zittel moved from the dense urban context of New York
to the spacious Californian desert, where she set up 'A–Z West',
a twenty-eight-hectare (seventy-acre) 'Institute of Investigative Living'
near Joshua Tree National Park. One of her projects here is the *Wagon
Station Encampment*, comprising a dozen small, metal-lined sleeping
pods, set up as an encampment on her land. These minimal living
units express the question central to much of Zittel's work: what
do we really need in order to live and feel free?

INDEX

Page numbers in *italic* refer
to the illustrations

A

Abakanowicz, Magdalena 16
  Agora 16
  The Group of Seven 16, *16*
Abbott, Berenice 17, 39
  Manhattan Bridge Looking Up 17, *17*
Abject art 363, 380
Abney, Nina Chanel 18
  Class of 2007 18, *18*
Abramović, Marina 19
  Rhythm 0 19, *19*
  The Artist is Present 19
Abstract Expressionism 42, 43, 44,
  114, 116, 142, 174, 186, 198, 224,
  228, 232, 265, 277, 300, 352, 358,
  361, 403, 407
Abstraction-Création 288, 397
Abts, Tomma 20
  Fenke 20, *20*
Academia Nacional de Belas-Artes,
  Lisbon 417
Académie Colarossi, Paris 102
Académie de la Grande Chaumière,
  Paris 306, 417
Académie Julian, Paris 53, *53*, 204,
  252, 400
Academie Minerva, Groningen 213
Académie Royale de Peinture et de
  Sculpture, Paris 126, 152, 282,
  402, 413
Academy of Art, Architecture and
  Design, Prague 52
Academy of Fine Arts, Belgrade 19
Academy of Fine Arts, Istanbul 444
Academy of Fine Arts, Vienna 206, 232
Academy of Fine Arts, Warsaw 16
Academy of the Society of Women
  Artists, Berlin 221
Accademia di Belle Arti, Palermo 21

Accademia di San Luca, Rome 89
Accardi, Carla 21
  Triple Tent 21, *21*
Ace Gallery New York 122
Adnan, Etel 22
  The Weight of the World 22, *22–3*
Advancing Women Artists
  Foundation 296
Aelst, Willem van 304, 347
af Klint, Hilma 24
  Group X, No. 1, Altarpiece 24, *24*
Africa Centre, London 188
Agar, Eileen 25
  Figures in a Garden 25, *25*
  Seashore Monster at Swanage 25
Ahtila, Eija-Liisa 26
  The House 26, *26*
A.I.R. Gallery, New York 42, 130,
  268, 322, 384
Akerman, Chantal 27
  *Jeanne Dielman, 23, Quai du
  Commerce, 1080 Bruxelles* 21, *27*
  News from Home 27
  No Home Movie 27
  Saute ma ville 27
Akunyili Crosby, Njideka 28
  Dwell: Aso Ebi 28, *28*
  Dwell: Me, We 28
Albers, Anni 12, 29, 168
  Wall Hanging 29, *29*
Albers, Josef 29, 41
  'Algorism' movement 283
Allori, Alessandro 329
Alloway, Lawrence 379
Altfest, Ellen 30
  The Back 30, *30*
Amaral, Olga de 31
  Alchemy 50 31, *31*
Amer, Ghada 32
  Portrait with One Earring 32, *32*
Anaxandra 9
Anderson, Laurie 33
  Duets on Ice 33
  United States 2: O Superman 33, *33*
Andersson, Mamma 34
  About a Girl 34, *34*
Andrade, Oswald de, *Manifesto
  of Anthropophagy* 400
Andre, Carl 112
André, Rogi 278
André Emmerich Gallery,
  New York 407
Andrea del Sarto 296
Anguissola, Amilcare 35
Anguissola, Sofonisba 9, 35, 249
  The Game of Chess 35, *35*
Antin, Eleanor 36
  *100 Boots Looking for a Job,
  San Clemente, California* 36, *36*
Antoni, Janine 37
  Gnaw 37, *37*
Apollinaire, Guillaume 133, 233

Applebroog, Ida 38
  Monalisa 38, *38*
Appropriation 25, 63, 103, 130, 138,
  234, 276, 393
Arab Cultural Gallery, Beirut 99
Arbus, Diane 39, 120, 278
  *Identical Twins, Roselle,
  N.J. 1966* 39, *39*
Arcos, Luis Antonio de los 340
Armleder, John 138
Armory Show, New York (1913) 233
Arnardóttir, Hrafnhildur
  ('Shoplifter') 40
  Nervescape V 40, *40*
Arp, Jean (Hans) 335, 397
Art Academy of Cincinnati 109
Art Club, Rome 21
Art Deco 239
Art Informel 232
Art Institute of Chicago 38, 62, 130,
  163, 277, 401
The Art Newspaper 320
Art Nouveau 161, 253
Art Students League of New York 125
Art of This Century, New York 351
Art21 Magazine 267
Artangel 430
Arte Povera 21, 269, 325
Artforum magazine 58
Asawa, Ruth 41
  *Untitled (S. 310, Hanging Five-Lobed
  Continuous Form)* 41
Assemblage 25, 73, 153, 173, 220, 250,
  263, 321, 349, 358, 365
Atelier Kvalnes, Lofoten Islands 121
Attie, Dotty 42, 223
  Skin Deep 42, *42*
Auerbach, Frank 332
Ayres, Gillian 43
  Remembrance of Things Past 43, *43*

B

Bacon, Francis 160
Baer, Jo 44
  Brilliant Yellow #9 44, *44*
Baker, Josephine 334
Baldwin, Alec 76
Balenciaga 158
Ballets Russes 156, 233, 389
Baltimore Museum of Art 12
Banner, Fiona 45
  Harrier 45, *45*
  The Nam 45
Bard, Joseph 25
Bard College, Annandale-on-Hudson,
  NY 373
Barlow, Phyllida 46
  folly 46
  untitled: GIG 46, *46*

Barnard College, New York 96
Barney, Tina 47
  Beverly, Jill, and Polly 47, *47*
  'Theater of Manners' 47
Barns-Graham, Wilhelmina 48
  *White, Black and Yellow (Composition
  February)* 48, *48*
Baroque art 35, 113, 140, 150, 340,
  402, 425
Barriball, Anna 49
  Mirror Window Wall III 49, *49*
Bartana, Yael 50
  ...And Europe Will Be Stunned 50, *50*
  Mary Koszmary ('Nightmares') *50*
  Mur i wieża ('Wall and Tower') *50*
  Zamach ('Assassination') *50*
Barth, Uta 51
  Field #3 51, *51*
Bartning, Ludwig 354
Bartolomeo, Fra 296
Bartusz, Juraj 52
Bartuszová, Mária 52
  Untitled I and *Untitled II* 52, *52*
Bashkirtseff, Marie 53
  In the Studio 53, *53*
Bateau-Lavoir group 233
Baudelaire, Charles 394
Bauhaus 11, 29, 110, 168, 401
Beale, Charles 54, *54*
Beale, Mary 54, 87
  Observations by MB 54
  *Self-Portrait with Husband Charles
  and Son Bartholomew* 54, *54*
Bearden, Romare 294, 404
The Beatles, *Happiness is a Warm
  Gun* 338
Becher, Bernd and Hilla 190
Beecroft, Vanessa 55
  VB55 55, *55*
Beert, Osias 315
Beethoven, Ludwig van, *Moonlight
  Sonata* 314
Behari, Benode 290
Bell, Clive 56
Bell, Vanessa 56
  Virginia Woolf 56, *56*
Belmore, Rebecca 57
  Fountain 57
  Mixed Blessing 57, *57*
Benglis, Lynda 58, 130
  Centrefold 58
  Contraband 58, *58*
Benoist, Marie-Guillemine 59
  Portrait of a Black Woman 59, *59*
Bertha Schaefer Gallery, New York
  71
Bertlmann, Renate 60
  *Knife-Dummy-Hands
  – Ambivalence* 60, *60*
  'Tender Hands' 60
Betty Parsons Gallery, New York
  265

Bhabha, Huma 61
  Benaam 61, *61*
  We Come in Peace 61, *61*
Bhimji, Zarina 62
  Out of the Blue 62, *62*
Birnbaum, Dara 63
  Technology/Transformation:
  Wonder Woman 63, *63*
Björk 40
Black Lives Matter 18, 213
Black Mountain College,
  NC 29, 41, 114
Blanchard, Maria 64
  Be Good 64, *64*
Blaue Reiter 292, 428
BLK Art Group 74
Blomdahl, Karl-Birger, *Aniara* 318
Bloomsbury Group 56
Blossfeldt, Karl 241
'Blue Stocking Society' 117
Boccaccio, Giovanni, *De Claris*
  Mulieribus 7
  Decameron 382
body art 19, 79, 203, 206, 268, 307,
  311, 341, 361, 364, 342
BOMB Magazine 96, 399
Bombay Art Society 369
Bond, Justin 305, *305*
Bonheur, Rosa 8, 65
  Ploughing in Nevers 65, *65*
Bonnie and Clyde (film) 342
Bonvicini, Monica 66
  Never Again 66, *66–7*
Bopape, Dineo Seshee 68
  Untitled (of Occult Instability)
  [Feelings] 68, *68*
Boty, Pauline 69
  Colour Her Gone 69, *69*
Boudry, Pauline & Lorenz, Renate 70
  Opaque 70, *70*
  To Valerie Solanas and Marilyn
  Monroe, In Recognition of their
  Desperation 70
Bourdelle, Antoine 291, 335, 417
Bourgeois, Louise 71
  Maman 71, *71*
Bourke-White, Margaret 72
  Dear Fatherland, Rest Quietly 72
  Prisoners at the Gates of the
  Buchenwald Concentration Camp
  Near the End of World War II 72, *72*
Bove, Carol 73
  La Pléiade 73, *73*
Bowdoin College, Maine 176
Bowie, David 317
  Ziggy Stardust 318
Boyce, Sonia 74
  She Ain't Holding Them Up, She's
  Holding On (Some English Rose) 74, *74*
BP Portrait Award 160
Bracquemond, Marie 285
Brancusi, Constantin 334

Braque, Georges 133, 335
Brassaï 335
Brătescu, Geta 75
  Self-Portrait – Mrs Oliver in Her
  Traveling Costume 75, *75*
  The Tree from the Neighbouring
  Courtyard 75
Brătescu, Mihai 75
Braunschweig University of Art 76
Bravo, Manuel Álvarez 198
Breitz, Candice 76
  Love Story 76, *76*
Breton, André 100, 106, 306
British Army 313
British Journal of Photography 83
British Surrealist Group 25, 106
Britten, Benjamin 169
Bronzino 329
Brooklyn Museum, New York 420
Brooklyn Museum Art School,
  New York 58
Brooks, Romaine 77
  Self-Portrait 77, *77*
Brown, Cecily 78
  Teenage Wildlife 78, *78*
Brown, Trisha 203
Die Brücke ('The Bridge') 388
Bruguera, Tania 79
  The Burden of Guilt 79, *79*
Bucher, Carl 80
Bucher, Heidi 80
  Raumhäute 80
  Small Glass Portal, Bellevue
  Kreuzlingen 80, *80*
Buddhism 284, 359
Buffalo State College 371
Bunka Fashion College, Tokyo 284
Burne-Jones, Edward, *Phyllis and*
  Demophoön 205

C

Cabaret Voltaire, Zürich 397
Cage, John 226, 387
Cahun, Claude 81
  Disavowals 81
  Self-Portrait 81, *81*
Calder Prize 122
California Institute of the
  Arts 305, 431
California State University, Fresno 431
Calle, Sophie 82
  The Hotel 82, *82*
  Room 26 (28 February) 82, *82*
Calypso, Juno 83
  12 Reasons You're Tired All
  the Time 83, *83*
  'The Honeymoon' 83
  'What to Do With a Million
  Years' 83

Camberwell School of Arts and Crafts,
  London 43, 160
Cameron, Julia Margaret 84, 382
  Iago – Study from an Italian 84, *84*
Campi, Bernardino 35
Cao Chong'en 85
Cao Fei 85
  Whose Utopia? 85, *85*
Capital Normal University, Beijing 441
Caravaggio, Michelangelo
  Merisi da 150
Cardiff, Janet 86
  The Forty Part Motet 86, *86*
Carlile, Joan 87
  Elizabeth Murray, Countess
  of Dysart 87, *87*
Carnegie Institute of Technology 93
Carnegie Prize 131
La Carpeta de los Diez ('Group
  of Ten') 180
Carr, Emily 88
  Big Raven 88, *88*
Carracci, Annibale 140
Carriera, Rosalba 89
  Self-Portrait Holding a Portrait of Her
  Sister 89, *89*
Carrière, Eugène 177
Carrington, Leonora 90, 414
  Down Below 90
  Penelope 90
  Temple of the Word 90, *90*
Carroll, Lewis 325 *Alice*
  in Wonderland 325
Carter, Lynda 63
Cartier-Bresson, Henri 141, 242
Cassatt, Mary 91, 201, 285, 358
  Little Girl in a Blue Armchair 91, *91*
Casteel, Jordan 92
  Q 92, *92*
Castro, Fidel 355
Catherine the Great, Empress
  of Russia 402, 418
Catlett, Elizabeth 93
  Woman Fixing Her Hair 93, *93*
Ceauşescu, Nicolae 251
Celmins, Vija 94
  'Ocean Surface' series 94
  Untitled (Ocean) 94, *94*
Centquatre, Paris 415
Central Academy of Fine Arts,
  Beijing 248, 438
Central Saint Martins,
  London 327, 410
Centre Georges Pompidou, Paris 13,
  254, 311, 334
Centro Diffusione Grafica,
  Florence 254
Cercle et Carré 397
Cézanne, Paul 22, 293, 331, 417
Chadwick, Helen 95
  Ego Geometria Sum:
  The Labours X 95, *95*

Chagall, Marc 141, 335, 444
Chanel, Coco 233
Charles, Prince of Wales 160
Charles I, King of England 54, 87, 282
Charles II, King of Spain 340
Charles V, Emperor 181
Charlesworth, Sarah 96
  Buddha of Immeasurable Light 96, *96*
  'Objects of Desire' series 96
Charlotte, Queen 286
Charpentier, Constance Marie 97, 419
  Melancholy 97, *97*
Chatillon, Henri de 199, *199*
Chelsea College of Art, London 46,
  49, 95, 104, 197
Chicago, Judy 98, 431
  The Dinner Party 98, *98*
China Academy of Art,
  Hangzhou 110, 209, 368
China National Art Gallery,
  Beijing 437
Chirico, Giorgio de 351
Choucair, Saloua Raouda 99
  Composition in Yellow 99, *99*
Christianity 57
Christo 275
Chryssa 100, 401
  Cycladic Books 100
  The Gates to Times Square 100, *100*
City College School of Liberal Arts,
  New York 36, 337
City Racing gallery, London 426
Civil War (English) 87
Clark, Lygia 101, 312, 359
  Máscara Abismo (Abyss Mask) 101, *101*
Claudel, Camille 102
  The Waltz 102, *102*
Claxton, Dana 103
  Buffalo Bone China 103
  Cultural Belongings 103, *103*
Clement of Alexandria, *Stromata* 9
Cleopatra 243, *243*
Cleveland Institute of Art 363
Clough, Prunella 104
  Midland Landscape II 104, *104*
Cocteau, Jean 17
Coenties Slip, New York 265, 401
Cohoon, Hannah 105
  The Tree of Life 105, *105*
Colgate University, Hamilton,
  New York 194
Colour Field movement 403
Colquhoun, Ithell 106
  The Dance of the Nine Opals 106, *106*
Columbia University, New York 119,
  203, 223, 363, 420
Communist Party (Mexico) 280
Communist Party (USA) 213
Conceptual art 9, 96, 119, 137, 191,
  220, 225, 241, 263, 272, 299, 302,
  306, 323, 392, 398
Concretism 101, 312

Conference for Women in the
 Visual Arts 130
Confrerie Pictura 347
Constructionism 266
Constructivism 133, 151, 266, 283,
 288, 312, 397
Cook, Captain James 333
Cooper Union, New York 356
Cossington Smith, Grace 107
 The Curve of the Bridge 107, *107*
Counter-Reformation 140, 249
Courbet, Gustave 404
Cox, Renee 108, 235
 'Flippin the Script' 108
 Yo Mamadonna and Child 108,
 108
 Yo Mama's Last Supper 108
Coyne, Petah 109
 Untitled Works 109, *109*
Crimean War 405
Cronenberg, David 61
Crumb, Robert 172, 423
The Crypt Group 48
Cubism 64, 125, 133, 233, 239, 363,
 400, 417
Cui Jie 110
 Corner Building 110, *110*
Cultural Revolution (China) 437,
 441
Cumming, Laura 13
Cunningham, Imogen 111
 Martha Graham 111, *111*
Cunningham, Merce 41, 114

D

Dada 189, 327, 397
Dali, Salvador 106
Daniel, Charles 125
Darboven, Hanne 112
 7 Panels, II (Panel 1) 112, *112*
Darwin, Charles 84
Dattilo-Rubbo, Antonio 107
David, Jacques-Louis 59, 97, 419
Davis, Angela 213, *213*
The Day the Earth Stood Still 61
de Bruyckere, Berlinde 113
 Marthe 113, *113*
de Kooning, Elaine 114, 174
 Untitled, Number 15 114, *114*
de Kooning, Willem 114, 134, 174
De La Warr Pavilion,
 Bexhill-on-Sea 439
Dean, Tacita 115
 Fernsehturm 115, *115*
Debussy, Claude 102
DeFeo, Jay 116
 The Rose 116, *116*
Degas, Edgar 91, 367, 411
Del Monte 214

Delany, Mary 117
 Physalis (Winter Cherry) 117, *117*
Delaunay, Robert 118
Delaunay, Sonia 99, 118, 184, 444
 Flamenco Singers 118, *118*
Delfina Foundation, London 178
Denes, Agnes 119
 *Tree Mountain – A Living Time
 Capsule* 119
 Wheatfield – A Confrontation 119,
 119
Denis, Maurice 239
Depp, Johnny 173
Deraismes, Maria 157
Designers Art School 204
Diaghilev, Serge 233
Dijkstra, Rineke 120
 'Beach Portraits' 120
 'Bull Fighters' 120
 *De Panne, Belgium,
 August 7 1992* 120, *120*
 'Parks' 120
 'Tiergarten' 120
Disney 41
Documenta, Kassel 257, 260, 275
Documentary photography 17, 72,
 376
Dolven, A K 121
 2am South 121, *121*
 The Kiss 121
 Puberty 121
 Self-Portrait with Cigarette 121
Donovan, Tara 122
 Untitled (Plastic Cups) 122, *122–3*
Dorich House Museum, London 161
Dostoyevsky, Fyodor 158
Dover School of Art 436
Drexler, Rosalyn 124
 Me and My Shadow 124, *124*
Driggs, Elsie 125
 Queensborough Bridge 125, *125*
Du Bois, W.E.B. 356
Duchamp, Marcel 138, 226, 241,
 306, 389
Ducreux, Joseph 126
Ducreux, Rose-Adélaïde 126
 Self-Portrait with a Harp 126, *126*
Dufour, Joseph 333
Dumas, Marlene 127, 136
 Genetic Longing 127, *127*
Dunaway, Faye 342
Dupont Theatre Art
 Gallery, Washington 403
Dupuy-Spencer, Celeste 128
 Early Snow – Rhinecliff Hotel 128, *128*
Duras, Marguerite 334
Dutch Golden Age 244, 362
Dutch Reformed Church 362
Duval, Jeanne 394
Dwight, Mabel 129
 Children's Clinic 129, *129*
Dyck, Anthony van 35, 54

E

East Slovak Gallery, Košice 52
Ebony magazine 147, 376
Eça de Queirós, Josè Maria de, *The Sin
 of Father Amaro* 332
École des Beaux-Arts, Paris 99, 102,
 252, 310, 369
École du Louvre, Paris 141
Edelson, Mary Beth 130
 *Some Living American Women
 Artists* 130, *130*
Edinburgh College of Art 48, 314, 321
Edo period 167, 210, 217
Ehrman, Marli 401
Eisenman, Nicole 131
 The Triumph of Poverty 131, *131*
Elizabeth, Princess (daughter
 of George III) 286
Emin, Tracey 78, 132, 250
 *Everyone I Have Ever Slept
 With 1963–1995* 132, *132*
Equipe 3 302
Ernst, Max 90, 100
Erró 361
Escola de Belas Artes,
 Rio de Janeiro 256
Eugénie, Empress 65
Evans, Walker 241, 242
Exposition Internationale des Arts
 Décoratifs et Industriels Modernes,
 Paris (1925) 239
Exposition Universelle,
 Paris (1878) 382
Expressionism 131, 279, 292, 363,
 388, 417, 428 *see also* Abstract
 Expressionism *and* German
 Expressionism
Exter, Alexandra 133, 291, 324
 Construction 133, *133*

F

Facebook 13, 410
Faiz, Faiz Ahmed 257
Fanon, Frantz 68
Färber, Helmut 390
Farmanfarmaian, Monir
 Shahroudy 134
 Decagon (Third Family) 134, *134*
Farocki, Harun 390
Farroukh, Moustafa 99
Fashion Institute of Technology,
 New York 237
Fassbinder, Rainer Werner 334
Fauve 88
Favaretto, Lara 135

 Gummo V 135, *135*
 'Momentary Monuments' 135
Fawcett, Millicent 426
Federal Art Project (US) 17, 129
feminist art 58, 98, 130, 137, 176,
 206, 358, 361, 379, 384, 431, 432
feminist art history 7, 11
Figgis, Genieve 136
 The Swing after Fragonard 136,
 136
Fine Art Society 154
Finn-Kelcey, Rose 137
 The Restless Image 137, *137*
Finnish Art Society 360
First World War 219, 221, 258,
 405
'The Five' 24
Flash Art (magazine) 94
Flavin, Dan 44
Fleury, Sylvie 138
 ELA 75/K (Go Pout) 138, *138*
 'Shopping Bag' series 138
Floyer, Ceal 139
 Solo 139, *139*
Fluxus 138, 185, 220, 226, 228,
 303, 361
Folk art 34, 153, 156, 207, 263, 287,
 348, 380
Fontana, Lavinia 35, 140
 Minerva Dressing 140, *140*
Fontana, Prospero 140
'Forma 1' 21
Fortune magazine 72
'The Four' 253
Fragonard, Jean-Honoré 152
 The Swing 136
Fragonard, Marie-Anne 152
Franck, Martine 141
 *Children's Library, Clamart,
 Hauts-de-Seine* 141, *141*
Frankenthaler, Helen 130, 142, 195
 Mountains and Sea 142, *142*
Fraser, Andrea 143
 *Museum Highlights:
 A Gallery Talk* 143, *143*
French Revolution 418
Freud, Lucian 357
Frink, Elisabeth 144
 Bird 144
 Goggle Head 144, *144*
Fritsch, Katharina 145
 Hahn/Cock 145
 Rat King 145
 *Tischgesellschaft
 (Company at Table)* 145, *145*
Fry, Roger 56
Fuller, Buckminster 41
Futurism 125, 133, 156, 324

G

Gainsborough, Thomas, *Mr and Mrs Andrews* 136
Gakushuin University, Tokyo 303
Galerie Philomene Magers, Bonn 406
Gallaccio, Anya 146
because nothing has changed 146, *146*
Gallagher, Ellen 147
Wiglette from Deluxe 147, *147*
Galleria Faber, Turin 330
Galleria degli Uffizi, Florence 13, 296
Garage magazine 235
Garbasz, Yishay 148
Footsteps (48) 148, *148*
'In My Mother's Footsteps' 148
Garvey, Marcus 213, 356
Gatti, Bernardino 35
Gaudi, Antoni 352
GEDOK 331
Geffroy, Gustave 285
Gego 149
Seven Icosidodecahedrons 149, *149*
Genet, Jean 334
Genthe, Arnold 230
Gentileschi, Artemisia 35, 98, 150, 378
Judith Beheading Holofernes 150, *150*
Gentileschi, Orazio 150
Genzken, Isa 151
Rose 151, *151*
Gérard, Marguerite 152
Sleep, My Child 152, *152*
Germain School of Photography, New York 138
German Expressionism 131, 292, 388
German, Vanessa L. 153
'ARThouse' 153
Delia on the Plane, or Cabbage Slicer 153, *153*
'Love Front Porch' 153
Giacometti, Alberto 73, 335, 423
Glamour magazine 39
Glasgow School of Art 253, 334, 357
Glasgow Style 253
Glissant, Édouard 70
Gluck 77, 154
Medallion [YouWe] 54, *154*
Goldin, Nan 155, 231
'The Ballad of Sexual Dependency' 155
Jimmy Paulette and Tabboo! Undressing, NYC 155, *155*
The Other Side 155
Goldsmiths College, London 62, 139, 146, 227, 250, 266, 327, 336, 426, 439
Gombrich, E.H., *The Story of Art* 9
Goncharova, Natalia 156
Cyclist 156, *156*

Gonzalès, Eva 157
A Box at the Théâtre des Italiens 157, *157*
La Matinée Rose 157
Gonzalez-Foerster, Dominique 158
Splendide Hotel 158, *158–9*
Goodman, Catherine 160
Sister 160, *160*
Gordine, Dora 161
Javanese Dancer 161, *161*
Gore, Al 173
Gørrill, Helen 12
Gowda, Sheila 162
What Yet Remains 162, *162*
Goya, Francisco 202
Graham, Martha 111, *111*
Grant, Duncan 56
Graves, Nancy 130
Green Leaf Award for Sculpture 308
Greenberg, Clement 174
Greenfield, Lauren 163
Cara, 31, from Batavia, Illinois… 163, *163*
Fast Forward 163
Generation Wealth 163
The Queen of Versailles 163
'THIN' 163
Gris, Juan 64
Grosse, Katharina 164
Rockaway! 164
Untitled Trumpet 164, *164*
Grosvenor Gallery, London 205
Group Ongaku 226
Grupo dos Cinco ('Group of Five') 400
Grupo Frente ('Front Group') 101, 312
Guangzhou Academy of Fine Arts 85
The Guardian 43
Guerrilla Girls 165
Do Women Have to be Naked to Get into the Met. Museum? 165
When Racism & Sexism are No Longer Fashionable… 165, *165*
Guggenheim, Peggy 17, 351
Guggenheim Fellowships 33, 51, 131, 230, 275, 375
Guild of St Luke, Haarlem 244
Guild of St Luke, Utrecht 362
Gulf War, First (1990–91) 208, 212
Gupta, Shilpa 166
Someone Else… 166, *166*
Gutai Art Association 398
Gyokuran, Ike 167
Autumnal Landscape 167, *167*

H

Haacke, Hans 143
Haarr, Elisabeth 168
Frustration Rug 168, *168*

Hadid, Zaha 264
Hall, Radclyffe, *The Well of Loneliness* 154
Halprin, Anna 427
Hals, Frans 244
Hambling, Maggi 169
Self-Portrait 169, *169*
Hamburg Kunsthalle 331
Hamilton, Ann 170
The Event of a Thread 170, *170–1*
Hammer Museum, Los Angeles 28
Handel, George Frideric 117
Hansson, Mie, *Where Pain Thrives* 32
'happenings' 185, 272, 352, 361
Haraway, Donna 390
Harcourt, Raoul d', *Textiles of Ancient Peru and Their Techniques* 186
Hare, Richard 161
Harlem Renaissance 204, 337, 356
Harper's Bazaar 278
Harrison, Margaret 172
Captain America 172, *172*
Harrison, Rachel 173
Alexander the Great 173, *173*
Hartigan, Grace 174
Billboard 174, *174*
Harvard University 163, 323
Hatoum, Mona 175
Greater Divide 175
Hot Spot III 175, *175*
Hauser & Wirth, Los Angeles 238
Hayes, Sharon 176
In the Near Future 176, *176*
Head, Bessie
A Question of Power 68
Heem, Jan Davidszoon de 304
Heemskerck, Jacoba van 177
Composition No. 23 177, *177*
Hefuna, Susan 178
Afaz Drawings 178, *178*
Heilmann, Mary 179
Primalon Balloon 179, *179*
Heinrich, Annemarie 180
Caprichos, Anita Grim 180, *180*
Hemessen, Catharina van 181
Self-Portrait at the Easel 181, *181*
Hemessen, Jan Sanders van 181
Henderson, Jerry 83
Henrietta Maria, Queen 54
Henrot, Camille 182
Grosse Fatigue 182, *182*
Hepworth, Barbara 48, 183
The Family of Man 183, *183*
Hepworth Prize for Sculpture 264
Heresies (journal) 223, 392
Heresies Collective 130
Hermitage, St Petersburg 190
Herrera, Carmen 184
Red & Blue 184, *184*
Hesse, Eva 185, 186
Accession II 185, *185*

Hicks, Sheila 186
Atterrissage (Landing) 186, *186*
Higgins, Eugene 129
Higonnet, Anne 419
Hildegard of Bingen 98
Hiller, Susan 187
Witness 187, *187*
Himid, Lubaina 74, 188
Naming the Money 188, *188*
Hirst, Damien 250
Hitler, Adolf 273
Höch, Hannah 189, 247, 294
The Journalists 189, *189*
Hochschule für bildende Künste, Hamburg 112
Hockney, David 160, 195, 332
Höfer, Candida 190
Hermitage, St. Petersburg VIII 2014 190, *190*
Hokusai *see* Katsushika Hokusai
Holiday, Billie 240
Hollywood films 45
Holocaust 148, 394, 395
Holt, Nancy 191
Boomerang 191
Sun Tunnels 191, *191*
Holzer, Jenny 192
'Truisms' series 192
Untitled ('Abuse of Power Comes As No Surprise') 192, *192*
Hongik University, Seoul 236
Horn, Rebecca 193
Concert for Anarchy 193, *193*
Einhorn 193
Der Eintänzer 193
Horn, Roni 194
'Still Water' 194
'To Place' 194
Water Double, V. 3 194, *194*
You Are the Weather 194
Howard University, Washington DC 93, 204, 403
Huang Yong Ping 368
Hughes, Shara 195
In the Clear 195, *195*
Hunterwali 328
Huxtable, Juliana 196
Untitled (Psychological Stuntin') 196, *196*
Huyghe, Pierre 182

I

Iglesias, Cristina 197
Laurel Leaves 197
Tres Aguas (Water Tower) 197, *197*
'Immaculates' 125
Imperial Art Academy, Tokyo 408
Impressionism 91, 157, 204, 219, 285, 360

Indiana, Robert 401
Indigenous Media Arts Group 103
Ingres, Jean-Auguste-
   Dominique 42, 239
   La Grand Odalisque 165
   The Turkish Bath 367, 379
Instagram 13, 410
Institute of Contemporary Art,
   London 188, 444
Institute of Contemporary
   Art, Washington DC 407
Institute for New Media,
   Frankfurt 178
institutional critique 143
Instituto de Artivismo Hannah Arendt
   (INSTAR) 79
International Art Prize 151
International Biennial of Prints,
   Bhopal, India 443
International Center of Photography
   School, New York 377
Internet 13–14, 83, 136, 182
Istanbul Biennial, 8th (2003) 353
Iturbide, Graciela 198
   Chickens, Juchitán, Mexico 198, *198*
   'Juchitán of the Women' 198
Izquierdo, Maria 199
   Portrait of Henri de Chatillon 199, *199*

J

Jacir, Emily 200
   'Where We Come From' 200, *200*
Jacob, Max 133
The Jarman Award 319
Jarry, Alfred, *Ubu Roi* 252
Jawlensky, Alexei 428
Jet magazine 376
Jewish Museum, New York 98, 407
Joan of Arc 64, 300
Joffe, Chantal 201
   Self-Portrait with Esme 201, *201*
Johann Wilhelm, Elector Palatine 347
John, Augustus 202
John, Gwen 202
   Girl with Bare Shoulders 202, *202*
John Moores Painting Prize 436
Johns, Jasper 393
Jonas, Joan 203
   Mirror Piece I 203, *203*
Jones, Loïs Mailou 204, 403
   Jennie 204, *204*
Jopling, Louise 205
   Phyllis 205, *205*
Joyce, James 17
Juchitán people 198
Judd, Donald 44
Jürgenssen, Birgit 206
   Housewives' Kitchen Apron 206,
   206

K

Kahlo, Frida 199, 207, 280, 358
   The Two Fridas 207, *207*
Kahraman, Hayv 208
   Strip Search 208, *208*
Kaiserring Goslar prize 193
Kamerny Theatre, Moscow 133
Kan Xuan 209
   Kanxuan! Ai! 209
   Millet Mounds 209, *209*
Kandinsky, Wassily 24, 292
Kanō school 217, 408
Kanō Tan'yū 217
Kaprow, Allan 185
Käsebier, Gertrude 111
Katsushika Hokusai 210
Katsushika Ōi 210
   *Three Women Playing Musical
   Instruments* 210, *210*
Kauffman, Angelica 211, 286
   Ariadne Abandoned 211, *211*
Kelly, Ellsworth 265
Kelly, Mary 176, 212
   Post-Partum Document 212, *212*
Kennedy, John F. 114
Kensmil, Iris 213
   Angela Davis #2 213, *213*
   'Study in Black Modernity' 213
   'Voices across the Ocean' 213
Kent, Corita 214
   The Juiciest Tomato of All 214, *214*
Kent State University 109
Kher, Bharti 215
   *An Absence Of Assignable
   Cause* 215, *215*
Kien, Yanagisawa 167
Kimsooja 216
   *Cities on the Move – 2727 km Bottari
   Truck* 216, *216*
King, Martin Luther Jr. 337, 349
The Kingpins 270
Kiyohara Yukinobu 217
   *Waxwings, Cherry Blossoms and
   Bamboo* 217, *217*
Klumpke, Anna 65
Kngwarray, Emily Kam 218
   Earth's Creation 218
   Ntange Dreaming 218, *218*
Knight, Laura 219, 286
   Fine Feathers 219, *219*
Knoll 29
Kolář, Jiři 220
Kolářová, Běla 220
   Variation: Two Triangles IV 220,
   220
Kollwitz, Käthe 9, 221
   'A Weavers' Revolt' 221
   Woman with Dead Child 221, *221*

Kootz Gallery, New York 174
Kora of Sicyon 7
Kosuth, Joseph 112
Kotátková, Eva 222
   Asylum 222, *222*
   *Behind Between Over Under In
   (the Flat)* 222
Kozloff, Joyce 223, 434
   Art Girl 223, *223*
   'Girlhood' 223
Krasner, Lee 130, 174, 224
   'Little Image' series 224
   Untitled 224, *224*
Kristallnacht (1938) 354, *354*
Kruger, Barbara 225, 234
   Picture/Readings 225
   *Untitled (Your Body
   is a Battleground)* 225, *225*
Kubota, Shigeko 226
   *Duchampiana: Nude Descending
   a Staircase* 226, *226*
   Vagina Painting 226
Kuffner, Raoul 239
Kunstakademie
   Düsseldorf 164, 190, 406
Künstlerhaus Bethanien, Berlin 139
Kurant, Agnieszka 227
   Air Rights 5 227, *227*
   Phantom Library 227
Kusama, Yayoi 228
   *All the Eternal Love I Have for the
   Pumpkins* 228, *228*
   'Infinity Rooms' 228
Kwade, Alicja 229
   Against the Run 229
   Big Be-Hide 229, *229*
Kyoto Prefectural Painting School 408
Kyoto School of Arts and Crafts 228

L

LA Rebellion 297
Labadists 362
Labille-Guiard, Adélaïde 89
Lac Seul First Nation community 57
LaChapelle, David 237
Ladies' Home Journal 278
Land art 119, 146, 191, 246, 251,
   392, 420
Lange, Dorothea 141, 230
   *Migrant Mother, Nipomo,
   California* 230, *230*
Lankton, Greer 155, 231
   Rachel 231, *231*
Larionov, Mikhail 156
Lassnig, Maria 232
   Du oder Ich (You or Me) 232, *232*
Latham, John 327
Laurencin, Marie 233
   The Dreamer 233, *233*

Lawler, Louise 234, 241
   Pollock and Tureen 234, *234*
Lawrence of Arabia (film) 45
Lawson, Deana 235
   Brother and Sister Soweto 235, *235*
Le Gray, Gustave, *Beech Tree, Forest
   of Fontainebleau* 259
Lebanese Civil War (1975–90) 99, 175
Lee Bul 236
   Abortion 236
   Majestic Splendor 236
   Willing To Be Vulnerable 236, *236*
Lee, Nikki S. 237
   The Ohio Project (7) 237, *237*
   'Projects' series 237
Léger, Fernand 99, 133, 288, 316,
   400, 417
Lehman, Emanuel 47
Leibovitz, Annie 238
   *Virginia Woolf's writing desk, Monks
   House, East Sussex, England* 238, *238*
Lempicka, Tamara de 239
   Young Woman in Green 239, *239*
Lennon, John 238, 303
Leo Castelli Gallery, New York 234
Leonard, Zoe 240
   'Analogue' project 240
   Strange Fruit 240, *240*
Leonardo da Vinci
   108, 130
   Last Supper 55
   Mona Lisa 307
Leopold II, King of the Belgians 341
Leopold Wilhelm, Archduke
   of Austria 425
Levin-Funcke studio, Berlin 388
Levine, Sherrie 234, 241, 393
   *Fountain (after Marcel
   Duchamp)* 241, *241*
Levitt, Helen 242
   *Four Boys in 'Beau Geste' Headgear,
   New York City* 242, *242*
Lewis, Edmonia 243
   The Death of Cleopatra 243, *243*
LeWitt, Sol 112, 323, 387
Leyster, Judith 244
   The Happy Couple 244, *244*
Lhote, André 239
Lichtenstein, Roy 393
Liebermann, Max 331
Life magazine 72, 174
Lijn, Liliane 245
   Time is Change 245, *245*
Lin, Maya 246
   Storm King Wavefield 246, *246*
Lincoln, Abraham 173
Linder 247
   Untitled 247, *247*
Lindsay, Lady 205
Lisiewski, Georg 402
Liu, Hung 248
   Mother and Daughter 248, *248*

Liverpool Biennial (2006) 262
Locke, Alain 204
Loewenthal, Jesse 184
London Group 43, 332
Longhi, Barbara 249
   Madonna and Child 249, *249*
   Saint Catherine of Alexandria 249
Longhi, Luca 249
Lonzi, Carla 21
Look magazine 278
Lorca, Federico García 64
Lorenz, Renate *see* Boudry,
   Pauline & Lorenz, Renate
Los Angeles County Museum of Art
   (LACMA) 12, 80
Los Angeles Museum
   of Contemporary Art 127
Louis XVI, King of France 418
Louis XVIII, King of France 59
Louvre, Paris 118, 152, 419
Louÿs, Pierre, *Les Chansons*
   de Bilitis 258
Lovell, Fenella 202, *202*
Lucas, Sarah 78, 250
   Au Naturel 250, *250*
Lupas, Ana 251
   Humid Installation 251
   The Solemn Process 251, *251*
Lyon Biennale, 12th (2013) 334

M

Maar, Dora 25, 252, 306
   Père Ubu 252, *252*
MacArthur Fellowship 51, 131
MacArthur Foundation 'Genius'
   Award 122
MacDonald, Frances 253
MacDowell Colony 435
Mackintosh, Charles Rennie 253
Mackintosh, Margaret
   MacDonald 253
   The Opera of the Wind 253, *253*
McNair, Herbert 253
Maharaja Sayajirao University,
   Baroda 290
Mahlangu, Esther 254
   Untitled 254, *254*
Maier, Vivian 255
   September 1953, New York,
   NY 255, *255*
Maiolino, Anna Maria 256
   Entrevidas ('Between Lives') 256, *256*
Malani, Nalini 257
   In Search of Vanished Blood 257, *257*
Malevich, Kazimir 133, 324
Malherbe, Suzanne 81
Mammen, Jeanne 258
   Carnival in Berlin N III 258, *258*
Manchester Polytechnic 247

Manet, Édouard 157, 285, 404
   Olympia 136
Mann, Sally 259
   'Deep South' 259
   'Immediate Family' 259
   Untitled (Scarred Tree) 259, *259*
Mannerism 128, 249, 329
Marakatt-Labba, Britta 260
   Historjá 260
   The Roots 260, *260*
Marcelle, Cinthia 261
   475 Volver (to come to) 261, *261*
Margolles, Teresa 262
   En El Aire (In The Air) 262, *262*
Marie Antoinette, Queen 126, 413,
   418, *418*
Marisol 263
   The Family 263, *263*
Marten, Helen 264
   The Cat from the Bacon 264, *264*
   'Drunk Brown House' 264
Martin, Agnes 265, 387, 401
   'Band' paintings 265
   'Grid' paintings 265
   The Tree 265, *265*
Martin, Jean-Hubert 254
Martin, Kenneth 266
Martin, Mary 266
   Rotation 3 266, *266*
Martin, Rosy 383
Mary of Hungary 181
Matisse, Henri 177, 179, 404
Mattress Factory, Pittsburgh 231
Max Mara Art Prize for Women 327
Maximilian II, Emperor 339
Medienkunstpreis Karlsruhe 193
Mehretu, Julie 267
   Empirical Construction,
   Istanbul 267, *267*
Mella, Julio Antonio 280
Mellor, David Alan 69
Mendieta, Ana 79, 268
   Silueta Works in Mexico 268, *268*
Merz, Mario 269
Merz, Marisa 269
   Untitled 269, *269*
Mesiti, Angelica 270
   The Calling 270, *270*
Messager, Annette 271
   My Vows: Circle – Triangle 271,
   271
Metabolism 110
#MeToo movement 192
Metropolitan Museum of Art,
   New York 61, 84, 419, 420
Metsu, Gabriel 152
Micas, Natalie 65
Michaelis School of Fine Art,
   Cape Town 364
Michelangelo Buonarroti 35
   David 108
Middlesex University 74

Milhazes, Beatriz 272
   Marotoloco 272, *272*
Millais, John Everett 84
Miller, George Bures 86
Miller, Lee 25, 273
   Fire Masks, Downshire Hill,
   London 273, *273*
Minimalism 37, 44, 98, 134, 146,
   151, 179, 185, 220, 228, 263, 265,
   302, 311, 323, 344, 355, 387, 392,
   406, 407
Minter, Marilyn 274
   Satiated 274, *274*
Minujín, Marta 275
   La Destrucción 275
   'The Fall of Universal Myths' 275
   Minuphone 275
   The Parthenon of Books 275, *275*
Mir, Aleksandra 276
   Cinema for the Unemployed 276
   First Woman on the Moon 276, *276*
   Newsroom 1986–2000 276
Mir Iskusstva 324
Mirbeau, Octave 102
Miro, Victoria 201
Mitchell, Joan 134, 277
   City Landscape 277, *277*
Model, Lisette 39, 96, 278
   Coney Island 278
Moderna Museet, Stockholm 24
Modernism 110, 128, 151, 161, 301
Modersohn, Otto 279
Modersohn-Becker, Paula 279, 331
   Self-Portrait on Sixth Wedding
   Anniversary 279, *279*
Modotti, Tina 280
   Untitled (Woman with
   Basket) 280, *280*
Moffatt, Tracey 281
   Night Cries 281
   Something More #4 281, *281*
Moillon, Louise 282
   Still Life with Fruit 282, *282*
Molenaer, Jan Miense 244
Molnar, Véra 283
   Four Items Distributed
   at Random 283, *283*
Mondrian, Piet 177, 179, 183, 213,
   283, 288
Monika Sprüth Galerie, Cologne 406
Monroe, Marilyn 69, 70, 393, *393*
Moore, Henry 183
Moore, Julianne 76
Moore, Marcel 81
Moore College of Art and Design,
   Philadelphia 295
Moraes, Henrietta 169
Mori, Mariko 284
   Enlightenment Capsule 284
   Last Departure 284, *284*
   Transcircle 1.1 284
Morikage, Kusumi 217

Morisot, Berthe 201, 285
   The Cradle 285, *285*
Morisot, Edma 285
Moser, George Michael 286
Moser, Mary 211, 286
   Joseph Nollekens 286, *286*
Moses, Anna Mary Robertson
   ('Grandma') 287
   Yellow House 287, *287*
Moss, Marlow 288
   Spatial Construction 288, *288*
Motif Editions Gallery, London 172
Mozart, Wolfgang Amadeus,
   Don Giovanni 154
Mueck, Ron 320
Muholi, Zanele 289
   'Faces and Phases' 289
   Sebenzile, Parktown 289, *289*
   'Somnyama Ngonyama' 289
Mukherjee, Mrinalini 290
   Adi Pushp II 290, *290*
Mukhina, Vera 291, 335
   Worker and Collective Farm
   Girl 291, *291*
Munch, Edvard 121, 232
Münter, Gabriele 292, 428
   Portrait of Marianne von
   Werefkin 292, *292*
Muralists, Mexican 199
Murasaki Shikibu, *The Tale*
   of Genji 408
Murray, Elizabeth 195, 293
   Arm-Ear 293, *293*
Musée National d'Art Moderne,
   Paris 13
Museo de Arte Latinoamericano
   de Buenos Aires 180
El Museo del Barrio, New York 325
Museo del Prado, Madrid 13, 315
Museum of Modern Art (MoMA),
   New York 12–13, 19, 29, 31, 36, 47,
   71, 116, 165, 174, 224, 226, 231,
   236, 242, 301, 322, 323, 389
Museum of Modern Art, Warsaw 52
Museum aan de Stroom, Antwerp 425
Mutu, Wangechi 294
   Beneath lies the Power 294, *294*
Myles, Eileen 334

N

Les Nabis 239
Napoleon I, Emperor 59
Napoleonic Wars 405
Nash, Paul 25
National Academy of Crafts and Art
   Industry, Oslo 168
National Art Museum, Kyoto 308
National Association of Women
   Painters and Sculptors (US) 356

National College of Art and Design, Dublin 136

National Gallery, London 115, 150, 169, 332

National Gallery of Modern Art, New Delhi 290

National Institute of Design, Ahmedabad 377

National Portrait Gallery, London 115, 160

National Women's Hall of Fame (US) 230

Nauman, Bruce 344

Nazis 29, 50, 81, 94, 119, 149, 189, 221, 258, 291, 331, 348, 354, 388, 394

Ndebele culture 254

Neel, Alice 295
Andy Warhol 295, *295*

Nelli, Plautilla 9, 13, 296, 329
Lamentation with Saints 296, *296*

Nengudi, Senga 297
R.S.V.P. 1 297, *297*

Neo-Classicism 97, 154, 239, 243, 291, 335

Neo-Concretism 101, 272, 302, 312

Neo-Cubism 224

Neo-Dada 173

Neo-Impressionism 204

Neshat, Shirin 298
Rebellious Silence 298, *298*
'Women of Allah' 298

Neue Sachlichkeit ('New Objectivity') 331

Neuenschwander, Rivane 299
I wish your wish 299, *299*

Nevelson, Louise 134, 300
Sky Cathedral 300, *300*

New Artists' Society, Munich 292

New Burlington Galleries, London 25

New Classicists 125

New Deal (US) 129

New Figuration movement 256

The New School, New York 119, 278

New York Graphic Workshop 325

New York Times 141

New York University 73

The New Yorker 20, 235

Newcastle Polytechnic 215

Newman, Barnett 407

Nicholson, Ben 48, 183

Nijhoff, Nettie 288

Nixon, Pat 342, *342*

Nochlin, Linda, 'Why Have There Been No Great Women Artists?' 10–11

Nollekens, Joseph 286, *286*

Nouveau Réalisme 352

Novembergruppe 388

O

Obama, Barack 317

Obama, Michelle 370, *370*

Oberlin College, Ohio 243

Obermer, Nesta 154

Oiticica, Hélio 312, 359

O'Keeffe, Georgia 11, 98, 130, 301, 389
Jimson Weed/White Flower No. 1 301, *301*

Okumura, Lydia 302
Untitled I 302, *302*

Old Masters 11, 78, 87, 224

Oliveros, Pauline 70

Omega Workshops 56

Los Once ('The Eleven') 355

Ono, Yoko 226, 238, 303
Cut Piece 303, *303*

Onsi, Omar 99

Oost, Jacob van 425

Oosterwijck, Maria van 304
Vanitas Still Life 304, *304*

Op art 20, 302, 336, 386, 429

Opie, Catherine 305
Justin Bond 305, *305*
'Portraits' series 305

Oppenheim, Meret 193, 306
Object 306, *306*

Oppenheimer, Margaret 419

Orchard gallery, New York 143

Orlan 307
Omnipresence 7th Surgery Performance. November 21st 1993 307, *307*
'The Reincarnation of Saint Orlan' 307

Orphism 118, 444

Orta, Jorge 308

Orta, Lucy 308
Body Architecture: Collective Wear × 8 308, *308*
'Refuge Wear' 308

Osborn, Emily Mary 309
Nameless and Friendless 309, *309*

Oslo Art Association 168

Otero, Alejandro 149

Our World 147

Outsider art 271

Outwin Boochever Portrait Competition 370

Ovid, 'Heroides' 205

Oxlade, Roy 436

Oz Magazine 172

P

Pace Gallery, New York 122, 124

Palaeolithic art 44

Palais de Tokyo, Paris 182, 327

Pan Yuliang 310
Chrysanthemum and Female Nude 310, *310*

Pane, Gina 311
Sentimental Action, 9 November, 1973 311, *311*

Pape, Lygia 101, 312
Divisor (Divider) 312, *312*
'Weaving' series 312

Parasol Unit, London 365

Paris Salon 59, 65, 91, 97, 126, 157, 205, 418, 419

Park, Kyong 298

Park Avenue Armory, New York 170

Parker, Cornelia 313
Cold Dark Matter 313, *313*
Mass (Colder Darker Matter) 313
The Maybe 313

Parreno, Philippe 158

Parsons School of Design, New York 18

Parveen, Abida 62

Paterson, Katie 314
Earth-Moon-Earth 314
Totality 314, *314*
Vatnajökull (the sound o movement 223, 358

Paul V, Pope 140

Paulette, Jimmy 155, *155*

Paxton, Steve 203

Pechstein, Max 388

Peeters, Clara 13, 315
Still Life with Cheeses, Artichoke and Cherries 315, *315*

Penland School of Crafts 401

Penrose, Roland 25, 106, 273

Penwith Society of Arts 48

Pepper, Beverly 316
The Gift of Icarus 316
Zig-zag 316, *316*

performance art 19, 98, 137, 203, 398, 409, 438

Peridot Gallery, New York 71

Peyton, Elizabeth 317
Live to Ride (E.P.) 317, *317*

Phalanx school, Munich 292

Philadelphia College of Art 42

Philadelphia Museum of Art 143

Philip II, King of Spain 35, 339

Philip V, King of Spain 340

Philipsz, Susan 318
A Single Voice 318, *318*

Phillipson, Heather 319
TRUE TO SIZE 319, *319*

Photojournalism 141, 230, 377

Photorealism 30, 94, 274

Picabia, Francis 306

Picasso, Pablo 25, 64, 133, 177, 233, 306, 337
Weeping Woman 252

Piccinini, Patricia 320
Skywhale 320
The Young Family 320, *320*

Pictures Generation 96, 234, 241

Piero della Francesca 125

Pierre Matisse Gallery, New York 90

Pieters, Geertje 304

Pietra, Count Alfonso 329

Pietra, Count Clemente 329

Pilkington, Cathie 321
Bill and Bob 321
Head Case 321, *321*

Pinchuk Foundation Future Generation Art Prize 440

Pindell, Howardena 322
Untitled #84 322, *322*

Piper, Adrian 143, 323
The Mythic Being: Sol's Drawing 323, *323*

Piper, Keith 74

Pistoletto, Michelangelo 269
Plastique (journal) 397

Pliny the Elder, *Natural Histories* 7

Pollock, Jackson 58, 142, 224, 234, 352, 387

Polytechnic of Central London 383

Pop art 69, 94, 100, 124, 172, 173, 174, 263, 274, 325, 393

Popova, Liubov 324
Painterly Construction 324, *324*

Porter, Liliana 325
Alice: The Way Out 325
Man with Axe 325, *325*
'Trabajo Forzado' series 325

Portland, Margaret Cavendish, Duchess of 117

Postcolonial art 57, 68, 103, 281, 289, 328, 333, 364, 372

Post-Impressionism 56, 88, 107, 411

Powers, Harriet 326
Bible Quilt 326, *326*
Pictorial Quilt 326

Prague Spring (1968) 220

Pratt Graphics Center, New York 409

Pratt Institute, New York 231, 409

Pre-Raphaelite 84, 205, 382

Precisionism 125

Primitivism 161

Prince, Richard 136, 241

Prinsep, Sara 84

Prix de Rome 310

Prouvost, Laure 327
The Artist 327
'Ring, Sing and Drink for Trespassing' 327
Wantee 327
We Will Feed You, Cooling Fountain 327, *327*

Prussian Academy of Arts, Berlin 221

Pushpamala N 328
'Return of the Phantom Lady (Sinful City)' 328, *328*

Q

Queer art 128, 155, 176, 196
Quistelli, Lucrezia 9, 329
 *The Mystical Marriage of Saint
  Catherine* 329, *329*

R

Rainer, Yvonne 203
Rama, Carol 330
 'Appassionata' 330
 Work No. 11 (Foxes) 330, *330*
Ranzan, Takai, *A Concise Dictionary
 of Sencha* 210
 *Illustrated Handbook for Daily Life
  for Women* 210
Rauschenberg, Robert 12
 'Combines' 264
Ray, Man 17, 25, 273, 306
Rayonism 156
Read, Herbert 90
Real Academia de Bellas Artes
 de San Fernando, Madrid 414
Realism 360, 367, 369, 405
 see also Socialist Realism
Redfern Gallery, London 43
Rée, Anita 331
 Self-Portrait 331, *331*
Rego, Paula 160, 332
 The Company of Women 332, *332*
Reihana, Lisa 333
 In Pursuit of Venus [Infected] 333, *333*
Reinhardt, Ad 407
Renaissance 10, 125, 128, 195, 249,
 296, 324, 378, 413, 434
Renoir, Auguste 411
Renoir, Jean 252
Repin, Ilya 428
Reynaud-Dewar, Lili 334
 *Live Through That?!
  (Atelier Brancusi)* 334, *334*
Reynolds, Sir Joshua 211
Rhode Island School of Design 37,
 131, 194, 195, 422, 435
Richier, Germaine 335
 The Mountain 335, *335*
Rie, Lucie 31
Riefenstahl, Leni 50
Riggs, Marlon 337
Rihanna 235
Rijksakademie Van Beeldende
 Kunsten, Amsterdam 209
Riley, Bridget 20, 336
 Current 336, *336*
Ringgold, Faith 337
 Echoes of Harlem 337
 Picasso's Studio 337, *337*

Rist, Pipilotti 338
 Ever is Over All 338, *338*
 I'm Not the Girl Who Misses Much 338
Rivera, Diego 64, 207, 300, 392
Rivolta Femminile 21
Robusti, Marietta 339
 Self-Portrait 339, *339*
Rococo painting 89, 136
Rodin, Auguste 102, 202, 423
Roldán, Luisa 340
 The Entombment of Christ 340, *340*
Roldán, Pedro 340
Rolleiflex camera 252, 255
Rolling Stone magazine 238
Roman Catholic Church 214, 271,
 299
Romantic movement 62
Rosano, Paul 379, *379*
Rose, Tracey 341
 Die Wit Man 341, *341*
Rosenthal 29
Rosenthal, Rachel 231
Rosler, Martha 342
 First Lady (Pat Nixon) 342, *342*
 'House Beautiful' 342
Rossi, Properzia de' 9, 343
 Joseph and Potiphar's Wife 343, *343*
Rothenberg, Susan 344
 Black in Place 344, *344*
Rottenberg, Mika 345
 Mary's Cherries 345, *345*
Rowling, J.K. 166
Royal Academy of Arts, London 115,
 132, 205, 211, 219, 286, 309, 313,
 321, 382
Royal Academy of Fine Arts,
 Stockholm 24
Royal Academy Schools, London 160,
 172, 286, 440
Royal College of Art, London 69,
 132, 162, 201, 266, 299, 321, 336,
 390, 436
Royal Drawing School, London
 160
Royal Female School of Art,
 London 405
Royal Museum of Fine Arts,
 Antwerp 197
Royal Society of British Artists 205
Rubell Contemporary Arts
 Foundation 18
Rubins, Nancy 346
 Airplane Parts & Hills 346, *346*
 Big Bil-Bored 346
Rubinstein, Helena 233
Rubinstein, Ida 77
Ruskin School of Drawing and Fine
 Art, Oxford 264
Russell, Ken, *Monitor: Pop Goes
 the Easel* 69
Russian Revolution (1917) 367
Ruysch, Frederik 347

Ruysch, Rachel 347
 *Still Life with Fruit, Bird's Nest
  and Insects* 347, *347*
Ryggen, Hannah 348
 Grini 348, *348*
Ryggen, Hans 348

S

Saar, Betye 349
 Black Girl's Window 349, *349*
Saatchi Gallery, London 357
Sadr Haghighian, Natascha 350
 I Can't Work Like This 350, *350*
Saffarzadeh, Tahereh 298
Sage, Kay 351
 The Upper Side of the Sky 351, *351*
St Ives' Society of Artists 48
Saint Phalle, Niki de 352
 Death 352, *352*
 'Nanas' 352
 'Tarot Garden' 352
Salazar, António de Oliveira 415
Salcedo, Doris 353
 Flor de Piel 353
 Noviembre 6 y 7 353
 Shibboleth 353
 *Untitled Installation for the 8th
  International Istanbul Biennial* 353, *353*
Salomon, Charlotte 354
 Kristallnacht 354, *354*
Salon *see* Paris Salon
Salon des Indépendants, Paris 233
Salon des Réalités Nouvelles,
 Paris 99, 184
Saltz, Jerry 12
Sámi community 260
San Francisco Art Institute 238
San Francisco Museum of Modern
 Art 163
San Francisco School of the Arts 41
Sánchez, Zilia 355
 Untitled 355, *355*
Sander, August 120
Sanderson, William, *Graphice* 87
São Paulo Biennial 216, 302
Sarah Lawrence College, New York
 303
Savage, Augusta 356
 Gamin 356, *356*
Savage Studio of Arts and Crafts,
 New York 356
Saville, Jenny 136, 357
 Plan 357, *357*
 Propped 357
Schapiro, Miriam 98, 358
 Wonderland 358, *358*
Schendel, Mira 359
 Untitled 359, *359*
Schjeldahl, Peter 269

Schjerfbeck, Helene 360
 *Self-Portrait with Black
  Background* 360, *360*
Schneemann, Carolee 361
 Cezanne: She was a Great Painter 361
 Eye Body 361, *361*
 Interior Scroll 361
School for American Craftsmen,
 Alfred, NY 434
School of Applied Arts, Zürich 80
School of Design, Basel 338
'School of London' 78, 160
School of the Museum of Fine Arts,
 Boston 155, 204
School of Visual Arts,
 New York 396, 438
Schurman, Anna Maria van 98, 362
 The Learned Maid 362
 Self-Portrait 362, *362*
Schutz, Dana 363
 Face Eater 363, *363*
 'Frank from Observation' 363
 'Sneeze' paintings 363
Schwitters, Kurt 327
Searle, Berni 364
 Snow White 364, *364*
Second World War 72, 144, 219, 230,
 273, 348, 433
The Secret Public magazine 247
Self, Tschabalala 365
 Bayo/Pink Soap/Red Soap 365, *365*
Semmel, Joan 366
 Intimacy-Autonomy 366, *366*
 'Self-Images' series 366
Sepia magazine 147
Serebriakova, Zinaida 367
 Bathhouse 367, *367*
Serpentine Gallery, London 178,
 264, 313
Serra, Richard 191
Sesshū school 408
Shakers 105
Shakespeare, William 84
Shanghai Art Academy 310
Sharjah Biennial, 11th (2013) 166
Shen Yuan 368
 Untitled 368, *368*
Sher-Gil, Amrita 369
 Three Girls 369, *369*
Sherald, Amy 370
 *Michelle Lavaughn Robinson
  Obama* 370, *370*
Sherman, Cindy 96, 234, 241, 328, 371
 Untitled Film Still #21 371, *371*
The Shop, London 250
Sibande, Mary 372
 *They Don't Make Them Like They
  Used To* 372, *372*
Siemens Art Program 85
Sillman, Amy 373
 Duel 373
 In Illinois 373, *373*

Simmons, Laurie 96, 374
First Bathroom/Woman
Standing 374, *374*
Simon, Taryn 375
'An American Index of the Hidden
and Unfamiliar' 375
Hymenoplasty, Cosmetic
Surgery 375, *375*
'The Innocents' 375
An Occupation of Loss 375
Simone, Nina 68
Simplicissimus (journal) 258
Simpson, Lorna 235, 376
'Earth & Sky' 376
Guarded Conditions 376, *376*
Singh, Dayanita 377
File Museum 377, *377*
Sent a Letter 377
Sirani, Anna Maria 378
Sirani, Barbara 378
Sirani, Elisabetta 378
Portia Wounding Her Thigh 378, *378*
Sirani, Giovanni Andrea 378
Skowhegan School of Painting and
Sculpture, Madison, MN 195
Slade School of Art, London 46, 62,
78, 106, 202, 314, 332, 430
Sleigh, Sylvia 379
Imperial Nude: Paul Rosano 379,
379
Turkish Bath 379
Smith, Ali, *Autumn* 69
Smith, Jennie 326
Smith, Kiki 380
Spinners (Moths and Spiders
Webs) 380, *380*
Smith, Lilo 219, *219*
Smith, Michelle 370
Smith, Zadie 235
Smithsonian Institution,
Washington 182
Socialist Realism 110, 291, 367, 395,
400, 428, 437, 441
Société Nationale des Beaux-Arts,
Paris 411
Society of Female Artists 309
Solanas, Valerie 70, 295
Sosnowska, Monika 381
1:1 381, *381*
Soto, Jesús Rafael 149
South African National Gallery,
Cape Town 341
Space Sciences Laboratory, Berkeley,
California 245
Sparrow, Walter Shaw, *Women Painters*
of the World 7–8
Spartali Stillman, Marie 84, 382
The Enchanted Garden of Messer
Ansaldo 382, *382*
Speer, Albert 291
Spence, Jo 383
Libido Uprising Part I 383, *383*

Spero, Nancy 384
Azur 384, *384–5*
'War' series 384
Sperone (Gian Enzo) Gallery,
Turin 269
Spoleto Festival 316
Stalin, Joseph 72
Stanley, Lady 117
Stanton, Eric 172
Stark, Frances 386
Chorus Girl Folding Self
in Half 386, *386*
My Best Thing 386
Stein, Gertrude 133, 233
Steiner, Rudolf 177
Steir, Pat 387
Sixteen Waterfalls of Dreams,
Memories, and Sentiment 387, *387*
Stella, Frank 293
Stern, Irma 388
The Flower Market,
Cape Town 388, *388*
Stettheimer, Florine 389
Family Portrait II 389, *389*
Steyerl, Hito 390
Factory of the Sun 390
How Not To Be Seen 390, *390*
Stieglitz, Alfred 241, 301
Stockholder, Jessica 391
Lay of the Land 391, *391*
Stölzl, Gunta 29
Storefront for Art and Architecture,
New York 298
Storm King, New York 246
Straight Photography movement 17
Streete, Delta 394
Stuart, Michelle 223, 392
'Rock Book' series 392
Serpent Mound, Ohio 392, *392*
The Studio Museum, Harlem,
New York 28, 92
Studio Orta 308
Studio Z collective 297
Sturtevant 393
Warhol Marilyns 393, *393*
Sublime 62, 121
Subramanyan, K.G. 290
subRosa 431
Sulter, Maud 74, 394
'Syrcas' series 394
Terpsichore from the series
'Zabat' 394, *394*
Sundance Film Festival 163
Suprematism 324
Surrealism 25, 81, 90, 106, 154, 199,
206, 252, 273, 306, 321, 351, 399,
400, 414, 441
Suzuki Shōnen 408
Symbolism 411
Szapocznikow, Alina 395
Lampe-Bouche
(Illuminated Lips) 395, *395*

Sze, Sarah 396
Triple Point (Pendulum) 396, *396*
Szeemann, Harald 341
Szenes, Árpád 417

T

T293 gallery, Naples 264
Tabboo! 155, *155*
Taeuber-Arp, Sophie 397
Composition of Circles and Overlapping
Angles 397, *397*
Dada Head 397
Taiga, Ike 167
Taipale, Martta 401
Tairov, Aleksandr 133
Tak van Poortvliet, Marie 177
Tallis, Thomas, *Spem in Alium* 86
Tanaka, Atsuko 398
Electric Dress 398, *398*
Work (Bell) 398
Tanaka, Min 270
Tanguy, Yves 351
Tanning, Dorothea 11, 399
Eine Kleine Nachtmusik 399, *399*
Taoism 387
Tarsila 400
Abaporú 400, *400*
Tassi, Agostino 150
Tate, London 52, 62, 71, 99, 144, 353, 444
Tate, Sue 69
Tatlin, Vladimir 324
Tawney, Lenore 265, 401
Dark River Wall Hanging 401, *401*
'Woven Forms' 401
Technische Hochschule, Stuttgart 149
Tennyson, Alfred Lord 84
Ter Borch, Gerard 152
Terry, Ellen 84
Théâtre du Soleil, Paris 141
Therbusch, Anna Dorothea 402
Self-Portrait 402, *402*
Thomas, Alma 403
Springtime in Washington 403, *403*
Thomas, Mickalene 404
Le Déjeuner sur l'Herbe: Les Trois
Femmes Noires 404, *404*
Thompson, Elizabeth, Lady Butler 405
Scotland Forever! 405, *405*
Thompson, Florence Owens 230, *230*
Tibor de Nagy Gallery, New York 142
Time-Life magazine 141
Time magazine 259
Tinguely, Jean 193, 352
Tintoretto 339
Titian 367
Venus and the Lute Player 411
Tokyo University of Education 226
Toledo, Francisco 198
Toulouse-Lautrec, Henri de 411

Trockel, Rosemarie 406
'Strickbilder' 406
Who Will Be In In '99? 406, *406*
Tropicália 272
Truitt, Anne 407
Daybook 407
Morning Choice 407, *407*
Turn 407
Truman, Harry S. 287
Tufts University, Massachusetts 191
Turner, J.M.W. 267
Turner Prize 20, 62, 95, 188, 264, 327,
426, 430, 439, 440
Twitter 13
Tyler School of Art, Philadelphia 442

U

Uemura Shōen 408
Yang Guifei 408, *408*
Ukeles, Mierle Laderman 409
Manifesto for Maintenance Art 1969! 409
Washing/Tracks/Maintenance 409, *409*
Ukiyo-e paintings 210
Ulay 19
Ulk (journal) 258
Ullstein Verlag 189
Ulman, Amalia 410
Excellences & Perfections 410, *410*
Universidad del País Vasco 197
Universidad Iberoamericana,
Mexico City 325
Universidad Nacional Autónoma
de México 93
Universidade Federal
de Minas Gerais 261
University of Applied Arts, Vienna 232
University of the Arts London 74
University of British Columbia 103
University of California, Berkeley 116
University of California, Los Angeles
(UCLA) 176, 298
University of California, Riverside 51
University of California,
San Diego 248
University of Cape Town 127
University of Central Lancashire 188
University of Chicago 391
University of Iowa 93
University of Johannesburg 372
University of Kansas 170
University of New South Wales 270
University of Tehran 134
University of Washington 111
University of the Witwatersrand 341
USC Roski School of Fine Arts,
Los Angeles 386
Utrecht University 362

V

The V-Girls 143
Val d'Ognes, Marie Joséphine
  Charlotte du 419, *419*
Valadon, Suzanne 411
  The Blue Room 411, *411*
VALIE EXPORT 206, 412
  Action Pants: Genital Panic 412, *412*
Vallayer-Coster, Anne 413, 419
  The Attributes of the Arts 413, *413*
Van Abbemuseum, Eindhoven 213
The Vanity Press 45
Varo, Remedios 414
  Woman Leaving the
  Psychoanalyst 414, *414*
Vasari, Giorgio 35, 249
  The Lives of the Most Excellent Painters,
  Sculptors, and Architects 9, 296, 343
Vasconcelos, Joana 415
  A Noiva [The Bride] 415, *415*
  Pop Galo 415
Velázquez, Diego 232
Venice Biennale
  32nd (1964) 348, 400
  36th (1972) 39
  46th (1995) 145
  49th (2001) 86, 341, 364
  50th (2003) 330
  51st (2005) 271, 415
  52nd (2007) 381
  53rd (2009) 262
  54th (2011) 50, 372, 386
  55th (2013) 30, 182, 209, 216, 232,
  269, 396
  56th (2015) 164, 334, 390
  57th (2017) 46, 73, 229, 333
  58th (2019) 40, 213, 270, 327, 350
Vermeer, Johannes 42
Versailles, Palace of 415
Vespucci, Amerigo 173
Victoria, Queen of England 309
Victoria & Albert Museum, London 84
Vicuña, Cecilia 416
  'Precarios' series 416
  Quipu Visceral 416, *416*
Vieira da Silva, Maria Helena 335, 417
  The Chess Game 417, *417*
Viennese Actionist movement 412
Vietnam War (1954–75) 172, 176,
  246, 384
Vigée-Lebrun, Élisabeth 59, 89,
  418, 419
  Marie Antoinette
  in Court Dress 418, *418*
Vigri, Caterina 8
Villa Arson, Nice 32
Villers, Marie-Denise 419
  Marie Joséphine Charlotte du Val
  d'Ognes 419, *419*

Virginia Commonwealth University,
  Richmond 122
Visconti, Fausta 329
Vogue 39, 141, 273
Vollard, Ambroise 91
Von Rydingsvard, Ursula 420
  Blackened Word 420, *420–1*

W

Wade, Cathleen and Colleen 39, *39*
Wadsworth Atheneum Museum of
  Art, Hartford, CT 407, 409
Waerndorfer, Fritz 253
Walker, Kara 422
  You Do 422, *422*
Wallpaper* magazine 73
WAR (Women Artists
  in Revolution) 384
War Relocation Authority (US) 230
Warhol, Andy 12, 134, 214, 263, 274,
  295, *295*, 393
Warren, Rebecca 423
  Hundemeister 423, *423*
Waser, Anna 424
  Self-Portrait at Twelve Years
  of Age 424, *424*
Waterloo, Battle of (1815) 405, *405*
Watteau, Jean-Antoine 367
Wautier, Charles 425
Wautier, Michaelina 425
  The Triumph of Bacchus 425, *425*
Wearing, Gillian 426
  I'm Desperate 426, *426*
  Rock 'n' Roll 426
Weems, Carrie Mae 235, 404, 427
  'The Kitchen Table' 427
  Untitled (Woman and Daughter
  with Makeup) 427, *427*
Weimar Academy 388
Wells, H.G. 158
Werefkin, Marianne von 292, *292*, 428
  The Country Road 428, *428*
Werner, Joseph 424
Wesleyan University,
  Middletown, CT 173
Wesselmann, Tom 393
Westermarck, Helena 360
Weston, Edward 280
Whistler, James McNeill 205
White, Clarence H. 230
White, Pae 429
  Untitled 429, *429*
Whitechapel Gallery, London 179, 266
Whiteread, Rachel 430
  House 430, *430*
Whitney, Gertrude Vanderbilt 129
Whitney Biennial 122, 195
Whitney Museum of American Art,
  New York 129, 176, 293, 295, 403

Wiener Werkstätte 253
Wilde, Oscar 169, 205
Wilding, Faith 431
  By Our Own Hands 431
  Crocheted Environment 431, *431*
Wilhelm II, Kaiser 221
Wilke, Hannah 432
  'Intra-Venus' 432
  S.O.S. – Starification Object
  Series 432, *432*
Wilson, Jane & Louise 433
  Azeville 433, *433*
  'Sealander' series 433
  Stasi City 433
Wilson, Richard 430
Wimbledon School of Art 69
Winsor, Jackie 396
Wolf, Christa, *Cassandra* 257
Wolfgang Hahn Prize 151
Wollstonecraft, Mary 169
Wolverhampton Art Gallery 69
Womanhouse, Los Angeles 98, 431
Women's Art Registry 392
Women's Liberation Art Group 172
Women's National Press Club
  Trophy 287
Wood, Grant 93
Woodman, Betty 434, 435
  A Single Joy of Song 434, *434*
Woodman, Francesca 435
  Self-Portrait Talking to Vince,
  Providence, Rhode Island 435,
  435
Woodman, George 435
Woolf, Virginia 56, *56*, 238
World's Fair, Paris (1937) 291
Wren, P.C. 242
Wylie, Rose 436
  Pink Skater (Will I Win,
  Will I Win...) 436, *436*
Wyntges, Geertgen 304

X

Xiamen Dada 368
Xiao Lu 437
  Dialogue 437, *437*
Xing Danwen 438
  Urban Fiction, Image 0 438, *438*

Y

Yale School of Art 28, 30, 92, 170, 185,
  186, 194, 246, 365, 391, 396, 442
Yass, Catherine 439
  'Corridors' 439
  Descent 439
  Lighthouse (East) 439, *439*

Yiadom-Boakye, Lynette 136, 440
  Complication 440, *440*
Yin Xiuzhen 441
  Portable Cities (Groningen) 441, *441*
Young British Artists (YBAs) 78, 132,
  146, 250, 357
Yuskavage, Lisa 442
  Day 442, *442*
Yuz Museum, Shanghai 365

Z

Zadkine, Ossip 93
Zappi, Paolo 140
Zarina 443
  Home is a Foreign Place 443, *443*
Zeid, Fahrelnissa 444
  Untitled 444, *444*
Zen Buddhism 359
Zhejiang Academy of Fine Arts,
  Hangzhou 437
Zionism 50
Zittel, Andrea 445
  Wagon Station Encampment at
  A–Z West, Joshua Tree, CA 445, *445*

PICTURE CREDITS

We would like to thank all those who gave their permission to reproduce the listed material. Every effort has been made to secure all permissions prior to publication. Phaidon apologizes for any inadvertent errors or omissions. If notified, the publisher will endeavour to correct these at the earliest opportunity.

All images © the artists. p.16 Courtesy Richard Gray Gallery. p.17 Metropolitan Museum of Art, New York. Gift of Phyllis D. Massar, 1971. Photo: Berenice Abbott/Getty Images. p.18 Courtesy of the artist. p.19 Courtesy of the Marina Abramović Archives. Photo: Donatelli Sbarra. p.20 Courtesy of the artist; greengrassi, London. Photo © Marcus Leith. p.21 © DACS 2019. Photo © Centre Pompidou, MNAM-CCI, Dist. RMN-Grand Palais / Georges Meguerditchian. p.22 Courtesy Galerie Lelong, Paris. Photo © Jerry Hardman-Jones. p.24 Bridgeman Images. p.25 Estate of Eileen Agar / Bridgeman Images. p.26 © 2002 Crystal Eye, Helsinki. p.27 Courtesy Chantal Akerman Fondation, Cinematek, Brussels. p.28 © Njideka Akunyili Crosby. Courtesy the artist and Victoria Miro, London/Venice p.29 © The Josef and Anni Albers Foundation/Artists Rights Society (ARS), New York and DACS, London 2019. Image © The Metropolitan Museum of Art/Art Resource/Scala, Florence. p.30 © Ellen Altfest. Courtesy White Cube. Photo © Todd-White Art Photography. p.31 Courtesy Olga de Amaral. Photo © Diego Amaral. p.32 © Ghada Amer. Courtesy Cheim & Read, New York. p.33 © Canal Street Communications. Courtesy the artist. Photo: Chris Harris. p.34 © Mamma Andersson. Courtesy the artist and David Zwirner. p.35 Museum Narodowe, Poznan, Poland / Bridgeman Images. p.36 Copyright the Artist. Courtesy of Richard Saltoun Gallery. p.37 Mrs. John Hay Whitney Bequest Fund,

MoMA. © Janine Antoni. Courtesy of the artist and Luhring Augustine, New York. p.38 Courtesy of Ida Applebroog and Hauser & Wirth. Photo: Alex Delfanne. p.39 © The Estate of Diane Arbus. p.40 Photo: Natasha Harth. p.41 © The Estate of Ruth Asawa. Courtesy The Estate of Ruth Asawa and David Zwirner. p.42 Courtesy of the Dottie Attie and P•P•O•W, New York. p.43 The Estate of Gillian Ayres. p.44 The Art Institute of Chicago, Gift of the Joel and Carole Bernstein Family. Bridgeman Images. p.45 Courtesy the artist and Frith Street Gallery, London. © Tate Photography/ Andrew Dunkley and Sam Drake. p.46 © Phyllida Barlow. Courtesy the artist and Hauser & Wirth. Photo: Fredrik Nilsen. p.47 © Tina Barney. Image courtesy of the artist and Kasmin Gallery. p.48 © Wilhelmina Barns-Graham Trust. p.49 Courtesy the artist and Frith Street Gallery, London. p.50 Courtesy of Annet Gelink Gallery, Amsterdam, and Sommer Contemporary Art, Tel Aviv. p.51 Courtesy the artist and Tanya Bonakdar Gallery, New York/Los Angeles. p.52 © The Archive of Maria Bartuszová, Košice. Courtesy The Estate of Maria Bartuszová, Košice and Alison Jacques Gallery, London. Photo: Boris Vaitovic. p.53 akg-images. p.54 The Geffrye Museum of the Home, London/Bridgeman Images. p.55 © 2018 Vanessa Beecroft. p.56 National Trust Photographic Library/ Bridgeman Images. p.57 Photo: Toni Hafkenscheid. p.58 Whitney Museum of American Art. Purchase with funds from the Painting and Sculpture Committee and partial gift of John Cheim and Howard Read. Courtesy Cheim & Read, New York. © Lynda Benglis/VAGA at ARS, NY and DACS, London 2019. p.59 Photo: Scala, Florence. p.60 Courtesy Renate Bertlmann/ Richard Saltoun Gallery, London © Renate Bertlmann / Bildrecht Wien. p.61 Courtesy of the artist and Salon 94, New York. © The Metropolitan Museum of Art. Photo: Hyla Skopitz. p.62 © Zarina Bhimji. All rights reserved, DACS 2019. p.63 Courtesy Electronic Arts Intermix, New York. Copyright: Dara Birnbaum. p.64 Photo © Centre Pompidou, MNAM-CCI, Dist. RMN-Grand Palais/Jacqueline Hyde. p.65 Photo: Josse/Scala, Florence. p.66 © Monica Bonvicini and VG-Bild Kunst. © DACS 2019. Photo: Rikke Luna/ARoS Aarhus Kunstmuseum. p.68 Courtesy of the artist and Sfeir-Semler Gallery Beirut/ Hamburg. Photo: Aurélien Mole. p.69 Purchased with the assistance of the Art Fund and the Friends of Wolverhampton Arts and Heritage. Wolverhampton Art Gallery, West Midlands, UK/Bridgeman

Images. © The Pauline Boty Estate. p.70 Photo: Andrea Thal. p.71 © The Easton Foundation/VAGA at ARS, NY and DACS, London 2019. Photo: Steve Taylor ARPS/ Alamy Stock Photo. p.72 Margaret Bourke-White/Time & Life Pictures/Getty Images. p.73 © Carol Bove. Courtesy the artist and David Zwirner. Photo: Maris Mezulis. p.74 Purchased with assistance from the V&A Purchase Grant Fund 1987/88. Image courtesy of Middlesbrough Institute of Modern Art. © Sonia Boyce. All rights reserved, DACS 2019. p.75 Courtesy the artist, Galerie Barbara Weiss, Berlin; Ivan Gallery, Bucharest; and Hauser & Wirth. Photo: Mihai Brătescu. p.76 Courtesy Goodman Gallery, Kaufmann Repetto + KOW. p.77 Photo: Smithsonian American Art Museum/Art Resource/Scala, Florence. p.78 Courtesy of Contemporary Fine Arts, Berlin. Photo: Robert McKeever. p.79 Courtesy Studio Bruguera. Photo: Museo de Bellas Artes, Caracas, Venezuela. p.80 © The Estate of Heidi Bucher. Courtesy the artist and Lehmann Maupin, New York, Hong Kong, and Seoul. Photo: Dhiyandra Natalegaw. p.81 Jersey Heritage Trust/ Bridgeman Images. p.82 Courtesy of the artist & Perrotin © Sophie Calle. © ADAGP, Paris and DACS, London 2019. p.83 Courtesy the artist and TJ Boulting. p.84 © National Science & Media Museum/Science & Society Picture Library. All rights reserved. p.85 Courtesy of the artist and Vitamin Creative Space. p.86 Sung by Salisbury Cathedral Choir. Recording and Postproduction by SoundMoves. Edited by George Bures Miller. Produced by Field Art Projects. © Janet Cardiff. Courtesy of the artist and Luhring Augustine, New York. Photo: Markus Tretter. p.87 National Trust Photographic Library/Bridgeman Images. p.88 Photo: Trevor Mills, Vancouver Art Gallery. p.89 akg-images/Rabatti & Domingie. p.90 © Estate of Leonora Carrington/ARS, NY and DACS, London 2019. Photo © Christie's Images/Bridgeman Images. p.91 National Gallery of Art, Washington DC, Collection of Mr. and Mrs. Paul Mellon. Photo: akg-images. p.92 Photo: Jason Wyche. p.93 © Catlett Mora Family Trust/VAGA at ARS, NY and DACS, London 2019. © 2019 The Metropolitan Museum of Art, Hortense and William A. Mohr Sculpture Purchase Fund/Art Resource/Scala, Florence. p.94 © Vija Celmins, Courtesy Matthew Marks Gallery. Digital image The Museum of Modern Art, New York/Mrs. Florene M. Schoenborn Fund/Scala, Florence. p.95 © The Estate of the Artist. Courtesy of Richard Saltoun Gallery. p.96 © The Estate of Sarah

Charlesworth. Image courtesy The Estate of Sarah Charlesworth; Paula Cooper Gallery, NY; Campoli Presti, London/Paris. p.97 Musee de Picardie, Amiens, France/ Bridgeman Images. p.98 Brooklyn Museum. Gift of the Elizabeth A. Sackler Foundation, 2002.10. © Judy Chicago. ARS, NY and DACS, London 2019. p.99 Image courtesy Barjeel Art Foundation. p.100 Albright Knox Art Gallery, Gift of Mr. and Mrs. Albert A. List/Art Resource, NY/Scala, Florence. p.101 © O Mundo de Lygia Clark-Associação Cultural, Rio de Janeiro. Courtesy of Alison Jacques Gallery, London. p.102 Musee Rodin, Paris/Philippe Galard/ Bridgeman Images. p.103 Courtesy of the artist. p.104 Bridgeman Images. © Estate of Prunella Clough. All rights reserved, DACS 2019. p.105 Collection of Hancock Shaker Village, Pittsfield, MA. p.106 The Sherwin Collection, Leeds, UK/Bridgeman Images. p.107 Art Gallery of New South Wales, Sydney, Australia. Purchased with funds provided by the Art Gallery Society of New South Wales and James Fairfax AO/ Bridgeman Images. p.108 Courtesy the artist. p.109 © Petah Coyne. Courtesy Galerie Lelong & Co., New York. Photo: J. Kotter. p.110 Courtesy the artist and The East West Bank Collection. On display at the Bank's Beverly Hills Private Banking Center, California. Photo: Damian Griffiths. p.111 © 2018 Imogen Cunningham Trust. All rights reserved. p.112 © DACS 2019. Photo Scala, Florence/bpk, Bildagentur fuer Kunst, Kultur und Geschichte, Berlin. p.113 © Berlinde De Bruyckere. Courtesy the artist and Hauser & Wirth. Photo: Mirjam Devriendt. p.114 Gift of Iris Cantor. Image © The Metropolitan Museum of Art/Art Resource/Scala, Florence. p.115 Courtesy the artist, Frith Street Gallery, London and Marian Goodman Gallery, New York/Paris. p.116 © The Jay DeFeo Foundation/DACS 2019. Photo: Ben Blackwell. p.117 © The Trustees of the British Museum. p.118 Calouste Gulbenkian Museum/Scala, Florence. © Pracusa 2017633. p.119 © Agnes Denes. Courtesy Leslie Tonkonow Artworks + Projects, New York. Photo: John McGrail. p.120 © Rineke Dijkstra. Courtesy of the artist and Marian Goodman Gallery. p.121 Courtesy Galleri Bo Bjerggaard, Copenhagen; OSLcontemporary, Oslo and Anthony Wilkinson Gallery, London. Photo: Vegar Moen. p.122 © Tara Donovan. Courtesy Jupiter Artland, Edinburgh, Scotland. Photo: Ruth Clark. p.124 © 2018 Rosalyn Drexler/Artists Rights Society (ARS), New York and Garth Greenan Gallery, New York. Private collection, Frankfurt, Germany. © ARS, NY and

DACS, London 2019. p.125 Montclair Art Museum, Lang Acquisition Fund, 1969.4. p.126 The Metropolitan Museum of Art, Bequest of Susan Dwight Bliss. Art Resource/ Scala, Florence. p.127 © Marlene Dumas. p.128 Courtesy of the artist and Marlborough Contemporary, New York and London. p.129 San Diego Museum of Art, Gift of Mr. Herbert Lerner/Bridgeman Images. p.130 Purchased with funds provided by Agnes Gund, and gift of John Berggruen by exchange. Digital image The Museum of Modern Art, New York/Scala, Florence. © 2018 Mary Beth Edelson. p.131 Image courtesy the artist, Anton Kern Gallery, New York, and Susanne Vielmetter Los Angeles Projects. p.132 Image courtesy White Cube © Tracey Emin. All rights reserved, DACS/ Artimage 2019. p.133 Digital image The Museum of Modern Art, New York/Scala, Florence. p.134 The Third Line Gallery, Dubai, UAE/Robert Divers Herrick. p.135 Fondazione Sandretto Re Rebaudengo Collection. Photo: Matthew Septimus. p.136 Courtesy the artist and Half Gallery, New York. p.137 Copyright and Courtesy The Estate of Rose Finn-Kelcey. p.138 Courtesy of the artist and Salon 94, New York. p.139 Courtesy Aspen Art Museum, Colorado. Photo: Tony Prikryl. p.140 Photo: Scala, Florence. Courtesy of the Ministero Beni e Att. Culturali e del Turismo. p.141 © Martine Franck/Magnum Photos. p.142 Courtesy National Gallery of Art, Washington DC. © Helen Frankenthaler Foundation, Inc./ARS, NY and DACS, London 2019. p.143 Photo: Kelly & Massa Photography. p.144 © Tate, London 2018. © The Executors of the Frink Estate and Archive. All rights reserved, DACS 2019. p.145 © Katharina Fritsch. © DACS 2019. p.146 Courtesy the artist and Lehmann Maupin, New York, Hong Kong and Seoul © Anya Gallaccio. All rights reserved, DACS 2019. p.147 © Ellen Gallagher. Courtesy Gagosian. p.148 Courtesy the artist and Ronald Feldman Gallery, New York. p.149 © Fundacion Gego. Courtesy Henry Moore Institute. Photo: Jerry Hardman-Jones p.150 Museo di Capodimonte, Naples, Italy/Bridge-man Images. p.151 © DACS 2019. p.152 akg-images. p.153 Courtesy of the artist and Pavel Zoubok Fine Art, New York. p.154 Photo © Christie's Images/ Bridgeman Images. p.155 © Nan Goldin. p.156 Photo: Scala, Florence/bpk, Bildagentur fuer Kunst, Kultur und Geschichte, Berlin. © ADAGP, Paris and DACS, London 2019. p.157 Photo: Josse/Scala, Florence. p.158 Courtesy the artist, Corvi-Mora, London and Esther Schipper, Berlin. Photo © Joaquín Cortés/

Román Lores – Museo Nacional Centro de Arte Reina Sofia. p.160 Photo: Dominic Brown. p.161 © Dorich House Museum. p.162 © Ikon Gallery. Photo: Stuart Whipps. p.163 Lauren Greenfield/INSTITUTE. © Lauren Greenfield. p.164 © Katharina Grosse. © DACS 2019. Courtesy of Barbara Gross, Munich, Galerie nächst St. Stephan/ Rosemarie Schwarzwälder, Vienna; König Galerie, Berlin; and Mark Müller, Zurich. Photo: Nic Tenwiggenhorn and VG Bild-Kunst, Bonn. p.165 © Guerrilla Girls. Courtesy guerrillagirls.com. p.166 Courtesy the artist and Gallery Chemould Prescott Road, Mumbai. Photo: Anil Ranc. p.167 Image © 2019 The Metropolitan Museum of Art/Art Resource/ Scala, Florence. p.168 Nordenfjeldske Kunst- industri-museum © Elisabeth Haarr/BONO 2018. Photo: Steffen W. Holden. p.169 © Maggi Hambling. p.170 Courtesy of Ann Hamilton Studio. Photo: Thibault Jeanson. p.172 Courtesy PayneShurvell London. p.173 MoMA Committee on Painting and Sculpture Funds. Courtesy the artist and Greene Naftali, New York. p.174 Minneapolis Institute of Arts, MN, The Julia B. Bigelow Fund/Bridgeman Images. p.175 © Mona Hatoum. Courtesy the artist and MdbK Leipzig. Photo: dotgain.info. p.176 © Sharon Hayes. p.177 Photo: Fine Art Images/ Heritage Images/Scala, Florence. p.178 Courtesy Sharjah Art Foundation, UAE. p.179 Courtesy of the artist; 303 Gallery, New York; and Hauser & Wirth. Photo © Stephen White. p.180 Courtesy Estudio Sanguinetti. p.181 Kunstmuseum Basel, Schenkung der Prof. J.J. Bachofen-Burckhardt-Stiftung. Photo: Kunstmuseum Basel, Martin P. Bühler. p.182 Courtesy the artist; Silex Films; Metro Pictures, New York; kamel mennour, Paris/London; and König Galerie, Berlin. p.183 Barbara Hepworth © Bowness. Clynt Garnham Suffolk/Alamy Stock Photo. p.184 © Carmen Herrera. Courtesy Lisson Gallery. p.185 © The Estate of Eva Hesse. Detroit Institute of Arts, Founders Society Purchase, Friends of Modern Art Fund and Miscellaneous Gifts Fund, 79.34. Courtesy Hauser & Wirth. Photo courtesy Detroit Institute of Arts. p.186 Courtesy of the artist, galerie frank elbaz and Alison Jacques Gallery. Photo: Zarko Vijatovic. p.187 © Susan Hiller. Courtesy the artist and Lisson Gallery. Photo © Tate. p.188 Courtesy of the artist, Hollybush Gardens and National Museums Liverpool. Photo courtesy Spike Island and Stuart Whipps. p.189 Erich Lessing/Art Resource, NY © DACS 2019. p.190 © Candida Höfer, Köln/ VG Bild-Kunst, Bonn and DACS, London 2019. p.191 © Estate of

Nancy Holt/VAGA at ARS, NY and DACS, London 2019. p.192 Jenny Holzer/Art Resource, NY. © Jenny Holzer. ARS, NY and DACS, London 2019. Photo: Lisa Kahane. p.193 © Tate, London 2018 © DACS 2019. p.194 Courtesy the artist, Hauser & Wirth, and Galleria Raffaella Cortese, Milan. Photo: Stefan Altenburger. p.195 Whitney Museum of American Art, New York, purchase with funds from Joel and Anne Ehrenkranz 2017.169. Courtesy of the artist and Rachel Uffner Gallery. p.196 Image courtesy of the artist and JTT, New York. p.197 Courtesy of the artist and Marian Goodman Gallery © DACS 2019. Photo: Attilio Maranzano. p.198 Courtesy of the artist. p.199 Photo © Christie's Images/ Bridgeman Images. Reproduced with the permission of Maria Rosenda López Posadas, legal representative of the intellectual property of Maria Izquierdo. p.200 © Emily Jacir. Courtesy Alexander and Bonin, New York. p.201 © Chantal Joffe. Courtesy the artist and Victoria Miro, London/Venice. p.202 A.Conger Goodyear Fund. Acc. no:124.1958. Digital image The Museum of Modern Art, New York/ A. Conger Goodyear Fund/Scala, Florence. p.203 © 2019 Joan Jonas. © ARS, NY and DACS, London 2019. p.204 Courtesy of Loïs Mailou Jones Pierre-Noel Trust. p.205 Russell-Cotes Art Gallery and Museum, Bournemouth, UK/ Bridgeman Images. p.206 Estate Birgit Jürgenssen, Bildrecht, Vienna, 2018. Courtesy Galerie Hubert Winter, Vienna. p.207 Photo: Schalkwijk/ Art Resource/Scala, Florence. © Banco de México Diego Rivera Frida Kahlo Museums Trust, Mexico, D.F./DACS 2019. p.208 © Hayv Kahraman. Courtesy of the artist and Jack Shainman Gallery, New York. p.209 © Kan Xuan. p.210 Museum of Fine Arts, Boston, Massachusetts/William Sturgis Bigelow Collection/Bridgeman Images. p.211 Photo: Scala, Florence/bpk, Bilda-gentur fuer Kunst, Kultur und Geschichte, Berlin. p.212 Courtesy the artist and Pippy Houldsworth Gallery, London. p.213 Photo: Gert Jan van Rooij. p.214 Reprinted with permission of the Corita Art Center, Immaculate Heart Community, Los Angeles. p.215 Courtesy the artist and Hauser & Wirth. Photo: Julie Lovens. p.216 © Kimsooja. Courtesy of the artists and KEWENIG, Berlin. p.217 Fishbein-Bender Collection, Gift of T. Richard Fishbein and Estelle P. Bender, Metropolitan Museum of Art. p.218 National Gallery of Australia, Canberra, Purchased 1989/Bridgeman Images. © Emily Karne Kngwarreye/ Copyright Agency. Licensed by DACS 2019. p.219 Nottingham City Museums and

Galleries (Nottingham Castle)/Bridgeman Images. © Reproduced with permission of The Estate of Dame Laura Knight DBE RA 2019. All rights reserved. p.220 © The Estate of the Artist. Courtesy Richard Saltoun Gallery. p.220 Courtesy Hunt Kastner, Prague and Meyer Riegger Berlin/ Karlsruhe. Photo: Michal Czanderle. p.221 akg-images/Erich Lessing. p.223 DC Moore Gallery. Courtesy of the Pennsylvania Academy of the Fine Arts, Philadelphia. Museum Purchase. Photo: Steven Bates. p.224 Gift of Alfonso A. Ossorio. Digital image The Museum of Modern Art, New York/ Scala, Florence. © The Pollock-Krasner Foundation ARS, NY and DACS, London 2019. p.225 Courtesy The Broad. p.226 Gift of Margot and John Ernst, Agnes Gund, and Barbara Pine/Digital image The Museum of Modern Art, New York/Scala, Florence. © Shigeko Kubota/VAGA at ARS, NY and DACS, London 2019. p.227 Courtesy the artist and Tanya Bonakdar Gallery, New York/Los Angeles. p.228 © YAYOI KUSAMA. p.229 Courtesy Alicja Kwade, KÖNIG GALERIE, Berlin/ London. Photo: Anders Sune Berg. p.230 Collection: Library of Congress. p.231 G.L.A.M. Greer Lankton Archives Museum p.232 © Maria Lassnig Foundation.Courtesy Hauser & Wirth. Photo: Stefan Altenburger Photography Zürich. p.233 © Fondation Foujita/ADAGP, Paris and DACS, London 2019. Photo: Josse/Scala, Florence. p.234 Courtesy of the artist and Metro Pictures, New York. p.235 © Deana Lawson. Courtesy of Sikkema Jenkins & Co., New York, and Rhona Hoffman Gallery, Chicago. p.236 Courtesy Studio Lee Bul and Lehmann Maupin, New York, Hong Kong, and Seoul. Photo: Algirdas Bakas. p.237 © Nikki S. Lee, courtesy of Sikkema Jenkins & Co., New York. p.238 © Annie Leibovitz. p.239 Album/Scala, Florence. © Authorized by Tamara Art Heritage/ADAGP, Paris and DACS London 2019. p.240 Photo Ron Amstutz. © Zoe Leonard. Philadelphia Museum of Art: Purchased with funds contributed by the Dietrich Foundation and with the partial gift of the artist and the Paula Cooper Gallery, 1998. p.241 © Sherrie Levine. Courtesy the artist and David Zwirner. p.242 © Helen Levitt Film Documents LLC. All rights reserved. Courtesy of Galerie Thomas Zander. p.243 Gift of the Historical Society of Forest Park, Illinois/Photo Smithsonian American Art Museum/Art Resource/Scala, Florence. p.244 Photo: Josse/Scala, Florence. p.245 © Liliane Lijn. All rights reserved, DACS 2019. Photo: Richard Wilding. p.246 © Maya Lin

Fund for the Twenty-First Century, MoMA. p. 346 Photo: Martin Siepmann. p. 347 National Trust Photographic Library/ Bridgeman Images. p. 348 © Hannah Ryggen/DACS 2018. 'Hannah Ryggen: Woven Histories' 2017 © Modern Art Oxford. Photo: Ben Westoby. p. 349 Museum of Modern Art, New York (MoMA) The Modern Women's Fund and Committee on Painting and Sculpture Funds. Inv.nr.:549.2013. Digital image The Museum of Modern Art, New York/Scala, Florence. © Betye Saar. Courtesy of the artist and Roberts Projects, Los Angeles. p. 350 Courtesy the artist and KÖNIG GALERIE, Berlin/London. p. 351 The Israel Museum, Jerusalem, Israel/Vera & Arturo Schwarz Collection of Dada and Surrealist Art/Bridgeman Images. © Estate of Kay Sage/DACS, London and ARS, NY, 2019. p. 352 © Niki de Saint Phalle Charitable Art Foundation/ADAGP, Paris and DACS, London 2019. Prisma by Dukas Presseagentur GmbH/Alamy Stock Photo. p. 353 © the artist. Courtesy Alexander and Bonin, New York and White Cube. Photo © Sergio Clavijo. p. 354 The Picture Art Collection/Alamy Stock Photo. p. 355 © Zilia Sánchez. Courtesy Galerie Lelong & Co., New York. p. 356 Photo: Smithsonian American Art Museum/Art Resource/Scala, Florence. p. 357 Courtesy the artist and Gagosian © Jenny Saville. All rights reserved, DACS 2019. p. 358 © 2019. Photo: Smithsonian American Art Museum/Art Resource/Scala, Florence. © Estate of Miriam Schapiro/ARS, NY and DACS, London 2019. p. 359 Museum of Modern Art, New York, Scott Burton Fund. © Mira Schendel Estate. Courtesy Estate of Mira Schendel, Hauser & Wirth Gallery. p. 360 Ateneum Art Museum, Finnish National Gallery, Helsinki, Finland/Bridgeman Images. p. 361 © C. Schneemann. Photo: Erró. p. 363 © Dana Schutz. Courtesy of the artist and Petzel, New York. p. 364 © Berni Searle. Courtesy of Stevenson, Cape Town and Johannesburg. p. 365 Courtesy of the artist and Pilar Corrias, London. p. 366 Brooklyn Museum of Art, New York/ Bridgeman Images. © ARS, NY and DACS, London 2019. p. 367 Photo: Scala, Florence. © ADAGP, Paris and DACS, London 2019. p. 368 © Shen Yuan. Courtesy the artist and kamel mennour, Paris/London. p. 369 The Picture Art Collection/Alamy Stock Photo. p. 370 National Portrait Gallery, Smithsonian Institution, Washington DC. Gift of Kate Capshaw and Steven Spielberg; Judith Kern and Kent Whealy; Tommie L. Pegues and Donald A. Capoccia; Clarence, DeLoise, and Brenda Gaines; Jonathan and Nancy Lee Kemper; The Stoneridge Fund of Amy

and Marc Meadows; Robert E. Meyerhoff and Rheda Becker; Catherine and Michael Podell; Mark and Cindy Aron; Lyndon J. Barrois and Janine Sherman Barrois; The Honorable John and Louise Bryson; Paul and Rose Carter; Bob and Jane Clark; Lisa R. Davis; Shirley Ross Davis and Family; Alan and Lois Fern; Conrad and Constance Hipkins; Sharon and John Hoffman; Audrey M. Irmas; John Legend and Chrissy Teigen; Eileen Harris Norton; Helen Hilton Raiser; Philip and Elizabeth Ryan; Roselyne Chroman Swig; Josef Vascovitz and Lisa Goodman; Eileen Baird; Dennis and Joyce Black Family Charitable Foundation; Shelley Brazier; Aryn Drake-Lee; Andy and Teri Goodman; Randi Charno Levine and Jeffrey E. Levine; Fred M. Levin and Nancy Livingston, The Shenson Foundation; Monique Meloche Gallery, Chicago; Arthur Lewis and Hau Nguyen; Sara and John Schram; Alyssa Taubman and Robert Rothman. p. 371 Courtesy of the artist and Metro Pictures, New York. p. 372 Photo: Carla Liesching. p. 373 © Amy Sillman. Courtesy of the artist and Gladstone Gallery, New York and Brussels. p. 374 Courtesy of the artist and Salon 94, New York. p. 375 Courtesy of the artist. p. 376 © Lorna Simpson. Courtesy the artist and Hauser & Wirth. p. 377 Courtesy the artist and Frith Street Gallery, London. Photo: Steve White. p. 378 The Picture Art Collection/Alamy Stock Photo. p. 379 Courtesy of Estate Sylvia Sleigh. p. 380 Courtesy Pace Gallery. Photo: Tom Barratt. p. 381 © Monika Sosnowska. Courtesy Foksal Gallery Foundation; Galerie Gisela Capitain; kurimanzutto; The Modern Institute; and Hauser & Wirth. p. 382 Pre-Raphaelite Inc., London/By courtesy of Julian Hartnoll/Bridgeman Images. p. 383 © The Estate of the Artist. Courtesy of Richard Saltoun Gallery. p. 384 © The Nancy Spero and Leon Golub Foundation for the Arts/VAGA at ARS, NY and DACS, London 2019. Photo © Centre Pompidou, MNAM-CCI, Dist. RMN-Grand Palais/Philippe Migeat. p. 386 Whitney Museum of American Art, New York, promised gift of Thea Westreich Wagner and Ethan Wagner P.2011.417. Photo: Robert Wedemeyer. p. 387 Collection of the Metropolitan Museum of Art, Kathryn E. Hurd Fund, by exchange. Courtesy of Pat Steir. p. 388 © The Irma Stern Trust, DACS 2019. Photo © Christie's Images/Bridgeman Images. p. 389 Gift of Miss Ettie Stettheimer/Digital image The Museum of Modern Art, New York/Scala, Florence. p. 390 Image CC 4.0 Hito Steyerl. Image courtesy of the artist; Andrew Kreps Gallery, New York; and Esther Schipper,

Berlin. p. 391 © Jessica Stockholder. Courtesy of the artist; Galerie nächst St. Stephan, Vienna; and Mitchell-Innes & Nash, New York. p. 392 © Michelle Stuart. Courtesy the Wexner Center for the Arts, The Ohio State University and Alison Jacques Gallery, London. p. 393 © Estate Sturtevant, Paris. Photo: Tom Carter. p. 394 Reproduced courtesy of The Estate of Maud Sulter. Photo: courtesy of Street Level Photoworks, Glasgow. p. 395 Courtesy The Estate of Alina Szapocznikow/ Piotr Stanislawski/ Loevenbruck, Paris/Hauser & Wirth. © ADAGP, Paris and DACS, London 2019. Photo: Fabrice Gousset, courtesy Loevenbruck, Paris. p. 396 Gift of the International Council of The Museum of Modern Art, Agnes Gund, Ronald S. and Jo Carole Lauder, and Sharon Percy Rockefeller, in honor of the 60th Anniversary of the International Council, 2014. Courtesy the artist and Tanya Bonakdar Gallery, New York/Los Angeles. p. 397 Digital image The Museum of Modern Art, New York/Scala, Florence. p. 398 © Kanayama Akira and Tanaka Atsuko Aesociation. p. 399 Photo © Tate, London 2018. © ADAGP, Paris and DACS, London 2019. p. 400 Christie's Images, London/ Scala, Florence. p. 401 Greta Daniel Design Fund, MoMA. Digital image The Museum of Modern Art, New York/Scala, Florence. Works © The Lenore G. Tawney Foundation. p. 402 akg-images. p. 403 Photo © Christie's Images/ Bridgeman Images. p. 404 © Mickalene Thomas. p. 405 Leeds Museums and Galleries (Leeds Art Gallery) UK/Bridgeman Images. p. 406 Courtesy Sprüth Magers. © Rosemarie Trockel © DACS 2019. p. 407 Saint Louis Art Museum, Missouri. Gift of Mrs. Marcella Louis Brenner © annetruitt.org/Bridgeman Images. p. 408 Historic Images/Alamy Stock Photo. p. 409 © Mierle Laderman Ukeles. Courtesy of the artist and Ronald Feldman Gallery, New York. p. 410 Courtesy the Artist and Arcadia Missa. p. 411 Photo © Centre Pompidou, MNAM-CCI, Dist. RMN-Grand Palais/Jacqueline Hyde. p. 412 Photo © Centre Pompidou, MNAM-CCI, Dist. RMN-Grand Palais/Philippe Migeat. © DACS 2019. p. 413 DeAgostini Picture Library/ Scala, Florence. p. 414 © Remedios Varo, DACS/VEGAP 2019. Photo: Schalkwijk/Art Resource/ Scala, Florence. p. 415 Luis Vasconcelos/Cour-tesy Unidade Infinita Projectos/Ajuda National Palace, Lisbon, 2013. p. 416 Courtesy the artist and Lehmann Maupin, New York, Hong Kong and Seoul. Photo: Matthew Herrmann. p. 417 © CNAC/MNAM/Dist. RMN-Grand Palais/Art Resource, NY. © ADAGP, Paris and DACS, London 2019. p. 418 Photo:

Austrian Archives/ Scala, Florence. p. 419 Metropolitan Museum of Art. Mr. and Mrs. Isaac D. Fletcher Collec- tion, Bequest of Isaac D. Fletcher, 1917. p. 420 Collection Albright-Knox Art Gallery, Buffalo, New York. Charles W. Goodyear Fund, by exchange and Bequest of Arthur B. Michael, by exchange, 2015 © Ursula von Rydingsvard. Courtesy Galerie Lelong & Co., New York. p. 422 © Kara Walker. Courtesy of Sikkema Jenkins & Co., New York. p. 423 © Rebecca Warren. Courtesy Maureen Paley, Matthew Marks Gallery and Galerie Max Hetzler. p. 425 Heritage Images/Fine Art Images/akg-images. p. 426 © Gillian Wearing. Courtesy Maureen Paley, London, Tanya Bonakdar Gallery, New York and Regen Projects, Los Angeles. p. 427 © Carrie Mae Weems. Courtesy of the artist and Jack Shainman Gallery, New York. p. 428 akg-images. p. 429 Courtesy of the artist and 1301PE, Los Angeles. Photo: Shaughn and John. p. 430 © Rachel Whiteread. Courtesy of the artist and Gagosian. Photo: Sue Omerod. p. 431 Institute of Contemporary Art, Boston. Gift of the artist. © Faith Wilding. Photo: Charles Mayer Photography. p. 432 Hannah Wilke © Marsie, Emanuelle, Damon & Andrew Scharlatt, Hannah Wilke Collection & Archive, Los Angeles/DACS, London 2019. Digital image The Museum of Modern Art, New York/Scala, Florence. p. 433 Courtesy the artists. p. 434 Courtesy of Charles Woodman/The Estate of Betty Woodman and David Kordansky Gallery, Los Angeles. Photo: Jeff Elstone. p. 435 Copyright and courtesy Charles Woodman/Estate of Francesca Woodman. p. 436 © Rose Wylie. Courtesy of Rose Wylie, David Zwirner and Choi&Lager. p. 437 Courtesy Xiao Lu. p. 438 The artist and Danwen Studio. p. 439 Courtesy of Alison Jacques Gallery, London. © Catherine Yass. All rights reserved, DACS 2019. p. 440 Courtesy the artist, Corvi-Mora, London, and Jack Shainman Gallery, New York. Photo: Marcus Leith. p. 441 © 2018 Yin Xiuzhen. Courtesy of Pace Gallery. p. 442 © Lisa Yuskavage. Courtesy the artist and David Zwirner. p. 443 © Zarina; Courtesy of the artist and Luhring Augustine, New York. p. 444 © Tate, London 2018. p. 445 Courtesy the artist and Sadie Coles HQ, London. Photo: Lance Brewer.

WRITER CREDITS

James Cahill: 25, 53, 129, 140, 150, 154, 155, 202, 244, 287, 291, 304, 340, 343, 351, 355, 367, 388, 389, 424, 425, 42

Louisa Elderton: 31, 41, 56, 58, 109, 110, 182, 194, 195, 212, 230, 239, 247, 270, 297, 307, 311, 327, 330, 337, 353, 365, 372, 390, 395, 434, 435

Elizabeth Fullerton: 22, 23, 57, 77, 105, 119, 124, 134, 153, 169, 173, 209, 214, 251, 263, 295, 312, 348, 387, 440

Orit Gat: 21, 84, 93, 219, 220, 306, 317, 326, 345, 356, 358, 359, 384, 885, 415, 417, 422, 429

Ferren Gipson: 36, 73, 74, 76, 85, 115, 141, 144, 187, 213, 217, 226, 236, 240, 310, 368, 408, 437, 438, 441

P L Henderson: 27, 33, 51, 89, 96, 99, 116, 131, 151, 167, 174, 178, 302, 321, 341, 403, 431

Katy Hessel: 34, 44, 52, 55, 68, 80, 83, 121, 158, 159, 179, 222, 257, 258, 273, 344, 346, 366, 379, 380

Catalina Imizcoz: 180, 199, 238, 349, 373, 416

Henry Little: 117, 120, 122, 123, 161, 211, 243, 253, 286, 402

Louisa Lee: 38, 42, 90, 95, 104, 137, 139, 170, 171, 172, 183, 250, 261, 272, 299, 336, 357, 430, 436

Helen Luckett: 28, 64, 71, 100, 111, 127, 142, 188, 197, 200, 231, 248, 252, 254, 262, 277, 288, 301, 331, 332, 347

Kathleen Madden: 17, 61, 63, 82, 98, 128, 130, 136, 165, 224, 241, 246, 275, 293, 294, 313, 316, 361, 386

Henry Martin: 18, 106, 114, 125, 164, 189, 221, 225, 232, 265, 271, 292, 334, 362, 400, 406, 407, 420, 421, 442

Tom Melick: 20, 37, 39, 45, 107, 143, 218, 228, 267, 281, 320, 333, 335, 423

Rebecca Morrill: 49, 163, 177, 314, 354, 375, 411, 426, 439

Yates Norton: 35, 40, 54, 59, 65, 75, 81, 87, 94, 97, 102, 126, 152, 157, 160, 249, 282, 285, 296, 350, 381, 409, 410, 413, 418, 419, 443

Matthew Price: 16, 32, 43, 69, 78, 132, 135, 162, 191, 266, 298, 305, 308, 338, 363, 371, 391, 398, 414

Cleo Roberts: 30, 50, 66, 67, 79, 112, 146, 166, 207, 208, 215, 216, 237, 245, 290, 369, 377, 444

Gabrielle Schwarz: 19, 46, 48, 92, 101, 103, 138, 149, 184, 185, 204, 223, 256, 274, 323, 360, 445

Robert Shane: 29, 47, 62, 148, 168, 175, 181, 186, 190, 193, 196, 201, 206, 233, 234, 235, 264, 268, 329, 339, 364, 378, 382, 396, 401

Mitch Speed: 24, 86, 145, 176, 203, 227, 269, 276, 283, 303, 324, 325, 342, 392, 404, 412, 428, 432

David Trigg: 26, 88, 113, 118, 133, 156, 205, 210, 260, 279, 300, 309, 315, 322, 328, 352, 370, 393, 397, 405

Ellen Mara De Wachter: 60, 70, 72, 91, 108, 192, 198, 229, 242, 255, 259, 278, 280, 284, 289, 318, 319, 374, 376, 383, 394, 399, 433

Phaidon Press Limited
2 Cooperage Yard
London E15 2QR

Phaidon Press Inc.
111 Broadway
New York, NY 10006

Phaidon SARL
55, rue Traversière
75012 Paris

phaidon.com

First published 2019
Reprinted 2020, 2021, 2022, 2025
Reprinted in this compact format 2026
© 2019 Phaidon Press Limited

ISBN 978 1 83729 143 4

Commissioning Editor: Rebecca Morrill
Consultant Editor: Karen Wright
Content Editor: Louisa Elderton
Assistant Editor: Catalina Imizcoz
Picture Researcher: Annalaura Palma
Production Controller: Rebecca Price
Design: Pentagram
Typesetting: Cantina

Printed in Malaysia

All dimensions are given height × width × depth unless otherwise specified.

The publishers would like to thank Karen Wright, who was instrumental to this book's conception, to the compilation of the long- and short-lists of artists, and to the selection of many of the artworks. We are indebted to Louisa Elderton and Guy Tindale for overseeing the commissioning, coordination, copy-editing and fact-checking of texts, and to Joanne Murray for her thorough proofreading. We are also grateful to all of the writers for their thoughtful texts and flexibility. The project benefited enormously from the knowledge and skills of Annalaura Palma who undertook the task of researching and acquiring images and clearing copyright with patience and good humour. Additional thanks go to the following for the various roles they played in inspiring, supporting and facilitating the creation of this publication: Deborah Aaronson, Caitlin Arnell Argles, Jane Beckett, Imogen Benson, Hilary Bird, Ella Boardman, Victoria Clarke, Nat Foreman, Diane Fortenberry, Hélène Gallois Montbrun, Jake Gilbert, Pedro Martin, Bridget McCarthy, Rosie Minney, Emily Paul, Emma Phillips, Julia Pollacco, Emma Ridgway, Michele Robecchi, Astrid Stavro, Rochelle Steiner, Pete Woronkowicz and Nayia Yiakoumaki. Finally, we would like to thank all of the great women artists and their representatives who greeted this project with enthusiasm and gave permission for their works to be reproduced.